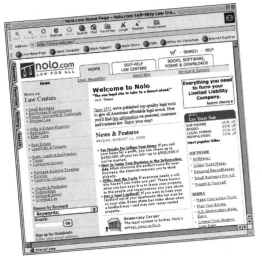

# LEGAL INFORMATION ONLINE ANYTIME
## 24 hours a day

## www.nolo.com

### AT THE NOLO.COM SELF-HELP LAW CENTER, YOU'LL FIND

- Nolo's comprehensive Legal Encyclopedia filled with plain-English information on a variety of legal topics
- Nolo's Law Dictionary—legal terms <u>without</u> the legalese
- Auntie Nolo—if you've got questions, Auntie's got answers
- The Law Store—over 200 self-help legal products including Downloadable Software, Books, Form Kits and eGuides
- Legal and product updates
- Frequently Asked Questions
- NoloBriefs, our free monthly email newsletter
- Legal Research Center, for access to state and federal statutes
- Our ever-popular lawyer jokes

## Quality LAW BOOKS & SOFTWARE FOR EVERYONE

Nolo's user-friendly products are consistently first-rate. Here's why:

- A dozen in-house legal editors, working with highly skilled authors, ensure that our products are accurate, up-to-date and easy to use
- We continually update every book and software program to keep up with changes in the law
- Our commitment to a more democratic legal system informs all of our work
- We appreciate & listen to your feedback. Please fill out and return the card at the back of this book.

### OUR "NO-HASSLE" GUARANTEE

Return anything you buy directly from Nolo for any reason and we'll cheerfully refund your purchase price. No ifs, ands or buts.

# Read This First

The information in this book is as up-to-date and accurate as we can make it. But it's important to realize that the law changes frequently, as do fees, forms and procedures. If you handle your own legal matters, it's up to you to be sure that all information you use—including the information in this book—is accurate. Here are some suggestions to help you:

**First,** make sure you've got the most recent edition of this book. To learn whether a later edition is available, check the edition number on the book's spine and then go to Nolo's online Law Store at www.nolo.com or call Nolo's Customer Service Department at 800-728-3555.

**Next,** even if you have a current edition, you need to be sure it's fully up-to-date. The law can change overnight. At www.nolo.com, we post notices of major legal and practical changes that affect the latest edition of a book. To check for updates, find your book in the Law Store on Nolo's website (you can use the "A to Z Product List" and click the book's title). If you see an "Updates" link on the left side of the page, click it. If you don't see a link, that means we haven't posted any updates. (But check back regularly.)

**Finally,** we believe accurate and current legal information should help you solve many of your own legal problems on a cost-efficient basis. But this text is not a substitute for personalized advice from a knowledgeable lawyer. If you want the help of a trained professional, consult an attorney licensed to practice in your state.

**2nd edition**

# New York Landlord's Law Book

by attorney Mary Ann Hallenborg
Edited by Marcia Stewart

Second Edition      JUNE 2003

Editor              MARCIA STEWART

Illustrations       LINDA ALLISON

Cover Design        TONI IHARA

Book Design         TERRI HEARSH

Proofreading        SUSAN CARLSON GREENE

Index               KATHERINE JENSEN

Printing            ARVATO SERVICES, INC.


Hallenborg, Mary Ann, 1956–
    The New York landlord's law book  /  by Mary Ann Hallenborg.--2nd ed.
        p.      cm.
    Includes index.
    ISBN 0-87337-927-6
    1. Landlord and tenant--New York (State)--Popular works.  I. Title.

KFN5145.Z9H35  2003
346.74704'34--dc21

                            2003042217

For information on bulk purchases or corporate premium sales, please contact the Special Sales Department. For academic sales or textbook adoptions, ask for Academic Sales. Call 800-955-4775 or write to Nolo at 950 Parker Street, Berkeley, CA 94710.

# Dedication

To my mother, Mary Hanlon. A perpetual source of inspiration.

# Acknowledgments

Thanks to Jake Warner and everyone at Nolo for their warmth and encouragement. Special thanks to my brilliant editor, Marcia Stewart, for her patience, good humor and unwavering commitment to making this book as useful as possible to our readers. Thanks to legal editor Janet Portman for her valuable insights on the legal issues presented in this book, and to Terri Hearsh for her work on the first edition, transforming a massive manuscript into a well-organized, visually appealing book. Thanks also to Margaret Livingston for meticulous production work on the second edition of this book, and to Toni Ihara for her creative cover design.

Thomas J. O'Hanlon, Vice President of the Real Estate Board of New York, graciously permitted us to reprint his organization's lease for rent-stabilized apartments in New York City. Michael Prinz, of the Rent Stabilization Association of New York, supplied helpful and relevant information about the RSA's myriad services to landlords. Thanks also to Daniel Finkelstein, Esq., of the Manhattan law firm of Finkelstein Newman LLP, and to Roberta Bernstein, President of the Small Property Owners of New York, for generously agreeing to review a manuscript the size of the New York City phone book. And special thanks to Lucas A. Ferrara, Esq., a member of the Manhattan law firm of Borah, Goldstein, Altschuler & Schwartz, P.C., for taking the time to answer dozens of arcane questions about New York landlord-tenant law as they arose during the writing of this book.

Finally, my gratitude to my family, especially my husband Neil and my daughter Kate, for their love and support.

# About the Author

Mary Ann Hallenborg is a New York attorney specializing in landlord-tenant law. She has represented New York landlords and tenants in a variety of matters for over ten years. Mary Ann gained a wealth of practical experience by managing a large portfolio of apartment buildings for a New York City real estate developer for several years prior to law school.

She is the author of *New York Tenants' Rights* (Nolo), a contributing author to the legal treatise *Landlord and Tenant Practice in New York* (West Group) and has contributed numerous articles on real property issues to regional and national trade periodicals. Mary Ann is also publisher and managing editor of *Landlord-Tenant Practice Reporter* (SideBar Press), a monthly law journal for the New York real estate community. In addition, she teaches landlord-tenant law at New York University's Real Estate Institute.

# Table of Contents

Introduction

## 1  How to Choose Good Tenants and Avoid Discrimination Complaints

## 2  Preparing Leases and Rental Agreements

# 3 Basic Rent Rules

# 4 Rent Regulation

# 5 Security Deposits

## 10 Landlord's Right of Entry and Tenant's Right to Privacy

## 11 Dealing with Environmental Hazards

## 12 Collecting Overdue Rent

# 13 Terminating Month-to-Month Tenancies

# 14 Grounds for Terminating Fixed-Term and Rent-Regulated Tenancies

# 15 How to Prepare and Serve Notices Terminating Leases and Rent-Regulated Tenancies

# 16 Returning Security Deposits and Other Move-Out Issues

# 17 Lawyers and Legal Research

# Appendix I

## Resources for New York Landlords

## Appendix II
### Sample Lease Forms and Riders for NYC Rent-Stabilized Units

## Appendix III
### How to Use the Forms CD

## Appendix IV
### Tear-Out Forms

Rental Application

Consent to Background and Reference Check

Tenant References

Month-to-Month Residential Rental Agreement

Fixed-Term Residential Lease

Guaranty Agreement

Rent Receipt

Agreement for Delayed or Partial Rent Payments

Rental Agreement Rider

Agreement to Rent Increase for New Equipment or Improvement

Notice of Security Deposit Transfer

Notice of No Security Deposit Record

Building Superintendent/Property Manager Agreement

Landlord-Tenant Checklist

Move-In Letter

Security Deposit Receipt

Request for Identity of Occupants Residing in Rental Unit

Letter Seeking Additional Sublet Information

Consent to Assignment of Lease

Resident's Maintenance/Repair Request

Time Estimate for Repair

Annual Safety and Maintenance Update

Notice of Intent to Enter Dwelling Unit

Disclosure of Information on Lead-Based Paint or Lead-Based Paint Hazards

Protect Your Family From Lead in Your Home Pamphlet

Three-Day Rent Demand Notice

Authorization to Issue Notices for Landlord

# Index

# Introduction

New York is a tough place to survive as a landlord. Few businesses on Earth are as regulated—many would say over-regulated—as is renting residential real property in New York. Landlords who don't understand the complicated web of laws and regulations that govern their relationship with tenants risk lost rental income, property damage, tenant lawsuits and fines. Today, a landlord either knows and follows the law or doesn't stay in business long.

Fortunately, armed with the knowledge in this book, you can cope with the law and get on with the real business of earning a decent return on your investment. Our goal is to explain legal rights and responsibilities of New York landlords in a clear and simple manner—from meeting your repair and maintenance responsibilities to complying with rent control and rent stabilization rules. In addition to covering key laws and regulations affecting landlords in New York State, this book covers important New York City laws and regulations affecting rental housing in the five boroughs. It provides a chronological treatment of subjects important to New York landlords, from taking rental applications for vacant apartments to returning security deposits when a tenant moves out, and everything in between—including preparing a lease, hiring a super or manager, providing notice when you need to enter a tenant's apartment and dealing with tenants who pay rent late, make too much noise or cause other problems. This book covers both straightforward procedures (such as how to run a credit check) and more tricky situations that may arise (such as what to do when you suspect a tenant is dealing drugs on the property).

Whenever possible, we give you the tools you need to head off legal headaches with tenants and government agencies alike, including dozens of form letters, notices and agreements—from a rental application to a security deposit itemization. These are usually included both in tear-out form (Appendix IV of this book) and on the Forms CD in the back of this book.

We have tried to suggest ways that you, as a conscientious landlord, can both comply with the law and at the same time make a decent profit. Stripped down to one sentence, we believe this involves choosing tenants carefully, staying on top of rent collections, keeping your property in good shape and being fair and reasonable with tenants. Some New York landlords view tenants as "the enemy" and provide only minimal services. But that's shortsighted. Meeting—and sometimes exceeding—the letter of the law will keep your tenants satisfied. And in the long run, satisfied tenants help profits by paying rent on time and taking care of their units.

Finally, establish a relationship with an experienced landlord-tenant lawyer. Inevitably, tricky legal questions and problems will come up. Before, not after, you get into legal hot water, you need to line up a lawyer. The lawyer should be willing to help you help yourself as much as possible and be readily available when you need more help. This book provides specific advice on how to find and work with an attorney, including a list of lawyer referral services.

**Note:** This book doesn't cover mobile homes, condominiums, co-operatives, hotels, lofts, commercial property, the preparation of eviction papers or the prosecution of eviction proceedings or bankruptcy.

## Abbreviations Used in This Book

Throughout this book, you will find references to various statutes, regulations and court decisions that delineate and explain your legal rights and responsibilities. Most of these legal references contain standard abbreviations that we explain below. If you want to read the complete law or case (or feel like digging deeper into a particular issue), Chapter 17 tells you where you can find relevant laws, cases and other legal resources.

### New York State Statutes

| | |
|---|---|
| BCL | Business Corporation Law |
| CPLR | Civil Practice Law and Rules |
| Corrections L. | Corrections Law |
| ETPA | Emergency Tenant Protection Act |
| Env. Cons. L. | Environmental Conservation Law |
| Exec. L. | Executive Law |
| GBL | General Business Law |
| GCL | General Construction Law |
| GOL | General Obligations Law |
| Lab. L. | Labor Law |
| Mil. L | Military Law |
| MDL | Multiple Dwelling Law |
| MRL | Multiple Residence Law |
| Partnership L. | Partnership Law |
| Pub. Health L. | Public Health Law |
| RPAPL | Real Property Actions and Proceedings Law |
| RPL | Real Property Law |
| Uncon. | Unconsolidated Laws |

### New York State Regulations

| | |
|---|---|
| NYCRR | New York Code of Rules and Regulations |
| ETPR | Emergency Tenant Protection Regulations |
| RSC | Rent Stabilization Code |
| Rent & Evict. Regs. | Rent and Eviction Regulations |

| | |
|---|---|
| NYC Rent & Evict. Regs. | New York City Rent and Eviction Regulations |

### New York City Laws and Regulations

| | |
|---|---|
| NYC Adm. Code | Administrative Code of the City of New York |
| RSL | New York City Rent Stabilization Law |
| NYCCR | New York City Compilation of Rules |

### Federal Statutes

| | |
|---|---|
| U.S.C. | United States Code |

### Federal Regulations

| | |
|---|---|
| CFR | Code of Federal Regulations |

### Cases

| | |
|---|---|
| N.Y. & N.Y.2d | *New York Reports*, New York Court of Appeals (New York State's highest court) |
| A.D. & A.D.2d | *Appellate Division Reports*, New York Appellate Division |
| Misc., & Misc. 2d | *Miscellaneous Reports*, New York County and Supreme Court, New York City Appellate Term, Civil and Criminal Court |
| N.Y.S. & N.Y.S.2d | *New York Supplement*, All New York Courts |
| U.S. | *United States Reports*, United States Supreme Court |
| F.2d, F.3d | *Federal Reports*, United States Court of Appeal |
| F. Supp. | *Federal Supplement*, United States District Court |
| N.Y.L.J. | *New York Law Journal*, New York Court of Appeals, Appellate Division, Appellate Term, and decisions from the trial courts of New York City and surrounding counties. |
| WL | *Westlaw*, an electronic database |

## Guide to Icons Used in This Book

This icon refers you to organizations, books and other resources for more information about the particular issue or topic discussed in the text.

This icon alerts you to material that applies exclusively to New York City properties.

This icon alerts you to special rules that apply only to rent-controlled or rent-stabilized rental units.

This icon refers you to related information in another chapter of this book.

This is a caution to slow down and consider potential problems you may encounter when renting out apartments and residential property.

This icon means that you may be able to skip some material that doesn't apply to your situation.

The form discussed in the text is on the Forms CD included with this book and a tear-out copy is in Appendix IV.

This icon alerts you to a practical tip or good idea.

This icon lets you know when you probably need the advice of a lawyer who specializes in landlord-tenant law.

## Get a Little Help From Your Friends

Many landlords and managers have discovered the value of belonging to an association of real estate professionals. These organizations, which range from small, volunteer-run groups of landlords to substantial organizations with paid staff and lobbyists, offer a wide variety of support and services to their members. Here are some services that may be available from your landlords' association:

- legal information and updates through newsletters, publications, seminars and other means
- tenant screening and credit check services
- training and practical advice on compliance with legal responsibilities, and
- a place to meet other rental property owners and managers to exchange information and ideas.

Appendix I lists several landlord organizations and associations in New York State and New York City. If you can't find an association of rental property owners on this list, check your phone book, ask other landlords for references or contact the National Apartment Association (listed in Appendix I) whose members include many individual associations from around the country.

Appendix I also lists dozens of government agencies, local bar associations and other organizations for more information on issues, laws and regulations affecting rental property owners in New York State and New York City.

# Chapter 1

# How to Choose Good Tenants and Avoid Discrimination Complaints

hoosing a tenant is the most important decision a landlord makes, and to do it well, you need a fair and reliable system. By following the steps in this chapter, you'll maximize your chances of selecting tenants who will pay their rent on time, keep their units in good condition and not cause you any legal or practical problems later. And, you'll minimize your risk of getting hit with fair housing complaints from prospective tenants whose rental applications you had to reject.

 **Before you advertise your property for rent, make a number of basic decisions—** including how much rent to charge, whether to offer a fixed-term lease or a month-to-month tenancy, how many tenants can occupy each rental unit under local overcrowding ordinances, how big a security deposit to require and whether you'll allow pets. Making these important decisions should dovetail with writing your lease or rental agreement (see Chapter 2).

## A. Avoiding Fair Housing Complaints and Lawsuits

Now and then, a rental applicant who gets rejected files a discrimination complaint of one sort or another against the landlord. While federal, state and local fair housing laws limit what you can say and do in the tenant selection process, you can't let a fear of lawsuits curtail your legitimate efforts to find the best possible tenants. In the sections that follow, you'll learn how to develop a system for screening and choosing tenants that's fair, reasonable and legal. As you read this chapter, bear in mind four important points:

1. **You are legally free to choose among prospective tenants as long as your decisions are based on legitimate business criteria.** You are entitled to reject applicants with bad credit histories, income that you reasonably regard as insufficient to pay the rent or past behavior—such as property damage or consistent late rent payments—that makes someone a bad risk. We discuss valid, nondiscriminatory reasons

for rejecting prospective tenants in Section B, below.

2. **Fair housing laws specify clearly illegal reasons to refuse to rent to a tenant.** Federal law prohibits discrimination on the basis of race, religion, national origin, sex, familial status and disability (including recovering alcoholics and people with a past drug addiction). New York State law adds marital status and age to the list of protected categories. And New York City law adds three more categories to the list: sexual orientation, lawful occupation and citizenship status. We review the details of these laws in Section C, below.

3. **Anybody who deals with prospective tenants must follow fair housing laws.** This includes owners, landlords, managers, building superintendents and real estate agents, and all of their employees. As the property owner, you may be held legally responsible for your employees' discriminatory statements or conduct, including sexual harassment. (Chapter 6, Section F, discusses how to protect yourself from your employees' illegal acts.)

**4. Consistency is crucial when dealing with prospective tenants.** If you don't treat all tenants more or less equally—for example, if you arbitrarily set tougher standards for renting to a member of a racial minority or other protected group—you are violating federal laws and opening yourself up to lawsuits. In Sections G, H and I, below, we'll show you some tenant screening procedures that will help you select great tenants and will prove (should you ever be challenged) that you treat applicants fairly and consistently.

---

### Housing Discrimination Laws Affect Every Aspect of Your Business

Housing discrimination laws don't just cover rental applicants and your process for choosing tenants. They also protect tenants during the course of their occupancy, and even affect your right to terminate a tenancy. Here's a sampling of the types of landlord conduct prohibited by housing discrimination laws:

- advertising or making any statement that indicates a limitation or preference based on race, religion or any other protected category
- falsely denying that a rental unit is available
- setting more restrictive standards for selecting tenants
- refusing to rent to members of certain groups
- before or during the tenancy, setting different terms, conditions or privileges for rental of a dwelling unit, such as requiring larger deposits of some tenants, or adopting an inconsistent policy of responding to late rent payments
- directing certain tenants to less desirable units, known as "steering"
- during the tenancy, providing different housing services or facilities, such as making a community center or other common area available only to selected tenants, or
- terminating a tenancy for a discriminatory reason.

---

## B. Legal Reasons for Rejecting a Rental Applicant

Only certain kinds of discrimination in rental housing are illegal, such as selecting tenants on the basis of religion or race (see Section C). You are legally free to choose among prospective tenants as long as your decisions are based on valid and objective business criteria, such as the applicant's ability to pay the rent and take good care of the property. For example, you may legally refuse to rent to prospective tenants with bad credit histories, frequent bouts of unemployment or even low incomes that you reasonably regard as insufficient to pay the rent. Why? Because these criteria for tenant selection are reasonably related to your right to run your business in a competent, profitable manner (sometimes called your "legitimate business interests"). And if a person who fits one or more obvious "bad tenant risk" criteria happens to be a member of a protected group, you are still on safe legal ground as long as:

- You are consistent in your screening and treat all tenants the same way—for example, you always require a credit report for prospective tenants.
- You are not applying a generalization about people of a certain group to an individual.
- You can document your legal reasons for not renting to a prospective tenant.

But pay attention to the fact that judges, tenants' lawyers and government agencies that administer and enforce fair housing laws know full well that some landlords concoct and document legal reasons to discriminate, when the real reason is that they just don't like people with a particular racial, ethnic or religious background. So, if you refuse to rent to a person who happens to be African-American, has children or speaks only Spanish, be sure you document your legitimate business reason specific to that individual (such as insufficient income or a history of eviction for nonpayment of rent). Be prepared to show that your tenant advertising, screening and selection processes have been based on objective criteria and that a more qualified applicant has always gotten the rental unit.

This section discusses some of the common legal reasons you may use to choose or reject applicants based on your business interests.

## 1. Poor Credit Record or Income

You can legitimately refuse to rent to a prospective tenant who has a history of nonpayment of rent or whom you reasonably believe would be unable to pay rent in the future. Here's some advice on how to avoid charges of discrimination when choosing tenants on the basis of income or credit history.

**Do a credit check on every prospective tenant and base your selection on the results of that credit check.** Accepting or rejecting tenants based on objective criteria tied to a credit report is the best way to protect yourself against an accusation that you're using a bad credit history as an excuse to illegally discriminate against certain prospective tenants. For example, if you establish rules saying you won't rent to someone with bad credit or who has been evicted by a previous landlord for nonpayment of rent (information commonly found in credit reports and court records), be sure you apply this policy to all tenants. Section H shows you how to check a prospective tenant's credit history and find out whether an applicant has ever been evicted, gone through bankruptcy or been convicted of a crime.

**Don't discriminate against married or unmarried couples by counting only one spouse or partner's income.** Always consider the income of persons living together, married or unmarried, in order to avoid the accusation of marital status discrimination or sex discrimination (discussed in Section C7).

## Do You Need to Accept Section 8 Tenants?

New York landlords need not accept "Section 8" tenants, even if they previously accepted such tenants. The U.S. Housing and Urban Development's Section 8 Housing Choice Voucher Program provides rental assistance to low-income tenants, senior citizens, disabled persons and displaced families. Landlord participation in the program is voluntary. Congress repealed the "take one, take all" law, which had obligated landlords who accepted one Section 8 tenant to accept them all. (See *Salute v. Stratford Greens Garden Apartments,* 136 F.2d 293 (2d Cir. 1998).)

Under the voucher program, the federal government pays a portion of the rent directly to the landlord for eligible low-income tenants. Some landlords opt into the program in order to fill vacancies. Other landlords set a "no Section 8 tenants policy" to avoid the government red tape (extra paperwork and site inspections) that comes with leasing to a Section 8 tenant. To avoid potential discrimination claims, you should develop a consistent policy at your property as to whether Section 8 tenants may apply, and stick to it. If you accept applications from Section 8 voucher-holders, you may nevertheless screen the tenant and reject applicants who fail to meet your non-income-related screening criteria, such as good landlord references, no prior criminal convictions or bankruptcies, and the like.

For more information on the Section 8 program, contact the New York State Division of Housing and Community Renewal (DHCR), which operates the Section 8 program. DHCR's Subsidy Services Unit, located at 25 Beaver Street, Room 673, New York, NY 10004 (212-480-6672) oversees the New York City program. Outside New York City, DHCR administers the Section 8 program through a network of Local Administrators, whose addresses and phone numbers may be found on the agency's website (www.dhcr.state.ny.us).

The New York City Housing Authority (NYCHA) and the New York City Department of Housing Preservation and Development (HPD) also operate Section 8 programs in New York City. To inquire about a NYCHA-issued voucher call the agency's leased housing office in your borough. (Bronx 718-329-7701; Brooklyn 718-250-9700; Manhattan 917-492-8900; Queens 212-797-4071; Staten Island 718-556-2682.) As of early 2003, the NYCHA website had no Section 8 information for landlords.

HPD has a special Web page for owners about the Section 8 program, found at www.nyc.gov/html/hpd/html/assistance/section-8-bldg-owner.html. New York City landlords who are interested in leasing their apartments to HPD Section 8 voucher clients may call HPD's "Section 8 Marketing and Outreach Unit" at 212-863-5501 to obtain additional information about the program.

## 2. Negative References From Previous Landlords

You can legally refuse to rent to someone based on what a previous landlord or manager has to say—for example, that the tenant was consistently late paying rent, broke the lease or left the place a shambles. (Section H1 discusses how to check references with previous landlords and managers.) But be sure that the information you get is truly relevant to whether the applicant will be a good tenant.

## 3. Money Judgments and Eviction Warrants

Credit reports typically indicate whether any money judgments or eviction warrants have been issued against the applicant. This should send up a red flag. Can you reject a tenant on this basis? It depends.

If a former landlord has won an eviction warrant against the applicant, for example, or if a credit card company won a money judgment for unpaid bills, you have solid grounds to reject this person. Be careful, however, if the court record indicates that the lawsuit was settled, or was won by the applicant. Getting sued doesn't mean the applicant did anything wrong, even though you may suspect that the person is a troublemaker who just got lucky. In most situations, however, if the applicant is truly a poor prospect, the information you get from prior landlords and employers will confirm your suspicions and you can reject the applicant on these more solid grounds (negative references).

Similarly, if the applicant was or is involved in a lawsuit that had nothing to do with paying debts on time or being a responsible tenant—a custody fight, for example, or a personal injury claim—you may be on shaky ground if you base a rejection solely on that basis.

## 4. Criminal Records

Understandably, many landlords wish to check an applicant's criminal record, and credit reports will sometimes include this information. New York law prohibits credit reporting agencies from disclosing an applicant's arrest record to you, unless the arrest either resulted in a criminal conviction or in criminal charges that are still pending. (GBL § 380-j (a)(1).)

You won't get "sealed" criminal records, either. New York criminal proceedings that get dismissed or result in an acquittal are sealed and aren't available to the public. (CPLR § 160.50.) New York usually doesn't seal conviction records and makes them available to the public. A few other states, however, permit criminal conviction records to be sealed if certain requirements are met. Keep this in mind when evaluating the criminal record of an out of state applicant.

### a. Convictions

If an applicant has been convicted for criminal offenses, you are probably, with one exception, entitled to reject him on that basis. After all, a conviction or guilty plea indicates that the applicant was not, at least in that instance, a law-abiding

individual, which is a legitimate criterion for prospective tenants. The exception, however, involves convictions for past drug use: As explained in Section C4, below, past drug addiction is considered a disability, and you may not refuse to rent to someone on that basis—even if the addiction resulted in a conviction. People with convictions for the sale or manufacture of drugs, or current drug users, are not, however, protected.

### b. Pending Charges

The person who's been arrested, but not convicted poses a more difficult problem. Under our legal system, a person is presumed not guilty until the prosecution proves its case or the arrestee pleads guilty. So, is it illegal to deny housing to someone whose arrest has not (yet) resulted in a conviction? Because "arrestees" are not, unlike members of a race or religion, protected under federal or state law, you could probably reject an applicant with an arrest history without too much fear of legal consequences. But there is an easy way to avoid even the slightest risk: Chances are that a previously arrested applicant who is truly a bad risk will have plenty of other facts in his or her background (like poor credit or negative references) that will clearly justify your rejection. In short, if you do a thorough check on each applicant, you should be able to get enough information on which to base your decision.

## 5. Incomplete or Inaccurate Rental Application

A carefully designed rental application form is a key tool in choosing tenants, and we include a rental application in Section G2, below. This (or any other) application form will do its job only if the applicant provides you with all the necessary information, such as references from previous landlords. Obviously, if you can reject applicants on the basis of negative references, you can reject them for failing to allow you to check their references, or if you catch them in a lie.

### 6. Inability to Meet Legal Terms of Lease or Rental Agreement

It goes without saying that you may legally refuse to rent to someone who can't come up with the security deposit or meet some other valid condition of the tenancy, such as the length of the lease or your occupancy limits. "The Roommate Law: Be Cautious When Setting Occupancy Limits," below, discusses occupancy restrictions.

### 7. Pets

You can legally refuse to rent to people with pets and you can restrict the types or size of pets you accept. You can also, strictly speaking, let some tenants keep a pet and say no to others—because pet owners, unlike members of a religion or race, are not as a group protected by housing discrimination laws. However, from a practical point of view, an inconsistent pet policy is a bad idea because it can only result in angry, resentful tenants. Also, if the pet owner you reject is someone in a protected category and you have let someone outside of that category rent with a pet, you are courting a discrimination lawsuit.

Keep in mind that you cannot refuse to rent to someone with a "service animal" that assists a sight-impaired, deaf or physically or mentally disabled person. (42 U.S.C. § 3604(f)(3)(B); Exec. L. § 296(18)(2); NYC Adm. Code § 8-102(18).) You may, however, ask the applicant or tenant for proof (in the form of a doctor's note, for instance) that the service animal is necessary to enable that person to live safely and comfortably in your rental property.

## C. Fair Housing Laws Define Illegal Grounds for Rejecting Tenants

Not so long ago, a landlord could refuse to rent to a prospective tenant for almost any reason—because of skin color or religion, or because the tenant had children, was elderly or disabled. Some landlords even discriminated against single women, believing that they would be incapable of paying the rent. So that everyone would have the right to live where they choose, federal, state and local legislatures passed laws prohibiting housing discrimination.

Fair housing laws prohibit intentional discrimination based on race, color, religion and other protected categories. Intentional discrimination is an outright refusal to rent to an applicant or provide services to a tenant because they belong to a certain race, religion or other protected category. That's easy to understand. Now here's the hard part: More subtle, unintentional forms of discrimination are illegal too, if they have the effect of unfairly impacting a protected group. For instance, a policy that requires single women to have a co-signer on their lease, but doesn't impose the same requirement for single men, unfairly impacts women (a protected category of applicants) and is illegal.

### Display Fair Housing Posters in Rental Office, Model Apartment

Federal and state regulations require you to put up special fair housing posters wherever you normally conduct housing-related business. You must display a HUD-approved poster saying that you rent apartments in accordance with federal fair housing law (24 CFR § 110 and following), and a New York State Division of Human Rights-approved poster saying that you follow state fair housing law (9 NYCCR § 466.3(a)).

While you're not legally required to hang a New York City fair housing poster, displaying one on the wall could help if a city investigator arrives to check out a discrimination complaint against you.

Hang the fair housing posters in a prominent spot in the office or area where you greet prospective tenants and take applications. If you have a model apartment, it's a smart idea to hang a poster there, too. To get free posters, available in English and Spanish, call the appropriate federal, state or local fair housing agency. For phone numbers, see "More Information: Fair Housing Laws and Agencies," in Section F, below.

**Federal law.** The Fair Housing Act and Fair Housing Amendments Act (42 U.S.C. §§ 3601-3619, 3631), which are enforced by the U.S. Department of Housing and Urban Development (HUD), address many types of housing discrimination. They apply to all aspects of the landlord-tenant relationship throughout the U.S. The Fair Housing Act prohibits discrimination on the following grounds (called protected categories):

- Race or color or religion (Section 1)
- National origin (Section 2)
- Familial status—includes families with children under the age of 18, pregnant women and elderly persons (Section 3)
- Disability or handicap (Section 4)
- Sex, including sexual harassment (Section 5).

**State law.** New York State's Human Rights Law (Exec. L. §§ 290 and following), which is enforced by the state Division of Human Rights, prohibits housing discrimination statewide. The only exception is within New York City, where the NYC Human Rights Law applies instead of state law. The state Human Rights Law echoes federal law by outlawing discrimination based on race, color, religion, national origin, familial status, disability and sex. It also adds three more protected categories:

- Age (Section 6)
- Marital status (Section 7), and
- Sexual orientation (Section 8).

**New York City law.** The New York City Human Rights Law (NYC Adm. Code § 8-107), which is enforced by the New York City Commission on Human Rights, prohibits housing discrimination anywhere within the five boroughs. Like state law, it bans landlords from discriminating because of race, color, religion, national origin, familial status, disability, sex, age, marital status and sexual orientation. In addition, it outlaws discrimination based on:

- Lawful occupation (Section 9), and
- Citizenship status or alienage (Section 10).

In some cases, federal, state and local fair housing laws will overlap or be interpreted differently. If you are accused of discrimination, you can usually expect to be held to the standard or interpretation that best favors the applicant or tenant.

In the sections that follow, we'll look at each of the categories of illegal discrimination and explore their obvious and not-so-obvious meaning.

## Rental Property Exempt From Fair Housing Laws

Fair housing laws are far-reaching and apply to almost every rental unit in the state. But there are a few exceptions:

- Owner-occupied buildings with two or fewer units are exempt from federal, state and New York City fair housing laws, unless the landlord makes the rental unit available to the public through advertising, real estate listings or public notice.
- Single-family housing is also exempt, so long as it's rented without the use of discriminatory advertising and without a real estate broker.
- Certain types of housing operated by religious organizations that limit occupancy to their own members are exempt from federal, state and New York City laws prohibiting religious discrimination.
- Single-sex housing accommodations (such as female- or male-only dormitories or rooming houses) are exempt from state and New York City laws prohibiting sex discrimination.
- Certain housing reserved exclusively for either senior citizens (persons 62 years of age or older) or households with at least one person 55 years of age or older are exempt from age discrimination laws.

## 1. Race or Religion

It goes without saying that you should not overtly treat tenants differently because of their race or religion—for example, renting only to members of your own religion or race is obviously illegal. So is requiring a higher security deposit from African-American tenants, for instance.

But more subtle forms of discrimination can also get you in hot water. Comments that are intended to discourage an applicant or steer him to another location—such as: "You wouldn't feel comfortable in this neighborhood," or "I have an apartment in another area where I'm sure you'd feel right at home"—are also illegal.

## 2. National Origin

Like discrimination based on race or religion, discrimination based on national origin is illegal, whether it's practiced openly and deliberately or unintentionally. Under state and New York City law, national origin specifically includes a person's "ancestry," that is, the national origin of a person's parents, grandparents and other ancestors. Obviously, asking a prospective applicant "What kind of name is that?" (even if you're only trying to make friendly conversation) can get you in trouble.

Even if you are motivated by a valid business concern, but choose tenants in a way that singles out people of a particular nationality, it's still illegal. Say, for instance, that two Haitian tenants recently skipped out on you, owing you unpaid rent. So you decide to make it a practice to conduct credit checks only on Haitians. A Haitian applicant may interpret your actions as sending a negative message to Haitians in general: Haitians are not welcome because you assume all of them skip out on debts. This sort of selective policy is illegal discrimination.

On the other hand, if you require all prospective tenants to consent to a credit check, (as well as meeting your other criteria), you will get the needed information but in a nondiscriminatory way.

Discriminatory comments as well as policies can get you in trouble too, as one New York owner learned the hard way. The landlord told a Honduran applicant that she couldn't rent an apartment because "Spanish people ... like to have loud music." The applicant sued the landlord for the discriminatory statement. A federal court ordered the landlord to pay $25,447 in damages: $7,000 to compensate her for her losses, $9,736 for attorneys' fees, $2,111 for court costs and $6,000 to penalize the landlord for making the discriminatory comment. (*Gonzales v. Rakkas*, 1995 WL 451034 (E.D.N.Y., 1995).)

## 3. Familial Status and Number of Occupants

Federal, state and NYC fair housing laws prohibit "familial status" discrimination, too. This type of discrimination includes openly refusing to rent to families with children under 18 or to pregnant women. It also targets a landlord who attempts the same goal by setting overly restrictive occupancy requirements (such as decreeing that children of a certain age must have separate rooms), thereby preventing families with children from occupying smaller units. Using this ploy, a landlord might rent a two-bedroom unit to a husband and wife and their one child, but would not rent the same unit to a mother with two children. This practice, which has the effect of keeping all (or most) children out of a landlord's property, would surely be found illegal in court and would result in monetary penalties.

To avoid discrimination complaints, it's essential to maintain a consistent occupancy policy. If you allow four adults to live in a two-bedroom apartment, you had better let a couple with two children (or a single mother with three children) live in the same type of unit, or you leave yourself open to charges that you are illegally discriminating. Finally, do not inquire as to the age and sex of any children who will be sharing the same bedroom. This is their parents' business, not yours.

It would also be illegal to allow children only to occupy ground-floor units, or to designate certain apartments or buildings within an apartment community as "family" units.

**State law sets strict penalties for discriminating against families with children.** In response to widespread discrimination against families with children in New York, the state legislature passed a special law making it a criminal misdemeanor for landlords to ban children from their properties or reject applicants solely because they have a child or children (no matter how old the child is). (RPL § 236-a; see also RPL § 235-f (permitting tenants to share rental units with members of their immediate family).) Watch out—this law has teeth! Landlords who ban kids (or reject applicants because they have kids) can not only get hit with criminal charges and penalties,

## The Roommate Law: Be Cautious When Setting Occupancy Limits

To prevent overcrowding, some landlords try to limit the number of persons who can occupy a rental unit. While setting occupancy limits might seem like a smart strategy, be careful: Federal and state laws restrict your ability to cap the number of occupants who may share a dwelling.

Federal fair housing law prohibits landlords from limiting the number of *children* who may live in a rental unit. You may, however, establish a "reasonable" restriction on the number of *occupants* per unit, to prevent overcrowding. (See Clause 3 of the form lease and rental agreement in Chapter 2.) While HUD has said that a policy of two persons per bedroom will, as a general rule, be considered reasonable, state law (which you must follow) is far more generous.

New York's "Unlawful Restrictions on Occupancy" law (commonly known as the "Roommate Law") prohibits landlords from limiting occupancy of a rental unit to just the tenant(s) named on the lease or rental agreement or to the tenant and the tenant's immediate family. (RPL § 235-f.) Here's how the state law works:

- If you sign a lease or rental agreement with one tenant, you must, at minimum, permit the tenant to share the unit with members of the tenant's immediate family, plus one additional occupant and the occupant's dependent children, so long as the tenant occupies the unit as a primary residence.
- If you sign a lease or rental agreement with two or more co-tenants, you must permit members of each co-tenant's immediate family to share the rental unit. And, if one or more of the co-tenants moves out, you must permit one or

more additional occupants to move in, provided that:

- the total number of tenants and additional occupants actually living in the unit (not counting the occupant's dependent children) does not exceed the total number of tenants listed on the lease or rental agreement, and
- at least one tenant (or a tenant's spouse) occupies the unit as a primary residence.

For detailed information on the Roommate Law, see Chapter 8, Section C.

While this may sound as though an infinite number of family members and other occupants may share a rental unit, there are limits. State law permits landlords to restrict occupancy in order to comply with local laws, regulations or ordinances. (RPL § 235-f(8).) Many localities have "overcrowding" ordinances that limit the number of people who can lawfully occupy a rental unit, based on the unit's available square footage. See, for example, NYC Adm. Code § 27-2075 (maximum number of persons who may occupy an apartment determined by dividing apartment's total livable floor area by 80 square feet); Rochester Property Code § 90-8 (every unit must have 120 square feet of habitable floor space for the first occupant, plus 70 square feet of habitable floor space for each additional occupant).

When setting occupancy limits for your property, your best bet is to use the maximum occupancy limits set under your local overcrowding law. Contact your municipal housing code enforcement office to get information about overcrowding laws or ordinances that apply where your property is located.

but can also get sued for money damages, including attorneys' fees. The only properties exempt from the law are owner-occupied one- or two-family dwellings; senior citizen housing that's subsidized, insured or guaranteed by the federal government; and mobile home parks exclusively for persons 55 or over.

## 4. Disability

You may not discriminate against people who:

- have a physical or mental disability that substantially limits one or more major life activities—including, but not limited to hearing, mobility and visual impairments, chronic alcoholism (but only if it is being addressed through a recovery program), mental illness, HIV-positive, AIDS, AIDS-Related Complex and mental retardation
- have a history or record of such a disability, or
- are regarded by others as though they have such a disability.

You may be shocked to see what is—and what is not—considered a disability. Although it may seem odd, alcoholism is classed as a protected disability. Does this mean that you must rent to a drunk? What about past, and current, drug addiction? Let's look at each of these issues.

### a. Recovering Alcoholics

You may encounter an applicant, let's call him Ted, who passes all your criteria for selecting tenants but whose personal history includes a disquieting note: Employers and past landlords let you know that Ted has a serious drinking problem that he is dealing with by attending AA meetings. As far as you can tell, Ted has not lost a job or a place to live due to his drinking problem. Can you refuse to rent to Ted for fear that he will drink away the rent, exhibit loud or inappropriate behavior or damage your property? No, you cannot, unless you can point to specific acts of misbehavior or financial shakiness that would sink any applicant, regardless of the underlying cause. Your fears alone that this might

happen (however well founded) will not legally support your refusal to rent to Ted.

In a nutshell, you may not refuse to rent to a so-called "recovering alcoholic" simply because of his status as an alcoholic—you must be able to point to specific facts other than his status as an alcoholic in recovery that render him unfit as a tenant.

Unfortunately, the agencies that enforce discrimination laws have not been very helpful in explaining what steps an alcoholic must take in order to qualify as "recovering." Regular attendance at AA meetings and counseling probably qualify, but an alcoholic who is less conscientious may not make the grade. In any event, you, as the landlord, are hardly in a position to investigate and verify an applicant's personal habits and medical history. So how can you choose tenants without risking a violation of law?

The answer lies in putting your energies into a thorough background check that will yield information that can unquestionably support a rejection at the rental office. If the applicant, recovering or not, is truly a bad risk, you'll discover facts (like job firings, bad credit or past rental property damage) independent of the thorny problem of whether the person has entered the "recovery" stage of his alcoholism.

### b. Drug Users

Under housing discrimination laws, a person who has a past drug addiction is classed as someone who has a record of a disability and, as such, is protected under fair housing laws. You may not refuse to rent to someone solely because he is an ex-addict, even if that person has felony convictions for drug use. Put another way, your fear that the person will resume his illegal drug use is not sufficient grounds to reject the applicant. If you do a thorough background check, however, and discover a rental or employment history that would defeat any applicant, you may reject the person as long as it is clear that the rejection is based on these legal reasons.

On the other hand, if the applicant has felony convictions for dealing or manufacturing illegal drugs, as distinct from convictions for possession of drugs for personal use, you may use that history as a basis of refusal. (New York law permits you to terminate a tenancy on the ground that the tenant uses the rental unit for the sale of illegal drugs or narcotics. For details, see Chapter 14, Section C.)

---

### No "Approved List of Disabilities"

The physical and mental disabilities that are covered by the Fair Housing Acts range from the obvious (wheelchair use and sensory disabilities) to those that may not be so apparent. The law protects applicants and tenants with invisible disabilities such as multiple chemical sensitivities, mental illness, past drug use and those who are HIV-positive (*Bragdon v. Abbott*, 524 U.S. 624 (1998).)

The list of groups protected by the law is not, however, set in stone. What may seem to you like an individual's hypochondria or personal quirk may become a legally accepted disability if tested in court. Tenants with hypertension have been known to ask for protection under the fair housing laws, as have tenants suffering from "building material sensitivity" (sensitivities to vapors emitted from paint, upholstery and rugs). Similarly, tenants who have a sensitivity or problem that is widespread throughout the population, such as asthma or allergies, may also win coverage under the fair housing laws.

If you have any questions as to whether a particular condition is a legally accepted disability, contact your local HUD office, the New York Human Rights Commission or the New York City's Human Rights Commission (see Appendix I for addresses and phone numbers).

---

### c.  Mental or Emotional Impairments

Like alcoholics or past drug users, applicants and tenants who had, or have (or appear to have) mental or emotional impairments must be evaluated and treated by the landlord and manager on the basis of their financial stability and histories as

tenants, not on the basis of their mental health status. Unless you can point to specific instances of past behavior that would make a prospective tenant dangerous to others, or you have other valid business criteria for rejecting the person, a refusal to rent could result in a fair housing complaint.

### d.  Questions and Actions That May Be Considered to Discriminate Against the Disabled

You may not ask a prospective tenant if she has a disability or illness, and may not ask to see medical records. If it is obvious that someone is disabled—for example, the person is in a wheelchair or wears a hearing aid—it is illegal to inquire how severely he is disabled.

Unfortunately, even the most innocuous, well-meaning question or remark can get you into trouble, especially if you decide not to rent to the person. What you might consider polite conversation may be taken as a probing question designed to discourage an applicant.

> EXAMPLE: Sam, a Vietnam veteran, was the owner of East Side Apartments. Jim, who appeared to be the same age as Sam and who used a wheelchair, applied for an apartment. Thinking that Jim might have been injured in the Vietnam War, Sam questioned Jim about the circumstances of his disability, intending only to pass the time and put Jim at ease. When Jim was not offered the apartment—because he did not meet the financial criteria that Sam applied to all applicants—he filed a complaint with HUD, alleging discrimination based on his disability. Sam's protestations that his questions were not intended to be discriminatory were unavailing and, on the advice of his attorney, Sam settled the case for several thousand dollars.

Your well-intentioned actions, as well as your words, can become the basis of a fair housing complaint. You are not allowed to steer applicants to units that you, however innocently, think would be more appropriate. For example, if you have two units for rent—one on the ground floor and one three stories up—do not fail to show both units to the applicant who is movement-impaired, however reasonable you think it would be for the person to consider only the ground-floor unit.

### e. State Law Permits Rent Discounts for the Disabled

While the general rule is that you can't discriminate against the disabled in the terms and conditions or privileges of a tenancy, you may, however, offer rent discounts to disabled tenants. (Exec. L. § 296(19).) That means you can offer the same rental unit to a qualified disabled applicant for less rent than you would charge a qualified nondisabled tenant.

### f. The Rights of Disabled Tenants to Live in an Accessible Place

You must also concern yourself with the fair housing laws after you have rented a unit to a disabled person. Under federal, state and New York City fair housing laws, landlords are required to:

- make "reasonable accommodation" for disabled tenants, at the landlord's expense. (42 U.S.C. § 3604(f)(3)(B); Exec. L. § 296(18)(3); NYC Adm. Code § 8-102(18)), and
- allow disabled tenants to make reasonable modifications of their living unit and the common areas at their expense if that is what is needed for the person to comfortably and safely live in the unit. (42 U.S.C. § 3604(f)(3)(A); Exec. L § 296(18); NYC Adm. Code § 8-102(18).)

**Accommodations.** To accommodate a disabled tenant, you're expected to adjust your rules, procedures or services where reasonable and necessary to give the tenant an equal opportunity to use and enjoy a dwelling unit or a common space. Reasonable accommodations include such things as:

- **Parking.** If you provide parking in the first place, providing a close-in, spacious parking

space for a disabled tenant. (See for example, *Shapiro v. Cadman Towers*, 51 F.3d 328 (2d Cir. 1995).) This case required a co-op to reasonably accommodate a shareholder-tenant with multiple sclerosis by providing an accessible parking spot.)

- **Service animals.** If you have a "no-pets" policy, making an exception for disabled tenants who need specially trained guide dogs, hearing dogs or emotional support pets.
- **Rent payment.** Allowing a special rent payment plan for a tenant whose finances are managed by someone else or by a government agency.
- **Reading problems.** Arranging to read all communications from management to a blind tenant.

Landlords are generally expected to pick up the tab for the costs of the accommodation unless the expense would place an undue hardship on their business. For example, a federal court ruled that a landlord could refuse a tenant's request for a wheelchair lift estimated to cost between $25,000 and $50,000 since the landlord had incurred financial losses in operating the building in the three years prior to the request. (*Rodriguez v. 551 West 157th Owners Corp.*, 992 F. Supp 385 (S.D.N.Y. 1998).)

**Modifications.** Allowing a disabled person to modify his living space to the extent necessary to make it safe and comfortable is also required, as long as the modifications will not make the unit unacceptable to the next tenant, or the disabled tenant agrees to undo the modification when he leaves. Examples of modifications undertaken by disabled tenants include:

- lowering counter tops for a wheelchair-bound tenant
- installing special faucets or door handles for persons with limited hand use
- modifying kitchen appliances to accommodate a blind tenant, and
- installing a ramp to allow a wheelchair-bound tenant to negotiate two steps up to a raised lobby or corridor.

The tenant must get your prior approval and bear all of the costs for modifications to the rental unit. You're entitled to ask for a detailed description of the proposed modifications, proof that they will be done in a workmanlike manner and evidence that the tenant will obtain any necessary building permits. If the tenant proposes to modify the rental unit to an extent that will require restoration later when the tenant leaves (such as repositioning the kitchen counters), you may request that the tenant pay into an interest-bearing escrow account the amount estimated for the restoration. (The interest belongs to the tenant.)

**Verification.** If a tenant asks for an accommodation or wants to modify his dwelling to accommodate a disability, you may ask for proof (for example, from the tenant's physician) that the proposed accommodation or modification is necessary for the tenant to live safely and comfortably on your rental property. Say, for example, that a tenant asks you to make an exception to your no-pets policy for Fifi, an "emotional support" poodle. You may legally request a letter or other proof from the tenant's doctor, psychologist or social worker that: 1) the tenant is a patient or client, and 2) that the tenant needs Fifi to accommodate his disability.

For more information on accessibility requirements for the disabled contact HUD or one of the fair housing agencies listed in "More Information: Fair Housing Laws and Agencies," below.

## 5.  Sex and Sexual Harassment

You may not refuse to rent to a person on the basis of gender—for example, you cannot refuse to rent to a single woman solely because she is female. Neither may you impose special rules on someone because of their gender—for example, limiting upper-story apartments to single females.

 **New York City landlords may not discriminate against transgendered individuals.** New York City has long prohibited housing discrimination based on actual or perceived gender. Since 2002, the definition of gender includes "a person's gender identity, self image, appearance, behavior or expression, whether or not that gender identity, self image, appearance, behavior or expression is differ-

ent from that traditionally associated with the legal sex assigned to that person at birth." Similar legislation has been enacted in Rochester and in Suffolk County.

Illegal sex discrimination also includes sexual harassment—refusing to rent to a person who resists your sexual advances, or making life difficult for a tenant who has resisted such advances. Suggestive comments, like "I'll rent you an apartment if you're *nice* to me," can lead to a valid complaint against you by an applicant.

## 6.  Age

We are reminded often that ours is an aging society. With the increase in the number of older adults comes the need for appropriate housing. Some older tenants may not, however, be able to live completely independently—for example, they may rely on the regular assistance of a nearby adult child or friend. Can you, as the landlord, refuse to rent to an older person solely because you fear that her frailty or dimming memory will pose a threat to the health or safety of the rest of your tenants? Or, can you favor younger tenants over equally qualified elderly tenants because you would like your property to have a youthful appearance?

The answer to these questions is "No." You may feel that your worry about elderly tenants is well founded, but unless you can point to an actual incident or to facts that will substantiate your concern, you cannot reject an elderly applicant on the basis of your fears alone. For example, you could turn away an older applicant if you learned from a prior landlord or employer that the person regularly forgot to lock the doors, failed to manage his income so that he was often late in paying rent or demonstrated an inability to undertake basic housekeeping chores. In other words, if the applicant has demonstrated that he or she is unable to live alone, your regular and thorough background check should supply you with those facts, which are legally defensible reasons to refuse to rent. As for your stylistic preference for youthful tenants, this is age discrimination in its purest form and it will never survive a fair housing complaint.

EXAMPLE 1: Nora's 80-year-old mother Ethel decided that it was time to find a smaller place and move closer to her daughter. Ethel sold her home and applied for a one-bedroom apartment at SoHo Lofts. Ethel had impeccable references from neighbors and employers and an outstanding credit history. Nonetheless, Armand, the manager of SoHo Lofts, was concerned about Ethel's age. Fearful that Ethel might forget to turn off the stove, lose her key or do any number of other dangerous things, Armand decided on the spot not to rent to her. Ethel filed a fair housing complaint, which she won on the basis of age discrimination.

Learning from his experience with Ethel, Armand, the manager at SoHo Lofts, became more conscientious in screening tenants. The following example shows how he avoided another lawsuit on age discrimination.

EXAMPLE 2: William was an elderly gentleman who decided to sell the family home and rent an apartment in the city after his wife passed away. He applied for an apartment at SoHo Lofts. Since William had no prior rental history, Armand, the manager, called each of William's personal references. From these sources, Armand learned that William had been unable to take care of himself the last few years, having been completely dependent on his wife. Armand also learned that, since his wife's death, William had made several desperate calls to neighbors and family when he had been unable to extinguish a negligently started kitchen fire, find his keys and maintain basic levels of cleanliness in his house. Armand noted these findings on William's application and declined to rent to him on the basis of these specific facts.

While the general rule is that you can't discriminate in the terms and conditions or privileges of a tenancy on the basis of an applicant's age, you may however offer rent discounts to people 65 years of

age or older. (Exec. L. § 296(17).) That means you can offer the same rental unit to a qualified senior citizen for less rent than you would charge a qualified applicant who is under 65.

And, remember, certain types of senior citizen housing are exempt from fair housing laws—that is, they can restrict tenants to only senior citizens. See "Rental Property Exempt From Fair Housing Laws," above.

## Renting to Minors

You may wonder whether the prohibition against age discrimination applies to minors (people under age 18). A minor applicant who is legally "emancipated"—is legally married, or has a court order of emancipation or is in the military—has the same status as an adult. This means you will need to treat the applicant like any other adult. In short, if the applicant satisfies the rental criteria that you apply to everyone, a refusal to rent to a minor could form the basis of a fair housing complaint. On the other hand, if the applicant is not emancipated, she lacks the legal capacity to enter into a legally binding rental agreement with you, and the prohibitions against age-related discrimination do not apply. (Exec. L. § 296(5)(f); NYC Adm. Code § 8-107(5)(g).)

## 7. Marital Status

Both New York State and New York City prohibit "marital status" discrimination. (Exec. L. § 296; NYC Adm. Code § 8-107.) Oddly though, protection extends only to married couples, meaning that you may not prefer single, platonic co-tenants (or one-person tenancies) over married couples. Not vice versa.

Strictly speaking, a "married couples only" policy won't expose the landlord to a charge of discrimination on the basis of marital status (*Hudson View Properties v. Weiss*, 59 N.Y.2d 733 (1983)), but such a policy may be found to be discriminatory on the basis of sexual orientation, which is now a protected category throughout New York State. For example, in *Levin v. Yeshiva University*, 96 N.Y.2d 484, 730 N.Y.S.2d 15, (N.Y. 2001), New York's highest court found that a school's policy of limiting housing to medical students, their spouses and children had a discriminatory impact on a lesbian couple who sought housing there.

A single tenant or unmarried couple might also get around a "married couples only" restriction under New York's "Roommate Law," which requires landlords to permit single tenants to share their units with an *unrelated* occupant. (RPL § 235-f; Chapter 8, Section C, covers the Roommate Law in detail.) If you sign a lease or rental agreement with one unmarried tenant, for instance, you can't stop that tenant from later inviting a friend or lover to move into the unit.

According to the New York State Attorney General's Office and the New York State Division of Human Rights, landlords should refrain from asking questions about a prospective tenant's past or present marital status or future plans for marriage. (Opinion of the N.Y. Att. Gen. 85-F45.) We recommend you follow this advice to avoid discriminating on the basis of marital status.

## 8. Sexual Orientation

"Sexual orientation" discrimination is prohibited statewide. (Exec. L. § 296(5); NYC Adm. Code 8-102).) However, the State and City laws define the term a little differently. The New York State Human Rights Law defines sexual orientation as "heterosexuality, homosexuality, bisexuality, or asexuality, whether actual or perceived." (Exec. L. § 292.) The New York City Human Rights Law defines sexual orientation as "heterosexuality, homosexuality, or bisexuality." (NYC Adm.Code § 8-107.)

Both laws prohibit landlords throughout New York State from refusing to rent to a single applicant, or to a couple, because the landlord knows or suspects that the applicants are gay, lesbian, straight or anywhere in between. You also can't ask about an applicant's (or tenant's) sex life, nor may you refuse to rent to someone whose sexual orientation you disagree with or don't understand.

New York City also prohibits landlords from discriminating against transgendered individuals (discussed in Section 5, above).

## 9. Lawful Occupation

New York City landlords may not reject prospective tenants based on their chosen occupation or the type of work they do. (NYC Adm. Code § 8-107(5)(n).) The law only applies to lawful occupations, which means that you may—and should—reject applicants who engage, or have engaged in illegal occupations such as prostitution, drug sales or gambling.

> EXAMPLE: Jane, a lawyer, applied for an apartment and returned her application to Lee, the landlord. Lee had spent the better part of the last year fighting a frivolous lawsuit brought by a former tenant who was also a lawyer, and the thought of renting to another lawyer was more than Lee could bear. Jane's credit, rental and personal references were excellent, but she was turned away.
>
> Under New York City law, Jane may file a complaint against the landlord with the NYC Human Rights Commission, and be entitled to the apartment she was denied, as well as to monetary compensation and attorney's fees.

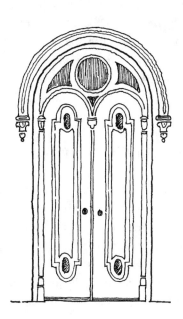

## Renting to Diplomats

Though New York City has the largest diplomatic community in the world, many New York landlords are reluctant to rent apartments to foreign states or missions for occupancy by diplomats. That's because federal courts have ruled that certain provisions of the Vienna Convention of 1961 protect diplomatic tenants from eviction, even when the tenant has violated a substantial lease obligation. (See *767 Third Avenue Associates v. Permanent Mission of the Republic of Zaire to the United Nations*, 988 F.2d 295 (2d Cir. 1993).) Some landlords will accept diplomats only if the proposed tenant agrees in the lease to waive diplomatic immunity in any summary proceeding or other legal action arising under the lease. Once diplomatic immunity is waived, a court may order the eviction of a diplomatic tenant if warranted.

Are landlords who require diplomats to waive their diplomatic immunity discriminating on the basis of "lawful occupation?" No, according to a state court judge who examined the issue. The case before the judge involved a Manhattan condominium board that refused to permit a Yugoslavian ambassador to the United Nations to rent a condo unit. The ambassador would not agree to waive diplomatic immunity with respect to any summary proceeding or other action to terminate the lease, as requested by the Board. The unit owner sued the condo board for discriminating against the ambassador on the basis of his lawful occupation, which is illegal in New York City. The judge ruled that the condo board was justi-

fied in conditioning its acceptance of the tenant on the tenant's waiver of diplomatic immunity, since otherwise, the terms of the Vienna Convention would prohibit the condo board from enforcing the lease against the diplomat. While New York City Human Rights Law makes it illegal to base a rejection of a tenant on the nature of the tenant's profession, in this case, the rejection was based on the tenant's refusal to waive diplomatic immunity, a reasonable legal protection sought by the condominium board. (*Park Tower Holding Corp. v. Board of Managers 500 Park*, N.Y.L.J., 8/5/99, p. 26, col. 5, (Sup.Ct., N.Y.County).)

**Get legal advice before renting to diplomats or foreign states.** Signing a lease with a foreign mission, consulate or state presents special legal issues. If the tenant doesn't pay rent or otherwise violates the lease, serving a foreign state with legal notices and getting around international laws that grant immunity to diplomatic missions can be problematic. In some cases, a diplomat or foreign state's occupancy could also raise special terrorism-related security issues. Fortunately, with the help of an experienced real estate attorney, you can avoid problems by adding special clauses to your lease that designate a local agent for the service of process, waive diplomatic immunity, and pass on security-related expenses to the tenant. Then, condition your acceptance of the applicant on the applicant's acceptance of the special lease clauses.

## 10. Alienage or Citizenship Status

New York City landlords may not prefer US citizens to non-citizens, nor may they base a rejection on an applicant's immigration status. (NYC Adm. Code § 8-107(5)(a).) According to the NYC Commission on Human Rights, questions such as "Do you have a green card?" or "Are you legally permitted to work in this country?" or other inquiries about whether an

applicant is an illegal alien are off-limits, even if you ask every applicant the same question.

The only exception is for public and government subsidized housing programs (such as the "Section 8 Housing Program") which require eligible tenants to be U.S. citizens or of eligible immigration status. (NYC Adm. Code § 8-107(14).) In such cases, inquiries about an applicant's citizenship and immigration status will not violate New York City law.

## D. Penalties for Housing Discrimination

An individual who suspects discrimination has one year to file a complaint with HUD, the New York State Division of Human Rights, or with the New York City Human Rights Commission. These agencies are authorized to investigate complaints and bring legal action against you, if necessary. Applicants and tenants may also file suit against you in federal court within two years or in state court within three years of the alleged discrimination. Guests of tenants may also sue landlords for housing discrimination under the federal Acts, according to one federal trial court. (*Lane v. Cole*, 88 F. Supp. 2d 402, E.D. Pa., 2000.) Landlords may always, however, impose reasonable restrictions on guest stays as discussed in Clause 3 of the form agreements in Chapter 2.

⚠ **Failure to stop a tenant from making discriminatory or harassing comments to another tenant may also get you into legal trouble.** If one tenant reports that another is making ethnic or racial slurs or threatening violence because of the their race, religion, ethnicity or other characteristic that is considered a protected category, act promptly. A simple warning may stop the problem. Depending on the situation, an eviction for tenant violation of the lease clause on quiet enjoyment of the premises (Clause 13 of the form lease and rental agreements in Chapter 2) may be warranted. If violence is involved, you'll need to act quickly and call the police. As with all tenant complaints, keep good records of conversations to protect yourself from tenant complaints that you acted illegally by failing to stop discrimination or harassment or that an eviction was illegal.

If a court housing agency finds that discrimination has taken place, it may order you to:

- rent a particular unit to the person who was discriminated against
- pay money damages to the applicant or tenant, including any additional rent the tenant had to pay elsewhere as a result of being turned down, and damages for humiliation or emotional distress
- pay the tenant punitive damages (extra money as punishment for especially outrageous discrimination) and the tenant's attorney fees
- in the case of a disability violation, retrofit your property or set up an escrow fund to be used for retrofitting in the future
- pay a penalty to the federal or local government. The maximum penalty under the federal Fair Housing Acts is $10,000 for a first violation and $50,000 for a third violation within seven years. (42 U.S.C. § 3613(g)(3).) In addition, New York State law provides for civil fines and penalties of up to $100,000 for acts found to be willful, wanton or malicious. (Exec. L. § 297.5(vi).) The New York City Human Rights Commission may order a penalty of up to $100,000 upon a finding of an unlawful discriminatory practice. (NYC Adm. Code § 8-126.)

You must defend fair housing complaints and lawsuits, even if you're innocent of the charges. In addition to your defense costs, you could be ordered to pay thousands of dollars in actual and punitive damages, civil and criminal penalties and the applicant or tenant's attorney's fees. Don't be too sure that your insurance policy will cover you here. While you can purchase insurance that will cover your costs to defend a fair housing complaint or lawsuit, if an agency or court finds that you discriminated and orders you to pay damages and penalties, you may not be covered. See "Insurance Policies and Housing Discrimination," below.

💼 **Get expert help to defend a housing discrimination lawsuit.** With the exception of a suit brought in small claims court, you should see an attorney if a tenant sues you or files an administrative complaint against you for discrimination. For more information on small claims court, see *Everybody's Guide to Small Claims Court* (National Edition) by Ralph Warner (Nolo). For advice on finding and working with an attorney or doing your own legal research, see Chapter 17.

## Insurance Policies and Housing Discrimination

Don't presume that your insurance policy will cover you for housing discrimination. The New York State Insurance Department prohibits liability insurance coverage for intentional acts of discrimination by the landlord, on public policy grounds. However, coverage is permitted for a landlord's *unintentional* acts of discrimination (known as discrimination claims based on disparate impact), and for your employees' acts of discrimination, regardless of intent. (NY State Insurance Department Circular Letter #6 (1994); see *American Management Assoc. v. Atlantic Mutual Insurance Company*, 168 Misc. 2d 971, 641 N.Y.S.2d 802 (N.Y. 1996) aff'd, 234 A.D.2d 112, 651 N.Y.S.2d 301 (1st Dep't 1996).)

Your insurer's duty to defend you (and pay all defense costs) depends on what the alleged victim of discrimination says happened. If the victim claims that you intentionally discriminated by say, refusing to rent to her because she is Latina, your insurer would have no duty to defend the suit; coverage for intentional acts of discrimination is against public policy. But if the victim says that your employee discriminated against her, or that one of your screening policies has a discriminatory effect on Latina women, your insurer will have a duty to defend, unless such coverage is specifically excluded from the policy.

Sometimes, instead of filing a lawsuit, the alleged victim will file a fair housing complaint with HUD, the New York State Commission of Human Rights, or a local fair housing agency. In such instances, the insurer's duty to defend will depend on the words of your insurance policy. Some policies exclude coverage for complaints or proceedings before administrative agencies.

## More Information: Fair Housing Laws and Agencies

If you need free fair housing posters or answers to specific fair housing questions, contact the appropriate agency listed below. Appendix I (at the back of this book) lists organizations that offer fair housing training programs for landlords and their employees.

**Federal housing law**. For more information on the rules and regulations of the Fair Housing Act (42 U.S.C. §§3601-3619, 3631), free copies of federal fair housing posters and technical assistance on accessibility requirements for the disabled, contact HUD's Information Distribution Center at 800-767-7468, or check the HUD website at www.hud.gov. You can also contact HUD's regional office by mail at 26 Federal Plaza, Room 3532, New York, NY 10278, or by phone at 212-264-5072.

**State housing law**. For more information on the rules and regulations of New York State's Human Rights Law (Exec. L. §§ 290 and following) or free copies of state fair housing posters, contact the New York State Division of Human Rights at 718-741-8400, or check their website at www.nysdhr.com. You can also contact the Division's main office by mail at One Fordham Plaza, Bronx, NY 10458.

**New York City law**. For more information on the rules and regulations of New York City's Human Rights Law (NYC Adm. Code § 8-107) or free copies of fair housing posters, contact the New York City Commission on Human Rights at 212-306-7500, or check their website at www.ci.nyc.ny.us/html/cchr/home. You can also contact the Commission's office by mail at 40 Rector Street, New York, NY 10006.

## E. Advertising Your Rental Property

You can advertise rental property in many ways:

- putting an "Apartment for Rent" sign in front of the building or in one of the windows
- taking out ads in newspapers and local magazines
- posting flyers on neighborhood bulletin boards, such as the local laundromat or coffee shop
- listing with an apartment-listing service that provides a centralized listing of rental units for a particular geographic area
- listing with a local real estate broker who handles rentals
- hiring a property management company that will advertise your rentals as part of the management fee (Chapter 6 discusses finding and hiring a property manager)
- posting a notice with a university, alumni or corporate housing office, or
- listing rental property on the Web (see "Online Apartment Listing Services," below).

### Online Apartment Listing Services

Dozens of online services now make it easy to reach potential tenants, whether they already live in your community or are moving from out of state.

**Community posting boards** allow you to list your rentals at no or low charge and are a good place to start. *Craigslist*, one of the most established community boards, has a site for New York City. Check out www.craigslist.org for details.

**National apartment listing services** are also available, with the largest ones representing millions of apartment units in the United States. Some of the most established are:

- www.homestore.com
- www.apartments.com
- www.rent.com
- www.apartmentguide.com, and
- www.forrent.com.

These national sites offer a wide range of services from simple text-only ads that provide basic information on a rental (such as the number of bedrooms), to full-scale virtual tours and floor plans of the rental property. Prices vary widely depending on the type of ad, how long you want it to run and any services you purchase (some websites provide tenant-screening services).

**Major newspapers** publish classified ads on their websites. Some of the most visited are:

- The *New York Times* (www.nyt.com). As we went to press in early 2003, it cost $75 to place a basic ad online for 14 days. Premium ads, with photos and a floor plan, cost $99.
- *The New York Daily News* (www.nydailynews.com). If you purchase a classified ad in the print edition of the *The New York Daily News*, the paper will also publish it on its website for free. In early 2003, it cost $120 to run a four-line classified ad for 14 days.
- *Village Voice* (www.villagevoice.com). If you purchase a classified ad in the weekly print edition of the *Village Voice*, the paper will also publish a color online ad. In early 2003, it cost $152 to run a four-line classified ad for two weeks. Display ads with photos and floor plans cost more.

## Make Sure Brokers and Apartment Listing Services Are Licensed

Don't give your rental listings to just any company. Real estate brokers collect commissions, application fees, security deposits and other monies from rental applicants. Sadly, some unscrupulous operators have been know to abscond with the funds they collect. To avoid problems, verify that anyone who purports to be a real estate broker or apartment listing service is, in fact, licensed. See "More Information: State Division of Licensing," in Section J, below.

## Fill Your Accessible Units

The National Accessible Apartment Clearinghouse maintains a website that connects owners of already accessible residential units with disabled tenants seeking housing: www.forrent.com/naac. To register your unit, visit their website; contact them at 201 North Union Street, Suite 200, Alexandria, VA 22314; fax 703-518-6191; or call 800-241-1221. The service is free to landlords and tenants.

The kind of advertising that will work best depends on a number of factors (such as rent, size, amenities), including the characteristics of the particular property, its location, your budget and whether you are in a hurry to rent. Many smaller landlords find that instead of advertising widely and having to screen many potential tenants in an effort to sort the good from the bad, it makes better sense to market their rentals through word-of-mouth—telling friends, colleagues, neighbors and current tenants. After all, people who already live in your property will want decent neighbors. For example, if you know a vacancy is coming up, you might visit or send a note to all tenants whom you or your manager think well of. Ask them to tell friends or relatives about the available apartment.

If you do advertise your units, try to target your ads as narrowly as possible to produce the pool of prospective tenants you want. For example, if you rent primarily to college students, your best bet is the campus newspaper or housing office.

To stay out of legal hot water when you advertise, just follow these simple rules:

**Describe the rental unit accurately.** Your ad should be easy to understand and scrupulously honest. Include basic details, such as:

- monthly rent (and if the unit is rent stabilized)
- size—particularly the number of bedrooms and baths
- location—either the general neighborhood or street address
- lease or rental agreement terms
- special features—such as river view, fireplace, big closets, remodeled kitchen, furnishings, elevator, doorman and garage
- phone number or email for more details (unless you're going to show the unit only at an open house and don't want to take calls), and
- date and time of any open house.

Read other ads to get good ideas. Some landlords find that writing a very detailed ad cuts down on the time they spend answering questions on the phone or taking calls from inappropriate tenants.

If you have any important rules (legal and nondiscriminatory), such as no pets, put them in your ad. Letting prospective tenants know about your important policies can save you or your manager from talking to a lot of unsuitable people. For example, your ad might say that you require credit checks in order to discourage applicants who have a history of paying rent late. For high-rent apartments, your ad could warn that tax returns, financial statements or pay stubs are required in order to discourage applicants who can't really afford the rent. However, rest assured that you need not list every rule in order to impose it. The wording of your ad does not legally obligate you to rent on any particular terms. In other words, just because your ad doesn't specify "no pets," you are not obligated to rent to someone with two Dobermans.

**Be sure your ad can't be construed as discriminatory.** The best way to do this is to focus only on the rental property—not on any particular type of tenant. Specifically, ads should never mention sex, race, religion, disability or age (unless your property is reserved exclusively for either senior citizens or households with at least one person age 55 or older). And ads should never imply through words, photographs or illustrations that you prefer to rent to people because of their age, sex, religion or race.

For instance, a Manhattan landlord ran six display ads for two luxury buildings in the *New York Times*. The ads, which appeared over a six-month period, featured all white models engaged in recreational activity at the landlord's buildings. Four African-Americans sued the landlord claiming that the ads violated the federal Fair Housing Act's prohibition against discriminatory advertising. A federal court agreed, ruling that the ads violated the law by suggesting a racial preference. The landlord was ordered to pay $20,000 in damages and to use non-white models in future advertising. *(Ragin v. Harry Macklowe Real Estate Co.*, 801 F. Supp. 1213 (S.D.N.Y.), modified on other grounds 6 F.3d 898 (2d Cir. 1993).)

**Quote the actual rent in your ad and stick to it.** Your ad should state the full monthly rent for the unit. Landlords who offer a discounted rent that only applies to students, for instance, or to tenants who pay rent early (before the 1st of the month), can violate consumer protection laws. Or, if a tenant who is otherwise acceptable (has a good credit history, impeccable references and meets all the criteria laid out in Section H, below), shows up promptly and agrees to all the terms set out in your ad, you may violate false advertising laws if you arbitrarily raise the price.

This doesn't mean you that you are always legally required to rent at your advertised price, however. If a tenant asks for more services or different lease terms that you feel require more rent,

it's fine to bargain and raise your price. And you can accept more rent if you're in the enviable position of having two or more applicants in a "bidding war" for a unit. Just make sure that your proposed increase doesn't violate rent stabilization laws, where applicable. (See Chapter 4 for details as to where rent stabilization laws may apply.)

**Don't advertise something you don't have.** Some large landlords, management companies and real estate brokers have advertised units that weren't really available in order to produce a large number of prospective tenants who could then be directed to higher priced or inferior units. Such bait-and-switch advertising is clearly illegal under consumer fraud laws, and many property owners have been prosecuted for such practices. So, if you advertise a sunny two-bedroom apartment next to a rose garden for $500 a month, make sure that the second bedroom isn't a closet, the rose garden isn't a beetle-infested bush and the $500 isn't the first week's rent.

Keep in mind that even if you aren't prosecuted for breaking fraud laws, your advertising promises can still come back to haunt you. A tenant who is robbed or attacked in what you advertised as a "high-security building" may sue you for medical bills, lost earnings and pain and suffering. Your best bet is not to make any oral or written representations as to security. Chapter 9, Section B16, explains this in more detail.

## F. Renting Property That's Still Occupied

Often, you can wait until the old tenant moves out to show a rental unit to prospective tenants. This gives you the chance to refurbish the unit and avoids problems such as promising the place to a new tenant, only to have the existing tenant not move out on time or leave the place a mess.

To eliminate any gap in rent, however, you may want to show a rental unit while its current tenants are still there. You can do this if your lease or rental agreement gives you access to show the unit to prospective tenants, or if the tenant consents (see Chapter 10 for details on access rules). But your current tenants are still entitled to their privacy. To minimize disturbing your current tenant, follow these guidelines:

- Before implementing your plans to find a new tenant, discuss them with outgoing tenants, so you can be as accommodating as possible.
- Give current tenants as much notice as possible before entering and showing a rental unit to prospective tenants. The tenant's lease may prescribe a minimum amount of notice. If it doesn't, at least 24 hours' notice is usually considered "reasonable." (See Chapter 10 for details.)
- Try to limit the number of times you show the unit in a given week, and make sure your current tenants agree to any evening and weekend visits.
- If possible, avoid putting a sign on the rental property itself, since this almost guarantees that your existing tenant will be bothered by strangers. Or, if you can't avoid putting up a sign, make sure any sign clearly warns against disturbing the occupant and includes a telephone number for information. Something on the order of "For Rent: Shown by Appointment Only. Call 555-1700. DO NOT DISTURB OCCUPANTS" should work fine.

If, despite your best efforts to protect their privacy, the current tenants are uncooperative or hostile, wait until they leave before showing the unit. Also, if the current tenant is a complete slob or has damaged the place, you'll be far better off to apply paint and elbow grease before trying to re-rent it.

# G. Dealing With Prospective Tenants

It's good business, as well as a sound way to protect yourself from future legal problems, to carefully screen prospective tenants.

## 1. Take Phone Calls From Prospective Tenants

➡️ If you show rental property only at open houses and don't list a phone number in your ads, skip ahead to Section 2.

### Getting a Unit Ready for Showing

It goes without saying that a clean rental unit in good repair will rent more easily than a rundown hovel. And, in the long run, it pays to keep your rental competitive. Before showing a rental unit, make sure the basics are covered:

- Clean all furnishings and rooms—floors, walls and ceilings—it's especially important that the bathroom and kitchen are spotless.
- Re-paint and re-finish floors where necessary.
- Remove all clutter from closets, cupboards and surfaces.
- Take care of any insect or rodent infestations. Remove any mousetraps, glue-boards or other pest-control devices, as they're sure to turn prospects off.
- Make sure that the appliances and fixtures work. Repair leaky faucets and running toilets, and check the unit for anything that might cause injury or violate health and safety codes, such as a broken heater or leaking roof. (Chapter 9 discusses state and local health and safety laws.)
- Consider updating old fixtures and appliances. If the unit is rent-stabilized, this is a great way to boost the legal regulated rent (see Chapter 4, for details).

If the previous tenant left the place in good shape, you may not need to do much cleaning before showing it to prospective tenants. To make this more likely, be sure to send outgoing tenants a move-out letter describing your specific cleaning requirements and conditions for returning a tenant's security deposit. (Chapter 16 discusses move-out letters.)

When prospective tenants call about the rental, it's best to describe all your general requirements—rent, deposits, pet policy, move-in date and the like—and any special rules and regulations up front. This helps you avoid wasting time showing the unit to someone who simply can't qualify—for example, someone who can't come up with the security deposit. Describing your general requirements and rules at the start may also help avoid charges of discrimination, which can occur when a member of a racial minority or a single parent is told key facts so late in the process that she jumps to the conclusion that you've made up new requirements just to keep her out.

Also be sure to tell prospective tenants about the kind of personal information they'll be expected to supply on an application, including phone numbers of previous landlords and credit and personal references.

![warning icon] **Show the property to and accept applications from everyone who's interested.** Even if, after talking to someone on the phone, you doubt that a particular applicant can qualify, it's best to politely take all applications. Refusing to take an application may unnecessarily anger a prospective tenant, and may make the applicant more likely to look into the possibility of filing a discrimination complaint. And discriminating against someone simply because you don't like the sound of their voice on the phone or on your answering machine (called linguistic profiling) is also illegal and may result in a discrimination claim. Accept applications from anyone who's interested and make decisions about who will rent the property later. Be sure to keep copies of all applications. (See discussion of recordkeeping in Section I, below.)

## 2. Have Interested Tenants Complete a Rental Application

To avoid legal problems and choose the best tenant, ask all prospective tenants to fill out a written rental application that includes information on the applicant's employment, income and credit, Social Security and driver's license numbers, past evictions or bankruptcies and references.

A sample Rental Application is shown below.

 The Forms CD includes the Rental Application. You'll also find a blank tear-out version in Appendix IV.

Before giving prospective tenants a Rental Application, complete the box at the top, filling in the property address and any deposit or credit check fee tenants must pay before moving in.

Here are some basic guidelines for accepting rental applications:

- Each prospective tenant—everyone age 18 or older who wants to live in your rental property —should completely fill out a written application. This is true whether you're renting to a married couple or to unrelated roommates, a complete stranger or the cousin of your current tenant.

- Always make sure that prospective tenants complete the entire Rental Application, including Social Security number, driver's license number or other identifying information, current employment and emergency contacts. You may need this information later to track down a tenant who skips town leaving unpaid rent or abandoned property. Also, you may need the Social Security number or other identifying information to request an applicant's credit report.

- Be sure all potential tenants sign the Rental Application, authorizing you to verify the information, contact references and run a credit report. (Some employers and others require written authorization before they will talk to you.) Although it's not legally required, it's also a good idea to obtain an applicant's okay for a credit report. You may also want to prepare a separate authorization, so that you don't need to copy the entire application and send it off every time a bank or employer wants proof that the tenant authorized you to verify the information. See the sample Consent to Background and Reference Check, below.

# Rental Application

*Separate application required from each applicant age 18 or older.*

## THIS SECTION TO BE COMPLETED BY LANDLORD

Address of Property to Be Rented: ___278 Henry St., Brooklyn, NY Apt. 2-A___

Rental Term: ☐ month-to-month ☒ lease from ___Feb. 1, 200X___ to ___Jan. 31, 200X___

### Amounts Due Prior to Occupancy

| | |
|---|---|
| First month's rent | $ 1,750 |
| Security deposit | $ 1,750 |
| Credit check fee | $ 40 |
| Other (specify): _____ | $ |
| TOTAL | $ 3,590 |

## Applicant

Full Name—include all names you use(d): ___Gustavo Rios___

Home Phone: ( 718 ) 555-1212        Work Phone: ( 212 ) 555-1212

Social Security Number: ___10-1000-1111___    Driver's License Number/State: ___NY #5555-2222-7200-55___

Other Identifying Information: _____

Vehicle Make: ___Volvo___    Model: ___700___    Color: ___Black___    Year: ___1998___

License Plate Number/State: ___NY XMG-707___

## Additional Occupants

List everyone, including children, who will live with you:

| Full Name | Relationship to Applicant |
|---|---|
| Ilsa Rios | Wife |
| Francisco Rios | Son |
| | |
| | |

## Rental History

Current Address: ___60 Cranberry St., Brooklyn, NY 11201___

Dates Lived at Address: ___2/1/00-present___    Reason for Leaving: ___Looking for bigger apt.___

Landlord/Manager: ___Paul S. Fogel___    Landlord/Manager's Phone: (718 )555-2222

Previous Address: ___235 Maple Ave., Marlton, NJ 08053___

Dates Lived at Address: ___10/30/98-1/31/00___    Reason for Leaving: ___Relocated to NYC___

Landlord/Manager: ___Arrowhead Realty Co.___    Landlord/Manager's Phone: (609 ) 555-6222

Previous Address: _5 Springfield Terr., Haddonfield, NJ 08050_

Dates Lived at Address: _8/1/96-9/30/98_     Reason for Leaving: _Too small_

Landlord/Manager: _Rev. Jack McBride_     Landlord/Manager's Phone: ( _609_ ) _555-1212_

## Employment History

Name and Address of Current Employer: _Silicon Alley Software, Inc._

_121 W. 18th St., NY, NY 10010_     Phone: ( _212_ ) _555-1212_ Ext. _121_

Name of Supervisor: _Chip Carmichael_     Supervisor's Phone: ( _212_ ) _555-1212 X121_

Dates Employed at This Job: _2/1/00-present_     Position or Title: _Web Page Designer_

Name and Address of Previous Employer: _Delaware Valley Software, Inc._

_7 Industrial Way, Mt. Laurel, NJ 08054_     Phone: ( _609_ ) _555-1212_

Name of Supervisor: _Freda Grey_     Supervisor's Phone: ( _609_ ) _555-1212_

Dates Employed at This Job: _2/1/97-12/31/97_     Position or Title: _Programmer_

## Income

1. Your gross monthly employment income (before deductions):     $ _8,000_

2. Average monthly amounts of other income (specify sources):     $ _0_

_Wife's income reported on separate application_

TOTAL:     $ _8,000/month_

## Credit and Financial Information

| Bank/Financial Accounts | Account Number | Bank/Institution | Branch |
|---|---|---|---|
| Savings Account: | 78093832 | Citibank | #46 |
| Checking Account: | 84976311 | " | " |
| Money Market or Similar Account: | 383-000343 | Chase | 100 William St., NYC |

| Credit Accounts & Loans | Type of Account (Auto loan, Visa, etc.) | Account Number | Name of Creditor | Amount Owed | Monthly Payment |
|---|---|---|---|---|---|
| Major Credit Card: | AMEX | 1010-222-28931 | | $1,000 | $1,000 |
| Major Credit Card: | MasterCard | 1213-777-68232 | Citibank | $4,300 | $120 |
| Loan (mortgage, car, student loan, etc.): | Auto Loan | 666-70-2390 | Chase | $7,500 | $319.02 |
| Other Major Obligation: | | | | | |

## Miscellaneous

Describe the number and type of pets you want to have in the rental property:     1 friendly Yellow
Labrador Retriever — 7 yrs. old

Describe water-filled furniture you want to have in the rental property:

None

Do you smoke?    ☐ yes   ☒ no

Have you ever:    Filed for bankruptcy? ☐ yes ☒ no     Been sued? ☒ yes ☐ no

                Been evicted? ☐ yes ☒ no     Been convicted of a crime? ☐ yes ☒ no

Explain any "yes" listed above:    I was sued by a former employer for prematurely ending my
employment contract. Settled pursuant to a confidential settlement agreement.

## References and Emergency Contact

Personal Reference:   Dr. Win Foley            Relationship:   College friend

Address: 101 Windam Way

        Chestnut Ridge, NY 10977        Phone: ( 914 ) 555-1212

Personal Reference:   May Lopez            Relationship:   Former co-worker

Address: 101 Greene St.

        NY, NY 10012        Phone: ( 212 ) 555-1212

Contact in Emergency:   Pedro Sanchez        Relationship:   brother

Address: 60 Pineapple St.

        Brooklyn, NY 11201        Phone: ( 718 ) 555-1212

I certify that all the information given above is true and correct and understand that my lease or rental
agreement may be terminated if I have made any false or incomplete statement in this application. I authorize
verification of the information provided in this application from my credit sources, credit bureaus, current and
previous landlords and employers and personal references.

1/8/0x           *Gustavo Rios*

Date                Applicant

Notes (Landlord/Manager):

The Forms CD includes the Consent to Background and Reference Check, and Appendix IV includes a blank, tear-out copy.

When you talk to prospective tenants, stick to questions on the application. Avoid asking questions that may discriminate, specifically any inquiries as to the person's birthplace, age, religion, marital status or children, physical or mental condition, sexual orientation, citizenship, immigration status or arrests. (See Section C for details on housing discrimination laws.) While that may seem to leave little room for conversation, you can always talk about the Yankees.

**Take your time to evaluate applications.** Landlords are often faced with anxious, sometimes desperate people who need a place to live immediately. On a weekend or holiday, especially when it's impossible to check references, a prospective tenant may tell you a terrific hard-luck story as to why normal credit- and reference-checking rules should be ignored in their case and why they should be allowed to move right in. Don't believe it. People who have planned so poorly that they will literally have to sleep in the street if they don't rent your place that day are likely to come up with similar emergencies when it comes time to pay the rent. Taking the time to screen out bad tenants will save you lots of problems later on.

Never, never let anyone stay in your property on a temporary basis. Even if you haven't signed a rental agreement or accepted rent, you give someone the legally protected status of a tenant by giving that person a key or allowing him or her to move in as much as a toothbrush. Then, if the person won't leave voluntarily, you will have to begin an eviction proceeding and get a warrant before you can get the person out.

---

## Consent to Background and Reference Check

I authorize ___Hannah Goren_____

to obtain information about me from my credit sources, court records, current and previous landlords and employers and personal references. I authorize my credit sources, credit bureaus, current and previous landlords and employers and personal references to disclose to _____Hannah Goren_____

_____ such information about me as

he or she may request.


Harmony Markowitz
_____
Name

765 Fifth Avenue, Apt. 19–C, NY, NY 10153
_____
Address

212-555-1212
_____
Phone Number

Feb. 2, 200X                        *Harmony Markowitz*
_____    _____
Date                               Applicant

## H. Checking References, Credit History and More

If an application looks good, your next step is to follow up thoroughly. The time and money you spend are some of the most cost-effective expenditures you'll ever make.

**⚠ Be consistent in your screening.** You risk a charge of illegal discrimination if you screen certain categories of applicants more stringently than others. Make it your policy, for example, to always require credit reports; don't just get a credit report for a single parent or older applicants. (Section B discusses legal reasons to refuse to rent to a tenant.)

Here are six steps of a very thorough screening process. You should always go through at least the first three to check out the applicant's previous landlords, income and employment, and run a credit check.

### 1. Check With Previous Landlords and Other References

Always call previous landlords or managers for references—even if you have a written letter of reference from a previous landlord. It's worth the cost of a long-distance phone call to weed out a tenant who may cause problems down the road. Also call previous employers and personal references listed on the application.

To organize the information you gather from these calls, use the Tenant References form, which lists key questions to ask previous landlords, managers and other references. A sample is shown below.

The Forms CD includes the Tenant References screening form, and Appendix IV includes a blank tear-out copy.

**💡 Check out pets, too.** If the prospective tenant has a dog or cat, be sure to ask previous landlords if the pet caused any damage or problems for other tenants or neighbors. It's also a good idea to meet the dog or cat, so you can make sure that it's well groomed and well behaved, before you make a final decision. You must, however, accommodate a mentally or physically disabled applicant whose pet serves as a support animal—no matter how mangy looking the pet might be. For more information on renting to tenants with pets and fair housing laws involving pets and the disabled, see Sections B7 and C4, above. Also, Clause 14 of the form lease and rental agreements in Chapter 2 discusses pet policies and legal issues.

Be sure to take notes of all your conversations and keep them on file. You may note your reasons for refusing an individual on this form—for example, negative credit information, insufficient income or your inability to verify information.

Occasionally, you may encounter a former landlord who is unwilling to provide key information. This reluctance may have nothing to do with the prospective tenant, but instead may reflect an exaggerated fear of lawsuits. And as landlords learn that their negative remarks about former tenants can be disclosed to rejected applicants if they request it (see Section H), one can expect that they will become even more circumspect. If a former landlord seems hesitant to talk, an approach that often works is to try to keep the person on the line long enough to verify the dates of the applicant's tenancy. If you get minimal cooperation, you might say something like this: "I assume your reluctance to talk about Julie has to do with one or more negative things that occurred while she was your tenant." If the former landlord doesn't say anything, you have all the answer you need. If she says instead "No, I don't talk about any former tenants—actually, Julie was fairly decent," you have broken the ice and can probably follow up with a few general questions.

### 2. Verify Income and Employment

Obviously, you want to make sure that all tenants have the income to pay the rent each month. Call the prospective tenant's employer to verify income and length of employment. Make notes on the Tenant References form, discussed above.

# Tenant References

Name of Applicant: _Linda Nichols_

Address of Rental Unit: _26 West 17th St., NY, NY 10010_

## Previous Landlord or Manager

Contact (name, property owner or manager, address of rental unit): _Michael Clark,_

_3 Hanover Square, NY, NY 10003 (212) 555-1212_

Date: _1/15/XX_

## Questions

When did tenant rent from you (move-in and move-out dates)? _12/98 thru 2/0X_

What was the monthly rent? _$1625_

Did tenant pay rent on time? _Paid late in month a few times_

Was tenant considerate of neighbors—that is, no loud parties and fair, careful use of common areas? _Yes, considerate_

Did tenant have any pets? If so, were there any problems? _Yes, she had a cat, contrary to lease._

Did tenant make any unreasonable demands or complaints? _No_

Why did tenant leave? _Don't know_

Did tenant give the proper amount of notice before leaving? _Yes_

Did tenant leave the place in good condition? Did you need to use the security deposit to cover damage?
_$100 or so applied to cover costs to fill holes in walls._

Any particular problems you'd like to mention? _No_

Would you rent to this person again? _Yes_

Other Comments: _____

**Employment Verification**

Contact (name, company, position): Keith Taylor, Cable News, Personnel Director

Date: 1/6/0X

Salary: $73,500/yr + bonus          Dates of Employment: 5/95 to present

Comments: Valued employee

**Personal Reference**

Contact (name and relationship to applicant): Susan B. Doherty, friend

Date: 1/11/0X          How long have you known the applicant? 12 years

Would you recommend this person as a prospective tenant? Yes

Comments: Former roommate. Linda is "neat as a pin," quiet, "bookish."

**Credit and Financial Information**

Mostly fine. See attached credit report.

**Notes, Including Reason for Rejecting Applicant**

Before providing this information, some employers require written authorization from the employee. You will need to mail or fax them a copy of the release included at the bottom of the Rental Application form or the separate Consent to Background and Reference Check form (Section G). If for any reason you question the income information you get by telephone—for example, you suspect a buddy of the applicant is exaggerating on his behalf—you may also ask applicants for copies of recent paycheck stubs.

It's also reasonable to require documentation of other sources of income, such as Social Security, disability, workers' compensation, public assistance, child support or alimony. To evaluate the financial resources of a self-employed person or someone who's not employed, ask for copies of recent tax returns or bank statements.

How much income is enough? Think twice before renting to someone if the rent will take more than one-third of their income, especially if they have a lot of debts.

## 3. Obtain a Credit Report

Private credit reporting agencies collect and sell credit files and other information about tenants. Many landlords find it essential to check a prospective tenant's credit history with at least one credit reporting agency to see how responsibly the applicant manages money.

**Get tenant's consent to run credit report.** Because many people think that you must have their written consent before pulling a credit report to evaluate a prospective tenant, we have included it in our consent forms (at the end of the Rental Application and in the separate Consent to Background and Reference Check form).

### a. How to Get a Credit Report

A credit report contains a gold mine of information for a prospective landlord. You may find out, for example, if a particular person has ever filed for bankruptcy or has been:

- late or delinquent in paying rent or bills, including student or car loans
- convicted of a crime
- evicted
- involved in another type of lawsuit such as a personal injury claim, or
- financially active enough to establish a credit history.

Information covers the past seven to ten years. To run a credit check, you'll need a prospective tenant's name, address and Social Security number.

If you own many rental properties and need credit reports frequently, you might consider joining one of the three largest consumer reporting agencies —Equifax, Trans Union or Experian (formerly TRW). (To contact them, see "More Information: Credit Reporting Resources," below.) Fees depend upon how many reports you order each month.

An attractive alternative to using one of the national agencies is the Rent Stabilization Association of New York City (RSA) Court and Credit tenant-screening service. This privately-run consumer reporting service is available to landlords statewide, regardless of whether their units are rent-regulated or not. The service offers up to three credit bureau reports, a New York State housing court records search, and employment, income and/or landlord verifications. The housing court search tells you whether the applicant has appeared in housing court anywhere in the state over the last seven years, and the current status of the case) Unlike the big three credit bureaus, there aren't any enrollment costs or annual fees for the service. Association members are entitled to discounts. To contact RSA, see "More Information: Credit Reporting Resources," below.

Here are phone numbers and website addresses for a few credit reporting services. You can find more tenant-screening companies in the Yellow Pages under "Credit Reporting Agencies."

**Court and Credit.** For information about the Rent Stabilization Association of New York City's tenant-screening service, call 212-214-9200 or visit the RSA's website at www.rsanyc.com.

**Equifax.** For information about joining Equifax, call 888-202-4025 or leave your name and number on its website (www.equifax.com) and a company representative will contact you.

**Trans Union.** For information about subscribing to Trans Union, call 800-888-4213; visit its website (www.tuc.com) to fill out a new subscriber application.

**Experian.** For information about membership with Experian, call 800-217-6064. For information about the company's other services, visit its website at www.experian.com.

related to your actual costs for the credit report and other application-related expenses. A fee of around $50–$75 is common.

Some landlords don't charge application fees, preferring to absorb the cost as they would any other cost of business. For low-end units, charging an extra fee can be a barrier to getting tenants in the first place, and a tenant who pays such a fee but is later rejected is likely to be annoyed and possibly more apt to try to concoct a discriminatory reason for the denial.

The Rental Application form in this book informs prospective tenants of your application fee. Be sure prospective tenants know the purpose of an application fee and understand that this fee is not a holding deposit and does not guarantee the rental unit.

**It is illegal to charge an application fee to cover the cost of processing an application and running a credit check if you do not use the money for the stated purpose and pocket it instead.** Return any application fees you don't use for that purpose.

If you do not rent to someone because of negative information obtained from a consumer reporting agency, or you charge someone a higher rent because of such information, federal and state fair credit laws require you to inform the applicant of three things:

- the reason why you rejected the applicant (or charged a higher rent)
- the name and address of the agency that reported the negative information, and
- the applicant's right to obtain a free copy of the report by requesting it from that agency within 60 days. (15 U.S.C. §§ 1681 and following; GBL § 380-i(a).)

## b. Application Fees

It's legal to charge rental applicants an "application fee" to cover the cost of a credit check and to process the application. The fee should be reasonably

## c. Investigative or Background Reports

Some credit reporting companies also gather and sell background reports about a person's character, general reputation, personal characteristics or mode of living. If you order a background check on a prospective tenant, it will be considered an "investigative consumer report" under federal and state fair credit reporting laws (15 U.S.C. §§ 1681 and following; GBL § 380-c.) You must tell the applicant, within three days of requesting the report, that the report may be made and that it will concern his character, reputation, personal characteristics and criminal history. You must also tell the applicant that more information about the nature and scope of the report will be provided upon request; and if asked, you must provide this information within five days.

If you turn down the applicant based wholly or in part on information in the report, you must tell the applicant that the application was denied based on information in the report, and give the applicant the name, address and phone number of the agency that prepared the report.

### d. What You're Looking for in a Tenant's Credit Report

In general, be leery of applicants with lots of debts—so that their monthly payments plus the rent obligation exceed 40% of their income. Also, look at the person's bill-paying habits, and, of course, pay attention to lawsuits and eviction warrants.

Sometimes, your only choice is to rent to someone with poor or fair credit. If that's your situation, you might also:

- require good references from previous landlords and employers
- require someone more creditworthy to co-sign the lease (Chapter 2 includes a guaranty agreement)
- make sure you get a good-sized deposit, as much as you can collect under New York law (see Chapter 5), and
- look at what steps the person has taken to improve credit—for example, enrolling in a debt-counseling group.

If the person has no credit history—for example, a student or recent graduate—you may reject them or consider requiring a guarantor to co-sign the lease before agreeing to rent to them.

### 4. Verify Bank Account Information

If an individual's credit history raises questions about financial stability, you may want to double-check the bank accounts listed on the rental application. If so, you'll probably need an authorization form such as the one included at the bottom of the Rental Application, or the separate Consent to Background and Reference Check (discussed in Section G, above). Banks differ as to the type of information they will provide over the phone. Generally, banks will at most only confirm that an individual has an account there and that it is in good standing.

**⚠ Be wary of an applicant who has no checking or savings account.** Tenants who offer to pay cash or with a money order should be viewed with extreme caution. Perhaps the individual bounced so many checks that the bank dropped the account or the income comes from a shady or illegitimate source—for example, from drug dealing.

### 5. Review Court Records

If your prospective tenant has lived in the state, you may want to review state court records to see if an eviction lawsuit has ever been filed against them. Checking court records may seem like overkill, since some of this information may be available on credit reports, but it's an invaluable tool, and doesn't violate housing discrimination laws as long as you check the records of every applicant. Because court records are kept for many years, this kind of information can supplement references from recent landlords. The RSA's Court and Credit service will search New York State housing records for the last seven years. (To contact RSA, see "More Information: Credit Reporting Resources," above.)

### 6. Use Megan's Law to Check State Database of Registered Sex Offenders

Not surprisingly, most landlords do not want tenants with criminal records, particularly convictions for violent crimes or crimes against children. Checking a prospective tenant's credit report, as we recommend above, is one way to find out about a person's criminal history. Self-reporting is another: Rental applications, such as the one in this book, typically ask whether the prospective tenant has ever been convicted of a crime, and, if so, to provide details.

"Megan's Law" may be able to assist you in confirming that some of the information provided in the rental application and revealed in the credit report is complete and correct. Named after a young girl who was killed by a convicted child molester who lived in her New Jersey neighborhood, this 1996 federal crime prevention law charged the FBI with keeping a nationwide database of persons convicted of sexual offenses against minors and violent sexual offenses against anyone. (42 U.S.C. §§ 14703 and following).

New York's version of Megan's Law is officially known as the New York State Sex Offender Registration Act. (Corrections L. § 168.) The law requires sexual offenders to register with the State's Division of Criminal Justice Services (DCJS) within 10 calendar days of being released from prison and to verify a home address annually for a period of at least ten years. High risk offenders must personally verify a home address with the local police every 90 days.

Prior to release from prison, offenders are evaluated as to their repeat offense risk and threat to public safety. Depending upon whether the risk is low, moderate or high, the offender receives a level one, two or three designation. Under the Act, the level of risk determines the amount of information that can be released to the public about the offender. If an offender is designated as "level one," the police are notified of his presence in the community. If the offender is "level two," the police can disseminate general information about the offender to the public. A "level three" designation authorizes the release of specific information about the offender, including his exact address.

To determine if a named individual is listed in the DCJS sex offender registry, landlords and other members of the public can call 1-900-288-3838 weekdays, between 8:00 AM and 5:00 PM. (There's a $5 fee that will appear on your telephone bill.) To be eligible to request information from the registry, you must be at least 18 years old and provide your name and address. To request a search of the registry, you must provide the name of the applicant and either her address and apartment number, driver's license number, Social Security number or birth date. Registry staff will search the database to determine whether the applicant is listed in the registry. And, if the offense was committed on or after 1996, you will also be told the applicant's re-offense risk (level one, two or three).

For more information, call the state Division of Criminal Justice Services at 518-485-7675, write them at 4 Tower Place, Albany, NY 12203-3702, or visit the DCJS website at www.criminaljustice.state .ny.us/nsor/index.htm. Inquiries to the sex offender registry can only be made through the telephone information line (900-288-3838). The DCJS will not accept inquiries about specific individuals through any other telephone number, the U.S. mail or by e-mail.

## I. Choosing—And Rejecting—An Applicant

After you've collected applications and done some screening, you can start sifting through the applicants. Start by eliminating the worst risks—people with negative references from previous landlords, a history of nonpayment of rent or poor credit or previous evictions. Section B discusses legal reasons for refusing to rent to a tenant, including convictions for criminal offenses. You'll want to arrange and preserve your information for two reasons: so that

1) you can survive a housing discrimination challenge, if a disappointed applicant files a complaint; and so

2) that you can comply with your legal duties to divulge your reasons for rejecting an applicant.

### 1. What Information Should You Keep on Rejected Applicants?

Be sure to note your reasons for rejection—such as poor credit history, pets (if you don't accept pets) or a negative reference from a previous landlord—on the Tenant References form or other paper so that you have a paper trail if an applicant asks for the reason for his rejection or accuses you of illegal discrimination. You want to be able to back up your reason for rejecting the person. Keep organized files of applications, credit reports and other materials and notes on prospective tenants for at least three years after you rent a particular unit. Keep in mind that if a rejected applicant files a complaint with a federal or state agency or files a lawsuit, your file will be made available to the applicant's lawyers. Knowing that, choose your words carefully, avoiding the obvious (slurs and exaggerations) and being scrupulously truthful.

## 2. How to Reject an Applicant

If you do not rent to someone (or you charge a higher rent) because of an insufficient credit report or negative information in the report, you must give the applicant the name and address of the agency that reported the negative information or furnished the insufficient report. This is a requirement of the federal Fair Credit Reporting Act. (15 U.S.C. §§ 1681 and following.) You must tell the applicant that the credit reporting company did not make the decision not to rent to them, and that the bureau cannot explain why the applicant was rejected. Tell the person that he has a right to obtain a free copy of his file from the agency that reported the negative information by requesting it within 60 days of being told that your rejection was based on the credit report. Finally, you have to tell applicants that they can dispute the report's accuracy and add their own "consumer statement" to their report.

The law doesn't require you to communicate an applicant's right to disclosure in writing, but it's a good idea to do so (and to keep a copy of the rejection letter in your files). That way, you'll have irrefutable proof that you complied with the law if you're ever challenged in court.

Exceptions: The federal requirements do not apply if you reject an applicant based on other sources, such as your review of his application or information you obtain from a former landlord.

Assuming you choose the best-qualified candidate (based on income, credit history and references), you have no legal problem. But what if you have a number of more or less equally qualified applicants? The best response is to use an objective tie-breaker: Give the nod to the person who applied first. If you cannot determine who applied first, strive to find some aspect of one applicant's credit history or references that objectively establishes that person as the best applicant. Be extra careful not to always select a person of the same age, sex or ethnicity. For example, if you are a larger landlord who is frequently faced with tough choices and who always avoids an equally qualified minority or disabled applicant, you are guilty of discrimination.

---

### Rating Applicants on a Numerical Scale

To substantiate your claim that you are fair to all applicants, you may be tempted to devise a numerical rating system—for example, ten points for an excellent credit report, 20 points for an excellent past landlord reference and the like. While this type of rating system may simplify your task, it has two significant drawbacks:

- Every landlord is entitled to rely on gut feelings regarding a potential tenant (as long as these are not illegally discriminatory—see Section C, above). You can decline to rent to an applicant you feel, instinctively, is a creep. You can decline to rent to him in spite of stellar recommendations or a solid financial report. Use of a numerical rating system should not limit your exercise of good sense.
- If a rejected tenant sues you, you will have to hand over your rating sheet. It will be easier to explain your decision by referring to the whole picture, rather than defending every "point" allocated in your system. You do want to be able to cite the many specific background checks you performed and used to arrive at your decision, but you do not want to lock yourself into a numerical straitjacket that you will be asked to defend.

---

### Changing Terms of the Tenancy Because of an Applicant's Credit Report

The Fair Credit Reporting Act requires that you provide an "adverse action report" to tenants whose credit report (or report from a tenant screening or reference service) affects the terms of their tenancy. (15 U.S.C. §§ 1681 and following.) For example, if you charge a higher deposit or rent, or require a cosigner on the lease because of an insufficient credit report or negative information in the report, you must provide an explanation similar to the one you give to an applicant whom you reject on these bases. For details on how to give proper notice, see the discussion in Section I2, above.

## J.  Commissions and Finder's Fees

Tenants in New York City and some other parts of the state sometimes pay real estate brokers and apartment listing services for help finding rental units. To be legally entitled to charge a brokerage commission or finder's fee from a tenant, the person collecting the fee must be licensed by the Department of State as a real estate broker, a real estate salesperson or as an apartment information vendor. (RPL § 442-d; § 446-b.)

## 1.  Real Estate Brokers

To qualify for a license, brokers must have at least one year of experience as a licensed real estate salesperson or at least two years of experience in the general real estate field—for instance, buying and selling their own property or managing property owned by their employer. Brokers must also satisfactorily complete both a 45-hour qualifying salesperson course and an additional 45-hour real estate broker course approved by the Secretary of State, and pass a qualifying examination administered by the Department of State.

There's no cap on the amount of the fee that a broker may charge a tenant. Depending on the strength of the market, brokers usually get a fee equal to one or two month's rent.

**Before giving your listings to a real estate broker, check two things:** First, make sure the broker is currently licensed by the state Division of Licensing. (For more information, see "More Information: State Division of Licensing," below.) Second, get assurances that the broker (and all salespersons who work under the supervision of the broker) understand and follow applicable fair housing laws. (Section C, above, describes the federal, state and New York City fair housing laws that must be followed by landlords and real estate brokers alike.)

## 2.  Apartment Listing Services

For a set fee (usually from around $150 to $500, up to a limit of one month's rent), apartment listing services provide apartment hunters with the addresses of available rentals in their price range and desired size and neighborhood. In order to collect a fee, apartment listing services, like brokers, must be licensed by the state Division of Licensing as "apartment information vendors." (RPL § 446-b.)

When deciding between listing with a broker and an apartment listing service, keep two considerations in mind. First, unlike brokers, apartment information vendors do not have to fulfill any educational requirements to be licensed. And second, only brokers may advertise your available unit. Vendors may not place ads for specific apartments—they may only advertise their services. (19 NYCRR § 190.8.)

## More Information: State Division of Licensing

The New York State Department of State, Division of Licensing, oversees the licensing of real estate brokers, salespersons and apartment information vendors.

To find out if a specific real estate broker or apartment listing service is currently licensed, contact a Division of Licensing Services customer service representative at 518-474-4429. For more information about real estate licenses, applications and exam schedules, call 518-474-4429, check the Department of State's website (www.dos.state.ny.us) or write to New York State Department of State, Division of Licensing Services, 84 Holland Avenue, Albany, NY 12208-3490.

**Don't charge fees to rent-stabilized tenants.** Neither the owner, nor the owner's employee, may collect a finder's fee or brokerage commission in connection with a rent-stabilized lease anywhere in the state. (RSL § 2525.1.) However, licensed brokers, salespersons and apartment information vendors who are unrelated to the owner may collect a finder's fee or commission from the tenant.

## K. Holding Deposits

Almost every landlord requires tenants to give a substantial security deposit. The laws concerning how much can be charged and when deposits must be returned are discussed in Chapters 5 and 16. Here we discuss some other fees and deposits.

Sometimes, if you make a deal with a tenant but don't actually sign a lease or rental agreement, you will want some type of cash deposit to hold the rental unit. This might happen when you want time to do a credit check or call the tenant's references. Or, it can happen if the tenant needs to borrow money (or wait for a paycheck) to come up with

enough to cover the rent and security deposit. For example, you might ask a for a few hundred dollars cash to hold the place until the tenant pays the first month's rent and any deposits you agreed on, pending the results of a credit check. Also, some tenants may want to reserve a unit while continuing to look for a better one.

While technically legal, accepting a deposit to hold a rental unit open for someone is almost always unwise. Holding deposits do you little or no good from a business point of view, and all too often result in misunderstandings or even legal fights.

EXAMPLE: A landlord, Jim, takes a deposit of several hundred dollars from a prospective tenant, Michael. What exactly is Jim promising Michael in return? To rent him the apartment? To rent Michael the apartment only if his credit checks out to Jim's satisfaction? To rent to Michael only if he comes up with the rest of the money before Jim rents to someone who offers the first month's rent and deposit? If Jim and Michael disagree about the answers to any of these questions, it can lead to needless anger and bitterness, and spill over into a small claims court lawsuit alleging breach of contract.

Another prime reason to avoid holding deposits is that the law is unclear as to what portion of a holding deposit you can keep if a would-be tenant decides not to rent or doesn't come up with the remaining rent and deposit money, or if the tenant's credit doesn't check out to your satisfaction. Some judges have ruled that the money must be held in trust for the prospective tenant, much like a security deposit. The landlord must refund the money in full if the deal doesn't work out. Other courts have ruled that you can keep an amount equal to your actual costs—for example, for more advertising and for prorated rent during the time the property was held vacant. Landlords who have tried to keep larger amounts as "liquidated damages" have been successfully sued, even when the rental application contained a clause authorizing the deduction. ("Liquidated damages" is an amount of damages agreed on in advance, say $250, which the tenant will pay to the landlord if the tenant changes his mind or doesn't qualify to rent the apartment.)

While you can accept checks for the first month's rent and the security deposit when an application is submitted to "hold" the apartment, don't cash them unless and until a lease is signed. If the deal falls through, either because you reject the application or the applicant changes her mind, give the checks back to the tenant.

You can lose precious time and rent by giving the nod to a specific applicant, only to find out that his credit is a disaster. Better to accept applications (and checks in advance) from more than one applicant. Just don't make any promises or cash any checks until you've identified the best-qualified applicant and are ready to sign a lease or rental agreement.

---

### What to Do If Your Apartment Is Hard to Rent

If you have a problem filling vacancies, resist the temptation to loosen up on your screening requirements. In the long run, a tenant who constantly pays rent late, disturbs other neighbors or damages your property is not worth the price of having your rental occupied. Instead of taking a chance on a risky applicant, consider whether the rent is too high as compared to similar properties. If so, lower it. Also, make sure the condition of the rental isn't affecting its desirability. New carpeting or linoleum may make a big difference. Some landlords have great success with resident referral programs in which you pay a premium to a tenant who refers someone to you whom you approve and sign up as a tenant. If all else fails, consider incentives such as a free month's rent or free satellite or cable TV service.

If you do provide incentives, be sure to offer them in a consistent and fair way to all eligible tenants in order to avoid charges of discrimination. Also, to avoid problems, be clear as to the terms of the freebies you're providing. For example, when exactly may the tenant use the "free" month's rent—after six months or beyond? How long will free satellite service last? How long must a referred tenant stay for you to award a premium?

## L. Landlords and the Fight Against Terrorism

In May 2002, the FBI told their field offices to alert local law enforcement, housing authorities, landlords and management personnel of a possible threat against residential rental properties from terrorists. Apparently, the FBI had vague information that terrorists had discussed rigging apartments with explosives. In particular, landlords were asked to be on the lookout for tenants who pay the entire rent in advance or who break a lease under suspicious circumstances and leave no forwarding address.

This and subsequent government advisories on possible terrorist attacks on apartment buildings have naturally engendered concern and lots of questions as to how to reduce the chances that terrorists may live in your properties. Careful tenant screening, as recommended in this chapter, is obviously the best strategy to weed out potentially dangerous tenants. As we've stressed many times in this book, however, you must not violate fair housing laws by targeting certain ethnicities—for example, people you perceive to be Moslem or from the Middle East. This chapter also discusses anti-discrimination laws and practices that apply to both potential and current tenants.

You should also keep a careful eye on your property and tenants and encourage residents and employees to report suspicious activity or materials (such as items that can be used for pipe bombs) to the local FBI as well as to you. At the same time, you should avoid violating your tenants' right to privacy as discussed in Chapter 10—unless you have been contacted by law enforcement. The USA PATRIOT ACT (PL 107-56) signed in 2001, authorizes the FBI to obtain "tangible things," including books, records or other documents for use in terrorism investigations. The FBI must, however, have an order issued by a U.S. magistrate. You may not be sued if you cooperate in good faith pursuant to this section. However, you may not disclose to anyone else that the FBI has gathered this information.

Landlords have even broader immunity against suits by tenants when they cooperate with law enforcement's anti-terrorism efforts. The PATRIOT ACT also amended the Foreign Intelligence Surveillance Act of 1978 (50 U.S.C. § 1805) to specifically assure landlords that they may not be sued by tenants when they "[furnish] any information, facilities or technical assistance in accordance with a court order or request for emergency assistance under this Act." (USA PATRIOT ACT, Title II, § 225.) While careful landlords will ask for a subpoena or warrant before they turn over tenant records or otherwise make their rental property or tenant belongings available to law enforcement, you need not do so if your only fear is a lawsuit from the affected tenants.

For more information on terrorism and rental properties, contact the local office of the FBI; a list is available at the FBI website www.fbi.gov/contact/fo/fo.htm, or by calling the FBI headquarters in Washington, D.C. at 202-324-3000.

The National Multi Housing Council (NMHC), a national landlords' membership organization, has recommendations on specific steps landlords can take to protect tenants and rental property from terrorist-related threats. These include guidelines on resident communications; rental unit inspections; screening and evaluating tenants, contractors and employees; cooperating with law enforcement and community security measures, such as keeping vacant units secured and reviewing parking lots for unattended or unauthorized vehicles. These guidelines are available to the public (not just NMHC members) at the NMHC website www.nmhc.org/Content/ServeContent.cfm?ContentItemID=2489. If you have trouble finding this section of the NMHC website, you can call the National Multi Housing Council at their Washington, D.C. office at 202-974-2300.

For additional information on preparing tenants for possible terrorist attacks, including issues for high-rise buildings, see the U.S. Department of Homeland Security website www.ready.gov. ■

# Preparing Leases and Rental Agreements

The rental agreement or lease that you and your tenant sign forms the contractual basis of your relationship. Taken together with the laws of New York State—and, in some areas, local and federal laws—it sets out almost all the legal rules you and your tenant must follow. Your rental agreement or lease is also an immensely practical document, full of crucial business details, such as how long the tenant can occupy your property and the amount of the rent.

Given their importance, there's no question that you need to create effective and legal agreements with your tenants. This chapter shows you how, by providing clearly written, fair and effective lease and rental agreement forms that are:

- legally accurate, based on careful research of New York landlord-tenant laws
- clearly written in plain English, with step-by-step instructions for each clause, and
- easily tailored to fit your own situation— whether you are upstate or down state, rent-regulated or not, with one exception: rent-stabilized units located in New York City.

 **Verify your prospective tenant's identity before signing a lease or rental agreement.** Before you sign this important document, be sure to verify that the person who completed the rental application (and whose credit and background you hopefully checked) is the same person who is signing the lease or rental agreement and taking occupancy of the rental unit. The best way to do this is to ask the tenant for a copy of her driver's license, or other form of government-issued photo identification, before you let the tenant sign the lease. Check to make sure the person sitting before you is the person whose name is on the identification card, the application you approved, and the lease or rental agreement. Many landlords make copies of the photo identification, and keep it in the tenant's file, along with the rental application and lease or rental agreement. The photo is good to have for security purposes.

 **Don't use our forms when preparing a lease for a rent-stabilized unit located in New York City.** Instead, we recommend using a special printed lease form developed by the Real Estate Board of New York, Inc. This popular lease form is tried and true, and fully complies with all laws and regulations that affect New York City rent-stabilized units. Section F, below, explains how to get and complete this lease form. Appendix II includes a sample.

# A. Which Is Better, a Lease or a Rental Agreement?

One of the key decisions you need to make is whether to use a lease or a rental agreement. To decide which is better for you, read what follows and carefully evaluate your own situation.

## 1. Month-to-Month Rental Agreement

**Skip ahead to Section 2 if the unit you wish to rent is covered by rent stabilization.** Both New York State (Emergency Tenant Protection Act or ETPA) and New York City rent stabilization laws require you to offer tenants a one- or two-year lease, at the tenant's option.

A written rental agreement provides for a tenancy for a short period of time. The law refers to these agreements as periodic, or month-to-month tenancies, although it is often legally possible to base them on other time periods—for example, if the rent were due every two weeks.

A month-to-month tenancy is automatically renewed each month unless you or your tenant gives the other the proper amount of written notice (typically 30 days) to terminate the agreement. The rental agreements in this book are month-to-month, although you can change them to a different interval.

Month-to-month rental agreements give landlords more flexibility than leases. You may increase the rent or change other terms of the tenancy on relatively short notice. You may also end the tenancy at any time, as long as you give the required amount of advance warning. (Chapter 13 discusses notice requirements and rules for changing or ending a month-to-month tenancy.) Not surprisingly, many landlords prefer to rent from month to month, particularly in urban areas with tight rental markets where new tenants can often be found in a few days and rents are trending upwards.

On the flip side, a month-to-month tenancy probably means more tenant turnover. Tenants who may legally move out with only a month's notice may be more inclined to do so than tenants who make a longer commitment. Some landlords base their rental business strategy on painstakingly seeking high-quality long-term renters. If you're one of those, or if you live in an area where it's difficult to fill vacancies, you will probably want tenants to commit for a longer period, such as a year. But, as discussed below, although a fixed-term lease may encourage tenants to stay longer, it is no guarantee against turnover.

## 2. Fixed-Term Lease

A lease is a contract that obligates both you and the tenant for a set period of time—usually a year. With a fixed-term lease, you can't raise the rent or change other terms of the tenancy until the lease runs out, unless the lease itself allows future changes or the tenant agrees in writing.

You can't ask a tenant to move out before the lease term expires unless the tenant fails to pay the rent or violates another significant term of the lease or the law, such as repeatedly making too much noise, damaging the rental unit or selling drugs on your property. (Chapter 14 discusses the reasons you may terminate a fixed-term lease.) This restriction can sometimes be problematic if you end up with a tenant you would like to be rid of but don't have sufficient cause to terminate or evict.

To take but one example, if you wish to sell the property halfway into the lease, the existence of long-term tenants—especially if they are paying less than the market rate—may be a negative factor. The new owner usually purchases all the obligations of the previous owner, including the obligation to

honor existing leases. Of course, the opposite can also be true—if you have good, long-term tenants paying a fair rent, it may be very attractive to potential new owners.

At the end of the lease term, you have several options. You can:

- decline to renew the lease—unless the lease contains a renewal option (which automatically renews the lease for a set period of time) or is covered by rent-stabilization (which provides tenants the option of renewing the lease for a one- or two-year term)
- sign a new lease for a set period, or
- do nothing—which means your lease will turn into a month-to-month tenancy if you continue to accept monthly rent from the tenant.

Chapters 14 and 15 discuss in detail how fixed-term leases end, including how to prepare and deliver termination notices. Section I, below, discusses renewal leases for rent-stabilized tenants.

Although leases restrict your flexibility, there's often a big plus to having long-term tenants. Some tenants make a serious personal commitment when they enter into a long-term lease, in part because they think they'll be liable for several months' rent if they leave early. And people who plan to be with you over the long term are often more likely to respect your property and the rights of other tenants, making the management of your rental units far easier and more pleasant.

**A lease guarantees less income security than you think.** As experienced landlords know well, it's usually not hard for a determined tenant to break a lease and avoid paying all of the money theoretically owed for the unused portion of the lease term. Some tenants, such as those in the military and certain senior citizens, may legally break a lease without penalty in specific circumstances (see Chapter 14, Section F). And in urban areas, judges sometimes require residential landlords to "mitigate" (minimize) the loss they suffer as a result of a broken lease—meaning that if a tenant moves out early, you must try to find another suitable tenant at the same or a greater rent. (This issue is discussed in Chapter 16, Section F2.)

As mentioned, you'll probably prefer to use leases in areas where there is a high vacancy rate or it is difficult to find tenants for one season of the year. For example, if you are renting near a college that is in session for only nine months a year, or in a vacation area that is deserted for months, you are far better off with a year's lease. This is especially true if you have the market clout to charge a large deposit, so that a tenant who wants to leave early has an incentive to find someone to take over the tenancy.

The Forms CD includes the Month-to-Month Residential Rental Agreement and the Fixed-Term Residential Lease. Appendix IV includes blank tear-out versions of these forms.

### Leases and Rental Agreements in a Nutshell

| Leases | Rental Agreements |
|---|---|
| You can't raise the rent or change other terms of the tenancy until the lease ends. | You may increase rent or change other terms of the tenancy on relatively short notice (subject to any restrictions of local rent control or stabilization ordinances). |
| You usually can't end the tenancy before the lease term expires, unless the tenant doesn't pay rent or violates another term of the lease. | You or the tenant may end the tenancy at any time (subject to any rent regulation restrictions) by giving the required amount of notice, typically 30 days. |

### Always Put Your Agreement in Writing

Oral leases or rental agreements are perfectly legal for month-to-month tenancies and for leases of a year or less. (GOL. § 5-703(2).) If you have an oral lease for a term exceeding one year, it becomes an oral month-to-month agreement after the first year is up. While oral agreements are easy and informal, it is never wise to use one. As time passes, people's memories (even yours) have a funny habit of becoming unreliable. You can almost count on tenants claiming that you made, but didn't keep, certain oral promises—for example, to repaint their kitchen or not increase their rent. Tenants may also forget key agreements, such as no pets. And other issues, like how deposits may be used, probably aren't covered at all. Oral leases are especially dangerous because they require that both parties accurately remember one important term—the length of the lease—over a considerable time. If something goes wrong with an oral rental agreement or lease, you and your tenants are all too likely to end up in court, arguing over who said what to whom, when and in what context.

## B. Using the Lease Forms in This Book

If the unit you wish to rent is covered by New York City rent stabilization laws, skip ahead to Section F, below.

The fill-in-the-blank lease and rental agreements in this section of the book are available in two forms:
- as files you can use with your computer, on the Forms CD enclosed with the book (see Appendix III for details on using this CD), and
- as tear-out forms in Appendix IV at the back of the book.

When you're ready to fill out a lease or rental agreement, go to Section C of this chapter for step-by-step instructions. The instructions explain how to fill in the blanks of each clause and also refer you to the chapter that discusses important issues that relate to your choices. Before you complete any clause for the first time, read the detailed discussion about it in the appropriate chapter. For example, before you complete Clause 5, which covers rent, be sure to read Chapter 3. Even if you have been a landlord for many years, reviewing the changing world of landlord-tenant law will be worthwhile.

**If any of your rental units are rent-controlled or rent-stabilized, be sure to read Chapter 4, which covers the various forms of rent regulation in New York.** There's no reason to prepare a lease for a rent-controlled tenant. But for rent-stabilized units, you'll need to prepare a so-called *vacancy lease* for the incoming tenant. A vacancy lease is the first lease you enter into with a tenant. Subsequent leases with the same tenant are called *renewal leases*. The terms of the vacancy lease must comply with applicable rent stabilization laws and regulations, and may not change or limit any of the protections or entitlements granted to rent-stabilized tenants. Section H, below, covers renewal leases.

You may want to modify our lease and rental agreement forms in some situations. The instructions suggest possible modifications for some of the clauses, as well as cautions about types of modifications likely to get you into hot water. (See "Avoid Adding Clauses That Are Unenforceable," at the end of Section C, below.) When you make changes, keep in mind that New York law requires leases and rental agreements to be written in plain English. (GOL § 5-702.) If you make extensive changes on your own, however, you may wish to have your work reviewed by an experienced landlords' lawyer. Also, see Appendix III at the end of this book for advice on editing the Forms CD.

**Don't reduce the type size on our agreements.** A residential lease or rental agreement must be printed clearly and legibly in eight point or larger type. Leases and rental agreements printed in smaller than eight point type may not be admitted as evidence in court. (CPLR § 4544.)

Don't be tempted to try to cram too many details into the lease or rental agreement. Instead, send new tenants a "move-in letter" that dovetails with the lease or rental agreement and highlights important terms of the tenancy—for example, how and where to report maintenance problems. You may also use a move-in letter to cover issues not included in the lease or rental agreement—for example, rules for use of a pool or laundry room or procedures for returning security deposits. (Chapter 7, Section C, covers move-in letters.)

**Help tenants understand the lease or rental agreement before they sign it.** Too many landlords thrust a lease or rental agreement at tenants and expect them to sign it unread. Far better to encourage tenants to ask questions about anything that's unclear, or actually review each clause with new tenants. It will save you lots of hassles later on.

## C. Completing the Lease or Rental Agreement Form

If the unit you wish to rent is covered by New York City rent stabilization laws, don't use the lease described here. Instead, skip ahead to Section F.

This section explains each clause in the lease and rental agreement forms provided in this book. A completed sample rental agreement is shown at the end of this chapter.

Except for the important difference in the term of the tenancy (see Clause 4 in the forms), leases and written rental agreements are so similar that they are sometimes hard to tell apart. Both cover the basic terms of the tenancy (such as amount of rent and date due). Except where indicated below, the clauses are identical for the lease and rental agreement. A filled-in sample rental agreement is included at the end of this chapter.

## How to Prepare Lease Riders

Although we have tried to leave adequate blank space on the lease and rental agreement forms, it's possible that you may run out of room in completing a particular clause, or you may want to add a clause. Space is obviously no problem if you use the Forms CD. But if you need to add anything to the tear-out copies of the lease or rental agreement forms, take the following steps:

1. If you want to add words to a clause, insert the words "Clause Continued on Attached Lease Rider." Similarly, if you want to add a new clause, insert the words "Lease Continued on Attached Lease Rider" after the last clause of the lease and before the place where the lease gets signed.

2. Make your own lease rider form, using a sheet of blank white paper. At the top of the form, write "Rider to Lease/Rental Agreement Between (insert the landlord and tenant's names)—Page 1 of 1." If you need more than one page, the first page of the rider is labeled "Page 1 of 2" and the second is labeled "Rider to Lease/Rental Agreement, Page 2 of 2," and so on.

3. Begin the rider with the number of the clause you're continuing or adding to the lease. Then add "a continuation of" if you're continuing a clause, or "an addition to" if you're adding a new clause.

4. Type or print the additional information on the rider.

5. You and each tenant should initial the rider at the bottom of each page, and sign the rider at the end.

6. Staple the rider to the lease or rental agreement.

## CLAUSE 1.  IDENTIFICATION OF LANDLORD AND TENANT

This Agreement is entered into on _____ , 200__, between _____ ("Tenant") and _____ ("Landlord"). Each Tenant is jointly and severally liable for the payment of rent and performance of all other terms of this Agreement.

Every lease or rental agreement must identify the tenant and the landlord or the property owner—often called the "parties" to the agreement. The term "Agreement" (a synonym for contract) refers to either the lease or rental agreement.

Any competent adult—at least 18 years of age—may be a party to a lease or rental agreement. (RPL § 11.) You can sign a lease with a minor, but be aware that within a reasonable time after turning 18, the tenant may "disaffirm," or cancel the lease. (GOL § 3-101.) A business may also be a tenant to a lease. Just make sure the business plans to use the rental unit for residential purposes only. (See Chapter 14, Section B1, for more information on permitted business uses for rental units.)

The last sentence of Clause 1 states that if you have more than one tenant, they (the co-tenants) are all "jointly and severally" liable for paying rent and abiding by the terms of the agreement. This essential bit of legalese simply means that each tenant is legally responsible for the whole rent and complying with the agreement. You can legally seek full compensation from any one of the tenants should the others skip out or be unable to pay, or evict all of the tenants even if just one has broken the terms of the lease—for example, by seriously damaging the property. Chapter 8, Section A, covers the concept of joint and several liability and discusses the legal obligations of co-tenants.

### How to Fill in Clause 1:

First, fill in the date you'll be signing the lease or rental agreement. This date is usually earlier than the date the tenancy will begin (see Clause 4). If you're not sure, leave a blank—you can easily fill in the date when you and the tenant sign the lease or rental agreement. If, however, you and the tenant are at different locations, or for some other reason you will sign the agreement on different dates, use the date of the second signature, since no contract is formed until you both sign.

Fill in the names of all tenants—adults who will live in the premises, including both members of a couple. Doing this makes everyone who signs responsible for all terms, including the full amount of the rent. Also, make sure the tenant's name matches his or her legal documents, such as a driver's license.

Take extra precautions if the tenant is a business. Be sure to include the full legal name for the business, including any endings like Inc., Corp., Ltd., Company, LLP and so on. To be on the safe side, verify the business name by asking for a copy of the company's partnership agreement or articles of incorporation. Then, make sure the person signing the lease or rental agreement is authorized to sign it on behalf of the business. Generally, corporate presidents, vice presidents and other officers can legally bind the business, as can any partner of a business organized as a partnership. (BCL § 202; Partnership L. §20.)

Also, for special issues when renting to diplomats, see Chapter 1, Section C.

## CLAUSE 2. IDENTIFICATION OF PREMISES

Subject to the terms and conditions in this Agreement, Landlord rents to Tenant, and Tenant rents from Landlord, for living purposes only, the Premises located at

_____, ("the Premises"), together with the following furnishings and appliances:

_____ .

Rental of the Premises also includes

_____ .

Clause 2 identifies the address of property being rented ("the Premises") and provides details on furnishings and extras such as a terrace or parking space. If parking is provided, the agreement should specify the number of the space provided and its exact location.

The words "for living purposes only" are included to prevent a tenant from using the property for conducting a business that might violate zoning laws, affect your insurance or adversely affect the residential character of your property. (See "Investigate Before Letting a Tenant Run a Home Business," below.)

### How to Fill in Clause 2:

Fill in the address of the unit or house you are renting, including its apartment number or other designation ("lower floor"). Also include the city, state and zip code.

Add as much detail as necessary to clarify what's included in—or excluded from—the rental premises, such as kitchen appliances. If the rental unit is fully furnished, state that here and provide detailed information on the Landlord-Tenant Checklist included in Chapter 7.

In some circumstances, you may want to elaborate on exactly what the Premises do or do not include. For example, if the rental unit includes a parking space, terrace or other area on or connected to the property, such as a gardening shed in the backyard or the use of a barn in rural areas, specifically include it in your description of the Premises. (See "How to Prepare Lease Riders" at the beginning of this section.)

### Possible Modifications to Clause 2:

If a particular part of the rental property that might be assumed to be included is not being rented, such as a garage or storage shed you wish to use yourself or rent to someone else, explicitly exclude it from your description of the Premises.

## Investigate Before Letting a Tenant Run a Home Business

Close to a million New Yorkers run a business from their house or apartment. If a tenant asks you to modify Clause 2 to allow him to operate a business, you have some checking to do—even if you are inclined to say yes.

For one, you'll need to check local zoning laws for restrictions on home-based businesses, including the type of businesses allowed (if any), the amount of car and truck traffic the business can generate, outside signs, on-street parking, the number of employees and the percentage of floor space devoted to the business. And if your rental unit is in a co-op or condominium, check the co-op by-laws or condo declaration.

You'll also want to consult your insurance company as to whether you'll need a different policy to cover potential liability of a tenant's employees or clients. In many situations, a home office will not be a problem—for example, if the tenant is a writer or artist, or someone who does solitary work at home. But if the tenant wants to operate a business, especially one with people and deliveries coming and going, such as a therapy practice, jewelry importer or small business consulting firm, you should seriously consider whether to expand or add coverage. You may also want to require that the tenant maintain certain types of liability insurance, so that you won't wind up paying if someone gets hurt on the rental property—for example, a business customer who trips and falls on the front steps.

Also be aware that if you allow a residence to be used as a commercial site, your property may need to meet the accessibility requirements of the federal Americans with Disabilities Act (ADA). For more information on the ADA, contact the Department of Justice, Office on the Americans With Disabilities Act, Civil Rights Division, in Washington, D.C., at 202-353-1555, or check their website at www.usdoj.gov/crt/ada/.

**Some child care and pet sitting businesses are okay.** Some judges have refused to evict tenants for running certain home-based businesses —even though their leases limited the tenant's permitted use of the premises to residential or living purposes only. For instance, courts have permitted tenants to conduct child care businesses from their units. The use of a rental unit for in-home family daycare furthers New York State policy favoring greater availability of in-home family daycare facilities. (*Haberman v. Gotbaum*, 698 N.Y.S. 2d 406, 182 Misc. 2d 267 (Civ. Ct., N.Y. County, 1999). When deciding if a tenant's business violates residential lease restrictions, courts look at the extent to which the business adversely affects the residential character of the building from which it's operated. (See Chapter 14, Section B, for more information on terminating a tenancy on this ground.)

## CLAUSE 3. LIMITS ON USE AND OCCUPANCY

The Premises are to be used for living purposes only for Tenant(s) listed in Clause 1 of this Agreement, by the immediate family members of the Tenant(s), and by additional occupants as defined in and only in accordance with RPL § 235-f. For purposes of this clause, immediate family members include a spouse, a sibling, a child, a stepchild, a grandchild, a parent, parent-in-law, stepparent or grandparent. In addition to the foregoing, the Premises may be occupied from time to time by guests of the Tenant(s) for a period of time not exceeding _____ days, unless a longer period is approved in writing by the Landlord. No immediate family members, additional occupants or guests may occupy the apartment unless one or more of the Tenants occupy the rental unit as a primary residence, or unless consented to in writing by the Landlord.

Clause 3 mirrors New York law by permitting the rental unit to be occupied only by the tenants and their immediate family members. (RPL § 235-f.) For purposes of this clause, immediate family members are defined as a spouse, a sibling, a child, stepchild, grandchild, a parent, parent-in-law, stepparent or grandparent. This definition is borrowed from the NYC rent stabilization law's definition of "immediate family," (9 NYCRR § 2520.2(n)) and applies to all rent-regulated units. If the rental unit is covered by rent regulation, your attempts to further limit the definition of immediate family may end up being unenforceable.

In addition to immediate family members, New York's "Roommate Law" entitles certain tenants to share their rental unit with a non-tenant roommate and their roommate's dependent children. However, the tenant must occupy the rental unit as a primary residence to be entitled to share the unit with immediate family members and non-tenant roommates. (Chapter 14, Section E, explains primary residence.) Clauses in rental agreements or leases that attempt to waive or modify a tenant's right to share a rental unit with a roommate or immediate family members are null and void. (RPL § 235-f (7).) For details on apartment

sharing and the Roommate Law, see Chapter 8, Section C.

**Avoid setting strict occupancy limits.** When setting limits on the number of occupants who may share a given rental unit, use your local "overcrowding" ordinance as a guide. Landlords who set occupancy limits that are stricter than those set by local ordinance are vulnerable to tenant lawsuits seeking damages, court costs and attorneys' fees. For more information, see "The Roommate Law: Be Cautious When Setting Occupancy Limits," in Chapter 1, Section C3.

Clause 3 also limits the length of time a tenant's guest may stay in the premises, and prohibits guests from staying there while the tenant is not in occupancy. We suggest a 30-day time limit for guests, since New York courts have often enforced such limits. Even if you do not plan to strictly enforce restrictions on guests, this provision will be very handy if a tenant tries to move in a subtenant or extra roommate without your permission by calling her a guest. It will give you the leverage you need to ask the guest to leave, request that the guest become a tenant with an appropriate increase in rent or, if necessary, evict the tenant for violating this lease provision. To avoid discrimination charges, don't make restrictions on guests that are based on the age or sex of the occupant or guest. Chapter 8, Section B, discusses guests in more detail.

**Don't discriminate against families with children.** While you can legally establish occupancy limits based on housing code or physical plant requirements, you cannot use overcrowding as an excuse for refusing to rent to tenants with children. Discrimination against families with children is illegal, except in limited situations, including certain housing reserved for senior citizens. (Chapter 1, Section C3, discusses fair housing laws and exemptions.) It's a criminal misdemeanor to insert a clause in a lease or rental agreement that requires the tenant to remain childless or not bear children during the course of the tenancy. (RPL § 237.)

### How to Fill in Clause 3:

Fill in the number of days you allow guests to stay without your consent. We suggest you allow up to 30 days, but of course you may want to modify this based on your own experience and preferences.

## CLAUSE 4. TERM OF THE TENANCY

This clause sets out the key difference between a lease and a rental agreement: how long a rent-paying tenant is entitled to stay.

### a. Lease Provision

The term of the rental will begin on _____, 200___, and end on _____ , 200___. If Tenant vacates before the term ends, Tenant will be liable for the balance of the rent for the remainder of the term.

The lease form sets a definite date for the beginning and expiration of the lease and obligates both you and the tenant for a specific term. Tenants signing leases for New York State (ETPA) rent-stabilized units have the right to select a one- or two-year lease term. (9 NYCRR § 2502.5(a).) Rent-stabilized tenants are entitled to one- or two-year renewal leases as discussed in Section H, below.

For unregulated units, most landlords offer one-year leases. This makes sense, because it allows you to raise the rent at reasonably frequent intervals if market conditions allow. Leases may be shorter (six months) or longer (24 months)—this, of course, is up to you and the tenants. A long period—two, three or even five years—can be appropriate, for example, if you're renting out your own house because you're taking a two-year sabbatical or if the tenant plans to make major repairs or remodel your property.

Chapter 16 discusses a tenant's liability for breaking a lease, what exactly happens at the end of a lease, monetary consequences if a tenant "holds over" or fails to leave after the lease ends, termination of fixed-term leases and your duty to mitigate damages. You may want to specify some of these issues in the lease or rental agreement or in a move-in letter you send new tenants (see Chapter 7).

### How to Fill in Clause 4 (Lease):

In the blanks, fill in the starting date and the expiration date.

### Possible Modifications to Clause 4 (Lease):

If you want to provide for a periodic rent increase, perhaps tied to a consumer price index or your operating expenses, you'll need to add language to this effect. Without this type of built-in increase, you can't raise the rent until the lease ends.

**Avoid liquidated damages provisions.** Some preprinted forms (not ours) include what lawyers quaintly call a "liquidated damages" clause. These require tenants who move out early to pay you a predetermined amount of money (damages) for breaking the lease. Unless the amount of liquidated damages is low, this approach is likely to be illegal. Some judges have ruled that residential landlords must do everything possible to minimize their losses and re-rent the unit. And most judges require residential tenants who move out before the lease expires to pay only for the actual losses they caused (such as rent lost). If a new tenant moves in immediately, this may be little or nothing. Chapter 16, Section F2, provides details on your responsibility to mitigate damages.

### b. Rental Agreement Provision

The rental will begin on _____, 200___, and continue on a month-to-month basis. Landlord may terminate the tenancy or modify the terms of this Agreement by giving the Tenant _____ written notice. Tenant may terminate the tenancy by giving the Landlord _____ written notice.

The rental agreement provides for a month-to-month tenancy and specifies how much written notice you must give a tenant to change or end a tenancy, and how much notice the tenant must provide you before moving out.

## How to Fill in Clause 4 (Rental Agreement):

In the first blank, fill in the date the tenancy will begin.

In the next blank, fill in the amount of written notice you'll need to give tenants to end or change a tenancy. If you are a New York City landlord, you must give tenants at least 30 days' notice. Landlords outside New York City must provide at least one month's notice. For optimal flexibility, we recommend that you fill in the minimum notice period (30 days' or one month's notice, depending where you live). You can always provide the tenant with more notice if the situation permits.

In the last blank, fill in the amount of written notice tenants must give you to end a tenancy. In New York City, month-to-month tenants are not statutorily required to give their landlords any advance written notice before moving out, unless their rental agreement requires it. We recommend requiring at least 30 days' written notice from New York City tenants. That will give you time to line up a new tenant for the unit before the departing tenant moves out. State law requires tenants outside New York City to provide at least one month's notice that they wish to end the tenancy. If you wish, you can require the tenant to give you more than the legal minimum notice. (Chapter 13 covers notice requirements for terminating a periodic rental agreement.)

Remember, you must offer tenants in rent-stabilized units the choice of a one- or two-year lease.

### Possible Modifications to Clause 4 (Rental Agreement):

This rental agreement is month-to-month, although you can change it to a different interval, such as week-to-week. If you do, also modify the notice requirements to change or end the tenancy so that all key notice periods are the same.

## CLAUSE 5. PAYMENT OF RENT AND ADDITIONAL RENT

### a. Regular monthly rent

Tenant will pay to Landlord a monthly rent of $_____, and additional rent as set forth below, payable in advance on the first day of each month, except when that day falls on a weekend or legal holiday, in which case rent is due on the next business day. Rent will be paid in the following manner unless Landlord designates otherwise.

### b. Additional rent

Tenant will pay to Landlord, as additional rent, the following monthly charges: _____, as well as any other fees or charges defined as additional rent under this Agreement.

### c. Delivery of payment

Rent and additional rent will be paid:
- ☐ by mail, to _____
- ☐ in person, at _____

### d. Form of payment

Landlord will accept payment in these forms:
- ☐ personal check made payable to _____
- ☐ cashier's check made payable to _____
- ☐ credit card
- ☐ money order
- ☐ cash
- ☐ electronic check or money transfer transmitted to:

_____

**e. Pro-rated first month's rent**

For the period from Tenant's move-in date, _____, 200__, through the end of the month, Tenant will pay to Landlord the pro-rated monthly rent of $_____. This amount will be paid on or before the date the Tenant moves in.

Clause 5 provides details on the amount of rent and when, where and how it's paid. *Monthly rent* is the rent payable by the tenant for use and occupancy of the rental unit. *Additional rent* is any extra rent or other charges the tenant agrees to pay for other services, such as parking or electricity. Clause 5 requires the tenant to pay rent and additional rent on the first day of the month, unless the first day falls on a weekend or a legal holiday, in which case rent is due on the next business day. (Extending the rent due date for holidays is legally required under New York law.) (GCL §§ 20, 24, 25, 25-a.)

We discuss how to set a legal rent and where and how rent is due in Chapter 3. Before you fill in the blanks, please read that chapter.

### How to Fill in Clause 5:

Here's how to fill in each section of Clause 5:
a. **Regular monthly rent.** State the amount of monthly rent in the first blank. For non-regulated units, you can legally charge as much rent as you want—or more practically speaking, as much as a tenant will pay. (For New York State (ETPA) rent-stabilized units, read Chapter 4 on calculating rents. For New York City rent-stabilized units, skip this section because you should not be using this lease. Go to Section F, below.)
b. **Additional rent.** Describe any fixed, monthly charges the tenant agrees to pay for services such as a parking or garage space or electricity costs.
c. **Delivery of payment.** Specify to whom and where the rent is to be paid—by mail (most common) or in person (if so, specify the

address, such as your office, to your manager or to a bank lock box).
d. **Form of payment.** Note all the forms of payment you'll accept, such as personal check and money order.
e. **Pro-rated first month's rent.** If the tenant moves in before the regular rental period—let's say in the middle of the month, and you want rent due on the first of every month—you can specify the pro-rated amount due for the first partial month. To figure out pro-rated rent, divide the monthly rent by 30 days and multiply by the number of days in the first rental period. That will avoid confusion about what you expect to be paid. Enter the move-in date, such as "June 21, 2000," and the amount of pro-rated monthly rent.

EXAMPLE: Meg rents an apartment for $900 per month with rent due on the first of the month. She moves in on June 21, so she should pay ten days' pro-rated rent of $300 when she moves in. ($900/30 = $30 X 10 days = $300.) The full $900 rent check is due on July 1.

If the tenant is moving in on the first of the month, or the same day rent is due, write in "N/A" or "Not Applicable" in the section on pro-rated rent, or delete this section of the clause.

### Possible Modifications to Clause 5:

Here are a few common ways to modify Clause 5:
**Rent due date.** You can establish a rent due date different from the first of the month, such as the day of the month on which the tenant moves in. For example, if the tenant moved in on July 10, rent would be due, in advance, on the tenth of each month, a system which of course saves the trouble of pro-rating the first month's rent.
**Frequency of rent payments.** You are not legally required to have your tenant pay rent on a monthly basis. You can modify the clause and require that the rent be paid twice a month, each week or by whatever schedule suits you.

## CLAUSE 6. LATE CHARGES

If Tenant fails to pay the rent or additional rent in full before the end of the _____ day after it's due, Tenant will pay Landlord, as additional rent, a late charge of $_____. Landlord does not waive the right to insist on payment of the rent or additional rent in full on the date it is due.

It is your legal right to charge a late fee if rent is not paid on time. This clause spells out details on your policy on late fees. For advice on setting a late charge policy, see Chapter 3, Section E.

### How to Fill in Clause 6:

In the first blank, specify when you will start charging a late fee and the amount of the late fee. You can charge a late fee the first day rent is late, but many landlords don't charge a late fee until the rent is ten or more days late.

### Possible Modifications to Clause 6:

If you decide not to charge a late fee (something we consider highly unwise), you may simply delete this clause, or write the words "N/A" or "Not Applicable" on it.

## CLAUSE 7. RETURNED CHECK AND OTHER BANK CHARGES

If any check offered by Tenant to Landlord in payment of rent or any other amount due under this Agreement is returned for lack of sufficient funds, a "stop payment" or any other reason, Tenant will pay Landlord, as additional rent, a returned check charge of $_____.

As with late charges, any bounced-check charges you require must be reasonable. Generally, you should charge no more than the amount your bank charges you for a returned check, probably $15 to $20 per returned item, plus a few dollars for your trouble.

Chapter 3, Section F, covers returned check charges.

### How to Fill in Clause 7:

In the blank, fill in the amount of the returned check charge. If you won't accept checks, you may simply delete this clause, or fill in "N/A" or "Not Applicable."

## CLAUSE 8. SECURITY DEPOSIT

On signing this Agreement, Tenant will pay to Landlord the sum of $_____ as a security deposit. Landlord will deposit this security deposit in _____ financial institution at _____. If the building in which the Premises is located contains six or more units, or if the unit is rent-stabilized, the security deposit will earn interest. Tenant may not, without Landlord's prior written consent, apply this security deposit to the last month's rent or to any other sum due under this Agreement.

If, within 60 days after Tenant has vacated and left the Premises in as good condition as it was found, except for normal wear and tear, Tenant has returned keys and provided Landlord with a forwarding address, Landlord will return the deposit in full or give Tenant an itemized written statement of the reasons for and dollar amount of any of the security deposit retained by the Landlord. Landlord may withhold all or part of Tenant's security deposit necessary to: (1) remedy any default by Tenant in the payment of rent; (2) repair damage to the Premises, except for ordinary wear and tear caused by Tenant; (3) clean the Premises if necessary, and (4) compensate Landlord for any other losses as allowed under law.

The use and return of security deposits is a frequent source of disputes between landlords and tenants. To avoid confusion and legal hassles, this clause is clear on the subject, including:
- the dollar amount of the deposit
- the name of the bank or financial institution where it will be deposited

- the fact that the deposit may not be used for the last month's rent without your prior approval
- when the deposit will be returned, and
- permitted deductions from the tenant's security deposit.

For non-regulated units, you may collect as large a deposit as you wish. For rent-stabilized units, the maximum deposit is one month's rent. You can't get around the strict security deposit rules—regardless of what your lease or rental agreement says. (GOL § 7-103(3).) That's why it's essential for landlords to know the laws on security deposits and to follow them carefully.

You must put tenant security deposits in a segregated bank account; you can't commingle, or mix, them with your own money or with your property's operating funds. Clause 8 identifies the financial institution where you will deposit the security deposit. If your building contains more than six units or if your units are rent stabilized, the security deposit account must earn interest. (GOL § 7-103.) Chapter 5 covers these rules in detail and discusses some considerations to make when setting a security deposit for both regulated and non-regulated rental units.

You have a "reasonable" time after the tenant leaves to return the tenant's deposit, adjusted for any deductions. While Clause 8 gives you up to 60 days to return the security deposit to the tenant, or to apply it to unpaid rent or other losses caused by the tenant, such as apartment repair costs, we recommend that whenever possible, you do so within 30 days after the tenant moves out. Chapter 16 discusses permitted security deposit deductions and procedures for returning security deposits.

### How to Fill in Clause 8:

Once you decide how much security deposit to charge (see Chapter 5), fill in the amount in the first blank. For non-regulated units, we suggest about two months as your rent deposit, assuming your potential tenants can afford that much. In no case is it wise to charge much less than one month's rent.

Next, fill in the name and address of the financial institution where you intend to deposit the tenant's security deposit. The rest of Clause 8 is fine as is.

### Possible Modifications to Clause 8:

If your building has fewer than six units, *and the unit is not rent-controlled or rent-stabilized,* you can delete the sentence that says that you will put the security deposit into an interest-bearing account. You may give yourself fewer than 60 days to refund the security deposit to the tenant, but giving yourself more than 60 days could be viewed by a judge as "unreasonable," and get you in trouble.

### CLAUSE 9. UTILITIES

Tenant will pay all utility charges, except for the following, which will be paid by Landlord:

_____.

This clause helps prevent misunderstandings as to who's responsible for paying utilities. Apartment building landlords normally pay for water, gas service (if there are gas appliances like stoves, laundry equipment or hot water heaters) and, in some parts of New York City, steam service. Tenants usually pay for their own electricity, phone and cable TV. When renting houses, tenants usually pay for all of the utilities themselves.

**Don't use shared meters.** So-called "shared meters," in which a tenant's gas, electric or steam meter services the tenant's rental unit as well as other areas outside the tenant's unit, are unlawful. (Public Service Law § 52(2)(a).) New York law requires landlords to eliminate shared meters by either sub-metering (so that the tenant's meter only measures service used within the tenant's unit) or by transferring the shared meter to the landlord's account.

In the blank, fill in the utilities you—not the tenants—will be responsible for paying. If you will not be paying for any utilities, simply delete the last part of the clause or write in "N/A" or "Not Applicable."

## CLAUSE 10. ASSIGNMENT AND SUBLETTING

a. **Assignment.** Tenant will not assign this Agreement without the Landlord's prior written consent. Prior to any assignment, Tenant must request permission to assign from the Landlord, in writing, and in the manner required by RPL § 226-b. Landlord may refuse to consent to an assignment for any reason or for no reason, but if the Landlord unreasonably refuses consent, Tenant may terminate this Agreement upon thirty days' notice.

b. **Subletting.** Tenant will not sublet any part of the Premises without the Landlord's prior written consent.

   1) If the building in which the Premises are located contains fewer than four (4) units, Landlord may refuse to consent to Tenant's sublet request for any reason or for no reason.

   2) If the building in which the Premises are located contains four (4) or more units, Tenant must request permission to sublet from the Landlord, in writing, and in the manner required by RPL § 226-b. Landlord may not unreasonably refuse to consent to Tenant's proper request to sublet.

c. **Fees.** Landlord may impose a reasonable fee on Tenant in connection with the review and processing of any Tenant request or application to assign or sublet.

Clause 10 prohibits tenants from assigning their agreements or subletting their units without your prior written permission.

**Assignments.** An assignment is a legal term that means your tenant transfers her entire tenancy to someone else. Clause 10 prevents your tenant from leaving in the middle of the month or lease term and moving in a replacement—maybe someone you wouldn't choose to rent to—without your consent.

By including this clause in your lease or rental agreement, you have the option not to accept the person your tenant proposes to take over the tenancy. If, however, you refuse to consent to an assignment for no reason, or unreasonably withhold consent, New York law (and Clause 10) give the tenant the option to be released from the agreement or lease upon 30 days' written notice. (RPL § 226-b.)

Chapter 8, Section E, discusses how to handle assignment requests.

**Sublets.** A sublet is a temporary arrangement where your tenant rents all or part of the Premises to someone else—who's known as the subtenant. Clause 10 requires the tenant to get your written permission before moving in a proposed subtenant. If the building in which the tenant's unit is located contains fewer than four units, the clause gives you the right to reject a proposed subtenant for any reason, or no reason.

If the building has four or more units, New York's "Sublet Law" applies and requires you to have a valid, nondiscriminatory reason for refusing to consent to a sublet. You can't reject a tenant's proper sublet request for no reason, or unreasonably withhold your consent.

If the unit is covered by New York State (ETPA) rent stabilization, a tenant may not sublet for more than a total of two years, including the term of the proposed sublease, out of the four-year period preceding the expiration date of the proposed sublease. (9 NYCRR § 2505.7(c).) The term of the sublease may, however, extend beyond the term of the rent-stabilized tenant's lease, and the landlord may not refuse to consent to a sublease on that basis.

Chapter 8 details how to respond to a tenant's sublet request, including special rules for rent-stabilized tenants.

You don't need to add anything to this clause. For month-to-month rental agreements, you may delete subparagraphs 1 and 2 from the Subletting paragraph.

## CLAUSE 11.  TENANT'S MAINTENANCE RESPONSIBILITIES

Tenant will: (1) keep the Premises clean, sanitary and in good condition and, upon termination of the tenancy, return the Premises to Landlord in a condition identical to that which existed when Tenant took occupancy, except for ordinary wear and tear; (2) immediately notify Landlord of any defects or dangerous conditions in and about the Premises of which Tenant becomes aware; and (3) reimburse Landlord, on demand by Landlord, for the cost of any repairs to the Premises damaged by Tenant or Tenant's guests or business invitees through misuse or neglect.

Tenant has examined the Premises, including appliances, fixtures, window coverings, and carpeting, if any, and has found them to be in good, safe and clean condition and repair, except as noted in the Landlord-Tenant Checklist.

Clause 11 makes the tenant responsible for keeping the rental premises clean and sanitary. This clause also makes it clear that if the tenant damages the premises (for example, by breaking a window or scratching hardwood floors), it's his responsibility for the damage. Clause 11 also requires the tenant to alert you to defective or dangerous conditions.

Before the tenant moves in, you and the tenant should inspect the rental unit and fill out the Landlord-Tenant Checklist in Chapter 7, describing what is in the unit and noting any problems.

Chapter 9 provides details on landlords' and tenants' repair and maintenance responsibilities, recommends a system for tenants to request repairs and offers practical advice on maintaining your rental property. Chapter 9 also covers tenant options (such as rent withholding) should you fail to maintain your property and keep it in good repair.

### How to Fill in Clause 11:

You do not need to add anything to this clause. If you are not using the Landlord-Tenant Checklist (described in Chapter 7), you can delete references to it in Clause 11.

⚠ **Don't fail to maintain the property.** Any words you stick into a lease or rental agreement saying a tenant gives up his right to habitable housing won't be effective. New York's warranty of habitability law obligates you to provide safe and livable housing, no matter what the agreement says. (RPL § 235-b.) And for buildings with three or more units, state law requires you to keep the unit (and common areas) in good repair. (MDL § 78; MRL § 174.) Avoiding your legal obligations to repair can lead to court-ordered rent abatements. And if your tenants or their guests suffer injury or property damage as a result of poorly maintained property, you may be held responsible for paying for the loss.

## Renters' Insurance

It is becoming increasingly popular, especially in high-end rentals, to require tenants to obtain renters' insurance. It covers losses to the tenant's belongings as a result of fire or theft. Often called a "Tenant's Package Policy," renters' insurance also covers the tenant if his negligence causes injury to other people or property damage (to his property or to yours). Besides protecting the tenant from personal liability, renters' insurance benefits you, too: If damage caused by the tenant could be covered by either his insurance policy or yours—for example, the tenant starts a fire when he leaves the stove on—a claim made on the tenant's policy will affect his premiums, not yours.

If you decide to require insurance, insert a clause like the following at the end of your lease or rental agreement, under Clause 26, Additional Provisions. This will help assure that the tenant purchases and maintains a renters' insurance policy throughout his tenancy.

⚠ **The issue of whether a landlord may require a new, rent-stabilized tenant to purchase renters' insurance is unclear.** It's possible that a court could interpret such a requirement as an illegal rent overcharge, if challenged by a tenant. There's no harm in suggesting renters' insurance to your rent-stabilized tenants. But to play it safe, stop short of mandating it. (Chapter 4 has more information on rent overcharges.)

> **Renters' Insurance**
>
> Within ten days of the signing of this Agreement, Tenant will obtain renters' insurance and provide proof of purchase to Landlord. Tenant further agrees to maintain the policy throughout the duration of the tenancy, and to furnish proof of insurance on a ☐ yearly ☐ semiannual basis.

## CLAUSE 12. REPAIRS AND ALTERATIONS BY TENANT

a. Except as provided by law, or as authorized by the prior written consent of Landlord, Tenant will not make any repairs or alterations to the Premises, including painting, wallpapering or nailing holes in walls. Tenant must not change the plumbing, ventilating, air conditioning or electric or heating systems.

b. If Tenant re-keys or installs any locks to the Premises or installs or alters any burglar alarm system, Tenant will provide Landlord with a duplicate key or keys capable of unlocking all such re-keyed or new locks as well as instructions on how to disarm any altered or new burglar alarm system.

Clause 12 makes it clear that the tenant may not make *any* alterations to the premises without your consent, from decorating walls to installing appliances and security systems. You can use this clause to end the tenancy if the tenant makes a substantial alteration without your prior consent. (Chapter 14, Section B, discusses the types of alterations that may justify termination of the tenancy.)

And to make sure you can take advantage of your legal right of entry in an emergency situation, Clause 12 obligates the tenant to provide duplicate keys for any locks that are re-keyed or installed, and to get your prior permission before installing a burglar alarm system. (State law also requires tenants in New York City and Buffalo properties with three or more units to supply you with duplicate keys to privately installed locks. (MDL § 51-c.) If you do permit tenant-installed burglar alarm systems, make sure your tenant gives you the name and phone number of the alarm company or instructions on how to disarm the alarm system so that you can enter in case of emergency. (See Chapter 10 for information on your right to enter rental property in an emergency.)

The "except as provided by law" language in Clause 12 is a reference to the fact that, in certain situations, tenants have a narrowly defined right to alter or repair the premises, regardless of what you've said in the lease or rental agreement. Examples include:

- **Alterations by a disabled person, such as lowering counter tops for a wheelchair-bound tenant.** Under the federal Fair Housing Acts, and New York's Human Rights Law, a disabled person may modify her living space to the extent necessary to make the space safe and comfortable, as long as the modifications will not make the unit unacceptable to the next tenant, or if the disabled tenant agrees to undo the modification when she leaves. (See Chapter 1, Section C4, for details.)

- **Use of the "repair and deduct" procedure.** Tenants have the right to repair defects or damage that make the premises uninhabitable or substantially interfere with the tenant's safe use or enjoyment of the premises. Usually, the tenant must first notify you of the problem and give you a reasonable amount of time to fix it. (See Chapter 9, Section D, for more on this topic.)

- **Installation of small satellite dishes and telecommunications antennas.** Federal law gives tenants limited rights to install wireless antennas and small satellite dishes. See Chapter 9, Section I, for details.

### How to Fill in Clause 12:

If you do not want the tenant to make any repairs or alterations without your permission, you do not need to add anything to this clause.

If you're renting a one- or two-family dwelling, you can make the tenant responsible for specified ongoing repairs. (But you still have an obligation under the warranty of habitability to ensure that the premises are safe and livable when the tenant moves in.) Provide enough detail so that the tenant knows what is expected and who will pay. For example, if you decide to allow the tenant to take over the repair of any broken windows, routine plumbing jobs or landscaping, give specific descriptions and limits to the tasks.

 **If you want the tenant to perform maintenance work for you in exchange for reduced rent, don't write it into the lease or rental agreement.** Instead, use a separate employment agreement and pay the tenant for her services. That way, if she doesn't perform, you still have the full rent and you can simply cancel the employment contract.

If the unit you're renting has three or more units, state multiple dwelling laws create an ongoing and "non-delegable" obligation keep the unit in good repair—even if the lease or rental agreement authorizes the tenant to make repairs. Chapter 9, Section A, includes a discussion about delegating repair and maintenance responsibilities.

### CLAUSE 13. VIOLATING LAWS AND CAUSING DISTURBANCES

Tenant is entitled to quiet enjoyment of the Premises. Tenant and guests or invitees will not use the Premises or adjacent areas in such a way as to: (1) violate any law or ordinance, including laws prohibiting the use, possession or sale of illegal drugs or controlled substances; (2) commit or permit waste (severe property damage); or (3) create a nuisance by annoying, disturbing, inconveniencing or interfering with the quiet enjoyment and peace and quiet of any other tenant or nearby resident, or their safety and comfort, or engage in any other objectionable conduct.

This type of clause is found in most form leases and rental agreements. It prohibits tenants (and their guests) from violating the law, damaging your property or disturbing other tenants or nearby residents. This clause also refers to tenants' right to "quiet enjoyment" of the premises. As courts define it, the "covenant of quiet enjoyment" amounts to an implied promise that you will not act (or fail to act) in a way that seriously interferes with the tenant's right to sole and exclusive use of the premises or that destroys the ability of the tenant to enjoy the premises.

Chapter 14, Section D, provides more detail on conduct that is considered a nuisance and grounds for termination. If you want more specific rules—for example, no loud music played after midnight—add them to Clause 18: Tenant Rules and Regulations, or to Clause 26: Additional Provisions.

### How to Fill in Clause 13:

You do not need to add anything to this clause.

---

## Waste and Nuisance: What Are They?

Committing **waste** means causing severe damage to real estate, such as a house or an apartment unit—damage that goes way beyond ordinary wear and tear. Punching holes in walls, pulling out sinks and fixtures and knocking down doors are examples of causing waste. Permitting waste means letting avoidable damage happen. Failing to close windows during a rainstorm, not putting out a small fire or letting a tub overflow are examples of permitting waste.

**Nuisance** means conduct that prevents tenants and neighbors from fully enjoying the use of their homes, or which threatens their health and safety. Continuous loud noise and foul odors are examples of legal nuisances that may disturb nearby neighbors. So, too, are selling drugs or engaging in other illegal activities that greatly disturb neighbors or put them at risk.

---

## CLAUSE 14. PETS

No animal, bird or other pet will be kept on the Premises without the Landlord's written consent, except service animals needed by blind, deaf or disabled persons and _____, under the following conditions: _____
_____.

This clause is designed to prevent tenants from keeping pets without your written permission. This is not necessarily to say that you will want to apply a flat "no-pets" rule. (Many landlords, in fact, report that pet-owning tenants are more appreciative, stable and responsible than the norm.) But it does provide you with a legal mechanism designed to keep your premises from being waist-deep in Irish wolfhounds. Without this sort of provision, particularly in a fixed-term lease that can't be terminated early, save for a clear violation of one of its provisions, there's little to prevent your tenant from keeping dangerous or non-housebroken pets on your property, except for city ordinances prohibiting tigers and the like.

You have the right to prohibit all pets, or to restrict the types of pets you allow. Exception: You can't ban "service animals" or companion pets required by blind, deaf or physically or mentally disabled people. For more on the legality of pet restrictions, see Chapter 1, Section B7, and Chapter 14, Section B1.

It is important to educate tenants from the start that you will not tolerate dangerous or even apparently dangerous pets, and that as soon as you learn of a worrisome situation, you have the option of insisting that the tenant get rid of the pet (or move). You may want to advise tenants that their pets must be well trained and non-threatening in the second blank of Clause 14; or you could set out your policy in your Rules and Regulations (if any). Your policy might look something like this:

"Tenant's pet(s) will be well-behaved, under Tenant's control at all times and will not pose a threat or apparent threat to the safety of other tenants, their guests or other people on or near the rental premises. If, in the opinion of Landlord, tenant's pet(s) pose such a threat, Landlord will serve Tenant with the appropriate notice to terminate the tenancy."

A policy against dangerous pets is only effective if it's enforced. To limit your liability if a tenant's pet injures someone on or even near your property, be sure that you or your manager follow through with your policy—by keeping an eye on your tenants' pets and by listening to and acting on any complaints from other tenants or neighbors.

### How to Fill in Clause 14:

If you do not allow pets, delete the words "and _____ under the following conditions: _____," or put the word "None" in the blanks.

If you allow pets, be sure to identify the type and number of pets in the first blank—for example, "one cat" or "one dog under 20 pounds." It's also wise to spell out your pet rules in the second blank or in an attached lease rider—for example, you may want to specify that the tenants will keep the grounds and street free of all animal waste, and that cats and dogs be spayed or neutered, licensed and up-to-date on vaccinations. (Your Rules and Regulations may be another place to do this. See Clause 18.)

See *Dog Law*, by Mary Randolph (Nolo), for more information on renting to pet owners. Also, see the Humane Society's website at www.rentwithpets.com.

**Enforce no-pets clauses.** When faced with tenants who violate no-pets clauses, landlords often ignore the situation for a long time, then try to enforce it later if friction develops over some other matter. This could backfire. In general, if you know a tenant has breached the lease or rental agreement (for example, by keeping a pet), and do nothing about it for a long time, you risk having legally waived—or given up—your right to object. Better to adopt a policy you plan to stick to and then preserve your right to object, by promptly giving any offending tenant a written warning notice to get rid of the animal—technically known as a notice to cure. Then follow through with a termination notice, subject to any rent regulatory requirements. (Chapter 15 explains how to prepare and serve a

notice to cure and a notice of termination.) In some localities, ignoring the situation for only a short time could preclude you from enforcing your no-pet clause. In both New York City and the County of Westchester, landlords have only three months to take action against a tenant who violates a no-pet rule. The three-month period begins to run as soon as you, or one of your employees, learns of the pet. If you wait more than 90 days to ask the tenant to remove the pet, these "pet laws" give the tenant permission to keep the pet—regardless of what your lease or rental agreement says. (NYC Adm. Code § 27-2009.1; Laws of Westchester County § 694.)

### Should You Require a Separate Security Deposit for Pets?

Some landlords allow pets but require the tenant to pay a separate deposit to cover any damage caused by the pet. This is legal as long as the tenant is not rent-controlled or rent-stabilized. But separate pet deposits can often be a bad idea because they limit how you can use that part of the security deposit. For example, if the pet is well-behaved, but the tenant trashes your unit, you can't use the pet portion of the deposit to clean up after the human. If you want to protect your property from damage done by a pet, you are probably better off charging a slightly higher rent or security deposit to start with.

It is illegal to charge an extra pet deposit for disabled people with trained "service animals," such as guide dogs, signal dogs or service dogs or emotional support pets.

### CLAUSE 15. LANDLORD'S RIGHT TO ACCESS

Landlord or Landlord's agents may enter the Premises in the event of an emergency, to make repairs or improvements or to show the Premises to prospective buyers or tenants. Landlord may also enter the Premises to conduct an annual inspection to check for safety or maintenance problems. Except in cases of emergency, Tenant's abandonment of the Premises, court order, or where it is impractical to do so, Landlord shall give Tenant reasonable notice before entering the Premises.

Clause 15 makes it clear to the tenant that you have a legal right of access to the property to make repairs or to show the premises for sale or rental, provided you give the tenant reasonable notice. In most cases, 24 hours is presumed to be a reasonable amount of notice for non-emergency access. Chapter 10 provides details on landlord's right to access rental property and how to give advance notice of entry.

### How to Fill in Clause 15:

You don't need to make any changes to this clause.

### CLAUSE 16. EXTENDED ABSENCES BY TENANT

Tenant will notify Landlord in advance if Tenant will be away from the Premises for _____ or more consecutive days. During such absence, Landlord may enter the Premises at times reasonably necessary to maintain the property and inspect for needed repairs.

This clause requires that the tenants notify you when leaving your property for an extended time. It gives you the authority to enter the rental unit during the tenant's absence to maintain the property as necessary and to inspect for damage and needed repairs. (Chapter 10 discusses your legal right to enter during a tenant's extended absence.)

This clause is especially important in leases for single-family home rentals, where undiscovered problems, like leaks, can quickly cause extensive damage. It's also helpful in leases for units upstate—where winter temperatures can rupture interior plumbing lines.

### How to Fill in Clause 16:

In the blank, fill in the time frame that you think is reasonable. Fourteen or more days is common.

### CLAUSE 17. POSSESSION OF THE PREMISES

a. **Tenant's failure to take possession.** If, after signing this Agreement, Tenant fails to take possession of the Premises, Tenant will still be responsible for paying rent and complying with all other terms of this Agreement.

b. **Landlord's failure to deliver possession.** If Landlord is unable to deliver possession of the Premises to Tenant for any reason not within Landlord's control, including, but not limited to, partial or complete destruction of the Premises, this Agreement shall remain in effect. Tenant's obligation to pay rent shall not begin, however, until such time as the Premises are made available to Tenant for occupancy. Landlord shall notify Tenant of the date that the Premises are available for occupancy. If Landlord fails to deliver possession to the Tenant within 30 days after the date this Agreement begins, Tenant, may elect to terminate the Agreement on written notice to the Landlord, and Landlord shall refund to Tenant any sums previously paid under this Agreement. Landlord shall not be responsible for Tenant's damages or expenses caused by any delay in delivering possession.

The first part of this clause (Part a) explains that a tenant who chooses not to move in after signing the lease or rental agreement will still be required to pay rent and satisfy other conditions of the agreement. This does not mean, however, that you can sit back and expect to collect rent for the entire lease or rental agreement term. If the tenant, without explanation, fails to move in within a month or so after the agreement begins, contact the tenant to make sure that she intends to move in. If it appears that the tenant has abandoned the agreement, you generally should take reasonably prompt steps to terminate it and re-rent the premises. Any rent you collect should then be credited against the first tenant's rent obligation.

If the unit is by covered New York State (ETPA) rent stabilization, the tenant is required to use the premises as a primary residence. Modify Part a of the clause to require the tenant to take occupancy of the unit. (See possible modifications to Clause 17, below.)

The second part of the clause (Part b) protects you if you're unable, for reasons beyond your control, to turn over possession after having signed the agreement or lease—for example, if the prior tenant doesn't move out on time or, despite your best efforts, the unit is not yet ready for occupancy. The clause gives you 30 days to deliver possession to the tenant, but suspends the tenant's rent obligation until the rental unit becomes ready for occupancy. If after 30 days the unit still isn't ready, the tenant may elect to cancel the agreement. The clause also limits your financial liability to the new tenant to the return of any prepaid rent and security deposits (the "sums previously paid" in the language of the clause).

### How to Fill in Clause 17:

You do not need to make any changes to the clause unless the unit is covered by New York State rent stabilization. In that case, make the modification suggested below.

### Possible Modifications to Clause 17:

If the unit is covered by New York State (ETPA) rent stabilization, delete the sentence in Part a and replace it with the following sentence: "Tenant must take occupancy of the Premises within 15 days after this Agreement begins."

Chapter 14, Section E3, discusses a rent-stabilized tenant's obligation to use the premises as a primary residence.

You can modify Part b if you want to extend the period of time you have to deliver possession to the tenant past 30 days. This might be a good idea if you're rehabilitating the premises, for instance, and you're not sure you can deliver possession on a certain date.

## CLAUSE 18. TENANT RULES AND REGULATIONS

☐ Tenant acknowledges receipt of, and has read a copy of, tenant rules and regulations, which are attached to and incorporated into this Agreement by this reference. Tenant agrees to obey and comply with these rules and all future reasonable tenant rules and regulations.

Many landlords don't worry about detailed rules and regulations, especially when they rent single-family homes or duplexes. However, in apartment buildings and complexes, rules are an effective way to control the use of common areas and equipment —both for the convenience, safety and welfare of the tenants and as a way to protect your property from damage. Rules and regulations also help avoid confusion and misunderstandings about day-to-day issues such as where bikes and strollers may (and may not) be kept.

Not every minor rule needs to be incorporated in your lease or rental agreement. But it is a good idea to specifically incorporate important ones (especially those that are likely to be ignored by some tenants). Doing so gives you the authority to evict a tenant who persists in seriously violating your code of tenant rules and regulations. Also, to avoid charges of illegal discrimination, rules and regulations should apply equally to all tenants in your rental property.

Because tenant rules and regulations are often lengthy and may be revised occasionally, we suggest you prepare a separate "rider" which gets attached to the lease. (See "How to Prepare Lease Riders" at the beginning of this section.) Be sure the rules and regulations (including any revisions) are dated on each page and signed by both you and the tenant.

### How to Fill in Clause 18:

If you have a set of Tenant Rules and Regulations, check the box. If you do not, simply delete this clause, or put a line through it or write the words "N/A" or "Not Applicable."

## What's Covered in Tenant Rules and Regulations

Tenant rules and regulations typically cover issues such as:

- storage of bikes, baby strollers and other equipment in halls, stairways and other common areas
- elevator use
- pool rules
- refuse and recycling
- keys and locks (lock-out and lost key charges)
- pet rules
- carpeting obligations
- specific details on what's considered excessive noise
- prohibitions on dangerous materials—nothing flammable or explosive should be kept on the premises
- specific tenant maintenance responsibilities (not permitting any acids or foreign objects to be placed in plumbing fixtures; replacing broken windows; lawn and yard maintenance)
- use of the grounds
- maintenance of fire escapes, terraces, balconies and decks—for instance, no storing property on fire escapes; no grilling or barbecuing
- display of signs in windows
- laundry room rules
- waterbed rules, and
- vehicles and parking regulations—for example, restrictions on repairs on the premises or types of vehicles (such as no RVs), or where guests can park.

### CLAUSE 19. TENANT DEFAULT

a. If Tenant fails to pay rent or additional rent after a personal demand for rent has been made by the Landlord or Landlord's agent, or within three days after a written demand for rent has been made by Landlord or Landlord's agent or attorney, Landlord may begin legal proceedings to evict Tenant and Tenant's occupants from the Premises.

b. If Tenant otherwise defaults under this Agreement by:

1) failing to comply with any other term or rule of this Agreement, or

2) permanently moving out before this Agreement expires

then Landlord must give Tenant notice of default stating the type of violation and directing Tenant to cure the violation within 10 days. If Tenant fails to cure the default within the time stated, Landlord shall terminate the Agreement by giving the Tenant a written termination notice. The termination notice will give the date the Agreement will end, which shall not be less than 10 days after the date of the notice. If Tenant and Tenant's occupants fail to move out on or before the termination date, Landlord may begin legal proceedings to evict the Tenant and Tenant's occupants from the Premises.

Clause 19 gives you the right to begin eviction proceedings against the tenant for violations (or "defaults") of the lease or rental agreement, such as not paying rent or illegally subletting the unit. It's critical to understand how this clause operates, since it sets the ground rules for dealing with tenants who violate your lease or rental agreement. This clause also describes the type of default notice (or notices) you must give to the tenant before resorting to legal action. If you don't carefully follow the notice requirements described in the default clause when demanding rent or terminating the lease, your later eviction proceeding is likely to be dismissed.

For rent defaults, Section a of the clause requires you to give the tenant a three-day rent demand, either orally or in writing. If the tenant doesn't pay up within three days after the demand is made, you can begin a "non-payment" summary proceeding to evict the tenant. (Chapter 12 tells you how to make a rent demand.)

Section b of the clause applies to all other types of default. It requires you to first give the tenant a notice of the violation, and ten days to remedy (or "cure") it. If the tenant doesn't remedy the violation in ten days, you can send the tenant a termination notice. The termination notice tells the tenant to move out within a certain time period, which may not be less than ten days. After that, you can begin a "holdover" summary proceeding to evict the tenant and any occupants. (Chapter 15 explains how to prepare and serve notices to cure and terminate.)

⚠ **If a New York State (ETPA) rent stabilized tenant violates a lease clause**, you must give the tenant a ten-day notice to cure, and if the tenant does not cure the default within the cure period, a *seven-day* notice of termination. (9 NYCRR § 2504.1(d)(1).) Chapter 15 explains how to prepare and serve notices on rent-regulated tenants.

### How to Fill in Clause 19:

You don't need to add anything to this clause.

### CLAUSE 20.  PAYMENT OF ATTORNEY FEES AND COURT COSTS

In any legal action or proceeding to enforce any part of this Agreement, the prevailing party ☐ shall not ☐ shall recover reasonable attorney fees and court costs.

Many landlords assume that if they sue a tenant and win, the court will order the losing tenant to pay the landlord's court costs (filing fees, service of process charges, deposition costs and so on) and attorney fees. But a court will order the losing tenant to pay your attorney fees only if a written agreement specifically provides for it.

If, however, you have an "attorney fees" clause in your lease, all this changes. If you hire a lawyer to bring a lawsuit concerning the lease and win, the judge will order your tenant to pay your court costs and attorney fees. (In rare instances, a court will order the loser to pay costs and fees on its own if it finds that the behavior of the losing party was particularly outrageous—for example, filing a totally frivolous lawsuit.)

But there's another important issue you may need to know about. By law, an attorney fees clause in a lease or rental agreement works both ways, even if you haven't written it that way. (RPL § 234.) That is, if the lease only states that you are entitled to attorney fees if you win a lawsuit, your tenants will be entitled to collect their attorney fees

from you if they prevail. The amount you would be ordered to pay would be whatever the judge decides is reasonable.

So, give some thought to whether you want to bind both of you to paying for the winner's costs and fees. Remember, if you can't actually collect a judgment containing attorney fees from an evicted tenant (which often happens), the clause will not help you. But if the tenant prevails, you will be stuck paying his court costs and attorney fees. In addition, the presence of a two-way clause will make it easier for a tenant to secure a willing lawyer for even a doubtful claim, because the source of the lawyer's fee (you, if you lose) will often appear more financially solid than if the client were paying the bill himself.

Especially if you intend to do all or most of your own legal work in any potential eviction or other lawsuit, you will almost surely be better off not to allow for attorney fees. Why? Because if the tenant wins, you will have to pay her fees; but if you win, she will owe you nothing since you didn't hire an attorney. You can't even recover for the long hours you spent preparing for and handling the case.

### How to Fill in Clause 20:

If you don't want to allow for attorney fees, check the first box before the words "shall not" and cross out (or delete on the disk) the words "shall."

If you want to be entitled to attorney fees and costs if you win—and you're willing to pay them if you lose—check the second box before the words "shall recover" and cross out (or delete on the disk) the words "shall not."

⚠ **Attorney fee clauses don't cover all legal disputes.** They cover fees only for lawsuits that concern the meaning or implementation of a rental agreement or lease—for example, a dispute about rent, security deposits or your right to access (assuming that the rental document includes these subjects). An attorney fee clause would probably not apply in a personal injury or discrimination lawsuit.

## CLAUSE 21. JURY TRIAL & COUNTERCLAIMS

a. **Jury trial.** Landlord and Tenant agree to give up their right to a trial by jury in any action or proceeding brought by either against the other for any matter concerning the Agreement or the Premises. This does not include actions for personal injury or property damage.

b. **Counterclaims.** Tenant agrees to give up the right to bring a counterclaim or set-off in any action or proceeding by Landlord against Tenant on any matter directly or indirectly related to the Agreement or the Premises.

Part a of this clause, known as a "jury waiver" clause, prevents the tenant and the landlord from demanding a jury trial in any legal action you bring for rent or possession of the premises. (You can't ask a tenant to give up the right to a jury trial in a personal injury or property damage lawsuit, however. (RPL § 259-c.) As a result, your eviction proceeding must be heard by a judge instead of a jury. Judges usually give landlords a fairer shake than jurors do, since many potential jurors are biased against landlords. And since the process of selecting a jury can drag on for days, our jury waiver clause translates into faster evictions and lower legal fees, too. If you don't have a jury waiver clause in your lease or rental agreement, the tenant is legally entitled to demand a jury trial.

Part b of this clause, known as a "counterclaim waiver" clause, prohibits the tenant from asserting any claims against you in a suit for rent or possession of the premises. If, for example, you sue the tenant for unpaid rent, the clause prevents the tenant from using your suit as an opportunity to sue you for something else.

Counterclaim waiver clauses aren't ironclad, though. Courts may disregard them when the tenant's claim is closely intertwined with the landlord's claim for rent or possession. For instance, tenants are usually permitted to make warranty of habitability counterclaims when sued for unpaid rent. That's because a tenant's obligation to pay rent is closely intertwined with a landlord's obligation to keep the premises livable. But a counterclaim waiver clause should shield you from unrelated tenant claims for discrimination or personal injury when you sue for rent or possession.

### How to Fill in Clause 21:

You don't need to add anything to this clause.

## CLAUSE 22. DISCLOSURES

Tenant acknowledges that Landlord has made the following disclosures regarding the Premises:

☐ Disclosure of Information on Lead-Based Paint and/ or Lead-Based Paint Hazards

☐ Other disclosures: _____

_____

Under federal law, you must disclose any lead-based paint hazards and must provide written notice of the possibility of such hazards in any housing constructed prior to 1978. Chapter 11, Section A, provides complete details on disclosing lead-paint health hazards including the specific form you must use. You should also disclose any other known dangerous or hazardous conditions, such as high levels of radon. (Chapter 11, Section D, discusses radon.)

**New York City law requires all landlords to distribute fire safety plans and notices to new tenants when they sign a lease or rental agreement.** For details, see "New York City Landlords Must Distribute Fire Safety Plans and Notices" in Chapter 9, Section B.

**If your building was constructed before 1960 and has three or more units, New York City law requires you to attach a lead hazard notice and pamphlet to the lease.** Chapter 11, Section A, provides details, including information on how to obtain and complete the required forms.

### How to Fill in Clause 22:

Check off the first box if you are providing the tenant with a lead hazard disclosure form under federal law. Check off the second box if you have made any other disclosure about a dangerous or hazardous condition on the rental property.

## CLAUSE 23. DAMAGE AND DESTRUCTION

If all or part of the Premises becomes unusable, in part or totally, because of fire, accident or other casualty, the following shall apply:

a. Unless the Agreement is terminated pursuant to Subparagraphs b or c, below, Landlord will repair and restore the Premises, with this Agreement continuing in full force and effect, except that Tenant's rent shall be abated based upon the part of the Premises which are unusable, while repairs are being made. Landlord shall not be required to repair or replace any property brought onto the Premises by Tenant.

b. In the event that Landlord wishes to demolish or substantially rebuild the building in which the Premises are located, the Landlord need not restore the Premises and may elect instead to terminate this Agreement upon written notice to Tenant within thirty (30) days after such damage. If the Premises are partially usable, this Agreement will terminate 60 days from the last day of the calendar month in which Tenant is given the Landlord's termination notice.

c. If the Premises are completely unusable and the Landlord does repair the Premises within 30 days, Tenant may, upon written notice, elect to terminate this Agreement, effective as of the date the damage occurred.

This clause addresses what would happen if the premises are seriously damaged by fire or other calamity. Without Clause 23, New York law permits tenants whose units are damaged or destroyed by no fault of their own to terminate the agreement and move out without any further obligation to pay rent. (RPL § 227.) Clause 23 changes this result by letting you elect either to hold the tenant to the agreement and restore the premises, or to terminate the agreement on written notice. If you elect to restore the premises, the clause entitles the tenant to a rent abatement in proportion to any unusable part of the premises. And if you don't repair the damage within 30 days after the damage occurs, the tenant may elect to terminate the agreement.

Chapter 14, Section F, explains a tenant's right to move out because of defective conditions at the property.

### How to Fill in Clause 23:

You don't need to add anything to this clause.

## CLAUSE 24. NOTICES

a. **Notices to Tenant.** Any notice from Landlord, or Landlord's agent or attorney will be considered properly given to Tenant if in writing; signed by or in the name of the Landlord or Landlord's agent; and addressed to Tenant at the Premises and delivered to Tenant personally, or sent by registered or certified mail to Tenant at the Premises. The date of service of any written notice by Landlord to Tenant under this Agreement is the date of delivery or mailing of such notice.

b. **Notices to Landlord.** Any notice from Tenant will be considered properly given to Landlord if in writing and delivered or sent to Landlord by registered or certified mail at the following address:

_____

or at another address for which Landlord or Landlord's agent has given Tenant written notice.

During the course of a tenancy, both you and your tenant may need to give the other an official notice to, say, exercise an option, cure a breach or terminate the tenancy. Clause 24 specifies the form and manner in which all required notices must be given, when the notice is deemed effective, who may issue or sign the notice, and to whom and where notices must be directed. Some landlords want to handle all of this themselves, while others delegate it to a manager or management company.

## Avoid Adding Clauses That Are Unenforceable

Many form leases include provisions that appear to benefit the landlord but, in actuality, are prohibited under state statute or public policy, making them unenforceable. A tenant cannot be bound to an unenforceable lease clause, even if the tenant read, acknowledged or signed the provision. Listed below are a variety of void and unenforceable clauses you should avoid putting into your lease or rental agreement.

- **Right to habitable housing.** Tenants may not waive or modify the protections of the warranty of habitability. (RPL § 235-b.) Chapter 9 explains the scope of your obligations under the warranty of habitability.
- **Right to share rental unit.** Tenants may not give up their right to share their unit with immediate family members and roommates, in accordance with RPL § 235-f. Chapter 8 details your tenant's apartment sharing rights.
- **Sublet and assignment rights.** In buildings with four or more units, a tenant with a lease has a right to your reasonable consent to a sublet or to terminate the lease if your consent to an assignment is unreasonably withheld. (RPL § 226-b.) Chapter 8 explains a tenant's right to sublet or assign.
- **Retaliatory eviction.** A tenant's legal protection against a landlord's retaliatory eviction cannot be waived. (RPL § 223-b.) Chapter 14, Section I, explains retaliation.
- **Right to form and join tenants' associations.** Landlords may not prohibit, restrict or interfere with a tenant's right to join or form a tenants' association or with the right of such organizations to meet in the property's common areas. (RPL § 230.)
- **Right to bear children.** It's a criminal misdemeanor to insert a clause in a lease or rental agreement that requires the tenant to remain childless or not bear children during the course

of the tenancy. (RPL § 237.) Chapter 1 covers illegal discrimination against families with children.

- **Exculpatory clauses.** Clauses which attempt to absolve you in advance from responsibility for all damages, injuries or losses caused by your negligence are void. (GOL § 5-321.) These clauses come in two varieties:
    - **Exculpatory:** "If there's a problem, you won't hold me responsible," and
    - **Hold-harmless:** "If there's a problem traceable to me, you're responsible."
    If a tenant is injured because of a dangerous condition you failed to fix for several months, no boilerplate lease language will protect you from civil and possibly even criminal charges.
- **Tenant's reciprocal right to attorneys' fees.** If your agreement gives you a right to recover legal fees and court costs from the tenant, a tenant may not waive a reciprocal right to recover these fees and costs. (RPL § 234.) Clause 20, above, covers attorney fees.
- **Jury trial in a personal injury or property damage action.** Neither landlords nor tenants can waive a right to a jury trial in a lawsuit or counterclaim for personal injury or property damage. (RPL § 259-c.) Clause 21, above, covers the topic of jury trials.
- **Shared meters.** A tenant's protections under the shared meter law cannot be waived. (Public Service Law § 52, as discussed in Clause 9, above.)
- **Rent control and rent stabilization benefits and protections.** A rent-regulated tenant may not give up any of the benefits or protections afforded under the rent control and rent stabilization laws and regulations. Chapter 4 specifies benefits and protections of a rent-regulated tenancy.

Make sure the person you designate to receive notices is almost always available to promptly transmit copies to you or your attorney. Be sure to keep your tenants up-to-date on any changes in this information.

Chapter 15 provides instructions on how to prepare and serve cure and termination notices, and discusses how to authorize your agent or attorney to sign notices on your behalf.

### How to Fill in Clause 24:

Fill in the address where you want notices from tenants to be delivered to you. Or, provide the name and street address of someone else you authorize to receive notices and legal papers on your behalf, such as a managing agent.

⚠ **Do you trust your manager?** It's unwise to have a manager you wouldn't trust to receive legal notices on your behalf. You don't, for example, want a careless apartment manager to throw away notice of a lawsuit against you without informing you. That could result in a judgment against you and a lien against your property in a lawsuit you didn't even know about. (For more information on hiring property managers, see Chapter 6.)

### CLAUSE 25. ABANDONED PROPERTY

When this Agreement expires or is terminated, Tenant must remove all personal property and belongings from the Premises. If any of Tenant's property remains in the Premises after the tenancy ends, Landlord may either discard the property or store it at Tenant's expense. Tenant agrees to pay Landlord for all costs and expenses incurred in removing and/or storing such personal property. The terms of this clause will continue to be in effect after the end of this Agreement.

This clause requires the tenant to remove furniture, belongings and other personal property from the rental unit at the end of the tenancy. If the tenant leaves something behind, this clause gives you two options: You may either store it or throw it out. And you may charge the tenant for any extra costs you incur removing property from the premises and/or storing it. (See "What to Do With Abandoned Belongings," Chapter 16, Section F.)

### How to Fill in Clause 25:

You don't need to add anything to this clause.

### CLAUSE 26. ADDITIONAL PROVISIONS

Additional provisions are as follows: _____
_____
_____ .

In this clause, you may list any additional provisions or agreements that are unique to you and the particular tenant signing the lease or rental agreement, such as a provision that prohibits waterbeds or smoking in the tenant's apartment or in the common areas. If you are adding any riders to the agreement, mention them here.

If you don't have a separate Rules and Regulations clause (see Clause 18, above), you may spell out a few rules under this clause—for example, regarding lost key charges or use of a pool on the property.

### How to Fill in Clause 26:

List additional provisions or rules here or in a lease rider. (See "How to Prepare Lease Riders" at the beginning of this section.) If you're using one or more riders, list them here. If there are no additional provisions or riders, delete this clause or write "N/A" or "Not Applicable."

 **There is no legal or practical imperative to put every small detail you want to communicate to the tenant into your lease or rental agreement.** Instead, prepare a welcoming, but no-nonsense "move-in letter" that dovetails with the lease or rental agreement and highlights important terms of the tenancy—for example, how and where to report maintenance problems. You may also use a move-in letter to cover issues not included in the lease or rental agreement—for example, rules for use of a laundry room. (Chapter 7 covers move-in letters.)

### CLAUSE 27.  VALIDITY OF EACH PART

If any portion of this Agreement is held to be invalid, its invalidity will not affect the validity or enforceability of any other provision of this Agreement.

This clause is known as a "savings" clause, and it is commonly used in contracts. It means that, in the unlikely event that one of the other clauses in this lease or rental agreement is found to be invalid by a court, the remainder of the agreement will remain in force.

### How to Fill in Clause 27:

You do not need to add anything to this clause.

### CLAUSE 28.  ENTIRE AGREEMENT; NO WAIVERS

a. **Entire agreement.** This document constitutes the entire Agreement between the parties, and no promises or representations, other than those contained here and those implied by law, have been made by Landlord or Tenant. Any modifications to this Agreement must be in writing signed by Landlord and Tenant.

b. **No waivers.** Only a written agreement between the Landlord and Tenant may waive an obligation or violation of this agreement. A waiver may not be implied by the Landlord's acceptance of rent, or failure to take immediate action against the Tenant, while the Tenant is violating one or more provisions of this agreement.

Part a of this clause establishes that the lease or rental agreement and any attached riders (covering things such as rules and regulations) constitute the entire agreement between you and your tenant. It means that oral promises (by you or the tenant) to do something different with respect to any aspect of the rental are not binding. Any changes or additions must be in writing.

Part b of this clause is known as an "anti-waiver clause." A waiver is a relinquishment, or giving up, of a right or enforcement remedy under an agreement. Landlords may inadvertently waive (or give up) their right to enforce a specific lease provision by accepting rent from a tenant who is violating the lease (say, by keeping a pet in violation of a no-pet clause). Landlords may also waive their right to enforce a lease clause if they fail to act promptly against a tenant who is violating the lease. Clause 28 says that the landlord's acceptance of rent or failure to take action will not operate to waive the landlord's right to hold the tenant to the lease. This clause may help if, when you try to evict a tenant for violating a substantial obligation of the lease, the tenant claims that you waived your right to enforce the lease. (Chapter 14 discusses how fixed-term tenancies are terminated.)

### How to Fill in Clause 28:

You do not need to add anything to this clause.

## D. Signing a Lease or Rental Agreement

You'll need to put together two copies of the lease or rental agreement: one for you and one for your tenant. If you are renting to more than one tenant, don't prepare a separate agreement for each co-tenant. After the agreement is signed, co-tenants may make their own copies of the lease or rental agreement.

Prepare two identical copies of the lease or rental agreement to sign, making sure all required riders are attached. Sections E, F and G discuss riders required for New York City rental units and for New York State rent-stabilized units.

Each tenant should sign both copies of the lease or rental agreement before you or another witness, such as your rental agent or manager. While witnesses aren't required for the lease to be legally valid, a witness could help you "authenticate" the lease in court later on, if you need to have it introduced as evidence in an eviction trial. You (or your authorized agent) should then sign both copies. Give one copy of the fully executed lease to the tenant(s) and keep the other one for your files.

If the tenant has a guarantor (sometimes known as a cosigner), you'll need to use a separate form. (Guarantors are discussed in Section G, below.)

If you alter our form by writing or typing in changes, be sure that you and all tenants initial the changes when you sign the document, so as to forestall any possibility that a tenant will claim you unilaterally inserted changes after he or she signed.

---

### Tips on Signing a Lease or Rental Agreement

- All of your expectations should be written into the lease or rental agreement or in attached riders that cover issues such as rules and regulations. Never sign an incomplete document assuming last-minute changes can be made.
- Ask all adults living in the rental units, including both members of a couple, to sign the lease or rental agreement.
- Check that the tenant's name and signature match his or her driver's license or other legal document.

---

## E. New York City Window Guard Notice

Skip this section if you're preparing a lease or rental agreement for premises located outside New York City, or for premises in New York City with only one or two units.

In buildings with three or more units, New York City law requires you to attach a Window Guard Notice to every lease and rental agreement, including renewal leases in a form approved by the Department of Health. A window guard is a metal device with bars that attaches to the exterior of the window and is designed to keep children from falling from windows. The notice tells the tenant that the landlord must install window guards in the rental unit if a child ten years of age or younger lives there or if the tenant requests. (NYC Adm. Code § 17-123; Department of Health Regs. § 12-02.) The tenant must check one of three boxes on the notice indicating whether a child ten or under is, or will be, residing in the rental unit, or if the tenant wants window guards, even if no young children are living in the apartment. After checking one of the boxes, the tenant must sign and date the notice. See the sample "Window Guards" notice, below.

**Window Guard Notice**

### WINDOW GUARDS REQUIRED

LEASE NOTICE TO TENANT

You are required by law to have window guards installed if a child 10 years of age or younger lives in your apartment.
Your Landlord is required by law to install window guards in your apartment:

- if you ask him to put in window guards at any time (you need not give a reason)

OR

- if a child 10 years of age or younger lives in your apartment.

It is a violation of law to refuse, interfere with installation, or remove window guards where required.

CHECK ONE

☐      CHILDREN 10 YEARS OF AGE
OR YOUNGER LIVE IN MY APARTMENT

☐      NO CHILDREN 10 YEARS OF AGE OR
YOUNGER LIVE IN MY APARTMENT

☐      I WANT WINDOW GUARDS EVEN
THOUGH I HAVE NO CHILDREN
10 YEARS OF AGE OR YOUNGER

_____

TENANT (PRINT)

_____

TENANT SIGNATURE

FOR FURTHER INFORMATION CALL:
Window Falls Prevention Program
New York City Department of Health
2 Lafayette Street, 20th Floor
New York, NY 10007
(212) 676-2137

The notice must be printed in not less that ten (10) point type, and must bear the title **"Window Guards Required"** underlined and in bold face. The words, size and layout of the notice must comply with New York City Department of Health regulations.

**Where to Get Copies of the Window Guard Notice.** You can obtain the Window Guard Notice from the New York City Department of Health, the New York City Rent Stabilization Association or the Real Estate Board of New York, Inc. Addresses, phone numbers and websites for these organizations are listed in Appendix I.

**New York City law prohibits you from changing any of the words, the size or the layout of Department of Health-approved Window Guard Notice.** Landlords who don't comply with New York City window guard notice and installation requirements are subject to civil and criminal penalties.

## F. Lease Forms and Riders for New York City Rent-Stabilized Units

If you own a rent-stabilized apartment in New York City, this section will guide you through the preparation of a vacancy lease and a renewal lease, including all necessary lease riders.

If your rental unit is located outside New York City and is covered by New York State ETPA rent stabilization, skip this section. You may use the lease form in this book with the modifications laid out in Section C, above.

### 1. NYC Rent-Stabilized Vacancy Lease

Since the 1980s, many New York City landlords have used the "Standard Form of Apartment Lease" (A1/88A) designed specifically for rent-stabilized units by the Real Estate Board of New York, Inc. This form of lease has withstood tenant challenges

to its various provisions and has been routinely enforced by both the New York courts and the Division of Housing and Community Renewal (DHCR), the state agency that enforces rent stabilization laws and regulations. Because its provisions are tried and true, we recommend that you use it whenever you lease a New York City rent-stabilized apartment.

A portion of the Real Estate Board of New York's Standard Form of Apartment Lease is shown here and the complete form is reprinted, with permission, in Appendix II. Do not use the sample copy in Appendix II. You will need to purchase copies of the form directly from the Board. (See "How to Purchase Lease Forms for New York City Rent-Stabilized Units," below.)

You don't need to add anything to most of the articles in this lease. There are only a handful of items you must fill in and these are fairly straightforward, including:

- the date the lease is signed and the names and addresses (as of the date the lease is signed) of the tenant(s) and owner (Preamble).
- the address of the rent-stabilized apartment being rented, including the apartment number, floor, building address and borough, such as Brooklyn or Manhattan (Article 1. Apartment and Use).
- the beginning and ending dates of the lease— this must equal a full one- or two-year term, at the tenant's option, under 9 NYCRR § 2522.5(a)(1) (Article 2. Length of Lease).
- the amount of monthly rent (this must agree with the rent computation included in Provision 4 of the Rent Stabilization Lease Rider, discussed in Section 2, below), when rent is due and where it must be paid (Article 3. Rent).
- the security deposit amount (this must be no greater than one month's rent under 9 NYCRR § 2525.4), where the deposit has been placed (this must be an interest-bearing trust bank account in New York State under GOL § 7-103, 9 NYCRR 2524.4) (Article 5, Security Deposit).
- utilities that are included in the rent (Article 13. Services and Facilities), and

**"ATTACHED RIDER SETS FORTH RIGHTS AND OBLIGATIONS OF TENANTS AND LANDLORDS UNDER THE RENT STABILIZATION LAW." ("LOS DERECHOS Y RESPON-SABILIDADES DE INQUILINOS Y CASEROS ESTÁN DISPONIBLE EN ESPAÑOL").**

---

### STANDARD FORM OF APARTMENT LEASE
**THE REAL ESTATE BOARD OF NEW YORK, INC.**
©Copyright 1988. All Rights Reserved. Reproduction in whole or in part prohibited.

---

**PREAMBLE:** This lease contains the agreements between You and Owner concerning Your rights and obligations and the rights and obligations of Owner. You and Owner have other rights and obligations which are set forth in government laws and regulations.

You should read this Lease and all of its attached parts carefully. If You have any questions, or if You do not understand any words or statements, get clarification. Once You and Owner sign this Lease You and Owner will be presumed to have read it and understood it. You and Owner admit that all agreements between You and Owner have been written into this Lease. You understand that any agreements made before or after this Lease was signed and not written into it will not be enforceable.

THIS LEASE is made on _____between
                                            month        day        year

Owner, _____

whose address is _____

and You, the Tenant, _____

whose address is _____

**1. APARTMENT AND USE**

☞ Owner agrees to lease to You Apartment _____on the _____floor in the Building at _____ Borough of _____, City and State of New York.

You shall use the Apartment for living purposes only. The Apartment may be occupied by the tenant or tenants named above and by the immediate family of the tenant or tenants and by occupants as defined in and only in accordance with Real Property Law §235-f.

**2. LENGTH OF LEASE**

☞ The term (that means the length) of this Lease is_____years,_____months _____days, beginning on _____

and ending on _____. If you do not do everything You agree to do in this Lease, Owner may have the right to end it before the above date. If Owner does not do everything that owner agrees to do in this Lease, You may have the right to end the Lease before ending date.

**3. RENT**

☞ Your monthly rent for the Apartment is $ _____

until adjusted pursuant to Article 4 below. You must pay Owner the rent, in advance, on the first day of each month either at Owner's office or at another place that Owner may inform You of by written notice. You must pay the first month's rent to Owner when You sign this Lease if the lease begins on the first day of the month. If the Lease begins after the first day of the month, You must pay when you sign this lease(l)the part of the rent from the beginning date of this Lease until the last day of the month and (2)the full rent for the next full calendar month. If this Lease is a Renewal Lease, the rent for the first month of this Lease need not be paid until the first day of the month when the renewal term begins.

**4. RENT ADJUSTMENTS**

If this Lease is for a Rent Stabilized apartment, the rent herein shall be adjusted up or down during the Lease term, including retroactively, to conform to the Rent Guidelines. Where Owner, upon application to the State Division of Housing and Community Renewal ("authorized agency") is found to be entitled to an increase in rent or other relief, You and Owner agree: a. to be bound by such determination; b. where the authorized agency has granted an increase in rent, You shall pay such increase in the manner set forth by the authorized agency; c. except that in the event that an order is issued increasing the stabilization rent because of Owner hardship, You may, within thirty (30) days of your receipt of a copy of the order, cancel your lease on sixty (60) days written notice to Owner. During said period You may continue in occupancy at no increase in rent.

**5. SECURITY DEPOSIT**

☞ You are required to give Owner the sum of $_____when You sign this Lease as a security deposit, which is called in law a trust. Owner will deposit this security in _____ _____bank at _____. If the Building contains six or more apartments, the bank account will earn interest. If You carry out all of your agreements in this Lease, at the end of each calendar year Owner or the bank will pay to Owner 1% interest on the deposit for administrative costs and to You all other interest earned on the security deposit.

If You carry out all of your agreements in this Lease and if You move out of the Apartment and return it to Owner in the same condition it was in when You first occupied it, except for ordinary wear and tear or damage caused by fire or other casualty, Owner will return to You the full amount of your security deposit and interest to which You are entitled within 60 days after this Lease ends. However, if You do not carry out all your agreements in this Lease, Owner may keep all or part of your security deposit and any interest which has not yet been paid to You necessary to pay Owner for any losses incurred, including missed payments.

If Owner sells or leases the building, Owner will turn over your security, with interest, either to You or to the person buying or leasing (lessee) the building within 5 days after the sale or lease. Owner will then notify You, by registered or certified mail, of the name and address of the person or company to whom the deposit has been turned over. In such case, Owner will have no further responsibility to You for the security deposit. The new owner or lessee will become responsible to You for the security deposit.

**6. IF YOU ARE UNABLE TO MOVE IN**

A situation could arise which might prevent Owner from letting You move into the Apartment on the beginning date set in this Lease. if this happens for reasons beyond Owner's reasonable control, Owner will not be responsible for Your damages

☞ Space to be filled in.

- details on any application you have pending with the DHCR for a buildingwide major capital improvement (MCI) rent increase (a subject discussed in Chapter 4, Section D) (Article 30. Rent Increase for Major Capital Improvement).

If a co-signer is signing the lease, fill in the "Guaranty" section at the bottom of the lease. For information on guarantors, see Section G, below.

If you have any question about a particular term or clause in the Real Estate Board's lease, review the discussion of the related lease clauses in Section C, above. Also, be sure to read the other chapters in this book which cover issues relevant to all rental properties, such as the warranty of habitability (Chapter 9), special rules for rent-stabilized apartments, such as how to calculate the rent after a vacancy (Chapter 4) and the grounds upon which a landlord may terminate a rent-stabilized tenancy (Chapter 14).

Once you've completed the rent-stabilized lease (in duplicate), there's more work ahead. You may also need to prepare the following documents:

- Two copies of the New York City "Rent Stabilization Lease Rider." The New York City Rent Stabilization Law requires you to complete this rider and attach it to all rent-stabilized vacancy leases. For details on this rider, see Section 2, below.

- Two copies of the New York City Window Guard Notice. New York City law requires you to attach this notice to every vacancy lease and have the tenant complete and sign it. For details on this notice, read Section E, above.

- If the building was constructed before 1978, one copy of the Disclosure of Information on Lead-Based Paint form and informational pamphlet "Protect Your Family From Lead in Your Home," as required by federal law. See Chapter 11, Section A, for details on how to get and complete the disclosure form and informational pamphlet.

- If the building was constructed before 1960, one copy of the New York City Department of Health lead hazard notice, which inquires whether a child under six will be residing in the apartment, and pamphlet, as required under New York City's lead law. See Chapter 11, Section A, for details on how to obtain the notice and pamphlet.

⚠️ **We don't recommend changing any of the words in the Real Estate Board's Standard Lease unless recommended by your attorney.** If however, you need to add words to an article to cover a special situation, or more likely, want to add extra articles to the lease, you'll need to prepare a rider. See "How to Prepare Lease Riders" at the beginning of Section C for advice. The Real Estate Board lease uses the word "article" instead of "clause," so edit the rider accordingly.

## How to Purchase Lease Forms for New York City Rent-Stabilized Units

You can get the Standard Form of Apartment Lease (Form A1/88A) from the Real Estate Board of New York, 570 Lexington Avenue, New York, NY 10022, or by calling 212-532-3100. As of early 2003, the six-page lease (including the required Rent Stabilization Lease Rider, the Window Guard Notice and lead-paint disclosure forms) was available as a set for $3.10 each.

Landlords with many rent-stabilized units (and an office computer) can save money by ordering the lease on electronic disk. With special software, which costs $140 for Real Estate Board members and $175 for non-members, you can put the lease on your computer's hard drive. You pay an additional fee based on the number of pages you actually print. For more information, call the Board at the phone number above, or visit its Internet website at: www.rebny.com.

## 2. New York City Rent Stabilization Rider

➡️ Skip this section if the unit you wish to lease is subject to New York State (ETPA) rent stabilization, rent control or is not rent-regulated.

The New York City Rent Stabilization Law requires you to attach a "Rent Stabilization Lease Rider For Apartment House Tenants Residing In New York City" (DHCR Form RA-LR1) to every vacancy lease signed by a new tenant and every renewal lease. (Section I explains how to offer a rent-stabilized tenant a renewal lease.) The eight-page rider describes the rights and obligations of tenants and landlords under the Rent Stabilization Law. The rider is only informational. Its provisions do not modify or become part of the lease.

A portion of the Rent Stabilization Lease Rider is shown here and the complete form is reprinted in Appendix II. Do not use the sample copy in Appendix II. You will need to obtain your own copies.

**Where to Get Copies of the Rent Stabilization Lease Rider.** You can obtain free copies of the Rent Stabilization Lease Rider directly from the DHCR. Your best bet is to download it from the DHCR's website (www.dhcr.state.ny.us). For a copy of the Rider written in Spanish, contact the DHCR's Central Public Information Office in Jamaica, Queens, or your Borough Rent Office.

Before attaching the Rent Stabilization Lease Rider to a vacancy lease, you must complete Provision 5, called "FOR VACANCY LEASES ONLY." (This section of the rider is shown below.) This provision informs the new tenant of the legal regulated rent in effect immediately prior to the vacancy, and explains how the present rent was computed. Fill out Provision 5 by checking the box corresponding to the rent-regulatory history of the apartment and the last tenant.

**Check box (A) if the apartment was rent stabilized when the last tenant moved out.** This is the most common situation and occurs when one rent-stabilized tenant moves out, and a new one moves in. Under the check box, fill in the last tenant's rent and detail the steps you took to arrive at the new vacancy rent. (Read Chapter 4, Section A5, to find out how to calculate a "vacancy" rent increase.) The

rent on the last line of Provision 5(A) ("New Tenant's Rent") must agree with the rent stated in the lease to which the rider is attached.

**Check box (B) if the apartment was rent-controlled when the last tenant moved out.** When a rent-controlled tenant (or tenant's successor) either dies or moves out, the unit goes from being rent-controlled to rent-stabilized if the building contains six or more units. Congratulations! You are finally permitted to charge a "fair market rent" for the unit. Fill in the blank with the amount of the fair market rent you are charging. This rent must agree with the rent stated in the lease to which the rider is attached. (For more information on setting a fair market rent and the tenant's right to challenge it, read Chapter 4, Sections A5 and G.)

**Check box (C) if the unit is covered by rent stabilization for the first time due to:**
- your participation in a government tax benefit program providing tax exemptions and abatements for the rehabilitation and new construction of housing. Fill in the name of the program and the initial rent (which is determined by the type of program you are participating in). Principal New York City programs are the "421-a" new construction program, the "423" redevelopment program and the "J-51" rehabilitation/improvement program.
- your receipt of insured rehabilitation loans through the State of New York Mortgage Agency (SONYMA) or the Private Housing Financing Law.

Fill in the initial or restructured rent and the name of the program. The rent you fill in must agree with the rent stated in the lease to which the rider is attached.

**Check box (D) if the unit is otherwise subject to rent-stabilization for the first time.**

When two rent-stabilized units are combined into one larger unit, or when an individual unit is reconfigured so that the total square footage has been changed, the unit remains subject to rent stabilization. However, you may charge the tenant a fair market rent for the unit, subject to the new tenant's right to later challenge it with the DHCR. Fill in the reason why the unit is newly subject to rent stabilization and the amount of rent you are changing the first rent-stabilized tenant.

## Sample Section of Rent Stabilization Lease Rider for Apartment House Tenants Residing in New York City

5.   **FOR VACANCY LEASES ONLY**:

If this Rider is attached to a **RENEWAL LEASE**, the owner is **NOT** obligated to complete this section.

If this Rider is attached to a **VACANCY LEASE**, the owner **MUST** show how the rental amount provided for in such vacancy lease has been computed above the prior legal regulated rent by completing the following chart. The owner is not entitled to a rent which is more than the legal regulated rent.   For additional information see DHCR Fact Sheet #5.

ANY INCREASE ABOVE THE PRIOR LEGAL REGULATED RENT MUST BE IN ACCORDANCE WITH ADJUSTMENTS PERMITTED BY THE RENT GUIDELINES BOARD AND THE RENT STABILIZATION

Status of Apartment and Last Tenant
(Owner to Check Appropriate Box - (A), (B), (C), or (D).)

☐   (A)  This apartment was rent stabilized when the last tenant moved out.

Last Legal Regulated Rent                                            $_____

1.   Statutory Vacancy Increase

(i)   Increase based on (1 year)  (2 year) lease (circle one)        (____%)   $_____

(ii)  Increase based on length of time (8 years or more)
since last vacancy allowance or if no vacancy alowance
has been taken, the number of years that the apartment
has been subject to stabilization.          (0.6%  x  number of years)   $_____

(iii) Increase based on low rental amount.  If applicable
complete (a) or (b), but not both.

(a)  Prior legal regulated rent was less than $300 -              $_____
additional $100 increase, enter 100

(b)  If the prior legal regulated rent was $300 or more
but less than $500                              (1)   $100
the sum of (i) and (ii)                         (2)   _____
(1) minus (2).  If less than zero, enter zero   (3)   _____

Amount from line(3)                 $_____

Vacancy Allowance, if permitted by NYC Rent Guidelines Board   (____%)   $_____

Guidelines Supplementary Adjustment, if permitted by NYC Rent
Guidelines Board                                                 $_____

New Equipment, Service, Improvement
for this apartment                                               $_____

New Legal Regulated Rent                                         $_____

Separate Charges or Credits:                                     $_____

Surcharge (e.g., 421-a)                                          $_____

Ancillary Service (e.g., garage)                                 $_____

Other (specify _____)                  $_____

New Tenant's Rent                                                $_____

or

☐   (B)  This apartment was Rent Controlled at the time the last tenant moved out. This tenant is the first rent
stabilized tenant and the rent agreed to and stated in the lease to which this Rider is attached is $_____.
The owner is entitled to charge a market rent to the first rent stabilized tenant. The first rent charged to
the first rent stabilized tenant becomes the initial legal regulated rent for the apartment under the rent
stabilization system. However, if the tenant has reason to believe that this rent exceeds a "fair market rent",
the tenant may file a "Fair Market Rent Appeal" with DHCR. The owner is required to give the tenant notice,
on DHCR Form RR-1, of the right to file such an appeal. The notice must be served by certified mail. A
tenant only has 90 days, after such notice was mailed to the tenant by the owner by certified mail, to file an
appeal. Otherwise, the rent set forth on the registration form becomes the initial legal regulated rent.

☐   (C)  The rent for this apartment is an Initial or Restructured Rent pursuant to a Government Program.
(Specify Program_____)   $_____.

- or -

☐   (D)  Other_____   $_____.
(Specify - for example, a market or "first" rent after renovation to an individual apartment where the outer
dimensions of the apartment have been substantially altered.)

⚠️ The following words must appear in bold print on the top of the first page of the lease to which the New York City Rent Stabilization Lease Rider is attached: **"ATTACHED RIDER SETS FORTH RIGHTS AND OBLIGATIONS OF TENANTS AND LANDLORDS UNDER THE RENT STABILIZATION LAW." ("Los Derechos y Responsabilidades de Inquilinos y Caseros Están Disponible en Español.")** If you are using the Real Estate Board of New York, Inc. "Standard Form Apartment Lease," (A1/88A) (discussed in Section 1 above), these words are already printed on the lease's first page. If you're using another lease, you may need to add them.

⚠️ **A tenant who does not receive a copy of the Rent Stabilization Lease Rider may file a complaint with the DHCR.** The agency usually responds by issuing an order directing the landlord to provide the tenant with the rider. If the landlord doesn't comply with the order within 20 days, the rent increases provided for in the new lease will be postponed until the rider is provided. The landlord may also be fined.

## G. About Guarantors

Some landlords require guarantors, also known as co-signers, on rental agreements and leases, especially when renting to students who depend on parents for much of their income. The guarantor signs a separate agreement, called a guaranty, under which he or she agrees to be jointly and severally liable with the tenant for the tenant's obligations— that is, to cover any rent or damage-repair costs the tenant fails to pay. (Clause 1 of the form agreements in this chapter discusses the concept of joint and several liability.) The guarantor retains responsibility regardless of whether the tenant sublets or assigns his agreement. (Clause 10 discusses sublets and assignments and Chapter 8 covers these issues in detail.)

💡 **Get a personal guaranty from a principal when renting to a business that's newly formed or thinly capitalized.** Landlords sometimes rent units to companies for use by their key employees or visitors. But companies can go out of business owing you rent. For extra security, require one of the business owners to personally guarantee the lease. That way, if the business can't pay rent, you can try and get it from one of its principals.

In practice, a guarantor's promise to guarantee the tenant's rent obligation may have less value than at first you might think. This is because the threat of eviction is the primary factor that motivates a tenant to pay the rent, and obviously you cannot evict a guarantor. Also, since the guarantor doesn't live in the rental unit, she must be sued separately in either a regular civil lawsuit or in small claims court. Filing a suit against the guarantor might be more trouble than it's actually worth, where, for example, the tenant stiffs you for a month's rent. This is especially true if the guarantor lives out-of-state, since the amount of money you are out may not justify hiring a lawyer to collect a judgment.

In sum, the benefits of having a lease or rental agreement guaranteed by someone who won't be living on the property are largely psychological. But these benefits may still be worth something: A tenant who thinks you can (and will) sue the guarantor—who is usually a relative or close friend—may be less likely to default on the rent. Similarly, a guarantor asked to pay the tenant's debts may persuade the tenant to pay.

If you decide to accept a guarantor, have that person fill out a separate rental application and agree to a credit check—after all, a guarantor who has no resources or connection to the tenant will be completely useless. Should the tenant and her prospective guarantor object to these inquiries and costs, you may wonder how serious they are about the guarantor's willingness to stand behind the tenant. Once you are satisfied that the guarantor can genuinely back up the tenant, add the guaranty agreement form we provide here. If you're using the Real Estate Board of New York's form lease for New York City rent-stabilized tenants, you don't need to add a separate agreement; there's one included at the bottom of the lease form.

# Guaranty Agreement

1. This Agreement is entered into on ___November 25, 200X___, between _____ ("Tenant"),
   __Mark O'Donnell__ _____ ("Tenant"),
   __Hudson View Properties, L.L.C.__ _____, ("Landlord")
   and __John D. O'Donnell__ _____ ("Guarantor").

2. Tenant has leased from Landlord the premises located at __377 Hudson Street, New York,__
   __NY 10014__ _____ ("Premises"). Landlord and Tenant signed a lease or
   rental agreement specifying the terms and conditions of this rental on ___November 25, 200X___.
   A copy of the lease or rental agreement is attached to this Agreement.

3. Guarantor guarantees to Landlord the full performance of the lease or rental agreement by the Tenant.
   Guarantor agrees to be jointly and severally liable with Tenant for Tenant's obligations arising out of
   the lease or rental agreement described in Paragraph 2, including but not limited to unpaid rent,
   property damage and cleaning and repair costs that exceed Tenant's security deposit. Guarantor further
   agrees to waive all notices about any default by Tenant, including nonpayment of rent. (For example, if
   Tenant fails to pay the rent on time or damages the premises, Landlord has no duty to warn or notify
   Guarantor, and may demand that Guarantor pay for these obligations immediately.)

4. This Guaranty shall remain in full force and effect and will not be changed by any extensions or
   renewals of the lease or rental agreement or by an assignment or sublet of the Premises. Guarantor
   shall remain liable under the terms of this Agreement for the performance of the Tenant, assignee or
   sublessee, unless Landlord relieves Guarantor by express written termination of this Agreement.

5. Owner and Guarantor agree to waive trial by jury in any action or proceeding brought against each
   other on any matter arising out of the lease, the rental agreement, or this guaranty.

6. If Landlord and Guarantor are involved in any legal proceeding arising out of this Agreement, the
   prevailing party shall recover reasonable attorney fees, court costs and any costs reasonably necessary
   to collect a judgment.

___Nov. 25, 200X___  _Matthew Wopat_  President, Hudson View Properties, L.L.C.
Date  Landlord  Title

___Nov. 25, 200X___  _Mark O'Donnell_
Date  Tenant

___Nov. 25, 200X___  _John D. O'Donnell_
Date  Guarantor

__123 East 75th Street, New York, NY 10021__
Guarantor's Address

_Elizabeth Bambrick_
Witness

A sample Guaranty Agreement is shown above. Simply fill in your name and your tenant's and guarantor's names, the address of the rental unit and the date you signed the agreement with the tenant. Attach the Guaranty Agreement to your lease or rental agreement.

The Forms CD includes a Guaranty Agreement form and Appendix IV includes a blank tear-out version of this form.

**If you change the lease, ask the guarantor to sign the new version.** Generally speaking, a guarantor is bound only to the terms of the exact lease or rental agreement he signs. If you later change a significant term, add a new tenant or otherwise create a new contract, the original guarantor will probably be off the hook, unless you again get him to sign.

## H. How to Prepare a Renewal Lease for Rent-Stabilized Tenants

As long as rent-stabilized tenants pay rent, they are legally entitled to successive renewals of their rent-stabilized lease. (9 NYCRR §§ 2503.5; 2523.5.) The renewal lease must be offered for a term of one or two years, at the tenant's option. The terms and conditions of the renewal lease must be the same as the expiring lease, except for any additional provisions permitted by law or under rent stabilization. Fortunately, you may increase the rent in accordance with the applicable order of your local rent guidelines board. In this section, we tell you how and when to offer a rent-stabilized tenant a renewal lease.

**Don't offer a rent-controlled tenant a renewal lease.** Leases for most rent-controlled tenants expired long ago. You are not legally required to offer a rent-controlled tenant a written renewal lease, nor is there any practical reason to do so. Rent control laws set the rights and obligations for rent-controlled landlords and tenants. Since a written lease will only serve to give the tenant additional rights, we do not recommend offering written renewal leases to rent-controlled tenants.

### When You May Refuse to Renew a Rent-Stabilized Tenant's Lease

While the general rule is that rent-stabilized tenants must be offered renewal leases, you may be able to refuse to renew the tenant's lease in the following limited circumstances:

- You seek the apartment in good faith for personal use as a primary residence by you or members of your immediate family.
- The tenant does not occupy the unit as his or her primary residence.
- You wish to demolish the building in which the unit is located.
- You require the apartment or land for your own use in connection with a business you own and operate.

In order to refuse to renew a tenant's lease on any of these grounds, you may be required to send special non-renewal notices to the tenant during the time period you would otherwise offer a renewal lease, or apply to the DHCR for a certificate of eviction. (Chapter 14 covers the permissible grounds for ending rent-stabilized tenancies. Chapter 15 describes the notice procedure you must follow, including whom to notify, how and when.)

### 1. How to Offer a Renewal Lease in New York City

*At least 90 days and not more than 150 days before a tenant's lease is set to expire,* you're required to notify the tenant in writing that the lease will soon expire (specify the date) and that the tenant may choose to renew for a term of one or two years. Your notice must also inform the tenant of the amounts by which the monthly rent (and required security deposit) will increase, based on the renewal rent increases authorized by the New York

## RENEWAL LEASE FORM

Owners and Tenants should read **INSTRUCTIONS TO OWNER** and **INSTRUCTIONS TO TENANT**
on reverse side before filling out or signing this form

**THIS NOTICE FOR RENEWAL OF LEASE AND RENEWAL LEASE FORM ISSUED UNDER SECTION 2523.5(a) OF THE RENT STABILIZATION CODE. ALL COPIES OF THIS FORM MUST BE SIGNED BELOW AND RETURNED TO YOUR LANDLORD WITHIN 60 DAYS.**

Tenant's Name: _Anthony Rosenthal_

Dated: _February 15_ 20 _2003_

Address: _4511 Sixteenth Avenue_   Apt. No. _6-B_

Owner's/Agent Name: _Burton T. Martin_

County: _Brooklyn (Kings), N.Y._   Zip Code _11204_

Mailing Address (No. & Street): _317 Madison Ave., Suite 2300_

City, State & Zip Code: _NY, NY 10017_

1. The owner hereby notifies you that your lease will expire on: _6 / 30 / 03_

### PART A - OFFER TO TENANT TO RENEW

2. You may renew this lease, for one or two years, at your option, as follows:

| Column a<br>Renewal Term | Column b<br>Legal Rent on Sept.30th Preceding Commencement Date of this Renewal Lease | Column c<br>Authorized Applicable Guideline Increase (If unknown, check box and see below)* ☐ | Column d<br>Applicable Guideline Supplement, if any | Column e<br>Lawful Rent Increase Adj. if any, effective after Sept. 30th indicated in Column b | Column f<br>Separate charge, if any (specify under item 4 below) | Column g<br>New rent (if lower rent is to be charged check box and see item 5 below)* ☐ |
|---|---|---|---|---|---|---|
| 1 Year | $ 1,500.00 | ( 2 %) $_____ | $____0__ | $___30.00__ | $____0__ | $1,530.00 |
| 2 Years | Same as above | ( 4 %) $_____ | $____0__ | $___60.00__ | $____0__ | $1,560.00 |

\*  If applicable guideline rate is unknown at time offer is made check box in column c and enter current guideline which will be subject to adjustment when rates are ordered.

\*\* The rent provided for in this renewal lease may be increased or decreased by order of the Division of Housing and Community Renewal (DHCR) or the Rent Guidelines Board (RGB).

3. Security Deposit:
   Current Deposit: $ _1,500.00_

   Additional Deposit Required - 1 year lease: $ _30.00_
   Additional Deposit Required - 2 year lease: $ _60.00_

4. Specify separate charges if applicable:
   Air conditioner - Electricity Charge: $ _N/A_ /mo.

   421 a(2.2%): $ _N/A_ /mo:
   Other: $ _N/A_ /mo:

5. Lower Rent to be charged, if any, $ _N/A_ .    Agreement attached:   Yes ☑   No ☐

6. This renewal lease shall commence on ____7/1/03____, which shall not be less than 90 days nor more than
   (month day year)

   150 days from the date of mailing or personal delivery of this Renewal Lease Form. This Renewal Lease shall

   terminate on ____6/30/04____ (1 year lease) or ____6/30/05____ (2 year lease.)
   (month day year)                          (month day year)

7. This renewal lease is based on the same terms and conditions as your expiring lease, except that ____0____ lawful

   provisions attached and ____0____ written agreements between owner and tenant have been added. (Indicate in

   the blank spaces as applicable, the number of additional provisions or written agreements attached).

This form becomes a binding lease renewal when signed by the owner below and returned to the tenant. A rider setting forth the rights and obligations of tenants and landlords under the Rent Stabilization Law must be attached to this lease when signed by the owner and returned to the tenant.

### PART B - TENANT'S RESPONSE TO OWNER

Tenant: Check and complete where indicated one of two responses below after reading instructions on reverse side. Then date and sign your response below. You must return this Renewal Lease Form to the owner in person or by regular mail, within 60 days of the date this Notice was served upon you by the owner. Your failure to do so may be grounds for the commencement of an action by the owner to evict you from your apartment.

   I (we) the undersigned tenant(s), agree to enter into a _____ year renewal lease at a monthly rent of $ _____.

This renewal lease is based on the same terms and conditions as my (our) expiring lease, and further attached lawful provisions and attached written agreements, if any (see item 7 under PART A above).

   I (we) will not renew my (our) lease and (we) intend to vacate the apartment on the expiration date of the present lease indicated above.

Dated: _____ 20 _____    Tenant's Signature(s): _____

Dated: _____ 20 _____    Owner's Signature(s): _____

RTP-8 (1/01) *INTERNET*

City Rent Guidelines Board. (For details on computing renewal rent increases, see Chapter 4, Section A5.) Finally, the notice should set out any additional provisions permitted by law or under the Rent Stabilization Code.

You must use a one-page DHCR form called Renewal Lease Form (RTP-8) for this purpose. (A sample is shown above.) You must use a Spanish version of the form if the tenant requests one, or if the expiring lease is in Spanish. After reading the instructions that come with the form, complete Part A ("Offer to Tenant to Renew") in duplicate by inserting the tenant's name, address, the date the lease will expire, the new rent and security deposit and the date the offered renewal lease will begin and end. One copy is for you and the other is for your tenant or tenants. (There's no need to make more than one tenant copy, even if the unit is occupied by more than one co-tenant.) Attach to both copies any additional provisions or written agreements between you and the tenant.

Mail or personally deliver both copies of the completed form (with any attachments) to your rent-stabilized tenant within the 150- to 90-day period before the lease expires.

**Where to Get Copies of the Renewal Lease.** You can get Renewal Lease forms from the DHCR. Your best bet is to download it from the DHCR website (www.dhcr.state.ny.us).

After receiving the renewal lease form, the tenant has 60 days to accept your offer by completing and signing Part B ("Tenant's Response to Owner") of the form and returning it to you. You then get 30 days to send a fully executed renewal lease form to the tenant, to which you must attach:

- a New York City Rent Stabilization Rider (see Section F, above)
- a New York City Window Guard Notice, with instruction to complete, sign and return it to you (see Section E above)

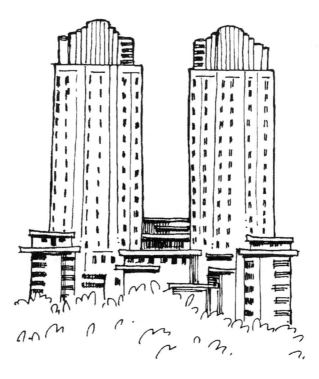

- if your building was constructed before 1974, an updated lead paint disclosure form, if required under federal law (see Chapter 11, Section A), and
- if your building was constructed before 1960, an updated New York City lead hazard form, inquiring whether a child under six will reside in the apartment, as required under New York City law (see Chapter 11, Section A, for an explanation of this requirement).

## 2. How to Offer a Renewal Lease Outside New York City

*At least 90 days and not more than 120 days before a tenant's lease is set to expire,* you're required to notify the tenant in writing that the lease will soon expire and that the tenant may renew the lease for a one- or two-year term. Your notice must also inform the tenant of the monthly rent (and security deposit) increase authorized by the county Rent Guidelines Board for one- and two-year renewal. (For details on computing renewal rent increases, see Chapter 4, Section A.) Finally, the notice should set out any additional provisions permitted by law or under the Rent Stabilization Code.

You must use a one-page DHCR form called Owner's Notice to Tenant for Renewal Lease (Form RTP-8 outside NYC) for this purpose. After reading the instructions that come with this form, complete

Part A in duplicate by inserting the tenant's name, address, the date the lease will expire, the amount that the rent and security deposit will increase and the dates that the offered renewal lease will begin and end. One copy is for you and the other is for your tenant or tenants. (There's no need to make more than one tenant copy, even if the unit is occupied by more than one co-tenant.) Attach any additional lawful provisions or written agreements between you and your tenant.

Send both copies of the form to the tenant within the 120- to 90-day period before the lease expires. The forms must be sent by certified mail, return receipt requested.

 **Where to Get Copies of the "Notice to Tenant for Renewal Lease."** You can get the ETPA Renewal Lease forms from the DHCR rent office in your county. Appendix I lists the addresses and phone numbers for each of the district rent offices.

After receiving the renewal form, the tenant has 60 days to accept your offer by completing and signing Part B of the form, and sending it back. The tenant must send the forms by certified mail, return receipt requested. You then get 30 days to send back to the tenant a fully executed renewal lease form, to which you must attach an updated lead paint disclosure form (discussed in Chapter 11, Section A).

## Month-to-Month Residential Rental Agreement

### Clause 1. Identification of Landlord and Tenant

This Agreement is entered into on _____April 1, 200X_____ between _____Marty Nelson_____

_____ ("Tenant") and

_Alex Stevens_____ ("Landlord"). Each

Tenant is jointly and severally liable for the payment of rent and performance of all other terms of

this Agreement.

### Clause 2. Identification of Premises

Subject to the terms and conditions in this Agreement, Landlord rents to Tenant, and Tenant rents

from Landlord, for living purposes only, the Premises located at _____Apartment 21-D,_____

_250 Park Ave, NY, NY 10177_____ ("the Premises"),

together with the following furnishings and appliances: _____

_____.

Rental of the Premises also includes _____

_____.

### Clause 3. Limits on Use and Occupancy

The Premises are to be used for living purposes only for Tenant(s) listed in Clause 1 of this

Agreement, by the immediate family members of the Tenant(s), and by additional occupants as

defined in and only in accordance with RPL § 235-f. For purposes of this clause, immediate family

members include a spouse, a sibling, a child, a stepchild, a grandchild, a parent, parent-in-law,

stepparent or grandparent. In addition to the foregoing, the Premises may be occupied from time to

time by guests of the Tenant(s) for a period of time not exceeding _____30_____ days, unless a

longer period is approved in writing by the Landlord. No immediate family members, additional

occupants or guests may occupy the apartment unless one or more of the Tenants occupy the rental

unit as a primary residence, or unless consented to in writing by the Landlord.

### Clause 4. Term of the Tenancy

The rental will begin on _____April 15_____, 200_X_, and continue on a month-to-month

basis. Landlord may terminate the tenancy or modify the terms of this Agreement by giving the

Tenant _____30 days_____ written notice. Tenant may terminate the tenancy by giving

the Landlord _____30 days_____ written notice.

### Clause 5. Payment of Rent

#### a. Regular monthly rent

Tenant will pay to Landlord a monthly rent of $_____2,500_____, and additional rent as set forth

below, payable in advance on the first day of each month, except when that day falls on a weekend

or legal holiday, in which case rent is due on the next business day. Rent will be paid in the following manner unless Landlord designates otherwise:

**b. Additional rent**

Tenant will pay to Landlord, as additional rent, the following monthly charges: _____, as well as any other fees or charges defined as additional rent under this Agreement.

**c. Delivery of payment**

Rent and additional rent will be paid:

☒ by mail, to _____ Alex Stevens, 28 Franklin St., NY, NY, 10013 _____

☐ in person, at _____

**d. Form of payment**

Landlord will accept payment in these forms:

☒ personal check made payable to _____ Alex Stevens _____

☒ cashier's check made payable to _____ Alex Stevens _____

☐ credit card

☒ money order

☐ cash

☐ electronic check or money transfer submitted to: _____

**e. Prorated first month's rent**

For the period from Tenant's move-in date, _____ April 15 _____, 200_ X _, through the end of the month, Tenant will pay to Landlord the prorated monthly rent of $_____ 1,250 _____. This amount will be paid on or before the date the Tenant moves in.

## Clause 6. Late Charges

If Tenant fails to pay the rent or additional rent in full before the end of the _____ tenth _____ day after it's due, Tenant will pay Landlord, as additional rent, a late charge of _____ $45 _____. Landlord does not waive the right to insist on payment of the rent or additional rent in full on the date it is due.

## Clause 7. Returned Check and Other Bank Charges

If any check offered by Tenant to Landlord in payment of rent or any other amount due under this Agreement is returned for lack of sufficient funds, a "stop payment" or any other reason, Tenant will pay Landlord a returned check charge of $_____ 15 _____.

## Clause 8. Security Deposit

On signing this Agreement, Tenant will pay to Landlord the sum of $_____ 2,500 _____ as a security deposit. Landlord will deposit this security deposit in _____ financial institution at _____. If the building in which the Premises is located contains six or more units, or if the unit is rent-stabilized, the security deposit will earn interest. Tenant may not, without Landlord's prior written consent, apply this security deposit to the last month's rent or to any other sum due under this Agreement.

If, within 60 days after Tenant has vacated and left the Premises in as good condition as it was found, except for normal wear and tear, Tenant has returned keys and provided Landlord with a forwarding address, Landlord will return the deposit in full or give Tenant an itemized written statement of the reasons for and dollar amount of any of the security deposit retained by the Landlord. Landlord may withhold all or part of Tenant's security deposit necessary to: (1) remedy any default by Tenant in the payment of rent; (2) repair damage to the Premises, except for ordinary wear and tear caused by Tenant; (3) clean the Premises if necessary, and (4) compensate Landlord for any other losses as allowed under law.

### Clause 9. Utilities

Tenant will pay all utility charges, except for the following, which will be paid by Landlord:

_gas and water_ _____

_____ .

### Clause 10. Assignment and Subletting

  a. **Assignment.** Tenant will not assign this Agreement without the Landlord's prior written consent. Prior to any assignment, Tenant must request permission to assign from the Landlord, in writing, and in the manner required by Real Property Law § 226-b. Landlord may refuse to consent to an assignment for any reason or for no reason, but if the Landlord unreasonably refuses consent, Tenant may terminate this Agreement upon thirty days' notice.

  b. **Subletting.** Tenant will not sublet any part of the Premises without the Landlord's prior written consent.

  1) If the building in which the Premises are located contains fewer than four (4) units, Landlord may refuse to consent to Tenant's sublet request for any reason or for no reason.

  2) If the building in which the Premises are located contains four (4) or more units, Tenant must request permission to sublet from the Landlord, in writing, and in the manner required by New York Real Property Law § 226-b. Landlord may not unreasonably refuse to consent to Tenant's proper request to sublet.

  c. **Fees.** Landlord may impose a reasonable fee on Tenant in connection with the review and processing of any Tenant request or application to assign or sublet.

### Clause 11. Tenant's Maintenance Responsibilities

Tenant will: (1) keep the Premises clean, sanitary and in good condition and, upon termination of the tenancy, return the Premises to Landlord in a condition identical to that which existed when Tenant took occupancy, except for ordinary wear and tear; (2) immediately notify Landlord of any defects or dangerous conditions in and about the Premises of which Tenant becomes aware; and (3) reimburse Landlord, on demand by Landlord, for the cost of any repairs to the Premises damaged by Tenant or Tenant's guests or business invitees through misuse or neglect.

Tenant has examined the Premises, including appliances, fixtures, window coverings and carpeting, if any, and has found them to be in good, safe and clean condition and repair, except as noted in the Landlord-Tenant Checklist.

### Clause 12. Repairs and Alterations by Tenant

a. Except as provided by law, or as authorized by the prior written consent of Landlord, Tenant will not make any repairs or alterations to the Premises, including painting, wallpapering or nailing holes in walls. Tenant must not change the plumbing, ventilating, air conditioning or electric or heating systems.

b. If Tenant re-keys or installs any locks to the Premises or installs or alters any burglar alarm system, Tenant will provide Landlord with a duplicate key or keys capable of unlocking all such re-keyed or new locks as well as instructions on how to disarm any altered or new burglar alarm system.

### Clause 13. Violating Laws and Causing Disturbances

Tenant is entitled to quiet enjoyment of the Premises. Tenant and guests or invitees will not use the Premises or adjacent areas in such a way as to: (1) violate any law or ordinance, including laws prohibiting the use, possession or sale of illegal drugs or controlled substances; (2) commit or permit waste (severe property damage); or (3) create a nuisance by annoying, disturbing, inconveniencing or interfering with the quiet enjoyment and peace and quiet of any other tenant or nearby resident, or their safety or comfort, or engage in any other objectionable conduct.

### Clause 14. Pets

No animal, bird or other pet will be kept on the Premises, without the Landlord's written consent, except service animals needed by blind, deaf or disabled persons and _____ under the following conditions: _____

_____ .

### Clause 15. Landlord's Right to Access

Landlord or Landlord's agents may enter the Premises in the event of an emergency, to make repairs or improvements or to show the Premises to prospective buyers or tenants. Landlord may also enter the Premises to conduct an annual inspection to check for safety or maintenance problems. Except in cases of emergency, Tenant's abandonment of the Premises, court order, or where it is impractical to do so, Landlord shall give Tenant reasonable notice before entering the Premises.

### Clause 16. Extended Absences by Tenant

Tenant will notify Landlord in advance if Tenant will be away from the Premises for _____14_____ or more consecutive days. During such absence, Landlord may enter the Premises at times reasonably necessary to maintain the property and inspect for needed repairs.

**Clause 17. Possession of the Premises**

   **a. Tenant's failure to take possession.** If, after signing this Agreement, Tenant fails to take possession of the Premises, Tenant will still be responsible for paying rent and complying with all other terms of this Agreement.

   **b. Landlord's failure to deliver possession.** If Landlord is unable to deliver possession of the Premises to Tenant for any reason not within Landlord's control, including, but not limited to, partial or complete destruction of the Premises, this Agreement shall remain in effect. Tenant's obligation to pay rent shall not begin, however, until such time as the Premises are made available to Tenant for occupancy. Landlord shall notify Tenant of the date that the Premises are available for occupancy. If Landlord fails to deliver possession to the Tenant within 30 days after the date this Agreement begins, Tenant, may elect to terminate the Agreement on written notice to the Landlord, and Landlord shall refund to Tenant any sums previously paid under this Agreement. Landlord shall not be responsible for Tenant's damages or expenses caused by any delay in delivering possession.

**Clause 18. Tenant Rules and Regulations**

   ☐ Tenant acknowledges receipt of, and has read a copy of, tenant rules and regulations, which are attached to and incorporated into this Agreement by this reference. Tenant agrees to obey and comply with these rules and all future reasonable tenant rules and regulations.

**Clause 19. Tenant Default**

   a. If Tenant fails to pay rent or additional rent after a personal demand for rent has been made by the Landlord or Landlord's agent, or within three days after a written demand for rent has been made by Landlord or Landlord's agent or attorney, Landlord may begin legal proceedings to evict Tenant and Tenant's occupants from the Premises.

   b. If Tenant otherwise defaults under this Agreement by:

   1) failing to comply with any other term or rule of this Agreement, or

   2) permanently moving out before this Agreement expires

   then Landlord must give Tenant notice of default stating the type of violation and directing Tenant to cure the violation within 10 days. If Tenant fails to cure the default within the time stated, Landlord shall terminate the Agreement by giving the Tenant a written termination notice. The termination notice will give the date the Agreement will end, which shall not be less than 10 days after the date of the notice. If Tenant and Tenant's occupants fail to move out on or before the termination date, Landlord may begin legal proceedings to evict the Tenant and Tenant's occupants from the Premises.

**Clause 20. Payment of Attorney Fees and Court Costs**

   In any legal action or proceeding to enforce any part of this Agreement, the prevailing party ☐ shall not ☒ shall recover reasonable attorney fees and court costs.

### Clause 21. Jury Trial and Counterclaims

**a. Jury trial.** Landlord and Tenant agree to give up their right to a trial by jury in any action or proceeding brought by either against the other for any matter concerning the Agreement or the Premises. This does not include actions for personal injury or property damage.

**b. Counterclaims.** Tenant agrees to give up the right to bring a counterclaim or set-off in any action or proceeding by Landlord against Tenant on any matter directly or indirectly related to the Agreement or the Premises.

### Clause 22. Disclosures

Tenant acknowledges that Landlord has made the following disclosures regarding the Premises:

☐ Disclosure of Information on Lead-Based Paint and/or Lead-Based Paint Hazards

☐ Other disclosures:_____

_____

_____

### Clause 23. Damage and Destruction

If all or part of the Premises becomes unusable, in part or totally, because of fire, accident or other casualty, the following shall apply:

a. Unless the Agreement is terminated pursuant to Subparagraphs b or c, below, Landlord will repair and restore the Premises, with this Agreement continuing in full force and effect, except that Tenant's rent shall be abated based upon the part of the Premises which are unusable, while repairs are being made. Landlord shall not be required to repair or replace any property brought onto the Premises by Tenant.

b. In the event that Landlord wishes to demolish or substantially rebuild the building in which the Premises are located, the Landlord need not restore the Premises and may elect instead to terminate this Agreement upon written notice to Tenant within thirty (30) days after such damage. If the Premises are partially usable, this Agreement will terminate 60 days from the last day of the calendar month in which Tenant is given the Landlord's termination notice.

c. If the Premises are completely unusable and the Landlord does repair the Premises within 30 days, Tenant may, upon written notice, elect to terminate this Agreement, effective as of the date the damage occurred.

### Clause 24. Notices

**a. Notices to Tenant.** Any notice from Landlord, or Landlord's agent or attorney will be considered properly given to Tenant if in writing; signed by or in the name of the Landlord or Landlord's agent; and addressed to Tenant at the Premises and delivered to Tenant personally, or sent by registered or certified mail to Tenant at the Premises. The date of service of any written notice by Landlord to Tenant under this Agreement is the date of delivery or mailing of such notice.

   **b. Notices to Landlord.** Any notice from Tenant will be considered properly given to Landlord if in writing and delivered or sent to Landlord by registered or certified mail at the following address:

_____

or at another address for which Landlord or Landlord's agent has given Tenant written notice.

## Clause 25. Abandoned Property

When this Agreement expires or is terminated, Tenant must remove all personal property and belongings from the Premises. If any of Tenant's property remains in the Premises after the tenancy ends, Landlord may either discard the property or store it at Tenant's expense. Tenant agrees to pay Landlord for all costs and expenses incurred in removing and/or storing such personal property. The terms of this clause will continue to be in effect after the end of this Agreement.

## Clause 26. Additional Provisions

Additional provisions are as follows: _____

_____

_____

## Clause 27. Validity of Each Part

If any portion of this Agreement is held to be invalid, its invalidity will not affect the validity or enforceability of any other provision of this Agreement.

## Clause 28. Entire Agreement; No Waivers

   **a. Entire agreement.** This document constitutes the entire Agreement between the parties, and no promises or representations, other than those contained here and those implied by law, have been made by Landlord or Tenant. Any modifications to this Agreement must be in writing signed by Landlord and Tenant.

   **b. No waivers.** Only a written agreement between the Landlord and Tenant may waive an obligation or violation of this Agreement. A waiver may not be implied by the Landlord's acceptance of rent, or failure to take immediate action against the Tenant, while the Tenant is violating one or more provisions of this agreement.

| April 1, 200X | *Alex Stevens* | Landlord |
|---|---|---|
| Date | Landlord or Landlord's Agent | Title |
| 28 Franklin St., 6th Floor | | |
| Street Address | | |
| New York, NY 10013 | | 212-555-1578 |
| City, State & Zip | | Phone |
| April 1, 200X | *Marty Nelson* | 718-555-8751 |
| Date | Tenant | Phone |
| | | |
| Date | Tenant | |
| | | |
| Date | Witness | |

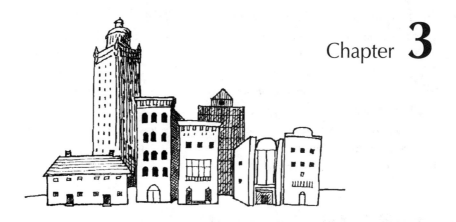

Chapter 3

# Basic Rent Laws

To state the obvious, one of your foremost concerns as a landlord is receiving your rent—on time and without hassle. It follows that you need a good grasp of the legal rules governing rent. This chapter outlines basic state laws affecting how much you can charge, as well as where, when and how rent is due. It also covers rules regarding grace periods, late rent, rent receipts, returned check charges and rent increases.

## Avoiding Rent Disputes

Here are three guidelines that can help you and your tenants have a smooth relationship when it comes to an area of utmost interest to both of you: rent.

1. Clearly spell out rent rules in your lease or rental agreement as well as in a move-in letter to new tenants.
2. Be fair and consistent about enforcing your rent rules.
3. If rent isn't paid on time, follow through as soon as possible with a legal rent demand notice telling the tenant to pay or move—the first legal step in a possible eviction proceeding.

**If you own one of the 1.2 million rental units in the state that are subject to rent control or rent stabilization laws and regulations, be sure to also read Chapter 4.** It covers issues of specific concern to landlords with rent-regulated properties, including registration, rent increases, decontrol, deregulation and tenant overcharge complaints. In this chapter, owners of rent-regulated units can find out about when rent is due (Section B), where and how rent is due (Section C), rent receipts (Section D), late charges and discounts for early payments (Section E), returned check charges (Section F) and how to deal with partial or delayed rent payments (Section G).

 Related topics covered in this book include:

- Lease and rental agreement provisions relating to rent: Chapter 2
- Collecting security deposits and keeping them in separate accounts: Chapter 5
- Compensating a manager with reduced rent: Chapter 6
- Highlighting rent rules in a move-in letter to new tenants and collecting the first month's rent: Chapter 7
- Co-tenants' and roommates' obligations for rent: Chapter 8
- How a landlord's responsibility to maintain the premises in good condition relates to a tenant's duty to pay rent: Chapter 9
- How to draft and serve a rent demand notice and deal with tenants who chronically pay rent late: Chapter 12, and
- Accepting rent after a termination notice is given: Chapter 15.

## A. How Much Can You Charge?

The general rule is that there's no limit to how much rent you can charge; you are free to charge what the market will bear. But there's a big exception to this rule: rental units that are covered by some form of government rent regulation. By far the biggest group falling under this exception is the 1.2 million rental units around the state that are subject to either "rent control" or "rent stabilization"—the two principal forms of rent regulation in New York. (The rules that determine how much you can charge rent-controlled and rent-stabilized tenants are examined in Chapter 4.)

If your rental unit is free from rent regulation, it's up to you to determine how much rent to charge. If you're unsure, you may wish to check newspaper apartment ads for rents of comparable properties in your area, and perhaps visit a few places that sound similar to yours. Local property management companies, real estate offices that handle rental property and apartment listing services can also provide useful advice. In addition, local apartment associations—or other landlords you meet at association functions—are a good source of pricing information.

Many wise landlords choose to charge just slightly less than the going rate as part of a policy designed to find and keep excellent tenants. As with any business arrangement, it usually pays in the long run to have your tenants feel they are getting a good deal. In exchange, you hope the tenants will be responsive to your business needs. This doesn't always work, of course, but tenants who feel their rent is fair are less likely to complain over trifling matters and more likely to stay for an extended period. Certainly, tenants who think you are trying to squeeze every last nickel out of them won't think twice before calling you about a clogged toilet at 11 PM.

**You may offer rent discounts for senior citizens and the disabled.** Fair housing laws prohibit you from offering different rental terms to applicants on the basis of their age or disability. (See Chapter 1.) But state law permits you to offer rent discounts to senior citizens and the disabled, without fear of violating fair housing laws. (Executive Law § 296(17), (19).) That means you can offer the same rental unit to a qualified disabled or senior citizen applicant for less rent than you would charge a tenant who is not disabled or who is under the age of 65.

## B. When Rent Is Due

Most leases and rental agreements, including the ones in this book, call for rent to be paid monthly, in advance, on the first day of the month. (See Clause 5 of the form agreements in Chapter 2.)

### 1. First Day, Last Day or In Between?

The first of the month is a customary and convenient due date for rent, at least in part because many

tenants get their paychecks on the last workday of the month. Also, the approach of a new month can, in itself, help remind people to pay monthly bills due on the first. With luck, your tenant will learn to associate flipping the calendar page with paying the rent on time.

It is perfectly legal to require rent to be paid on a different day of the month, and may make sense if the tenant is paid at odd times. Some landlords make the rent payable each month on the date the tenant first moved in. Generally, it's easier to pro-rate rent for a short first month and then require that rent be paid on the first of the next month. But if you have only a few tenants and don't mind having different tenants paying you on different days of the month, it makes no legal difference.

Whatever you decide, be sure to put the day of the month that rent is due in your lease or rental agreement. If you don't, state law could do it for you. The law presumes that rent is not due until *after* it has been earned, unless the lease or rental agreement says otherwise. (*Smathers v. Standard Oil Co.*, 233 N.Y. 617, 135 N.E. 942 (1922).) If you want a tenant to pay rent in advance on the first day of the month, your lease or rental agreement must expressly provide for advance payments. You would probably never deliberately allow a tenant who moved in on the first day of the month to wait to pay rent until the 31st. Make sure you don't accidentally allow it.

### Collecting Rent More Than Once a Month

If you wish, you and the tenant can agree that the rent be paid twice a month, each week, or on whatever schedule suits you. The most common variation on the standard monthly payment arrangement is having rent paid twice a month. This is a particularly good idea if you have tenants who have relatively low-paying jobs and get paid twice a month, because they may have difficulty saving the needed portion of their mid-month check until the first of the month.

## 2. When the Due Date Falls on a Weekend or Holiday

The lease and rental agreements in this book state that when the rent due date falls on a weekend day or legal holiday, the tenant must pay it by the next business day. (See Clause 5 of the form agreements in Chapter 2.) This extension of the due date is legally required under state law (Gen.Const. L §§ 20, 24, 25, 25-a). That means that you can't insist that the tenant always get the rent check to you on the first, no matter what.

> EXAMPLE: If your lease or rental agreement says that a tenant's rent is due on the first day of each month, and April 1 falls on a Saturday, rent isn't due until Monday, April 3. If April 3 is a legal holiday, rent isn't legally due until Tuesday, April 4.

Figuring out the exact date when rent is due is important if you plan on serving a rent demand on the tenant. (Chapter 12 covers starting a non-payment eviction proceeding with a rent demand.) If your rent demand is made too soon, it won't be legally enforceable. (And if you commence an eviction lawsuit following a premature rent demand, your tenant will be able to toss it out, making you start over.)

## 3. Grace Periods for Late Rent

Lots of tenants are absolutely convinced that if rent is due on the first, but they pay by the 5th (or sometimes the 7th or even the 10th) of the month, they have legally paid their rent on time because they are within a legal grace period. This is simply not true. It is your legal right to insist that rent be paid on the day it is due (unless that day falls on a weekend or holiday). As we recommend in Clause 5 of our form agreements in Chapter 2, use your lease or rental agreement and move-in letter to disabuse tenants of this bogus "grace period" notion.

In practice, many landlords do not get upset about late rent or collect a late fee (discussed in Section E), until the rent is a few days past due. Nevertheless, your best approach is to consistently stress to tenants that rent must be paid on the due date.

In our opinion, if you wait more than ten days or so to collect your rent, you are running your business unwisely and just extending the time a non-paying tenant can stay. Be firm, but fair. Any other policy will get you into a morass of special cases and exceptions and will cost you a bundle in the long run. If you allow exceptions only in extreme circumstances (see Section G), tenants will learn not to try and sell you sob stories.

## Evictions for Non-Payment of Rent

Failure to pay rent on time is by far the most common reason landlords go to court and evict tenants. First, however, a landlord must issue a "rent demand" notifying the tenant to either pay within a few days or move out. How long the tenant is allowed to stay depends on what the lease or rental agreement says. The legal minimum is three days. Our form agreements require three days' notice. (See Chapter 2, Clause 19(a).) Some leases and rental agreements require landlords to give the tenants as much as ten days' notice. (Chapter 12 describes how to make a rent demand.)

In most instances, the tenant who receives a rent demand pays up, and that's the end of it. But if the tenant doesn't pay the rent (or move) within the time provided in the notice, you can begin a "non-payment" eviction proceeding against the tenant.

If you find yourself delivering too many rent demands to a particular tenant, you may want to end the tenancy—even if the tenant always comes up with the rent at the last minute. For month-to-month tenants, this is easy. (Chapter 13 tells you how to terminate a monthly tenancy.) It's more difficult (but not impossible) to end a fixed-term tenancy for chronic late rent payment—especially if the tenant is protected by rent control or rent stabilization. (Chapter 14, Section D, discusses terminating a fixed-term tenancy for chronic late payment of rent.)

## C. Where and How Rent Is Due

You should specify in your lease or rental agreement where the tenant should pay the rent and how you want it paid—for example, by check, money order or electronic transfer only. (See Clause 5 of the form agreements in Chapter 2.)

## 1. Where Rent Must Be Paid

You have several options for where the tenant pays you rent:

**By mail.** Allowing tenants to mail you the rent check is the most common method of payment, by a long shot. It's pretty convenient for everyone, and you can make it even easier by giving tenants pre-addressed (and stamped, if you're feeling generous) envelopes. The small amount you spend on postage and supplies may save you money in the long run, because this will help assure that you'll get paid on time.

**At your office.** Requiring the rent to be paid personally at your place of business or manager's office is feasible only if you have an on-site office. Asking tenants to drive across town is both unreasonable and counterproductive, because inevitably some of them just won't get around to it. This approach does have certain advantages. It makes the tenant responsible for getting the rent to you at a certain time or place, and avoids issues such as whether or not a rent check was lost or delayed in the mail. It also guarantees at least a bit of personal contact with your tenants, and a chance to air little problems before they become big ones.

**At home.** You can send someone to each unit, every month, to pick up the rent. But this more old-fashioned way of collecting the rent isn't well suited to modern life, when in most households it's hard to find someone at home during the day. It may be useful, however, if you think face-to-face contact might prompt a tenant to come up with the rent more quickly.

If your lease or rental agreement doesn't specify where you want tenants to pay you rent, the law presumes that you'll go to the tenant's rental unit to pick up the rent. (*M & E Design Co. v. Whitney's Cadillac Rental Inc.*, 75 N.Y.S.2d 924 (Sup. Ct., Queens County, 1947).)

## New Ways to Pay the Rent

More and more landlords, especially those with large numbers of rental units, are looking for ways to ensure that rent payments are quick and reliable. Here are three new methods:

**Credit card.** If you have enough tenants to make it worthwhile, explore the option of accepting credit cards. You must pay a fee—a percentage of the amount charged—for the privilege, but the cost may be justified if it results in more on-time payments and less hassle for you and tenants. Keep in mind that you'll need to have someone in your office to process the credit card payments and to give tenants receipts (Section D explains what receipts must say). And if your tenant population is affluent enough, consider requiring automatic credit card debits.

**Automatic bank debit.** You can get a tenant's permission to have rent payments debited automatically each month from the tenant's bank account and transferred into your account. Tenants may be leery of this idea, however, and it's not worth insisting on. Tenants who travel a lot, however, or are too busy to write monthly checks, may appreciate this alternate payment option. For more details on this option, contact your bank.

**Electronic payment.** You can give tenants permission to transfer rent payments directly into your bank account "electronically" via personal computer. Unlike automatic debits, there's no set date for the payment. The tenant decides when to transfer the funds to you. Electronic payments are growing in popularity as more and more New York banks offer free online banking to their customers. Ask your bank for details on how you can make this form of payment available to your tenants.

## 2. Form of Rent Payment

You should also specify in your lease or rental agreement how rent must be paid: by cash, check, money order or electronic transfer. (See Clause 5 of the form agreements in Chapter 2.)

For most landlords, rental checks are routine. If a tenant doesn't have a checking account or has bounced too many checks, you may want to require a certified check or money order.

You should never accept post dated checks. The most obvious reason is that the check may never be good. You have absolutely no assurance that necessary funds will ever be deposited in the account, or be available when the time comes to cash the check. Far better to tell the tenant that rent must be paid in full on time and to give the tenant a late notice if it isn't.

⚠️ **Don't accept cash unless you have no choice.** You are a likely target for robbery if word gets out that you are taking in large amounts of cash once or twice a month. And if you accept cash knowing that the tenant earned it from an illegal act, such as drug dealing, the government could seize it from you under criminal forfeiture laws. If you do accept cash, be sure to provide a written receipt (see Section D, below).

## 3. Changing Where and How Rent Is Due

If you've been burned by bounced checks from a particular tenant, you may want to decree that from now on, you'll accept nothing less than a certified check or money order, and that rent may be paid only during certain hours at the manager's office.

Be careful. It may be illegal to suddenly change your terms for payment of rent without proper notice to the tenant—unless you are simply enforcing an existing term. For example, if your rental agreement states that you accept only money orders, you are on solid ground when you tell a check-bouncing tenant that you'll no longer accept her checks, and that your previous practice of doing so was merely an accommodation not required under the rental agreement.

If, however, your lease or rental agreement doesn't say where and how rent is to be paid, your past practice may legally control how rent is paid until you properly notify the tenant of a change. If you want to require tenants to pay rent at your office, for example, you must formally change a written periodic rental agreement with a written "rider" (see Section H2, below, for a sample Rental Agreement Rider). You may modify an oral rental agreement orally—no written notice is required. If your tenant has a lease, you will have to wait until the lease runs out.

## D. Rent Receipts

If a tenant pays rent by cash, money order or any form *other than* a personal check, state law requires you to give the tenant a written receipt. (RPL § 235-e(a).) The rent receipt must contain the following information:

- the date rent was paid
- the amount of rent paid
- the address of the tenant's rental unit
- the time period for which rent is paid
- the signature and title of the person who accepted the rent, and
-  for NYC tenants only, the name and New York City address of the owner or managing agent. (NYC Admin. Code § 27-2105; 9 NYCRR § 2525.2(b)(3).)

If requested in writing, you must give rent receipts to a tenant who pays by personal check, too. (RPL § 235-e(b); 9 NYCRR § 2525.2(b)(2).) The rent receipt requirement applies to all tenants, including those covered by rent control and rent stabilization laws.

A sample Rent Receipt is shown below.

 The Forms CD includes a Rent Receipt form, and a blank tear-out copy is in the Appendix.

Be sure to keep copies of rent receipts in tenant files. These may be important evidence if you and the tenant end up in court in a rent dispute.

 **The Housing Maintenance Code requires New York City landlords to provide either a rent bill or a rent receipt to every tenant each month.** (NYC Admin. Code §27-2105.) Unlike state law, there's no exception for tenants who pay by check. Most landlords satisfy this requirement by generating monthly rent bills for their buildings and having building staff slide them beneath the entrance door to each rental unit. All rent bills and receipts for payment must state the name and New York City address of the "managing agent," as listed on the registration for the building with the City. A "managing agent" is a natural person (not a business) over the age of 21 who is in control of and responsible for the maintenance and operation of the building, and who may authorize emergency repairs. The managing agent must either live or have an office in New York City. Alternatively, an owner or corporate officer who meets these requirements may be registered as the managing agent. (Chapter 6 covers supers and property managers.)

What happens if you don't issue rent receipts as required? Technically, nothing. There's no penalty under either the Real Property Law or the Housing Maintenance Code for failing to provide a rent receipt. But not having a copy of a receipt could hurt you down the road if you end up in court with the tenant. That happened to one Wayne County landlord who sued a tenant for $783 in back rent. The tenant, who paid his rent in cash each month, claimed that he only owed "about $200." Since the landlord violated the law by failing to issue rent receipts for the tenant's cash rent payments, the court resolved the case in favor of the tenant. The landlord ended up unable to collect $583 in back rent that he claimed was owed. If the landlord had been able to show that he consistently issued receipts for rent, he might have fared better. (*Brinkman v. Cahill*, 143 Misc. 2d 1048, 543 N.Y.S. 2d 636 (Justice Ct., Wayne Cty., 1989).)

Set a written management policy as to which of your employees are authorized to accept rent from tenants and sign rent receipts. Use your move-in letter to notify tenants as to which building employees, if any, are authorized to accept rent. (Chapter 7 covers tenant move-in letters.)

---

## Rent Receipt

ABC Management Corporation

202 Madison Avenue

New York, NY 10016

Receipt No. ___1008___

Date: ___November 8, 200X___

Premises address: ___202 Madison Ave, NY, NY___

_____ Unit #: ___Apt. 5-B___

Amount of rent received: ___$1,250.00___

Rental period: ___November, 200X___

Form of payment (check one):

[X] Personal check        [ ] Certified check     [ ] Cash

[ ] Postal money order    [ ] Bank check          [ ] Other: (specify)_____

Received by: ___Paul Ruiz___

Recipient's name and title: ___Paul Ruiz, Managing Agent___

---

## E. Late Charges and Discounts for Early Payments

If you're faced with a tenant who hasn't paid rent on the due date, you probably don't want to immediately hand out a formal rent demand notice telling the tenant to pay the rent or leave. After all, it's not going to do anything positive for your relationship with the tenant, who may have just forgotten to drop the check in a mailbox. But how else can you motivate tenants to pay rent on time?

A fairly common and sensible practice is to charge a reasonable late fee. You can base your late fee on a percentage of the overdue rent, or impose a flat fee instead.

New York landlords have no statutory right to a late fee, so you must establish a late fee policy in your lease or rental agreement. (See Clause 6 of the form agreements in Chapter 2.) *If it's not if the lease or rental agreement, you can't collect a late fee.* It's a good idea to highlight your late fee policy when you review the lease with rental applicants. Also mention it in your move-in letter to new tenants. (Chapter 7 covers tenant move-in letters.)

While New York has no set limit on how big a late fee you can charge, you're still bound by general legal principles that prohibit unreasonably high fees. Contracts that call for a late fee that is disproportionate and way beyond the amount of money you have lost (in interest and time spent reminding the tenant to pay) are not enforceable. If a tenant challenges a big late fee in court (either in a non-payment eviction proceeding or a separate case brought by the tenant), you could lose. And obviously, excessive late fees generate tenant hostility, anyway.

⚠ **Never use the term "penalty" to describe your late fee.** While courts will usually enforce late fees that bear a realistic relationship to your actual losses, courts steadfastly refuse to enforce "penalties" that are intended to punish late-payers. To make your late fee stick, avoid using the words "penalty" or "penalize" when referring to your late fees in a lease, rental agreement or move-in letter.

How big a late fee can you charge? You should be on safe ground if you adhere to these principles:

- The late fee should not apply until at least seven days after the due date—especially if you accept rent by mail. Imposing a stiff late charge if the rent is only a few days late probably won't be upheld in court.
- The total late charge should not be much higher than five percent of the monthly rent. That's $50 on a $1,000-per-month rental.

💡 **State law permits mobile home landlords to collect a 5% late fee when the rent is ten or more days late.** (RPL § 233(r).) A late fee policy that reflects this formula should be enforceable for other types of rental housing, too.

If the late fee increases each day the rent is late, it should be moderate and have an upper limit. A late charge that increases without limit each day could be considered interest charged at an illegal ("usurious") rate. Under New York law, interest charged at a rate exceeding 25% per year constitutes criminal usury. (Penal L. § 190.40.) (Ten dollars a day on a $1,000-per-month rent is 3,650% annual interest.) A more acceptable late charge would be $10 for the first day rent is late, plus $5 for each additional day, up to a maximum of 5% of the rental amount.

⚠ **Don't try to disguise excessive late charges by giving a "discount" for early payment.** Courts usually see the discount for what it really is—a late fee in disguise. And if the amount of the "discount" is excessive—that is, more than 5% or so of the monthly rent—it won't be enforceable. One landlord we know concluded he couldn't get away with charging a $100 late charge on a $850 rent payment, so instead, he designed a rental agreement calling for a rent of $950 with a $100 discount if the rent was not more than three days late. Ingenious as this ploy sounds, it is unlikely to stand up in court, unless the discount for timely payment is very modest. Giving a relatively large discount is in effect the same as charging an excessive late fee, and a judge is likely to see it as such.

Anyway, fooling around with late charges is wasted energy. If you want more rent for your unit, raise the rent (unless the unit is rent-regulated). If you are concerned about tenants paying on time—and who isn't—put your energy into choosing responsible tenants. (See Chapter 1 for advice.)

If you have a tenant with a month-to-month tenancy who drives you nuts with late rent payments, and a reasonable late charge doesn't resolve the situation, terminate the tenancy with the appropriate notice, as explained in Chapter 13. See Chapter 12, Section I, for advice on dealing with tenants who chronically pay rent late.

## F. Returned Check Charges

It's legal to charge the tenant an extra fee if a rent check bounces, so long as the lease or rental agreement authorizes the charge. (See Clause 7 of the form agreements in Chapter 2.) If you're having a lot of trouble with bounced checks, you may want to change your policy to accept only money orders for rent. (See Section C2, above.)

Like late charges, bounced check charges must be reasonable. You should charge no more than the amount your bank charges you for a returned check charge, probably $15 to $20 per returned item, plus a few dollars for your trouble.

It is a poor idea to let your bank redeposit rent checks that bounce. Instead, tell the bank to return bad checks to you immediately. Getting a bounced check back quickly alerts you to the fact that the rent is unpaid much sooner than if the check is resubmitted and returned for nonpayment a second time. You can use this time to ask the tenant to make the check good immediately. If the tenant doesn't come through, you can promptly serve a rent demand notice on the tenant demanding that he pay the rent or move. If the tenant doesn't make the check good by the deadline, you can start non-payment eviction proceedings.

## G. Partial or Delayed Rent Payments

On occasion, a tenant suffering a temporary financial setback will offer something less than the full month's rent, with a promise to catch up as the month proceeds, or at the first of the next month. You're not legally required to accept less than the full month's rent. (*335 West 38th Street Cooperative Corp. v. Anchev*, N.Y.L.J., 12/17/97, p. 21, col. 1 (App. Term, 1st Dep't).) You may nevertheless wish to make a rare exception where the tenant's financial problems truly appear to be temporary and you have known the person for a long time.

### 1. Don't Routinely Accept Partial or Late Payments

There is generally no legal problem if you accept partial rent payments or late payments now and then. If you occasionally accept less than a full month's rent from a tenant, you don't give up your right to collect the balance. But if you regularly accept rent in installment payments or accept full payment on, say, the 15th of the month (despite a written agreement that rent is due in one payment in advance), you may unwittingly "waive," or give up, your right to insist on full payment of the rent on the first of the month.

**EXAMPLE:** You routinely permit your tenant Howard, whose $1,200 rent is due on the first of the month, to pay $600 on the first and the other $600 on the 15th. Nine months later, you grow tired of this arrangement. After receiving $600 on the first day of the month, you direct your manager to serve Howard with a three-day rent demand on the second of the month to pay the rest of the rent or move out. This may not work. You may be stuck with getting $600 on the first and $600 on the 15th for the balance of the lease term or, in the case of a month-to-month rental agreement, until you give Howard written notice of change in the terms of the tenancy. (See Section H2, below.)

Why? Because a judge in a non-payment eviction proceeding may rule that, by giving Howard this break for almost a year, coupled with his reliance on this custom, you in effect waived your right to demand full payment on the first of the month. In effect, you changed the terms of the lease or rental agreement. Viewed this way, your three-day rent demand would be premature because the second $600 isn't due until the 15th.

### 2. Accepting Partial Payment After a Rent Demand Notice

If your tenant offers partial payment after receiving a rent demand notice, you're not required to accept partial payment. But you may accept the partial payment and then serve a new rent demand on the tenant for the new balance of rent due. Or, you can refuse to accept the partial payment and begin a non-payment eviction proceeding if the tenant doesn't pay up by the time provided in the rent demand notice.

 **Don't accept partial payment and then sue for the balance without serving a new rent demand.** Once you accept partial payment, your original rent demand is no longer correct or valid. Any subsequent lawsuit based on the original rent demand would probably fail. (Chapter 12 covers rent demands.)

## 3. Written Agreements to Accept Delayed or Partial Rent

If you do give a tenant a little more time to pay some or all of the rent, establish a schedule, in writing, for when the rent will be paid. Then monitor the situation carefully. Otherwise, the tenant may try to delay payment indefinitely, or make such small and infrequent payments that the account is never brought current. A signed agreement—say for a one-week extension—lets both you and the tenant know what's expected. If you give the tenant two weeks to catch up and she doesn't, the written agreement precludes any argument that you had really said "two to three weeks." A sample Agreement for Delayed or Partial Rent Payments is shown below.

The Forms CD includes the Agreement for Delayed or Partial Rent Payments, and the Appendix includes a blank tear-out copy of this form.

---

### Agreement for Delayed or Partial Rent Payments

This Agreement is made between _____Allison Morris_____ "Tenant(s),"

and _____James J. Cannon_____ "Landlord/Manager."

1. _____Allison Morris_____ "Tenant(s)" has/have paid

_____one-half of her $2,800 rent for Apt. 3B at 100 Water St., NY, NY_____

_____

on _____March 1_____, 200_X_, which was due _____March 1_____, 200_X_.

2. _____James J. Cannon_____ (Landlord/Manager)

agrees to accept all the remainder of the rent on or before _____March 15_____, 200_X_,

and to hold off on any legal proceeding to evict _____Allison Morris_____

_____ (Tenant(s)) until that date.

| _____3/2/0X_____ | _James J. Cannon_ |
|---|---|
| Date | Landlord/Manager |

| _____3/2/0X_____ | _Allison Morris_ |
|---|---|
| Date | Tenant |

| _____ | _____ |
|---|---|
| Date | Tenant |

| _____ | _____ |
|---|---|
| Date | Tenant |

If the tenant does not pay the rest of the rent when promised, you can follow through with the appropriate legal steps to collect the rent, starting with a written rent demand notice as discussed in Chapter 12.

## H. Raising the Rent

Except for rent-regulated units, your freedom to raise the rent (or modify other terms of the tenancy) depends primarily on whether the tenant has a lease or a month-to-month rental agreement.

 **Rent control and rent stabilization laws limit your right to increase the rent.** Chapter 4 details permissible rent increases under New York State and New York City rent regulatory laws.

### 1. Fixed-Term Tenancies

Fixed-term tenants sign leases. For the most part, the lease fixes the terms of tenancy for the length of the lease. You can't change anything until the lease ends unless the lease itself allows it or the tenant agrees to the change. When the lease expires, you can present the tenant with a new lease with a higher rent or other changed terms. While not legally required, it's usually best to give tenants one or two month's notice of any rent increase before negotiating a new lease.

### 2. Month-to-Month Tenancies

It's easy to change the rent or other term of a month-to-month rental agreement. But the procedure to follow depends on whether the rental agreement is oral or written.

**If the rental agreement is oral,** simply tell the tenant that you intend to raise the rent for the next monthly period. If the tenant agrees to the rent increase (or to any other change in term), you're finished. You're not legally required to provide the

tenant with a prescribed amount of notice or to put the agreement is writing. If the tenant doesn't agree to the rent hike (or other change), you can terminate the tenancy on 30 days' notice within New York City and one month's notice outside New York City. (Chapter 13 explains how to terminate a month-to-month tenancy.)

**If the rental agreement is in writing,** you may need to draw up a "rider" to the rental agreement in order to raise the monthly rent and security deposit, or otherwise change your agreement. That's because many written rental agreements, like the one in this book, contain a clause that requires all modifications of the agreement to be made in writing and signed by the landlord and tenant (see Chapter 2, Clause 28). A sample Rental Agreement Rider you can use for this purpose appears below.

 The Forms CD includes the Rental Agreement Rider and the Appendix includes a blank tear-out version of the form.

If the tenant refuses to sign the rider, you can terminate the tenancy on 30 days' notice if the property is within New York City or one month's notice if it's outside New York City. Chapter 13 explains how to terminate a monthly tenancy.

### 3. How Much Can You Raise the Rent?

For month-to-month tenants (and other periodic tenants), there's no limit on the amount you can increase the rent. Similarly, there is no restriction on the period of time between rent increases. You can legally raise the rent as much and as often as good business dictates. Of course, common sense should tell you that if your tenants think your increases are unfair, you may end up with vacant units or a hostile group of tenants looking for ways to make you miserable. As a courtesy, you may wish to tell your tenants of the rent increase personally, perhaps explaining the reasons—although reasons aren't legally necessary.

# Rental Agreement Rider

This Rider shall be attached to and form a part of the Rental Agreement dated ___March 1, 200X___

between ___White Street Associates_____,

as Landlord, and _____Michael Bloome,_____,

as Tenant, for the Premises located at _____Apartment 3A, 65 White Street, New York, NY 10013___

_____.

1. It is hereby agreed that the monthly rent for the Premises shall be increased to $____1,750____

    as of ___January 1, 200x._____.

2. Tenant agrees to post additional security for the premises in the amount of $____500____ on

    or before___January 1, 200X_____. Upon receipt of the additional security by landlord,

    the full amount of tenant's security deposit for the premises shall total $____1,750_____.

3. There are no other changes to the Rental Agreement.

____December 12, 200X_____    _Perry Aziz_, General Partner, White Street Associates, Landlord
Date                                          Landlord/Manager

____December 12, 200X_____    _Michael Bloome_____
Date                                          Tenant

Chapter **4**

# Rent Regulation

Rent laws and regulations do not affect every locality in New York. But some cities, towns and villages with local rental housing shortages have elected to opt in to a system of state-administered rent laws. More than 1.2 million rental units in 55 localities across the state are subject to either "rent stabilization" or "rent control"—the two principal forms of "rent regulation" in New York.

*Rent stabilization*, which first began in 1969, now affects over one million units in New York City and in the suburban counties of Nassau, Rockland and Westchester. Tenants who move into vacant rent-stabilized units are entitled to one- or two-year "vacancy" leases at regulated rents and are generally entitled to "renewal" leases for successive one- or two-year terms. When a rent-stabilized tenant moves out, the unit usually remains subject to rent stabilization. That means that the next incoming tenant will also be entitled to the benefits and protections of rent stabilization.

*Rent control*, which began after World War II, now only affects around 96,000 units scattered around the state. Rent-controlled tenants seldom have a current lease for their units. They are often called "statutory tenants" since a rent control statute, not a lease, entitles them to remain in occupancy at regulated rents (which are generally far lower than stabilized rents). Generally, when a rent-controlled tenant dies or moves out, the unit becomes "de-controlled" and is no longer subject to rent control.

Trying to understand rent stabilization and rent control is a little like trying to understand the Internal Revenue Code. So prepare to feel baffled, daunted (and more than a little angry) by the arcane web of rent laws and regulations that follow.

Rent laws and regulations control far more than how much rent a landlord may charge. They also govern security deposits, required services, sublet rights, your right to access, how and under what circumstances you can end a tenancy and, for rent-stabilized units, the lease itself.

This chapter examines the basic rent control and rent stabilization rules that are in effect throughout the state and in New York City, specifically those that cover rent, rent increases, rent registration, vacancy decontrol, "high-rent/high-income" deregulation and rent overcharge proceedings.

 Other chapters discuss rules that affect rent-controlled and rent-stabilized units:

- Writing rent-stabilized leases, riders and renewal offers: Chapter 2 and Appendix II, which includes a sample copy of a New York City rent-stabilized lease
- Rules covering when, where and how rent is due, rent receipts, late fees and accepting partial or delayed rent payments: Chapter 3
- Dealing with security deposits: Chapter 5
- Apartment sharing, subletting and assignments, including special subletting rules for rent-stabilized units: Chapter 8
- Providing and maintaining services and making repairs: Chapter 9
- Getting access to a rent-regulated tenant's unit for repairs, improvements, inspections and showings: Chapter 10
- Making a rent demand for overdue rent: Chapter 12
- Grounds for terminating rent-controlled and rent-stabilized tenancies and succession rights to rent-regulated units: Chapter 14
- Preparing and serving notices terminating rent-regulated tenancies: Chapter 15
- Division of Housing and Community Renewal (DHCR) office addresses, telephone numbers, website and publications: Appendix I
- Rent Guidelines Board addresses, phone numbers and websites: Appendix I
- New York City Housing Preservation and Development (HPD) Office of Code Enforcement addresses and phone numbers: Appendix I.

## Municipalities Subject to Rent Regulation

The counties, cities, towns and villages listed below have adopted some form of rent regulation. Not all units within these municipalities are subject to rent control or rent stabilization. Only those units in buildings that meet certain requirements are covered. We detail those requirements (and describe which units are exempt from rent regulation) in Sections A and B of this chapter.

**Localities Covered by New York City Rent Control**

- Bronx County
- Kings County (Brooklyn)
- New York County (Manhattan)
- Queens County
- Richmond County (Staten Island)

**Localities Covered by State Rent Control**

- Albany County: Cities of Albany and Watervliet; Towns of Bethlehem, Green Island and New Scotland; Villages of Green Island and Voorheesville
- Erie County: City of Buffalo; Town of Cheektowaga; Villages of Depew and Sloan
- Nassau County: Cities of Glen Cove and Long Beach; Towns of Hempstead, North Hempstead and Oyster Bay
- Rensselaer County: City of Rensselaer; Towns of Hoosick and North Greenbush; Village of Hoosick Falls
- Schenectady County: Towns of Niskayuna and Princeton
- Westchester County: Cities of Mount Vernon, New Rochelle, White Plains, Yonkers; Towns of Eastchester, Greenburgh, Harrison and Mamaroneck; Villages of Ardsley, Dobbs Ferry, Hastings-on-Hudson, Larchmont, Mamaroneck, Sleepy Hollow, Tarrytown and Tuckahoe

**Localities Covered by New York City Rent Stabilization**

- Bronx County
- Kings County (Brooklyn)
- New York County (Manhattan)
- Queens County
- Richmond County (Staten Island)

**Localities Covered by State ("ETPA") Rent Stabilization***

- Nassau County: Cities of Glen Cove and Long Beach; Town of North Hempstead; Villages of Cedarhurst, Floral Park, Flower Hill, Freeport, Great Neck, Great Neck Plaza, Hempstead, Lynbrook, Mineola, Rockville Centre, Russell Gardens, Thomaston and Baxter Estates
- Rockland County: Town of Haverstraw and Village of Spring Valley
- Westchester County: Cities of Mount Vernon, New Rochelle, White Plains and Yonkers; Towns of East Chester, Greenburgh, Harrison and Mamaroneck; Villages of Dobbs Ferry, Hastings-on-Hudson, Irvington, Larchmont, Mamaroneck, Mt. Kisco, Sleepy Hollow, Pleasantville, Port Chester and Tarrytown

*Rent stabilization may continue in these municipalities only as long as there is a rental vacancy rate of less than 5% for the area.

## Where to Find Rent Stabilization and Rent Control Laws and Regulations

Throughout this chapter, we provide legal citations for key sections of rent stabilization and rent control laws and regulations. Here are the citations for the full text of these laws and regulations:

- **New York City Rent Stabilization Law:** The full text of the law can be found at § 26-501 of the Administrative Code of the City of New York. (NYC Adm. Code § 26-501 and following.)
- **New York City Rent Stabilization Regulations:** Officially titled the "New York City Rent Stabilization Code," you may find these regulations at Volume 9 of the Official Compilation of Codes, Rules and Regulations of the State of New York, beginning at § 2520.1. (9 NYCCR § 2520.1 and following).
- **New York State ("ETPA") Rent Stabilization Law:** Officially called the "Emergency Tenant Protection Act (ETPA) of 1974," you can find this law in New York's Unconsolidated Laws, beginning at § 8621. (NY Uncon. § 8621 and following.)
- **New York State Rent Stabilization Regulations:** Officially called the "Emergency Tenant Protection Regulations," they may be found at Volume 9 of the Official Compilation of Codes, Rules and Regulations of the State of New York, starting at § 2500.1. (9 NYCRR § 2500.1 and following.)
- **New York City Rent Control Law:** Officially called the "New York City Rent and Rehabilitation Law," you may find the full text of this law in the Administrative Code of the City of New

York, beginning at § 26-401. (NYC Adm. Code § 26-401.)
- **New York City Rent Control Regulations:** Officially called the "New York City Rent and Eviction Regulations," you may find these regulations in Volume 9 of the Official Compilation of Codes, Rules and Regulations of the State of New York, beginning at § 2200.1. (NYCRR § 2200.1 and following.)
- **New York State Rent Control Law:** Officially called the "Emergency Housing Rent Control Law," you may find the full text of this law in New York's Unconsolidated Laws, beginning at § 8581. (NY Unconsol. § 8581 and following.)
- **New York State Rent Control Regulations:** Officially called the "State Rent and Eviction Regulations," you can find these in Vol. 9 of the Official Compilation of Codes, Rules and Regulations of the State of New York, beginning at § 2100.1. (9 NYCRR § 2100.1 and following.)

You can find full copies of these laws and regulations in the reference section of most public libraries. If you have access to the Internet, you can find the latest version of New York's *Unconsolidated Laws* at the New York Assembly's website (www.assembly.state.ny.us./ALIS). Many of the agencies and organizations listed in "More Information: Rent Laws and Regulations," below can answer your questions on rent control. Also, Chapter 17, Section F, explains how to do your own legal research.

## More Information: Rent Laws and Regulations

The following agencies and organizations can help answer questions about rent control and stabilization. See Appendix I for a listing of addresses, phone numbers and websites for these organizations and agencies.

**New York State Division of Housing and Community Renewal (DHCR), Office of Rent Administration.** This state agency administers and enforces rent stabilization and rent control laws and regulations. Unfortunately, the DHCR doesn't publish a comprehensive guide or form book for landlords. The following publications, however, are available free to the public:

- *DHCR Fact Sheets* review the law, regulations and agency's policies on various rent policies on 38 specific issues. Of all DHCR's publications, these are the most helpful—especially to new landlords.

- *DHCR Operational Bulletins* explain how the agency will implement various provisions of rent laws and regulations.

- *DHCR Policy Statements* explain how the agency will interpret various provisions of the rent laws and regulations.

- *DHCR Forms.* The DHCR publishes dozens of official forms that landlords may use to access rent records, register apartments, obtain rent increases, request deregulation and more.

Appendix I lists all available *DHCR Fact Sheets*, *Operational Bulletins* and *Policy Statements* issued to date. For a specific DHCR publication or form, call the DHCR's InfoLine at 718-739-6400 (copies will be mailed to you) or visit your local DHCR office. Fact sheets, operational bulletins, policy statements and some forms are also available on the DHCR's website (www.dhcr.state.ny.us).

**Special help for small landlords**: DHCR's Small Building Owners' Assistance Unit provides special assistance to owners of rent-regulated buildings with a total of 50 units or fewer. The Unit offers advice on preparing forms for allowable rent increases; lease renewal procedures; applying for major capital improvement rent increases; responding to tenant objections to building registration information, fair market rent appeals and other tenant complaints; rent registration and preparing appeals to a rent administrator's orders.

**Rent Guidelines Boards in New York City and the counties of Nassau, Rockland and Westchester.** These agencies provide information on allowable rent increases for rent-stabilized units. Each board also maintains data on local housing costs and expenses. For details, see "Rent Guidelines Boards" in Section A5, below.

**New York City Rent Stabilization Association (RSA).** This private membership organization represents over 25,000 landlords of both rent-controlled and rent-stabilized units. The RSA provides the latest updates on rent laws, regulations and court cases; offers educational seminars and workshops and publishes information about rent regulations and management practices in its monthly newsletter. Other membership benefits include individual assistance with rent increase applications, rent overcharge complaints and other rent regulation problems and a computerized rent registration service.

**Real Estate Board of New York, Inc.** This private membership organization consists of major residential and office owners, builders, brokers, managers and other professionals interested in Manhattan real estate. Among other services, it publishes a residential lease designed specifically for rent-stabilized units in New York City. See Appendix II for a sample copy.

**Small Property Owners of New York (SPONY).** This private, nonprofit, self-help organization of small property owners was founded in 1984. Its purpose is to inform, educate and provide networking opportunities for small property owners, in addition to lobbying on behalf of small property owners in New York City and Albany.

**Community Housing Improvement Program (CHIP).** This trade association represents over 2,500 New York City landlords and managers with rent-regulated units. It provides information, advice, seminars, educational programs and newsletters to members.

**Apartment associations.** Outside New York City, your local apartment association can also give you general information on rent regulation for the areas that they serve. For a listing of New York State landlord associations, see Appendix I.

**Local attorneys** can be an additional resource as discussed in Chapter 17, Section A.

**Tenant/Net (www.tenant.net)** is a website designed for tenants and has lots of useful information for landlords too. Look here for the text of the rent control and rent stabilization laws and regulations, state Real Property Law, housing court decisions and DHCR opinions and orders.

⚠ **Stay current on laws, regulations and DHCR filing requirements.** You should read the material here to get a broad idea of how rent regulation works. But keep in mind that rent laws and regulations change frequently, and court decisions also affect them. If the property you rent is subject to rent control or rent stabilization, it is imperative that you get an up-to-date copy of all relevant laws and regulations. You must also keep current on the latest forms and filing instructions issued by the State Division of Housing and Community Renewal (DHCR), the agency that enforces rent control and rent stabilization laws statewide. The DHCR regularly updates the forms owners need to properly register their units, apply for rent increases and seek other forms of relief. Getting the latest DHCR forms and carefully following the filing instructions and deadlines will go a long way toward maximizing the amount of rent you collect from rent-regulated tenants. This chapter discusses key forms, where to get them and how to fill them out.

## A. Rent Stabilization

Rent stabilization affects over one million units in New York City and certain cities, towns and villages in the neighboring counties of Nassau, Westchester and Rockland. Tenants who move into rent-stabilized units may opt for either one- or two-year vacancy leases and are generally entitled to renew their leases for successive one- or two-year terms. When rent-stabilized tenants move out, their units usually remain subject to rent stabilization. As a result, subsequent tenants are also entitled to the benefits and protections of rent stabilization.

Throughout this book, we refer to the law and regulations that affect rent-stabilized units in New York City as "NYC Rent Stabilization." And we call the separate system of laws and regulations that affect units outside New York City as "State (Emergency Tenant Protection Act or ETPA) Rent Stabilization." When we use the general term "rent stabilization," we are referring to both New York City and State (ETPA) rent stabilization.

### 1. What Units Are Covered by NYC Rent Stabilization?

Within New York City, there are three categories of units that are covered by rent stabilization:

- Units in buildings with six or more units built between February 1, 1947, and January 1, 1974 (NYC Adm. Code § 26-504(a)(1))
- Units in buildings with six or more units built before February 1, 1947, and occupied by tenants who moved in after June 30, 1971 (NYC Adm. Code § 26-504(b)), and
- Units in buildings with three or more units constructed or extensively renovated since 1974 under real property tax benefit programs that mandate rent stabilization during the term of the tax abatement or exemption (NYC Adm. Code § 26-504(c)(1)); these include the "421-a" new construction program, the "423" redevelopment program and the "J-51" rehabilitation program. Generally, these buildings are only subject to stabilization while the tax benefits continue, or in some cases, until the tenant vacates (NYC Adm. Code 26-504). (For more information on these property tax benefit programs, call the NYC Office of Tax Incentive Programs at 212-863-5517.)

### 2. What Units Are Covered by State ("ETPA") Rent Stabilization?

Outside New York City, state rent stabilization (also known as the Emergency Tenant Protection Act (ETPA)) applies to units in buildings that meet the following three requirements:

- the unit is located in a community in Nassau, Rockland or Westchester county that has adopted rent stabilization (see Localities Covered by State ("ETPA") Rent Stabilization in Municipalities Subject to Rent Regulation, above)
- the unit was built before 1974, and
- the building in which the unit is located contains at least six units. Some municipalities limit coverage to buildings of a specific size—

for instance, buildings with 20 or more units—but it is never applicable to buildings with fewer than six units (9 NYCRR § 2500.8).

Also covered are units that were formerly rent-controlled and vacated on or after June 30, 1971 ("decontrolled units," as described in Section B5, below). (NY Unconsol. L. § 8623(a).)

### Tenants Can't Give Up Rent Stabilization Rights

In a tight rental market, you'll encounter tenants who are willing to "give up" their rent stabilization rights to land an apartment. They might offer to pay more than the legal regulated rent each month, for instance, or offer to give you money on the side. While this might seem like a sweet deal, don't do it. You could end up owing the tenant excess rent and be on the hook for stiff penalties, too.

Any agreement by a tenant to waive the benefits or protections of the rent stabilization laws and regulations is absolutely void. (9 NYCRR §§ 2500.12, 2520.13.) And it's unlawful for landlords to "directly or indirectly" evade rent stabilization laws and regulations—for example, by requiring tenants to pay illegal fees, charges or rent or by arbitrarily making changes in required services. (9 NYCRR §§ 2205.1(a); 2525.2(a).)

Landlords who collect more than the legal regulated rent for a rent-stabilized unit can be ordered to refund any overcharge to the tenant with interest and be ordered to pay triple damages as a penalty (overcharges are discussed in Section G, below).

## 3.　What Units Are Exempt From Rent Stabilization?

There are a number of statewide exemptions to rent stabilization. (9 NYCRR §§ 2500.9, 2520.11.) They include:

- rent-controlled units (see Section B1, below)
- units in buildings newly constructed or substantially rehabilitated after December 31, 1973
- units owned, operated or leased by charitable and educational institutions on a nonprofit basis (such as hospitals, monasteries or school dormitories), so long as they are occupied by tenants who are affiliated with the institution when they move in
- units in cooperatives and condominiums (except those still occupied by rent-stabilized tenants who elected not to purchase their units when the building was converted to cooperative or condominium ownership)
- units not occupied as a tenant's "primary residence," that is, occupied fewer than 183 days per year
- units used exclusively for professional, commercial or other non-residential purposes
- units that have been deregulated under so-called high-rent/high-income deregulation (Section F explains deregulation), and
- units currently occupied by servants, superintendents, janitors, managers or other employees to whom the unit is provided rent free, as all or part of the employee's compensation.

## How to Find Out If a Unit Is Rent Stabilized or Rent Controlled

If you have any question whether or not a specific unit is covered by rent stabilization or rent control, ask DHCR for a copy of the most recent "Rent Registration Building-Wide Rent Roll" for that address. The rent roll will list every registered rent-stabilized and rent-controlled unit at the address, including details on past rent increase applications, rent restoration orders and the like.

To get a copy of the rent roll, you must obtain and complete a DHCR form called Request for Access to Public Records (FOIL-1). The one-page form is easy to complete using the instructions on the back of the form. A sample form is shown below. You may download the form from the DHCR website (www.dhcr.state.ny.us), order it from the DHCR InfoLine (718-739-6400) or pick one up at your local DHCR office. If the property is located in New York City, the completed form should be mailed to the following address: Records Access Officer, Division of Housing and Community Renewal, Gertz Plaza, 92-31 Union Hall Street, Jamaica, New York 11433. If the property is located outside New York City, mail it to the Records Access Officer for the DHCR Rent Office serving your area. Appendix I has a list of addresses. Copies of records cost 25 cents a page.

If the registration rent roll says that the unit is not registered, you'll need to do a little more legwork to determine for sure whether or not the unit is rent stabilized or rent controlled. Some units don't appear on the DHCR's registration rolls because they're exempt from coverage. But others don't appear because a prior owner never bothered to properly register the unit. If the unit doesn't clearly fall into one of the rent stabilization or rent control exemptions listed in Section A3 or B2, you might consider hiring an experienced landlord-tenant attorney to analyze the unit's tenant history and make a determination as to whether the unit is subject to rent regulation.

## 4. Registration Requirements for Rent-Stabilized Units

State law requires all rent-stabilized units to be registered annually with the DHCR. (NY Unconsol. L. § 8632(a).) An "initial registration" of the rent, services and room count is required within 90 days after a unit first becomes occupied by a rent-stabilized tenant. (9 NYCRR §§ 2509.1(c), 2528.1.) Each year thereafter, you must file an "annual registration" updating the registration information for all of your rent-stabilized units. (9 NYCRR § 2509.2, § 2528.3.) Many municipalities charge landlords a registration fee. (As of early 2003, the maximum fee a municipality can set is $10 per unit.)

The procedure for filing initial and annual registration statements is explained below. For your registration to be effective, you'll need to be diligent about following all the steps and keeping the right records. Before you begin, obtain current registration forms from the DHCR (new forms are published each April). You can pick them up, along with that year's "Instruction for Registration" booklet, at your local DHCR office (addresses and phone numbers are listed in the DHCR Directory, Appendix I), call DHCR's Infoline (718-739-6400) and ask for forms to be mailed to you, or download them from the DHCR website (www.dhcr.state.ny.us). Make sure to obtain the Registration Instructions from DHCR, too. They are very detailed and helpful.

⚠ **Don't forget to register.** Neglecting to file an initial or annual registration form, even for a single year, can result in a "rent freeze." That means that you may not apply for, charge or collect any rent increase over the legal regulated rent in effect on the date that the last preceding registration statement was filed. If the unit has never been registered, the legal regulated rent is frozen as of the date that the unit became subject to the registration requirements. (9 NYCRR §§ 2509.3, 2528.4.) However, rent increases may again be taken once initial or annual registration forms covering the missing year or years are filed.

State of New York
**Division of Housing and Community Renewal**
Office of Rent Administration

**Reference Number:**

Office use only.

### Request For Access to Public Records

**Please read instructions on the back of this application before completing the request form.
Type or clearly print all information requested. This request must be dated and signed.
Mail or deliver the original and all attachments to DHCR at the address listed above.**

1. **Mailing Address of Requester:**                    **Subject Building:**

_____        _____
Name                                                          Address                    (No. & Street)

_____        _____
Address                              Apt. No.                 City, State & Zip Code

_____        _____
City, State & Zip Code                                   Owner's/Managing Agent's Name

_____
Daytime Telephone No. (          )

2. **Have you previously requested this specific information?** ☐ Yes  ☐ No
   If "yes," enter previous reference number _____

3. **I am the** ☐ Owner ☐ Prospective buyer ☐ Managing Agent ☐ Subtenant

   ☐ Tenant Representative ☐ Owner Representative ☐ Tenant ☐ Other (specify): _____

**If this information is needed for a court appearance, please give date and attach court papers. Court date: _____**

**Access may be denied on grounds stated in the Freedom Of Information Law; obtaining such access could be an
unwarranted invasion of personal privacy. You must provide proof of identity. (See instructions on page 2.)**

**Only one category may be selected per request form, as the purpose of this form is to facilitate the processing of each category
requested.**

4. ☐ **Copy of Order(s)**
   Docket/Order # (limit of four (4) per request form.)
   1. _____
   2. _____
   3. _____
   4. _____

5. ☐ **Record Review - Case File**                    6. ☐ **Record Review**
                                                             **Rent Control Records Only:**
   ☐ Docket/Order Number _____              Apartment Number(s) _____

   ☐ Copy of Entire File _____              ☐ Registration Card

   ☐ Copy of Specific Document _____        ☐ MBR Profile

                                                        ☐ Fuel Cost Adjustment

7. ☐ **Rent Registration**
   ☐ Building-wide Rent Roll, (specify years) _____ (Rent Roll information can only be provided
     to the building owner; authorized representative of owner or authorized representative of all tenants in the subject
     building or anyone operating with the express consent of the foregoing.)
   ☐ Initial Building-wide Services Registration
   ☐ Individual Apartment(s) Rent History (specify years) _____ Apt. #'s. _____
   ☐ Initial Apartment Services Registration. Apt. #'s. _____
   ☐ Print-out of cases for subject building.

8. ☐ **Status Request**
   Please provide an update on the status of the pending case.
   Docket Number(s) _____

Date: _____/_____/_____                    Signature: _____

FOIL - 1 (6/96) *INTERNET*

## How to Get Help With Registration

The registration process can be a big paperwork headache for landlords and managers. Here are three ways to get help with the registration process.

- The Rent Stabilization Association of New York City (RSA) offers a rent registration service for members and nonmembers. RSA counselors help to complete registration forms, and have the forms properly mailed and filed with DHCR. For initial registration, the fee is $10 per unit for members and nonmembers. The fee for annual registration varies, depending on the number of units and whether you belong to RSA. As of early 2003, the annual registration fee for a landlord with 110 units, for example, was $5.45 per unit for nonmembers and $3.40 per unit for members.
- DHCR's Small Building Owner (SBO) Assistance Unit offers registration help to owners of rent-stabilized buildings with a total of 50 units or fewer. The Unit provides services at DHCR's main office and at DHCR offices throughout the state. (Appendix I lists the addresses and phone numbers for all DHCR offices.)
- The DHCR provides PC-based rent registration software free of charge to landlords as an alternative method to filing manually. According to the agency, the software is easy to use, streamlines the data entry process, produces laser printed forms, and creates a generated diskette for submission to DHCR. The software automatically creates a database which may be updated as changes occur during the year (making it easier to register next year). You can obtain the software by downloading it from the agency website (www.dhcr.state.ny.us), contacting the DHCR Processing Services Unit via email at pcreg@dhcr.state.ny.us or calling DHCR at 518-486-3367.

### a. Initial Registration

Back in 1984, state law required landlords to initially register with DHCR the rent and services for all of their occupied rent-stabilized units. Chances are you or a prior owner filed an "Initial Apartment Registration" and a corresponding "Initial Building Services Registration" for your rent-stabilized buildings then. You can find out which units at a given property are registered by going to your local DHCR office and requesting a copy of the "Rent Registration Building-Wide Rent Roll," as described in Section A4, above.

You must complete, serve and file your initial registration forms within 90 days from the date that the first rent-stabilized tenant moves in. So whenever possible, start early.

To register a newly rent-stabilized unit, complete these five steps:

### Step 1: Complete Initial Apartment Registration (DHCR Form RR-1(i))

Fill in all of the required information about the unit, including the new rent, equipment, services and room count. If the unit was rent-controlled immediately prior to initial registration under rent stabilization, also include the last maximum rent-controlled rents in the registration data.

### Step 2: Serve Tenant With Initial Apartment Registration Form

You must serve the rent-stabilized tenant with the tenant's copy of the initial apartment registration form by certified mail, return receipt requested. For initial registrations, regular mail won't cut it with the DHCR. If there's more than one rent-stabilized tenant named on the lease for the unit, you need only mail one of them the registration form.

### Step 3: Complete Initial Building Services Registration (DHCR Form RR-3(i))

If this if the first unit in your building to become rent-stabilized, you'll also need to complete this form which summarizes the building services provided by the landlord, and identifies the managing agent.

⚠️ **Post building services registration in lobby.** A copy of the Initial Building Services Registration form must be posted in a public area of the property. Frame the form and hang it in your lobby. Most owners find that the area around tenant mailboxes is a good place to hang required notices and forms like these.

### Step 4: Complete Initial Registration Summary (DHCR Form RR-2(i))

Once the tenant is served and the Initial Building Services Registration form has been completed, it's time to fill out the Initial Registration Summary; this is the last form you need to complete the initial registration of one or more rent-stabilized units. This initial registration form requires you to identify the owner and managing agent and summarize the number of units in the building subject to rent stabilization and rent control. The owner must sign this form before a notary public.

### Step 5: File Forms With DHCR

Once the tenant is served, you can file your Initial Apartment Registration form and summary with DHCR. If this is the first rent-stabilized unit in the building, you must also file your Initial Building Services Registration form at the same time. Mail or hand deliver the forms to this special address:

    DHCR Processing Services Unit
    Hampton Plaza, 38-40 State St.
    Albany, NY 12207

If you file by mail, use certified mail, return receipt requested, so that you have proof that you filed the forms on time. If you file by hand, have your copy of the registration forms date-stamped by the DHCR clerk who accepts them.

## b. Annual Registration

You must update your registration information as of April 1 with the DHCR each year between April 1 and July 31. (If July 31 falls on a weekend or federal or state holiday, the deadline gets extended to the next business day. (NY GCL § 25-1.) Here are the steps to follow:

### Step 1: Complete Annual Apartment Registration (DHCR Form RR-2A)

Fill in this form updating your registration information as of April 1 for each of your rent-stabilized units.

### Step 2: Serve Tenants With Annual Apartment Registration Form

You must serve tenants with the tenant's copy of the Annual Apartment Registration form between April 1 and July 31. The form may be served by regular mail or hand delivery. If you mail the forms, your envelope must be postmarked by the post office by July 31. While not required, it's a good idea to get a certificate of mailing from the post office in case you later need to prove that you registered the unit on time. If you hand deliver the form, ask the tenant to sign and date a receipt for it.

If there's more than one tenant on the lease, you must serve the form to at least one of the tenants named on the lease. If the unit was vacant on April 1, and has since been re-rented, deliver the registration form to the current tenant. If the tenant who occupied the unit on April 1 has moved out, you're supposed to try to forward the registration form to that tenant (who lived in the unit on April 1). Using the prior tenant's forwarding address, if you have one, or by addressing it to the unit in hopes that the post office will forward it to the tenant's new address. If the post office returns the form to you, save the copy with the envelope it was returned in. That's your proof that you tried to forward the form to the prior tenant.

### Step 3: Complete Annual Registration Summary (DHCR Form RR-2S)

After you've mailed or delivered apartment registration forms to all of the rent-stabilized tenants in your building, complete an Annual Registration Summary. You must complete a separate summary form for each building you own that contains at least one rent-stabilized tenant. This form must be signed before a notary public.

### Step 4: File Forms with DHCR

File the DHCR copy of each apartment registration form you served on a tenant in your building, along with the DHCR copy of the Annual Registration Summary form by July 31. Follow the directions for filing Initial registration forms with DHCR in Section 4a, Step 5, above.

**Keep registration records and receipts.** If a rent-stabilized tenant files a rent overcharge complaint with DHCR, the agency may order you to submit proof of proper registration, including proof of service on the tenant, for up to four years prior to the date of the tenant's complaint. If you don't have mailing receipts or delivery receipts from the tenant, you could stand to lose a prior rent increase and be ordered to refund any rent overcharges to the tenant. (Section G, below, discusses rent overcharge complaints.)

## 5. How Do You Increase Rent for Rent-Stabilized Units?

There are four main ways to increase the rent for a rent-stabilized unit:

1. Sign a renewal lease with a current tenant (see subsection a, below).

2. Sign a vacancy lease with a new tenant after a tenant moves out or is evicted (see subsection b, below).
3. Improve the unit (see Section C, below).
4. Complete a buildingwide major capital improvement (see Section D, below).

**Get a rent hike for adding a roommate to rent-stabilized lease.** You may be entitled to collect a vacancy lease rent hike if you add a co-tenant to a current tenant's rent-stabilized lease. For details, see Chapter 8, Section C5.

**Never accept rent from non-tenant occupants.** Don't demand, collect or accept any rent from any person other than the rent-regulated tenant. Accepting rent from a tenant's family member, roommate, subtenant or other non-tenant occupant can entitle that person to certain tenant rights that she wouldn't otherwise be entitled to. For details, see Chapter 8, Section B1.

### a. Renewal Lease Rent Increases for Rent-Stabilized Units

When a rent-stabilized tenant's lease expires, the general rule is that the tenant is automatically entitled to renew the lease for a one- or two-year term. There are, however, a few narrow exceptions to this rule that permit the landlord, under certain circumstances, to refuse to renew a rent-stabilized tenant's lease. Upon proper notice, you may refuse to renew on any of the following grounds:

- You (or one of your immediate family members) want to occupy the unit as a primary residence.
- The tenant is not using the unit as his or her primary residence.
- You wish to withdrawal the unit from the rental market.
- You plan to demolish the building.

Chapter 14 details these grounds for non-renewal. Chapter 15 provides instructions for drafting and serving required non-renewal and termination notices, and/or applying for a certificate of eviction.

If you don't have grounds to refuse to renew the lease, you are obligated to offer the current tenant a one- or two-year renewal lease, at the tenant's option. (Chapter 2, Section H, shows how.) If the tenant elects to renew, you're entitled to a "renewal" rent increase. Maximum renewal rent increases are determined annually by local Rent Guidelines Boards. (There's a separate Board established for New York City and for each of the counties of Nassau, Rockland and Westchester (see "Rent Guidelines Boards," below).) To figure out how much you can raise the rent, look at the current Rent Guidelines Board Order. To obtain a copy of the current or past orders, contact the applicable Rent Guidelines Board or DHCR.

EXAMPLE: Mary, a NYC landlord, has a tenant whose lease expires November 31, 2002. Because Mary has no grounds upon which to refuse to renew the tenant's lease, she must offer her tenant a renewal lease for a term of either one or two years. The tenant's current rent is $1,300 per month. To determine the maximum permitted rent increase for a renewal lease, Mary must look at NYC Rent Guidelines Order #34, which covers leases that begin between October 1, 2002 and September 30, 2003. That Order authorizes rent increases of 2% for one-year renewal leases and 4% for two-year renewal leases. That means that Mary can charge a renewal rent of $1,326 on a one-year renewal lease (2% x $1,300 = $26; $1,300 + $26 = $1,326); or $1,352 on a two-year renewal lease (4% x $1,300 = $52; $1,300 + $52 = $1,352).

⚠ **Landlords of New York State (ETPA) rent-stabilized units must complete and certify an annual Property Maintenance and Operations Cost Survey Schedule.** DHCR sends the survey to landlords with instructions on how to complete and file it. The DHCR shares this information with the County Guidelines Board, which keeps tabs on changes in owners' costs and expenses from year to

year. Late filing or a failure to return a completed survey could make you ineligible for guideline rent increases. For more information, take a look at DHCR Fact Sheet #31, "Guide to Rent Increases for Rent-Stabilized Apartments in Nassau, Rockland and Westchester Counties" available from agency offices and its website.

## Rent Guidelines Boards

The Rent Stabilization Laws provide for the establishment of Rent Guidelines Boards in New York City, and in the counties of Nassau, Westchester and Rockland. (Appendix I lists phone numbers, address and websites.) The Boards independently set the maximum allowable rent increase rates for rent-stabilized units.

Each Board consists of nine members who are appointed by the Commissioner of the Division of Housing and Community Renewal (DHCR) based on recommendations from local legislators. The members include tenant representatives, landlord representatives and public members with at least five years' experience in finance, economics or housing. The Commissioner selects the Chair of each Board from among the public members.

The Boards serve part-time, meeting throughout the year to review cost and the availability of financing, cost-of-living indexes and other relevant factors to arrive at the annual guidelines for rent increases. They also consider the economic condition of the residential real estate industry including current and projected real estate taxes, supply of housing, vacancy rates, sewer and water rates, governmental fees and fuel and labor costs.

After a series of public hearings, each board issues an annual "Rent Guidelines Order" setting out maximum rates for rent increases affecting rent-stabilized units. Customarily, the Order affects leases commencing October 1 of that year through September 30 of the following year.

## b. Vacancy Lease Rent Increases for Rent-Stabilized Units

There's good news and bad news when a rent-stabilized tenant moves out or is evicted. The bad news is that the unit remains subject to rent stabilization. The good news is that when you rent the unit to a new tenant, you're entitled to a hefty vacancy rent increase. The rent hike is made up of four components:

  (*i*)  the "Vacancy Bonus"
  (*ii*)  the "Additional Vacancy Bonus"
  (*iii*)  the "Low-Rent Apartment Bonus," and
  (*iv*)  the "Rent Guidelines Board Vacancy Increase."

Here are the details on each component.

### i. *Vacancy Bonus*

The "vacancy bonus" was established by the 1997 Rent Regulation Reform Act (NYC Adm. Code § 26-511(c) (5-a); ETPA ch. 576 §§ 44, 10(a-1)). The size of the bonus depends on the length of the lease your new tenant is signing (either one or two years).

• For a two-year vacancy lease, the vacancy bonus is a 20% rent hike.
• For a one-year vacancy lease, the vacancy bonus is a 20% increase *minus* the difference between rates set by the Rent Guidelines Board for two- and one-year renewal rent increases. For instance, NYC Rent Guidelines Order #34, which covers leases that begin between October 1, 2002, and September 30, 2003, authorized rent increases of 2% for one-year renewal leases and 4% for two-year leases. Since the difference between the rates set for one- and two-year renewal leases is 2% (4% – 2%); the rent hike for a one-year vacancy lease signed between 10/1/02 and 9/30/03 is 18% (20% – 2%).

### ii. *Additional Vacancy Bonus*

In addition to the vacancy bonus, you can collect an additional vacancy bonus if you haven't taken one on the unit for the eight years prior to the date of the new vacancy lease. To figure out how much of a rent increase you can take, multiply the number of years since you took your last vacancy increase by .006 of the rent charged to the last tenant.

> EXAMPLE: After a ten-year tenancy, Mrs. Hecht finally moves out of her studio apartment in Queens. Mrs. Hecht's last monthly rent was $600. Because you haven't taken a vacancy rent increase on the unit in over eight years (you've only been allowed to take renewal rent increases during Mrs. Hecht's tenancy), you're entitled to an "additional vacancy bonus." To calculate the additional vacancy bonus for the apartment, multiply the number of years since your last vacancy increase, in this case, ten, by .006 (10 x .006 = .06) and multiply that figure by the monthly rent (.06 x $600 = $36.00) to arrive at the additional vacancy rent increase of $36 per month. You can add this to the vacancy bonus and any other allowable increases when you calculate the new rent for the apartment.

### iii. *Bonus for Low-Rent Apartments*

If your previous tenant's legal rent was less than $300 per month, in addition to the bonuses described above, you can collect an extra $100 per month. Or, if your previous tenant's legal rent was between $300 and $500 per month, you can collect either a) the combined vacancy bonus and additional vacancy bonus described above, or b) $100 per month, whichever is higher.

### iv. *The Rent Guidelines Board Vacancy Increase*

In addition to the vacancy bonuses described above, the "Rent Guidelines" vacancy increase lets you add the vacancy rent increase authorized by your local

Rent Guidelines Board for that year. Each year, each Rent Guidelines Board authorizes vacancy rent increases for one- and two-year leases that begin on or after October 1 of that year and on or before September 30 of the following year. This is often referred to as a "guidelines year."

⚠️ **Since the vacancy bonus was established by the State Legislature in 1997, local Rent Guidelines Board vacancy increases have been set at zero.** However, the boards have discretion to set such an increase if local economic conditions necessitate it. Check your local Rent Guidelines Order before computing any vacancy leases to see whether you are entitled to this rent hike.

The following example may make this complicated system a bit clearer.

**EXAMPLE:** After ten years as a rent-stabilized tenant, Mary's tenant elects not to renew the lease on her apartment and moves out at the end of her lease term. Mary finds a new tenant for the apartment who wants to sign a two-year lease. Here's how Mary calculates the rent for the new tenant:

Previous Legal Rent:                               $1,020
*This is the last registered rent payable by Mary's old tenant.*

Vacancy Bonus                        +        $204
*Since the new tenant is signing a two-year lease, Mary is entitled to a 20% vacancy bonus (20% x $1,020 = $204).*

Additional Vacancy Bonus        +      $61.20
*Since Mary hasn't collected a vacancy increase on this unit for eight or more years, she can collect an additional vacancy bonus equal to .006 of the old rent, multiplied by 10—the number of years since Mary last collected a vacancy increase for the unit (.006 x $1,020 = $6.12; $6.12 x 10 =$61.20).*

Bonus for Low-Rent Apartment  +           $0
*Since Mary's old tenant paid more than $500 per month, Mary doesn't qualify for the bonus for low rent apartments.*

Rent Guidelines Board Vacancy
Rent Increase                          +      $40.80
*In addition to the vacancy bonuses, Mary can collect the applicable Rent Guidelines Board increase. Say, for instance, that the vacancy rate increase for that year is 4%. That entitles Mary to increase the rent by an additional $40.80 (4% x $1,020 = $40.80).*

New Rent For Two-Year
Vacancy Lease                          = $1,326.00
*(a $306 per month total rent increase)*

**Use the New York City Rent Guidelines Board's "Vacancy Lease Calculator" to check your math.** The Calculator is actually a computer program which you may download from the Board's website (www.housingnyc.com) onto your computer at no charge. It is compatible with most computer spreadsheet programs such as Microsoft Excel.

### c. Telling NYC Rent-Stabilized Tenants About Rent Increases

When a tenant signs a lease for a NYC rent-stabilized unit, you must put into writing the prior regulated rent for the unit. Within New York City, you must include a Rent Stabilization Lease Rider (DHCR Form RA-LR1) with your tenants' vacancy and renewal leases. (9 NYCRR § 2522.5(c).) The rider informs the tenant of the legal regulated rent in effect immediately prior to the vacancy or renewal, and explains how the present rent was calculated. If you fail to provide the rider, you're not entitled to take the vacancy or renewal rent increase. (9 NYCRR § 2522.5(c)(3).)

A portion of the Rent Stabilization Lease Rider form, with instructions for completing it, appears in Chapter 2, Section G2. A full copy of this form is reprinted, in Appendix II.

## B. Rent Control

Rent control affects units within and outside New York City. Most rent-controlled tenants have no current lease for their units. Rent-controlled tenants are sometimes called "statutory" tenants because rent control laws and regulations establish the maximum rent and security deposits they pay, the level of services they receive and the grounds upon which they may be evicted. Tenancy issues that aren't covered by rent control laws, such as pets, are resolved by looking at the lease, rental agreement or policy that was in effect when the unit first became subject to rent control. When a rent-controlled tenant dies, moves out or is evicted, the

unit generally becomes "de-controlled" and is no longer subject to rent control.

Throughout this book, we'll refer to the system of laws and regulations that affect rent-controlled units in New York City as "NYC Rent Control." And we'll call the separate system of laws and regulations that affect units outside New York City "State Rent Control." In many instances, the rules relating to rent, services and eviction under both schemes are the same. When we use the general term "rent control," we are referring to both New York City and state rent control laws and regulations.

### 1. What Units Are Covered by Rent Control?

To be rent-controlled, a unit must meet all of the following four requirements:
- The premises must be located in an area. where rent control is in effect (see "Municipalities Subject to Rent Regulation," above).
- The premises must have been built *before* February 1, 1947.
- The unit must have been continuously occupied by the same tenant (or by the original tenant's legal successor) since July 1, 1971.
- It must be located in a building with three or more units. (NY Unconsol. L. § 8582.2; NYC Adm. Code § 26-403(e).) *Exception:* Units in buildings with fewer than three units are subject to rent control if they've been occupied by the same tenant (or the tenant's legal successor) continuously since April 1, 1953.

As of early 2003, there were around 96,000 rent-controlled units in New York, with over 50,000 units located within New York City. Each year, the number of rent-controlled units statewide falls as units become decontrolled through vacancies (see Section 5, below) and through "high-rent/high-income" deregulation (discussed in Section F, below).

The main difference between NYC and state rent control is the manner in which landlords must apply for operating cost rent increases. We detail both procedures in Section 3, below. Rent-controlled tenants under both systems enjoy similar protections from eviction. (Chapter 14 describes the limited grounds upon which a rent-controlled tenancy may be terminated.)

## 2. What Units Are Exempt From Rent Control?

Some units which would otherwise be covered by rent control are actually exempt, thanks to special regulations (9 NYCRR §§ 2100.9, 2100.10; 2200.2). Exempt units include:

- government-operated and subsidized units
- hotel rooms (not rooming houses)
- units in charitable and educational nonprofit institutions, such as hospitals, convents, monasteries, asylums, colleges and dormitories
- units in summer resorts or vacation rentals
- units in nonprofit clubs, such as college fraternity or sorority houses
- units occupied by farming tenants, and
- units occupied by service employees, such as building superintendents, property managers, caretakers or janitors, who receive housing as part or all of their compensation.

Units that are exempt from rent control may, nevertheless, be covered by rent stabilization. We discuss which units are subject to rent stabilization in Section A, above.

## 3. How Can You Raise Rent on a Rent-Controlled Unit?

There are three main ways to boost the rent for a rent-controlled unit:

1. Apply for a rent increase based on increased operating costs (see Subsections a and b, below).
2. Make improvements to the unit with the tenant's consent (see Section C, below).
3. Complete a building-wide major capital improvement to the premises (see Section D, below).

**Get a rent increase for roommates.** You're also entitled to apply for a rent increase if your rent-controlled tenant shares the unit with an additional occupant who is not a member of the tenant's immediate family (see Chapter 8, Section C5 for details).

**Never accept rent from non-tenant occupants.** Don't demand, collect or accept any rent from any person other than the rent-regulated tenant. Accepting rent from a tenant's family member, roommate, subtenant or other non-tenant occupant can entitle that person to certain tenant rights that she wouldn't otherwise be entitled to. For details, see Chapter 8, Section B1.

### a. Getting an Operating Costs Rent Increase under the NYC Rent Control "MBR" System

Rent control in New York City operates under the Maximum Base Rent (MBR) system. (NYC Local L. 1970, No. 30.) Under this complex system, an MBR rent is established for each of your rent-controlled units. Every two years, the state Division of Housing and Community Renewal (DHCR) determines how much you can increase the rent for your rent-controlled units. (9 NYCRR § 2201.5(b).) The rent hikes are based on the DHCR's assessment of what it costs landlords to operate their buildings, and are supposed to allow enough for a reasonable profit.

The rent actually paid by the tenant is called the Maximum Collectible Rent (MCR) and is generally lower than the MBR. The DHCR is entitled to order annual increases in the MCR of up to 7.5% until the unit's MCR reaches the MBR. (See 9 NYCRR § 2201.6.)

Unfortunately, you can't just take the rent increase DHCR orders for that two-year cycle. There's a lot of complicated paperwork involved. You have to apply for and get a DHCR Order of Eligibility first. DHCR publishes a detailed set of forms and instructions you can use to obtain the Order of Eligibility. The instructions give deadlines for filing the forms and tell you how and where to file them. The forms you need to apply for the rent increase should arrive in the mail well before the deadline (the DHCR mails them out semi-annually). If the forms don't arrive, you can get them by calling DHCR's Infoline (718-739-6400) and requesting an MBR packet.

Your forms must be filed within the deadlines indicated in the instructions in order to be eligible to collect the rent increase on January 1 of the next two-year cycle. If you file your forms late, you won't be able to collect the increase until later in the year. Here is an overview of the process:

## Step 1:   File Violation Certification (DHCR Form VC)

DHCR won't let you increase the rent if there are serious code violations at your building. By signing this form, you certify that that you have cleared, corrected or abated all "rent-impairing" violations issued against your building as of the previous January 1st, and at least 80% of all nonrent-impairing violations. The DHCR instructions give you the deadline for filing this form. The NYC Department of Housing Preservation and Development (HPD), Division of Code Enforcement, keeps track of the violations it issues after inspections and decides which ones are serious enough to be rent-impairing. (Chapter 9 discusses code requirements and rent-impairing violations.) The DHCR should send you a list of pending violations with its forms. Or, you can get a printout of outstanding violations for your building by visiting your local HPD office (see Appendix I for a list of HPD offices).

If no violations were on record for your building as of the previous January 1, you're not required to file a violation certification. You can skip to Step 2.

## Step 2:   File Operation and Maintenance and Essential Services Certification (DHCR Form OMESC)

By signing this form, you certify (swear as real) your operating expenditures and that you are maintaining all essential services. The deadline for filing this form is included in the instructions. If possible, send this form, together with your violation

certification form, by June 30. At the latest, the DHCR Form OMESC must be filed by October 6.

## Step 3:   Pay MBR Fee

After you file the above forms at your local DHCR office, the DHCR sends you a bill for the MBR fee (now $30) for each rent-controlled apartment in the building. There's an exception to the fee for owner-occupied buildings with eight or fewer units.

Once you pay the fee, the DHCR issues an Order of Eligibility and sends copies to you and each of your rent-controlled tenants. The Order of Eligibility authorizes you to calculate, on official forms, the MBR and MCR for each rent-controlled unit in the premises. The official forms should arrive in the mail about a week after you receive the Order of Eligibility. If they don't, call DHCR's Infoline at 718-739-6400 and ask for these forms:

(1) Notice of Increase in MBR and MCR Computation—DHCR Form RN 26 (long and short forms), together with the Attachment form (RMBR-ATT), and

(2) Maximum Base Rent Master Building Rent Schedule (DHCR Form RMB).

By law, the Order of Eligibility cannot raise your MCRs by more than 7.5% per year for each year of the two-year MBR cycles, with the following exceptions:

- if you are eligible for an "individual apartment improvement" rent increase (see Section C below), or
- if you are eligible for a "major capital improvement" rent increase (see Section D below).

Both tenants and landlords may challenge the DHCR's order of eligibility.

**Tenant challenges.** Your rent-controlled tenants can challenge the rent increase on three grounds: 1) that you've failed to provide essential services, 2) that the building has serious code violations, or 3) that your expenses don't warrant the rent increase.

**Landlord challenges.** Landlords may challenge the rent increase as too low, based on the assessed value of the building, the amount of commercial income it realizes or the amount of operating expenses. (Landlords may use two forms for this purpose: a DHCR RA-94MBR and an MBR Building Application form.)

Any challenges to the order of eligibility must be filed within 33 days of the date the order was issued. The DHCR usually takes at least several months to process and decide these challenges.

### Step 4:  Deliver Notice of Increase in MBR and MCR Computation (DHCR Form RN-26) to Tenants

DHCR sends out two versions of this form: a long and short form for the current year. You'll need to make enough copies of the forms for all of your rent-controlled tenants. (You'll also get a long and short version of the form for the following year, since your order of eligibility covers a two-year period. File next year's forms in a safe place so you can take another rent increase next year.)

Most landlords need to use the long form. You are required to use the long form if: 1) you previously used the long form for the unit, 2) DHCR granted a labor cost adjustment for the unit during the last MBR cycle, 3) the landlord pays for gas or electricity for the unit, or 4) since August 1, 1970, DHCR adjusted the rent for the unit—for example, as a result of a buildingwide major capital improvement, an individual apartment improvement, or a decrease in the level of services provided to the building or to the unit. Otherwise, you may use the short form. Use the instructions on the appropriate form to compute the unit's new MBR and the MCR, and sign and date the back of the form.

If you are filing the long form, you may also need to fill out, sign and annex the Attachment form (DHCR Form RMBR-ATT) to the RN-26 (long or short) form. If you pay for the unit's gas or electricity, you must complete the Attachment to adjust the MBR to reflect your utility payments. You must also complete the Attachment form if you received a labor cost adjustment during the last MBR cycle, so that there is a corresponding MBR adjustment. Make extra copies of the Attachments, since you'll need to file them with DHCR when you file your Master Building Rent Schedule (Step 5, below).

Next, you must deliver the completed RN-26 form (and the Attachment if required) to the tenant. Your delivery deadline is set by the order of eligibility you received from DHCR. You have 60 days after the issue date or effective date on the order of eligibility—whichever is later—to get the form(s) to your tenant.

The instructions tell you to deliver the form to the tenant, but don't specify any special method. If you hand deliver the notices, ask the tenant to sign and date a receipt. If you use regular mail, get a certificate of mailing for each one from the post office. (A certificate of mailing lists the addressee, the date mailed and the postage. It's proof of mailing, not proof of receipt. If you want a receipt, you must send it certified mail, return receipt requested. It's not legally required, however.)

 **If you're not sure about the maximum rent you can collect for a rent-controlled unit,** you can file a Request for Calculation of Maximum Collectible Rent (DHCR Form RA-1) with DHCR. However, if you're collecting more than the MCR, the DHCR will direct the tenant to sue you in court for a refund of the overcharge.

### Step 5:  File Master Building Rent Schedule (DHCR Form RMB) with DHCR

This form must be filed with DHCR within 60 days after the notice of eligibility is issued. To complete this form, you must list the new MBRs and MCRs for each rent-controlled unit in your building. You can get this information from the notices you delivered to tenants (Step 4). You must include a copy of each Attachment used with a long form RN-26 with the schedule (but not the RN-26 forms themselves). By signing and dating the schedule, you certify that the information on it is true and accurate and that you delivered the required notices to your tenants. To file the schedule (and any attachments), mail it to the DHCR at the address given on the form. We recommend that you send it certified mail, return receipt requested. The postmark must be within 60 days of the date the order of eligibility was issued.

## New York City "Fuel Cost Rent Adjustment"

New York City permits you to adjust a rent-controlled tenant's rent based on the changes, up or down, in the prices of heating fuels. (NYC Adm. Code § 26-405(n).) The rent adjustment is based on fuel price changes between the beginning and end of the prior year. The law states that the fuel cost adjustment is not to be incorporated in the rent on which maximum base rent increases are computed.

To compute the rent adjustment, the quantity of fuel delivered to your building during the previous year is divided by the number of rooms in the building, up to an annual maximum consumption standard per room set by DHCR for the type of fuel used. This figure is then multiplied by the price change, divided by 12 months and multiplied by 75%. Seventy-five percent of the annual fuel cost per room is passed along to the tenant.

To apply, landlords must certify that they are maintaining heat, hot water and other essential services. Buildings that have not qualified for maximum base rent increases may nevertheless be eligible for fuel cost adjustments. To obtain the adjustment, the owner must complete, certify and deliver to each rent-controlled tenant a copy of DHCR's Owner's Report, Certification, and Notice of Fuel Cost Adjustment Eligibility (DHCR Form RA-33.10). Then, a master copy of the report, together with a schedule of monthly rent increases for all the rent-controlled tenants who were served with copies of the report, must be filed with the DHCR. The rent adjustment is collectible when the tenant and DHCR are served with the completed report forms and schedules. No order from the Rent Administrator is required.

When the cost of fuel decreases, the owner must file a report and pass the decrease on to the tenants. Failure to serve the tenants and DHCR within 60 days after the fuel consumption and price change standards are released by DHCR will result in the suspension and revocation of all previous fuel increases for a period of 12 months.

For more information or to obtain application forms, call the DHCR Infoline at 718-739-6400.

## Step 6: Collect the Rent Increase

You may begin to collect the new MCR (the number on line 6 of the short form and line 14 on the long form) on the next rent payment date after delivery of the RN-26 form to your tenant. Add any fuel cost adjustments you may be entitled to (see "New York City 'Fuel Cost Rent Adjustment'"). If you completed all of your paperwork (Steps 4 and 5) by the deadlines, you are also entitled to collect the rent increase retroactive to the effective date of your order of eligibility. The tenant has the option of paying the retroactive portion of the rent increase in a lump sum or in monthly installments. The installments must equal the number of months that elapsed between the effective date of the order of eligibility and the next rent payment date after getting the RN-26 form.

> EXAMPLE: The DHCR issues Judy an order of eligibility that is effective January 1. On May 1, Judy mails a RN-26 form advising Bob, her rent-controlled tenant, about a $15 MCR increase for his unit. On May 5, Judy files the rent schedule with DHCR. Since Judy completed her MBR paperwork on time, she is entitled to collect the rent increase retroactively to January 1. Bob may choose to pay the retroactive portion of the rent increase ($15 per month for January through May) in a lump sum payment of $75 with his June rent, or he may elect to pay it in five monthly installments of $15, over the next five months.

**Copy and save your MBR paperwork.** Make copies of all MBR paperwork that you deliver to tenants or send to DHCR. This agency has been known to misplace and lose documents filed by landlords. Also save your post office mail receipts for at least four years from the date you start collecting the rent increase.

## b. Getting Operating Costs Rent Increases for Non-NYC Rent-Controlled Units

Landlords of rent-controlled units outside New York City may periodically adjust maximum rents up a percentage set by the rent administrator. (9 NYCRR § 2102.3.) As of early 2003, landlords could apply for 9.5% rent increases every two years. To qualify, you must be prepared to prove that there has been a "significant and unavoidable" increase in operating costs such as real estate taxes, heating fuel, utility charges, repairs, replacements or labor, with no corresponding rent increase for the same two-year period.

It's relatively simple to apply for this rent increase. You can apply at any time, so long as it's been at least two years since the last operating costs rent increase. Here are the basic steps:

### Step 1: Complete an Owner's Sixty-Day Notice of Maximum Rent Adjustment (DHCR Form R-33.8)

This one-page form notifies the tenant of your rent increase. You'll need to complete one form for each of your rent-controlled tenants. To obtain copies of the form, call or visit your county DHCR office. At the top of the form, complete the name and address boxes for the Owner or Agent and the Tenant. List only the name or names of the rent-controlled tenant (or the tenant's legal successor) living in the unit—don't include the names of any family members, roommates or subtenants who might occupy the unit. (For a discussion on succession rights, see Chapter 14.)

Complete Part A of the form by filling in the current rent and the new rent for the unit. By signing this form, you certify that:

- You have owned the building for the last two years.
- There has been a "significant and unavoidable increase in operating costs" for the building in the preceding two-year period. DHCR will consider costs relating to real estate taxes,

heating fuel, utility charges, repairs, replacements and labor. You don't need to supply any records of increased costs at this point. But DHCR may order you to produce them if a tenant challenges your rent increase.

- All essential services are being maintained and will continue to be maintained. An "essential service" means any service that was furnished or required to be furnished to the tenant on May 1, 1950, including any increased services ordered by DHCR thereafter, with a corresponding rent increase. Examples include repairs, light, heat, hot and cold water, elevator service, kitchen and bath facilities, janitor service, refuse removal, a refrigerator, stove, air conditioning equipment or painting.
- There are no outstanding municipal, county, state or federal violations in effect regarding building services.
- The tenant's rent, after the increase, will not exceed:
    i. the average legal regulated rent for rent-stabilized apartments in the same building with the same number of rooms, services and equipment, or
    ii. the rent for any non-regulated unit in the same building, with the same number of rooms, services and equipment.

After you have completed and signed the form, date the form as of the date you intend to deliver or mail a copy of the notice to tenants. Then make three copies of each form.

### Step 2: Deliver or Mail Original and One Copy of Notice to Tenants

You must deliver the original notice and one copy to the tenant by personal delivery or certified mail at least 60 days before the proposed rent increase. The date you deliver or mail the notice should match the date you filled in at the bottom of the notice. If you hand deliver the notice, ask the tenant to sign and date a receipt. If you mail the notice, hold onto your certified mail receipts.

### Step 3: Deliver or Mail One Copy of Notice to DHCR

You must deliver or mail a copy of each notice to the DHCR office in the county where the property is located. If you hand deliver the copy, ask the DHCR clerk who accepts it to date-stamp your copy of the notice. If you send it, your best bet is to use certified mail, return receipt requested. While not technically required, this method will assure you of a receipt. A copy of the notice must be delivered or mailed to DHCR at least 60 days prior to the date that the rent increase goes into effect.

### Step 4: Be Prepared to Deal With Tenant Objections to Rent Increase

Once a rent-controlled tenant receives your notice of rent increase, the tenant has only seven days from receipt to challenge it. To do so, the tenant must complete Part B of the notice (Tenant Response to Owner) with specific questions or objections. Tenants usually object on the ground that there are pending violations or service problems, or that your costs didn't really go up much in the prior two years.

If a tenant objects to the rent increase, you must respond directly to the tenant, in writing, within seven days of the date you receive the notice back from the tenant. This is your opportunity to show the tenant, for instance, that an alleged violation has been cleared or that a service problem has been remedied. If you don't respond to the tenant, the DHCR can cancel your rent increase.

If the tenant thinks that your response is unsatisfactory (or if it doesn't arrive in seven days), the tenant may complete and sign Part C of the notice (Tenant Complaint to DHCR) and deliver or mail it to DHCR. To decide the matter, the DHCR may request copies of your records relating to operating expenses, violations and repairs for the preceding two-year period. Upon receipt, the DHCR can affirm, reduce or cancel your rent increase and order you to refund any overpayments to the tenant.

## 4. DHCR Registration Requirements for Rent-Controlled Units

Back in the 1950s, state law required most landlords to file registration statements for their rent-controlled units with their local housing authority. (9 NYCRR §§ 2103.1, 2103.2, 2103.9.) In 1984, New York City law required landlords to file new registration statements with the State DHCR for those rent-controlled units in buildings *with rent-stabilized units*. Chances are you or a prior owner complied with the registration requirements then. Unlike rent-stabilized units (discussed in Section A4, above), which must be registered with the DHCR annually, there's no ongoing registration requirement for rent-controlled units.

If you have any question whether a specific unit is registered, ask DHCR for a copy of the most recent "Rent Registration Building-Wide Rent Roll" for that address. See "How to Find out If a Unit Is Rent-Stabilized or Rent-Controlled," above.

## 5. Vacancy Decontrol

When a rent-controlled tenant dies (leaving behind no legal successors), voluntarily moves out or is lawfully evicted, the unit automatically becomes "vacancy decontrolled" (see "Terminating a Rent-Controlled Tenancy," below). A unit that's decontrolled is no longer subject to rent control laws and regulations.

After a unit is vacancy decontrolled, it may, however, become subject to rent stabilization if it is:

- located in an area such as New York City, where rent stabilization laws are in effect (see "Municipalities Subject to Rent Regulation," above)
- located in a building built before 1974, and
- contains six or more units.

If the unit doesn't qualify for rent stabilization coverage, it is completely removed from regulation. That means that you're free (at last!) to rent the unit on whatever terms you see fit.

## Terminating a Rent-Controlled Tenancy

So long as the tenant pays rent, rent-controlled tenancies may only be terminated on specific grounds. Generally, you can end a rent-controlled tenancy if the tenant:

- violates a substantial obligation of the tenancy by, for instance, subletting the unit without your permission
- uses or occupies the rental unit for an illegal or immoral use, such as drug sales
- commits objectionable conduct or permits a nuisance that threatens the safety and well-being of neighboring tenants
- refuses to provide access to the unit for necessary repairs or improvements, or
- fails to use the rental unit as a primary residence.

In some cases, landlords may end rent-controlled tenancies where the rental unit is required for the landlord's use, is being withdrawn from the rental market or where the property is being demolished. Chapter 14 details the various grounds upon which you may terminate a rent-controlled tenancy. Chapter 15 describes the notices that must be delivered to the tenant to effectuate the termination.

### a.    Report Rent Control Vacancies to DHCR

When a rent-controlled unit becomes vacant, you must report the vacancy to the DHCR. (9 NYCRR §§ 2103.3; 2203.2.) File an Owner's Report of Vacancy Decontrol (DHCR Form RA-42V) with DHCR within 30 days of the date the unit is re-rented. Keep a copy for your files.

What happens if you forget to file the form? There aren't any penalties for failing to report the vacancy. And the filing omission won't affect the unit's decontrolled legal status. But it's a good idea to file the form anyway so DHCR will take the unit off its list of rent-controlled units.

### b.    When Decontrolled Units Become Rent Stabilized

When a decontrolled unit becomes rent stabilized, you may negotiate the rent with the first rent-stabilized tenant. Then you must register the unit with the DHCR by filing an Initial Registration for the unit within 90 days of the date the first rent-stabilized tenant moves in. (See Section A4, above, for details on registration.)

Does the idea of finally being able to collect a negotiated rent for the unit sound too good to be true? Well—it is. The rent you negotiate with the new tenant is subject to the tenant's right to file a Fair Market Rent Appeal with the DHCR, contending that the negotiated rent exceeds the unit's "fair market rent." (9 NYCRR §§ 2502.3, 2522.3.) The tenant must file the appeal with the DHCR within 90 days of receiving your Initial Apartment Registration form. If the appeal is filed too late, the rent you set sticks, and becomes the lawful regulated rent for the unit.

To determine a unit's fair market rent, the DHCR considers special guidelines for rent increases issued annually by the Rent Guidelines Board (see "Rent Guidelines Boards," above), rents for comparable rent-stabilized units in the same area and the cost of any improvements added to the unit while it was vacant. If the DHCR determines that the rent you set exceeds the fair market rent, it adjusts the legal rent for the unit downward and orders you to reimburse (or credit) the tenant for any excess rent collected.

 **If your tenant files a Fair Market Rent Appeal, you may want to hire an attorney to prepare and file your answer.** The DHCR's formula for calculating "fair market rent" is pretty complicated, and an experienced attorney will know what evidence to submit to establish comparable rents. When deciding on whether to retain legal counsel, keep the "high-rent/high-income" deregulation rules in mind (see Section F, below). The sooner you can get the regulated rent for the unit over $2,000 per month, the sooner you can get the unit deregulated once and for all, if the tenant's income meets the threshold. (See Section F, below.)

While landlords who lose Fair Market Rent Appeals must pay back any excess rent collected from the tenant, they can't be hit with any other penalties. Unlike "overcharge" cases (discussed in Section G, below), you can't be ordered to pay triple damages, interest or attorneys' fees to the tenant.

## C. Individual Apartment Improvement Rent Increases

When you make improvements to rent-regulated units by, say, installing a new refrigerator or replacing a wood floor, you may be entitled to an individual apartment improvement rent increase. The amount of the rent hike is equal to 1/40th of the improvement's cost. This type of rent increase is one of the easiest for landlords to get—especially for vacant units. You don't need the prior consent of the DHCR or the incoming tenant to improve a vacant apartment. You just perform the work and raise the legal rent—permanently. (NY Uncon. § 8626(d); NYC Adm. Code § 26-511.)

If the unit is occupied, the rent hike is a little harder to get. You need the tenant's consent. (9 NYCRR §§ 2502.4, 2522.4; 9 NYCRR §§ 2102.3(b), 2204.2(a).)

### 1. What Improvements Qualify?

As a general rule, you can't take an individual apartment improvement rent increase for ordinary repairs, maintenance or decorating work. Fixing a dishwasher or replacing a broken window sash won't qualify for a rent hike, since that type of work is considered ordinary maintenance. But if you upgrade the condition of the unit by, say, installing a new dishwasher or a completely new window, you'll probably be allowed to take a rent increase.

Here are the kinds of improvements that have qualified for an individual apartment improvement rent increase: New appliances, such as air condi-

tioners, refrigerators, ranges, range hoods and dishwashers; new kitchen cabinets; vanities and/or countertops; bathroom improvements like toilets, sinks, tubs, shower doors, faucets, medicine cabinets and new tiling; new light fixtures; new doors; new windows, window blinds or shades and replacement flooring (not repairs).

For rent-controlled units, DHCR considers painting to be an apartment improvement when painting was not one of the services provided to the unit when it became subject to rent control. For all other tenants, painting work is not considered an improvement. (For details on the landlord's obligation to paint apartments, see Chapter 9, Section B14.)

Here are some work items which, according to the DHCR, don't qualify for a rent increase: scraping and refinishing wood floors; replacing cracked or broken tiles and replacing light bulbs, entrance door locks or window panes.

If you have any question about whether a specific improvement qualifies for a rent increase, ask DHCR to issue a written opinion letter. See "How to Request a DHCR Opinion Letter," below. Alternatively, you can ask an experienced landlord-tenant lawyer to give you an opinion as to whether a specific individual apartment improvement will qualify for a rent increase.

### How to Request a DHCR Opinion Letter

To request a written opinion—for example, as to whether a specific individual apartment or capital improvement qualifies for a rent increase—write down your question as specifically as possible and send to the DHCR at this address:

NY State Division of Housing and Community Renewal
Office of Rent Administration
Gertz Plaza
92-31 Union Hall Street
Jamaica, Queens, NY 11433
Phone 718-739-6400

## 2. Calculating the Rent Increase

When you make apartment improvements you can collect a monthly rent increase of 1/40th of the cost of the equipment or improvement. The rent hike is a permanent addition to the base rent for the unit—you don't have to stop taking it after 40 months. When figuring out the cost of the improvements, you can include charges for labor, materials, equipment, sales tax and delivery fees. You can also include your costs for removing an old appliance before a new one is installed, or for demolition and debris removal.

> **EXAMPLE:** You install a new refrigerator in a vacant rent-stabilized unit. Your total expense is $440 including tax, delivery and removal charges. You may permanently increase the monthly rent for the unit by $11 (1/40th of $440).

When calculating the vacancy lease rent for vacant units, add the individual apartment improvement rent increase *after* you apply the applicable vacancy lease rent increases. You can't add the increase, and then compound it by the vacancy bonuses or rent guidelines vacancy increase. (See Section A5b, above.)

⚠ **Include individual apartment improvement rent increases in annual registration.** Any rent increase for a rent-stabilized unit based on apartment improvements must be listed on your next annual apartment registration form (DHCR Form RR-1A). Registration requirements for rent-stabilized units are detailed in Section A4.

## 3. Getting Tenant Consent

You'll need the tenant's written consent for the improvement and the rent increase. Don't rely on a tenant's oral promise to pay more rent. Get it in writing. Otherwise, a tenant could later claim that she agreed to the improvement, but never consented to pay a rent increase.

A sample Agreement to Rent Increase for New Equipment or Improvement is shown below. After the agreement is signed, keep it in the tenant's file along with other important papers, especially the lease.

The Forms CD includes the Agreement to Rent Increase for New Equipment or Improvement, and Appendix IV includes a blank tear-out copy.

If the unit is vacant, you don't need anyone's consent to perform improvements. You just do the work and add 1/40th of the cost to the new tenant's rent. The new tenant may, however, challenge the rent increase by filing a later rent overcharge complaint with DHCR (Section G, below, discusses rent overcharge complaints). At that point, you may need to prove the cost of the improvements. So keep your receipts.

## 4. Keep the Right Receipts

If a tenant files a rent overcharge complaint after you raise the rent, you may need to substantiate the costs of the equipment or improvements you added to the apartment. According to DHCR Policy Statement 90-10, any one of the following four documents is acceptable proof:

- cancelled checks dated around the same time the improvement was installed
- invoice receipts marked "paid in full"
- a signed and dated written contract, or
- a sworn statement from a supplier or contractor describing the improvement made to the unit and that you paid in full for the equipment or improvement.

For more details on proof of costs, see "Submit Proof of Costs with MCI Application," below. (The requirements for proving individual apartment improvements costs are the same as those for proving MCI Costs. (DHCR Policy Statement 90-10).)

## Agreement to Rent Increase for New Equipment or Improvement

Landlord's Name: 302 Fifth Associates

Address: Suite G

302 Fifth Avenue

New York, NY 10001

Tenant's Name: Anne F. Hannemann

Address: Apartment 8-D

302 Fifth Avenue

New York, NY 10001

Tenant hereby acknowledges that on or about __March 1, 200X__, the Landlord will install into the Tenant's Unit, the new equipment and/or improvements described below:

| Item | Cost |
| --- | --- |
| New, white 34" General Electric stove | $648.50 |
| New, white 34" General Electric range hood | $129.32 |
| | |
| | |
| | |
| | |
| Total Cost: | $777.82 |

Pursuant to applicable law, the Landlord may increase the Unit's legal regulated rent, as of the date of installation, by $__19.45__ per month, which represents 1/40th of the total cost of the equipment and improvements.

2/15/0X     302 Fifth Associates

Date     Landlord's Name

*Sidney Levy*       General Partner

Signature     Title

2/15/0X     Anne F. Hannemann

Date     Tenant's Name

*Anne F. Hannemann*

Signature

## D. Major Capital Improvement (MCI) Rent Increases

When you make a buildingwide major capital improvement to a property, such as installing new windows in each unit or putting a new roof on the building, you may be permitted to take a "Major Capital Improvement" (MCI) rent increase. MCI rent hikes permit you to recoup the cost of an eligible MCI in seven years. The rent hike is permanent and affects both rent-controlled and rent-stabilized units. (9 NYCRR §§ 2102.3(b)(1); 2202.3(a), (b); 2502.4(a)(2); 2522.4(a)(2).)

### 1.  What Work Qualifies as an MCI?

To qualify as an MCI, the improvement or installation must:

- relate to the operation, preservation and maintenance of the property
- benefit all tenants, and
- be depreciable under the Internal Revenue Code as something other than an ordinary repair.

For example, you can get an MCI increase for installing a new boiler in your building, but not for a having an existing boiler repaired or rebuilt.

Here are some items that qualify as MCIs: new air conditioners, aluminum or vinyl siding on all exposed sides of building, complete bathroom modernization in every unit, new boiler room or expansion to accommodate new boiler, complete catwalk replacements, new chimneys, complete courtyard/walkway resurfacing, new fire escapes, new gas heating units in every unit, new hot water heaters, incinerator upgrading, new intercom systems, parapet replacements, brick pointing and exterior waterproofing, re-piping, re-roofing with single-ply rubber roofs or multi-ply asphalt, new solar heating systems, structural steel replacement, new television security monitor systems, new waste compactors, new water tanks, new aluminum-framed windows (wood framed windows are allowed only for landmark buildings). (See 9 NYCRR § 2522.4(a).)

If you have any question as to whether an improvement qualifies as an MCI, ask DHCR to issue a written opinion letter. See "How to Request a DHCR Opinion Letter," above. Alternatively, you can ask an experienced landlord-tenant attorney for a legal opinion as to whether a specific improvement project will qualify as a major capital improvement with DHCR.

### 2.  When to Apply for an MCI Rent Increase

You may apply for an MCI rent hike after you have completely installed and paid for the improvement. If the improvement is completely installed, but is not fully paid for because of an installment agreement or loan, you may still apply for a rent increase, as long as you submit proof of the loan or installment agreement. You may not include finance charges, however, when calculating the cost of the improvement.

Window replacement, new roofs, boiler replacement and extensive electrical or structural work usually require some sort of written approval from a local building inspector or department. If your improvement requires an approval, sign-off or certificate of operation from a government agency, you must apply for it before you file an MCI application. DHCR will begin processing your application when it's filed, but won't order a rent increase until all final approvals are received.

To obtain an MCI rent increase for rent-stabilized units, your MCI application must be filed no later than two years after completion of the MCI. The rent hike is retroactive to the date DHCR notifies tenants about your MCI application.

### 3.  How to Apply for an MCI Rent Increase

To get an MCI rent increase, you must complete and file an Owner's Application for Rent Increase Based on Major Capital Improvements (MCI)

## Submit Proof of Costs With MCI Application

To be eligible for the largest possible rent increase, you must prove each of your MCI costs to the DHCR. To help landlords prove their costs, the DHCR issued a policy statement detailing what it considers adequate proof (DHCR Policy Statement 90-10). If you fail to submit any evidence of payment, the claimed cost of the item will be disallowed and your potential rent increase will be reduced. According to the policy statement, you should submit *at least one* of the following four documents with your MCI application to prove your costs:

• **Cancelled checks.** Submit copies of your cancelled checks (front and back) for the work. The checks should be dated around the same time that the MCI work was ordered or completed.

• **Invoice receipts marked "paid in full."** Another acceptable way to prove the cost of your MCI is to submit copies of your paid invoices and receipts. The dates on the invoice receipts are supposed to be "contemporaneous" with the completion of the MCI work. Ask your contractors and suppliers to furnish as much detail as possible on the receipt about the materials, labor or services provided, including the make,

model and serial number of any appliance or equipment and where it was installed.

• **Signed contract agreement for the work.** If you entered into a written agreement with a contractor for the MCI work, submit that. Make sure that the description and cost of the work matches the description and cost data you furnish in your application. In other words, make sure that the contract answers more questions than it raises.

• **Sworn statement from supplier or contractor stating that installation was completed and paid in full.** A supplier or contractor's affidavit, or sworn statement, is helpful when you have no other proof of payment. The affidavit should cover these points: the name of the person signing the affidavit, his or her relationship to the contractor, the name of the contracting company, the address of the property where the MCI work was performed, a description of the MCI work performed, a statement that the work has been completed, the total cost of the work and a statement that the owner has paid the cost in full. The contractor must sign and date the affidavit before a notary public.

State of New York
**Division of Housing and Community Renewal**
Office of Rent Administration
Web Site: www.dhcr.state.ny.us

Gertz Plaza
92-31 Union Hall Street
Jamaica, NY  11433
(718) 739-6400

| For DHCR use only |
| --- |
| **Docket Number:** |
| **MCI Package Returned to** |
| **Owner:**_____ |

## Owner's Application for Rent Increase
## Based on Major Capital Improvements (MCI)

Subject Building: _____
                     Number            Street

_____
              Municipality/Borough and Zip Code

R.E. Tax Block Number: _____ Lot Number: _____

Building(s) Registration Number: _____

Total Number of Apartments: _____

Total Number of Rent Regulated Apts.: _____

Number of Residential Rooms:     _____

**Mailing Address of Owner/Agent:**

Name:     _____

Number/Street: _____

City: _____

State, Zip Code:     _____

Telephone No.: (     ) _____

Telefax No.:     (     ) _____

### Request for Increase

1. I request an increase in the rent for the subject premises of $_____ per room per month

2. Improvements were done with: a. government loan/grant agreement ☐ Yes ☐ No   If yes, attach a copy of the agreement, including Orders restructuring any or all rents or Tax Abatement Certificate.
   b. tax abatement ☐ Yes ☐ No

3. The affected apartments are:   ☐ Rent Controlled   ☐ Rent Stabilized   ☐ Both

4. If there is an application pending for tax abatement, submit a copy of the application.

### Affirmation of Owner

1. I am submitting two complete identical applications with two copies of all required supplements and supporting documentation.

   ☐ a.   After I receive the DHCR date stamped package, I will make the complete package, including all supplements and documentation, available for tenant review in the office of the superintendent or resident manager at the building or conveniently close at:

   _____

   I will also make available any additional information related to this application which is required by DHCR.

   ☐ b.   As such office is not available, tenants may request appointments at DHCR to review the package.

   I am maintaining all required services and will continue to provide such services.  I affirm that there are no current immediately hazardous violations on the premises issued by any municipality, county, state or federal agency.  However, if there still is such a violation of record, the violation has been corrected; if it is a tenant induced violation, I believe it should be waived for the purposes of this application.

2. I affirm under the penalties provided by law that the contents of this application are true to the best of my knowledge.

Owner/Agent:_____        Date: _____
                     Type or Print

   By: _____        Title: _____
                     Signature

   It is not necessary that the above be sworn to, but false statements may subject you to the penalties provided by law.

(DHCR Form RA-79). This form is several pages long. (Some key sections are shown below.) You can request that application forms be mailed to you by calling DHCR's Infoline (718-739-6400) or you may download the application and instructions from the DHCR's website (www.dhcr.state.ny.us). File an original and one copy of the application (and supplements), copies of all necessary approvals from applicable government agencies for the work done and "proof" of your MCI costs (see "Submit Proof of Costs with MCI Application," below) with the DHCR.

You can apply for a rent increase based on an MCI completed by a previous landlord, so long as the previous landlord never obtained a rent increase based on the same improvements and you can prove the previous landlord's MCI costs.

After you file your MCI rent increase application with the DHCR, the agency notifies your tenants of the application. Tenants get an opportunity to respond to the application. Tenants sometimes challenge MCIs by claiming that the improvement didn't benefit all of the building's tenants or that the MCI work wasn't properly performed or fully completed. You get a chance to respond to or refute the tenants' challenges. Then the DHCR makes a final determination on your MCI rent increase application by issuing an order granting the rent increase you requested (in part or in full) or denying it. Both landlords and tenants are entitled to appeal the order (instructions for filing an appeal are included with the DHCR's order).

The MCI application process is slow. Depending on the size of the MCI project and the number of affected tenants, the DHCR can take a year or more to process your application.

For New York City rent-stabilized tenants, the rent increase is retroactive to the first rent payment date 30 days after DHCR notifies the tenants about your MCI application. The DHCR order granting the rent increase explains how to collect the retroactive

portion from rent-stabilized tenants. MCI rent increases are not retroactive for rent-stabilized tenants outside New York City or for any rent-controlled tenants. The landlord may begin to collect the rent increase on the first rent payment date following the DHCR's issuance of the MCI rent increase order.

**No rent increase may be charged or collected unless anduntil DHCR issues an order approving the increase.** Unauthorized rent hikes are unlawful and expose you to liability for triple damages.

**Landlords must follow two notice requirements for units that become exempt from rent regulation due to a monthly rent that has reached $2,000 after a vacancy.** Local Law No. 12 of 2000 requires you to provide the initial deregulated tenant with two separate notices:

- A written notice certifying the last regulated rent for the unit, the reason the unit is not subject to regulation, a calculation of how the new rent was computed so as to reach $2,000 or more per month and a statement advising the tenant that the rent may be verified by contacting the DHCR. This notice must be delivered to the tenant when the lease is signed, or sent to the tenant by certified mail within 30 days after the tenancy begins.
- A copy of the registration statement form filed with DHCR, certified by the owner, showing that the rental unit became exempt from rent regulation and the last regulated rent. The statement must be sent to the tenant within 30 days after the tenancy begins or after the registration is filed, whichever occurs later.

The Rent Stabilization Association of New York City (RSA) has prepared two helpful forms you can use to comply with this requirement. The forms may be downloaded, free of charge, from the RSA's website (www.rsanyc.com; click "resources" then "Local Law 12").

## 4. Computing and Collecting the Rent Increase

Eventually, DHCR will issue an order either granting your MCI increase in whole or in part or denying the increase. The monthly rent hike for each rent-regulated tenant is calculated by taking the total cost of the MCI (as allowed by DHCR) and dividing it by 84—the number of months in seven years. That sum is then divided by the number of rooms in the building. This yields the cost of the MCI the landlord can collect per room per month.

**For all units subject to NYC rent stabilization:** The rent increase collectible in any one year may not exceed 6% of the tenant's rent, as listed on the schedule of monthly rental income filed with the owner's application. Increases above the 6% cap can be spread forward to future years

**For all rent-controlled apartments and for stabilized apartments outside NYC,** the increase collectible in any one year may not exceed 15% of the tenant's rent as of the issue date of the order. There is no retroactive portion.

Units occupied by senior citizens with a valid Senior Citizen Rent Increase Exemption (SCRIE) are exempt from paying the MCI over the amount of their exemption. (Section E, below, covers this exemption.)

## 5. When an MCI Rent Increase Begins

For rent-stabilized units, you can't collect an MCI rent increase until the end of the current lease *unless* the tenant's lease contains a special clause that allows for an MCI rent increase during the lease term. Your rent-stabilized leases should contain a provision alerting the tenant to any pending MCI applications and specifically describing the improvement. If that provision isn't part of a tenant's lease, you can't collect the increase from that tenant until the unit is vacated.

If an apartment is vacant or becomes vacant while an application to DHCR for an MCI rent in-crease is pending, notify the incoming tenant about the pending MCI application, and that the rent will be increased if the application is approved. Your failure to include this notice in the vacancy leases can result in your loss of an MCI increase for that apartment during the term of the vacancy lease. Landlords who charge MCI increases without this notification can be subject to overcharge penalties.

Here is a sample MCI notification clause you can add to your vacancy lease:

"An application for a major capital improvement rent increase has been filed under Docket No._____ with DHCR based upon the following work:_____. Should DHCR issue an order granting the rent increase, the rent provided for in this lease will be increased accordingly."

The New York City rent-stabilized lease, written by the Real Estate Board of New York, (discussed in Chapter 2) contains a clause like this. Landlords of rent-stabilized units outside New York City should add this clause to their lease.

If the tenant's lease contains such a clause, you may begin charging the MCI rent hike as of the next rent payment date.

There are three situations in which landlords are generally prohibited from collecting an MCI rent increase. You can't collect an MCI rent hike:

- from a tenant for whom DHCR has determined that required services are not being maintained or from a tenant who has a rent reduction order in place (Chapter 9 covers required services and DHCR rent reduction orders)
- in a building that has an outstanding DHCR buildingwide rent reduction order in effect, unless the owner has filed an application with DHCR to restore the rent, or
- if you're a landlord against whom DHCR had issued an outstanding finding of harassment.

## E. Senior Citizen Rent Increase Exemption (SCRIE)

Tenants who are 62 years old or older may qualify for full or partial exemption from rent increases under the state's Senior Citizen Rent Increase Exemption (SCRIE) program. The SCRIE program applies to rent-regulated tenants who live in New York City and in 18 other municipalities in Westchester and Nassau Counties (see "Municipalities with SCRIE Programs," below).

---

### Municipalities With SCRIE Programs

- *New York City* (all counties)
- *Nassau County:* Glen Cove, Town of North Hempstead; Villages of Hempstead, Great Neck Plaza, Thomaston and Great Neck
- *Westchester County:* Cities of Mount Vernon, New Rochelle, White Plains and Yonkers; Towns of Greenburgh and Mamaroneck; Villages of Mamaroneck, Tarrytown, Irvington, Pleasantville, Larchmont and Sleepy Hollow

---

Under the SCRIE program, senior citizens are eligible for a full or partial exemption from rent increases if their disposable incomes are below a maximum limit set by the municipality ($20,000 as of early 2003) and they are paying at least one-third of their income for rent. Landlords with SCRIE tenants are issued certificates that entitle them to property tax abatements equal to their tenants' rent increase exemptions. If the rent abatement is greater than the amount of property tax due on your building, you're eligible for a cash reimbursement for the excess.

It's the tenant's responsibility to apply for and get the exemption.

**In New York City,** the Department for the Aging (2 Lafayette Street, 6th Floor, New York, NY 10007, 212-442-1000) administers the SCRIE program. For more information, see the Department's website at www.ci.nyc.ny.us/html/dfta.

**Outside NYC,** the SCRIE program is run by the DHCR. Contact the appropriate agency if you think that your tax abatement certificate is incorrect.

## F. High-Rent/High-Income Deregulation

Owning a rent-regulated unit doesn't have to be a life sentence. Once a unit's rent rises to $2,000 per month, you may be entitled to have the unit permanently freed from rent regulations—thanks to the so-called "high-rent/high-income" deregulation laws. The rules on deregulation depend on whether the unit is vacant or occupied.

### 1. Vacant Units

Rent-stabilized units that become vacant can be deregulated if the rent after vacancy reaches $2,000 or more. To see if a unit meets this rent threshold, be sure to apply all applicable vacancy lease rent increases and bonuses (see Vacancy Lease Rent Increases for Rent-Stabilized Units, Section A5 above) and rent increases for improvements you've made to the unit (see Section C above).

> EXAMPLE: After a three-year occupancy, a rent-stabilized tenant of Apt. 23F moves out. The New York City tenant's last monthly rent was $1,600. While the unit is vacant, you spend $12,000 upgrading the bathroom and kitchen. A new tenant signs a one-year vacancy lease starting November 1, 2002, for $2,188 (calculated by taking the old rent ($1,600), adding a $288 vacancy bonus (18%* x $1,600) and then adding a $300 individual apartment improvement rent increase (1/40th of $12,000). Because the new rent exceeds $2,000, Apt. 23-F has become exempt from rent regulation.
>
> *NYC Rent Guidelines Order #34, which covers leases that begin between October 1, 2002, and September 30, 2003, authorizes rent increases of 2% for one-year renewal leases and 4% for two-year renewal leases. Since the difference between the rates set for one- and two-year renewal leases is 2% (4% − 2%); the vacancy bonus for a one-year vacancy lease signed between 10/1/02 and 9/30/03 is 18% (20% − 2%). The Order authorizes a 0% increase

for vacancy leases. (For more information on how to calculate a rent increase, see Vacancy Lease Rent Increases for Rent-Stabilized Units, Section A5, above.)

## 2. Occupied Units

Occupied units renting for $2,000 or more can become deregulated, too. Here's the hitch: The tenant's adjusted income must hit or exceed $175,000 for two consecutive years. For occupied units, you need "high rent" and "high income."

How are you supposed to know how much your tenant earns? When the rent-stabilized or rent-controlled rent reaches $2,000 or more on a given unit, you may serve an Income Certification Form (DHCR Form RA-93 CF) to at least one of the rent-stabilized or rent-controlled tenants who live in the unit. A sample is shown below. The form asks tenants to confirm or deny that their combined adjusted gross income (including that of any occupants who live full-time at the unit) was at least $175,000 for each of the last two calendar years.

The income certification form must be served on the tenant before May 1st of a given year. If you serve the form on the tenant personally, ask the tenant to sign (not initial) a copy of the form which acts as a receipt. You can also mail the form to the tenant by certified mail, return receipt requested, or by regular mail. Make sure you get a mailing receipt (either a receipt for certified mail or a certificate of mailing for regular mail).

Tenants get 30 days to complete and return the income certification form to you. You can ask the DHCR to deregulate the unit if a tenant fails to return the certification, if the tenant admits that adjusted income was at least $175,000 for the last two years or if you dispute your tenant's claim that adjusted income is lower than $175,000. To do so, file a Petition by Owner for High Income Rent Deregulation (DHCR Form RA-93-OPD) by June 30 of a given year (late petitions will be dismissed). The DHCR will notify the tenant of your application, and give the tenant 60 days to respond. If the tenant doesn't answer, the DHCR will usually rule in your favor.

The DHCR will verify the tenant's income from the tenant's state income tax return. For rent-controlled units, a final DHCR determination deregulating an apartment becomes effective as of June 1 of the year following the application. For rent-stabilized units, deregulation becomes effective when the current tenant's lease ends. After deregulation, the tenant must either pay market rent for the unit or move out.

## 3. Units Exempt From High-Rent/High-Income Deregulation

Certain units are exempt from the deregulation rules—even when the rent rises to $2,000. Exemptions include units that are rent regulated solely because the owner receives tax benefits under the Multiple Dwelling Law 7-c, "421-a", "489" or "J-51" tax benefit programs and units covered by the New York City Loft Law. For more information on these programs, call the city's Office of Tax Incentive Programs at 212-863-5517, or check its website at www.ci.ny.us/html/hpd/html/tax_incentives/tax_incentives.html.

## G. How to Deal With a Rent-Stabilized Tenant's Rent Overcharge Complaint

Landlords are prohibited from charging or collecting sums over the legal regulated rent for rent-stabilized units. (9 NYCRR §§ 2525.1, 9 NYCRR § 2505.1(a).) Tenants who believe they are paying more than the legal regulated rent for their apartments may file a complaint of rent overcharge with the DHCR. (They may also have their complaints of rent overcharge heard by a court, instead.)

If your tenant files a rent overcharge complaint with DHCR, you get 30 days to respond by filing a written answer to the tenant's complaint. Your answer should itemize the amount of rent payable under the current lease and under each prior lease for the unit for the four-year period prior to the most recent DHCR rent registration filed for the unit. This is known as a rent history. If you're found

State of New York
**Division of Housing and Community Renewal**
Office of Rent Administration
Web Site: www.dhcr.state.ny.us

Gertz Plaza
92-31 Union Hall Street
Jamaica, NY  11433
(718) 739-6400

## Income Certification Form - 2003 Filing Period
## (New York City)

The New York City Rent Stabilization Law ("rent stabilization") and the New York City Rent and Rehabilitation Law ("rent control") permit an owner to make an annual application to exempt from rent regulation housing accommodations having a "maximum rent" (rent controlled) or "legal regulated rent" (rent stabilized) of $2,000.00 or more per month. If the tenant(s) timely respond to a separate notice of the deregulation application from the NYS Division of Housing and Community Renewal (DHCR), the NYS Department of Taxation and Finance will review whether the housing accommodation is occupied by persons who have a total annual income in excess of $175,000.00 in each of the two preceding calendar years.  Annual income means federal adjusted gross income as reported on the New York State income tax return.  For housing accommodations subject to rent stabilization, total annual income means the sum of the annual incomes of all persons whose names are recited as the tenant or co-tenant on a lease who occupy the housing accommodation, whether or not as a primary residence, and of all other persons who occupy the housing accommodation as their primary residence on other than a temporary basis.  For housing accommodations subject to rent control, total annual income means the sum of the annual incomes of all persons who occupy the housing accommodation as their primary residence on other than a temporary basis.  For both rent-stabilized and rent-controlled housing accommodations, the incomes of bona fide employees of such tenants, co-tenants, and occupants residing in the housing accommodation in connection with their employment are not included.  In addition, where a housing accommodation is sublet, the annual income of a bona fide subtenant is not included.  In all cases, the operative date for determining the nature of any person's status or occupancy is the date that this form is served upon the tenant.  The incomes of otherwise qualifying tenants or occupants who temporarily vacated the housing accommodation during the 2001, 2002 or 2003 calendar years will be included in total annual income.  This form, when served upon a tenant, initiates the process of determining whether this housing accommodation qualifies for deregulation based upon the above criteria.  This housing accommodation can only be deregulated **pursuant to a separate order issued by the Division of Housing and Community Renewal** in response to an owner's filing a petition for deregulation based on the tenant's (s') income.

### Part A
(To be completed by the owner or the owner's managing agent)

1. **Mailing Address of Owner or Managing Agent:**

    Name: _____

    Number/Street: _____

    City,
    State, Zip Code: _____

    _____
        (Name of Owner if different from above.)

2. **Mailing Address of Tenant(s):  (as named on lease)**

    Name: _____

    Number/Street: _____ Apt. No.: _____

    City,
    State, Zip Code: _____

3. List the docket number(s) of all DHCR proceeding(s) involving the subject housing accommodation of which you are aware:

    _____

4. Signature of Owner or Managing Agent: _____

    Name (printed): _____ Date: ____/____/____

### Part B

**(To be completed by the tenant(s) named in the existing lease or by statutory tenant(s) and returned to the owner, not to DHCR. Also, where the tenant named in the lease is a corporation, consulate, institution or a business entity, all occupants must complete this form.)**

**Tenants are not required to complete this form if the legal regulated rent or maximum rent of their housing accommodation is not $2,000.00 or more per month.**

RA-93 CF NYC (10/02)                                           -1-

5. List the names of all tenants of this housing accommodation. Include all persons whose names are recited as the tenant or co-tenant on any lease (for rent-stabilized housing accommodations) as well as "statutory tenants" (those without a current lease) if this is a rent-controlled housing accommodation. In the "status" column, enter: "a" for those tenants who occupy this housing accommodation as a primary residence on other than a temporary basis or who have sublet this housing accommodation to another person; "b" for those tenants who occupy it as a non-primary residence; "c" for those tenants who have temporarily vacated this housing accommodation (other than those listed under "a" above who have sublet the housing accommodation), and "d" for those tenants who have permanently vacated the housing accommodation. If you entered "c" or "d" for any tenant, enter the date upon which that tenant vacated the apartment. For each tenant listed, indicate by writing "Yes" or "No" in the space provided, whether the tenant filed New York State income tax returns for 2001 and 2002. If any tenant did not file a return for one or both years, give the reason(s) for not filing. **(Attach an additional sheet if necessary.)**

| Name of Tenant | Status (a), (b), (c), or (d) | Vacancy Date for status (c) or (d) (mo./day/yr.) | N.Y.S. Income Tax Return Filed? 2001 | 2002 | Reason for not filing |
|---|---|---|---|---|---|
| _____ | _____ | ___/___/___ | _____ | _____ | _____ |
| _____ | _____ | ___/___/___ | _____ | _____ | _____ |
| _____ | _____ | ___/___/___ | _____ | _____ | _____ |
| _____ | _____ | ___/___/___ | _____ | _____ | _____ |

6. List all the names of all other persons who occupy this housing accommodation as a primary residence on other than a temporary basis as of the date this form was served upon you by the owner, or who occupied it as a primary residence on other than a temporary basis at any time during the period from January 1, 2001 through the date this form was served upon you by the owner (include children and other relatives). In the "status" column, enter "a" for such persons who occupy the housing accommodation as a primary residence on other than a temporary basis as of the date this form was served upon you by the owner; "b" for such persons who now occupy the apartment as other than a primary residence; "c" for such persons who have temporarily vacated the housing accommodation, and "d" for such persons who have permanently vacated the housing accommodation. For all persons whose status you entered as "b," "c," or "d," enter the date such persons ceased maintaining the accommodation as their primary residence or vacated the accommodation. If any person listed is a child, a bona fide employee of an occupant residing in the housing accommodation in connection with such employment, or a bona fide subtenant in occupancy pursuant to the provisions of Section 226-b of the Real Property Law, check the appropriate box. For each person listed (other than a bona fide employee or a bona fide subtenant), indicate, by writing "Yes" or "No" in the spaces provided, whether such person was required to file New York State income tax returns for 2001 and 2002 and whether such persons did file such returns.

| Name Occupant | Status (a, b, c, or d) | Date of Vacancy or of Change in Use (mo./day/yr.) for status b, c, or d | Employee | Subtenant | Child | Age of Child | N.Y.S. Income Tax Return Required? 2001 | 2002 | NYS Income Tax Return Filed? 2001 | 2002 |
|---|---|---|---|---|---|---|---|---|---|---|
| _____ | ____ | ___/___/___ | ☐ | ☐ | ☐ | ____ | ____ | ____ | ____ | ____ |
| _____ | ____ | ___/___/___ | ☐ | ☐ | ☐ | ____ | ____ | ____ | ____ | ____ |
| _____ | ____ | ___/___/___ | ☐ | ☐ | ☐ | ____ | ____ | ____ | ____ | ____ |
| _____ | ____ | ___/___/___ | ☐ | ☐ | ☐ | ____ | ____ | ____ | ____ | ____ |
| _____ | ____ | ___/___/___ | ☐ | ☐ | ☐ | ____ | ____ | ____ | ____ | ____ |

If any occupant listed (other than a bona fide employee or bona fide subtenant) did not file a N.Y.S. income tax return for either or both years, indicate that occupant's name and explain (**attach an additional sheet if necessary**): _____

_____

7. List the docket number(s) of all DHCR proceeding(s) involving the subject housing accommodation: _____

_____

8.  **Income Certification**

I (we) hereby certify that the total annual income (the total federal adjusted gross incomes as reported on the New York State income tax returns) of all persons identified in Items 5 and 6 above, **excluding** (for rent-stabilized and rent-controlled apartments):

- those persons listed in Item 5 under status "d";

- those persons designated as employees or subtenants in Item 6;

- those persons listed in Item 6 under status "b" and "d"; and

- for rent-controlled apartments **only**, also excluding those persons listed in Item 5 under status "b," is

(Check one)

☐  in excess of $175,000.00 in each of the two preceding calendar years.

☐  $175,000.00 or less in either of the two preceding calendar years.

| _____ | _____ | _____ |
|---|---|---|
| Signature of Tenant | Name (printed) | Date |
| _____ | _____ | _____ |
| Signature of Tenant | Name (printed) | Date |

**Return the completed form to the owner, at the address indicated in Part A, Item 1 on page 1 of this form. Do not return this form to DHCR.**

It is not necessary that the statements made in this form be notarized. However, intentionally false statements may subject you to the penalties provided by law.

### Notice to Tenant(s)

By serving you with this form for completion, the owner is asking for information which may result in the elimination of rent control or rent stabilization protections for your apartment, such as the protections against unlimited rent increases and eviction. **The income level certified to by you may be subject to verification by the New York State Department of Taxation and Finance pursuant to Section 171b of the Tax Law.** You are not required to provide any information regarding your income except that which is requested on this form. You have protections available to you to prevent harassment by the owner.

You must return this completed certification **to the owner** (not to DHCR) at the address indicated on this form **within thirty days** after the owner served you with the form. You should retain a copy of the completed form. Failure to reply may ultimately result in the deregulation of the subject housing accommodation.

You **must** keep photocopies of the preprinted mailing labels or the first page of the New York State income tax returns (**with social security numbers and income figures deleted**) for each tenant or occupant listed on this form for **both** tax years 2001 and 2002 for future submission to DHCR when requested.

### Notice to Owner

DHCR shall dismiss an owner's petition for deregulation where the owner cannot prove that the Income Certification Form was served upon the tenant **on or before May first of each calendar year.** The owner is required to serve the Income Certification Form by any of the following methods:

1) Personal delivery, where accompanied by a copy of the Income Certification Form signed (not initialed) by the tenant upon receipt; and/or

2) Certified mail where accompanied by a United States Postal Service receipt; and/or

3) Regular first-class mail where accompanied by a United States Postal Service Certificate of Mailing.

It is suggested that the owner retain proof of service, together with a copy of the form served on the tenant.

- - - - - - - - - - - - - - - - - - - - - - - - - - - - - - - - - - - - - - - - -

Quienes deseen más información o asistencia, pueden llamar a la Línea de Información de Alquileres de la DHCR a (718) 739-6400.

RA-93 CF NYC (10/02)                                    -3-

to have charged the tenant more than the legally regulated rent for the unit, you're on the hook for the amount of any overcharge collected during that four-year period, plus interest and attorneys' fees. If the DHCR finds that the overcharge was "willful," you can be ordered to pay triple damages to the tenant, for the two-year period prior to the complaint.

To decide the complaint, the DHCR may order you to produce copies of prior vacancy and renewal leases, proof of proper rent registration, and copies of any DHCR orders raising or restoring the rent covering the four-year period prior to the filing of the tenant's complaint. Nevertheless, your liability for rent overcharge is limited to the four-

year period preceding the most recent annual registration. (9 NYCRR §§ 2506.1(a)(2), (3); 2526.1(a)(2).)

 **Small owners qualify for free help with answering overcharge complaints.** The DHCR Small Building Owner's Assistance Unit provides special assistance to owners of rent-regulated buildings with a total of 50 units or less. The Unit can help you prepare and file your answer. For more information call the DHCR Infoline at 718-739-6400 or visit your borough or county DHCR office. (Appendix I lists phone numbers and addresses for all DHCR offices.)

---

### Gathering the Right Documents For Your Answer to a Rent Overcharge Complaint

To answer a tenant's rent overcharge complaint, you must provide a rent history for the unit illustrating that all rent increases collected for the unit were lawful during the four-year period prior to the filing of the complaint.

These are the rent records you'll need to gather in order to prepare and substantiate the unit's rent history:

**Rent registration forms.** Pull out and copy the initial and/or annual registration statements that were filed for the unit during the four-year period prior to the most recent registration. (Registration requirements are covered in Section A4, above).

**Leases.** Gather all vacancy and renewal leases for the unit. You'll only need records that go back four years before the date that the unit was most recently registered.

**Rent ledgers.** If you're missing an old lease, you can use rent ledgers to show how much rent was collected during that time period.

**DHCR MCI rent orders.** If you took a rent increase for the unit in accordance with a DHCR major capital improvement rent increase order, you'll

need a copy of the order or, at minimum, the docket number for the order, to prepare your answer (Section D, above, covers MCI rent increases).

**Individual apartment improvement records.** If you took a rent increase in connection with an individual apartment improvement, you'll need to itemize what improvements were made, the date they were completed and the cost. Whenever possible, submit proof of your costs with the answer. (Section C, above, covers individual apartment improvement rent increases.)

**DHCR rent orders.** Pull from your file any DHCR orders which reduced the rent for the unit (in response to a tenant complaint of a decrease in required services) or which restored the rent to its prior level (in response to your certification that required services had been restored). Since these orders have the effect of lowering the rent and later, restoring it to its former level, they are relevant to the unit's rent history. (Chapter 9 discusses required services.)

Chapter **5**

# Security Deposits

Tenant security deposits perform two important functions. First, security deposits give tenants an incentive to fulfill their lease obligations. Tenants who are paid up in rent and leave a clean, undamaged rental unit get rewarded with a full security deposit refund after they move out. Second, security deposits safeguard your real estate investment. After a tenant moves out, you can use the security deposit to cover unpaid rent, to pay for extraordinary cleaning and repairs or to replace rental unit property taken by the tenant.

But it's easy to get into legal trouble over security deposits. Strict state laws dictate how much you can collect, where you must put the money and how much interest to pay. If you break the laws, you can end up forfeiting your tenants' security deposits, paying penalties or even facing criminal action. You can't get around the strict security deposit rules—regardless of what your lease or rental agreement says. (GOL § 7-103(3).) That's why it's essential for landlords to know the laws on security deposits and to follow them carefully.

This chapter explains how to set up a clear, fair system of setting, collecting and holding deposits. It may exceed the minimum legal requirements affecting your property, but it will ultimately work to your advantage, resulting in easier turnovers, better tenant relations and fewer legal hassles.

  Related topics covered in this book include:
- Charging prospective tenants credit check fees, finder's fees or holding deposits: Chapter 1
- Writing clear lease and rental agreement provisions on security deposits: Chapter 2
- Highlighting security deposit rules and procedures in move-in and move-out letters to the tenant: Chapters 7 and 16
- Terminating a lease or rental agreement for a tenant's failure to post a security deposit: Chapter 14, and
- Returning deposits and deducting for cleaning, damages and unpaid rent; how to handle legal disputes involving deposits: Chapter 16.

## A. What's a Security Deposit?

Under New York law, a security deposit is defined as anything of value—money, usually—that's "deposited" by a tenant to secure performance of the tenant's lease obligations, or "advanced" for use as a later rental payment. (GOB § 7-103(1).) Because the legal definition of the term security deposit is so broad, it includes so-called pet deposits or key deposits, since they are intended to secure a tenant's promise to keep the pet from damaging the property or to return the keys at the end of the tenancy.

The "first month's rent," which is customarily paid by tenants when a lease is signed, is not considered a security deposit. That's because it's applied right after the lease is signed. But rent paid in advance for any subsequent month, including the "last month's rent," is subject to the strict security deposit laws. (Section B, below, covers last month's rent.)

> **EXAMPLE:** A Manhattan landlord collected prepaid rent from three tenants. Since they often traveled abroad, the tenants elected to pre-pay several months' rent out of convenience, and to avoid falling into arrears. A judge ruled that the pre-paid rent was a type of security deposit. That meant that the landlord had to handle the funds under the strict rules that apply to security deposits. (*The Yasuda Trust and Banking Co. v. Carven Associates*, N.Y.L.J., 6/28/95, p. 29, col. 3 (Sup. Ct., N.Y. County, 1995).)

## B. Last Month's Rent

Avoid labeling all or part of a security deposit as the tenant's "last month's rent." Landlords who collect last month's rent tend to treat this money as just another security deposit, and use it to cover not only the last month's rent but also other expenses such as repairs or cleaning. But the law restricts the use of money labeled as "last month's rent" to its stated purpose: the rent for the last month of the tenant's occupancy.

EXAMPLE 1: Fernando charged his tenant, Liz, a total deposit of $2,400, calling $1,200 a security deposit and $1,200 last month's rent. As a result, Liz did not pay rent for the last month when she gave her notice to Fernando. This left Fernando with the $1,200 security deposit. Unfortunately, when Liz moved out, she left $1,500 worth of damages, sticking Fernando with a $300 loss.

The security deposit clause in our lease and rental agreement forms (see Clause 8 in Chapter 2) specifically prohibits the tenant's use of any part of the security deposit for last month's rent. This gives landlords more flexibility in their use of the deposit.

EXAMPLE 2: Learning something from his unhappy experience with Liz (Example 1, above), Fernando charged his next tenant a simple $2,400 security deposit, not limiting any part of it to last month's rent. This time, when the tenant moved out, after paying his last month's rent as legally required, the whole $2,400 was available to cover the cost of any repairs or cleaning.

## C. Dollar Limits on Deposits

For non-regulated rental units, there's no legal limit on the amount you can collect as a deposit. (Dollar limits for rent-stabilized and rent-controlled units are discussed in Section D, below.) Normally, the best advice is to charge as much as the market will bear, usually one to two month's rent. The more the tenant has at stake, the better the chance your property will be respected. And, the larger the deposit, the more financial protection you will have if a tenant leaves owing you rent.

⚠ **Make sure you set a big enough security deposit for fixed-term renters.** Once you've signed a lease with a tenant, you're stuck with the security deposit amount set in the lease. You can't arbitrarily raise the security deposit—even if the tenant turns out to be a sloppy housekeeper. (Section H, below, covers the rules on raising the security deposit.)

The market, however, often puts a practical limit on how big a security deposit you may charge. Your common sense and your business sense need to work together in setting security deposits. Here are a number of considerations to keep in mind:

- **Charge as much as you can in high-risk situations**—for example, where there's a lot of tenant turnover, if the tenant has a pet and you're concerned about damage or if the tenant's credit is shaky and you're worried about unpaid rent.
- **Consider the psychological advantage of a higher rent rather than a high deposit.** Many tenants would rather pay a slightly higher rent than an enormous deposit. Also, many acceptable, solvent tenants have a hard time coming up with several months' rent, especially if they are still awaiting the return of a previous security deposit. And, remember, unlike the security deposit, the extra rent is not refundable.

EXAMPLE: Lenora rents out a lavish, three-bedroom furnished unit in Westchester for $3,500 a month. Since there's no legal limit to the security deposit amount she can charge, Lenora would like to charge $7,000—an amount she feels would adequately protect her against unpaid rent or property damage. This is in addition to the first month's rent of $3,500 that Lenora can (and should) insist on before turning the property over to a tenant. But, realistically, Lenora would probably have difficulty finding a tenant if she insisted on receiving a $7,000 deposit plus the first month's rent, for a total of $10,500. So she decides to charge only one month's rent for the deposit but to increase the monthly rent by a few hundred dollars. That gives Lenora the protection she feels she needs without imposing an enormous initial financial burden on her tenants.

• **Single-family homes call for a bigger deposit.** Unlike multi-unit residences, where close-by neighbors or a manager can spot, report and quickly stop any destruction of the premises, the single-family home is somewhat of an island. The condition of the interior and even the exterior may be hard to assess. And, of course, the cost of repairing damage to a house is likely to be higher than for an apartment. Unless you live next door or can frequently check the condition of a single-family rental, a substantial security deposit is a good idea.

• **Gain a marketing advantage by allowing a deposit to be paid in installments.** If rentals are plentiful in your area, with comparable units renting at about the same price, you might give yourself a competitive edge by allowing the tenant to pay the deposit in several installments over a few months, rather than one lump sum.

**Require renters' insurance as an alternative to a high security deposit.** If you're worried about damage, but don't think you can raise the deposit any higher, require renters' insurance. Renters' insurance, which may cover fire or water damage caused by the tenant or the tenant's guests, gives your property an extra measure of protection. While you're at it, evaluate your own insurance policy to make sure it is adequate. If the tenant's security deposit is inadequate to cover any damage and there is no renters' insurance (or it won't cover the loss), you may be able to collect from your own carrier. (Chapter 2 contains an optional clause requiring the tenant to maintain renters' insurance which you can add to your leases or rental agreements.) You can request, but can't require, a rent-controlled or rent-stabilized tenant to buy renters' insurance.

**In multi-unit buildings, it's best to set a policy on security deposits and stick to it.** An inconsistent security deposit policy is an invitation to a lawsuit. Even if your motives are good—for example, collecting a smaller deposit from a student tenant—you risk a charge of illegal discrimination by other tenants who didn't get the same break. (Chapter 1 explains fair housing laws and their impact on your renting practices.)

## D. Dollar Limits on Deposits for Rent-Regulated Units

For rent-regulated units, the security deposit you collect from the tenant may not exceed one month's rent. (9 NYCRR §§ 2505.4; 2105.5; 2205.5; 2525.4.) The state Division of Housing and Community Renewal (DHCR), the agency that enforces rent laws, can hit landlords who demand or collect a bigger security deposit with penalties of up to three times the amount of the security deposit overcharge, plus interest.

There's a narrow exception to the one-month rule: If the tenant had more than one month's rent on deposit when the unit first became subject to regulation, then that sum may remain on deposit, as long as it's not more than two months' rent.

## E. Where to Put the Money

You can't mix a tenant's security deposit with your other money or spend it as you wish. That's because, legally speaking, a security deposit belongs to the tenant until it's later refunded or applied to cover unpaid rent, extraordinary repairs or cleaning costs or other fees authorized by the lease. (See Chapter 16 for details on how you can apply tenant deposits.)

You're required to hold a tenant's security deposit "in trust" for the tenant. (GOL § 7-103(1).) That means keeping the money safe and separate from your other funds. While one landlord we know got away with keeping a tenant's security deposit funds in a sealed envelope, we strongly recommend that you open a special segregated New York bank account for your tenants' security deposits. In many cases, you'll be required to do this anyway (see Section 1, below). Only one account is necessary. You won't need to open a separate account for each tenant.

Landlords who "commingle," or mix tenant security deposit funds with their personal or business funds risk forfeiting the security deposits. Some judges have ruled that commingling entitles the tenant to the immediate recovery of the deposit—before the tenant moves out. (*LeRoy v. Sayers*, 217 A.D.2d 63, 635 N.Y.S.2d 217 (1st Dep't 1995).) Borrowing from your tenant's security deposit, or pledging the funds as an asset to get a loan are also off limits.

## 1. When a New York Bank Account Is Required

**Security deposits for tenants of rent-stabilized and rent-controlled units must be deposited into a New York bank.** (GOL § 7-103; 9 NYCRR §§ 2505.4; 2105.5; 2205.5.) To find out what units are covered by rent control and rent stabilization, see Chapter 4.

New York bank accounts are also required for security deposits collected from tenants who live in buildings with six or more units. (GOL § 7-105(2-a).) This rule applies even if you own fewer than six units in the building. It's the building's size—not the number of units you own in the building—that's determinative.

EXAMPLE 1: Todd moves to New Jersey and rents out his New York City apartment. The apartment is in a 200-unit high-rise. Even though he's only renting a single unit in the building, the building's size requires Todd to put his tenant's security deposit in a New York bank.

EXAMPLE 2: Paul owns a four-unit building that's not covered by rent regulation. Paul can put his tenants' security deposits in a savings and loan association account, an out-of-state bank, or any other segregated account he wishes. Because his building contains fewer than six units, he's not required to use a New York bank.

## 2. Notify Tenants of Bank Location

Whenever security deposit funds are deposited in a bank or other financial institution, regardless of the building's size or rent-regulatory status, the landlord must notify the tenant in writing of the amount of the deposit and the name and address of the bank or financial institution. (GOL § 7-103(2).) You can put this information in the security deposit clause of your lease to avoid having to send out a separate notice after the money is deposited. Our rental agreement and lease forms have places to insert the amount of the deposit and name and address of the bank or other financial institution where the funds are deposited. (See Clause 8, Chapter 2.)

## F. When the Deposit Must Bear Interest

In some cases, you must pay interest on tenant security deposits. Of course, you may find that it helps your relationship with tenants to pay interest on all deposits, even if there's no law requiring it. It's up to you. Here are the rules.

**If the rental unit is located in a building with five or fewer units,** you're not required to pay interest on your tenants' security deposits, unless the tenant's unit is rent-regulated. (*Williams v. Brand*, N.Y.L.J., 5/3/96, p. 32, col. 3 (App. Term, 2d Dep't).)

**If the premises are rent-stabilized or rent-controlled,** you *must* deposit the tenant's security deposit in an interest-bearing account in a New York bank. (9 NYCRR §§ 2505.4; 2105.5; 2205.5; GOL 7-103(2-a).)

**If the premises are in a building with six or more units,** you must deposit the tenant's security deposit in an interest-bearing account in a New York bank. (GOL § 7-103(2-a).)

Interest-bearing accounts must earn interest at the "prevailing rate," that is, the same rate earned on similar deposits at other banks in the area. Land-lords who deposit security deposits in interest-bearing accounts are entitled annually to 1% of the deposit. This is an "administrative expense" for handling the account.

> EXAMPLE: Peter deposits $1,000 into a tenant security deposit account that earns 4% interest in the first year. Of the $40 interest earned in Year 1, Peter keeps $10 (1% of $1,000) and his tenant keeps $30 (3% of $1,000).

## G. When Interest Must Be Paid

When must you pay out the interest earned on the security deposit? The answer depends on whether or not the unit is rent-regulated.

**If the unit is not covered by rent regulations,** you have the option of depositing the security deposit in an interest-bearing or non-interest-bearing account. If the account earns interest, you may pay interest to the tenant annually, hold it on deposit or apply it to unpaid rent. (GOL § 7-103(2a).) It's your call. Keeping the interest on deposit in the security account is easiest—since there's no annual paperwork required between you, your bank and your tenants.

**If the unit is rent-stabilized or rent-controlled,** tenants have three options—technically. They can elect to have the interest 1) paid to them annually, 2) held in trust until the tenancy ends, or 3) applied to outstanding rent for the unit. (9 NYCRR §§ 2505.4; 2105.5; 2205.5; 2505.4.) As a practical matter, though, most landlords instruct their banks to send rent-regulated tenants a check for their share of the interest at the end of the year. This arrangement satisfies most tenants. You can make alternate arrangements if the tenant insists.

## H. Changing the Security Deposit Arrangement

Once you negotiate the amount of a security deposit with a tenant and state the amount in a lease or rental agreement, you can't change it by whim. While you might wish you had an extra month's security on deposit when you discover that your tenant's a slob, you're stuck with the arrangement until the lease ends. You can't change the amount of the security deposit unless the tenant agrees.

With month-to-month tenants, this isn't a big problem. You can change the amount of the security deposit, as well as other terms of the agreement such as rent, by giving the tenant a written Rental Agreement Rider, as discussed in Chapter 3, Section H.

With fixed-term tenants, you can't raise the security deposit during the term of the lease, unless either the lease allows it or the tenant consents to pay more. When you renew a fixed-term lease, however, you may change your security deposit arrangement by, say, instituting a security deposit for the first time, or raising it to a higher amount.

 **Rent-stabilized renewal leases must be offered on the same terms and conditions as the tenant's initial lease.** That means that if a rent-stabilized tenant's initial lease required no security deposit, for example, the renewal lease may not require a deposit either. However, when a rent-stabilized lease is renewed at a higher rent, the landlord may collect enough money from the tenant to bring the security deposit up to the new monthly rent.

## I. Handling Deposits When You Buy or Sell Rental Property

When rental property is sold, what should you do with deposits already collected? After all, when the tenant moves out, she'll be entitled to get her deposit back. Who owes her the money—the buyer or the seller? Here are the rules (and exceptions) for handling tenant security deposits when you buy and sell rental property.

## 1. When Selling or Leasing Rental Premises

If you're selling (or assigning) the premises, the general rule is that you must transfer all tenant security deposits to the new owner or assignee *within five days* of the sale. After you turn the security deposits over to the new owner, you must notify your tenants, by registered or certified mail, of the name and address of the new owner. (GOL § 7-105 (1).)

A sample Notice of Security Deposit Transfer is shown below.

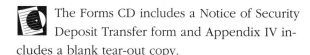 The Forms CD includes a Notice of Security Deposit Transfer form and Appendix IV includes a blank tear-out copy.

By law, the full amount deposited by the tenant, including any earned interest, must be turned over to the new owner. You're not entitled to take security deposit deductions for back rent owed or for any damage in excess of wear and tear that you know about at the time of transfer.

**Notice is critical.** You're relieved of legal responsibility for the tenants' deposits only after you notify tenants that you've transferred their security deposits to the new owner. After notices are delivered, the new landlord is legally liable for holding the security deposits in trust for the tenants.

The only exception to the general rule applies when the tenant's lease calls for a different procedure upon the sale (or lease) of the premises. Say, for example, that the lease says that security deposit proceeds are to be refunded to the tenant upon a sale of the premises. In that case, instead of following the general rule, the seller must follow the procedure authorized by the lease and distribute the deposit proceeds to the tenant.

The New York City rent-stabilized apartment lease reprinted in Chapter 2 gives landlords the option of either refunding the tenant's security deposit or turning it over to the new landlord within five days of a sale or lease of the building.

Sellers who fail to turn over tenant security deposits or to notify tenants of a security deposit transfer may be found guilty of a misdemeanor (a minor crime). (GOL § 7-105.)

## Notice of Security Deposit Transfer

TO:

Tenant: _____Nadia Lebov_____ ("Tenant")

Premises: _____100 Grand Street, White Plains, NY 10601_____ ("Premises")

Rental Unit: _____Apt. 3-B_____ ("Rental Unit")

Security Deposit Amount: _____$1,206.20_____ ("Security Deposit")

PLEASE BE ADVISED, that in connection with the transfer and sale of the Premises from

___William F. Hanlon_____, as Seller,

to ___ABC Realty Corp._____, as Purchaser,

which sale occurred _____November 1, 200X_____, your Security Deposit for the Rental

Unit, in the amount set forth above, has been transferred and turned over to the Purchaser.

PLEASE BE FURTHER ADVISED that the new Owner and Landlord for the Premises,

___ABC Realty Corp., 9 East 40th St., New York, NY 10016 (212) 555-1212_____

is now legally responsible to you for the Security Deposit, and, pursuant to General Obligations Law

§ 7-105, the undersigned has no further responsibility to you for the Security Deposit.

| | |
|---|---|
| November 2, 200x | *William F. Hanlon* |
| Date | Seller's Signature |
| | |
| White Plains, New York | William F. Hanlon, Seller |
| Place | Seller's Name (Printed) |

## Buyers Must Be Diligent About Tenant Security Deposits

When purchasing a rental property, it's easy to overlook tenant security deposit issues. Here are some key points to bear in mind as you prepare for closing:

- Find out the total dollar amount of security deposits held by the seller and the amount on deposit for each tenant.
- If there is no record of a security deposit for any tenant, require the seller to establish an escrow account equal to one month's rent for every tenant for which there is no record of a security deposit. (This is legally required if the property has one or more rent-controlled units or has six or more unregulated units. (GOL § 7-108(d).) In all other cases, you'll need to negotiate this point.)
- Find out in advance of the closing whether the seller will be transferring security deposits to you (to be held in trust for the tenants in a separate account) or refunding them to tenants instead before the sale. If the seller will be refunding security deposits, you may wish to negotiate an appropriate reduction in the sales price, since you'll be losing the financial protection security deposits afford against rent defaults and property damage.
- Where possible, have the seller agree to transfer the deposits to you instead of refunding them to tenants. That way, you'll begin ownership of the property with tenant security deposits already in place.
- Review the seller's security deposit transfer notices to tenants to ensure that the security deposit amounts listed in the notices match the amounts being transferred to you. If the transfer amount is less than the amount listed in the seller's notice, the tenant could look to you for the difference.
- If the seller refunds security deposits to tenants before closing, get proof (in the form of copies of cancelled checks or a sworn statement from the seller) that the refunds were actually made.

## 2. When Buying Rent-Stabilized Units

When buying rent-stabilized units, make sure that you account for every tenant's security deposit. (See Chapter 4 for details on which units are covered by rent stabilization.) Once you buy the premises, you become absolutely responsible for a rent-stabilized tenant's security deposit—whether or not you actually received it from the seller! (GOL § 7-107.) Lease clauses attempting to modify or waive a rent-stabilized tenant's security deposit rights are void.

## 3. When Buying Rent-Controlled Units or Units in Buildings With Six or More Unregulated Units

Upon the sale of a building with rent-controlled tenants or with tenants who have written leases in buildings with six or more non-stabilized units, the seller must either transfer the security deposits to you within five days of the sale, or, where required by the lease, refund the security deposits to the tenants.

Once you buy the premises, you're responsible for those security deposits as to which you have "actual knowledge." But this term's normal meaning doesn't apply here. You are deemed to know about any tenant security deposit which is either:

1. deposited in a bank at any time during the six months immediately prior to the sale
2. acknowledged in any lease in effect at the time of the sale, or
3. supported by "documentary evidence" provided by the tenant. (GOL § 7-108.)

You'll need to do your homework in advance of the sale to avoid liability for tenant security deposits you may never get (see "Buyers Must Be Diligent About Tenant Security Deposits," above). Specifically, you must check to make sure that every tenant's security deposit has been deposited in a New York bank. Then, if any security deposit records are missing, demand that the seller establish an escrow account equal to one month's rent for every unit for which there is no record of a security deposit. State law entitles you to this protection from the seller. (GOL § 7-108.)

Then, within 30 days after closing, prepare a special notice to tenants for whom you could find no record of a security deposit. The notice should inform the tenant that there is no record of a security deposit for their rental unit, and give the tenant 30 days to prove otherwise. The statute doesn't specify how the notice should be delivered. If you hand deliver it, get a receipt from the tenant. If you mail it, get a receipt from the post office. That way, you'll be able to show that you gave the notice to the tenant, if the issue comes up when the tenant moves out.

The Forms CD includes the Notice of No Security Deposit Record form and Appendix IV includes a blank tear-out copy.

If the tenant doesn't respond within 30 days after getting the special notice, you are not responsible for the tenant's security deposit. If, however, the tenant comes forward with a receipt signed by a former owner of the premises, a cancelled check for the security deposit endorsed by a former owner, or a lease signed by any former landlord, the new owner is responsible for the tenant's security deposit—even if it wasn't actually received from the former owner. You may use the money the seller deposited in the escrow account in the event that a tenant comes forward with documentary evidence of the deposit. (GOL § 7-108.)

**If you fail to notify the tenant that there is no record of the security deposit** within 30 days after the closing, then the tenant may come forward with documentary evidence of the security deposit *at any time* thereafter.

## Notice of No Security Deposit Record

TO:

Tenant: _____ Marcus Roberts _____ ("Tenant")

Premises: _____ 100 Grand Street, White Plains, NY 10601 _____ ("Premises")

Rental Unit: _____ Apt. 2-A _____ ("Rental Unit")

PLEASE BE ADVISED, that in connection with the transfer and sale of the Premises from

_____ William F. Hanlon _____, as Seller,

to _____ ABC Realty Corp. _____, as Purchaser,

which sale occurred _____ November 1, 200X _____, YOU ARE HEREBY NOTIFIED

THAT THERE IS NO RECORD OF ANY SECURITY DEPOSIT FOR YOUR UNIT.

PLEASE BE FURTHER ADVISED, that if you posted a Security Deposit for your Rental Unit, you must, within 30 days of receipt of this Notice, submit proof of your Security Deposit payment to the landlord at the following address: _____ ABC Realty Corp., 9 East 40<sup>th</sup> St., New York, NY 10016 _____

_____. Acceptable proof of payment includes: a receipt from a prior landlord for payment of the security deposit; a cancelled check for the security deposit payment endorsed by a former owner, or a lease for the Rental Unit signed by a former landlord acknowledging security deposit payment. Pursuant to General Obligations Law 7-108, your failure to submit proof that you posted a Security Deposit for the Rental Unit within 30 days from receipt of this Notice, will release _____ ABC Realty Corp. _____

as Owner and Landlord, from any responsibility or liability for a Security Deposit at the end of your tenancy.

| November 20, 200x | *Paul Shilowitz, President, Owner/Landlord* |
|---|---|
| Date | Purchaser's Signature |

| White Plains, New York | ABC Realty Corp. |
|---|---|
| Place | Purchaser's Name (Printed) |

■

Chapter **6**

# Hiring Supers, Resident Managers and Management Companies

Many landlords hire a live-in super or manager to handle the everyday details of running a rental building, including fielding tenants' routine repair requests, cleaning the building and collecting rent. Landlords who own several rental buildings (large or small) may contract with a property management company instead, to act as managing agent for the properties. Hiring a manager can free you from many of the time-consuming (and tiresome) aspects of being a residential landlord. But it can also create some headaches of its own: lots of paperwork for the IRS, worries about liability for a manager's acts and the responsibility of finding, hiring and supervising an employee.

This chapter reviews the nuts and bolts of hiring and working with a super, manager or management company, including:

- when you're legally required to hire a super or manager
- how to select a manager or super, decide the details of their job and prepare a written agreement
- your legal and tax obligations as an employer
- how to comply with special municipal rules that apply to supers and managers, including registration and certification requirements
- how to protect yourself from liability for a manager or super's illegal acts, and
- how to fire or evict a manager or super.

## A. Legal Reasons for Hiring a Super or Manager

State law requires all landlords to keep their properties clean and in good repair. (RPL § 235(b); MDL §§ 78, 80; MRL § 174.) Landlords who fail to keep up with their building maintenance responsibilities stand to lose rent, in the form of court-ordered rent reductions, and may also be ordered to pay penalties to housing code enforcement agencies. Common sense dictates that if you can't handle the work yourself, you must hire a building superintendent or manager to do it for you.

Sometimes you won't have a choice on whether to enlist help. You may be legally required to hire a

live-in super or manager (or else move into the building yourself). It depends how big your building is, and where it's located.

For NYC buildings with *nine or more* units, you must either:

- live in the building and perform janitorial services yourself
- hire a super or manager to live in the building or find one who lives within 200 feet or one block of the building (whichever is greater) to perform janitorial services, or
- hire a 24-hour-a-day janitorial service for the building. (NYC Adm. Code §§ 27-2053, 2054.)

Janitorial services include cleaning and maintaining the building's systems and common areas, making minor repairs, furnishing heat and hot water, removing refuse and keeping sidewalks clear of snow, ice and debris. (NYC Adm. Code § 27-2052.)

For buildings located in Buffalo that contain *13 or more* units, you must either:

- live in the building and perform janitorial services yourself, or
- provide a super or manager who lives in the building or lives within 200 feet of the building to perform janitorial services. (MDL § 83.)

## B. Hiring Your Own Super or Manager

Before you hang out your "Help Wanted" sign, you should decide what kind of "help" you actually need and want. First, you'll need to understand the difference between a building superintendent (super) and a manager. While there aren't any hard and fast rules, here's the distinction:

- **Property managers** usually have more tenant-relations responsibilities than supers do, such as taking apartment applications, accepting rent and responding to tenant problems and complaints. You might also authorize a trusted manager to purchase building supplies and hire outside contractors for specialized repairs—up to an agreed upon spending limit, of course.
- **Building supers,** on the other hand, usually concentrate on building repairs and mainte-

nance tasks. They often possess special skills and are experienced at running complicated heating plants and air conditioning systems. Customarily, supers don't collect rent or take rental applications.

If you put some thought into writing a job description, and some effort into recruiting and hiring a good super or manager, you'll avoid problems down the road. Don't hurry the process, or jump into an informal arrangement with a tenant who offers to help out if you'll take a little off the rent—you'll almost surely regret it. The employment rules and recommendations covered within this chapter apply equally to supers or resident managers. We discuss management companies in Section E, below.

## 1. Decide Duties, Hours and Pay

Why do you want to hire help? You need to answer this question in some detail as your first step in the hiring process. Here are the key issues you need to decide:

**What are the responsibilities?** Selecting tenants, collecting rents and hiring and paying contractors are some of the duties you may want to delegate to a manager or super. But finding an on-site employee who can handle all these key management responsibilities is a tall order—so tall that many owners restrict the job (especially for supers) to handling routine repair and maintenance chores. Listing the job duties and skills you're looking for in a super or manager will make the hiring process more objective and will give you ready standards for measuring which applicants are most qualified. The

Building Superintendent/Property Manager Agreement (Section C, below) includes a complete list.

**Is the job full- or part-time?** How many hours per week will it take to get the work you require done? During what hours of the day or night do you expect the employee to be on the rental property or available (for example, by beeper)?

**If your building has three or more units, you must supply the City with your managing agent's 24-hour phone number.** The NYC Department of Housing Preservation and Development requires you to provide a 24-hour telephone number within the New York City metropolitan area at which your "managing agent" can reasonably be expected to be reached in case of emergencies. A managing agent is someone over age 21 who's responsible for the maintenance and operation of the building, and who can authorize emergency repairs. (NYC Adm. Code § 27-2097 and following.)

**Will the employee live on the rental property or out?** Obviously, you need a vacant apartment for a resident super or manager. If you just want someone to handle minor repairs and janitorial work, he or she may not necessarily need to live in. But depending on the size of the building and where it's located, you might be required to hire a live-in super or manager. See Section A, above, for details.

**How much do you plan to pay the super or manager?** You may pay an hourly wage, generally ranging from $10 to $25 per hour, or a flat salary. Salaries run from around $35,000 per year for smaller buildings outside Manhattan, to an average salary of $60,000 to $80,000 for large luxury buildings in Manhattan. How much you pay depends on the job responsibilities, the number of hours, time of day and regularity of the schedule, benefits and the going rate in your locality. You can get an idea how much supers and managers are paid by asking other landlords or checking want ads for supers and managers. (See Section D5, below, for guidance on minimum wage requirements.) Offering slightly above the going rate in your area should allow you to hire the best, most experienced candidates. On the other hand, the value of a great apartment may make it easier to offer a live-in a lower wage.

## How and When Collective Bargaining Agreements Apply

Some apartment buildings are bound by collective bargaining agreements that cover the resident manger or building superintendent, as well as other building staff members. For example, some 3,000 New York City buildings are covered by an "apartment house agreement" with Service Employees International Union Local 32B-J. If your building is covered by a collective bargaining agreement, get and keep a full copy of the current agreement. It sets wages, hours and work responsibilities for supers and resident managers, as well as your mandatory contributions to the union's pension and welfare fund. Collective bargaining agreements usually entitle building superintendents and resident managers to vacation pay and several paid holidays each year.

Under some collective bargaining agreements, you're required to give the super or resident manager a free apartment (in addition to wages). It's part of the employee's compensation package. Under such circumstances, the worker may occupy the unit only as long as he or she is employed by you. When employment ends, the worker must move out (unless the worker was previously or is currently a tenant under a separate lease or rental agreement).

**If your super or manager belongs to a labor union, check the collective bargaining agreement before taking any action to discipline or terminate the employee.** Some collective bargaining agreements set procedures that employers must follow to properly discipline, suspend or terminate a union member. Collective bargaining agreements usually limit the reasons why you may fire a union employee. In many cases, the terminated employee will have the right to contest an unfair suspension or termination before a labor arbitrator. If the arbitrator agrees with the employee, the super or manager you thought you fired could be reinstated with back pay.

**Should you give the super or manager reduced or free rent?** Some landlords give their supers or managers reduced or free rent instead of, or in addition to, a separate salary. Your obligations as an employer are the same whether you compensate the worker with reduced rent or a paycheck—for example, you must still pay Social Security and payroll taxes as discussed in Section D. Also, if you end up firing a manager who has a free or reduced rent arrangement, your (now) ex-employee may have a right to stay in your property as discussed in Section I.

 **Be careful if you are planning to move the super or manager into a rent-stabilized unit.** If you give the super or manager a lease or rental agreement or collect any rent (even a reduced rent), a court or NYS Division of Housing and Community Renewal (DHCR) could find that the super or manager is entitled to stay on as a rent-stabilized tenant after the job ends. The unit will be exempt from rent-stabilization only as long as the employee 1) pays no rent, 2) gets the apartment as all or part of his job compensation and 3) works in the building where the apartment is located (9 NYCRR §§ 2520.11(m), 2500.9(o)). That's important if you want to be able to evict a manager or super after their employment ends.

Several other Nolo books provide useful information on hiring, managing and firing employees.

- *The Employer's Legal Handbook*, by Fred Steingold is a complete guide to the latest workplace laws and regulations. It covers everything you need to know about hiring and firing employees, drug tests of employees, personnel policies, employee benefits, discrimination and other laws affecting small business practices.
- *Everyday Employment Law: The Basics*, by Lisa Guerin & Amy DelPo has excellent information about hiring employees.
- *Federal Employment Laws*, by Amy DelPo & Lisa Guerin has extensive discussions on relevant federal laws, including the Fair Labor Standards Act, Americans With Disabilities Act, Equal Pay Act, Immigration Reform and Con-

trol Act, Fair Credit Reporting Act and Occupational Safety and Health Act, as well as state and federal employment discrimination laws.

- *Dealing with Problem Employees*, by Amy DelPo & Lisa Guerin, includes chapters on evaluating, disciplining and firing employees.

These Nolo books are available at bookstores and public libraries. They may also be ordered directly from Nolo's website (www.nolo.com) or by calling 800-728-3555.

For free general information on employment law, see Nolo's Legal Encyclopedia at www.nolo.com.

## 2. Advertise the Job

➡️ If you already know someone, such as a current tenant, who you think will be perfect for the manager's or super's job, skip ahead to Section 5.

Next, determine the best way to advertise the position. Some landlords find great supers and managers via word-of-mouth by talking to other landlords, tenants, friends and relatives. Others run a newspaper ad, use an employment agency or advertise online. What will work best depends on your particular property and needs. In writing an ad, stick to the job skills needed and the basic responsibilities—for example, "Fifty-unit apartment complex seeks full-time resident manager with experience in selecting tenants, collecting rent and apartment maintenance." Your ad should also say whether you're looking for any special licenses or certifications. (See "Special Credentials for Supers and Managers," below.)

If you do advertise, provide an address for applicants to send resumés or a phone number to call for more information.

⚠️ **Be sure your help wanted ad can't be interpreted as discriminatory.** The best way to do this is to focus on the type of skills you're looking for—not on any particular personal characteristics. Specifically, your ad should never mention sex, race, religion, disability, age or nationality. When

### Illegal Discrimination in Hiring

Federal, state and local laws prohibit many kinds of discrimination in hiring. The federal laws—Title VII of the Civil Rights Act, the Age Discrimination in Employment Act and the Americans with Disabilities Act—apply only if you employ 15 or more people. (42 U.S.C. § § 12101, 2000(e); 29 U.S.C. § 701.) New York State and New York City's Human Rights Law kicks in if you have four or more employees. (Exec. L. § 291 ; NYC Adm. Code, Title 8.)

Pay attention to these laws even if they do not specifically bind your business. Doing so will not hinder you from making a decision based on sound business reasons—skills, experience and references. The laws only forbid making a decision based on a factor that isn't reasonably related to the applicant's ability to do the job. Following the laws will protect you from accusations of discrimination.

Federal laws prohibit employment discrimination on the basis of race, color, gender, religious beliefs, national origin, age or disability. New York State law also prohibits discrimination based on marital status and sexual orientation. In addition, New York City law makes it illegal to discriminate on the basis of immigration or citizenship status. Many stationery stores sell outdated employment application forms that contain questions that are now prohibited under discrimination laws. As a general rule, avoid forms that are more than a few years old or haven't been specifically designed for New York employers, since they may run afoul of New York law.

Much of the advice in Chapter 1, which deals with illegal discrimination against tenants, will also be of help when you're hiring a super or manager.

📖 If you have any questions about employment discrimination laws, illegal questions or related issues, you can check with the New York State Division of Human Rights at 718-741-8400, the New York City Commission of Human Rights at 212-306-7500, or with an employment law attorney.

## Special Credentials for Supers and Managers

Here are some specialized technical and management certification credentials sometimes held by supers and managers.

**Technical certifications.** Property owners with large or sophisticated building systems often need supers or managers with special expertise to operate them. And in some cases, owners are legally required to use only specially certified or licensed personnel. Here are a few required technical certifications. Call your local government to find out if there are any others.

- EPA Technician Certification. Anyone on your staff who services or repairs refrigerators or air conditioning equipment with HCFC/CFCs must be certified as a "technician" by the U.S. Environmental Protection Agency (EPA). (For more information see Chapter 11, Section C.)
- New York City Certificate of Fitness. If your New York City property building has a fire standpipe system, your super or manager must hold a Certificate of Fitness, issued by the NYC Fire Department. For more information about Certificates of Fitness and fire protection equipment inspection requirements, call the Fire Department's Fire Prevention Unit at 718-999-1986.
- New York City No. 6 Oil Burner License. If your building's heating system runs on No. 6 grade fuel oil, your super or manager must hold a special license to operate the system. For more information about license requirements, call the Fire Department's Fire Prevention Unit at 718-999-1986.
- While not required, certifications that are issued by technical schools, unions and government agencies, such as NYC's Division of Housing Preservation and Development, are also a great asset. These are given to supers who have completed building maintenance skills courses that cover topics like heating plant operations, minor repairs and housing standards.

**Management certifications.** National and local trade organizations offer certifications to property managers who complete educational programs covering topics such as leasing, financial operations, building operations and risk management, and who have attained a prescribed experience level. Here are some of the more common certification designations:

- Certified Property Manager (CPM) is a certification awarded by the Institute of Real Estate Management to commercial and residential real estate managers. The Institute also awards its Accredited Residential Manager (ARM) certification to those who specialize in residential management.
- Certified Apartment Manager (CAM) is a certification offered by the National Apartment Association to residential leasing agents, resident managers and property managers.
- Registered Apartment Manager (RAM) is a national certification program sanctioned by the National Association of Home Builders and approved by HUD.
- New York Accredited Realty Manager (NYARM) is a certification awarded by the New York Association of Realty Managers, in association with New York University's School of Continuing and Professional Studies, The Real Estate Institute. This certification is recognized and approved by the New York State Division of Housing and Community Renewal and the New York City Department of Housing Preservation and Development. Managers are required to complete a professional realty management program that provides training and practical knowledge in finance, supervision, management and operation of building systems, local laws, renovation construction and dealing with tenants. Courses are taught by industry professionals.

writing your ad, avoid words that could be viewed as discriminatory, such as "handyman" or "mature worker."

## 3. Screen Potential Supers and Managers Over the Phone

When people call about the job, be ready to describe the responsibilities, pay and hours. Then ask some questions yourself—you'll be able to quickly eliminate unlikely candidates and avoid wasting time interviewing inappropriate people. Use the phone call to get information on potential applicants, including their:

- experience and qualifications
- interest in the position and type of work
- job-related certifications
- current employment, and
- ability to work at the proposed pay and schedule.

Jot down notes of your conversation so you can follow up later in a personal interview.

## 4. Interview Strong Candidates

Limit your interviews to people you're really interested in hiring. There's no point meeting with someone who's unqualified or unsuitable for the job. When setting interviews, ask potential supers or managers to bring a resumé (or a written list) with relevant experience and names and phone numbers of four or five references.

A face-to-face meeting provides the opportunity to get in-depth information about a person's background, work experience and ability to handle the job, and allows you to assess an individual's personality and style.

Before you begin interviewing, write down questions focusing on the job duties and the applicant's skills and experience. To avoid potential charges of discrimination, ask everyone the same questions and don't ask questions that are not clearly job-related—for example, steer clear of the applicant's age, medical condition, religion, marital status or plans for having children. (See "Illegal Discrimination in Hiring," above.)

Here are some examples of questions that are appropriate to ask potential managers or supers:

- "Tell me about your previous jobs running rental properties."
- "Have you ever been responsible for operating a heating plant before?"
- "How much experience do you have collecting rents? Doing general repairs? Keeping records of tenants' complaints of repair problems?"
- "What have you liked most about previous jobs? What have you liked least?"
- "What kinds of problems have you encountered as a property super or manager? How did you solve them?"
- "Why do you want this job?"

You might also ask some more direct questions, like:

- "What would you do if a tenant who had paid rent on time for six months asked for a ten-day extension because money was short as a result of a family problem?"
- "What would you do if a tenant called you at 11 PM with a complaint about a clogged sink?"

## Character Traits of a Good Super or Manager

Look for a person who is:

- **Honest and responsible.** This is especially important if the manager will be entitled to receive legal documents and papers on your behalf. (See Section G.)
- **Patient.** Predictably, dealing with tenants, repair people and guests will have its share of hassles. A person with a short fuse is a definite liability.
- **Financially responsible.** This should be demonstrated by a good credit history (See Chapter 1, Section H, for information on ordering and evaluating credit reports.)
- **Mechanically inclined.** Operating an apartment building takes mechanical know-how, whether you expect the worker to do-it-herself or to oversee the work of outside contractors.
- **Personable yet professional.** Good communication skills are a must, both with you and your current and prospective tenants and any other workers the manager may supervise (for example, a cleaning crew).
- **Fastidious about keeping the building and common areas neat, clean and secure.**
- **Meticulous about maintaining records.** This is particularly important if collecting rent will be part of the job.
- **Fair and free of biases.** This is a must if the super or manager will be showing apartments, taking rental applications or selecting tenants.
- **Unafraid of minor confrontations with tenants.** This is particularly important if the super or manager will be collecting overdue rents, delivering eviction notices and handling disputes between tenants (for example, complaints over noise).

**Don't offer the job yet.** Even if an applicant seems perfect, hold off on making an offer. You'll need at least to review his or her application and check references. These issues are covered in Steps 5, 6, 7 and 8, below.

## 5. Get a Completed Application

If your super or manager will also be a tenant, make sure he or she (like all other tenants) completes a rental application (as discussed in Chapter 1) and that you check references and other information carefully. Be sure the applicant signs a form authorizing you to check credit history and references. This can be either part of the application form itself or a separate document, such as the Consent to Background and Reference Check form in Chapter 1.

If your super or manager is not also a tenant, prepare your own employment application (you can use the Rental Application in Chapter 1 and cross out what's not relevant) or ask prospective applicants to bring a resume with their employment and educational background.

 **When you check a prospective super's or manager's application or resumé, be sure to look for holes**—dates when the person didn't indicate an employer. The applicant may be covering up a bad reference. Insist that the applicant explain any gaps in employment history.

## 6. Check References

No matter how wonderful someone appears in person or on paper, it's essential to contact former employers. Ideally, you should talk with at least two former employers or supervisors with whom the applicant held similar positions.

Before calling any references, make a list of key questions. Ask about the applicant's previous job responsibilities, character and personality traits, strengths and weaknesses and reasons for leaving the job. Review your interview notes for issues you want to explore more—for example, if you sense that the applicant really doesn't seem organized enough to handle all the details of the manager's job, ask about it. Take your time and get all the information you need to determine whether the applicant is the best person for the job.

Employers are often reluctant to say anything negative about a former employee for fear of being hit by a lawsuit for defamation. Many may refuse to give any information other than the dates the person worked and the position held. It may be helpful to send the former employer a copy of the applicant's signed consent to disclosure of employment information. (See the Consent to Background and Reference Check form in Chapter 1.) If a former employer is still not forthcoming, you'll need to learn to read between the lines. If a former employer is neutral, offers only faint praise or overpraises a person for one aspect of a job only—"always on time"—he may be hiding negative information. Ask former employers: "Would you hire this person back if you could?" The response may be telling. If a reference isn't glowing and doesn't cover all aspects of the job, check several other references—or hire someone else.

## 7. Check Credit History and Background

Checking an individual's credit history is especially important if you want a super or manager to handle money. Someone with large debts may be especially tempted to skim money from your business. And a prospective employee with sloppy personal finances is probably not a good choice for managing rental property. Before you order a credit report, be sure to get the applicant's consent, as discussed in Chapter 1, Section G.

You may also wish to ask a credit bureau to do a background report. Investigators will talk to friends, neighbors and employers and get information about the applicant's character, reputation and lifestyle. A report like this is considered an "investigative consumer report" under the Fair Credit Reporting Act (15 U.S. Code §§ 1681 and following.) If you decide to order a background report, you must:

- inform the applicant, in writing, within three days of your requesting the report
- include a statement of the applicant's right to make a written request—to you or the credit agency—for a description of the nature and scope of the investigation you have requested, and
- provide that description within five days of receiving the applicant's request.

Chapter 1, Section H, provides more information on investigative reports.

## 8. Check Criminal Records

Supers and managers occupy positions of trust, often having access to tenants' apartments as well as to your money. Obviously, it's essential that the super or manager not present a danger to tenants. You should check an applicant's criminal history; credit reports and background investigations often include this information. Another reason for thoroughness is your personal liability—if your employee commits a crime, you may be held responsible.

**Use Megan's Law to check state database of registered sex offenders.** "Megan's Law" may be able to help you find out if a job applicant has been convicted of a sexual offense against a minor or a violent sexual offense against anyone. For details on how to check the database, see Chapter 1, Section H6.

Our best advice is check carefully and consider the type, seriousness and dates of any prior convictions and how they relate to the job. Under state law, it's unlawful to refuse employment based on an individual's arrest record or to ask questions about that record prior to employment. However, you may deny employment on the basis of an applicant's prior conviction record if there's a direct relationship between the criminal offenses and the specific employment being sought, or where employing the applicant would present an unreasonable risk to your tenants or your property. (Corrections L. § 752.) Obviously, if the applicant's record reveals that the applicant was convicted of a prior theft, burglary, assault or rape, you could legally deny employment since the applicant could pose a risk to your tenants, your tenants' property or your own. But if the applicant had been convicted of, say, writing a bad check 15 years ago, it probably wouldn't be reasonable to deny employment to the applicant on that ground.

## 9. Offer the Position and Put Your Agreement in Writing

Once you make your decision and offer someone the super or manager's job, you may need to do some negotiations. The potential employee may, for example, want a higher salary, different hours, more vacation, a different rental unit or a later starting date than you offer. It may take some compromises to establish mutually agreeable work arrangements. When all terms and conditions of employment are mutually agreed upon, you and the super or manager should complete a Building Superintendent/Property Manager Agreement (discussed in Section C).

### How to Reject Applicants

It used to be a matter of simple courtesy to inform unsuccessful applicants that you'd hired someone else for the job. Sending a quick but civil rejection letter cut down on post-interview calls, too. You didn't owe rejected applicants an explanation, however, and were usually better off saying as little as possible.

Is this approach still legal? It depends on why you have rejected the applicant. If your decision is based on information that the applicant himself has provided, or if the applicant simply doesn't have the qualifications for the job, you can still use the courteous-but-minimalist approach. For example, if the applicant tells you that she has never managed real estate property (but experience is one of your job criteria), or if the interview reveals that the applicant obviously doesn't have the "people skills" the position requires, you can (if you wish) simply say that you have chosen someone more qualified for the job.

However, if your rejection is based on information from a credit reporting agency that collects and sells credit files or other information about consumers, you must comply with requirements of the Fair Credit Reporting Act (15 U.S. Code §§ 1681 and following), as discussed in Chapter 1, Section H.

### Why Do You Need a Written Agreement?

Landlords and supers and managers often agree orally about job responsibilities and compensation, never signing a written agreement.

Even though oral agreements are usually legal and binding, they are not advisable. Memories fade, and you and your employee may have different recollections of what you've agreed to. If a dispute arises between you and the manager for instance, the exact terms of an oral agreement are difficult or impossible to prove if you end up arguing about them in court. It is a far better business practice to put your understanding in writing. If you're providing your super or manager with an apartment, a written agreement also serves to clarify the employee's right of occupancy upon termination of employment.

**Don't promise long-term job security.** When you hire someone, don't give assurances that you may not be able to honor and that may give an applicant a false sense of security. Your best protection is to make sure your Building Superintendent/Property Manager Agreement emphasizes your right to fire an employee at will—and have the applicant acknowledge this in writing. (See Clause 6 of the agreement in Section C, below.) This means you'll have the right to terminate the employment at any time for any reason that doesn't violate the law. (See Section I for information on how to fire a manager.)

## C. How to Prepare a Building Superintendent/Property Manager Agreement

Below is an example of a sound written agreement that spells out the employee's responsibilities, hourly wage or salary, hours, schedule and other terms.

The step-by-step instructions that follow take you through the process of completing your own agreement.

# Building Superintendent/Property Manager Agreement

## 1. Parties

This Agreement is between ___Diane M. Marten___,

Owner of residential real property at ___209 East 73rd St., NY, NY 10021___,

_____, and

___Ned O'Grady, Superintendent___, (Employee).

## 2. Beginning Date

Employee will begin work on ___April 1, 200X___.

## 3. Responsibilities

Employee's duties are set forth below:

**Renting Units**

☑ answer phone inquiries about vacancies

☑ show vacant units

☑ accept rental applications

☐ select tenants

☑ accept initial rents and deposits

☐ other (specify) _____

☐ _____

**Vacant Apartments**

☑ inspect unit when tenant moves in

☑ inspect unit when tenant moves out

☑ clean unit after tenant moves out, including:

    ☑ floors, carpets and rugs

    ☑ walls, baseboards, ceilings, lights and built-in shelves

    ☑ kitchen cabinets, countertops, sinks, stove, oven and refrigerator

    ☑ bathtubs, showers, toilets and plumbing fixtures

    ☑ doors, windows, window coverings and mini-blinds

    ☐ other (specify) _____

    ☐ _____

**Rent Collection**

☐ collect rents when due

☐ sign rent receipts

☐ maintain rent collection records

☐ collect late rents and charges

☐ inform Owner of late rents

☐ prepare late rent notices

☐ serve late rent notices on tenants (when directed by Owner)

☐ serve rent increase and tenancy termination notices

☐ deposit rent collections in bank

☐ other (specify) _____

☐ _____

## Maintenance

☑ remove garbage, refuse and recycling materials from building for collection

☑ inspect heating/hot water system daily

☑ inspect fire standpipe/sprinkler system monthly, and complete inspection report

☑ vacuum and clean hallways, stairwells and entryways

☐ replace lightbulbs in common areas

☐ drain water heaters

☑ clean exterior stairs, decks, patios, facade and sidewalks

☐ clean garage oils on pavement

☐ mow lawns

☑ rake leaves

☐ trim bushes

☑ clean up garbage and debris on grounds

☑ shovel snow from sidewalks and driveways or arrange for snow removal

☑ other (specify)  _lubricate roof fans and pumps, change belts when needed_

☐ _____

## Repairs

☑ accept tenant complaints and repair requests

☑ inform Owner of extraordinary or unusual maintenance and repair needs

☑ maintain written log of tenant complaints

☑ handle routine maintenance and repairs, including:

    ☑ plumbing stoppages

    ☑ garbage disposal stoppages/repairs

    ☑ faucet leaks/washer replacement

    ☑ toilet tank repairs

    ☑ toilet seat replacement

    ☑ stove burner repair/replacement

☑ stove hinges/knobs replacement

☑ dishwasher repair

☑ light switch and outlet repair/replacement

☑ heater thermostat repair

☐ window repair/replacement

☑ painting (interior)

☐ painting (exterior)

☑ replacement of keys

☐ window guard installation

☐ other (specify)

☑ _Change air conditioner filters, as needed_

**Other Responsibilities**

_Inform owner about any pets in the building._

_Inform owner about any new occupants in the building._

_____

_____

**4. Hours and Schedule**

Employee will be available to tenants during the following days and times: _Monday through Friday, 8AM until 4PM (with ½ hour lunch break)_. If the hours required to carry out any duties may reasonably be expected to exceed _40_ hours in any week, Employee shall notify Owner and obtain Owner's consent before working such extra hours, except in the event of an emergency. Extra hours worked due to an emergency must be reported to Owner within 24 hours.

**5. Payment Terms**

a. Employee will be paid:

☑ $ _20_ per hour

☐ $ _____ per week

☐ $ _____ per month

☐ Other: _____

b. Employee will be paid on the specified intervals and dates:

☑ Once a week on every _Thursday_

☐ Twice a month on _____

☐ Once a month on _____

☐ Other: _____

**6. Ending the Employee's Employment**

Owner may terminate Employee's employment at any time, for any reason that isn't unlawful, with or without notice. Employee may quit at any time, for any reason, with or without notice.

**7. Rental Unit Occupancy**

Owner shall provide Apt. __B-2__ at the property for Employee's occupancy during the term of his or her employment. Employee agrees to occupy the Apartment solely as an incident to employment. Employee's right to occupy the Apartment shall expire when the Employee's employment is terminated or otherwise ends.

**8. Additional Agreements and Amendments**

a. Owner and Employee additionally agree that: __1. Employee shall keep current his NYC Fire Department "Certificate of Fitness".__

__2. Employee shall be entitled to 5 (five) vacation days after six months of continuous employment.__

b. All agreements between Owner and Employee relating to the work specified in this Agreement are incorporated in this Agreement. Any modification to the Agreement must be in writing and signed by both parties.

**9. Place of Execution**

Signed at __New York City__ , __New York State__

__3/15/0X__
Date

__Diane M. Marten__
Owner

__3/15/0X__
Date

__Ned O'Grady__
Employee

⚠ **If your building is bound to a labor union agreement that covers resident managers or building superintendents, you may not use the agreement included in this chapter.** The collective bargaining agreement sets the terms of workers' employment.

💿 The Forms CD includes the Building Superintendent/Property Manager Agreement which you can modify to fit your exact needs. Appendix IV includes a blank tear-out copy of this form.

## 1. Parties

Here you provide details about you and the employee, including their title, such as manager or super, the location of the rental property and the rental unit that the employee will occupy, if any, during the course of his employment.

## 2. Beginning Date

Fill in the month, day and year of the super or manager's first day of work.

## 3. Responsibilities

This form includes a broad checklist of duties, such as rent collection, maintenance and repair. Check all the boxes that apply to your situation. In the space provided, spell out what is required, with as much detail as possible, particularly regarding maintenance responsibilities. (Read Chapter 9 for details on your repair and maintenance responsibilities.)

## 4. Hours and Schedule

To save on overtime pay, the super or manager should be scheduled to work no more than 40 hours per week, not including lunch breaks, paid holidays or vacation days. Giving time off instead of providing overtime pay is illegal unless the time off is given during the same pay period in which the overtime work was put in by the employee and is given at the rate of one and one-half hours for each hour of overtime worked.

## 5. Payment Terms

Here you state how much and when you pay your manager. The federal and state minimum wage is currently $5.15 per hour. You generally must pay all employees overtime pay (time and one-half) for all hours actually worked over 40 in the work week. For this purpose, lunch breaks, paid sick days, holidays, vacations and other time off are not considered as hours worked. (Some employees, such as bona fide executives, administrative and professional employees, are exempt from the overtime requirement provided they are paid on a salary basis.)

Specify what day of the week the super or manager will get a paycheck. New York's Labor Law requires that employees be paid regularly and no less frequently than semimonthly. To be on the safe side of the law, pay your super or manager on a weekly basis. For more information on state laws relating to wages and hours, contact the state Department of Labor (see "New York State Department of Labor Services for Employers," below).

### Should You Pay Benefits?

No law requires you to pay a manager for vacations, holiday and sick pay, premium pay for weekend or holiday work (unless it's for overtime) or fringe benefits such as health insurance. You may, however, want to provide your manager with some extras, if you can afford to do so.

## 6. Ending the Employee's Employment

This clause gives you the right to fire a manager any time for any legal reason. It makes clear that you are not guaranteeing a year's, or even a month's, employment to your new hire. You can legally fire your manager or super any time for any or no reason—as long as it's not for an illegal reason. In return, your manager can quit at any time, for any reason—with or without notice. (See Section I.)

## 7. Rental Unit Occupancy

If you're not providing a rental unit to the super or manager, skip this clause. (You can also delete it from the electronic version of the form on the Forms CD or cross it out of the printed version of the form in Appendix IV.)

This clause says that you are providing a rental unit at the property to the super or manager for occupancy during the term of the employment. The employee agrees to occupy the unit "solely as an incident to employment." It also clarifies that the employee's right to occupy the unit expires when the employment ends.

When the job ends, you have two options. If you have a good relationship with the former employee and think that she would make a good tenant, you can offer the employee a lease or rental agreement for the unit. But if there's bad blood between you and your former employee, or you simply don't want to the employee to become a tenant, you can begin eviction proceedings to remove the employee from the property.

## 8. Additional Agreements and Amendments

Here you provide details about any areas of the super or manager's employment that weren't covered elsewhere in the agreement, such as the number of vacation or sick days, or any paid holidays the employee is entitled to each year, how you plan to reimburse her for the cost of materials purchased for repairs, or any job-related certifications the worker is required to keep current. If you want the super or manager to obtain or keep current a

specific license or certification, such as a New York City Fire Department "Certificate of Fitness," include that obligation here.

The last part of this section is fairly standard in written agreements. It states that this is your entire agreement about the manager's employment, and that any changes to the agreement must be in writing. Together, these provisions prevent you or your manager from later claiming that additional oral or written promises were made, but just not included in the written agreement.

## 9. Place of Execution

Here you specify the city and state in which you signed the agreement. If there's any legal problem with the agreement later, it may be resolved by the courts where it was signed. Be advised, however, that the laws where the work is to be performed may be applied instead. So if, for example, you sign the agreement at your office in New Jersey, but your rental property and the super or manager's work place is in New York, the different laws of New York may be applied by a court.

**Make changes in writing.** If you later change the terms of your agreement, write the new terms down and have each person sign.

## D. Your Legal Obligations As an Employer

Whether or not you compensate a super or manager with reduced rent or a regular salary, you have specific legal obligations as an employer, such as following laws governing minimum wage and overtime. If you don't pay Social Security and meet your other legal obligations as an employer, you may face substantial financial penalties. See "Tax Resources for Small Business Employers," below, for useful federal and state tax forms and publications.

## Tax Resources for Small Business Employers

Start out by getting IRS Publication 334 (*Tax Guide for Small Businesses*), which provides details about the records you must keep on your employees. Contact the IRS at 800-829-1040 or check its website at www.irs.gov, to obtain a free copy of this and other IRS publications and forms. For guidance on state tax issues, get the NYS Department of Taxation and Finance's Publication 20 (New York State Tax Guide for New Businesses), which also includes many of the necessary tax forms you'll need. Contact the Department at 800-462-8100 or visit its website at www.tax.state.ny.us for a free copy of this and other New York forms and publications.

*Tax Savvy for Small Business*, by Frederick W. Daily (Nolo), covers strategies that will help you minimize taxes and stay out of legal trouble, including how to deduct business expenses, write off or depreciate long-term business assets, keep the kinds of records that will satisfy the IRS, get a tax break from business losses and handle a small business audit.

## Most Resident Managers Are Employees, Not Independent Contractors

The IRS and other government agencies will probably consider a resident manager your employee. Employees are guaranteed a number of workplace rights that are not guaranteed to people who work as independent contractors. To be considered an independent contractor, a person must offer services to the public at large and work under an arrangement in which he or she controls the means and methods of accomplishing a job. Most tenant-managers are legally considered to be employees because the property owner who hires them sets the hours and responsibilities and determines the particulars of the job. Only a manager who works for several different landlords might qualify for independent contractor status.

## 1. Employer Identification Number

As an employer, you need a federal identification number for tax purposes. If you are a sole proprietor without employees, you can use your Social Security number. Otherwise, you need to get an "employer identification number" (EIN) from the IRS. To obtain an EIN, complete Form SS-4 (Application for Employer Identification Number), available free from the IRS. See "Tax Resources for Small Business Employers," above.

## 2. Income Taxes

The IRS considers a super's or manager's compensation as taxable income to the employee. For that reason, your new super or manager must fill out a federal W-4 form (Employee Withholding Allowance Certificate) when hired. Within 20 days after your new employee completes a W-4, you must mail a copy to the New York State Department of Taxation and Finance, New Hire Notification, PO Box 15119, Albany NY 12212-5119. Or, you may fax it to 518-438-3715. For information on filing new hire information electronically over the Internet, visit this special website (www.nynewhirecom/index/jsp). You must deduct federal taxes from each paycheck, and turn over the withheld funds each quarter to the IRS.

In addition to federal withholding, you are required to deduct New York State income taxes (and, where applicable, municipal taxes too) from each paycheck, and pay them quarterly to each appropriate tax agency. For tax tables and instructions on withholding state income tax (as well as NYC and Yonkers income tax) get Publication NYS-50 (*New York State Tax Guide to Withholding Tax and Wage Reporting*) from the NYS Department of Taxation and Finance. See "Tax Resources for Small Business Employers," above.

You must provide the super or manager with a W-2 form (Wage and Tax Statement) for the previous year's earnings by January 31. The W-2 form lists the employee's gross wages and provides a breakdown of any taxes that you withheld.

## 3. Social Security and Medicare Taxes

Every employer must pay to the IRS a "payroll tax," currently equal to 7.65% of the employee's gross compensation—or paycheck amount—before deductions. You must also deduct an additional 7.65% from the employee's wages and turn it over (with the payroll tax) to the IRS quarterly. These Federal Insurance Contributions Act (FICA) taxes go toward the employee's future Social Security and Medicare benefits.

If you compensate your manager with reduced rent, you must still pay the FICA payroll tax. For example, an apartment owner who compensates a manager with a rent-free $500/month apartment must pay 7.65% of $500, or $38.25, in payroll taxes each month. The manager is responsible for paying another 7.65% ($38.25) to the IRS.

**Always pay payroll taxes on time.** If you don't, the IRS will fine you—and you could be forced out of business by the huge penalties and interest charges that will be added to the delinquent bill. And unlike most other debts, you must pay back payroll taxes even if you go through bankruptcy.

### Help With Paperwork

Employers are responsible for a certain amount of paperwork and recordkeeping, such as time and pay records. If you hate paperwork, your accountant or bookkeeper can probably handle it for you. Or, a reputable payroll tax service that offers a tax notification service will calculate the correct amount of Social Security, unemployment, workers' compensation and other taxes due, produce the check to pay your manager and the taxes and notify you when the taxes are due.

Payroll services can be cost-effective even if you employ only one or two people. But when you look for one, it pays to shop around. To get cost quotes, check the Web or your Yellow Pages under Payroll Service or Bookkeeping Service. Avoid services that charge set-up fees—basically, a fee for putting your information into the computer—or extra fees to prepare W-2 forms or quarterly and annual tax returns.

## 4. Unemployment Taxes

A manager who is laid off, quits for good reason, or is fired for anything less than gross incompetence or dishonesty is entitled to unemployment benefits. These benefits are financed by unemployment taxes paid by employers. You must pay a federal unemployment tax (FUTA) at a rate of 6.2% of the first $7,000 of the employee's wages for the year.

You may receive a credit of up to 5.4% of FUTA wages for the state unemployment tax you pay.

In addition to contributing to FUTA, you're also responsible for quarterly contributions to the New York State unemployment insurance fund. For new employers, the tax starts out at a rate, as of early 2003, of 4.1% of the first $8,500 of the worker's wages. After that, your unemployment tax rate gets adjusted annually, based on the number of claims made by your employees. The highest rate (as of early 2003) was 8.9%.

**For publications and forms on FUTA and unemployment insurance,** either call the IRS (800-829-1040) or visit its website (www.irs.gov). For more information on New York State unemployment insurance tax, call the Department of Labor (518-457-5806 or 5807) or visit its website (www.labor.state.ny.us).

## 5. Minimum Wage and Overtime

However you pay your manager—by the hour, with a regular salary, or by a rent reduction—you should monitor the number of hours worked to make sure you're complying with the federal Fair Labor Standards Act (FLSA) (29 U.S.Code §§ 201 and following) and state wage and hour laws. The federal and state minimum hourly wage is currently $5.15. Wage and hour laws also require employers to pay time-and-a-half if an employee works more than 40 hours a week (with a few exceptions).

**For information on minimum wage laws, over-time rules and recordkeeping requirements,** contact the nearest office of the U.S. Labor Department's Wage and Hour Division, or your local office of the New York State Department of Labor (see "New York State Department of Labor Services for Employers," below).

---

### New York State Department of Labor Services for Employers

Federal and state employment law requirements can be daunting, particularly to new employers. The State Department of Labor (DOL) offers a variety of free services that can help. Here are a few:

**Labor exchange.** You can list job openings at no charge on DOL's computer system, which is linked to colleges, high schools, libraries and self-search terminals located in shopping malls and other public places. DOL also allows job seekers to browse employment openings via the Internet.

**Tax credit programs.** You can get up to $8,500 in federal tax credits when you hire employees who are from certain employment-disadvantaged targeted groups, who are long-term public assistance recipients or who are disabled New Yorkers who have received vocational rehabilitation services.

**Human resource consultants.** Ask to speak to a consultant for help writing employee handbooks and reviewing individual employer personnel policies and problems. You can also get information about state laws on minimum wage, hours of work, child labor, payment of wages and wage supplements.

For more information call your local NYS Department of Labor Employer Services Offices at 800-447-3992, or visit the DOL's website at: www.labor.state.ny.us.

---

### Equal Pay for Equal Work

You must provide equal pay and benefits to men and women who do the same job or jobs that require equal skills, effort and responsibility. This is required by the Equal Pay Act, an amendment to the Fair Labor Standards Act.

---

## 6. Workers' Compensation Insurance

Workers' compensation provides replacement income and pays medical expenses for employees who are injured or become ill as a result of their job. It's a no-fault system—an injured employee is entitled to receive benefits whether or not you provided a safe workplace and whether or not your worker's own carelessness contributed to the injury. (You are, of course, required by federal and state laws to provide a reasonably safe workplace.) But you, too, receive some protection, because the worker is limited to fixed types of compensation—basically, partial wage replacement and payment of medical bills. Employees may also get money for retraining or special equipment if they are "permanently disabled." The super or manager can't sue you (nor get paid) for pain and suffering or mental anguish.

To cover the costs of workers' compensation benefits for employees, you're legally required to buy a workers' compensation insurance policy—even if you only have one employee. You can purchase a policy from one of the 800 private insurance carriers authorized to write such insurance in New York State (contact your insurance broker or insurers listed in the Yellow Pages of your telephone directory). There's no use shopping around for the best price. Premiums are set by the New York Compensation Insurance Rating Board based upon the worker's specific job functions and the employer's history of work-related accidents.

 For more information, call the State Workers' Compensation Board Bureau of Compliance at 800-628-3331 or visit its website at www.wcb.state.ny.us.

## 7. Immigration Laws

When you hire someone, even someone who was born and raised in the city where your rental property is located, you must review documents such as a passport or naturalization certificate that prove the employee's identity and employment eligibility. You and each new employee are required to complete BCIS Form I-9, Employment Eligibility Verification. These rules come from the Immigration Reform and Control Act (IRCA), a federal law that prohibits hiring undocumented workers. The law, now enforced by the Bureau of Citizenship and Immigration Services (BCIS), prohibits hiring workers who don't have government authorization to work in the U.S.

 For more information, obtain a copy of the free BCIS publication *Handbook for Employers: Instructions for Completing Form I-9 (m-378),* by calling 800-375-5283 or visiting the BCIS website at www.immigration.gov.

## 8. Reporting of Newly Hired Employees

Within 20 days after you hire a new super or manager, you must submit information about the employee to the State Tax Department. (Ch. 81, Laws of 1995.) The information becomes part of the National Directory of New Hires, used primarily to locate parents so that child support orders can be enforced. Government agencies also use the data to prevent improper payment of workers' compensation and unemployment benefits or public assistance benefits.

To comply, send a legible photocopy of the new employee's fully completed federal form W-4 (Employee's Witholding Allowance Certificate) to this address: New York State Tax Department, New Hire Notification, P.O. Box 15119, Albany, NY 12212-5119. Alternatively, you may fax the form to: 518-463-4514. For more information on your responsibilities under the new-hire reporting program, you can call the Department's business tax information center toll free at 800-225-5829.

 **Some building service workers get temporary protection from termination when the building is sold or transferred.** If you purchase a New York City residential building with 50 or more units, a 2002 New York City ordinance requires you to retain the previous employer's service workers for a trial period of ninety days, after which time each worker can be dismissed. If you determine that you need fewer employees than you inherited from the prior owner, you must only retain the number of satisfactory existing employees you need, in order of seniority. (NYC Adm. Code § 22-505.)

## E. Management Companies

Property management companies are often used by owners of large apartment buildings or complexes and by absentee owners too far away from the property to be directly involved in everyday details. Management companies act as the owner's agent and generally take care of renting units, collecting rent, taking tenant complaints, arranging repairs and maintenance and evicting troublesome tenants. Of course, some of these responsibilities are often shared with or delegated to the resident managers or building superintendent who, in some instances, may work for the management company.

A variety of relationships between owners and management companies are possible, depending on your wishes and how the particular management company chooses to do business. Depending on the size and location of your building, the management company will probably recommend (and state multiple dwelling laws may require) hiring a live-in super or manager. (See Section A, above for details on when you must hire a live-in super or manager.) But if your rental property has only a few units, or you own a number of small buildings spread over a good-sized geographical area, the management company will probably suggest simply responding to tenant requests and complaints from its central office.

One advantage of hiring a management company is that you avoid all the legal hassles of being an employer: paying payroll taxes, buying workers' compensation insurance and withholding income tax. The management company is an independent contractor, not an employee. It hires and pays the people who do the work. Typically, you sign a contract spelling out the managing agent's duties and fees. Most companies charge a fixed percentage—about 4% to 10%—of the total rent collected. (The salary of any resident super or manager is extra.) This gives the company a good incentive to keep the building filled with rent-paying tenants.

Another advantage is that management companies are usually well informed about the law, keep good financial records and are adept at staying out of legal hot water in such areas as discrimination, invasion of privacy and returning deposits.

The primary disadvantage of hiring a management company is the expense. For example, if you pay a management company 5% of the $18,000 you collect in rent each month from tenants in a 20-unit building, this amounts to $900 a month and $10,800 per year. Also, if the management company works from a central office with no one on site, tenants may feel that management is too distant and unconcerned with their day-to-day needs.

Management companies have their own contracts, which you should read thoroughly and understand before signing. Be sure you understand how the company is paid and its exact responsibilities.

A management contract is not a take it or leave it deal. You should negotiate the company's fee, obviously, as well as any extra charges you can expect to pay during the length of the contract. You may also specify spending limits for ordinary repairs. The contract is a good place to spell out insurance requirements, too. Most landlords require the management company to be insured under a comprehensive general liability policy which names them as an "additional insured." Extra coverage for errors and omissions and employee dishonesty is also a good idea. Your insurance broker or agent should be able to recommend how much insurance to require.

Policies on screening tenants, maintenance and repairs and letting contracts aren't usually part of the management contract itself, but should be clearly communicated, so that the management company knows what you expect.

## F. Your Liability for a Super or Manager's Acts

Depending on the circumstances, you may be legally responsible for the acts of a super, manager or management company. For example, you could be sued and found liable if your super, manager or management company:

- refuses to rent to a qualified tenant who is a member of a protected group or has children, or otherwise violates antidiscrimination laws (see Chapter 1)
- sexually harasses a tenant
- makes illegal deductions from the security deposit of a tenant who has moved out, or does not return the departing tenant's deposit within a reasonable period of time (see Chapter 16)
- ignores a dangerous condition, such as substandard wiring that results in an electrical fire, causing injury or damage to a tenant or security problems that result in a criminal assault on a tenant (see Chapter 9), or
- invades a tenant's privacy by flagrant and damaging gossip or trespass (see Chapter 10).

In short, a landlord who knows the law but has an employee (or management company) who doesn't, could wind up in a lawsuit brought by prospective, current or former tenants.

Here's how to protect your tenants and yourself:

**Choose your super or manager carefully.** Legally, you have a duty to protect your tenants from injury caused by employees you know or should know pose a risk of harm to others. If someone gets hurt or has property stolen or damaged by an employee whose background you didn't check carefully, you could be sued. So it's crucial that you be especially vigilant when hiring a super or manager who will have easy access to rental units. (See Section B, above, for advice on checking the references and background of a prospective manager.)

## Questions to Ask When You Evaluate a Management Company

- Who are its clients: owners of single-family houses, small apartment buildings or large complexes? Look for a company with experience handling properties like yours. Also, ask for client references, and check to see whether other landlords are satisfied with the management company. (Don't forget to ask these landlords how their tenants feel about the service they get. Unhappy tenants are bad business.)
- What services are provided?
- Is the management company equipped to take tenant calls 24 hours a day, seven days a week?
- Is the company located fairly close to your property?
- Will there be an individual property manager assigned to your property? How frequently will the property manager visit and inspect the building? How many other units is the property manager responsible for?
- What are the costs? What services cost extra?
- Will you be able to take advantage of any of the management company's bulk purchasing agreements or discounts on items like fuel oil, building supplies or insurance coverage?
- Is the management company licensed? (Management companies that collect rent on behalf of the landlord must be licensed by the NYS Division of Licensing, described in Chapter 1, Section J.)

- Are the management company employees bonded?
- How early in the month are late rent notices sent to tenants?
- Will the management company prepare an annual budget for the building and furnish monthly financial reports on rent collections, cash disbursements and accounts payable? How early in the month will financial reports on the previous month's financial activities be provided?
- Are employees trained in landlord-tenant law? Will the company consult an attorney qualified in landlord-tenant matters if problems arise, such as disputes over rent? If so, who will select and pay for the attorney?
- If your property is covered by rent control or rent stabilization laws, are company personnel familiar with DHCR's rent regulations and filing requirements? Is there an extra charge for preparing and filing DHCR forms for rent increases or apartment registrations? Will the company answer routine tenant complaints filed with the DHCR?
- Are large contracts put to bid? Ask what bid procedures are in effect to discourage bid-rigging and kickback schemes between contractors and management company employees.
- Can you terminate the management agreement without cause upon reasonable notice?

Make sure your super or manager is familiar with the basics of landlord-tenant law, especially if she'll be taking rental applications from tenants or serving eviction notices. One approach is to give your super or manager a copy of this book to read and refer to. In addition, you'll want to provide detailed instructions that cover likely trouble areas, such as the legal rules prohibiting discrimination in tenant selection.

Train new employees about fair housing laws and the types of questions and comments that are discriminatory or that could trigger a fair housing complaint from a rental applicant or tenant. You can conduct the training yourself, or enroll employees in a fair housing training course or program. Appendix I (at the end of this book) lists organizations that offer fair housing training courses for New York landlords, managers, supers and real estate agents.

Make sure your insurance covers illegal acts of your employees. No matter how thorough your precautions, you may still be liable for your manager's illegal acts—even if your manager commits an illegal act in direct violation of your instructions. To really protect yourself, purchase a good comprehensive general liability insurance policy with an employee dishonesty endorsement.

## G. Notifying Tenants of the Super or Manager

Make sure new tenants know your super or manager's name, address and phone number. A move-in letter (discussed in Chapter 7) is a good place to do this. Whenever you replace a super or manager, or hire a new building staff member, send tenants a notice introducing the new employee and describing her job functions. A sample letter of introduction is shown below. You should give each tenant a copy and post another in a prominent place in the building.

### Emergency Contacts and Procedures for Your Employees

It's an excellent idea to prepare a written set of emergency procedures for the super or manager, including:

- owner's name and emergency phone number, so your employee can contact you in case of emergency
- names and phone numbers of nearest hospital and poison control center
- ambulance, police and fire departments and a local taxi company
- names and phone numbers of contractors who can respond to a building emergency on a 24-hour basis, including any licensed plumber, electrician, locksmith, boiler mechanic, elevator service company and air conditioner maintenance company with whom you have set up an account.
- procedures to follow in case of a fire, flood, hurricane, tornado or other disaster, including how to safely shut down elevators, water, electricity and gas.

### Sample Letter of Introduction of New Staff Member

November 1, 200x

Dear Tenants,

We are pleased to introduce our new resident manager for The Montana, Muhammad Azziz. Mr. Azziz, who has moved into Apartment 1-A, will be on duty in the building between the hours of 8AM and 4 PM each weekday. Mr. Azziz, whose office is the building's basement, can be reached at 212-555-1212. If Mr. Azziz is not in his office, you can leave a voice message for him. In the event of an emergency, you can also call our special 24-hour emergency number: 212-555-1213.

If you have any complaints about the condition of your unit or common areas, please notify Mr. Azziz immediately. He is authorized to act for and on behalf of the owner of the premises for the purpose of receiving all notices from you, including rent checks or money orders. Unfortunately, Mr. Azziz is not authorized to accept cash rent payments.

Very truly yours,

*Pamela Logan*

Owner and Landlord

## 1. Post Sign Identifying Super or Manager

Some municipalities, such as New York City, legally require landlords to post a permanent sign in the lobby or entrance hall of their buildings giving the super or manager's name, address and phone number. Installing a sign like this is a good idea whether or not your local government requires it.

**Landlords of New York City buildings with nine or more units must display a sign giving the name, address and phone number for the person who performs janitorial services.** (NYC Adm. Code § 27-2053.) The lettering on the sign must be at least 3/16 of an inch tall, and be large enough to include a 1/4 inch border around the lettering.

## 2. Identify Managing Agent in Rent Bills and Receipts for NYC Tenants

All rent bills and receipts for payment of rent given to New York City tenants must state the name and NYC address of the "managing agent," as listed on the registration for the building with the City (see Section H, below, for New York City registration requirements). (NYC Adm. Code § 27-2105.) A managing agent is a natural person (not a corporation, partnership or other business entity) over the age of 21 who is in control of and responsible for the maintenance and operation of the building, and who may authorize emergency repairs. The managing agent must either live or have an office in New York City. Alternatively, an owner or corporate officer who meets these requirements may be registered as the managing agent.

## H. Municipal Registration Requirements

Owners of buildings with three or more units are generally required to periodically register their rental properties with the local housing code enforcement office. This helps the municipality track down the owner or manager when there's a complaint filed with the office about conditions at the property. To register, you usually must furnish the name, address and phone number of the owner and manager, and pay a fee. When you hire a new manager, you must amend the registration, usually within a specific period of time. Call your local housing code enforcement office to see if there's a rental property registration requirement in the city or town where your property is located.

Each year, New York City rental property owners with three or more units must complete and file a Property Registration Form (RHM Form 521) and pay a fee. (Owners of one-

and two-unit rental buildings must register only if they live outside New York City.) A sample of this Property Registration Form is shown below.

The Property Registration Form gets filed with the City's Department of Housing Preservation and Development (HPD) Office of Rent and Housing Maintenance. Required information includes the names, home and business addresses and phone numbers for the owner, managing agent (discussed in Section G2, above) and on-site super or manager. Also required is a confidential 24-hour phone number in the NYC metropolitan area where the owner or a "responsible person" can be reached in the event of an emergency regarding the property. The form must be signed by the building's owner and the managing agent. You must file an amended form whenever any registration information changes.

Upon registration, HPD assigns a permanent multiple-dwelling registration (MDR) number to the property. You must post a sign over the entrance door to your property with the MDR number and the building's address. A New York City landlord's failure to file a Property Registration Form can result in a fine from $250 to $500. More importantly, your failure to register the property can prevent you from being able to bring an eviction proceeding against a tenant for non-payment of rent. If you forget to post the sign, you can get hit with a code violation and fine of between $10 and $50. For more information or to get registration forms, call HPD's Property Registration Assistance Unit at 212-863-7000, or check their website at www.nyc.gov.html/hpd.

**Post Multiple Dwelling Registration sign.** If your building has three or more units, you must post a sign identifying the property's HPD multiple dwelling number, owner and managing agent. The sign should also identify the rent collections agent, if different from the managing agent. (NYC Adm. Code 27-2104.)

## I. Firing a Super or Manager

Unless you have made a commitment (oral or written contract) to employ a super or manager for a specific period of time, you have the right to terminate a non-unionized employee at any time. But you cannot do it for an illegal reason, such as:

- race, age, gender or other prohibited form of discrimination, or
- retaliation against the manager for calling your illegal acts to the attention of authorities.

EXAMPLE: You order your manager to dump 20 gallons of fuel oil at the back of your property. Instead, the manager complains to a local environmental regulatory agency, which fines you. If you now fire the manager, you will be vulnerable to a lawsuit for illegal termination.

To head off the possibility of a wrongful termination lawsuit, be prepared to show a good business-related reason for the firing. It's almost essential to back up a firing with written records documenting your reasons. Reasons that may support a firing include:

- performing poorly on the job—for example, not depositing rent checks promptly, or continually failing to respond to tenant complaints
- refusing to follow instructions—for example, allowing tenants to pay rent late, despite your instructions to the contrary
- possessing a weapon at work without a permit
- being dishonest or stealing money or property from you or your tenants
- endangering the health or safety of tenants
- engaging in criminal activity, such as drug dealing
- arguing or fighting with tenants
- behaving violently at work, or
- unlawfully discriminating or harassing prospective or current tenants.

Ideally, a firing shouldn't come suddenly or as a surprise. Give your manager ongoing feedback about job performance and impose progressive

City of New York
**DEPARTMENT OF HOUSING PRESERVATION AND DEVELOPMENT**
Office of Housing Preservation

**PROPERTY REGISTRATION FORM**

| For Office Use Only | |
|---|---|
| MIN # | |
| REG ID # | |

| House No. | Street Name | Boro |
|---|---|---|
| | | |

Type or print new information in block letters and numbers. Use black or blue ink only.

**1(B). IS THE OWNER OF THE PROPERTY THE SAME AS PREVIOUSLY REGISTERED?**
(Check One): ☐ YES (Go to 2)    ☐ NO (Go to 2)

**2. INDICATE FORM OF OWNERSHIP:**
(Check One): ☐ Individual (Go to 3)   ☐ Joint (Go to 5B)   ☐ Corporation (Go to 5)   ☐ Partnership (Go to 5)   ☐ Condo (Go to 5)   ☐ Co-Op (Go to 5)   ☐ Other _____ Specify

**3. INDIVIDUAL OWNERSHIP**
A person who is the sole owner of the property. (Enter only ONE name)

| Owner's Name: First | M.I. | Owner's Name: Last | | | | | Currently in Active Military Service? ☐ YES ☐ NO |
|---|---|---|---|---|---|---|---|
| Bldg. No. (BUSINESS) | Street Name | | Suite/Room | City | State | Zip Code | Telephone/Extension ( ) |
| House No. (RESIDENCE) | Street Name | | Apartment | City | State | Zip Code | Telephone ( ) |

**4. IS THE INDIVIDUAL IN SECTION 3 ALSO THE MANAGING AGENT OF THE PROPERTY SPECIFIED ABOVE?**
(Check One): ☐ YES (Go to 7)    ☐ NO (Go to 6)

**5. OTHER THAN INDIVIDUAL OWNERSHIP**
Property owned jointly, or by two or more individuals, or by an entity other than an individual. Enter Corporation/Partnership/Other (Estate, Trust) Name in Section 5A.
Enter Responsible Person(s) Information in Sections 5B, 5C, and 5D.

| 5A. Corporation/Partnership/Other Name | | | Tax ID Number | | County Where Certificate of Doing Business Filed | Are One or More Partners a Corporation? ☐ YES ☐ NO |
|---|---|---|---|---|---|---|
| Bldg. No. (BUSINESS) | Street Name | Suite/Room | City | State | Zip Code | Telephone/Extension ( ) |

| 5B. Responsible Person #1 (First Name) | M.I. | (Last Name) | Title | Currently in Active Military Service? ☐ YES ☐ NO |
|---|---|---|---|---|
| Bldg. No. (BUSINESS) | Street Name | Suite/Room | City | State | Zip Code | Telephone/Extension ( ) |
| House No. (RESIDENCE) | Street Name | Apartment | City | State | Zip Code | Telephone ( ) |

| 5C. Responsible Person #2 (First Name) | M.I. | (Last Name) | Title | Currently in Active Military Service? ☐ YES ☐ NO |
|---|---|---|---|---|
| Bldg. No. (BUSINESS) | Street Name | Suite/Room | City | State | Zip Code | Telephone/Extension ( ) |
| House No. (RESIDENCE) | Street Name | Apartment | City | State | Zip Code | Telephone ( ) |

| 5D. Responsible Person #3 (First Name) | M.I. | (Last Name) | Title | Currently in Active Military Service? ☐ YES ☐ NO |
|---|---|---|---|---|
| Bldg. No. (BUSINESS) | Street Name | Suite/Room | City | State | Zip Code | Telephone/Extension ( ) |
| House No. (RESIDENCE) | Street Name | Apartment | City | State | Zip Code | Telephone/Extension ( ) |

OHP Form 521
(Rev. 5/99)

NOTE: PROPERTY REGISTRATION FORM MUST BE SUBMITTED AS ONE PAGE (2-SIDED). HPD WILL NOT ACCEPT TWO SEPARATE SHEETS.

Side 1

## 6. MANAGING AGENT INFORMATION
Designated by the Owner to oversee the operation of the property.

| Company Name (If Applicable) | Tax ID Number | First Name | M.I. | Last Name | Currently in Active Military Service? YES [ ] NO [ ] |
|---|---|---|---|---|---|
| Bldg. No. (BUSINESS)   Street Name | | Suite/Room | City | State | Zip Code | Telephone/Extension ( ) |
| House No. (RESIDENCE)  Street Name | | Apartment | City | State | Zip Code | Telephone ( ) |

## 7. SITE MANAGEMENT INFORMATION
Enter the name and telephone number of a nearby Responsible Individual (superintendant, building manager) who can be contacted in the event of an emergency regarding this property.

| Site Manager's Name: First | M.I. | Site Manager's Name: Last | Telephone/Extension ( ) |
|---|---|---|---|

## 8. IS THE ENTIRE PROPERTY LEASED TO ONE INDIVIDUAL OR CORPORATION?
Refers to a single lease for the entire property and does not refer to the rental of individual units.   (Check One): YES [ ] (Go to 9)   NO [ ] (Go to 10)

## 9. LESSEE INFORMATION
Enter information about the Corporation/Partnership (if appropriate) and/or the individual leasing the entire property.

| Corporation/Partnership Name | First Name | M.I. | Last Name |
|---|---|---|---|
| Bldg. No. (BUSINESS)  Street Name | Suite/Room  City | State  Zip Code | Telephone/Extension ( ) |

## 10. CONFIDENTIAL 24 HOUR TELEPHONE NUMBER(S)
Enter the names and confidential 24 hour telephone numbers (in the NYC metropolitan area) of the Owner and/or one or more Responsible Persons who can be contacted in the event of an emergency regarding this property.

| Telephone/Extension ( ) | First Name | Last Name | Telephone/Extension ( ) | First Name | Last Name |
|---|---|---|---|---|---|

This Property Registration Form must be SIGNED AND DATED BY **BOTH** the MANAGING AGENT indicated in Section 6 and the PROPERTY OWNER indicated in Sections 3 or 5.

## 11. MANAGING AGENT SIGNATURE _____ Date _____
I CONSENT TO THE DESIGNATION AS MANAGING AGENT OF THE ABOVE PROPERTY. I AM AT LEAST 21 YEARS OLD.

## 12. OWNER SIGNATURE _____ Date _____
I AM A PERSON WITH DIRECT OR INDIRECT CONTROL OVER THIS PROPERTY. I AM SIGNING IN MY CAPACITY AS:

[ ] Individual Owner  [ ] Joint Owner  [ ] Officer  [ ] General Partner  [ ] Limited Partner  [ ] Receiver  [ ] Executor  [ ] Trustee  [ ] Other_____ Specify

If you have the Owner's Power of Attorney and are signing for the Owner, a copy of the notarized Power of Attorney must accompany the Registration Form.

*I CERTIFY THAT ALL STATEMENTS MADE HEREIN ARE TRUE AND CORRECT.*
**False Statements Are Punishable Under Section 27-2096 of the NYC Housing Maintenance Code.**

RETURN THIS FORM TO: HPD, P.O. BOX 9020, CHURCH STREET STATION, NEW YORK, NY 10256.
TELEPHONE (212) 863-7000 FOR ASSISTANCE IN COMPLETING THIS FORM, MONDAY THROUGH FRIDAY BETWEEN 9:15 A.M. AND 4:30 P.M.

For Office Use Only — Do Not Write Below This Line

| Agent | Owner |
|---|---|
| 1 | 2 |

OHP Form 521 (Rev. 5/99)

*NOTE: PROPERTY REGISTRATION FORM MUST BE SUBMITTED AS ONE PAGE (2-SIDED). HPD WILL NOT ACCEPT TWO SEPARATE SHEETS.*

Side 2

discipline, such as an oral or written warning, and/or a suspension before termination. Do a six-month performance review (more often, if necessary) and keep copies. Solicit comments from tenants once a year, and if comments are negative, keep copies.

---

### Handling Requests for References

One of your biggest problems after a super or manager quits or has been fired may be what to tell other landlords or employers who inquire about the former employee. You may be tugged in several directions:

- You want to tell the truth—good, bad or neutral—about the former manager.
- You want to help the former manager find another job for which he is better suited.
- You don't want to be sued for libel or slander because you say something negative.

Legally, you're better off saying as little as possible, rather than saying anything negative or untrue. Just say that it's your policy not to comment on former managers. Besides, if you politely say, "I would rather not discuss Mr. Jones," the caller will get the idea.

---

## J. Evicting a Manager

If you fire a manager, you may often want the ex-employee to move out of your property, particularly if there is a special manager's unit or the firing has generated (or resulted from) ill will. However, in some cases, your ex-employee may have a right to continue in occupancy.

- If you hire a current tenant (including a rent-stabilized or rent-controlled tenant) as the super or manager, that individual will revert back to being a tenant when the job ends. (*Gottlieb v. Adames*, N.Y.L.J., 9/23/94, p. 21,

col. 2 (App.T., 1st Dep't).) The tenant's employment doesn't annul or end the tenancy, even if the tenant moves from a rent-regulated unit into a different unit in the same property as a condition of employment. When the job ends, the ex-employee usually has the right to remain as a tenant.

- If the employee moved into the rental unit under a month-to-month rental agreement, termination of the employment will not terminate the rental agreement. You will need to end the tenancy by giving the super or manager a written 30-day notice of termination (give one month's oral or written notice outside New York City). (See Chapter 13 for instructions on how to prepare and serve this notice.)

- If the ex-employee has a fixed-term lease for the rental unit, generally, the tenancy won't end until the lease expires. (Chapter 14 describes the grounds upon which fixed-term tenancies may be terminated.)

- If the super or manager took occupancy of the rental unit under a written or oral employment agreement (such as the Building Superintendent/Property Manager Agreement contained in Section C, above), not a lease or rental agreement, the employee is generally considered to be a "licensee," not a tenant. (RPAPL § 713.) Terminating employment works to terminate the employee's right to occupy the unit. If the ex-employee refuses to move out, you can begin an eviction proceeding to remove the ex-employee. There's no need to serve a termination notice first. (RPAPL § 713(11).)

**If the ex-employee refuses to move out, get an experienced landlord-tenant attorney to draft the notices and handle the eviction proceeding**—especially if the employee is claiming to have a right to continue in occupancy under the rent control or rent stabilization laws. An experienced lawyer should be able to bring the matter to a conclusion faster than you could on your own. ■

# Getting the Tenant Moved In

Legal disputes between landlords and tenants have gained a reputation for being almost as emotional as divorce court battles. Many disputes are unnecessary and could be avoided if—right from the very beginning—tenants knew their legal rights and responsibilities. A clearly written lease or rental agreement, signed by all adult occupants, is the key to starting a tenancy. (See Chapter 2.) But there's more to establishing a positive attitude when new tenants move in. You should also:

- inspect the property, fill out a Landlord-Tenant Checklist documenting the condition of the rental property and photograph the rental unit, and

- prepare a move-in letter highlighting important terms of the tenancy and your expectations.

While you're not legally required to give new tenants a written statement on the condition of the rental premises at move-in time, doing so will make your job a lot easier when the tenant moves out.

## A. Inspect the Rental Unit

To eliminate the possibility of all sorts of future arguments, it is absolutely essential that you (or your representative) and prospective tenants (together, if possible) check the place over for damage and obvious wear and tear before the tenant moves in. The best way to document what you find is to jointly fill out a Landlord-Tenant Checklist form.

## 1. Fill Out the Landlord-Tenant Checklist

A Landlord-Tenant Checklist, inventorying the condition of the rental property at the beginning and end of the tenancy, is an excellent device to protect both you and your tenant when the tenant moves out and wants the security deposit returned. Without some record as to the condition of the unit, you and the tenant are all too likely to get into arguments about things like whether the kitchen linoleum was already stained, the garbage disposal was broken, the stove was filthy or the bathroom

mirror was already cracked when the tenant moved in.

The checklist provides good evidence as to why you withheld all or part of a security deposit. And coupled with a system to regularly keep track of the rental property's condition, the checklist will also be extremely useful to you if a tenant withholds rent, breaks the lease and moves out or sues you outright, claiming the unit needs substantial repairs.

A sample Landlord-Tenant Checklist is shown below.

 The Forms CD includes the Landlord-Tenant Checklist, and a blank, tear-out copy is in Appendix IV.

## 2. How to Fill Out the Checklist

You and the tenant should fill out the checklist together. If that's impossible, complete the form and then give it to the tenant to review. The tenant should note any disagreement and return it to you.

The checklist is in two parts. The first side covers the general condition of each room. The second side covers furnishings, such as a living room lamp or bathroom shower curtain.

You will be filling out the first column—*Condition on Arrival*—before the tenant moves in. The last two columns—*Condition on Departure* and *Estimated Cost of Repair or Replacement*—are for use when the tenant moves out and you inspect the unit again. At that time the checklist will document your need to make deductions from the security deposit for repairs or cleaning, or to replace missing items. (See Chapter 16 for details on returning security deposits.)

When you look at the checklist included here, you'll see that we have filled out the first column (*Condition on Arrival*) with rooms and elements in these rooms. If you happen to be renting a one-bedroom, one-bath unit, our pre-printed form will work just fine. However, chances are that your rental has a different number of rooms, or elements in those rooms, than those on the checklist form. Changes are no problem if you use the CD-ROM

# Landlord-Tenant Checklist

## GENERAL CONDITION OF RENTAL UNIT AND PREMISES

922 West End Avenue         18-F     NY, NY 10025

Street Address                   Unit Number   City

| | Condition on Arrival | Condition on Departure | Estimated Cost of Repair/Replacement |
|---|---|---|---|
| **LIVING ROOM** | | | |
| Floors & Floor Coverings | OK | | |
| Drapes & Window Coverings | Mini-blinds discolored | | |
| Walls & Ceilings | OK | | |
| Light Fixtures | OK | | |
| Windows, Screens & Doors | Window rattles | | |
| Front Door & Locks | OK | | |
| Fireplace | NA | | |
| Other | | | |
| Other | | | |
| **KITCHEN** | | | |
| Floors & Floor Coverings | Cigarette burn hole on linoleum | | |
| Walls & Ceilings | OK | | |
| Light Fixtures | OK | | |
| Cabinets | Two cabinet doors don't close completely | | |
| Counters | Stain near sink | | |
| Stove/Oven | Burners filthy (grease) | | |
| Refrigerator | OK | | |
| Dishwasher | OK | | |
| Garbage Disposal | N/A | | |
| Sink & Plumbing | OK | | |
| Windows, Screens & Doors | OK | | |
| Other | | | |
| Other | | | |
| **DINING ROOM** | | | |
| Floors & Floor Covering | Scrape on wood floor near kitchen | | |
| Walls & Ceilings | Crack in ceiling | | |
| Light Fixtures | OK | | |
| Windows, Screens & Doors | OK | | |
| Other | | | |

| | Condition on Arrival | | Condition on Departure | | Estimated Cost of Repair/Replacement |
|---|---|---|---|---|---|
| **BATHROOM(S)** | Bath 1 | Bath 2 | Bath 1 | Bath 2 | |
| Floors & Floor Coverings | OK | | | | |
| Walls & Ceilings | Mold on ceiling | | | | |
| Windows, Screens & Doors | OK | | | | |
| Light Fixtures | OK | | | | |
| Bathtub/Shower | Tub chipped near faucet | | | | |
| Sink & Counters | | | | | |
| Toilet | OK | | | | |
| Other | Base of toilet very dirty | | | | |
| Other | | | | | |

| | Bdrm 1 | Bdrm 2 | Bdrm 3 | Bdrm 1 | Bdrm 2 | Bdrm 3 | |
|---|---|---|---|---|---|---|---|
| **BEDROOM(S)** | | | | | | | |
| Floors & Floor Coverings | | | | | | | |
| Windows, Screens & Doors | OK | OK | | | | | |
| Walls & Ceilings | OK | OK | | | | | |
| Light Fixtures | Dented | OK | | | | | |
| Other | Mildew in closet | | | | | | |
| Other | | | | | | | |
| Other | | | | | | | |
| Other | | | | | | | |

| | Condition on Arrival | Condition on Departure | Estimated Cost of Repair/Replacement |
|---|---|---|---|
| **OTHER AREAS** | OK | | |
| Heating System | OK | | |
| Air Conditioning | N/A | | |
| Lawn/Garden | N/A | | |
| Stairs and Hallway | N/A | | |
| Patio, Terrace, Deck, etc. | N/A | | |
| Basement | N/A | | |
| Parking Area | OK | | |
| Intercom | | | |
| Other | | | |
| Other | | | |
| Other | | | |
| Other | | | |

☐ Tenants acknowledge that all smoke detectors and fire extinguishers, if any, were tested in their presence and found to be in working order, and that the testing procedure was explained to them. Tenants agree to test all detectors at least once a month and to report any problems to Landlord/Manager in writing. Tenants agree to replace all smoke detector batteries as necessary.

## FURNISHED PROPERTY

| | Condition on Arrival | | Condition on Departure | | Estimated Cost of Repair/Replacement |
|---|---|---|---|---|---|
| **LIVING ROOM** | | | | | |
| Coffee Table | Two scratches on top | | | | |
| End Tables | OK | | | | |
| Lamps | OK | | | | |
| Chairs | OK | | | | |
| Sofa | | | | | |
| Other | | | | | |
| Other | | | | | |
| **KITCHEN** | | | | | |
| Broiler Pan | new | | | | |
| Ice Trays (4) | new | | | | |
| Other | | | | | |
| Other | | | | | |
| **DINING AREA** | | | | | |
| Chairs | OK | | | | |
| Stools | N/A | | | | |
| Table | Leg bent slightly | | | | |
| Other | | | | | |
| Other | | | | | |
| **BATHROOM(S)** | Bath 1 | Bath 2 | Bath 1 | Bath 2 | |
| Mirrors | OK | | | | |
| Shower Curtain | Torn | | | | |
| Hamper | N/A | | | | |
| Other | | | | | |
| **BEDROOM(S)** | Bdrm 1 | Bdrm 2 | Bdrm 3 | Bdrm 1 | Bdrm 2 | Bdrm 3 |
| Beds (single) | OK | N/A | | | | |
| Beds (double) | N/A | OK | | | | |
| Chairs | OK | OK | | | | |
| Chests | N/A | N/A | | | | |
| Dressing Tables | OK | N/A | | | | |
| Lamps | OK | OK | | | | |
| Mirrors | OK | OK | | | | |
| Night Tables | OK | N/A | | | | |
| Other | | | | | | |

|  | Condition on Arrival | Condition on Departure | Estimated Cost of Repair/Replacement |
|---|---|---|---|
| Other |  |  |  |
| **OTHER AREAS** |  |  |  |
| Bookcases | N/A |  |  |
| Desks | N/A |  |  |
| Pictures | Hallway picture frame chipped |  |  |
| Other |  |  |  |
| Other |  |  |  |

Use this space to provide any additional explanation:

_____
_____
_____
_____
_____
_____
_____
_____
_____
_____
_____
_____
_____

Landlord-Tenant Checklist completed on moving in on _____ May 1 _____, 200_X_, and approved by:

*Bernard Cohen* _____ and ___ *Marcia Crose* _____
Landlord/Manager                                         Tenant

                                                        ___ *Sandra Martino* _____
                                                        Tenant

                                                        _____
                                                        Tenant


Landlord-Tenant Checklist completed on moving out on _____, 200____, and approved by:

_____ and _____
Landlord/Manager                                         Tenant

                                                        _____
                                                        Tenant

                                                        _____
                                                        Tenant

that comes with this book. You can change the entries in the *Condition on Arrival* column of the checklist, and you can add or delete rows. For example, you may want to add a row for another bedroom or a service porch, or add room elements such as a trash compactor or fireplace. You may also delete items, such as a dishwasher. See the instructions for your word processing program for advice on how to edit a table.

If you want to use the checklist form as is, and make only a few changes, make a copy of the tear-out form in Appendix IV. Simply handwrite in changes or put "N/A" (not applicable) in the appropriate section. If necessary, you can attach a separate sheet of paper with additional items, such as furnishings, and staple it to the checklist.

The following sections explain how to complete the checklist.

### a. General Condition of Rental Unit and Premises

In the *Condition on Arrival* column, make a note—as specific as possible—on items that are not working or are dirty, scratched or simply in bad condition. For example, don't simply note that the refrigerator "needs fixing" if an ice maker doesn't work—it's just as easy to write "ice maker broken, should not be used." If the tenant uses the ice maker anyway and causes water damage, he cannot claim that you failed to tell him. Be sure to note any mildew, pest or rodent problems.

Mark "OK" next to items that are in satisfactory condition—basically, clean, safe, sanitary and in good working order.

If your rental unit does not have a particular item listed, such as a dishwasher or kitchen broiler pan, put "N/A" (not applicable) in the *Condition on Arrival* column.

**Make repairs and clean thoroughly before a new tenant moves in.** To get the tenancy off to the best start, and avoid all kinds of hassles over repairs, handle problems before the start of a new tenancy. See "Getting a Unit Ready for Showing," in Chapter 1, Section G. You may often be able to cover your repair and cleaning costs by deducting expenses from the outgoing tenant's security deposit (assuming the tenant is reponsible for the problem). Chapter 16 discusses how you may use security deposits for this purpose.

### b. Furnishings

The second part of the checklist covers furnishings, such as lamps or shower curtains. Obviously, you can simply delete this section of the checklist if your unit is not furnished.

If your rental property has rooms or furnishings not listed on the checklist, edit the form as explained above. If you are renting out a large house or apartment or providing many furnishings, be sure to include this information.

### 3. Sign the Checklist

After you and your new tenant agree on all of the particulars of the rental unit, you each should sign and date every page of the checklist, including any attachments. Keep the original and give the tenant a copy. If the tenant filled out the checklist on his own, make sure you review his comments, note any disagreement and return a copy to him. You should make the checklist part of your lease or rental agreement, as we recommend in our form agreements in Chapter 2, Clause 11.

Be sure the tenant also checks the box on the bottom of the second page of the checklist stating that smoke detectors (and any fire extinguishers) were tested in his presence and shown to be in working order. This section on the checklist also requires the tenant to test smoke detectors monthly and to replace the batteries when necessary. By doing this, you'll limit your liability if a smoke detector fails and an undetected (or tardily detected) fire results in damage or injury. (See Chapter 9 for details on your responsibility to maintain the property.)

**Be sure to keep the checklist up to date if you repair, replace, add or remove items or furnishings after the tenant moves in.** Both you and the tenant should initial and date any changes.

# B. Photograph the Rental Unit

Taking photos or videotapes of the unit before a new tenant moves in is another excellent way to avoid disputes over security deposit deductions. In addition to the checklist, you'll be able to compare "before" and "after" pictures when the tenant leaves. This should help refresh your tenant's memory, which may result in her being more reasonable. Certainly, if you end up in mediation or court for not returning the full security deposit, being able to document your point of view with photos will be invaluable. In addition, photos or a video can also help if you have to sue a former tenant for cleaning and repair costs above the deposit amount.

It's best to take "before" photographs with a Polaroid camera that develops pictures on the spot. This will allow both you and the tenant to date and sign the pictures, each keeping a set. Otherwise, use a camera that automatically imprints the date on each photo. If you don't have access to either type of camera, photograph the tenant or yourself during the inspection. Then develop the pictures promptly and sign and date them on the back. If you're doing the inspection on your own, bring a copy of that day's newspaper and photograph the front page as part of one of the photos.

If you make a video, get the tenant on tape stating the date and time so that you can prove when the video was made.

You should repeat this process when the tenant leaves, as part of your standard move-out procedure. Chapter 16 discusses inspecting the unit when a tenant leaves.

# C. Send New Tenants a Move-In Letter

A move-in letter should dovetail with the lease or rental agreement and provide basic information such as the manager's and super's phone numbers (day and night) and office hours. You can also use a move-in letter to explain any procedures and rules that are too detailed or numerous to include in your lease or rental agreement—for example, how and where to report maintenance problems, details on garbage disposal and recycling and location and use of laundry rooms. Consider including a brief list of maintenance do's and don'ts as part of the move-in letter—for example, how to avoid overloading circuits and proper use of the garbage disposal. (Alternatively, large landlords may use a set of Rules and Regulations to cover some of these issues. See Clause 18 of the form agreements in Chapter 2.)

Because every situation is different, we cannot supply you with a generic move-in letter that will work for everyone. We can, however, give you a template for a move-in letter that you can easily fill in with your own details, using the Forms CD. You can use the sample Move-In Letter shown below as a model in preparing your own move-in letter.

 The Forms CD includes the Move-In Letter, and a blank, tear-out copy is in Appendix IV.

We recommend that you make a copy of each tenant's move-in letter for yourself and ask him to sign the last page, indicating that he has read it. (As an extra precaution, ask him to initial each page.) Although this step may seem paranoid now, you won't think so later if a tenant sues you over something he claims you never told him (like the importance of promptly reporting any lost or stolen keys).

## Move-In Letter

March 1, 200x
_____
Date

Laureen Robbins
_____
Tenant

232 West 41st Street
_____
Street address

New York, NY 10018
_____
City and State


Dear_____ Ms. Robbins, _____,


Welcome to _____ 232 West 41st Street _____

_____. We hope you will enjoy living here. This letter is to explain what you

can expect from the management and what we'll be looking for from you:

**1. Rent:** _____ Rent is due on the first day of the month. There is no grace period for the payment of rent.

(See Clauses 5 and 6 of the lease for details, including late charges.) Also, we don't accept postdated

checks. Mail or deliver your rent check to our office at NoHo Realty, 693 Broadway, NY, NY 10012.

Members of the building staff are not authorized to accept rent checks from tenants.

**2. Maintenance/Repair Problems:** _____ We are determined to maintain a clean and safe building in which all

systems are in good repair. To help us make repairs properly, we will give you Maintenance/Repair

Request Forms to report to the superintendent any problems in your unit or elsewhere on the property.

(Extra copies are available just outside the super's office.) If the super does not respond to your request

or if you are unhappy with any work done, please report the problem to management. For emergency

service, call NoHo Management's 24-hour emergency answering service at 212-555-1234.

**3. Manager or Building Superintendent:** _____ Jim Murray (Apartment 1-B, telephone 212-555-1212) is the

building superintendent. Promptly let him know of any maintenance or repair problems. His office is

located in the basement of the building (next to the laundry room). If he's not in his office, you can slide

a note under the office door (repair request forms are provided on the shelf next to the door to the

super's office). Management also maintains a 24-hour answering service where you can report

emergencies: 212-555-1234.

**4. Landlord-Tenant Checklist:** _____ By now, Jim Murray should have taken you on a walk-through of your

apartment to check the condition of all walls, floors, fixtures and appliances, and to test the smoke

detector/s. These are all listed on the Landlord-Tenant Checklist, which you should have reviewed

carefully and signed. When you move out, we will ask you to check each item against its original condition

as described on the Checklist.

**5. Annual Safety Inspection:** _Once a year, we will ask to inspect the condition of your apartment and update the Landlord-Tenant Checklist. We will give you reasonable notice before the inspection, and encourage you to be present for it._

**6. Insurance:** _We highly recommend that you purchase renters' insurance. The building property insurance policy will not cover the replacement of your personal belongings if they are lost due to fire, theft or accident. In addition, you could be found liable if someone was injured on the premises as a result of your negligence. If you damage the building itself—for example if you start a fire in the kitchen and it spreads—you could be responsible for large repair bills._

**7. New Occupants:** _Under New York law, you must give us written notice of the names of any additional occupants (including immediate family members) who move into the unit with you within 30 days after they move in. Upon request, we would be happy to supply you with a form you may use for this purpose. Please be reminded that under the terms of your lease, you may share your unit with "immediate" family, which includes your spouse, a sibling, children, stepchildren, parents and parents-in-law, only._

**8. Notice to End Tenancy:** _Your lease obligates you to pay rent for the premises through the end of the lease term, whether or not you remain in occupancy. If you intend to move out of the rental unit before your lease ends, please contact me._

**9. Security Deposit:** _Your security deposit may be applied to the cost of damages, extraordinary cleaning or unpaid rent after you move out. You may not apply any part of the deposit toward any part of your rent in the last month of your tenancy (see Clause 8 of your rental agreement)._

**10. Moving Out:** _It's a little early to bring up moving out, but please be aware that we have a list of items that should be cleaned before we conduct a move-out inspection. If you decide to move, please ask for a copy of our Move-Out Letter, explaining our procedures for inspection and returning your deposit._

**11. Telephone Number Changes:** _Please notify us if your home or work phone number changes, so we can reach you in an emergency._

Please let us know if you have any questions.

Sincerely,

_9/1/0X_                          _Byron Burton_
Date                              Owner

I have read and received a copy of this statement.

_9/1/0X_                          _Laureen Robbins_
Date                              Tenant(s)

## D. Cash Rent and Security Deposit Checks

Every landlord's nightmare is a new tenant whose first rent or deposit check bounces and who must be dislodged with time-consuming and expensive legal proceedings. To avoid this, never sign a rental agreement, or let a tenant move furniture into your property or take a key until you have the tenant's cash, certified check or money order for the first month's rent and security deposit. An alternative is to cash the tenant's check at the bank before the move-in date. (While you have the tenant's first check, photocopy it for your records. The information on it can be helpful if you ever need to sue to collect a judgment from the tenant.) Be sure to give the tenant a signed receipt for the deposit (see sample receipt below).

 The Forms CD includes the Security Deposit Receipt form, and a blank tear-out copy is in Appendix IV.

Set a written management policy as to which of your employees are authorized to accept security deposits from tenants and sign receipts.

Clause 5 of the form lease and rental agreements in Chapter 2 requires tenants to pay rent on the first day of each month. If the move-in date is other than the first day of the month, rent is pro-rated between that day and the end of the month.

---

### Security Deposit Receipt

BIG APPLE MANAGEMENT CORP.

185 Madison Avenue

New York, NY 10016

(212) 555-1212

Receipt No. ___1008___

Date: ___November 8, 200x___

Premises address: _2 Madison Ave., NY, NY_____

_____ Unit #: _Apt. 5-B___

Amount of security deposit received: ___$2,000.00___

Form of payment (check one):

☐ Personal check        ☑ Certified check        ☐ Cash

☐ Postal money order    ☐ Bank check            ☐ Other: (specify)_____

Received by: ___Thelma Simkins_____

Recipient's name and title: ___Thelma Simkins, Leasing Agent_____

# E. Organize Your Tenant Records

A good system to record all significant tenant complaints and repair requests will provide a valuable paper trail should disputes develop later—for example, regarding your right to enter a tenant's unit to make repairs or the time it took for you to fix a problem. Without good records, the outcome of a dispute may come down to your word against your tenant's—always a precarious situation.

Set up a file folder on each property with individual files for each tenant. Include the following documents:

- tenant's rental application, references, credit report and background information, including information about any co-signers
- a signed lease or rental agreement, plus any changes made along the way
- Landlord-Tenant Checklist and photos or video made at move-in, and
- a signed move-in letter.

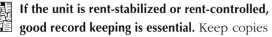 **If the unit is rent-stabilized or rent-controlled, good record keeping is essential.** Keep copies of annual rent registration forms for rent-stabilized units, rent increase notices to rent-controlled tenants, copies of invoices for any individual apartment improvements you made (such as installing a new refrigerator) for which you took a rent increase and DHCR complaints filed by the tenant (and your answer). (Chapter 4 has detailed information on rent-regulated units.)

After a tenant moves in, add these documents to the individual's file:

- rent receipts
- your written requests for access into the tenant's unit

- rent demand notices
- rent increase notices
- records of repair requests, and details of how and when they were handled (Chapter 9, Section F, suggests ways to set up an effective system for keeping track of repairs.)
- safety inspection reports
- move-out letter, security deposit itemizations and other documents related to the end of a tenancy
- correspondence, and
- other relevant information.

Your computer can also be a valuable tool to keep track of tenants. Set up a simple database for each tenant with spaces for the following information:

- address or unit number
- move-in date
- home phone number
- name, address and phone number of employer
- information as to where tenant banks
- monthly base rent amount and rent due date
- additional rent for garage space, etc.
- security deposit information, including location of deposit and interest payments
- vehicle make, model, color, year and license plate number
- emergency contacts, and
- whatever else is important to you.

Once you enter the information into your database, you can sort the list by address or other variables and easily print labels for rent bills, rent increases or other notices.

There are several commercial computer programs that allow you to keep track of every aspect of your business, from the tracking of rents to the follow-up on repair requests. Especially if you own many rental properties, these programs are well worth the cost. ■

Chapter **8**

# Apartment Sharing, Subletting and Assignments

Keeping track of exactly who is living in your rental units can be a tough job. Tenants often open their doors to guests, roommates, family members and other occupants. And state laws giving tenants the right to share, sublet and assign their rental units don't make your job any easier.

Fortunately, there are ways to exert some control over who moves into your rental property, despite the tenant-friendly laws on apartment sharing, subletting and assignment. This chapter helps you understand your options when your tenant asks questions like these:

- "Can I bring in a roommate?"
- "Can I add my girlfriend to my lease?"
- "Can I sublet my apartment?"
- "May I get someone else to take over the rest of my lease?"

We also advise you on what to do if your tenant attempts to do any of the above *without* consulting you. Because, as with so much of life, the best defense is a good offense, we prepare you in advance for these situations with a thorough examination of New York law on co-tenancies, roommates, sublets and assignments. In particular, this chapter covers:

- how to find out exactly who's living at your property
- strategies on handling co-tenancies
- how the "Roommate Law" works
- your tenants' right to share with immediate family members
- how to handle a tenant's request to sublet under the "Sublet Law," and special rules for rent-stabilized tenants
- the legal differences between sublets and assignments
- your right to refuse to consent to an assignment, and
- how to collect a rent increase when rent-regulated tenants share or sublet their rental units.

 Related topics covered in this book include:

- Setting occupancy restrictions: Chapter 1
- Writing rental agreement and lease clauses on subletting and assignment: Chapter 2
- Terminating a tenancy for a tenant's subletting or assigning without your consent: Chapter 14
- Which tenant "family members" are protected from eviction under succession laws when a rent-controlled or rent-stabilized tenant dies or moves out: Chapter 14
- Releasing a tenant or co-tenant from a lease: Chapter 14, and
- Returning security deposits when one tenant leaves but the others stay: Chapter 16.

## A. Dealing with Co-Tenants

Co-tenants are two or more people who rent a unit together and all sign the same lease or rental agreement, sharing the same rights and responsibilities. A co-tenancy can also arise when two or more people enter into the same oral rental agreement with you and move in at the same time.

### 1. Joint and Several Liability

Among themselves, co-tenants may split the rent equally or unequally, depending on their own personal arrangement. However, any co-tenant who signs a lease or rental agreement with you is independently liable for all of the rent and abiding with the rules of the tenancy. Landlords often remind co-tenants of this obligation by inserting into the lease a chunk of legalese which says that the tenants are "jointly and severally" liable for paying rent and adhering to terms of the agreement. (See Clause 1 of the form agreements in Chapter 2.) But co-tenants are still bound by this principle even if the lease or rental agreement doesn't mention it.

When two or more tenants are "jointly and severally liable," you can choose to hold all of them, or just one of them, responsible for lease violations. If a co-tenant leaves, the remaining co-tenants stay

## Glossary of Terms Used in This Chapter

What's the difference between a co-tenant and a roommate? Believe it or not, there's a legal distinction between these two terms. Here is a list of terms you'll encounter as you read through this chapter, along with their legal meanings under New York law.

- **Tenant.** Someone who has signed a lease or a rental agreement entitling that person to exclusive possession of a rental unit, or who has gained the status of a tenant because the landlord has accepted his presence on the property or has accepted rent from him. A tenant has a legal relationship with the landlord that creates various rights and responsibilities for both parties.

- **Co-tenants.** Two or more tenants who rent the same rental unit under the same lease or rental agreement. (Sometimes co-tenants sign at the same time, or a co-tenant may be added later to an existing lease.) As far as the landlord is concerned, each tenant is 100% responsible for carrying out the agreement (in legal jargon, "jointly and severally liable"), including paying all the rent (see Section A1). When one co-tenant leaves, the remaining co-tenants remain fully responsible for carrying out the agreement.

- **Subtenant.** Someone who rents the rental unit from a tenant under an agreement called a

sublease. Most leases and rental agreements require the landlord's consent to a subtenant. A subtenant has the right to occupy the rental unit for the length of the sublease, whether or not the tenant continues to live in the rental unit. However, the tenant remains 100% responsible for all tenant obligations, including paying all the rent to the landlord. When the subtenant leaves, the tenant is still bound to her lease with the landlord. (See Section D, below.)

- **Roommate.** An immediate family member or unrelated occupant invited by the tenant to live permanently in the rental unit with the tenant. A roommate does not sign a lease and is not a tenant. While a roommate may share expenses with the tenant, there is no obligation to pay rent to the landlord. As far as the landlord is concerned, the tenant remains 100% responsible for the rent. A roommate may leave at any time without any responsibility to the landlord. However, a roommate has no right to remain in the rental unit after the tenant moves out (see Section C, below).

- **Assignee.** The person to whom a tenant transfers and assigns all of his rights of tenancy. After a lease assignment, the old tenant becomes the "assignor." Unlike a subtenant, an assignee rents directly from the landlord (see Section E, below.)

fully responsible for rent and abiding by the lease or rental agreement. (Chapter 14 discusses your options when a co-tenant leaves.) That means you may demand the entire rent from just one tenant, should the others skip out or be unable to pay their share for a particular month. You may also evict all of the tenants even if just one has broken the terms of the lease, for example, by damaging property or violating a "no pets" clause.

If you must evict a tenant for a breach other than for nonpayment of rent (in which case you would evict all the tenants), it's not a good idea to evict only the offending co-tenant. While you have no legal obligation to evict a blameless co-tenant (for example, one who has no control over a dog-owning co-tenant), it's a good idea to do so. New York's liberal roommate law entitles tenants to invite non-tenant occupants to move in. (See

Section C, below.) You don't want to evict a co-tenant on Monday, only to have that person move back in on Tuesday as the "roommate" of the innocent co-tenant you didn't evict. Because co-tenants are "jointly and severally liable," you also have the legal right to evict all co-tenants (even those who claim not to have caused the difficulty) and start over. Chapters 13, 14 and 15 provide details on terminating tenancies.

---

### Treat Married Couples Just Like Other Co-Tenants

Every adult who intends to move into a rental unit—including both members of a married couple—should sign the lease or rental agreement. This underscores your expectation that each individual is responsible ("jointly and severally liable") for the rent and the proper use of the rental property.

Don't presume that if you neglect to have either the husband or wife sign the lease, that person will still be directly responsible to you. It is no longer the rule in New York that a spouse is financially responsible for the necessities of life of the other, including rent. Husbands aren't automatically bound by their wives' lease obligations, and vice versa. (GOL § 3-305.)

You can sue either spouse for rent if both names are on the lease or rental agreement, making them co-tenants. (And if one of your tenants gets married during the lease term, prepare a new agreement and have both bride and groom sign it.) Listing both the husband and wife as co-tenants on the lease or rental agreement also protects you if the couple splits up during their tenancy. That way, if one spouse moves out, you will have the other spouse on the hook for 100% of the rent.

---

## 2. Disagreements Among Co-Tenants

Usually, co-tenants make only an oral agreement among themselves concerning how they will split the rent, occupy bedrooms and generally share their joint living space. For all sorts of reasons, their arrangements may go awry. If you have been a landlord for a while, you surely know all about tenants who play the stereo too loud, are slovenly, pay their share of the rent late, have too many overnight guests or create some other problem that their co-tenants can't abide. If the situation gets bad enough, the tenants may start arguing about who should leave, whether one co-tenant can keep another out of the apartment or who is responsible for what part of the rent.

The best advice we can give landlords who face serious disagreements among co-tenants is this: Don't get involved in spats between co-tenants, as a mediator or otherwise. The reasons for our advice are both practical and legal.

On the practical side, you probably do not have the time to get to the bottom of financial or personal disputes; and even if you do, you have no ability to enforce any decisions among your tenants. (How could you enforce a ruling that one tenant must occupy the smaller of the two bedrooms?)

On the legal side, too, you are largely helpless. For example, you cannot threaten eviction if a tenant violates an agreement with the other tenant and occupies the larger bedroom, unless you put that particular "offense" into the lease as a ground for eviction. And since it's impossible to design a lease that will predict and list every possible co-tenant disagreement, attempting to use a legal solution will be of little help.

If one or more co-tenants approach you about a dispute, explain that they must resolve any disagreements among themselves. Remind them that they are each legally obligated to pay the entire rent, and that you are not affected by any rent-sharing agreements they have made among themselves. If one co-tenant asks you to change the locks to keep another co-tenant out, tell the tenant that you cannot legally do that—unless a court has issued an order that the particular tenant stay out. The wisdom of remaining aloof during tenants' squabbles stops at the point that you fear for the physical safety of one of your tenants. (See "Dealing With Abuse Between Tenants," below.)

## Dealing With Abuse Between Tenants

Call the police immediately if you hear or witness violence between co-tenants or neighboring tenants, or if a reliable source tells you about it. If you have any reasonable factual basis to believe that a tenant intends to harm another tenant, you may also have a legal duty to warn the intended victim (who probably already knows) and begin proceedings to evict the aggressor. Failure to sensibly intervene where violence is threatened might result in a finding of liability if the aggressor carries through with the threat.

In the meantime, if one tenant fears violence from another tenant, consider taking the following steps:

- Suggest mediation if you think there is a potential for a reasoned resolution. Low-cost mediation services are often available through local colleges and bar associations.
- Contact the local police department or court clerk's office on behalf of the intended victim for information on obtaining a temporary restraining order, and urge the victim to apply for one. If the judge decides that the situation merits it, he or she will issue an order forbidding the aggressor tenant from coming near the other.

- Evict the aggressor or all co-tenants on the lease. If you choose to allow a blameless tenant to stay, keep in mind the remaining tenant's ability to pay the rent may be severely curtailed by the absence of a paying co-tenant.

EXAMPLE: Andy and his roommate Bill began their tenancy on friendly terms. Unfortunately, it soon became clear that their personal habits were completely at odds. Their arguments regarding housekeeping, guests and their financial obligations to contribute to the rent escalated to a physical fight. As a result, they each asked their landlord, Anita, to evict the other.

After listening to Andy and Bill's complaints, Anita referred them to a local mediation service, and they agreed to participate. The mediator's influence worked for a while, but Andy and Bill were soon back at loud, unpleasant shouting matches. Anita initiated eviction proceedings against both tenants, on the grounds that their disruptive behavior interfered with the rights of the other tenants and created a nuisance.

# B. Subtenants and Other Occupants

While most landlords would prefer that only tenants occupy their rental property, state law prohibits you from restricting occupancy of a rental unit to only the tenant or co-tenants. New York law generously gives tenants the right to open their apartment doors to subtenants, roommates, family members and guests—none of whom get added to the tenant's lease or rental agreement. But don't throw up your hands. There are limits to your tenant's right to share a rental unit with others, as well as legal remedies that permit you to remove illegal occupants from your property.

Unfortunately, it's not always a simple matter to determine who has the legal right to live in your rental property. In some cases, such as when a tenant has an occasional guest, you may not care. But if you turn a blind eye to long-term unlawful occupants, you can unintentionally bestow tenant rights upon the occupant, including protection from eviction under rent control and rent stabilization laws. (See "Don't Accept Rent From Non-Tenant Occupants," Section 1, below.)

In the sections that follow, we take a close look at New York's "Roommate Law," which permits tenants to share rental units with certain immediate family members and unrelated occupants, and we suggest ways you can keep sharing to a legal minimum. (See Section C, below.) Your tenants' right to sublet is covered in Section D, below, with emphasis on your right to screen (and reasonably reject) prospective subtenants. Special sublet rules for rent-stabilized tenants are covered there, too. This chapter concludes with a look at a tenant's statutory right to assign a lease (Section E, below).

## 1. Don't Accept Rent From Non-Tenant Occupants

Taking rent from anyone whose name is not on the lease or rental agreement for the unit is a dangerous practice. That applies equally to your tenants' family members, roommates and subtenants. Accepting rent from a non-tenant occupant can create a landlord-tenant relationship between you and that

person. And since you don't get a chance to screen tenants' family members and roommates, you may not want to enter into a tenancy with them. A Manhattan case illustrates how this can happen.

EXAMPLE: A tenant shared her rental unit with a roommate. The tenant moved out on August 31, but the roommate stayed. From September 1 forward, the roommate paid the rent to the landlord with checks in his own name. The landlord cashed the first few checks but made a notation that the checks were accepted "without prejudice" for "use and occupancy only"—that is, not as "rent." The landlord accepted checks for the next three years from the roommate without making any notation on the check. When the landlord sued to evict the roommate, the court dismissed the case. The judge found that because the landlord knew that the tenant had moved out, but continued to accept rent from the roommate, the landlord intended to create a landlord-tenant relationship with the roommate. (*640 Broadway Renaissance Co. v. Eisner*, N.Y.L.J., 3/18/98, p. 30, col. 5 (Civ. Ct., N.Y. County).)

**If the unit is rent-stabilized or rent-controlled, you definitely do not want to create a tenancy by accepting rent from a non-tenant occupant.** For rent-stabilized units, accepting rent from a family member or roommate after the tenant moves out can operate to entitle the occupant to a rent-stabilized renewal lease and deprive you of a hefty vacancy rent hike for the unit. Accepting rent from a rent-controlled tenant's family member or roommate can backfire, too. By taking rent, you could create a rent-controlled tenancy with the occupant and end up forfeiting your right to have the unit vacancy decontrolled when the tenant moves out.

## 2. Guests You Haven't Approved

A "guest" is someone who stays temporarily with the tenant, but who is not a regular occupant of the rental unit. (*Black's Law Dictionary*, 6th ed. 1990.) Our form rental agreement and lease include a clause requiring your written consent for guests to stay overnight more than a reasonable amount of time. We recommend that you allow guests to stay up to 30 days without your written permission. (See Clause 3 of the form lease and rental agreements in Chapter 2.) The value of this clause is that a tenant who tries to move someone in for a longer period has clearly violated a defined standard, which gives you grounds for eviction.

If it appears that a guest has moved in clothing and furniture and begun to receive mail at your property, it's best to take decisive action right away. First, request information as to the identity of all occupants in the unit (Section 3, below, tells you how to do this). Then, determine whether the guests' occupancy exceeds the occupancy limit in your lease or rental agreement and the tenant's entitlement to share the unit with additional occupants under state law. (Occupancy limits are covered in Chapter 1, Section C3.) Section C, below, covers your tenants' right to share their unit with certain immediate family members and additional non-tenant occupants under the Roommate Law.)

If the extra occupant violates the occupancy limit in the tenant's lease or rental agreement and is not covered under the Roommate Law, you should object to the extra occupant. If you allow the situation to continue without taking action, though, you run the risk that the extra occupant could assert a right to stay in the unit. Depending on your relationship with the tenant, you can start with an informal discussion or, if the tenant has a lease, you can use a formal "notice to cure" to advise the tenant that the extra occupant must go. (Chapter 15 covers notices to cure.) If the tenant refuses to remove the extra occupant, you can send the tenant a notice of termination. (Chapter 13 covers termination notices for month-to-month tenancies; Chapter 15 covers termination notices for tenants with leases or who are rent-controlled or rent-stabilized.)

### 3. How to Find Out Who Lives in a Rental Unit

All landlords have the right to know who lives at their rental property. It doesn't matter if the unit is

rent regulated or not. For landlords, this information is vital to maintain security, prevent overcrowding and to take prompt action to remove unauthorized occupants.

### a. Your Legal Right to Request Information on Occupants

State law requires tenants to inform you of any additional occupants within 30 days after they move into the rental unit. (RPL § 235-f(5).) Most tenants will voluntarily tell you when someone is moving into their unit because they want an extra set of keys or to ensure that the occupant's mail and packages are accepted at the building.

If the tenant doesn't volunteer this information, you have the right to demand it. State law requires tenants to respond to your request for the names of any occupants who occupy the rental unit within 30 days of your request. (RPL § 235-f.) While there's no requirement that you put your request in writing, we recommend that you do so. Tenants respond better to written requests from their landlords. And if the tenant refuses to give you occupant information, you'll have a record of your request if you decide to take steps to terminate the tenancy. (For details on how to terminate a tenancy, see Chapters 13, 14 and 15.)

A sample Request for Identity of Occupants Residing in Rental Unit form is shown below.

 The Forms CD includes the Request for Identity of Occupants Residing in Rental Unit form, and Appendix IV includes a blank, tear-out copy.

 Use an official form to demand occupant information from New York City tenants. See "How to Request Occupant Information in New York City," below.

# Request for Identity of Occupants Residing in Rental Unit

February 22, 200x
Date
Jayne E. Reiner
Tenant
Apt. 12-F, 9 East 40th Street
Rental Unit Address
New York, NY 10016
City and State

Dear Ms. Reiner ,
Tenant

New York Real Property Law § 235-f (5) requires you to inform the landlord of the identity of any and all persons, other than yourself, who are living in the rental unit.

Please complete the bottom portion of this letter by inserting the names of all adults and children living in the rental unit and their relationship to you. Then, sign and date this letter where indicated and mail it back to the landlord in the envelope provided. State law (RPL § 235-f) requires you to respond to this request within 30 days of your receipt of this letter.

Thank you in advance for your anticipated cooperation. If you have any questions, feel free to call the undersigned.

Very truly yours,

*Veda Zuponic*

Owner and Landlord

8 Washington Square South

New York, NY 10013

212-555-1212

- - - - - - - - - - - - - - - - - - - - - - - - - - - - - - - - - - - - - - - - - - - - - - - - - - - - - - - - - - - - - -

## Statement of Tenant

**Names of adults and names and ages of children
(under age 18) other than tenant residing in rental unit**    **Relationship to tenant (family or otherwise)**

1. _____    _____

2. _____    _____

3. _____    _____

For additional persons, check box and attach separate sheet. ☐

Signature of Tenant(s): _____

Date: _____

### b. How to Request Occupant Information in New York City

The NYC Housing Maintenance Code authorizes landlords "at any time" to demand a tenant to complete a sworn statement listing the names and relationship of all occupants residing in the rental unit and the ages of any minor children. The Division of Code Enforcement in the NYC Department of Housing Preservation and Development publishes an official form called a "Demand" you may use for this purpose. A sample is shown below. For copies of the Demand form, call the Division of Code Enforcement at 212-316-8184.

### c. Requesting Occupant Information From Rent-Regulated Tenants

Rent-controlled and rent-stabilized tenants may use an official form to tell you about occupants. DHCR publishes a Notice To Owner Of Family Members Residing With The Named Tenant In The Apartment Who May Be Entitled To Succession Rights/Protection From Eviction (DHCR Form RA-23.5). This form includes information on people (other than the tenant) currently residing in the apartment, the date they began their primary residence in the apartment, their family relationship to the tenant, and whether or not they are a senior citizen or disabled. The DHCR form is designed to be used by tenants, but owners may use it, too. The only limit is that you may not send this form to a tenant more than once in any 12 month period.

The form asks tenants to provide information that, if true, could entitle occupants to be named as tenants on a renewal lease for the unit or become entitled to protection from eviction under succession laws. Some landlords don't like using this form, though. They think that its instructions could prompt a tenant to give less-than-truthful answers about how long an occupant has lived in the unit or about the tenant's relationship to an occupant that could entitle the occupant to succession rights. (See Chapter 14 for more information about how occupants attain succession rights to rent-controlled and rent-stabilized

units.) For that reason, we recommend that you use the Request for Identity of Occupants Residing in Rental Unit form included in this chapter. (You are not legally required to use the official DHCR form.)

If the tenant refuses to answer the notice, any occupant seeking succession rights to a rent-controlled or rent-stabilized unit has an "affirmative obligation" to establish such a right. That means that the occupant would need to provide documents proving his "family member" status, the date he moved into the rental unit, and that he used the unit as a "primary residence" for the applicable residency period.

## C. Additional Occupants and the Roommate Law

The law is stacked in favor of tenants when it comes to sharing their units with additional occupants. Try as you might, you can't restrict occupancy of a unit to just tenants who sign the lease or rental agreement, or even to just tenants and their immediate family members.

### 1. Overview of the Roommate Law

New York's "Unlawful Restrictions on Occupancy" law (RPL § 235-f (3)), commonly known as the "Roommate Law," was originally enacted to protect "live-in lovers" from eviction. The Roommate Law prohibits landlords from limiting occupancy of a rental unit to just the tenant named on the lease or rental agreement or to the tenant and the tenant's immediate family. It permits tenants to share their rental units with their immediate family members and, in many cases, with unrelated, non-tenant occupants, too, so long as a tenant (or tenant's spouse) occupies the unit as a primary residence.

The Roommate Law applies across the board. It covers:

- every tenant with a lease or rental agreement, including all rent-stabilized tenants, and
- all rent-controlled tenants, even if they have no current lease (RPL § 235-f (1)(a)).

OHP Form AMO-1
(Rev. 11/94)

*(FOR DEPARTMENT USE ONLY)*

Return this form to Chief Inspector of appropriate Borough only if signed by Department (otherwise tenant is to return form to managing agent making demand).

Date Requested: _____     _____
                                                        Chief Inspector or Deputy

Address: _____     Borough _____ Badge No. _____

**THE CITY OF NEW YORK**
**DEPARTMENT OF HOUSING PRESERVATION AND DEVELOPMENT**
**DIVISION OF CODE ENFORCEMENT**

# Demand

**(PURSUANT TO SECTION 27-2075 OF THE HOUSING MAINTENANCE CODE)**

1. Mailing Address of Landlord:
*(Complete only if owner is making demand)*

Name _____
(Managing agent, Natural person only, registered with the Division of Code Enforcement)

Tel. No. ( ___ ) _____

Business Address _____

Borough & Zip Code _____

2. Mailing Address of Tenant:

Name _____ Apt. No. _____

Address _____

Borough & Zip Code _____

3. Address of Building _____
*(Complete only if different from Mailing Address of Tenant)*

4. Multiple Dwelling Registration No. _____

**TO THE ABOVE TENANT**

PLEASE TAKE NOTICE, that pursuant to Section 27-2075 of the Housing Maintenance Code, Subchapter III, Article 4 of Title 27 of the Administrative Code of the City of New York, the Department or the owner of a dwelling may require a tenant to submit an affidavit setting forth the names and relationship of all persons living in an apartment and the ages of all such persons under the age of twenty-one years.

Failure to comply with the request may subject you to criminal penalties, and other sanctions pursuant to the Housing Maintenance Code.

NOTE TO TENANT: This affidavit must be completed, notarized and returned to the party requesting the information. If the owner is the requesting party, his name and address is listed above. If the Department is the requesting party, return this form to the borough office listed above.

**AFFIDAVIT**

STATE OF NEW YORK   } ss:
County of

_____ , being duly sworn, deposes and says:
*(Print Name)*

1. That (s)he is the tenant occupying apartment _____ of _____
                                                                *(Address of Building)*

2. That the following adults (21 years of age or older) reside within the aforesaid apartment:

3. That the following minors (under 21 years of age) reside within the aforesaid apartment:

| Name | Relationship | Name | Age | Relationship |
|---|---|---|---|---|
| _____ | _____ | _____ | ___ | _____ |
| _____ | _____ | _____ | ___ | _____ |
| _____ | _____ | _____ | ___ | _____ |
| _____ | _____ | _____ | ___ | _____ |
| _____ | _____ | _____ | ___ | _____ |
| _____ | _____ | _____ | ___ | _____ |
| _____ | _____ | _____ | ___ | _____ |
| _____ | _____ | _____ | ___ | _____ |

Sworn to me before this _____ day of _____ , 19 ___     _____
                                                                        *(Signature of Tenant)*

_____
*(Notary Public)*

The only tenants who aren't covered by the Roommate Law are those who don't use their unit as a primary residence (see Section 4, below).

⚠ **Don't try to reduce or limit a tenant's apartment sharing rights.** Clauses in rental agreements or leases that attempt to waive or modify a tenant's Roommate Law rights are null and void. (RPL § 235-f (7).)

Under the Roommate Law, tenants don't need your prior consent to ask an immediate family member or an additional occupant to move in. Nor do you get the opportunity to put a family member or other occupant through your screening process. Hopefully, good tenants will bring in good people. But if you're faced with an occupant who is creating a nuisance or using the unit illegally, you can direct the tenant to remove the occupant or face termination and eviction. (Chapter 13 explains how to terminate a month-to-month tenancy; Chapter 15 covers terminating tenants with leases and rent-regulated units.)

The Roommate Law requires tenants to notify you within 30 days after anyone new moves in or within 30 days of your request for information about occupants living in the rental unit. (Section B3, above, explains how you can request occupant information from tenants.)

While the Roommate Law prohibits any "unlawful" occupancy restrictions by landlords, there are some limits you can impose on apartment sharing. In the following sections, we'll look at some of the ways you can legally restrict apartment sharing in your building, without running into legal trouble.

## 2. How Many Roommates and Family Members May Live in a Unit?

The number of occupants allowed under the Roommate Law depends on how many tenants signed the lease or rental agreement.

### a. When Only One Tenant Is on the Lease

If you sign a lease or rental agreement with one tenant, you must permit the tenant to share the unit with members of the tenant's immediate family, plus one additional occupant and the occupant's dependent children, so long as the tenant occupies the unit as a primary residence.

> EXAMPLE: Linda signs a lease for a one-bedroom unit. The following month, Linda invites her boyfriend Ralph to move into the unit, along with Ralph's five-year old twins, Jet and Sky. You may not object to this arrangement, since Linda is entitled to share her unit with an additional occupant (Ralph) and the occupant's dependent children (Jet and Sky).

### b. When Two or More Tenants Are on the Lease

If you sign a lease or rental agreement with two or more co-tenants, you must permit members of each co-tenant's immediate family to share the rental unit. And, if one or more of the co-tenants moves out, you must permit one or more additional occupants to move in, provided that the total number of tenants and additional occupants actually living in the unit (not counting the occupant's dependent children) does not exceed the total number of tenants listed on the lease or rental agreement. In addition, at least one tenant (or a tenant's spouse) must continue to occupy the unit as a primary residence.

> EXAMPLE: Artie, Max and Murphy sign a lease as co-tenants on a two-bedroom unit. Murphy quickly becomes disenchanted with his co-tenants' housekeeping habits and moves out. Artie and Max then invite Helga to move in, along with her daughter Brittany. Two months later, Daisy, Max's mom moves in too. You may not object to this arrangement either. Because Daisy is Max's immediate family member, she may share the unit with her son. And because the total number of tenants and occupants

(Artie, Max and Helga) does not exceed three, the total number of tenants on the lease, Helga and Helga's dependent child Brittany may share the unit with Artie, Max and Daisy.

### c. Overcrowding Statutes Put Legal Limits on Occupancy

While this may sound as though an infinite number of family members and other occupants may share a rental unit, there are limits. State law permits landlords to restrict occupancy in order to comply with local laws, regulations or ordinances that deal with health and safety. (RPL § 235-f(8).) Many localities have "overcrowding" ordinances that limit the number of people who can lawfully occupy a rental unit, based on the unit's available square footage. For example, NYC Adm. Code § 27-2075 sets the maximum number of persons who may occupy an apartment by dividing the apartment's total livable floor area by 80 square feet. And the Rochester Property Code § 90-8 requires every unit to have 120 square feet of habitable floor space for the first occupant, plus 70 square feet of habitable floor space for each additional occupant.

Local health and safety laws that limit occupancy based on a rental unit's size are a landlord's best weapon against the effects of the Roommate Law. Contact your local code enforcement office for information about overcrowding laws or ordinances that apply where your property is located.

### 3. Limit Sharing to Immediate Family Members

There are other ways besides the welcome sanity of local overcrowding laws to curb the number of roommates in a given rental unit. You have a powerful tool right in your word processor: the lease or rental agreement. Here's how to use it.

The Roommate Law permits tenants to share their units with members of their immediate family. But it doesn't define the term "immediate family." For non-regulated units, courts look to the rental agreement for the meaning of the term "immediate

family." (See, for example, *Mitchell Gardens No. 1 Co-Op Corp. v. Cataldo*, 175 Misc.2d 493, 670 N.Y.S.2d 190 (App.T., 1998).) Our form agreements (Clause 3 in Chapter 2) define "immediate family members" as the tenant's spouse, a sibling, child, stepchild, parent or parent-in-law.

If a tenant's lease or rental agreement doesn't define the term "immediate family member," a judge could end up doing it for you. And the judge's definition could be generous and include relatives such as cousins, aunts or uncles.

**Rent Regulations define "immediate family."** While the Roommate Law does not define the term "immediate family," New York's rent regulations do. Under rent stabilization and rent control, immediate family members include one's "husband, wife, son, daughter, stepson, stepdaughter, father, mother, stepfather, stepmother, brother, sister, grandfather, grandmother, grandson, granddaughter, father-in-law, mother-in-law, son-in-law or daughter-in-law ... ." (9 NYCRR §§ 2500.2(m); 2520.6(n); 2104.5(a)(1); 2204.5(a).) While there's no written requirement that landlords apply this definition when deciding whether an additional occupant qualifies as a rent-regulated tenant's immediate family member under the Roommate Law, it does provide some guidance to judges. In other words, it would be prudent to apply this definition when dealing with rent-regulated tenants.

Remember that this definition is different from the definition of "family member" for apartment succession purposes. (Chapter 14, Section H, discusses a family member's succession rights to rent-controlled and rent-stabilized apartments.)

Here's an example that illustrates how you can legally limit a tenant's right to share her rental unit with immediate family members.

EXAMPLE: Paul invites his cousin, and his cousin's wife to move into his two-bedroom unit, which he already shares with his co-tenant wife, Rena, and their child. You may object to this arrangement, on the ground that it violates the occupancy restriction in Paul's and Rena's lease. While Paul's cousin is clearly related to

Paul, his cousin doesn't qualify as an immediate family member. And because there are two tenants on the lease who are both in occupancy, neither Paul nor his wife are entitled under the Roommate Law to move in a non-tenant "roommate" occupant.

**Let tenants know which family members are welcome.** Use your Move-In Letter to Tenants to describe which relatives a tenant may share the rental unit with under the Roommate Law. You can't expect your tenants to know which relatives are included in the definition. And doing so may reduce the number of unauthorized occupants in your building. (Chapter 7, Section C, discusses how to put together a Move-In Letter for your tenants.)

## 4. Don't Permit Sharing by Tenants Who Live Elsewhere

To be entitled to share a rental unit with immediate family members or a roommate, a tenant, or the tenant's spouse, must use the unit as a "primary residence." (RPL § 235-f (3).) Tenants who spend most of their time at another residence aren't entitled to move non-tenants into their rental unit unless their lease permits it.

EXAMPLE: Phoebe signs a lease on a Manhattan apartment that limits occupancy of the unit "to the tenant, immediate family members and additional occupants as defined in and only in accordance with RPL Section 235-f." Phoebe uses the apartment only when she's in town for a social event or appointment. Phoebe lives in a large house in Greenwich, Connecticut, where she raises her family, pays taxes, registers her cars and votes. Phoebe asks Mike, her Manhattan landlord, for an extra set of keys for Millie, her new roommate. Mike says no, and reminds Phoebe that under the terms of her lease, she can only share the unit with family members. Since Phoebe's primary residence is in Connecticut, the Roommate Law does not cover her. So Mike can prohibit Millie from moving into Phoebe's unit.

**Rent-stabilized and rent-controlled tenants who maintain a primary residence elsewhere are subject to eviction.** Rent-regulated tenants are legally required to use their apartments as their primary residence. You may terminate a rent-controlled tenant who doesn't occupy the rental unit as a primary residence. And you may refuse to renew a rent-stabilized tenant's lease if the tenant actually lives somewhere else. Chapter 14 covers your right to terminate rent-regulated tenancies on this ground. Chapter 15 details notices of non-renewal and termination notices.

If you suspect that a non-regulated tenant who has moved in additional occupants actually lives elsewhere, explain to the tenant that only primary residents are entitled to share their rental units. Hopefully, the tenant will arrange for the extra occupant to move out. But in some cases, you'll need to get tough and to take steps to evict the tenant for violating the occupancy clause of the lease or rental agreement. To determine whether a rental unit is a tenant's primary residence, judges presiding over eviction proceedings look at the address listed on various records belonging to the tenant, including the tenant's driver's license, car registration, voter registration, credit card records, bank statements, utility bills and tax returns. (*Pendias v. 3 East 69th Street Assoc.*, 119 A.D.2d 467, 500 N.Y.S.2d 679 (1st Dep't 1986).) Chapter 14, Section E, covers the details of terminating a rent-regulated tenancy when a tenant has failed to use the premises as a primary residence.

## 5. Don't Permit NYC Rent-Stabilized Tenants to Profiteer from Roommates

There are legal limits on the amount of rent a rent-stabilized tenant may charge her roommate. The rule is that tenants may not charge unrelated, non-tenant roommates a rent that exceeds a "proportionate share "of the legal regulated rent for the unit. (RSC § 2525.7.)

A roommate's proportionate share is calculated by dividing the unit's regulated rent by the total number of tenants and occupants residing in the unit. The tenant's spouse, family members and dependent children are not counted as occupants under the formula.

> EXAMPLE: Lauren, a rent-stabilized tenant, shares her two-bedroom apartment with her ten-year old daughter, Amanda, and her friend Ben. Lauren's legal rent is $1650. To compute Ben's proportionate share of the monthly rent, Lauren must divide the monthly rent ($1650) by the total number of tenants and occupants living in the unit (two). (Since Amanda is Lauren's family member, she isn't counted as an occupant.) The maximum rent Lauren may collect from Ben is $825 per month.

If a rent-stabilized tenant is charging a roommate more than his proportionate share of rent, the landlord may terminate the lease and begin eviction proceedings against both the tenant and the roommate. While that may not seem fair to the roommate, that is how judges have interpreted this rule. (Chapter 14, Section E7, details this ground for eviction. Chapter 15 explains the type of notice required to terminate a tenancy on this ground.)

## 6. Increasing the Rent for Additional Roommates

For landlords of rent-regulated units, additional occupants can translate into additional rent. You can get a rent hike if a rent-controlled tenant moves in an additional occupant, provided the occupant isn't a member of the tenant's immediate family. Subsection a, below, explains how to apply. And if a rent-stabilized tenant asks to add a roommate's name to the lease at renewal time, saying yes could entitle you to take a hefty vacancy rent increase. Subsection b, below, explains how.

⚠ **Never accept rent from non-tenant occupants.** Don't demand, collect or accept any rent from a person who is not listed on the lease or rental agreement as a tenant. Doing so can entitle that person to certain tenant rights that she wouldn't otherwise be entitled to. For details, see Section B1, above.

### a. Apply for Rent Increase If Rent-Controlled Tenant Gets Roommate

When your rent-controlled tenant brings in a roommate who is not a member of the tenant's immediate family, you can apply to the New York Division of Housing and Community Renewal (DHCR) for a rent-increase. (9 NYCRR § 2102.3(b)(3); 9 NYCRR §§ 2202.3(f)(1), 2202.6.) The rent increase is available to landlords of rent-controlled units within and outside New York City. Chapter 4, Section A, explains how to get copies of DHCR forms.

To apply for the rent increase, file an Owner's Application for Increase of Maximum Rent (Increased Occupancy) with the DHCR (DHCR Form RA-33.3). A sample is shown below. Instructions for filing this form are on the form itself. The amount of the rent hike is determined by the agency and can be as high as 10%. The rent hike isn't permanent, though. It remains in effect only as long as the roommate or her replacement lives with the tenant in the unit.

### b. Collect Rent Hike for Adding Roommate to Rent-Stabilized Lease

At lease renewal time, rent-stabilized tenants often ask to add a roommate to their lease as a co-tenant. In some cases, it pays for you to consent to the new co-tenant. According to the DHCR, you may issue a "vacancy" lease to the current rent-stabilized tenant and her new co-tenant. That entitles you to collect a hefty vacancy rent increase. (See, for example, *839 West End Avenue, Apt. 4D*, DHCR Adm. Rev. Docket No. DH 410524-RO (11/17/94).) For details on calculating vacancy rent hikes for rent-stabilized units, see Chapter 4, Section A5.

## 7. Make Sure Non-Tenant Occupants Leave When Tenant Moves Out

When a tenant moves out, any family members or roommates living with the tenant must move out too, unless they've signed a lease or rental agreement. (RPL § 235-f (6).) Non-tenant occupants do not have any independent right to continue living in

| STATE OF NEW YORK DIVISION OF HOUSING AND COMMUNITY RENEWAL OFFICE OF RENT ADMINISTRATION | Gertz Plaza 92-31 Union Hall Street Jamaica, NY 11433 | Docket No. (For Office Use Only) |
| --- | --- | --- |

**Owner's Application For Increase Of Maximum Rent (Increased Occupancy)**
(See Section 2202.6 of the Regulations printed below)

MAILING ADDRESS OF TENANT:

Name: _____
Number and Street: _____  Apt. No. _____
City, _____
State, Zip Code: _____

MAILING ADDRESS OF OWNER:

Name: _____
Number and Street: _____
City, _____
State, Zip Code: _____

Subject Building: _____

(Number and Street)          (Apt. No.)          (City, State, Zip Code)

1. The maximum rent for the housing accommodations is: $ _____ per _____

2. Amount of increase requested for the housing accommodations is: $ _____ per _____

3. Date tenant first took occupancy: _____
(Month)          (Day)          (Year)

**Instructions:** An original and one copy of this application and accompanying documents, if any, must be filed with the Borough Office by delivery or mailing. Before filing the application, be sure to sign and date the application on the reverse side.

An increase in the maximum rent is requested on the following grounds:

There has been since March 1, 1959 a subletting without the written consent of the owner or an increase in the number of adult occupants who are not members of the immediate family of the tenant, and the owner has not been compensated by adjustment of the maximum rent by lease or order of the Administrator or pursuant to the State Rent Act or the Federal Act. (Section 2202.6 of the Regulations.)

**Statement of Owner**

4. (Check either A or B and give the information requested.)
There has been since March 1, 1959:

☐ A. A subletting without the written consent of the owner, and the owner has not been compensated by adjustment of the maximum rent by lease or pursuant to the State Rent Act or the Federal Act.

☐ B. An increase in the number of adult occupants who are not members of the immediate family of the tenant, and the owner has not been compensated by adjustment of the maximum rent by lease or order of the Administrator or pursuant to the Federal Act.

- 1 -

RA-33.3 (8/92)

On March 1, 1959 the number of adult occupants who were not members of the immediate family of the tenant was _____ persons.

Today the number of adult occupants who are not members of the immediate family of the tenant is _____ persons.

5. **Additional Information:**

Set forth in detail in the space provided below all additional facts necessary to establish that an increase of the maximum collectible rent is warranted under this section of the Regulations.

**Note:** If an increase in the maximum collectible rent had previously been granted because of such additional occupants or subtenants, no further adjustment of the maximum collectible rent will be granted under this section of the Regulations.

**Affirmation**

I have read the application and I affirm under the penalties provided by law that the contents are true of my own knowledge.

It is not necessary that the application be sworn to, but false statements may subject you to the penalties provided by law.

_____
(Signature of Owner)

Dated _____ 19 _____

- 2 -

RA-33.3 (8/92)

**Owner's Application for Increase of Maximum Rent (Increased Occupancy)**

the rental unit after the tenant vacates, nor do they earn any tenancy rights by sharing the unit with the tenant.

If a tenant's family member or roommate refuses to leave after the tenant moves out, you have two options. You could offer the occupant a lease or rental agreement for the unit (with a rent increase, if the market will bear it). Or you could serve the occupant with a legal notice called a "Ten-Day Notice to Quit." This notice requires the occupant to vacate the rental unit within ten days after the notice is served or face eviction. If the occupant ignores your notice to quit, you can begin eviction proceedings to remove the occupant from the rental unit.

 **Some non-tenant occupants are protected from eviction from rent-controlled and rent-stabilized units under "succession laws."** Certain occupants have so-called "succession rights" which entitle them to a renewal lease, if the unit is rent-stabilized, or to protection from eviction if the unit is rent-controlled. To qualify, the occupant must be a "family member" or demonstrate a "financial and emotional interdependence" with the tenant. Chapter 14 details the way in which rent-regulated units may be "passed on" under the succession rules.

## D. Sublets and the Sublet Law

Ideally, you want to rent to tenants who will stay a long time, or at least the entire term of the lease. But despite your best efforts, you will encounter tenants who, for various reasons will want to leave before the expiration of their lease. It's fairly straightforward if the tenant wants to completely end a lease (see "Consider Releasing Tenant From Lease," below). But what about tenants who want to leave temporarily—say, to care for an ailing relative or to pursue a job-related opportunity—and then return and reoccupy the rental unit? Must you permit tenants to sublet their units while they're away?

---

### What's a Sublet?

A sublet is a rental arrangement in which your tenant agrees to rent his unit for a specific time period to another person, called a subtenant. Under this arrangement, your original tenant keeps the right to return and reoccupy the rental unit when the arrangement ends.

Usually, your tenant signs an agreement with the subtenant called a sublease. The subtenant is bound by both the terms of the sublease and by the terms of the tenant's lease with you. Your tenant can enforce the sublease in the same way that you can enforce the lease. If the subtenant violates the sublease, your tenant can sue to evict the subtenant.

You have no direct legal relationship with the subtenant. So if a subtenant violates the lease, you must act against your tenant. To avoid a termination of the tenancy, your tenant must then take action against the subtenant. If the tenant doesn't act and the lease violation continues, you can terminate the lease—which causes the sublease to lapse—and sue to evict the tenant and the subtenant.

---

Sublets are often a pain in the neck for landlords. Besides the obvious hassles of dealing with extra people moving in and out, you can't enforce the lease against the subtenant without getting the tenant involved. This means, for instance, that you may not sue the subtenant for money damages if he leaves the place a mess and the security deposit is insufficient to cover your loss. You must sue the original tenant. And for rent-stabilized units, permitting sublets translates into a far lower rent increase than you could get if the tenant permanently moved out instead. (Section 5d, below, details the "surcharge" you can collect when you permit a rent-stabilized tenant to sublet. Chapter 4 covers vacancy rent increases for rent-stabilized units.)

## Consider Releasing Tenant From Lease

Suppose a tenant asks to sublet her apartment for six months while she is out of town. If the proposed subtenant passes your standard screening process, consider offering to release the tenant from the lease and signing a new lease with the proposed subtenant. This strategy may work if the tenant really wants to get out from under the lease early. A lease with a new tenant gives you the opportunity to boost the rent for the unit. And it gives you the most direct legal relationship with the new tenant.

The way to accomplish this is to first release your original tenant from her obligations under the lease by having her sign a Lease Surrender Agreement. You'll find a sample in Chapter 14, Section G. Then begin a new tenancy with the substitute tenant in the same way that you begin any tenancy: sign a lease, present a move-in letter, and so on.

In some cases, you can prohibit subletting. Month-to-month rental agreements may ban subletting, as may leases for single family houses, duplexes and small buildings with fewer than four units. Our form agreements (Clause 10 in Chapter 2) prohibit subletting in these instances. But despite the downsides, there are three situations when you must consent to a tenant's request to sublet:

- When a tenant has no lease or rental agreement, or has a lease or rental agreement that is silent on the issue of subletting, the tenant has a right to sublet without your prior consent.
- When the tenant's lease or rental agreement permits subletting and any applicable qualifications, such as getting your consent, have been met.
- When a tenant's lease prohibits subletting, but the tenant is nevertheless entitled to sublet under New York's "Sublet Law" (RPL § 226-b).

The Sublet Law gives eligible tenants in buildings with four or more units the right to sublet—even if the lease prohibits it. But there are strings attached: 1) the tenant needs your consent to sublet, and

| | **Comparing Subleases and Assignments** | |
|---|---|---|
| | **Sublease** | **Assignment** |
| **Rent** | Subtenant is liable to the tenant, not to the landlord. Tenant is liable to landlord. | New tenant (assignee) is liable to the landlord. Old tenant is liable if new tenant doesn't pay. |
| **Damage to premises** | Tenant is liable for damage caused by subtenant. | Absent an agreement to the contrary, old tenant is not liable for damage caused by new tenant (assignee). |
| **Violations of lease** | Landlord can't sue subtenant for money losses caused by violating lease, because subtenant never signed lease. Subtenant can't sue landlord for lease violations, either. | New tenant (assignee) and landlord are bound by all terms in lease except those that were purely personal to the landlord or old tenant. |
| **Eviction** | Landlord can sue to evict subtenant for any reason old tenant could have been evicted. But to evict subtenant, landlord must also evict old tenant. | Landlord can sue to evict new tenant (assignee) for any reason old tenant could have been evicted. |

2) you can't withhold your consent without a very good reason.

Section 1, below, describes which tenants are eligible for coverage under the Sublet Law. Section 2 details the manner in which eligible tenants must request permission to sublet. And the balance of this section examines your options when faced with a sublet request, including special limits you can place on a rent-stabilized tenant's ability to sublet.

Assignments are covered in Section E, below.

## 1. What Tenants Are Covered by the New York Sublet Law?

The Sublet Law covers all New York tenants who:
- have a current lease for the unit, and
- live in a building with four or more residential units.

The Sublet Law protects rent-stabilized tenants throughout the state since they have current leases. However, special restrictions apply. (See Section 5, below, for a rundown on two important limitations on a rent-stabilized tenant's right to sublet.)

The following groups of tenants are not covered by the Sublet Law:

- **Tenants with leases in properties with three or fewer units.** For these tenants, the lease governs the right to sublet. If the lease is silent on the issue of subletting, the tenant is presumed to have the right to sublet the apartment.
- **Tenants with periodic rental agreements, such as month-to-month tenants.** Their right to sublet is governed by their written rental agreement, if they have one. Our form rental agreement prohibits sublets for month-to-month tenants without your prior consent (see Clause 10, Chapter 2).
- **Rent-controlled tenants, unless they have a current lease.** Leases for most rent-controlled tenants expired long ago. Landlords don't need a valid reason to refuse to a sublet request from a rent-controlled tenant without a current lease.

## 2. What Tenant's Sublet Request Must Cover

Tenants who are eligible to sublet under the Sublet Law must first ask your permission. The Sublet Law requires tenants to follow a set procedure when making a request to sublet and to furnish you with particular information about the proposed sublet. If the tenant doesn't make the sublet request the right way, you can reject it. That's why it's essential for you to know exactly how the tenant's sublet request must be made.

To be valid, the tenant's sublet request must be in writing and be sent to you by certified mail, return receipt requested, no less than 30 days prior to the proposed sublet. The tenant's request must include the following information about the proposed sublet:
- the length of the proposed sublease
- the name of the proposed subtenant
- the business and home address of proposed subtenant
- the tenant's reason for subletting
- the tenant's address during the sublease term
- written consent from any co-tenant or guarantor of the lease, and
- a copy of the tenant's lease, attached to a copy of the proposed sublease, acknowledged by both the tenant and subtenant as being a true copy of the sublease. (RPL §226-b (2)(b).)

## 3. Responding to the Sublet Request

The amount of time you have to respond to a tenant's sublet request depends on your proposed course of action and whether you need additional information to make a decision. After reviewing the request, you have three options. You can:
1. **Accept or reject the sublet within 30 days.** If the tenant's sublet request contains all the information you need to make an informed decision about the sublet, you must send the tenant a notice either accepting or rejecting the sublet request within 30 days of the date the tenant mailed the request to you. (Section 6, below, explains what your rejection letter might say.)

2. **Ask the tenant for more information about the sublet within ten days.** You must send a request for more information within ten days after the tenant sends you the written request to sublet. Section 4, below, tells you what information you may ask about the sublet. Once the tenant sends you the information you requested, you have 30 days from the date the tenant sent you additional information to consent to or reject the sublet.

3. **Reject sublet request as defective within ten days.** Because the sublet rules are complicated, it's easy for tenants to make mistakes. Technically, you can reject a sublet request if it omits required information. But the most practical response, and the one we recommend, is to simply ask the tenant for the missing information (as well as any other information you need to make your decision) within ten days after the mailing of the tenant's request to sublet.

**Ignoring the time deadlines can be fatal.** It's critical for landlords to follow the time deadlines when responding to a tenant's sublet request. If you miss the ten-day deadline to request more information, you must make your decision based on the information that the tenant sends you. If you miss the 30-day deadline to reject, it's as though you consented, and the tenant may go ahead with the sublet.

## 4. Requesting Additional Information From the Tenant

When you get a tenant's sublet request, your best bet is to evaluate the proposed subtenant by exactly the same standards that you use in selecting any other new tenant: financial stability, credit history, references and other criteria described in Chapter 1. If the prospective subtenant passes your tests, consent to the sublet. If he fails the test that you apply to all potential tenants, you will be legally justified in saying "No." (We explain how to reject a sublet in Section 6, below.)

But chances are, you won't be able to make an informed decision about the subtenant based only on the information that's included in the tenant's sublet request. Fortunately, the sublet law lets you demand additional information about the proposed subtenant's finances, rental history and the terms of the sublease. Before reaching a final decision on a sublet request, we recommend taking this extra step. It's a good way to screen out potential trouble.

To request additional information, you must, within ten days after the tenant makes the sublet request, send the tenant a written list of questions about the sublet. While you're not required to send your request for additional information to the tenant by certified mail, it's a good idea to do it anyway. You can use your certified mail receipt as proof of the date you responded to the tenant's sublet request.

Your request should begin with a letter informing the tenant that the Sublet Law authorizes you to ask the tenant for more information about the proposed subtenant (see the sample Letter Seeking Additional Sublet Information, below). Your letter can list specific questions about the proposed subtenant's finances and rental history. Or, to save time, you may attach a rental application form to your letter, and direct the tenant to have the proposed subtenant complete and sign it. (You'll want the proposed subtenant's written consent if you want to obtain an investigative report on the subtenant. A sample authorization form and rental application you can use for this purpose are in Chapter 1.

In addition to the rental application, you may include a list of questions for the tenant to answer. Ask for the tenant's address and phone number during the proposed sublease period. You'll need an address to send rent bills and other notices to the original tenant during the sublease period. And you'll need a telephone number to contact the original tenant in case of an emergency.

If the rental unit is rent-stabilized, you should ask some special questions about the tenant's primary residence, and the tenant's intent to return to the unit to use it as a primary residence at the end of the sublease term. Section 5, below, supplies some sample questions on these points.

**Avoid burdensome requests for additional information.** The Sublet Law specifically prohibits landlords from making "unduly burden-

## Letter Seeking Additional Sublet Information

November 10, 200x

Paul Wiggins

450 East 51st Street, Apt. 15-C

New York, NY 10021


Dear     Paul

I have received your request to sublet your apartment, dated _____ November 3, 200x _____.
The New York Sublet Law (Real Property Law Section 226-b) permits landlords to ask for information in addition to that submitted by the tenant in the sublet request.

Accordingly, please instruct your proposed subtenant to complete and sign the attached rental application. In addition, please provide answers to the following questions:

1. Where will you be residing during the term of the sublease?

2. At what telephone number may we contact you during the term of the sublet?

3. Where should rent bills be sent during the term of the sublet?

4. Do you intend to return and reoccupy the rental unit when the sublease ends?


Upon receipt of the requested information, your sublet request will be processed.

Sincerely,

*John L. Hiatt*

Landlord/Manager

450 East 51st Street, Apt. 1-A

New York, NY 10021

some" requests for additional information about the sublet. Avoid asking repetitive or irrelevant questions, or requiring the tenant to fill out 20-page question-naires. Tactics like these, which are intended to discourage the tenant from subletting, can backfire.

A sample cover letter requesting more information about a tenant's sublet request is shown above. Fill in any questions that are relevant.

The Forms CD includes the Letter Seeking Additional Sublet Information, and Appendix IV includes a blank, tear-out copy.

## 5. Special Rules for Rent-Stabilized Tenants

Landlords of rent-stabilized units within and outside of New York City need to know about two special sublet rules, discussed below, which operate to limit a rent-stabilized tenant's right to sublet.

### a. Primary Residence Rule

In order to sublet, a rent-stabilized tenant must:
- use the rental unit as a primary residence when the request is made, and
- intend to return to the unit and occupy it as a primary residence at the end of the sublease term. (9 NYCRR § 2505.7(a); 9 NYCRR § 2525.6(a).)

A tenant's "primary residence" is generally considered to be the dwelling in which the tenant has an ongoing and physical nexus. That means the place where the tenant actually spends the night more often than not. (Tenants who fail to use their rent-stabilized apartment as a primary residence are not entitled to renewal leases, and are subject to eviction at the end of the current lease term. For details, see Chapter 14.)

You may reject a rent-stabilized tenant's sublet request if you have good reason to believe that the tenant does not use the rental unit as a primary residence, or that the tenant does not intend to use the rental unit as his primary residence at the end of the lease term.

Here are two examples that illustrate this point.

EXAMPLE 1: Peter and Mae rent a rent-stabilized unit on the Upper West Side. After their baby arrives, they realize that their one-bedroom apartment is too small. So the family buys a spacious three-bedroom co-op apartment on the East Side. Peter and Mae move all of their belongings out of their one-bedroom unit and then request permission to sublet it. Their landlord may reasonably refuse to consent to the sublet. Peter and Mae's primary residence is at their new, East Side apartment. They have no real intention of squeezing back into their one-bedroom unit at the end of the sublease.

EXAMPLE 2: Emma, an investment banker, lives in a rent-stabilized apartment in Brooklyn Heights. Emma gets transferred to Tokyo for a 14-month job assignment. Emma wants to hold onto her apartment, and feels lucky when she finds a suitable subtenant who is willing to sublet it for the 14-month period that Emma will be in Tokyo. If Emma's subtenant meets the landlord's screening criteria, Emma's landlord may not reasonably refuse to consent to Emma's request to sublet her rental unit while in Tokyo. Emma fully intends to move back into her apartment when she returns from Japan, and use it as her primary residence.

### b. Tenants Can't Continuously Sublet

The Sublet Law prohibits tenants from continuously subletting their apartments. The rule is that a rent-stabilized tenant can't sublet for more than two years, including the term of the proposed sublet, out of the four-year period preceding the termination date of the proposed sublease. (9 NYCRR § 2505.7(c); 9 NYCRR § 2525.6(c).) The term of the sublease may, however, extend beyond the prime tenant's lease term. That's because rent-stabilized tenants have a "vested" right to a renewal lease. A sublet does not affect the tenant's right to be offered a renewal lease.

**EXAMPLE:** Ravi asks his landlord for permission to sublet his rent-stabilized apartment for two years starting January 1, 2003. Ravi's lease expires on December 31, 2003. The two-year sublet would expire December 31, 2004. Unless Ravi has already sublet the apartment for any period of time between January 1, 2001, and December 31, 2002, his landlord may not refuse to consent to Ravi's request on the ground that the proposed sublet exceeds the limit.

### c. Request Additional Information About Primary Residence and Prior Sublets

When a rent-stabilized tenant requests permission to sublet, you may request additional information from the tenant about the proposed sublet before making a final decision. We discuss the advantages and mechanics of requesting additional information on sublets in Section 4, above, including the importance of not making "unduly burdensome" requests for additional information.

Use this opportunity to ask your tenant questions about his or her primary residence, and her intention to return to the apartment at the end of the proposed sublet term. Also ask about other sublets during the prior four-year period. (See "Sample Questions for Rent-Stabilized Tenants Wishing to Sublet," below.) If it turns out that the tenant has already moved to a new permanent residence, or is planning such a move, you can refuse a tenant's request to sublet on this ground.

---

### Sample Questions for Rent-Stabilized Tenants Wishing to Sublet

- State in detail why you are requesting to sublet (employment, vacation, etc.).
- Are there any other dwellings you own or lease? If so, please provide the addresses and the names of any occupants.
- Will you be removing all of or most the furnishings from the subject apartment before the sublease begins?
- List the primary dwelling address where you will reside during the sublease period.
- Is the primary dwelling address where you will reside during the period of the sublease a co-op, condominium, private home or rental?
- Who will own or rent the primary dwelling address which you will occupy during the sublet period?
- Where do you intend to live at the end of the sublease?
- Have you sublet the subject apartment during the last four-year period? If so, supply the dates that the subletting occurred, the rent charged, and the name of the subtenant.
- Does the subtenant have the option to renew the sublease for an additional term? If yes, state the term of the subtenant's renewal option.

### d. NYC Landlords May Collect Sublet Surcharge During Sublet Term

If you approve a rent-stabilized tenant's sublet which commences during the term of a renewal lease (as opposed to the tenant's initial rent-stabilized lease), you may collect a sublet surcharge from the tenant. The amount of the surcharge is equal to the NYC Rent Guidelines Board "sublet allowance" in effect on the date the sublease begins. In early 2003, the allowance equalled 10% of the legal rent. The surcharge may remain in effect only as long as the sublease in effect. You must discontinue collecting the surcharge at the end of the sublease. (9 NYCRR § 2525.6(e).) (For more information about Rent Guidelines Board vacancy allowances, see Chapter 4, Section A5.)

⚠ Landlords outside New York City are not entitled to collect a sublet surcharge from their rent-stabilized tenants.

### e. Rent-Stabilized Tenants May Collect Surcharge for Fully Furnished Units

Tenants who rent their rent-stabilized units fully furnished may collect a rent surcharge from the subtenant. (NYCRR §§ 2504. 7(b); 2525.6(b).) The surcharge may not exceed ten percent of the legal rent for the apartment. The surcharge is payable to the tenant, not the landlord. You may not reject a sublet application because the tenant intends to charge the subtenant a surcharge of ten percent or less for a fully furnished unit.

## 6. Making a Final Decision

Within 30 days after a tenant requests permission to sublet, or submits additional information that you've requested, you must notify the tenant that you're consenting to or rejecting the proposed sublet. A landlord's failure to respond to the tenant within 30 days constitutes consent to the sublet. (RPL § 226-b (2)(c).)

### a. Reasonable Grounds for Rejection

The Sublet Law says that you can't unreasonably withhold consent to an eligible tenant's sublet request. You can only reject if you have reasonable grounds for refusal, such as valid concerns about the subtenant's financial stability, credit history, rental history or personal references. (The legitimate, nondiscriminatory grounds for rejecting rental applicants described in Chapter 1, Section B, are reasonable grounds upon which you could reject a proposed subtenant.) If the tenant is rent-stabilized, you could also reasonably reject the sublet request on the basis of prior sublets or primary residence. (See Section 5, above, for details.)

If you withhold consent, you must state your reason or reasons for rejecting the tenant's request. Courts have consistently ruled that a landlord's failure to state a reason for the refusal of a sublet request is, in essence, consent to the sublet. (See, for example, *Conrad v. Third Sutton Realty Co.*, 81 A.D.2d 50, 439 N.Y.S.2d 376 (1st Dep't 1981).)

If the tenant challenges your sublet rejection, you may have to prove to a court that your reasons were legitimate and well founded. Your best bet is to evaluate the proposed subtenant by exactly the same standards that you use in evaluating any other new tenant: financial stability, credit history, references and other criteria described in Chapter 1. If the prospective subtenant passes your tests, consent to the sublet. If he fails the test that you apply to all potential tenants, you will be legally justified in saying "No."

### Don't Discriminate Illegally in Handling Sublet and Assignment Requests

If you turn down a proposed sublet or assignment for an illegal reason (racial discrimination against the subtenant, for example), you are vulnerable to a lawsuit under federal, state, and New York City law (see Chapter 1, Section C, for an extended discussion of illegal discrimination).

### b. Notifying Tenant of Sublet Rejection

If you have reasonable grounds to reject a tenant's sublet request, you must notify the tenant in writing. Prepare a letter setting out specific reasons why you're rejecting the sublet. State as many possible rejection grounds as possible. That way, your refusal is more apt to withstand judicial scrutiny, if necessary.

A sample letter rejecting a sublet request, in this case, a rent-stabilized tenant, is shown below.

⚠ **Sign rejection letters yourself.** Some tenants have successfully challenged the validity of sublet rejection letters because they were signed by

## Sample Sublet Rejection Letter

December 10, 200x

Paul Wiggins
450 East 51st Street
New York, NY 10021

Re:  Apartment 15-C, 450 East 51st Street, New York, New York 10021
     (the "Rental Unit")

Dear Paul,

I have carefully considered your request to sublet the above-referenced Apartment, dated November 3, 200X, and the additional sublet information you provided on November 20, 200x. Unfortunately, I must deny your request for several reasons.

First, the credit report furnished on your proposed subtenant, Rena Andrews, revealed that she filed for personal bankruptcy two years ago. It is our policy to reject any rental applicant who has declared bankruptcy in the five-year period prior to the date of the rental application. Your subtenant may receive a free copy of the credit report upon which this decision was made by contacting my office, or by requesting it directly from the credit reporting agency, ABC Credit Reporting Company, 373 Broadway, New York, NY 10013, (212) 555-1212.

The second reason your sublet request is being denied is because of a negative reference from one of your proposed subtenant's prior landlords.

Finally, Section 2525.6(a) of the Rent Stabilization Code says that in order to sublet, a rent-stabilized tenant must be able to establish at all times that he has maintained the rental unit as his primary residence, and intends to occupy it as such at the expiration of the sublease. I do not believe that you satisfy this legal requirement. According to the additional information you furnished with your sublet request, you have purchased a home in Short Hills, New Jersey, removed all your furniture from the Rental Unit, and moved there with your family. This strongly suggests that your primary residence is now in Short Hills, New Jersey, and that you have no intention to return to the Rental Unit with your family at the end of the sublease term.

Based on these reasons, I am rejecting your sublet request and believe that said rejection is based upon reasonable grounds under the Real Property Law and Rent Stabilization Code.

Sincerely,

*John L. Hiatt*

Owner and Landlord

the landlord's attorney or agent instead of the landlord. To be on the safe side, put your sublet rejection letter on your letterhead and sign the letter yourself. That way, the tenant can't raise the claim that the person who rejected their sublet request lacked authority to do so.

## E.  When a Tenant Wants to Assign the Lease

An assignment is a transfer of all of a tenant's remaining lease rights and obligations, including the right to occupy the rental unit, to another person, known as an assignee. When a lease is assigned, the assignee steps into the tenant's shoes and is bound to all of the terms of the lease. The tenant loses the right to reoccupy the rental unit.

Unless a greater right is provided under a tenant's lease, New York law prohibits tenants from assigning their lease without your prior written consent. (RPL § 226-b(a).) The form lease in this book follows New York law by prohibiting assignments without your consent (see Chapter 2, Clause 10). But the law gives tenants a loophole. If you unreasonably refuse to consent to the tenant's request to assign the lease, you must release the tenant from the lease upon 30 days' notice from the tenant.

Unlike sublets, you *may* withhold your consent to a tenant's request to assign for no reason or any reason. (RPL § 226-b.) This means that you can respond to a tenant's assignment request by simply saying "No." You needn't state your reasons for rejecting the assignment. Remember, though, that if you just say no, you must release the tenant from the lease upon 30 days' notice from the tenant. But if you "reasonably" withhold consent, that is, if you say no for a good reason, the lease may not be assigned and the tenant will not be released from the lease.

 **If the rental market is brisk, simply say no to a tenant's request to assign without giving a reason.** This is deemed an "unreasonable" rejection,

and entitles the tenant to be released from the lease. Once the tenant moves out, you can boost the rent when you lease the unit to a new tenant.

If you want to bar an assignment and keep the tenant, you'll need a reasonable ground for your rejection. If the tenant challenges your rejection in court, you may have to prove to a judge that your reasons were legitimate and well founded. Play it safe by evaluating the proposed assignee by exactly the same standards that you use in evaluating any other new tenant: financial stability, credit history, references and other criteria described in Chapter 1. If the prospective assignee fails the test that you apply to all potential tenants, you will be legally justified in saying "No."

From a landlord's point of view, assignments are usually preferable to subleases. With an assignment, the tenant moves out permanently and you have a direct legal relationship with the assignee (the person to whom the tenant turns over the entire lease). The assignee not only moves into the rental unit formerly occupied by the original tenant, but into her legal shoes as well. Unlike a subtenant, whose legal relationship is with the original tenant, not you, the assignee rents directly from you. If things go wrong with respect to behavior or money matters under the lease, the assignee can sue or be sued by the landlord.

Assignment doesn't, however, completely sever the legal relationship between you and the original tenant. Oddly enough, the original tenant remains responsible for the rent if the assignee fails to pay. Absent an agreement to the contrary, however, the tenant is not liable for damage to the premises caused by the assignee. (The Consent to Assignment of Lease form, discussed in Section E, below, protects you by incorporating this promise.)

Generally, the landlord and assignee are bound by promises made in the lease signed by the original tenant. For example, the lease provision in which the landlord agreed to return the security deposit in a certain manner is still in effect; it now benefits the assignee. And the assignee must honor

# Consent to Assignment of Lease

Carolyn Friedman _____ ("Landlord") and

Joel Oliver _____ ("Tenant") and

Sam Parker _____ ("Assignee")

agree as follows:

1. Tenant has leased the premises at ____ Apt. 18-F, 922 West End Avenue, NY, NY 10025 ____

   _____ from Landlord.

2. The lease was signed on _____ April 1 _____, 200 X , and will expire on

   ____ March 31 _____, 200 X .

3. Tenant is assigning the balance of Tenant's lease to Assignee, beginning on ____ November 1 ____

   _____, 200 X , and ending on _____ March 31 _____, 200 X .

4. Tenant's financial responsibilities under the terms of the lease are not ended by virtue of this
   assignment. Specifically, Tenant understands that:

   a. If Assignee defaults and fails to pay the rent as provided in the lease, namely on

      _____ the first of the month _____, Tenant will be obligated to do so within

      ____ three __ days of being notified by Landlord; and

   b. If Assignee damages the property beyond normal wear and tear and fails or refuses to pay
      for repairs or replacement, Tenant will be obligated to do so.

5. As of the effective date of the assignment, Tenant permanently gives up the right to occupy the
   premises.

6. Assignee is bound by every term and condition in the lease that is the subject of this assignment.


| October 1, 200X | *Carolyn Friedman* |
|---|---|
| Date | Landlord |

| October 1, 200X | *Joel Oliver* |
|---|---|
| Date | Tenant |

| October 1, 200X | *Sam Parker* |
|---|---|
| Date | Assignee |

the previous tenant's promise to abide by the lease's noise rules and use restrictions.

## 1. How to Assign a Lease

Typically, to accomplish an assignment, the landlord and the tenant write "Assigned to John Doe" on the lease at each place where the tenant's name appears. The new occupant, John Doe, then signs at each place where the original tenant signed. If this is all that's done, the original tenant remains liable for the rent, but not for damage to the property.

## 2. Use Consent Agreement

We suggest that a formal Consent to Assignment of Lease document also be used, such as the sample shown. Using this form protects you in two additional respects:

- it educates the tenant to the fact that he will remain liable for the rent if the assignee defaults, and

- it obligates the tenant to cover damages to the property beyond normal wear and tear if the assignee refuses or is unable to do so.

You will find a Consent to Assignment of Lease form on the Forms CD and a blank, tear-out copy in Appendix IV.

**Collect rent increase when rent-stabilized lease is assigned.** If you consent to the assignment of a rent-stabilized lease, you can collect a vacancy rent increase from the assignee as of the date of the assignment, including any applicable Rent Guidelines Board vacancy allowance in effect at the time of the commencement date of the lease being assigned. (See Chapter 4 for details on calculating the vacancy allowance.) The rent increase remains a part of the legal regulated rent for the unit, and may be used to calculate rent increases for subsequent renewal and vacancy leases. (9 NYCRR §§ 2525.6(e), 2505.7(f).) ∎

Chapter **9**

# Landlord's Duty to Repair and Maintain the Premises

Landlords are required by law to provide rental property that meets basic structural, health and safety standards for heat, garbage removal, security and the like. This chapter describes the specific housing standards and laws landlords must follow under the state's warranty of habitability, multiple dwelling laws and various New York City ordinances. Every landlord needs to know that if he doesn't meet his duties, tenants may legally respond in a variety of ways. Tenants may have the legal right to:

- reduce or withhold rent
- file complaints with state and local housing agencies to trigger an inspection
- pay for repairs themselves and deduct the cost from the rent (called repair and deduct)
- sue you in court for a rent reduction (retroactive and prospective) or damages, or
- move out without notice.

This chapter outlines strategies for dealing with tenants who withhold rent or pursue other legal remedies because of the property's condition. Finally, we provide advice on how to stay on top of your repair and maintenance needs and minimize financial losses and legal problems with your tenants.

 Related topics in this book include:

- Writing clear lease and rental agreement provisions for repair and maintenance and tenant alterations and improvements to rental property: Chapter 2
- Getting "MCI" rent increases for rent-regulated units for buildingwide major capital improvements, such as new windows or a new roof: Chapter 4
- Setting valid occupancy limits: Chapter 8
- Delegating maintenance and repair responsibilities to a manager or super: Chapter 6
- Highlighting repair and maintenance procedures in a move-in letter to new tenants and using a Landlord-Tenant Checklist to keep track of the condition of the premises before and after the tenant moves in: Chapters 7 and 16

- Following rules of entry to make repairs or conduct inspections: Chapter 10
- Landlord's responsibility for cleaning up environmental hazards, such as asbestos, lead and mold: Chapter 11
- Conducting a final inspection of the rental unit for cleaning and damage repair before the tenant moves out and making deductions from the security deposit: Chapter 16
- The tenant's right to terminate if the premises are seriously damaged or destroyed: Chapter 14
- How to terminate a tenancy for major property damage caused by the tenant: Chapters 13, 14 and 15, and
- How to research state laws, local ordinances and court cases on landlord repair and maintenance responsibilities: Chapter 17.

## A. Landlord's Legal Responsibility for Repairs and Maintenance

Almost all of your repair and maintenance obligations arise out of one or more of the following four legal sources:

1. The warranty of habitability, which applies to all landlords (see Section 1, below)
2. State multiple dwelling laws, which apply to properties with three or more rental units (see Section 2, below)
3. Local housing codes and ordinances that apply to residential rental property (see Section 3, below), and
4. Landlord promises—either written (in leases, rental agreements or brochures) or oral (see Section 4, below).

While specific housing standards and penalties may vary depending on the source of your legal obligation, the bottom line remains the same: Put your rental units in good condition before renting them, and keep them that way while people live there.

## 1. The Warranty of Habitability

The cornerstone of landlord responsibility for repairing and maintaining rental premises is a legal doctrine called the warranty of habitability. The warranty is your promise, implied by law, that the property is livable, usable and safe—and will stay that way throughout the rental term. (RPL § 235-b.)

Now, wait a minute, you may say—I haven't promised anything. Sorry, but here the law steps in and decrees that whenever housing is offered, the landlord has impliedly guaranteed that it's fit. If this is a promise you never intended and don't want to keep, your best bet is to look for another line of work, because courts will hold you to the warranty of habitability very strenuously.

To comply with the warranty, the landlord must keep the rental unit and common areas free of any conditions that would be dangerous, hazardous, or detrimental to the occupants' life, health or safety. The warranty's purpose is to not only protect tenants from dangerous conditions, but also to give them a legal remedy if there is a lack of essential services. A tenant can seek money damages (often awarded in the form of a rent reduction, called "abatement" in legalese), punitive damages, attorney's fees, interest and court costs from a landlord who violates the warranty of habitability.

### A Brief History of the Warranty of Habitability

Under early common law, a tenant's obligation to pay rent was completely independent of the condition of any structures built on the land. It was the land—not the condition of its structures—that was of paramount importance. With the growth of cities, and the shift away from an agricultural economy, the condition of the structures grew in importance as tenants needed to rent shelter, not land. Yet, landlords continued to have no obligation to deliver or keep the premises in good repair. A strict "buyer beware" rule applied to tenants when it came to rental premises. (See *Park West Management Corp. v. Mitchell,* 47 N.Y.2d 316, 418 N.Y.S.2d 310, 391 N.E.2d 1288 (1979) cert. denied, 444 U.S. 992, 100 S. Ct. 523, 62 L. Ed. 2d 421 (1979) (hereafter, "*Park West*").)

In the early 1970s, judges began to reject the harsh rule of buyer beware. One by one, they imposed an implied warranty of habitability when a landlord rents property for residential use. In 1975, the judge-made warranty of habitability made its way into the New York State code books, when a statute was passed and signed into law.

### a. Who's Affected by the Warranty of Habitability?

With two exceptions (noted below), the warranty of habitability applies to every landlord and every tenant who rents residential property in New York State. (RPL § 235-b(1).) It doesn't matter how few (or how many) units are in the building or where the building is located. If you rent a residential rental unit to a tenant, you're bound by the warranty.

New York courts have, however, refused to extend the warranty of habitability to two types of tenants:

- "Holdover" tenants, who remain in a unit without your permission after the lease or rental agreement expires. (*Dean v. Korkidis*, N.Y.L.J., 3/18/92, p. 26, col. 1 (App. Term, 2d Dep't).) (See Chapter 14 for a discussion of holdover tenants.)

- Tenants who move out but are still responsible for rent, such as tenants who sublet or who assign their lease. A tenant must actually occupy the unit to be protected by the warranty. (*Leventritt v. 520 East 86th St. Inc.*, 266 A.D.2d 45, 698 N.Y.S.2d 20 (1st Dep't 1999).) The subtenant, however, may assert a warranty of habitability claim against the actual tenant.

## Who's Financially Responsible for Habitability Problems?

It is important to understand the difference between being legally obligated for the habitability of rental property and financially responsible to keep it fit. In most situations—for example, when a unit is rented in the first place—the owner is on the hook for both responsibilities. What happens, however, if the tenant does something to make the property unfit—for example, by negligently breaking the water main? If damage beyond regular wear and tear is caused by a tenant or his guest, the financial burden of fixing it properly falls on the tenant. (See "Make the Tenant Financially Liable for Damage to Your Property," in Section C, below.) The landlord, however, remains responsible for seeing that the work gets done and the property returned to a habitable state. In this situation, the landlord could rightly bill the tenant for the repair. (Clause 11 of the form lease and rental agreements in Chapter 2 alerts the tenant to this responsibility.) If, however, a third party (such as a vandal or burglar) does the damage, or if it is the result of normal wear and tear, the landlord bears the burden of fixing and paying for the damage.

### b. Key Concepts of the Warranty of Habitability

As you might expect, understanding how courts have interpreted the warranty of habitability is much more difficult than understanding the square footage requirements or minimum hot water temperatures that are typical of housing codes (discussed in Section A4, below). Nevertheless, it's possible to identify a few key concepts, as follows.

- The warranty of habitability doesn't require you to provide a rental unit that's in "perfect" or "aesthetically pleasing condition." (*Park West*, cited in "A Brief History of the Warranty of Habitability," above.) It simply needs to be fit, livable and safe.

- The warranty applies to conditions caused by "latent" (that is, hidden or dormant conditions) defects in the premises, as well as those that are plainly visible or discoverable. (*Park West.*) That means that you can't avoid responsibility for problems such as a concealed water leak that weren't obvious or that you couldn't foresee when the tenancy began.

- The warranty also applies to defects in the premises caused by conditions that are beyond the landlord's control, such as acts of third parties and natural disasters. (*Department of Housing Preservation and Development of the City of New York v. Sartor*, 109 A.D.2d 665, 487 N.Y.S.2d 1 (1st Dep't 1985).)

- The warranty of habitability requires landlords to provide basic security devices such as good locks and adequate lighting (see Section B16, below).

- Tenants are not entitled to a heightened degree of protection under the warranty by virtue of the "luxury" status of a particular building or unit, or by the amount of rent they pay. When tenants of luxury apartments in a fashionable Manhattan high-rise claimed to be entitled to higher service standards under the warranty of habitability, the State's highest court turned them down. (*Solow v. Wellner*, 154 Misc.2d 737, 595 N.Y.S.2d 619 (App. Term, 1st Dep't, 1992) aff'd as modified by

205 A.D.2d 339, 613 N.Y.S.2d 163 (1st Dep't 1994) aff'd 86 N.Y.2d 582, 658 N.E.2d 1005, 635 N.Y.S.2d 132 (1995) (hereafter, "*Solow*").)

- Tenants who cause uninhabitable conditions are not entitled to the protections of the warranty of habitability. (RPL § 226-b (1).)
- Tenants who refuse to let you inspect or repair a defective condition can't seek the protections of the warranty of habitability, either. (*Ansonia Assoc. v. Moan*, N.Y.L.J., 8/21/92, p. 24, col. 3 (Civ. Ct., N.Y. County).)

While each case turns on its own facts, specific conditions which tenants have claimed to violate the warranty of habitability are discussed in Section B, below.

### c. Don't Try to Evade Your Legal Responsibilities

Some landlords have attempted to get around the implied warranty of habitability by advancing one or both of the following theories:

**Tenant waiver.** Landlords may argue that, if the housing was substandard when the lease or rental agreement began, or it became so during the tenancy, the fact that the tenant nevertheless moved in (or stayed) indicated that he waived the protections of the implied warranty.

**Landlord disclaimer.** Some lease or rental agreements include a clause stating that the landlord will not satisfy the implied warranty's requirements. You may argue that a tenant who signs a lease with this type of clause has effectively absolved you from the responsibility of the implied warranty of habitability.

Don't rely on either theory. Neither a tenant waiver (at the beginning of the tenancy or during its life) nor a disclaimer in the lease will relieve you of the responsibility to provide housing that begins— and remains—fit and habitable. (RPL § 235(b)(2).)

### Delegating Repair and Maintenance Responsibilities to Tenants

Any lease or rental agreement clause in which a tenant agrees to give up her right to a habitable rental unit is illegal and unenforceable. (RPL § 235(b)(2).) Nor can a landlord escape his duty to keep the property fit and livable by trying to make it the tenant's responsibility.

In addition, state multiple dwelling laws, which apply to buildings with three or more units, require landlords to keep rental units reasonably safe and free of defects. New York courts have ruled that landlords may not delegate these statutory duties to residential tenants. So even if a tenant agrees to be solely responsible for repairs and maintenance, the landlord remains responsible for the property's compliance with housing laws and regulations.

While you can ask the tenant to handle minor jobs—like repainting a wall or moving refuse to the curb in exchange for rent reduction—it's up to you to make sure the work actually gets done. If it doesn't, you—not the tenant—will be the one hit with a fine.

**Never delegate major repairs or maintenance tasks to tenants.** These jobs will generally involve a significant amount of money and will require expertise that the average tenant is not likely to possess. And if the job comes out wrong, you'll be responsible for fixing it.

See Section E, below, for a discussion of a tenant's rights to sue for a rent reduction, called an abatement, when a landlord fails to keep the rental property in a habitable condition. For a related topic, setting repair and maintenance responsibilities for a live-in super or manager, see Chapter 6.

## 2. State Multiple Dwelling Laws

In addition to the warranty of habitability, landlords of buildings with three or more units must follow the repair and maintenance requirements set by state multiple dwelling laws, specifically, either the "Multiple Dwelling Law" or the "Multiple Residence Law."

The Multiple Dwelling Law (MDL § 1 and following) applies to buildings with three or more residential rental units in cities with populations of 325,000 or more. As of early 2003, only Buffalo and New York City met this population standard.

Buildings with three or more units outside New York City and Buffalo are subject to the Multiple Residence Law (MRL § 1 and following).

➡ **Owners of single-family rentals and duplexes can skip this section.** Properties with three or fewer units aren't subject to the Multiple Dwelling Law or the Multiple Residence Law. That doesn't mean, however that anything goes in these properties. The warranty of habitability applies to single-family homes and duplexes. (See Section 1, above.) And in many cases, such as in New York City, municipal housing codes apply to one- and two-family rental properties as well as to multiple dwellings. (See Section 3, below.)

The Multiple Dwelling Law and the Multiple Residence Law both set specific minimum construction requirements for room size, light, ventilation, water and electrical service, heat and fire protection. They mandate specific minimum security devices (detailed in Section B, below) and lay out certain ongoing maintenance requirements. State and local codes also have a catch-all provision that prohibits "public nuisances." A public nuisance is something that is dangerous to human life, detrimental to health or immoral—for example, overcrowding a room with occupants, providing insufficient or inadequate ventilation, illumination, sewage or plumbing facilities or using the premises for prostitution. (See, for example, NY MDL § 309.) When referring to both sets of laws, we use the term multiple dwelling laws.

The most sweeping obligation under both laws is the one requiring you to keep your multiple dwelling in "good repair." (MDL § 78; MRL § 174.) This repair obligation extends to each unit in the building, as well as to corridors, stairwells, courtyards, parking lots and other common areas in the building or on your lot. Also significant is the requirement in the Multiple Dwelling Law (which applies only in New York City and Buffalo) that landlords provide certain basic security devices to tenants, such as self-closing, self-locking entrance and exit doors, elevator mirrors and, in some buildings, intercom systems.

Your duty to keep multiple dwellings in good repair doesn't transform you into an absolute "insurer" of your tenants' safety, however. Rather, it requires you to act reasonably to protect tenants from dangerous or defective conditions that you know of or should know about. Section B, below, gives you specific examples of the kind of repairs and maintenance required under state multiple dwelling laws.

---

### Housing Code Exemptions for Older Buildings

When a state or local housing code changes, it doesn't necessarily mean that all existing buildings are illegal because they are not "up to code." Especially when it comes to items that would involve major structural changes, lawmakers will often exempt certain older buildings. They do it by writing a "grandfather clause" into the code, exempting all buildings constructed before a certain date (sometimes that date is the same as when the new code takes effect, but not always). Such exemptions will often not apply if you undertake significant renovations or remodeling, meaning that, over the years, you may eventually have to comply with these new rules. Contact your local housing authority for information on any grandfather clauses that may apply to your rental property.

There are, however, many types of code changes—for example, those involving smoke detectors—that must be made regardless of the age of the building and irrespective of the fact that the owner wasn't intending to remodel or renovate.

Tenants may also point to a violation of a housing or maintenance code if they do not pay the rent, or attempt to pay less, on the grounds that the premises are substandard. If you sue a tenant for eviction on the basis of nonpayment of rent, the tenant may use code violations as the justification for her action. See Section D, below, for information on these types of responses.

## 3. Local Housing Codes

Some municipalities enact their own housing codes. The Rochester Property Code, for instance (Roch. Code Chap. 90), sets heating, lighting, ventilation, fire safety and occupancy standards that apply to all residential buildings, regardless of size. Call your municipality's building or health department to find out if there's a local housing code in effect in the locality where your property is located.

**The New York City Housing Maintenance Code applies to all New York City properties, including single-family homes and duplexes.** (NYC Adm. Code Tit. 27, Ch.2.) It sets repair and maintenance standards that cover cleaning, heat and hot water at specified times and temperatures, lighting and required safety and security measures. Section B, below, also details some of these responsibilities.

One- and two-family properties are not subject to state multiple dwelling laws, but may be covered under local housing codes. (These properties are covered by the warranty of habitability, though, which applies to all rental units.) It is not unusual for local codes to permit landlords of one- and two-family properties to transfer their maintenance and repair responsibilities to the tenant, under the terms of a lease or rental agreement. This is permitted in New York City, under the Housing Maintenance Code. (HMC § 27-2005(c).)

In some cases, state and local codes may conflict. That happens when one code sets a stricter mainte-nance or repair standard than the other. In such cases, you will be held to the stricter of the two standards.

## 4. Enforcement of Housing Codes

New York does not have one state agency that enforces state multiple dwelling laws. That job is left to local building, health and fire departments, which are authorized to enforce state multiple dwelling laws, as well as any applicable local housing codes. In New York City, the Department of Housing Preservation and Development (HPD) enforces the state Multiple Dwelling Law as well as the City's Housing Maintenance Code.

Local inspectors discover code violations through routine checks or when they inspect in response to complaints from tenants or neighboring owners. Local authorities may issue violations against rental buildings that fail to comply with state multiple dwelling laws and/or local housing codes—for example, due to lack of adequate heat, trash in the hallways, hazardous electrical wiring, a leaking roof, broken toilet or other defective conditions.

The local enforcement agency typically requires the property owner to remedy all violations found within a given time period. The amount of time you get to correct a violation depends on how hazardous it is. For example, a landlord would be required to quickly repair a fire stair door that doesn't close properly, since it poses a fire hazard, but would get more time to repair a minor leak or peeling paint problem. If you fail to make repairs within the time allowed, the municipality may bring a civil lawsuit against you. A failure to comply with certain cited violations of state and local housing laws is a criminal misdemeanor punishable by hefty fines or even imprisonment. In some cases, local officials may require that the building be vacated, with the landlord providing tenants with temporary housing, until the violation is corrected.

## All Violations Are Not Created Equal

Most local code enforcement offices rank housing code violations by the degree of hazard posed to the property's occupants. For example, the New York City Department of Housing Preservation and Development (HPD), the agency that enforces the multiple dwelling law and the HMC in New York City, has sorted possible violations into three classifications:

- **Class "A" Non-Hazardous.** These include minor leaks, chipping or peeling paint when no children under the age of six live in the home or a lack of signs designating floor numbers. An owner has 90 days to correct an "A" violation.
- **Class "B" Hazardous.** These include orders requiring public doors to be self-closing, adequate lighting in public areas, lack of a posted Certificate of Occupancy or removal of vermin. An owner has 30 days to correct a "B" violation.
- **Class "C" Immediately Hazardous.** These cover dangerous conditions such as inadequate fire exits, rodents, lead-based paint where a child under six resides or lack of heat, hot water, electricity or gas. An owner has 24 hours to correct a "C" violation. If the owner fails to comply with emergency "C"

violations such as lack of heat or hot water, HPD is authorized to initiate corrective action or emergency repairs.

- **"Rent-Impairing" Violations.** A "rent-impairing" violation refers to a condition in a multiple dwelling that constitutes a fire hazard or a serious threat to the life, health or safety of occupants. In New York City and Buffalo, it's up to local code enforcement offices to classify which violations are rent-impairing and to make a full list of possible violations available to the public. (MDL. § 302-a.) In New York City, all Class "C" and some Class "B" violations are rent-impairing violations.

**Uncorrected rent-impairing violations may disqualify you from certain rent increases.** A New York City rent-controlled tenant's maximum base rent may not be increased unless the landlord certifies that he has corrected all rent-impairing violations against the building and 80% of the non-rent-impairing violations recorded against the property. (NYC Adm. Code § 26-405(h)(6).) Outstanding rent-impairing violations may also disqualify a landlord from collecting a major capital improvement rent hike. For more information on rent increase rules, see Chapter 4.

---

**More Information on State and Local Housing Codes**

For more information on the Multiple Dwelling Law and the Multiple Residence Law, call your municipal housing authority. The laws may also be viewed or downloaded from the New York State Assembly website (www.assembly.state.ny.us). In addition, most public libraries have copies of the Multiple Dwelling Law and the Multiple Residence Law in the reference section.

New York City landlords may call the Department of Housing Preservation and Development's Office of Code Enforcement at 212-863-8000; visit HPD's website by logging onto the New York City site (www.nyc.gov) and clicking HPD. Most New York City public libraries have copies of the Housing Maintenance Code (it's part of the New York City Administrative Code) in the reference section. The code may also be viewed or downloaded from the New York City Rent Guidelines Board website (www.housingnyc.com).

## 5. Housing Codes and the Warranty of Habitability

In New York, the warranty of habitability is considered by courts to be independent of any housing and maintenance codes. So, a condition that violates an applicable housing code does not necessarily constitute automatic breach of the warranty. (*Park West*, see cite in "A Brief History of the Warranty of Habitability," above.) Under this approach, the legal question is not merely whether the building meets specific state or local housing codes, but whether it is also fit, habitable and safe. Although a breach of the housing code does not automatically determine that a unit is uninhabitable (nor does compliance alone mean that it is habitable), usually a serious housing code violation will also qualify as a breach of the warranty of habitability.

The independence of the implied warranty of habitability from the housing code has particular importance to landlords because it:

- imposes duties of maintenance or repair on the landlord in situations where the housing or building codes are poorly written or non-existent, and
- allows a court to require more of a landlord than the letter of the law as contained in the housing or building codes.

EXAMPLE: The elevator in Russell's ten-story building was old, but managed to pass the city-mandated annual elevator inspection test. Tenants in the building claimed that elevator service had gotten slow and unreliable, and began to withhold rent. Unable to afford a new elevator, Russell sued the tenants for back rent. He assumed that since his elevator satisfied local building codes, the tenants were wrong to withhold rent. Russell was dismayed when the judge awarded a rent abatement to the tenants. Under New York case law, a decrease in elevator service is a breach of the warranty of habitability—even if the elevator complies with applicable codes.

## 6. Your Promises for Services and Repairs

A tenant can hold you to a repair or maintenance promise you made in the lease or rental agreement —even if the work is not required under the warranty of habitability or by state or local laws or regulations. Your ads and brochures can also create special repair and maintenance obligations, as can promises made in the rental office.

We use the term "bargained-for service" to refer to something you have agreed to provide either in writing or orally.

### a. Promises in the Lease or Rental Agreement

When it comes to legal responsibility for repairs, your own lease or rental agreement is often just as important (or more so) than the warranty of habitability and housing codes. If your written agreement describes or lists items such as drapes, washing machines, swimming pools, saunas, parking places, security systems, intercoms or dishwashers, you must provide them in decent repair. And the promise to provide them carries with it the implied promise to maintain them.

If you violate an express or implied promise relating to the condition of the premises, the tenant may sue you (usually in small claims court) or countersue you in housing court, for money damages for breach of contract, and may be able to pursue other legal remedies discussed in Sections D and E, below.

## b.   Promises in Ads and Brochures

If an advertisement for your unit described or listed a feature, such as a cable TV hookup, especially if the feature is emphasized, you must follow through with these promises, even if your written rental agreement says nothing about cable TV. You must repair promised items such as dishwashers, clothes washers and dryers, garbage disposals, microwave ovens, security gates and Jacuzzis if they break through no fault of the tenant.

> EXAMPLE 1: Tina sees Joel's ad for an apartment, which says "heated swimming pool." After Tina moves in, Joel stops heating the pool regularly, because his utility costs have risen. Joel has violated his promise to keep the pool heated.
> The promise doesn't have to be in words.

> EXAMPLE 2: Tom's real estate agent showed him a glossy color photo of an available apartment, which featured a smiling resident in front of a working fireplace. The fireplace in the apartment Tom rented had a broken damper, and didn't work. Tom complained to the management, arguing that the advertisement implied that all units had fireplaces that worked. The landlord realized that he would have to fix the fireplace.

## c.   Promises Made Before You Rented the Unit

It's a rare landlord or manager who refrains from even the slightest bit of puffing when showing a rental to a prospective tenant. It's hard to refrain from announcing rosy plans for amenities or services that haven't yet materialized: "We plan to redo this kitchen—you'll love the snappy way that trash compactor will work!" Whenever you make promises like these, even if they're not in writing, your tenant can legally hold you to them.

⚠️ **Your promises about crime or security can come back to haunt you.** A tenant who is robbed or attacked in what you call a "high-security building" may sue you for medical bills, lost earnings and pain and suffering. Your best bet is not to make any oral or written representations as to security; if you do, be sure to conscientiously maintain promised security measures in working order.

> EXAMPLE: The manager of Ivette's apartment building gave her a thorough tour of the "very secure" building before she decided to move in. Ivette was particularly impressed by the doorman, closed-circuit camera system and apartment alarm system. One night, Ivette discovered an intruder in her apartment. Though she hit the emergency button on her alarm system, nothing happened and Ivette was assaulted by the intruder. Ivette sued the landlord for her injuries. Ivette's landlord was held liable because he failed to maintain the alarm system and level of security that had been promised.

## d.   Implied Promises

Suppose your rental agreement doesn't mention a garbage disposal and neither did any of your advertising. And you never pointed it out when showing the unit. But there is a garbage disposal and it was working when the tenant moved in. Now the garbage disposal is broken—do you have to fix it? Many courts will hold you legally responsible for maintaining all significant aspects of the rental unit. If you offer a unit that already has certain features—light fixtures that work, doors that open and close smoothly, faucets that don't leak, tile that doesn't fall off the wall—many judges reason that you have made an implied contract to keep them in workable order throughout the tenancy.

The flip side of this principle works in your favor. Look at it this way: When your tenant has paid for a hamburger, the waiter—you—doesn't have to deliver a steak. In other words, if the rental was shabby, but legally fit, when the tenant moved in, and you never gave the tenant reason to believe that it would be spruced up, he has no legal right to demand improvements—unless, of course, he can point to health hazards or code violations. As when you offer secondhand goods "as is" for a low price, legally your buyer/tenant is stuck with the deal.

Another factor that is evidence of an implied contract is your past conduct. If you have consistently fixed or maintained a particular feature of a rental, you have an implied obligation to continue doing so.

> EXAMPLE: Robin's apartment has a built-in dishwasher. When she rented the apartment, neither the lease nor her landlord Doug said anything about the dishwasher or who was responsible for repairing it. The dishwasher has broken down a few times and whenever Robin asked Doug to fix it, he did. By doing so, Doug has established a "practice" that the landlord—not the tenant—is responsible for repairing the dishwasher.

## B. How to Meet Your Repair and Maintenance Responsibilities

What must you do to meet your legal obligations to tenants? The following sections examine specific services, repairs and maintenance that landlords are required to provide under state multiple dwelling laws, the warranty of habitability, and where applicable, under New York City local law. The list is arranged alphabetically, from "Appliances and Amenities" to "Window Guards."

**A landlord may not reduce or suspend any services that were furnished to a rent-regulated unit when it first became subject to rent control or rent stabilization, unless the service reduction has been approved by the DHCR, the state agency that enforces the rent laws.** For rent-controlled units, these are known as "essential" services. For rent-stabilized units, they are called "required" services. Such services may include repairs, painting, maintenance, the furnishing of light, heat, hot and cold water, telephone, elevator service, kitchen, bath and laundry appliances, such as refrigerators, stoves, dishwashers and air conditioners and amenities such as mail delivery, linen service, janitor service and garbage removal. Landlords who reduce essential or required services to a rent-regulated unit are subject to rent cuts and or rent freezes. For more information, see DHCR Fact Sheet #3, "Required and Essential Services." You can get it by calling the DHCR InfoLine at 718-739-6400 or downloading it from the DHCR's website at www.dhcr.state.ny.us (click Rent Administration, then click Fact Sheets).

### 1. Appliances and Amenities

Most landlords supply tenants with appliances like refrigerators, stoves, microwave ovens and garbage disposals. In addition, many properties offer "amenities"—nonessential features that make life a little nicer or easier for tenants, such as air conditioning, window coverings, swimming pools and special services like valet parking.

 **While not legally required, it's a good idea to install window blinds anyway.** They're an inexpensive apartment amenity. And they can make your building look better from the outside. If you don't supply window blinds, tenants tend to improvise, at least temporarily, by hanging unsightly sheets, flags, or blankets in the windows. Window treatments like these can definitely reduce your building's "curb-appeal." If you install mini-blinds, make sure they are free of lead paint—especially in units where small children reside. (For details on which blinds to avoid, see Chapter 11, "Dealing with Environmental Hazards.")

### a. Statutory Requirements.

State multiple dwelling laws and local housing codes only cover essential services such as heat, hot water and plumbing. They don't provide standards for appliances and amenities. However, once you have agreed to provide certain appliances and amenities, your duty to keep the rental unit and property in "good repair" would probably extend to maintaining appliances and amenities, too. (MDL § 78; MRL § 174.)

⚠ **Use certified technicians for air conditioning repairs and maintenance.** For environmental reasons, federal law requires landlords to take certain precautions when repairing or servicing air conditioning equipment. Chapter 11, Section C, covers these federal requirements.

### b. Warranty of Habitability

A defective appliance can breach the warranty of habitability when the defect creates a dangerous condition, such as the hazard posed by a stove with a broken gas valve. And where air conditioning is a "bargained-for" service, its absence during the summer months may well violate the warranty of habitability. But innocuous defects, like broken window blinds, do not affect habitability (*Solow,* cited above).

You'll be relieved to learn that the warranty of habitability does not cover service amenities. A group of Manhattan tenants in a luxury high-rise claimed that the landlord's "package room" service at their building had become inefficient, and that the service reduction was a breach of the warranty. (Package room service entails signing, accepting and storing packages, deliveries and dry cleaning for tenants who are not at home. It also includes notifying tenants about deliveries that have been accepted on their behalf and stored in the building's package room.) An appeals court ruled that amenities and conveniences, such as package room ser-

vice, are not within the intended scope of the warranty of habitability. (*Solow.*)

## 2. Asbestos

Structures built before the mid-1970s often contain asbestos insulation around heating systems and plumbing lines, and in ceilings and other areas. Until 1981, asbestos was also widely used in many other building materials, such as vinyl flooring and tiles. The mere presence of asbestos or asbestos-containing material in a rental unit or common area isn't considered dangerous or hazardous. However, asbestos is particularly dangerous in its "friable" state, when it is easily crumbled or flaked by hand. Friable asbestos fibers that become airborne—for example, when it is disturbed during renovation work—have the potential to become a significant health problem to tenants.

### a. Statutory Requirements

State multiple dwelling laws don't contain any specific asbestos-related obligations. However, federal and state laws require landlords to take special precautions before undertaking renovation or demolition work in buildings with asbestos-containing materials. Those requirements are detailed in Chapter 11, Section B.

### b. Warranty of Habitability

Since asbestos is a known carcinogen, courts have found a violation of the warranty where there is proof of asbestos dust or "friable" asbestos (which could become airborne) in the tenant's apartment or in the building's ventilation system. For instance, a Manhattan judge ruled that asbestos dust in a unit's bathroom ventilation system and in a closet violated the warranty. (*Ansonia Assoc. v. Moan,* N.Y.L.J., 8/21/92, p. 24, col. 3 (Civ. Ct. N.Y. County), aff'd. N.Y.L.J. 7/13/95, p.12, col. 2 (App.Term, 1st Dep't).)

## 3.  Common Areas

Your property's common areas include the lobby, laundry and trash compactor rooms, all corridors, stairwells and elevator cabs. Exterior walkways, parking lots, courtyards, lots and alleys and roofs are considered common areas, too, if they are accessible to tenants.

### a.  Statutory Requirements

State multiple dwelling laws require you to keep common areas "clean" and in "good repair." (MDL §§ 78, 80; MRL § 174.) Common areas must also be kept adequately lit. Service areas, which include mechanical rooms, shops or other areas used by service personnel, must also be kept clean and in good repair. In addition to regularly cleaning these areas, landlords must repair paint, wallpaper and carpeting when needed, replace burned-out light bulbs and fix broken light fixtures. Exterior sidewalks and other walkways must be kept clean and smooth, to avoid trips and falls.

Some properties are legally required to have a live-in super or manager whose duties include cleaning and maintaining common areas. See Chapter 6, Section A, for details.

### b.  Warranty of Habitability

The warranty of habitability specifically applies to "all areas used in … common with other tenants or residents." (RPL § 235-b.) Courts have found a breach of the warranty where:
- tenants were denied use of "environmental common areas," including a park and playground (*Forest Hills No. 1 Co. v. Schimmel,* 110 Misc.2 d, 429, 440 N.Y.S.2d 471 (Civ. Ct., Queens County, 1981))
- tenants were denied use of an apartment complex swimming pool (*Tower Club v. Matheny,* N.Y.L.J., 8/8/90, p. 23, col. 3 (Just. Ct., Village of Tuckahoe))

- fire-damaged common areas went unrepaired (*55 Midlock Tenants Corp. v. Nesselson,* N.Y.L.J., 4/29/92, p. 22, col. 6 (Civ. Ct., N.Y. County)), and
- mailboxes were in disrepair or missing and garbage receptacles were removed from common areas (*Mali Realty Corp. v. Rivera,* N.Y.L.J., 8/9/95, p. 24, col. 4 (Civ.Ct., Kings County))

Deteriorated common area carpeting will not violate the warranty of habitability, so long as it doesn't pose a trip hazard. Tenant complaints of worn hallway carpets "are not within the intended scope of RPL § 235-b." (*Solow.*) For more on the subject of carpeting and flooring, see Section 7, below.

## 4.  Electricity

Electrical service includes supplying electricity to your property's common areas and mechanical systems, supplying electrical fixtures and outlets in your tenants' units and supplying electricity to the tenant's unit or to an electrical meter that serves your tenants' units.

### a.  Statutory Requirements

State multiple dwelling laws require owners to supply and maintain electricity to every room of every rental unit. (MDL § 64, MRL § 103.) In addition, electrical outlets and fixtures must be kept in good repair. Local housing and electrical codes may set minimum standards as to the number of electrical outlets which must be supplied to each room.

NYC landlords must provide and maintain light fixtures in every room of every rental unit (including the bathroom and kitchen), and a sufficient number of outlets to comply with the electrical code. (NYC Adm. Code § 27-2037.)

### b.  Warranty of Habitability

Temporary interruptions in electrical service will not breach the warranty of habitability so long as the landlord takes steps to restore power as quickly as possible. However, the longer the time period during which electricity service is discontinued, the more likely it is that a tenant could assert a successful claim against the landlord for a breach of the warranty.

## 5.  Elevator Service

Elevator service includes repairing and maintaining the passenger elevators which serve your tenants on a 24-hour basis.

### a.  Statutory Requirements

State multiple dwelling laws require you to keep all elevators in good repair. (MRL § 174; MDL § 78.) In addition, most municipalities require periodic elevator inspections and testing.

 **NYC landlords must have an elevator maintenance contract with a city-approved private elevator repair company which authorizes emergency work.** (NYC Adm. Code § 27-1000.) In addition, passenger and freight elevators must be inspected a total of five times every two years (three times by the city's Department of Buildings (DOB), and twice by a private DOB-approved inspector). Periodic safety tests are also required. For more information, contact the DOB, 280 Broadway, New York, NY 10007, 212-227-7000, or visit it by logging onto the New York City website (www.nyc.gov) and clicking Department of Buildings.

### b.  Warranty of Habitability

Chronic elevator problems or lengthy shutdowns can violate the warranty of habitability. For instance, courts have ruled that slow and unreliable service, prolonged and unexplained delays and/or "skipping" of floors are problems which, if uncorrected, can violate the warranty. (*Solow.*)

## 6.  Exterminating Service

The presence of rodents and insects in your rental property is a health hazard. Here are your legal obligations to exterminate.

### a.  Statutory Requirements

State multiple dwelling laws, as well most local housing laws, require you to keep your premises free of rodents, such as mice and rats, and infestation by cockroaches and other insects like ants, bedbugs, bees, beetles, houseflies, mosquitoes, moths, silverfish and spiders. (MRL § 174; MDL § 78; NYC Adm. Code § 27-2018.) While you're generally not required to have a licensed exterminator visit your building at any set time interval (say, monthly), you are required to exterminate active infestations in tenants' units and in common areas.

### b.  Warranty of Habitability

A severe infestation of insects or vermin violates the warranty of habitability, if the tenant has requested extermination service from you. But what about the occasional cockroach? The warranty isn't violated by the presence of one or more roaches on 30 or 40 occasions during a tenant's two-year occupancy, according to an appeals court in a case where extermination services weren't requested by the tenant. (*Solow.*) But once a tenant does request an exterminator, your best bet is to keep working on an infestation problem until it has been abated. In some cases, this will require sealing up holes in walls, cracks around pipes or other points of entry for rodents or insects.

In some cases, a tenant's poor housekeeping can contribute, or even create, an infestation problem.

Technically, a tenant can't hold you responsible for a condition she's created. But ignoring infestation problems is a very bad idea, since you can expect the infestation to spread to neighboring units. Your best bet in these situations is to show the sloppy tenant what they must do to help rectify the problem. If the tenant's bad housekeeping habits persist and pose a health hazard to other tenants, you can terminate the tenancy on the ground of nuisance. (To terminate a rental agreement, see Chapter 13. Chapters 14 and 15 discuss terminating fixed-term and rent-regulated tenants on the ground of nuisance.)

## 7. Flooring

Flooring includes vinyl, ceramic, tile and wood parquet floors, strip wood flooring and carpeting located in rental units and common areas.

### a. Statutory Requirements

State multiple dwelling laws require you to keep all flooring in "good repair." (MDL § 78; MRL § 174.) That means fixing "buckled" tile and wood floors and repairing carpeting that has loosened or could otherwise pose a safety hazard to tenants or guests. You must clean all carpets and rugs in the common areas of your building at least once a year or as often as the local code enforcement agency deems necessary. (MDL § 81(3).)

### b. Warranty of Habitability

Broken floor tiles violate the warranty of habitability when they present a hazardous condition. (*Pleasant East Assoc. v. Cabera*, 125 Misc. 2d 877, 480 N.Y.S.2d 693 (Civ.Ct., N.Y. County, 1984).) So long as rugs and carpets are not sufficiently damp or mildewy to constitute a health hazard, and so long as carpets don't have dangerous holes that could cause someone to trip and fall, you aren't legally required to replace them. What about floor tiles that have grown old and tired looking? Floor tiles that are discolored from age or other reasons don't violate the warranty, so long as they are safe to walk on. (*Solow.*) Water-damaged carpeting may pose a hazard if mold begins to form. (Chapter 11 discusses mold and other environmental hazards in detail.)

### 8. Garbage Removal

Garbage removal includes supplying receptacles in your building for the disposal of trash and recyclables by tenants. It also includes removing trash and recyclables from the building to a designated area for collection by a local sanitation department or private carting service. In buildings that are equipped with trash compacting systems and incinerators, garbage removal service also includes keeping refuse chutes operational and clear of debris.

### a.  Statutory Requirements

State multiple dwelling laws require landlords to keep their buildings free of garbage and other health hazards. You're required to provide receptacles for garbage (and for recycling, in municipalities where recycling is mandated) and to empty them on a daily basis. Receptacles must be large enough to hold a day's worth of refuse. (MRL § 174; MDL § 81.) Local housing and sanitation codes may contain other requirements.

**NYC landlords must provide receptacles for tenant refuse and recyclables, place refuse and recyclables out for collection at the appointed times and, in multiple dwellings, post a notice telling tenants of the hours and method of waste collection for the building.** (NYC Adm. Code § 27-2021; § 27-2022). For more information, contact the New York City Department of Sanitation, 125 Worth St., New York, NY 10013, 212-219-8090, or visit its website (www.nyc.gov/html/dos/home/html).

### b.  Warranty of Habitability

A temporary accumulation of garbage in your basement won't affect habitability—even if it causes a stench—so long you can show that the building's garbage is regularly removed by a local sanitation department or private carting service. (*Solow*, cited above.) Failing to remove garbage on a regular basis, of course, will violate the warranty because it threatens the health and safety of tenants.

## 9.  Heat

Heating service includes providing sufficient heating elements and units within your tenants' units and making sufficient heat available during the "heating season." Here are specific legal standards on heating service.

### a.  Statutory Requirements

State multiple dwelling laws require landlords to provide heat to tenants from October 1st through May 31st each year. How much heat? Between the hours of 6:00 AM and 10:00 PM, whenever the outside temperature drops below 55 degrees Fahrenheit, landlords must keep the temperature in their tenants' units to at least 68 degrees Fahrenheit. (MDL § 79; MRL § 173.) This is the minimum—local laws may set higher standards.

For buildings in New York City and Buffalo, there's a nighttime standard too. Between 10:00 PM and 6:00 AM, you must keep units at a minimum temperature of 55 degrees Fahrenheit, when the outside temperature dips below 40 degrees Fahrenheit. (MDL § 79; NYC Adm. Code § 27-2709.)

### b.  Warranty of Habitability

Repeated or lengthy interruptions in heating service can violate the warranty of habitability. For instance, a Manhattan judge found that a lack of heat on 13 instances during a three-month period breached the warranty of habitability. (*Parker 72nd Associates v. Isaacs,* 109 Misc. 2d 57, 436 N.Y.S.2d 542 (Civ. Ct., N.Y. County, 1980).)

Sometimes, short interruptions in the supply of heat to tenants are inevitable. You may need to shut down your heating system for a few hours in order to perform needed repairs or maintenance work. Fortunately, an occasional and temporary service interruption won't get you in trouble. Service interruptions that are necessary to service or adjust a newly installed boiler, for instance, won't violate the warranty. (*Toomer v. Higgins,* 161 A.D.2d 347, 554 N.Y.S.2d 921 (1st Dep't 1990).)

## 10. Janitorial Service

Janitorial services generally include common area cleaning, building system maintenance, minor repairs and waste collection (removing garbage and recyclables from the building to a designated pick-up area).

### a. Statutory Requirements

State multiple dwelling laws require you to keep clean and maintain every part of the building, including roofs, yards, courts and alleys. (MDL § 78, MRL § 174.) Garbage removal is also a required service. (See Section 8, above.) You can hire a building superintendent or resident manager to perform this work or you can do it yourself. Some landlords are legally required to either hire a resident super or manager or move into the building themselves and perform janitorial services. It depends how big your building is and where it's located. Chapter 6, Section A, details these requirements.

### b. Warranty of Habitability

The warranty of habitability requires you to provide adequate janitorial services for tenants. Discontinuing or reducing janitorial services can violate the warranty of habitability.

> EXAMPLE: A Manhattan landlord discharged a building's superintendent and handyman and replaced them with part-time staff. The part-timers didn't keep the building as clean as the former employees did and didn't regularly remove the garbage. Tenants in the building withheld rent, and the landlord sued them in housing court. The housing court ruled that the reduction of services violated the warranty and reduced the tenants' rent to compensate for the reduction in service. (*111 East 88th Partners v. Simon,* 106 Misc. 2d 693, 434 N.Y.S.2d 886 (Civ. Ct., N.Y. County, 1980) aff'd as modified 127 Misc. 2d 74, 489 N.Y.S.2d 139 (App. Term, 1st Dep't, 1985).)

## 11. Leaks and Water Damage

The general rule is that a tenant is entitled to a watertight rental unit. But despite your best efforts, leaks from roofs and exterior walls happen. And when they do, you're obliged to act.

### a. Statutory Requirements

State multiple dwelling laws require you to keep your property's roofs and exterior walls in good repair. (MDL § 78; MRL § 174.) That means repairing roofs and parapets, waterproofing masonry walls and painting brickwork as needed. In addition, local laws may impose special building facade inspection and repair requirements (see "NYC 'Local Law 11' Building Facade Inspections," below).

### b. Warranty of Habitability

When a roof fails, sending water cascading through the building each time it rains, you're expected to act immediately to fix the roof and to start making damaged units livable again. But if a corner of a tenant's ceiling is stained by a slow, occasional trickle of water from the roof, it may be reasonable for you to postpone the roof repair until spring— when you can do the job right.

Sometimes, careless tenants cause leaks and water damage. Bathtub overflows, for instance, can seriously damage units on lower floors. Even though the damage is not your fault, you're responsible—as one Yonkers landlord learned the hard way.

> EXAMPLE: On several occasions, a tenant's basement unit had been flooded by water coming from a problem tenant on the third floor who intentionally filled up her kitchen sink so that the water would overflow onto the kitchen floor. Each time, the water worked its way down to the basement unit and damaged the tenant's property. The landlord knew that his third-floor tenant was responsible for the flooding but did nothing to have the disruptive tenant legally evicted. A court ordered the landlord to pay the basement tenant $500 for water-damaged property, $300 for the inconvenience and aggravation and $500 in punitive damages. (*Benitez v. Restifo*, N.Y.L.J., 3/27/96, p. 36, col. 3 (City Ct., Yonkers).)

Minor, temporary leaks do not violate the warranty of habitability. For example, a judge rejected a tenant's claim that a constant drip onto his bedroom windowsill, lasting between one- and two-and-one-half weeks, didn't affect habitability, even though the drip disrupted the tenant's sleep and kept him from using the entire windowsill. (*Solow.*)

---

### NYC "Local Law 11" Building Facade Inspections

New York City's Local Law 11 requires periodic inspections of facades of buildings taller than six stories. (NYC Adm. Code § 27-129 as amended by Local Law 11 of 1998.) The law was designed to better protect pedestrians and tenants from falling masonry. Every five years, owners must hire licensed engineers to perform "critical examinations" of all of their buildings' exterior walls (not just the front side), including cast iron and terra cotta cornices and other decorations that project from the building. If the engineer deems any portion of a facade "unsafe," the owner must make immediate repairs.

For more information about your responsibilities under Local Law 11, contact the New York City Department of Buildings, 280 Broadway, New York, NY 10007, 212-227-7000, or visit its website by logging onto the New York City site (www.nyc.gov/html/dob/home.html) and clicking Department of Buildings.

---

## 12. Lighting Common Areas

Lighting your property's common areas is not only an essential service but is also an inexpensive way to beef up security at your building. The legal requirements described below set absolute minimal lighting requirements. We recommend that, where practicable, you exceed these lighting standards so as to enhance the safety and security of your tenants. You can be held liable for personal injuries and deaths due to inadequate lighting in common areas.

### a. Statutory Requirements

State multiple dwelling laws require you to provide and maintain at least one exterior light fixture at or near your building's entrance. (MDL § 35.) The light must burn between sunrise and sunset. In addition, owners of multiple dwellings built after 1955 must provide and maintain electrical light fixtures at all building exits. (MDL § 64.) Inside multiple dwellings, you must provide and maintain light fixtures in vestibules, public halls, stairs (including any fire stairs) and above your mailboxes (if needed). (MDL § 37, MRL § 32.) Interior lighting must be lit between sunset and sunrise, as well as during daylight hours if the amount of natural light from windows, skylights or other sources is inadequate.

**Owners of NYC buildings with two or more units must provide and maintain electrical light fixtures in every room of every unit, at the building's entrance, and in all public parts of a building.** (NYC Adm. Code § § 2037-2040.) For more information about your obligation to provide lighting, contact the Department of Housing Preservation and Development (HPD) Division of Code Enforcement at 212-863-8000, or visit HPD's website (www.nyc.gov/html/hpd/home.html).

### b. Warranty of Habitability

Tourists might like New York City's bright lights and neon glare, but tenants don't—especially if the lights are shining right into their bedroom window. Illumination from a light source outside the tenant's unit may violate the warranty of habitability if it's intrusive enough. Usually though, it's not.

EXAMPLE: A tenant withheld rent claiming that an illuminated awning from a commercial street-level store directly below and outside the tenant's bedroom window caused physical ailments and claustrophobia. The landlord sued for unpaid rent. The housing court ruled that the lighting didn't breach the warranty of habitability, observing that: "people who live in a crowded urban environment must expect less than pristine, bucolic conditions and have

## Your Responsibility to Deal With Noise

Some localities have established legal standards on excessive noise. (See for example, NYC Adm. Code § 24-201 ("New York City Noise Code").) Landlords who ignore tenant noise complaints can get hit with code violations, court-ordered rent reductions and even punitive damages. Here are the some types of noise that have gotten landlords into hot water:

- **Noisy neighbors.** Unfair as it may seem, you're responsible for tenant-created noise disturbances. In one case, a tenant in a New York City building complained about loud noise from a neighboring apartment in the late night and early morning hours. But neither the owner nor manager took any effective steps to stop it. A court ruled that the continuous, excessive noise violated the warranty of habitability, and entitled the tenant to a 50% rent abatement. (*Nostand Gardens Co-Op v. Howard*, 221 A.D.2d 637, 634 N.Y.S.2d 505 (2d Dep't, 1995).)

- **Construction work.** When a landlord's extensive construction work to convert a garden apartment complex into one- and two-family homes created excessive noise, the court held that the landlord violated the warranty of habitability. (*Forest Hills No. 1 Co. v. Schimmel*, 110 Misc. 2d, 429, 440 N.Y.S.2d 471 (Civ.Ct., Queens County, 1981).) But when the construction is not the landlord's fault, there's no violation of the warranty of habitability—at least in New York City. As one judge put it: "Demolition and construction are lawful activities and part of the economic development and life cycle of New York City." (*Mantica R. Corp. NV v. Malone*, 106 Misc. 2d 953, 436 N.Y.S.2d 797, (Civ. Ct., N.Y. County, 1981).)

- **Mechanical equipment.** Too much noise from building machinery or from a commercial tenant in the same building will breach the warranty. For example, a Manhattan court awarded a tenant a 40% percent rent reduction for noise caused by a defectively mounted industrial exhaust fan situated above the tenant's living room. (*Little v. Robinson*, N.Y.L.J., 4/13/93, p. 25, col. 1 (App. Term, 1st Dep't).) A Bronx judge gave tenants a 50% rent reduction for disruptions caused by noise and vibration levels coming from their building's laundry room equipment. And in another case, a tenant got a 15% rent reduction due to excessive noise coming from a ground-floor bakery. (*Regency Joint Venture v. Goodman*, N.Y.L.J., 5/12/93, p. 30, col. 2 (Civ. Ct., N.Y. County).)

- **Pets.** Excessive noise created by another tenant's pet will breach the warranty if you have notice of the noisy pet but fail to act. (*Central Park Gardens, Inc. v. Klein*, 107 Misc. 2d 414, 434 N.Y.S.2d 125 (Civ. Ct., N.Y. County, 1980).)

Tenants who continuously create too much noise may be terminated on the ground of nuisance (Chapter 14 discusses your right to terminate on this ground. Chapter 15 shows you how to draft a "notice to cure," which officially notifies the tenant that the tenancy will be terminated if the noise doesn't stop by a certain date.)

universally been held to expect a certain 'annoyance factor' not experienced by their country cousins[.]" (*169 East 69th Street Owners Corp. v. Leland,* 156 Misc. 2d 669, 594 N.Y.S.2d 531 (Civ. Ct., N.Y. County, 1992).)

## 13. Light and Ventilation

Windows are the principle source of light and ventilation into your tenants' units.

### a. Statutory Requirements

The multiple dwelling laws specify minimum standards for natural light and ventilation within a unit. (MDL § 26, MRL § 103.) You may not alter your building so as to diminish the amount of light or air supplied to a tenant's unit. In addition, landlords are required to keep mechanical ventilation systems in working order.

Local building codes usually set standards as to minimum window sizes in relationship to the unit's square footage. And in some areas, windowless kitchens and bathrooms are required to have mechanical ventilation systems.

### b. Warranty of Habitability

Insufficient light or ventilation in a unit may violate the warranty of habitability.

> EXAMPLE: The bedroom in a Manhattan apartment had one window that faced a lot on an adjacent property. When a building was constructed on the adjacent lot, this window was closed off. When the tenant stopped paying rent, the landlord sued. The housing court ruled that the loss of the window deprived the tenant of necessary light and ventilation, made the bedroom unfit for the use reasonably intended by the parties and therefore violated the warranty of habitability. (*Department of Housing Preservation and Development of the City of New York v. Sartor*, 109 A.D.2d 665, 487 N.Y.S.2d 1 (1st Dep't 1985).)

## 14. Painting

Here's a rundown of your painting responsibilities inside a rental unit.

### a. Statutory Requirements

There's no state law obligating landlords to completely repaint units at specific time intervals. But local law may impose this requirement.

 **In New York City buildings with three or more units, landlords must completely repaint their units once every three years.** (NYC Adm. Code § 27-2013.) Landlords and managers are urged to keep painting records for each of their dwelling units that show the date the unit was last repainted, and by whom.

Your obligation under state multiple dwelling laws to keep rental units in good repair requires you to fix peeling paint conditions, and to repaint areas where necessary after they have been patched—for instance, after a behind-the-wall plumbing repair. State law prohibits the use of lead-based paint on all interior surfaces and outside porches. (Chapter 11 details state lead prohibitions). Lead-based paint in a unit where small children reside may also violate local housing codes.

 **In NYC buildings with three or more units, landlords must correct "lead hazards" in any unit in which a child under six years of age resides.** (NYC Adm. Code § 27-2056 and following.) (See Chapter 11, Section A, for more information about this requirement and lead paint abatement work.)

 **Federal and state law requires you to warn tenants about possible lead paint risks in your building.** (See Chapter 11, "Dealing With Environmental Hazards," for a full discussion of your lead-paint disclosure and abatement responsibilities.) The disclosure requirement applies when you rent an apartment, renew a lease or perform certain renovations.

### b. Warranty of Habitability

Ignoring local painting ordinances is also a breach of the warranty of habitability. (*DeVito v. Potts,* N.Y.L.J., 3/4/92, p. 25, col. 2 (Civ. Ct., N.Y. County).) If there's no local repainting requirement, you need only paint when there's a habitability problem—for example, to fix water-damaged walls or repair paint that's so thick around a window that the window can't be opened.

The existence of lead-based paint in apartments where small children reside violates the warranty of habitability. (*German v. Federal Home Loan Mortg. Corp.,* 885 F. Supp. 537 (S.D.N.Y. 1995) clarified on reargument in part, 896 F. Supp. 1385 (S.D.N.Y. 1995).) In such cases, courts are authorized to order the landlord to abate the lead paint condition. (*Laura Goldberg Mgmt. v. Rivera,* N.Y.L.J., 7/28/94, p. 23, col. 1 (Civ. Ct., N.Y. County).)

### 15. Plumbing Maintenance and Repairs

The plumbing system is generally considered to include a property's water pumps, supply and drain lines, sewage lines and fixtures, such as toilets, baths, showers, sinks and faucets.

### a. Statutory Requirements

State multiple dwelling laws set plumbing construction standards and require landlords to keep the plumbing system in good repair. (MDL § 78, MRL § 174.) Most local laws contain similar requirements.

### b. Warranty of Habitability

Defective plumbing lines and fixtures can breach the warranty of habitability. For example, a toilet that doesn't flush violates the warranty (*City of New York v. Rodriguez,* 117 Misc. 2d 986, 461 N.Y.S.2d 149 (App. Term, 1st Dep't, 1983), as does an inoperative shower.

Defective waste lines threaten tenants' health and safety. When a malfunctioning septic system caused a spillage of raw sewage along the interior and

exterior of one rental unit, this condition was found to trigger a breach of the warranty of habitability. (*People ex rel. Higgins v. Peranzo,* 179 A.D.2d 871, 579 N.Y.S.2d 453 (3d Dep't 1992).)

The warranty of habitability law does not apply to conditions caused by a tenant's misconduct. That's fortunate, since many blockages are commonly the tenant's fault—for example, when a tenant's child drops a small toy into the toilet which gets lodged in a drain line. Most leases, including ours, authorize you to charge the tenant for the cost of repairs like these. (See Clause 11 of the lease agreements in Chapter 2.)

### 16. Security

State and local laws impose basic security duties upon landlords. As you read this section, bear in mind these laws set minimum standards for security at your property. By exceeding these standards, you'll make your property safer for tenants and reduce the likelihood of a tenant getting robbed or assaulted at your property and subsequently suing you for injuries and property losses.

### a. Statutory Requirements

Multiple dwellings in New York City and Buffalo must, at minimum, be equipped with the following protective devices.

**Self-closing, self-locking building doors.** Owners of buildings built after 1967 must equip their buildings with self-closing and self-locking entrance doors. These doors must be kept locked at all times, except when a doorman or other attendant is on duty at the entrance. This requirement doesn't just apply to your lobby. It also applies to entrances from side streets, passageways, courts and yards, as well as entrances to your building's cellar, if any. (MDL § 50-a.)

**Self-closing roof doors.** All roof doors must be self-closing and secured. But they can't be self-locking. They must be fastened on the inside with movable bolts, hook or keyless lock. (MDL § 50-a.)

**Intercom systems.** Intercoms are required in all buildings with eight or more units built or converted after 1967. Older buildings with eight or more units must also have an intercom if requested by a majority of the tenants. The intercom must be located at the self-closing, self-locking entrance door, and must give the tenants of each unit the ability to talk to visitors and buzz them into the building. (MDL § 50-a.)

**Elevator mirrors.** There must be a mirror in each self-service elevator so tenants may see—prior to entering—if anyone is already in the elevator. (MDL § 51-b; NYC Adm. Code § 27-2042.)

Local ordinances may require you to install additional protective devices.

All NYC landlords must install the following additional protective devices to the entrance doors to tenant apartments:

- **peepholes,** unless the rental unit is located in a one- or two-family home where it is possible to see from the inside, any person immediately outside the entrance door. (NYC Adm. Code § 27-2041.) (The peephole requirement described above applies to buildings with three or more units, only.)
- **chain guards,** so as to permit partial opening of the door. (NYC Adm. Code § 27-2043(b).)
- **key locks** in the entrance door and at least one key, and
- **in buildings with three or more units, a heavy-duty latch set and a heavy-duty dead bolt** operable by a key from the outside and a thumb-turn from the inside. (NYC Adm. Code § 27-2043(a).)

## b. Warranty of Habitability

Courts are likely to consider the prevalence of crime in urban areas when determining what constitutes habitable housing. Good locks, security personnel, exterior lighting and secure common areas may, in some areas, be seen as an absolute necessity, as important to the tenants as are water and heat. As a result, your failure to take simple precautions, such as fixing broken locks and windows and re-keying front door locks when new tenants move in, can breach the warranty of habitability. (*Carp v. Marcus*, 112 A.D.2d 546, 491 N.Y.S.2d 484 (3d Dep't 1985).) Here's how:

**Defective unit door locks.** A secure door lock is essential to a tenant's safety. A landlord's failure to secure a rental unit compromises security and violates the warranty of habitability. (*610 West 142nd St. Corp. v. Braxton*, 137 Misc. 2d 567, 521 N.Y.S.2d 370 (Civ. Ct., N.Y. County, 1987) affirmed as modified, 140 Misc. 2d 826, 535 N.Y.S.2d 870 (App. Term, 1st Dep't, 1988).) When a tenant reports that an entrance door lock isn't working, act immediately. Otherwise, the tenant may seek damages for breach of the warranty. (*Jangla Realty v. Gravagna*, 112 Misc. 2d 642, 447 N.Y.S.2d 338 (Civil Ct., Queens County, 1981).) Or if a break-in occurs and the tenant is assaulted or robbed, the tenant can sue you for negligence.

**Inoperable building door locks and buzzer systems.** Dysfunctional building entry door locks and buzzer systems affect habitability. In one case, the landlord installed a front door lock and buzzer system, and obtained a rent increase for the installation. When a tenant was subsequently killed in the building's lobby, a Brooklyn court found a breach of warranty had occurred, since security had become an "essential service affecting habitability." (*Brownstein v. Edison*, 103 Misc. 2d 316, 425 N.Y.S.2d 773 (Sup. Ct., Kings County, 1980).)

**Drug-dealing neighbors.** When a landlord fails to protect tenants from threats and harassment from known drug dealers or other criminals in the building, a breach of the warranty of habitability may exist. (*Auburn Leasing Corp. v. Burgos*, 160 Misc. 2d 374, 609 N.Y.S.2d 549 (Civ. Ct., Queens County, 1994).) You may immediately terminate a tenancy when a unit is used for drug selling or other illegal activities. (For details, see Chapter 14.) And increasingly, courts are looking to landlords to evict drug-dealing tenants.

**Thefts and burglaries.** Usually, a landlord isn't legally responsible for crimes on the premises. But there's a legal trend that makes landlords responsible to tenant crime victims when a crime on the premises is foreseeable, and the landlord does nothing to warn or protect tenants. A landlord of a 366-unit garden apartment complex on Long Island, for example, was found to have breached the warranty by failing to take steps to protect tenants in the face of ten known thefts and burglaries committed in a one-year period. (*Highview Assoc. v.*

*Koferl*, 124 Misc. 2d 797, 477 N.Y.S.2d 585 (Dist. Ct., Suffolk County, 1984).) The court found that it was reasonable for a tenant of the complex, after an attempted burglary of her apartment, to end her lease without liability to the landlord for costs incurred in re-renting the unit.

## Drug-Dealing Problems in the Building or Neighborhood

State law imposes a statutory duty on landlords to evict tenants and other occupants who are known to be engaging in illegal drug sales or manufacturing on the property. (RPL § 231(2).) Landlords who fail to take steps to remove tenants whom they know are engaging in commercial drug activity are liable for any resulting damage, including money damages for injuries to other tenants, guests and employees that occur on the property.

A neighboring tenant who lives within 200 feet of a rental unit used for illegal or immoral purposes is authorized under state law to bring an eviction proceeding against the tenant. (RPAPL § 715(1).) In practice, tenants rarely use this power—probably fearing reprisals from the tenant conducting illegal drug business.

The same law authorizes the District Attorney's office to order a landlord to evict a tenant who uses a rental unit illegally. Ordinarily, this is triggered by the arrest of the tenant on drug charges at or near the property. You can help move this process along by providing a tip to the police about the drug activities of a tenant. Many police departments accept anonymous tips. In New York City, you may call the NYPD's Narcotics Division (888-374-DRUG) to report any illegal activity involving drugs or drug gangs.

## 17. Smoke Detectors

Smoke detectors save lives and property. More than one smoke detector may be required in a unit, depending on its size and layout. Install the device so that its alarm is clearly audible in every bedroom.

### a. Statutory Requirements

All multiple dwellings throughout the state must be equipped with at least one battery-operated smoke detector. (MRL § 15; Buffalo Code Ch. 395; NYC Adm. Code § 27-2045, § 27-2056.)

 You can charge New York City tenants a one-time reimbursement fee of $10 per battery-operated detector purchased or installed in a tenant's unit. The device must be installed so that its alarm is clearly audible in every bedroom. More than one smoke detector may be required in a unit, depending on its size and layout.

Once you install a smoke detector, it must be maintained. That means testing the device at least annually and replacing batteries whenever a new tenant moves in. Tenants are responsible for replacing batteries during their occupancy. To help limit your liability if the smoke detector fails and results in fire damage or injury, our Landlord-Tenant Checklist in Chapter 7 requires the tenant to check a box stating that the smoke detector was tested in his presence and shown to be in working order. The checklist also requires the tenant to test the smoke detector monthly and to replace the battery when necessary. As an additional safeguard, our annual safety and maintenance update (see Section G, below) reminds you to test rental unit smoke detectors each year.

### b. Warranty of Habitability

Courts have reached mixed conclusions as to whether a landlord's failure to maintain a smoke detector violates the warranty of habitability. But whether a tenant can move out, withhold rent or use the repair and deduct remedy should be the least of your worries. If a missing or defective smoke detector results in the spread of a fire that causes damage or injuries, you could pay dearly if the tenant sues and proves that the damage could have been avoided or minimized if you had followed through with your legal obligation to providing a working detector.

## New York City Landlords Must Distribute Fire Safety Plans and Notices

New York City's "Residential Fire Safety Plans and Notices Rule" (3 RCNY § 43-01) requires all residential landlords to prepare a fire safety plan and distribute it to all building occupants and staff, and to prepare and post fire safety notices in the building. The rule, adopted pursuant to New York City Local Law 10 of 2000, took effect April 13, 2000. The New York City Fire Department has prepared forms and notices for landlords to complete and reproduce in order to comply with this rule. Here are the details.

**Distribute Fire Safety Plans to Tenants and Building Staff.** A fire safety plan identifies your building's construction ("combustible" or "non-combustible"), fire safety system, means of egress, evacuation and other procedures to be followed in the event of a fire in the building. You must prepare a separate plan for each building address which consists of two sections: a building information section and a fire emergency section.

To prepare the building information section, obtain and complete a "Fire Safety Plan (Part I—Building Information Section" form from the Fire Department (a sample form is reproduced below). To prepare the fire emergency section, obtain and complete a "Fire Safety Plan Part II—Fire Emergency Information" form. This form is seven pages long. You must reproduce the completed forms (in at least 11 point type) on standard letter- or legal-sized paper and staple or bind them into booklet format.

You must give new tenants a copy of the booklet when they sign a lease or rental agreement. If you don't use a written agreement, give tenants a booklet when they move in. Thereafter, you must redistribute an updated copy of the booklet to your tenants on an annual basis, by hand delivery or first-class mail during Fire Safety Week (the first week of the month of October of each year) or with the New York City required window guard notices (between January 1 and January 16). If there's more than one tenant in the rental unit, you only need to send the booklet to one of the tenants. If you hand deliver the booklet, ask the tenant to sign a receipt for it. If you mail the booklets, get a certificate of mailing or other proof that you sent

them to each of your rental units.

In addition, you must provide a copy of the plan to building service employees when they begin employment at the building.

You must also post a copy of Part I—Building Information Section in the mailbox area of your lobby.

Finally, you must retain a copy of your building's fire safety plan (with proof of mail or delivery to tenants and employees) for at least five years.

**Post Fire Safety Notices in Rental Units and Common Areas.** A Fire Safety Notice describes evacuation procedures to be followed in the event of a fire. This one-page, 8.5" by 5.5" notice must be posted on the inside of the entrance door to each of your rental units and in the mailbox area of your lobby. The Fire Department has issued two versions of this notice: one for noncombustible buildings and one for combustible buildings. Obviously, you must obtain the form that's appropriate for your building's construction.

Once you've obtained the correct fire safety notice, you may reproduce and post it in one of two ways. You can simply copy the notice onto a single-sided sheet of letter-sized paper, frame it under clear plexiglass, and attach the frame to the inside front door of your rental units with hardware or adhesive. Or you can have the notice reproduced onto a matte-finish vinyl adhesive backed decal (at least 3 mils thick), using thermalprinting, screenprinting, or a similar permanent water-resistant printing technique, and stick them onto the doors.

Tenants and occupants are required by law to permit access to their rental units for the posting of this notice.

**Where to Get Forms.** The New York City Fire Department can provide you with the official forms. The easiest way to obtain them is to download them from the Department's website (www.nyc.gov/html/fdny/html/rcny_legal/rcny_forms.html). Or you may request forms from the Department's Bureau of Fire Prevention, 9 MetroTech Center, Brooklyn, NY 11201, 718-999-0096.

# FIRE SAFETY PLAN
## PART I -- BUILDING INFORMATION SECTION

**BUILDING ADDRESS:** _____

**BUILDING OWNER/REPRESENTATIVE:**

**Name:** _____
**Address:** _____
_____
**Telephone:** _____

**BUILDING INFORMATION:**

**Year of Construction:** _____

**Type of Construction:** ☐ Combustible   ☐ Non-Combustible

**Number of Floors:** _____ Above ground   _____ Below ground

**Sprinkler System:** ☐ Yes   ☐ No

**Sprinkler System Coverage:** ☐ Entire Building   ☐ Partial *(complete all that apply)*:

☐ Dwelling Units: _____
☐ Hallways: _____
☐ Stairwells: _____
☐ Compactor Chute: _____
☐ Other: _____

**Fire Alarm:**   ☐ Yes   ☐ Transmits Alarm to Fire Dept/Fire Alarm Co   ☐ No

Location of Manual Pull Stations: _____
_____

**Public Address System:**   ☐ Yes   ☐ No

Location of Speakers: ☐ Stairwell ☐ Hallway ☐ Dwelling Unit ☐ Other:_____
_____

**Means of Egress** (e.g., Unenclosed/Enclosed Interior Stairs, Exterior Stairs, Fire Tower Stairs, Fire Escapes, Exits):

| Type of Egress | Identification | Location | Leads to |
|---|---|---|---|
| | | | |
| | | | |
| | | | |
| | | | |
| | | | |
| | | | |

**Other Information:** _____
_____
_____

**DATE PREPARED:** _____

## 18. Snow Removal

This service includes removing ice and snow from exterior sidewalks, parking lots and other walkways used by tenants and pedestrians.

### a.  Statutory Requirements

State multiple dwelling laws do not contain any specific snow-removal obligations or standards. However, most local ordinances require you to remove snow or ice from public sidewalks on your property within a specified time period after the snow has stopped falling.

**Remove snow from the public sidewalks and gutters on your property within four hours after the snow stops falling.** If ice on a sidewalk is frozen so hard that it can't be removed, the NYC landlord may place sand, sawdust or other suitable material on the sidewalk within four hours of the end of the snowfall. If it snows between 9 PM and 7 AM, the four-hour rule doesn't apply. (NYC Adm. Code § 16-123.)

### b.  Warranty of Habitability

It's unclear as to whether shoveling snow from common areas is covered by the warranty of habitability. In one case, a Brooklyn tenant stopped paying rent, claiming that her landlord's failure to remove snow from the walkway outside her unit breached the warranty. When the landlord took her to housing court for unpaid rent, the judge rejected the tenant's claim for lack of evidence as to how deep the snow was or of any snow-related obstacle which impeded the tenant's access in or out of her unit. (*Steltzer v. Spesaison,* 161 Misc. 2d 507, 614 N.Y.S.2d 488 (Civ. Ct., Kings County, 1994).) This case suggests that the warranty could be violated if snow or ice impedes a tenant's access.

## 19. Water Service

As used here, the term "water service" means supplying hot and cold water to every bath, shower, washbasin and sink in your tenants' rental units. State laws set standards as to when water service must be provided and sets minimum temperatures for hot water.

### a.  Statutory Requirements

State multiple dwelling laws require owners of multiple dwellings at least three stories high built between 1929 and 1950, and all multiple dwellings built after 1950, to provide hot and cold water service 24 hours a day, every day of the year. (MDL § 75(3).) Hot water must be supplied at a minimum temperature of 120 degrees Fahrenheit. (Buildings constructed before 1929 must supply hot water 24 hours per day only if it was supplied or was required at the time the building was constructed.) Landlords who are exempt under the state laws may, however, be covered under local law.

 **Landlords who are not covered by the state law are subject to the NYC hot-water law.** It requires that hot water be provided at 120 degrees Fahrenheit between the hours of 6AM and midnight. (NYC Adm. Code § 27-2031.)

### b.  Warranty of Habitability

Short interruptions in water service are inevitable. Water shutdowns for plumbing repairs or water tank cleanings are often necessary. And hot water service may be affected whenever you need to service or fine-tune your heating system. Fortunately, courts have ruled that short interruptions in water service are not a breach of the warranty of habitability. A Manhattan court ruled, for instance, that insufficient hot water three or four times during a tenancy, for example, does not trigger a breach of the warranty of habitability. (*Solow.*)

Repeated or lengthy interruptions in hot or cold water service may breach the warranty.

> EXAMPLE: One Bronx apartment was without water during 13 of the hottest days of the year. Excessive use of fire hydrants in surrounding areas reduced water pressure in the building. The tenant stopped paying rent, and the landlord went to court. The judge found that the lack of water could have been remedied by the installation of a stronger water pump in the building, and ruled that the landlord violated the warranty of habitability. (*H. and R. Bernstein v. Barrett*, 101 Misc. 2d 611, 421 N.Y.S.2d 511 (Civ. Ct., Bronx County, 1979).)

## 20. Window Guards

Window guards are metal bars that attach to the outside of the apartment window. They are designed to prevent children from falling from windows. Window guards are different from so-called burglar bars that are intended to keep intruders out.

### a. Statutory Requirement

There's no state law that requires window guards. But in some localities, landlords are required to install window guards in units where young children live.

NYC landlords must install and maintain window guards in every window of a unit in which a child under the age of 11 resides, or at the request of a tenant. (NYC Adm. Code § 17-123; NYC Health Code § 131.15(a).) All New York City leases must contain a Window Guard Rider. Chapter 2, Section E, details this requirement. In addition, NYC landlords are required to deliver an annual notice to each tenant advising of the landlord's obligation to install window guards and inquiring whether children ten years of age or younger live in the unit.

### b. Warranty of Habitability

If you are subject to a local ordinance requiring the installation of window guards in units where young children reside, your failure to provide them will generally be considered a breach of the warranty of habitability. (*Ramos v. 600 West 183rd Street,* 155 A.D.2d 333, 547 N.Y.S.2d 633 (1st Dep't 1989).)

## C. Tenant Repair and Maintenance Obligations

Landlords aren't the only ones who are obligated to repair and maintain the rental premises. Tenants have responsibilities, too, that arise under ancient law, modern housing codes and the lease or rental agreement

### 1. Common Law Duty to Avoid Waste

Tenants have an implied obligation to protect the premises from becoming damaged or destroyed and to preserve it for the landlord. This is the concept of "waste," developed under early English common law. It occurs when a tenant or a tenant's family member or guest:

- intentionally damages the premises—for example, by punching a hole through a wall
- carelessly damages the unit—for example, by not cleaning fixtures and appliances or by letting a pet scratch walls or soil carpets
- permits the unit to be damaged by the elements, say by failing to fix or notify the landlord about a broken window, or
- performs alterations that change the essential character of the premises or reduce its value, such as by adding a wall to create an extra bedroom, or removing a closet without the landlord's permission.

Landlords may sue tenants who permit or commit waste. You may sue for compensatory damages, and, in some cases, for the tenant's removal. (RPAPL § § 801, 815.) In addition, most modern leases contain a clause that permits termination if the tenant is responsible for deterioration or destruction of rental property. Our lease and rental agreement contain such a clause. (See Chapter 2, Clause 13.)

 **Tenants have a narrowly defined right to alter or repair the premises in specific situations.** Examples include:

- alterations by a disabled person (see Chapter 1, Section 4, for details)
- use of the "repair and deduct" procedure (discussed in Section D, below), and
- installation of wireless antennas and small satellite dishes (see the end of this chapter for details).

## 2. Tenant Duties Under Modern Housing Codes

State and local housing and maintenance codes also address the age-old duty to avoid waste by making tenants responsible for violations in rental units and common areas of the building that are:

- caused by the willful act of the tenant, a guest or a member of the tenant's family or household, or
- the result of the gross negligence, neglect or abuse of the tenant, a guest or a member of the tenant's family or household. (See, for example, HMC § 27-2006(a)(1)-(2).)

In addition to an obligation to keep the premises from becoming damaged or destroyed, state (and most local) housing maintenance codes require tenants to keep their rental units clean and sanitary. Under the multiple dwelling laws and the HMC, these include:

- keeping the rental unit clean and free from vermin, dirt, filth, garbage and any other thing that endangers life or health
- not keeping garbage or trash in the apartment for so long as to create a public nuisance, and
- only placing garbage and trash in the receptacles or compactor trash chutes provided by the landlord. (MDL § 81.)

Local housing maintenance codes may include additional obligations. For example, under the HMC § 27-2007, tenants shall not:

- remove, disable or prop open any self-closing door device which is required by law to be self-closing, such as a stairwell door in a common area
- obstruct access to any public hall or fire escape, for example, with a baby carriage, bike or potted plant
- remove or disable any showerhead installed by the landlord, such as a water-saving showerhead, or
- unreasonably refuse to afford access to the landlord to make repairs or improvements required under the HMC.

## 3. Duties Arising Under the Lease or Rental Agreement

Most leases and rental agreements, including ours, obligate the tenant to:

- take good care of the rental unit during the tenancy and not damage it, and
- restore and repair the rental unit to its original condition before moving out, except for ordinary wear and tear that may occur during the tenancy.

In addition, most leases and rental agreements require tenants to notify the landlord of repair problems or defective conditions. And even if it's not a lease requirement, landlord notification is a condition for exercising any of the tenant's repair-related legal remedies, as explained in Section D, below.

If a rental unit is rendered uninhabitable due to the tenant's failure to keep up his end of the bargain, the tenant will have a difficult, if not impossible, time convincing a judge that he is not a suitable candidate for eviction and the repair bill. (If a tenant doesn't pay, the landlord can deduct the expense from the security deposit.) A tenant can't withhold rent, or use "repair and deduct" for conditions she caused.

## Make the Tenant Financially Liable for Damage to Your Property

Be sure your lease or rental agreement makes the tenant financially responsible for repair of damage caused by the tenant's negligence or misuse. (See Clause 11 of the form agreements in Chapter 2.) That means that where the tenant or his friends or family cause damage—for example, a broken window or a freezer that no longer works because the tenant defrosted it with a carving knife—it's the tenant's responsibility to make the repairs or to reimburse you for doing so. If a tenant refuses to repair or pay for the damage he caused, you can add the repair costs to the tenant's rent bill as "additional rent." If he refuses, he's a candidate for a nonpayment eviction proceeding. Or you can sue, perhaps in small claims court, for the cost of the repairs. You can't tap the security deposit for any tenant-caused repairs, however, until the tenant moves out. (Chapter 16 discusses small claims court and security deposit deductions.)

## D. Tenant Responses to Unfit Premises: Paying Less Rent

If you fail to live up to your legal duty to maintain your property, your tenants have a variety of options, each one designed to pressure you into compliance. Hopefully, you will run your business in such a way that your tenants will have no reason to take legal action. But even the most conscientious landlord may encounter a tenant who attempts to avoid his responsibility to pay the rent by claiming that the premises are unfit. If you are a victim of a scam like this, you'll need to know how to defend yourself.

Your tenants' options will probably include one or more of what we call the "big sticks" in a tenant's self-help arsenal. These include:

- repairing the problem (or having it repaired by a professional) and deducting the cost from the rent (this is called "repair and deduct," see Section 2, below)

- withholding the rent and if you sue, seeking a "rent abatement" from the court (see Section 3, below)
- organizing a "rent strike" in which a group of tenants withholds rent (see Section 3)
- calling state or local building or health inspectors (see Section E)
- filing suit against you for damages or for the appointment of a court-appointed rent administrator (see Section E), or
- moving out (see Section E).

**Rent-regulated tenants may seek a rent cut from the State Division of Housing and Comunity Renewal (DHCR) for decreased building-wide or individual apartment services.** This issue is discussed in Section F, below.

If you haven't fixed a serious problem that truly makes the rental unit uninhabitable—a severe infestation of mice in the kitchen, for example—you can expect that a savvy tenant will successfully use more than one of these options. In this section, we'll explain the two options that involve paying less rent; in Section E, below, we'll explain the others. Finally, in Sections G and H, we'll discuss how careful adherence to a high quality maintenance system should help you avoid problems with tenants paying less rent in the first place.

## 1. Conditions for Paying Less Rent

A tenant can't point to a trivial problem, like a dripping water faucet or a broken kitchen drawer, as an excuse to pay less rent. Generally, three conditions must be met before a tenant is justified in withholding rent or using the repair and deduct remedy.

1. **The problem is serious, not just annoying, and imperils the tenant's health or safety.** Not every building code violation or annoying defect in a rental home (like the water heater's ability to reach only 110 degrees F, short of the code-specified 120 degrees) justifies paying less rent.

2. **The tenant told you, either orally or in writing, about the problem and gave you a reasonable**

**opportunity to get it fixed.** What's "reasonable" will depend on the nature and urgency of the problem. A broken door lock should be fixed as soon as possible after notice and certainly within 24 hours. A stubborn roach problem in the kitchen, on the other hand, may take weeks to completely abate. "Reasonable opportunity" also means that the tenant must have provided access to the rental unit to you or your workers in order to make needed repairs.

3. **The tenant (or a guest) did not cause the problem, either deliberately or through carelessness or neglect.** A tenant can't pay less rent based on a window he broke himself.

## 2. Repair and Deduct

If you let your rental property fall below the fit and habitable standard, tenants may use a legal procedure called "repair and deduct." It works like this: Under certain conditions the tenant can, without your permission and without filing a lawsuit, have the defect repaired and subtract the cost of the repairs from the following month's rent. Section 1, above, describes three conditions that must be met before a tenant is justified in using the repair and deduct remedy.

EXAMPLE: When Mary got home, she discovered that her Queens apartment had been burglarized. The thieves broke the lock on her front door. At 7 PM, Mary reported the burglary to the building super and asked him to replace the lock. By the following afternoon, the landlord still hadn't fixed the lock, so Mary hired a locksmith to do it and deducted the $120 cost from her monthly rent. A judge found that the urgent circumstances entitled the tenant to use the repair and deduct remedy to remove the code violation and secure the tenant's safety and peace of mind. (*Jangla Realty Co. v. Gravagna*, 112 Misc. 2d 642, 447 N.Y.S.2d 338 (Civ.Ct., Queens County, 1981).)

A tenant's use of the repair and deduct remedy can have unpleasant consequences. The tenant may not hire the kind of skilled, reasonably priced repair person whom you would have chosen. Consequently, the chances for a needlessly expensive job or a shoddy one are great.

EXAMPLE: When Matt opened the cupboard underneath his bathroom sink, he saw that the flexible hose connecting the pipe nipple to the sink was leaking. He turned off the water and called his landlord, Lee, who promised to attend to the problem right away. After three days without a bathroom sink, Matt called a plumber, who replaced the hose for $100. Matt deducted this amount from his next rent check. Lee thought no more about this until he got a frantic call from the tenant in the apartment beneath Matt's. She described her ceiling as looking like a giant, dripping sponge. Lee called his regular plumber to check the problem out. His plumber told Lee that the repair on Matt's sink had been done negligently, resulting in a major leak into the walls. If Lee had called his own plumber, the job would have been done right in the first place, saving Lee lots of money and hassle.

Chances are you'll be less than thrilled to learn that your tenant has repaired his unit and sent you a short rent check. But consider the circumstances when deciding if a tenant acted unreasonably. Ask yourself how much it would have cost you to make the same repair, Obviously, a tenant who pays $400 for a simple lock repair that should have cost only $100 is acting more unreasonably than someone who paid $150 for a repair you could have accomplished for $100.

Whether the tenant gave you reasonable notice of the problem before making a repair, or spent too much money, are issues that are ultimately decided by a judge, not you. A judge will weigh the severity of the problem against the ease with which it could have been fixed. But even if you think that a judge would conclude that a tenant acted precipitously (or spent too much), going to court over this sort of dispute is rarely productive, unless the tenant's conduct was outrageous. The cost of dragging the tenant to court can easily offset or outweigh any additional rent a judge may think you're entitled to.

## 3.  Rent Withholding and Rent Strikes

While there isn't any statute that explicitly authorizes New York tenants to withhold rent, it's quite common for some tenants to withhold all or part of their monthly rent when they believe that you're ignoring a serious problem in their rental unit or in the building's common areas. Section 1, above, describes three conditions that may compel rent withholding by tenants.

A "rent strike" refers to the withholding of rent by either a group of tenants or by a tenants' association in response to a landlord's failure to provide essential buildingwide services or necessary repairs. The tenants' goal is usually to coerce the landlord to address conditions that breach the warranty of habitability and/or violate state or local housing codes, such as rodent infestation or problems that affect all tenants, such as malfunctioning elevators, a lack of heat or inoperable security systems. (So-called "7-A proceedings," in which rent-striking tenants sue to have a rent administrator appointed for the building, are discussed in Section E2, below.)

⚠ **Tenants are legally entitled to organize.** Landlords may not inhibit or otherwise restrict tenants from forming, joining or participating in tenant groups (RPL § 230). Landlords are specifically prohibited from evicting tenants due to their organizational activities or efforts. (RPL § 223(b).) Landlords may, however, bring nonpayment eviction proceedings against tenants who withhold rent.

## 4.  Options When a Tenant Pays Less Rent

When a tenant or group of tenants withholds rent, you basically have two options:

- Go to the tenant or tenants and attempt to resolve the problem yourself. This is the fastest, cheapest route. Subsection a, below, suggests ways to work out a compromise.
- Demand the rent, go to court and let a judge resolve it. But when tenants have a legitimate gripe, this is rarely the best strategy. Subsection b, below, explains why.

While the focus here is on dealing with a tenant who withholds rent, many of the strategies are useful if a tenant uses the repair and deduct remedy.

### a.  Working Out a Compromise With Rent-Withholding Tenants

If you think the tenant is wrong, but sincere—that is, she probably isn't trying to make up an excuse for not paying rent, but thinks that she is entitled to do so—your best course is usually to try and work things out with the tenant either over the phone or in a face-to-face meeting. If, for example, your tenant withheld rent but you were never given adequate notice of the problem, it may make sense to agree to perform any needed work as soon as possible, in exchange for the tenant's promise to pay all or most of the overdue rent upon completion. It may be painful to make this sort of compromise, but not nearly as bad as trying to evict the tenant and risk that a judge might give her a bigger rent reduction than you could have negotiated yourself with the tenant.

Sometimes, despite your best efforts to keep on top of repair and maintenance issues, a repair job falls through the cracks. It could happen while you are on vacation and your backup system doesn't work, or maybe you simply need a better manager. If, in all fairness, a tenant was justified in using rent withholding or repair and deduct, admit it and take steps to rectify the situation. For example, after getting the necessary work done, you might try to make use of the compromise procedure outlined here. Once the immediate problem is behind you, treat what happened as an opportunity to review, revise and improve your maintenance and repair procedures. (See Section G, below.)

## Sample Letter Suggesting Compromise on Rent Withholding

May 3, 200X

Tyrone McNab
Villa Arms, Apt. 4
200 Main Street
Buffalo, NY 14203

Dear Mr. McNab:

I am writing you in the hope we can work out a fair compromise to the problems that led you to withhold rent. You have rented a unit at the Villa Arms for the last three years and we have never had a problem before. Let's try to resolve it.

To review briefly, on May 1, Marvin, my resident manager at Villa Arms, told me that you were temporarily withholding your rent because of several conditions in your apartment. Marvin said you had asked him to correct these problems two weeks ago, but he hasn't as yet attended to them. Marvin states that you listed these problems as some peeling paint on the interior wall of your bedroom, a leaky kitchen water faucet, a running toilet, a small hole in the living room carpet and a cracked kitchen window.

I have instructed Marvin to promptly arrange with you for a convenient time to allow him into your apartment to repair all these problems. I am sure these repairs would already have been accomplished by now except for the fact that Hank, our regular repair person, has been out sick for the last ten days.

I understand that these problems are annoying and significant to you. However, I do not believe that they justify rent withholding under state law. My first wish is to come to an amicable understanding with you that we can live with and use to avoid problems like this in the future.

Because of the inconvenience you have suffered as a result of the problems in your apartment, I am prepared to offer you a prorated 50% rebate on your rent for ten days, this being the estimated length of time it will have taken Marvin to remedy the problems from the day of your complaint. As your monthly rent is $1,200, equal to $40 per day, I am agreeable to your paying only $1,000 rent this month.

If this is not acceptable to you, please call me at 555-1234 during the day. If you would like to discuss any aspect of the situation in more detail, I would be pleased to meet with you at your convenience. I will expect to receive your check for $1,000, or a call from you, before May 10.

Sincerely,

*Sandra Schmidt*

Sandra Schmidt
Owner, Villa Arms

The chances for resolving a conflict will be greater if you have a compromise system in place when you need it. When you find yourself dealing with a tenant who is not an obvious candidate for eviction (and especially if the tenant has some right on her side), consider taking the following steps:

1. Call or meet with the tenant (or tenants) to negotiate. You should be interested in establishing a good solution to avoid problems in the future and not in determining who was right. If you're reluctant to call, write a letter instead. See the Sample Letter Suggesting Compromise on Rent Withholding, above.

2. If negotiation fails, suggest mediation by a neutral third party. Colleges, law schools and bar associations in many areas run low-cost mediation programs for landlord-tenant disputes. Check out how this works in advance so you can move quickly should the need arise again.

3. Put your solution in writing.

4. If the process indicates a larger problem with tenant dissatisfaction, encourage the tenant or tenants to meet with you regularly to solve it.

In many cases, it may be possible for you and the tenant to come to a mutually acceptable agreement using this system. On your end, this might mean promptly having the necessary work done and better maintaining the unit in the future. You might also give the tenant a prorated rent reduction for the period between the time the tenant notified you of the defect and the time it was corrected. In exchange, the tenant might promise to promptly notify you of problems before resorting to the same tactic in the future.

EXAMPLE: A leaky roof during a rainy month deprives a tenant, Steve, of the use of one of his two bedrooms. If Steve gave his landlord, Joe, notice of the leak, and Joe did not take care of the problem quickly, Steve might be justified in deducting $600 from the $1,600 rent for that month. However, if Steve didn't tell Joe of the problem until the next month's rent was due, a compromise might be reached where Steve bears part of the responsibility, by agreeing to deduct only $200 from the rent.

In Section G, below, we give detailed suggestions of how to set up and implement a maintenance program designed to identify repair needs before they become repair problems.

## b. Going to Court Against Rent-Withholding Tenants

When tenants improperly withhold rent, you're entitled to demand the unpaid rent and, if necessary, begin "nonpayment" eviction proceedings in court. (Chapter 12 covers rent demands.) But from a practical standpoint, going to court isn't always the best strategy.

If you're faced with rent-striking tenants especially, it's wise to craft a solution outside of a courtroom. Rent strikers can usually get their individual nonpayment proceedings "consolidated" into a single proceeding which permits them to hire big legal guns. You'll be pressured to "arm" yourself accordingly—and you can forget trying to use quick, inexpensive small claims court.

**Get a lawyer to represent you in rent strikes.** It makes economic sense to have an experienced landlord-tenant lawyer handle a nonpayment case against a group of rent-striking tenants. When tenants' cases are consolidated, there's a lot of unpaid and future rent at stake.

If the tenant (or tenants) can convince a judge that their rental unit is uninhabitable or that there are serious violations of state or local housing laws, the judge may 1) order you to repair any defects within a set period of time, 2) require you to come back to court to show proof that repairs have been made, 3) retroactively reduce the rent by granting a "rent abatement," usually based on a percentage formula that relates to the loss of rental value in the unit caused by the defect, 4) reduce the future rent that the tenant will have to pay by the same formula until repairs are made and 5) order you to pay the tenant's (or tenants') legal fees, if authorized under the lease or rental agreement. (Chapter 2, Clause 20, covers attorneys' fees.) So unless you're absolutely sure of your position, going to court can leave you worse off than where you started.

EXAMPLE 1: One Manhattan judge awarded a 20% rent abatement to a tenant for 17 instances of no hot water, and a 30% rent abatement for a lack of heat on 13 instances during a three-month period. (*Parker 72nd Associates v. Isaacs*, 109 Misc. 2d.57, 436 N.Y.S. 2d 542 (Civ.Ct., N.Y. County, 1980).)

EXAMPLE 2: A Manhattan court ruled that a landlord's failure to provide heat and hot water to a tenant for 31 days violated the warranty of habitability and reduced the value of the unit—and the tenant's rent—from $450 to $275 per month. (*Leris Realty Corp. v. Robbins*, 95 Misc. 2d 712, 408 N.Y.S.2d 166 (Civ.Ct., N.Y. County, 1978).)

EXAMPLE 3: In a Watertown case, a landlord was ordered to pay $10,000 in punitive damages for failing to remedy a severe vermin infestation. (*Smithline v. Monica,* 1987 WL 14296 (City Ct., Watertown, 1987).)

On the other hand, if you have kept your rental properties in good shape and properly handle repair and maintenance problems, your best bet may be to serve a rent demand on any tenant who pays you less or no rent telling the tenant to pay or leave. (Chapter 12 provides details on rent demands.) If the tenant ignores your notice, you can begin a nonpayment eviction proceeding.

If you do end up in court, the tenant normally has the burden of convincing a judge that the withholding was justified. (Section 1, above, describes the three conditions the tenant must prove to justify rent withholding.) Then the burden falls on the landlord to prove that the tenant was wrong to withhold rent by raising one or more of the following points:

- The claimed defect was nonexistent and nothing justified the tenant's failure to pay the rent.
- The tenant caused the defect himself.
- The tenant is merely trying avoid paying rent.
- The claimed defect was not really serious or substantial enough to entitle the tenant to a rent abatement for a breach the warranty of habitability.

- Even if the defect was substantial, you were never given adequate notice and a chance to fix it. (At this point you should present a detailed complaint procedure to the court as we recommend in Section G, below. You should show, if possible, that the tenant didn't follow your complaint procedure.)
- The tenant failed to provide access to you or your workers to inspect and fix the defect. (You should present copies of any notes or letters to the tenant requesting access. If you don't have these, bring notes from any of your telephone conversations or meetings with the tenant regarding access.)

# E. Tenant Responses: Calling Inspectors, Filing Lawsuits or Service Complaints and Moving Out

Tenants who are faced with unfit rentals are not limited to rent withholding or repairing the defects themselves and deducting the cost from their rent. Other options that do not involve paying less rent include calling government inspectors (Section 1, below), suing you for money damages, an order requiring you to make repairs or for the appointment of a "rent administrator" (Section 2, below), or surrendering the lease or rental agreement and moving out (Section 3, below).

Rent-regulated tenants have another option if you fail to provide required or essential services; they may apply to the Division of Housing and Community Renewal (DHCR) for a rent reduction as discussed in Section F, below.

## 1. Reporting Code Violations to Housing Inspectors

A tenant may complain to a local building, health or fire department about problems such as inoperable plumbing, a leaky roof or bad wiring. If an inspector discovers code violations, you will be issued an order to correct the problem.

The local enforcement agency typically requires the property owner to remedy all violations found (within a certain amount of time, such as five to 30 business days). If you fail to make any repairs demanded by local officials within the time allowed, the municipality may bring a civil lawsuit against you. Moreover, failure to comply with certain cited violations of state and local housing laws is a criminal misdemeanor punishable by hefty fines or even imprisonment. In some cases, local officials may require that the building be vacated, with the landlord providing tenants with temporary housing, until the violation is corrected.

## 2. Lawsuits by the Tenant

A landlord who fails to maintain his property can be sued by a tenant who has not withheld rent and is not defending a nonpayment eviction proceeding. By failing to repair defective conditions, the landlord breaches the warranty of habitability—an implied-by-law term in every lease and rental agreement. The tenant (whether she is still in occupancy of the unit or has moved out) can sue you for violating your promise to provide a habitable dwelling and ask for the following:

- money damages based on the difference between the rental value of the premises in substandard condition and the rent you've charged
- repair costs incurred by the tenant due to the landlord's failure, after reasonable notice, to make a repair affecting habitability
- replacement costs for personal property damage caused by your negligence, such as replacing a water-soaked Persian rug ruined by a leaking roof
- compensation for personal injuries—including pain and suffering—caused by your negligence

- interest on money damages the tenant is awarded, calculated as of the date the breach occurred
- "punitive" damages to punish you for especially outrageous or egregious violations of the warranty of habitability, and
- attorneys' fees, if authorized by the tenant's lease or rental agreement (Clause 20 of the form agreements in Chapter 2 discusses attorneys' fees).

Tenants may also seek a court order directing you to make repairs, with rent reduced until you show proof to the court that the defects have been remedied. And in some cases, a group of tenants may sue for the appointment of an administrator to collect rents and make needed repairs (see "When Tenants Sue for a 'Rent Administrator,'" below).

If the total money damages sought by the tenant are at or under $3,000, the tenant may sue you in the municipal "small claims" court that serves your area. For claims over $3,000, the tenant must file a state court action. Chapter 16, Section I, discusses small claims court.

**NYC tenants may commence "Housing Part" (HP) proceedings against you to compel you to correct housing violations.** Tenants may bring an HP proceeding alone or together with other tenants in Housing Court for conditions in your building that violate housing codes. (NYC Adm. Code § 27-2115(h); NYCCCA § 110(a).) The tenant may ask for a court-ordered inspection by HPD, the City agency that enforces housing codes, if HPD hasn't already issued a violation against the property for the defective condition. If one or more violations are found, the Court will order the landlord to correct them by a certain date. If you fail to do so, you may be penalized or even imprisoned for being in contempt of a court order.

## Your Liability for Dangerous Conditions

As a property owner, you are responsible for keeping your premises reasonably safe for tenants and guests. For example, you may be liable (legally responsible) for physical injuries caused by a broken step or defective wiring that you knew about (or should have known about) and failed to fix. Injured tenants can seek financial recovery for medical bills, lost earnings, pain and other physical suffering, permanent physical disability and disfigurement and emotional distress. Tenants can also look to you for the cost of property damage that results from faulty or unsafe conditions. In extreme cases, a single personal injury verdict against your business has the potential to wipe you out.

Contact your insurance company as soon as you know about a tenant's injury (your policy probably requires you to immediately report any claim or *expected* claim). Your insurer will tell you what to do, such as preparing a report on details of the accident. Similarly, if you're served with legal papers that threaten legal action or notify you about a personal injury lawsuit, get copies of the papers to your insurer right away.

A tenant who is injured on your property may have a good legal claim against you. That doesn't necessarily mean you'll end up in court. The majority of tenant claims against landlords are settled without trial—usually through negotiations with your insurance company. If your tenant does end up filing a personal injury lawsuit, you (or your insurance company) will need to hire a lawyer.

**You may not retaliate against a tenant who files a lawsuit and stays in the property.** (See Chapter 14 for a discussion of retaliatory eviction.) It may seem inconsistent for a tenant to take the extreme step of suing you and expecting to remain on the property. Nevertheless, a tenant who sues and stays is exercising a legal right. Retaliation, such as delivering a rent increase or a termination notice, is illegal and will give the tenant yet another ground on which to sue.

## When Tenants Sue for a "Rent Administrator"

Under certain circumstances, tenants in buildings with serious habitability problems or multiple housing code violations may join together to begin a legal process known as an "Article 7-A proceeding." This proceeding asks the court to appoint an administrator to collect unpaid and future rents from all tenants at the building and to use the money to fix building defects.

This remedy is available only to tenants of buildings with three or more units, in both regulated and non-regulated units statewide. And, at least one-third of the building's tenants must be willing to join in the proceeding. (RPAPL § 770(1).) The landlord may ask the court to dismiss the case (or at least some of the claims made by the tenants) on any of the following grounds:

- Fewer than one-third of the building's tenants in occupancy have joined in the proceeding.
- A claimed defect is nonexistent or has been fixed.
- A tenant, tenant's family member or guest caused one or more of the claimed defects.
- You were refused entry or access to a tenant's unit so that repairs could be made. (RPAPL § 775).

If the tenants convince the judge that the building has serious defects, a judge may order that all unpaid and future rent due from the building's tenants be deposited with a court-appointed administrator and used to remedy the defective conditions. The rent administrator controls the purse strings until necessary repairs or improvements get made. Upon completion of the work and/or correction of all code violations, any surplus rent is released to the landlord, together with a complete accounting of rents deposited and costs incurred. (RPAPL § 776.)

If you're served with legal papers notifying you of a 7-A proceeding (officially called Petition for the Appointment of an Administrator, Pursuant to Article 7-A), go to an experienced landlord-tenant attorney for help. These proceedings have been known to drag on for years and have bankrupted many landlords. Effective legal representation can save you from a similar fate.

## 3. Moving Out

In certain circumstances, tenants are entitled to move out—either temporarily or permanently—because of defective conditions at the property.

### a. Asking Tenants to Move So Repairs Can Be Made

Unsafe conditions at your building may require you to voluntarily relocate one or more tenants while repairs are made. Similarly, a state or local authority could issue a "vacate" order in response to an unsafe condition (such as a hazardous structural or environmental condition) that requires all of your tenants and occupants to temporarily move out. In such cases, the landlord is generally required to provide the tenant with comparable housing or to reimburse the tenant for alternate housing expenses.

 **Notify your insurance carrier immediately if you are required to relocate tenants.** Depending on the nature of the unsafe condition, your insurance policy may cover your tenant relocation expenses (as well as related repair work).

### b. Tenant's Right to Move Out of Uninhabitable Unit

When a landlord has allowed his property to become uninhabitable, the tenant may move out without any further obligation to pay rent. The law, of course, has a shorthand phrase to describe this situation. It's called a "constructive eviction," and it means that conditions on the property are so bad that the landlord has indirectly "evicted" the tenant by making it impossible to live there. (*Barash v. Pennsylvania Terminal Real Estate Corp.*, 26 N.Y.2d 77, 308 N.Y.S.2d 649, 256 N.E.2d 707 (1970); RPL § 227.) A tenant who has been constructively evicted (that is, he has a valid reason to move out) has no further responsibility for rent.

Tenants who move out permanently because of habitability problems may also be entitled to money from you to compensate them for out-of-pocket losses. For example, the tenants may be able to recover for moving expenses and the cost of a hotel for a few days until they find a new place. Also, if the conditions were substandard during prior months when the tenants did pay the full rent, you may be sued for money damages equal to the difference between the value of the defective dwelling and the rent paid.

EXAMPLE: Susan signed a one-year lease for an apartment with a river view. She thought it was a great deal because the monthly rent of $1,400 was considerably less than similar properties in the neighborhood. Susan's dream of an apartment began to turn into a nightmare when she discovered, soon after moving in, that the bedroom was full of mildew that attacked every surface and interfered with her breathing. After numerous complaints to the landlord, which were ignored, Susan moved out at the end of four months, and rented a comparable apartment nearby for $1,600. She then sued the landlord for money damages. The judge decided that Susan was entitled to:

**Compensation for the months she had endured the defective conditions.** Susan asked for the difference between the agreed-upon rent and the real value of the apartment (the apartment with its defects), times four (the number of months she paid rent). The judge ruled that the mildew problem, which had forced Susan to sleep in the living room, had essentially reduced the one-bedroom apartment to a studio apartment, which would have rented for $1,000 per month. Accordingly, Susan was entitled to a refund of $400 for each of the four months, or $1,600.

**Moving costs.** Susan asked for the $250 cost of hiring a moving company to transport her belongings to her new home. The judge ruled that Susan's moving costs of $250 were reasonable, and ordered the landlord to pay them.

### c. Tenant's Right to Move Out After a Fire or Other Calamity

If your property is seriously damaged or destroyed as a result of a fire, hurricane or other calamity, tenants whose units are damaged or destroyed by no fault of their own may cancel their lease or rental agreement and move out without any further obligation to pay rent. (RPL § 227.) However, landlords and tenants are free to change this result, and usually do, by way of a special clause in their lease or rental agreement.

For instance, the lease and rental agreements in this book provide that in the event that the premises are destroyed or seriously damaged, the landlord may elect either to hold the tenant to the agreement and restore the premises, or to terminate the agreement on written notice. (See Clause 23 of the agreements in Chapter 2.) However, if you elect to restore the premises, our clause entitles the tenant to a rent abatement in proportion to any unusable part of the premises. And if you don't repair the damage within 30 days after the damage occurs, the tenant gets the right to terminate the agreement.

Depending on the cause of the damage and the terms of your lease or rental agreement, a tenant who moves out may have a viable claim for relocation expenses and related costs. Obviously, the tenant whose rental unit is destroyed by a natural disaster has less reason to expect assistance from you than one whose home is destroyed by fire caused by your botching an electrical repair job. And the tenant whose home burns down because he left the stove on all night will probably find himself at the other end of a lawsuit.

**Natural or third-party disasters.** If a fire, flood, hurricane, tornado or other natural disaster renders the dwelling unlivable, or if a third party is the cause of the destruction (for instance, a fire due to an arsonist), your best bet is to look to your insurance policy for help in repairing or rebuilding the unit and to cover any claims made by tenants for relocation costs. While waiting for the insurance coverage to kick in, give month-to-month tenants a termination notice (see Chapter 13). For tenants with leases, you may be obligated to pay for substitute housing for a longer period, depending on the terms of the lease. To be prudent, when you purchase or renew your insurance policy, ask your insurance broker if your policy will cover tenant relocation costs in the event of a fire or natural disaster so that you know exactly where you'll stand.

**Destruction that is traceable to the landlord.** If it can be shown that you or your employees were even partially responsible for the damage, your legal responsibility to the tenant is likely to increase. You may be expected to cover a longer period of temporary housing and, if the substitute housing is more expensive, you may be stuck with paying the difference between the new rent and the old rent. The insurance issue will also take on a different cast: Some policies exclude coverage for natural disasters, but include (as is standard) coverage for the owner's negligent acts. The facts surrounding the property damage or destruction, the wording of your insurance policy and the terms of the tenant's lease or rental agreement will determine how each situation is handled.

If a tenant moves out due to damage or destruction of the premises, for whatever cause, it will be important for you and the tenant to sign a written agreement surrendering all rights to the rental unit once the tenant is relocated. (See the sample Lease Surrender Agreement in Chapter 14, Section G.) This allows you to proceed with the repair or rebuilding without the pressure of tenants waiting to move in immediately. If you want to re-rent to the same tenant, a new lease or rental agreement can be drawn up at that time.

## F. Rent-Regulated Tenant's Right to a DHCR Rent Reduction for Decreased Services

Rent-stabilized and rent-controlled tenants have another option at their disposal if you fail to provide required or essential services. They may apply to the Division of Housing and Community Renewal (DHCR), the state agency that enforces rent regulations, for a rent reduction due to decreased "individual apartment" or "buildingwide" services. If the DHCR finds that you have indeed decreased services, it will issue a rent reduction lowering the amount of rent you may collect for the apartment. The rent reduction remains in effect until you correct the problem and obtain a DHCR "rent restoration order," which permits you to again charge and collect the full, regulated rent from the tenant. Be forewarned: While rent is reduced for a failure to provide services, you are ineligible for any future rent increases for the apartment until rents are restored by DHCR order.

 **DHCR offers expedited mediation for new service complaints.** If you consent, all newly filed service complaints are eligible for telephone mediation. Here's how it works. If your tenant requests mediation, the complaint will be handled by a counselor who will contact you by phone. The counselor will attempt to have you make repairs within 14 days. If you restore services during this time period, the case is over. The tenant can't get any rent reductions for the time period in which the case was pending. But if you fail to restore services, the tenant's service complaint will be processed through the ordinary channels (requiring you to file a written answer, inviting the tenant's reply, and dispatching an inspector, if necessary, for an on-site inspection) that take an average of 12 months to complete. If the DHCR finds that you decreased services, the tenant (or tenants) who filed the complaint is entitled to a rent reduction until you restore services and the DHCR issues a rent restoration order.

## 1. What Services Are Required?

Landlords may not reduce or suspend any services that were furnished to a rent-controlled or rent-stabilized unit when the unit first became subject to rent regulation. These "base-date services" are also called "required services" for rent-stabilized units and "essential services" for rent-controlled units. Such services may include repairs, painting, maintenance, the furnishing of light, heat, hot and cold water, telephone, elevator service, kitchen, bath and

laundry facilities and amenities such as maid service, linen service, janitor service and garbage removal. Landlords who reduce services to rent-regulated tenants are subject to rent cuts.

A tenant can't sandbag you by filing a service complaint over a condition you were never notified about. The tenant must request necessary repairs or maintenance from you or your agent, in writing, at least ten—and no more than 60—days before the date she files a service complaint. The tenant must attach a copy of her letter to you, to the DHCR complaint, along with a U.S. Post Office certificate of mailing, certified mail receipt or signed delivery receipt acknowledging personal delivery to you or your agent. The only exception to the prior notification rule is for heat and hot water complaints, emergency repairs or if a fire requires the tenant to move from the premises.

## 2. Minor Problems That Do Not Qualify for a Rent Reduction

Under regulations issued in December, 2000, DHCR may not order a rent reduction in response to certain *de minimus* conditions in the building or in individual units.

### a. Buildingwide Conditions

Here is a list of buildingwide conditions that will generally *not* constitute a failure to maintain a required service and qualify for a rent reduction:

- **Air conditioning.** Failure to provide in lobby, hallways, stairwells and other nonenclosed public areas.
- **Building entrance door.** Removal of canopy over unlocked door leading to vestibule; changes in door-locking devices, where security or access is not otherwise compromised.
- **Carpeting.** Change in color or quality under certain circumstances; isolated stains on otherwise clean carpets; frayed areas that do not create a tripping hazard.
- **Cracks.** Sidewalk cracks that do not create a tripping hazard; hairline cracks in walls and ceilings.

- **Decorative amenities.** Modification (for example, fountain replaced with rock garden); removal of some or all for aesthetic reasons.
- **Elevator.** Failure to post elevator inspection certificates; failure to provide or maintain amenities in elevator, such as an ashtray, fan or recorded music.
- **Floors.** Failure to wax floors; discrete areas in need of cleaning or dusting, where there is evidence that janitorial services are being regularly provided and most areas are clean (See "Janitorial services," below.)
- **Garage.** Any condition that does not interfere with the use of the garage or an assigned parking space, such as peeling paint where there is no water leak.
- **Graffiti.** Minor graffiti inside the building; any graffiti outside the building where the owner submits an "affidavit of ongoing maintenance" indicating a reasonable time period when the specific condition will be next addressed.
- **Janitorial services.** Failure to clean or dust discrete areas, where there is evidence that janitorial services are being regularly provided because most areas are, in fact, clean.
- **Landscaping.** Modification; failure to maintain a particular aspect of landscaping where the grounds are generally maintained.
- **Lighting in public areas.** Missing light bulbs where the lighting is otherwise adequate.
- **Lobby or hallways.** Discontinuance of fresh cut flowers; removal of fireplace or fireplace andirons; modification of furniture; removal of some furnishings (determined on a case-by-case basis); removal of decorative mirrors; reduction in lobby space where reasonable access to tenant areas is maintained; elimination of public area doormat; failure to maintain a lobby directory that is not associated with a building intercom; removal or replacement of window coverings (See "Decorative amenities," above).
- **Mail distribution.** Elimination of door-to-door or other methods of mail distribution where mailboxes are installed in a manner approved by the U.S. Postal Service.

- **Masonry.** Minor deterioration; failure to paint exterior bricks where there is no interior leak damage.
- **Painting.** Change in color in public areas; replacement of wallpaper or stenciling with paint in the public areas; isolated or minor areas where paint or plaster is peeling, or other similarly minor areas requiring repainting, provided there are no active water leaks; any painting condition in basement or cellar areas not usually meant for or used by tenants; any painting condition that is limited to the top-floor bulkhead area provided there is no active water leak in such area.
- **Recreational facilities.** Modifications, such as reasonable substitution of equipment, combination of areas, or reduction in the number of items of certain equipment where overall facilities are maintained (see "Roof," below).
- **Roof.** Discontinuance of recreational use (for example, sunbathing on the roof) unless a lease clause provides for such service, or formal facilities (such as a solarium) are provided by the owner; lack of repairs where water does not leak into the building or the condition is not dangerous.
- **Sinks.** Failure to provide or maintain in compactor rooms or laundry rooms.
- **Storage space.** Removal or reduction of, unless storage space service is provided for in a specific rider to the lease (not a general clause in a standard form residential lease), or unless the owner has provided formal storage boxes or bins to tenants within three years of the filing of a tenant's complaint alleging an elimination or a reduction in storage space service.
- **Superintendent or maintenance/staff/management.** Decrease in the number of staff, other than security, provided there is no decrease in janitorial services; elimination of on-site management office; failure to provide an on-site superintendent, provided there is no decrease in janitorial services.
- **Television.** Replacement of individual antennas with master antenna; visible cable, television wires or other technologies.

• **Windows**. Sealed, vented, basement or crawl space windows, other than in areas used by tenants (for example, laundry rooms); cracked fire-rated windows; peeling paint or other nonhazardous condition of exterior window frames.

## b. Individual Apartment Conditions

Here is a list of individual apartment conditions that will generally *not* constitute a failure to maintain a required service and qualify for a rent reduction:

• **Appliances and fixtures.** Chips on appliances, countertops, fixtures or tile surfaces; color-matching of appliances, fixtures or tiles.

• **Cracks.** Hairline cracks; minor wall cracks, provided there is no missing plaster or no active water leak.

• **Doors.** Lack of alignment, provided condition does not prevent proper locking of entrance door or closing of interior door.

• **Floor.** Failure to provide refinishing or shellacking.

• **Noise.** Caused by another tenant.

• **Window furnishings.** Failure to re-tape or re-cord venetian blinds.

## 3. How Individual Apartment Complaints Are Handled

Tenants may file an Application for a Rent Reduction Based on Decreased Service(s)—Individual Apartment (DHCR Form RA-81) to complain about reduced services to their individual apartments, such as a malfunctioning fixture or appliance, broken tile or falling plaster. When you get a copy of a tenant's complaint from DHCR, make sure the tenant has attached a copy of his letter notifying you of the conditions, along with proof of delivery. If not, raise that in your answer.

For heat and hot water complaints, tenants must attach an inspection report from a local municipal agency (such as the New York City Department of Housing Preservation and Develop-

ment (HPD)), showing a lack of heat and hot water, to a special complaint form, entitled Failure to Provide Heat and/or Hot Water—Tenant's Application for Rent Reduction (DHCR form HHW-1). If the inspection report is missing, or the tenant used the wrong complaint form, point that out in your answer and ask DHCR to dismiss the complaint.

## 4. How Buildingwide Service Complaints Are Handled

Rent-stabilized and rent-controlled tenants may complain about problems that affect the common areas of the property, or that affect all of the tenants in the building, by filing a form called Tenant's Application for Rent Reduction Based Upon Decreased Building-Wide Services (DHCR Form RA-84). A tenant may file this complaint individually or together with other tenants in the building. The complaint may relate to any service decrease that affects all or substantially all tenants, such as a reduction in elevator service or security, or dangerous conditions in a common area of the building.

Not every tenant in your building must sign the complaint. To be eligible for a rent reduction, all rent-stabilized tenants in your building must sign the complaint. If you receive a complaint that lacks a signature of one or more of your rent-stabilized tenants named on the complaint, point that out in your answer and ask the DHCR to deny rent reductions for those tenants who failed to sign. If DHCR finds that a building-wide hazardous condition exists, all rent-stabilized tenants who signed the complaint are eligible for rent reductions, as are all affected rent-controlled tenants in the building, even if they (the rent-controlled tenants) didn't sign the complaint.

## 5. Answering the Complaint

When DHCR receives a tenant complaint, it assigns a docket number and sends you a copy of the complaint with a notice to answer the tenant's charges.

You get 45 days from the date DHCR mails you a copy of the docketed complaint to submit an answer to the tenant's complaint. To avoid a rent reduction order, you should answer the tenant's complaint promptly. If you need more time to respond, say, because a certain repair or replacement will take longer than 45 days to complete, then you may request a time extension of another 45 days by sending a letter to DHCR and mailing it before the original 45-day deadline. Make sure your extension request bears the complaint docket number.

**Don't misplace the docket number!** This number is the only way the DHCR can identify your complaint. You can use this number to check on the status of your complaint by calling the DHCR's InfoLine 718-739-6400 or visiting the DHCR's website at www.dhcr.state.ny.us.

If the complaint is legitimate, your best bet is to make the necessary repairs or provide the needed services as soon as possible. Then, answer the complaint within the deadline period. Your answer should detail what repairs, needed services or other work you did in response to the tenant's complaint and the date work was completed. If you used an outside contractor, attach a copy of the contractor's work order or invoice as additional proof that the work was done.

**There's no "double dipping" for tenants.** What's to keep a tenant who wins a rent abatement in court for a condition that violates the warranty of habitability from also seeking a DHCR rent reduction for the same condition? Until June of 1997, nothing. A tenant could seek both types of relief. Fortunately, DHCR now offsets rent reductions by the value of any rent abatement the tenant may have received from a court for the same condition. (See, for example, 9 NYCRR 2523.4(h).) It's up to you to point out that the tenant already received a rent abatement, credit or offset for the same condition, though. Your answer should identify the court, the index number for the case, and if possible include a copy of the court papers. (Correspondingly, you can ask a court to offset a tenant's

warranty of habitability claim if the DHCR has already issued a rent reduction order for the same condition.)

If the tenant complained about a minor problem that doesn't merit a rent reduction, you can ask the DHCR to deny a rent reduction on that ground. (See Section 2, above). Your answer might go something like this:

*The tenant has asked for a rent reduction based on three alleged conditions: 1) excessive noise from the apartment above, 2) the wearing away of shellac on some areas on the wooden floor and 3) hairline cracks in the living room wall. I respectfully request that DHCR deny the tenant's application for a rent reduction on the ground that all of the tenant's complaints are* de minimis, *or minor in nature and do not constitute a failure to maintain a required service under applicable rent regulations.*

## Access Problems: When Tenants Refuse Entry for Repairs

Some tenants file a decreased services complaint with DHCR, and then refuse entry to their apartments for inspection or repair. If you experience access problems with a tenant, follow this procedure to avoid an unfair rent decrease.

Within the 45-day period you have to answer the complaint, write at least two letters to the tenant requesting access to the apartment on a specific date. Each letter must be mailed at least eight days prior to the proposed access date, and must be mailed by certified mail, return receipt requested.

If the tenant refuses to provide access on both dates, answer the complaint by stating that you have attempted, but have been unable to obtain access to the tenant's apartment to correct the service or equipment deficiency. Refer to your written letters in your answer and submit copies of your letters to the tenant with your answer.

In response, the DHCR will schedule a "no access inspection" with the tenant to verify that the conditions exist. Landlords are entitled to be present during the inspection. If the tenant again fails to provide access, DHCR will deny the tenant's application for a rent decrease. (See, for example, 9 NYCRR 2523.4(d)(2).)

level in effect prior to the last guidelines increase. For example, if the most recent guideline increase was 2% for a one-year lease and the legal regulated rent was $1,020 per month under a one year renewal lease beginning on October 1, 2003, a rent reduction ordered on December 1, 2003 would reduce the rent to $1000 per month.

For rent-controlled tenants, the rent is reduced by a fixed dollar amount, using a DHCR formula. For example, the DHCR reduced one rent-controlled tenant's rent by $17.00 per month based on a loose kitchen sink, peeled paint in plaster in one room, and rotted window sills in the unit. (*Matter of Mai*, DHCR Admin. Rev. Dckt. No. DF 110315RO.)

On average, it takes DHCR twelve months to process a service complaint. Rent-stabilized tenants get relief from the delay, since rent reduction orders become effective as of the first day of the month following the date when you were mailed a copy of the complaint. That means that the tenant is entitled to a retroactive rent reduction.

For rent-controlled tenants, the rent reduction order becomes effective the first day of the month *following* DHCR's issuance of the order—which could be over a year after the tenant files the complaint. For that reason, many rent-controlled tenants prefer to withhold rent and defend themselves in court, instead of filing a services complaint with DHCR.

The tenant may get an opportunity to respond to your answer. If the conditions are in dispute, the DHCR may order an inspection to obtain on-site evidence. If the evidence demonstrates that you failed to maintain required services, DHCR will direct you to restore services and may issue a rent reduction if the tenant has requested one (which tenants almost always do). Any ordered rent reduction continues in effect until you complete the repairs and file an application to restore the rent to its former level

## 6. Calculating the Rent Reduction

If the DHCR finds that you have decreased services to a rent-stabilized unit, the rent is reduced to the

## 7. Getting the Rent Restored

To have the rent restored, complete and file an Owner's Application to Restore Rent (DHCR form RTP-19); a sample is shown below. You may order the one-page (two-sided) form from the DHCR InfoLine (718-739-6400) or download it from the DHCR website (www.dhcr.state.ny.us). If the rent reduction order affects only one tenant, complete and sign the form, and file an original and one copy of the form with DHCR together with a copy of the rent reduction order.

If the rent reduction order affects more than one tenant, the procedure is a bit more complicated. The DHCR requires that you make and submit a

| | | |
|---|---|---|
| **New York State**<br>**Division of Housing and Community Renewal**<br>Office of Rent Administration<br>www.dhcr.state.ny.us | Gertz Plaza<br>92-31 Union Hall St.<br>Jamaica, NY 11433<br>(718) 739-6400 | **Docket Number:**<br>(For DHCR Use Only) |

### Owner's Application to Restore Rent

**Mailing Address of Tenant:**

Name: _____
Number/
Street: _____ Apt.
                                    No.
City,
State, Zip: _____
Telephone
Number: ( )

**Mailing Address of Owner/Agent:**

Name: _____
Number/
Street: _____
City,
State, Zip: _____
Telephone
Number: ( )

_____    _____    _____
Number and Street                  Apartment Number                City, State, Zip Code

### Instructions:

**Individual: Where only one (1) tenant is affected by the order,** one (1) original and one (1) copy of this application and supporting documents must be signed in two (2) places, dated, and filed at the DHCR office noted above, **together with a complete copy of the rent reduction order or order directing restoration of service.**

**Building-Wide: Where more than one tenant is affected by the order,** one (1) original (master) application must be signed in two (2) places, dated and filed with supporting documents at the DHCR office noted above, **together with a complete copy of the rent reduction order or order directing restoration of service,** and the owner must also submit the following:

1. A copy of the application and supporting documents, including a copy of the order, **for each apartment affected by the Reduction Order, or Order Directing Restoration of Service, including vacant apartments,** with each tenant's name and mailing address filled in;

2. The list of all affected apartments, from the Rent Reduction Order or Order Directing Restoration of Services; and

3. A 4" by 1" self-sticking mailing label, unaffixed, addressed to each affected apartment.

Applications **must** be filed for all apartments affected by an Order.

**Note: Applications will be rejected if they are not completed and filed correctly.**

Building Status (check one):  ☐ Condominium   ☐ Cooperative   ☐ Not Applicable

Date of most recent registration of subject apartment/building with DHCR: _____

Multiple Dwelling Registration Number: _____.

Docket Number of order reducing rent and/or directing restoration of service: _____

Number of tenants affected by the order: _____

Have any other orders been issued denying or granting in part an owner's application to restore rent on the same underlying docket number? ☐ Yes ☐ No    If "yes," list the docket numbers: _____

**Please check the applicable box below.  Box A, B or C must be checked:**

☐ A.  The owner has restored all services for which a rent reduction order was issued on ____/____/____, under Order or Docket Number _____. Attach a complete copy of the Order.

☐ B.  The owner has restored all services for which an order was issued directing restoration of services, under Order or Docket Number _____. No rent reduction was given. Attach a complete copy of the Order.

☐ C.  The tenant has unreasonably refused to permit owner/agent to restore service which was the basis for a rent reduction order or an order directing restoration of service issued ____/____/____, under Order or Docket Number _____. **Attach a complete copy of the order. Please give explanation on reverse side as to circumstances and attach required documentation. See Policy Statement 90-5 for further information.**

Check box D, E, or F if applicable:

☐ D.  The above named tenant of subject unit agrees and consents to same **(PART III - Tenant's Statement of Consent must be signed)**

☐ E.  For building-wide orders only (except those finding inadequate heat and/or hot water): An affidavit of an independent licensed architect or engineer is included stating that the conditions that are the subject of the order referenced above do not exist. The affidavit is signed by the person investigating the condition(s) and indicates when the investigation was conducted and findings with respect to each condition. See Policy Statement 96-1 for further information.

☐ F.  A Major Capital Improvement (MCI) application has been filed for the subject building and is pending under Docket Number _____.

list of all affected tenants, a 4" by 1" mailing label for each tenant, and a copy of the DHCR rent reduction order for each tenant. Then, complete and sign a "master" copy of the form, omitting the tenant's name and mailing address from the top of the form and making enough copies of the form for each tenant affected by the order. On each copy, fill in an affected tenant's name and address. File the signed master form, attached to a copy of the rent reduction order with the tenant copies of the form, with DHCR, along with the tenant list and mailing labels.

 **For more information, read DHCR Fact Sheet #14, "Rent Reduction Due to Decreased Services."** To obtain the fact sheet, stop into a borough or district DHCR office, call the DHCR InfoLine (718-739-6400) or download it from the DHCR's website (www.dhcr.state.ny.us).

## G. Avoiding Problems by Adopting a Good Maintenance and Repair System

Your best defense against rent withholding hassles and other disputes with tenants is to establish and communicate a clear, easy-to-follow procedure for tenants to use to ask for repairs. Also, you should document all complaints, respond quickly when complaints are made and schedule annual safety inspections. And, if you employ a live-in super or manager or hire a management company, make sure they follow your guidelines as well.

### 1. Recommended Repair and Maintenance System

Follow these steps to avoid maintenance and repair problems with tenants:

1. Clearly set out your and the tenant's responsibilities for repair and maintenance in your lease or rental agreement. (See Clauses 11 and 12 of the form agreements in Chapter 2.)

2. Use the written Landlord-Tenant Checklist form in Chapter 7 to check over the premises and fix any problems before new tenants move in.

3. Don't assume your tenants know how to handle routine maintenance problems such as a clogged toilet or drain. Make it a point to explain the basics when the tenant moves into the unit. In addition, include a brief list of maintenance dos and don'ts as part of your move-in materials. For example:
   - how to avoid overloading circuits
   - proper use of garbage disposal, if any
   - how to test the smoke detectors, and
   - problems tenant should definitely not try to handle, such as electrical repairs.

4. Encourage tenants to immediately report plumbing, heating, weatherproofing or other defects or safety or security problems—whether in the tenant's unit or in common areas such as hallways and parking garages. A Maintenance/Repair Request form (discussed in Section 3, below) is often useful in this regard.

5. Keep a written log (or have your property manager keep one) of all complaints (including those made orally). This should include sections to record your immediate and any follow-up responses (and subsequent tenant communications), as well as space to enter the date and brief details of when the problem was fixed. The Maintenance Repair/Request form, below, can serve this purpose.

6. Keep a file for each rental unit with copies of all complaints and repair requests from tenants and your response. As a general rule, you should respond in writing to every tenant repair request (even if you also do so orally).

7. Handle repairs (especially urgent ones) as soon as possible. Notify the tenant by phone and follow up in writing if repairs will take more than 72 hours, excluding weekends. Keep the tenant informed—for example, if you have problems scheduling a plumber, let your tenant know with a phone call or a note.

8. Once a year, inspect all rental units, using the Annual Maintenance and Safety Update as a guide, below. (Keep copies of the filled-in update in your file.)

9. In multiple dwellings, place conspicuous notices in several places around your property about your determination to operate a safe, well-maintained building, and list phone numbers for tenants to call with maintenance requests.

10. Remind tenants of your policies and procedures to keep your building in good repair in every written communication by printing it at the bottom of all routine notices, rent increases and other communications.

---

### Sample Notice to Tenants Regarding Complaint Procedure

Tenants will be more likely to keep you apprised of maintenance and repair problems if you remind them that you are truly interested. A notice such as the following will be helpful:

*Empire Towers wants to maintain all apartment units and common areas in excellent condition so that tenants enjoy safe and comfortable housing. If you have any questions, suggestions or requests regarding your unit or the building, please direct them to the superintendent between 8 AM and 4 PM, Monday through Friday, either by calling 555-9876 or by dropping off a completed Maintenance/Repair Request form at the super's office any time. In case of an emergency, please call 555-1234 at any time.*

---

## 2. Benefits of Establishing a Repair and Maintenance System

The recommendations in this chapter reflect our belief that you will be better off in the long run if you offer and maintain housing in excellent condition—that is, you go beyond satisfying the letter of the law. Here's why:

- While state and local housing codes set high standards, comfortably exceeding these standards will help you avoid expensive legal trouble.

- Tenants who are given an added measure of care are likely to be more satisfied—and, as a result, easier to deal with. More importantly, happy tenants are likely to stay longer, resulting in fewer turnovers and interruptions of your stream of income.

- Landlords who know that they are well within the legal requirements can be confident that their housing is not likely to be found wanting if they are challenged by a disgruntled tenant. You can negotiate from a position of strength (and get more sleep at night), since you know you are likely to win if a dispute ends up in court.

- Landlords who maintain their property well are far less likely to face the risk of tenant lawsuits based on habitability problems or injuries resulting from defective conditions. A good record in this regard can, of course, translate into lower insurance premiums.

In addition to a thorough and prompt system for responding to problems after they have been brought to your attention, you should establish a good, nonintrusive system of frequent and periodic maintenance inspections. In short, encouraging your tenants to report problems, and following the guidelines we suggest here will give you several advantages:

**Prevention.** First, the system we recommend allows you to fix little problems before they grow into big ones. For example, you would want to replace the washer in the upstairs bathtub before the washer fails, the faucet can't be turned off and the tub overflows, ruining the floor and the ceiling of the lower unit.

**Good tenant relations.** Communication with tenants who have legitimate concerns with the property creates a climate of cooperation and trust that can work wonders in the long run. Making tenants happy and keeping them is really an investment in your business.

**Rent withholding defense.** At least as important as damage prevention and good tenant relations, a responsive communication system provides you with an excellent defense when it comes to those few unreasonable tenants who seek to withhold or reduce rent for no reason other than their disinclination to pay. (In addition, if you need to establish as part of an eviction proceeding that a claimed repair problem is phony, you may want to have the repair person who looked at the supposed "defect" come to court to testify as to why it was phony.) In short, you may still have to go to court to evict the tenant, but your carefully documented procedures will constitute a paper trail to help you accomplish this with a minimum of time and expense. And, a tenant who doesn't pay the rent because you "failed" to fix a problem will have a hard time making his case if you can show that he never availed himself of your repair procedures. If you make it your normal business practice to save all repair requests from tenants, the absence of a request is evidence that the tenant has made no complaints.

**Limit legal liability.** Finally, an aggressive repair policy backed up by an excellent recordkeeping system can help reduce your potential liability to your tenants in lawsuits based on injuries suffered as a result of defective conditions on your property. There are two reasons for this. First, it is less likely that there will be injuries in the first place if your property is well maintained. Second, in many situations an injured person must prove not only that they were hurt but that you were negligent (careless) in allowing the situation to develop. You may be able to defeat this claim by demonstrating that you actively sought out and quickly fixed all defects.

EXAMPLE: Geeta owns a 12-unit building and regularly encourages her tenants to request repairs in writing on a special form she's prepared. Several prominent signs, as well as reminders on all routine communications with tenants, urge tenants to report all problems. Most tenants do so. One month, Ravi simply doesn't pay his rent. After her phone calls are not answered, Geeta serves a Rent Demand Notice. Still Ravi says nothing.

When Geeta files an eviction suit, Ravi claims he withheld rent because of a leaky roof and defective heater Geeta supposedly refused to repair. At trial, Geeta testifies that she routinely saves all tenants' filled-out forms for at least one year, and that she has no record of ever receiving a complaint from Ravi, even though she supplied him with blank forms and sent notices twice a year asking to be informed of any problems. She also submits her complaint log, which has a space to record oral requests. The judge has reason to doubt Ravi ever complained, and rules in Geeta's favor.

## 3. Resident's Maintenance/Repair Request Form

One way to assure that defects in the premises will be reported by conscientious tenants—while helping to refute bogus tenant claims about lack of repairs—is to include a clause in your lease or rental agreement requiring that tenants notify you of repair and maintenance needs. (See Clause 11 in the form agreements in Chapter 2.) Make the point again and describe your process for handling repairs in your move-in letter to new tenants (see Chapter 7).

Many tenants will find it easiest (and most practical) to call you or your manager with a repair problem or complaint, particularly in urgent cases. Make sure you have an answering machine or voice mail available at all times to accommodate tenant calls. Check your messages frequently when you're not available by phone.

We also suggest you provide all tenants with a Maintenance/Repair Request form (see the sample below). Give each tenant five or ten copies when they move in, explain how the form should be used to request specific repairs. Be sure that tenants know to describe the problem in detail and to indicate the best time to make repairs. Make sure tenants know how to get more copies. Your manager (if any) should keep an ample supply of the Maintenance/Repair Request form in her rental unit or office.

You (or your manager) should complete the entire Maintenance/Repair Request form or keep a

## Resident's Maintenance/Repair Request

Date: _____ February 9, 200X _____

Address: _____ 103–20 Queens Blvd., Forest Hills _____

_____ Unit Number _____ 6–E _____

Resident's Name: _Ida Hechtman_ _____

Phone (home): _718-555-1212_ _____ Phone (work): _212-555-1212_ _____

Problem (be as specific as possible):_____

  1. Bedroom closet bi-fold doors off track.

  2. Bathroom door knob needs adjustment.

_____

_____

_____

Best time to make repairs: _____ Thursdays or Fridays, during the day. _____

Other comments: _____ Please call me at home and leave a message as to approximately when

  workers will arrive at my apartment. _____

_____

I authorize entry into my unit to perform the maintenance or repair requested above, in my absence, unless stated otherwise above.

_Ida Hechtman_ _____

Resident

- - - - - - - - - - - - - - - - - - - - - - - - - - - - - - - - - - - - - - - - - - - - - - - -

FOR MANAGEMENT USE

Work done: _Tightened door knob; re-hung doors to closet_ _____

Time spent: _1 1/2_ _____ hours

Date completed: _____ 2/13 _____, 200 _X_ By: _Paulie_ _____

Unable to complete on _____, 200___, because: _____

_____

Notes and comments: _____

_February 13, 200X_ _____    _Ed Rosenbloom, Superintendent_ _____

Date                          Landlord/Manager/Superintendent

separate log for every tenant complaint, including those made by phone. (See the discussion below.) Keep a copy of this form or your log in the tenant's file along with any other written communication. (Chapter 7, Section E, discusses recordkeeping systems.) Be sure to keep good records of how and when you handled tenant complaints, including reasons for any delays and notes on conversations with tenants. For a sample, see the bottom of the Maintenance/Repair Request form (labeled For Management Use, shown below). You might also jot down any other comments regarding repair or maintenance problems you observed while handling the tenant's complaint.

The Forms CD includes a copy of the Resident's Maintenance/Repair Request form, and Appendix IV includes a blank, tear-out copy.

## 4. Tracking Tenant Complaints

Most tenants will simply call you when they have a problem or complaint, rather than fill out a Maintenance/Repair Request form. For recordkeeping purposes we suggest you always fill out this form, regardless of whether the tenant does. And, in addition, it's also a good idea to keep a separate chronological log or calendar with similar information on tenant complaints. A faithfully kept log will qualify as a "business record," admissible as evidence in court, that you can use to establish that you normally record tenant communications when they are made. By implication, the absence of an entry is evidence that a complaint was not made. This argument can be important if your tenant has reduced or withheld rent or broken the lease on the bogus claim that requests for maintenance or repairs went unanswered.

## 5. Responding to Tenant Complaints

You should respond almost immediately to all complaints about defective conditions by talking to the tenant and following up (preferably in writing). Explain when repairs can be made or, if you don't

yet know, tell the tenant that you will be back in touch promptly. This doesn't mean you have to jump through hoops to fix things that don't need fixing or to engage in heroic efforts to make routine repairs. It does mean you should take prompt action under the circumstances—for example, immediate action should normally be taken to cope with broken door locks or security problems. Similarly, a lack of heat or hot water (especially in frigid winter days) and safety hazards such as broken steps or exposed electrical wires should be dealt with on an emergency basis.

One way to think about how to respond to repair problems is to classify them according to their consequences. Once you consider the results of *inaction*, your response time will be clear:

- **Personal security and safety problems = injured tenants = lawsuits.** Respond and get work done immediately if the potential for harm is very serious, even if this means calling a 24-hour repair service or having you or your manager get up in the middle of the night to put a piece of plywood over a broken ground floor window.
- **Major inconvenience to tenant = seriously unhappy tenant = tenant's self-help remedies (such as rent withholding) and vacancies.** Respond and attempt to get work done as soon as possible, or within 24 hours, if the problem is a major inconvenience to tenants, such as a plumbing or heating problem or other repair that could make the unit unlivable.
- **Minor problem = slightly annoyed tenant = bad feelings.** Respond in 72 hours (on business days) if not too serious.

Yes, these deadlines may seem tight and, occasionally, meeting them will cost you a few dollars extra, but in the long run you'll be way ahead.

If you're unable to take care of a repair right away, such as a dripping faucet, and if it isn't so serious that it requires immediate action, let the tenant know when the repair will be made. It's often best to do this orally (a message on the tenant's answering machine or voice mail should serve), and follow up in writing by leaving a notice under the tenant's door. See the sample Time Estimate for Repair form, below. If there's a delay in handling the problem (maybe the part you need to fix the oven has to be ordered), explain why you won't be able to act immediately.

 **Respect tenant's privacy.** To gain access to make repairs, the landlord can enter the rental premises only with the tenant's consent, or after having given reasonable notice, usually 24 hours. See Chapter 10 for rules and procedures for entering a tenant's home to make repairs and how to deal with tenants who make access inconvenient for you or your maintenance personnel.

 The Forms CD includes the Time Estimate for Repair form, and Appendix IV includes a blank, tear-out copy.

 **If you can't attend to a repair right away, avoid possible rent withholding.** Some landlords voluntarily offer a small "rent rebate" if a problem can't be corrected in a timely fashion, especially if it's serious, such as a major heating or plumbing problem. A rebate builds goodwill and avoids rent withholding.

If, despite all your efforts to conscientiously find out about and make needed repairs on a timely basis, a tenant threatens to withhold rent, move out or pursue another legal remedy discussed in Sections D and E above, you should respond promptly in writing, telling him either:

- when the repair will be made and the reasons why it is being delayed—for example, a replacement part may have to be ordered to correct the running sound in a bathroom toilet, or
- why you do not feel there is a legitimate problem that justifies rent withholding or other tenant action—for example, point out that the running sound may be annoying, but the toilet still flushes and is usable (see "Sample Letter Suggesting Compromise on Rent Withholding," above).

At this point, if you feel the tenant is sincere, you might also consider suggesting that you and the tenant mediate the dispute. If you feel the tenant is

trying to concoct a phony complaint to justify not paying the rent, take action to evict him.

## H. Landlord's Regular Safety and Maintenance Inspections

In addition to a thorough and prompt system for responding to problems after they have been brought to your attention, you should establish a good, nonintrusive system of frequent and periodic maintenance inspections. In short, encouraging your tenants to promptly report problems as they occur should not be your sole means of handling your maintenance and repair responsibilities. Here's why: If the tenant is not conscientious, or if he simply doesn't notice that something needs to be fixed, the best reporting system will not do you much good. To back it up, you need to take stock at specified intervals by getting into the unit and taking a look yourself.

We put together a form you can use to list any problems in the rental unit. (See the sample Annual Safety and Maintenance Update form, below). As with the Maintenance/Repair Request form, be sure to note how you handled the problem on the bottom of the form.

 The Forms CD includes the Annual Safety and Maintenance Update form, and Appendix IV includes a blank, tear-out copy.

At least once a year, use the Safety and Maintenance Update to make sure smoke detectors, heating and plumbing systems and major appliances are in fact safe and in working order. If a problem develops with one of these items, causing injury to a tenant, you may be able to defeat a claim that you were negligent by arguing that your periodic and recent inspection of the item was all that a landlord should reasonably be expected to do.

You may reserve the right to enter a tenant's home for the purpose of a safety inspection by inserting a special clause in your lease. Our rental agreements and leases permit you to gain access, upon reasonable notice, for such inspections. (See

## Time Estimate for Repair

_____ Metrotech Towers _____

September 19, 200X
Date

Anne Castro
Tenant

189 Willoughby Street
Street Address

12-C
Unit Number

Brooklyn, NY
City and State

Dear_____ Ms. Castro _____,
                    Tenant

Thank you for promptly notifying us of the following problem with your unit:

Dishwasher doesn't work

_____

_____

_____

_____

_____

We expect to have the problem corrected on _____ Sept. 26 _____, 200 X , due to

the following:

Dishwasher part is out of stock locally, but has been ordered and will be delivered next week.

_____

_____

_____

_____

We regret any inconvenience this delay may cause. Please do not hesitate to point out any other problems that may arise.

Sincerely,

Ed Cohen

Landlord/Manager/Superintendent

## Annual Safety and Maintenance Update

Please complete the following checklist and note any safety or maintenance problems in your unit or on the premises.

Please describe the specific problems and the rooms or areas involved. Here are some examples of the types of things we want to know about: ceiling leaks, fuses blow out frequently, door lock sticks, water comes out too hot in shower, exhaust fan above stove doesn't work, broken window locks, smoke alarm malfunctions, peeling paint and mice infestation.

Please indicate the approximate date when you first noticed the problem and list any other recommendations or suggestions for improvement.

Please return this form with this month's rent check. Thank you.—THE MANAGEMENT

Name: _____ Susan and Charlie Biesenhouse _____

Address: _____ 349 West 73rd St., NYC _____

Unit Number: _5-B_ _____


Please indicate (and explain below) problems with:

☐ Floors and floor coverings _____

☒ Walls and ceilings _____ Peeling plaster in rear bedroom _____

☒ Windows, screens and doors _____ Doors stick in summer _____

☐ Window coverings (drapes, mini-blinds, etc.) _____

☐ Electrical system and light fixtures _____

☐ Plumbing (sinks, bathtub, shower or toilet) _____

☐ Heating or air conditioning system _____

☐ Major appliances (stove, oven, dishwasher, refrigerator) _____

☐ Locks or security system _____

☐ Smoke detector _____

☐ Fireplace _____

☐ Cupboards, cabinets and closets _____

☐ Furnishings (table, bed, mirrors, chairs) _____

☒ Laundry facilities _____ Should be cleaned regularly! _____

☐ Elevator _____

☐ Stairs and handrails _____

☐ Hallway, lobby and common areas _____

☐ Garage _____

☒ Patio, terrace or deck _____ Broken tile work on east side of terrace ___

☐ Lawn, fences and grounds _____

☐ Pool and recreational facilities _____

☐ Roof, exterior walls, and other structural _____

☐ Driveway and sidewalks _____

☐ Basement or attic _____

☐ Other _____

_____

Specifics of problems: _____

_____

_____

_____

_____

Other comments: _____

_____

_____

_____

_____

_____

June 1, 200X _____     *Susan Biesenhouse* _____
Date                               Tenant

- - - - - - - - - - - - - - - - - - - - - - - - - - - - - - - - - - - - - -

FOR MANAGEMENT USE

Action/Response: _____

• Repaired plaster in rear bedroom on June 10.

• Repainted bedroom ceiling on June 12.

• Terrace tile work completed on June 20.

• Spoke to Herman about cleaning laundry room on daily basis.

• Tenant will call when door-sticking problem arises.

_____

_____

_____

_____

_____

June 23, 200X _____     *Frank Garcia* _____
Date                               Landlord/Manager/Superintendent

Chapter 10 for a discussion of your right of entry.) This does not mean, however, that you can just let yourself in unannounced. You must give "reasonable notice." To be on the safe side, allow at least 24 hours' notice.

What should you do if your tenant objects to your safety inspection? If your lease lets you enter for this purpose (and if you have given adequate notice and have not otherwise abused your right of entry by needlessly scheduling repeated inspections) the tenant's refusal is grounds for eviction. But real-istically, a court would probably order the tenant to provide access on a specified date and time, instead of evicting the tenant for refusing to let you in.

There may be, however, a practical way around the uncooperative tenant who bars the door. Point out that you take your responsibility to maintain the property very seriously. Remind her that you'll be checking for plumbing, heating, electrical and struc-tural problems that she might not notice, which could develop into bigger problems later if you're not allowed to check them out. Most tenants will not object to yearly safety inspections if you're courteous about it—giving plenty of notice and try-ing to conduct the inspection at a time convenient for the tenant. (You might offer to inspect at a time when she is home, so that she can see for herself that you will not be nosing about her personal items.)

## I.  Permissible Limits on Tenant-Installed Satellite Dishes

The Federal Communications Commission (FCC) prohibits landlords from imposing restrictions that unreasonably impair a tenant's ability to install, maintain or use an antenna or satellite dish that meet criteria described below. Here's a brief over-view of the FCC rule.

**For complete details on the FCC's rule on satellite dishes and antennas,** see www.fcc.gov /csb/facts/otard.html or call the FCC at 888-CALLFCC (toll free) or 202-418-7096. The FCC's rule

was upheld in *Building Owners and Managers Assn. v. FCC*, 254 F.3d 89 (D.C. Cir. 2001).

### 1.  Devices Covered by the FCC Rule

The FCC's rule applies to video antennas, including direct-to-home satellite dishes that are less than one meter (39.37 inches) in diameter, TV antennas and wireless cable antennas. These pieces of equipment receive video programming signals from direct broadcast satellites, wireless cable providers and television broadcast stations. Antennas up to 18 inches in diameter that transmit as well as receive fixed wireless telecom signals (not just video) are also included.

Exceptions: Antennas used for AM/FM radio, amateur (ham) and Citizen's Band (CB) radio or Digital Audio Radio Services (DARS) are excluded from the FCC's rule. Landlords may restrict the in-stallation of these types of antennas, in the same way that they can restrict any modification or alter-ation of rented space.

### 2.  Permissible Installation of Satellite Dishes and Antennas

Tenants may place antennas or dishes only in their own, exclusive rented space, such as inside the rental unit or on a balcony, terrace, deck or patio. The device must be wholly within the rented space (if it overhangs the balcony, you may prohibit that placement). Also, you may prohibit tenants from drilling through exterior walls, even if that wall is also part of their rented space.

Tenants *cannot* place reception devices in com-mon areas, such as roofs, hallways, walkways or the exterior walls of the building. Exterior windows are no different that exterior walls—for this reason, placing a dish or antenna on a window by means of a series of suction cups is impermissible under the FCC rule (obviously, such an installation is also un-safe). Tenants who rent single-family homes, how-ever, may install devices in the home itself, on pa-tios or in yards, gardens or similar areas.

## 3. Restrictions on Installation Techniques

Landlords are free to set restrictions on how the devices are installed, as long as the restrictions are not unreasonably expensive, or if the restrictions are imposed for safety reasons or to preserve historic aspects of the structure. You may insist that your maintenance personnel (or professional installers) do the work.

### a. Expense

You may not impose a flat fee or charge additional rent to tenants who want to erect an antenna or dish. On the other hand, you may be able to insist on certain installation techniques that will add expense—as long as the cost isn't excessive and reception will not be impaired. Examples of acceptable expenses include:

- insisting that an antenna be painted green in order to blend into the landscaping, or
- requiring the use of a universal bracket which future tenants could use, saving wear and tear on the building.

### b. Safety Concerns

You may insist that tenants place and install devices in a way that will minimize the chances of accidents and will not violate safety or fire codes. For example, landlords may prohibit placement of a satellite dish on a fire escape, near a power plant or near a walkway where passers-by might accidentally hit their heads. You may also insist on proper installation techniques, such as those explained in the instructions that come with most devices. What if proper installation (attaching a dish to a wall) means that you will have to eventually patch and paint a wall? Can you use this as reason for preventing installation? No—unless you have a legitimate reason for prohibiting the installation, such as a safety concern. Tenants may, however, be charged for the cost of repairing surfaces if they remove the device when you move.

## 4. Placement and Orientation of Antennas and Reception Devices

Tenants have the right to place an antenna where they'll receive an acceptable quality signal. As long as the chosen spot is within the exclusive rented space, not on an exterior wall or in a common area as discussed in Section 2, above, you may not set rules on placement—for example, by requiring that an antenna be placed only in the rear of the rental property—if this results in a substantially degraded signal or no signal at all.

Reception devices that need to maintain line-of-sight contact with a transmitter or view a satellite may not work if they're stuck behind a wall or below the roofline. In particular, a dish must be on a south wall, since satellites are in the southern hemisphere. Faced with a reception problem, tenants who have no other workable exclusive space may want to mount their devices on a mast, in hopes of clearing the obstacle. They may do so, depending on the situation.

- **Single-family rentals.** Tenants may erect a mast that's 12 feet above the roofline or less without asking for the landlord's permission first—and the landlord must allow it if the mast is installed in a safe manner. If the mast is taller than 12 feet, you may refuse permission if you have legitimate safety concerns about the installation.
- **Multi-family rentals.** Tenants may use a mast as long as it does not extend beyond their exclusive rented space. For example, in a two-story rental a mast that is attached to the ground-floor patio and extends into the air space opposite the tenant's own second floor would be permissible. On the other hand, a mast attached to a top-story deck, which extends above the roofline or outward over the railing, would not be protected by the FCC's rule—you could prohibit this installation because it extends beyond the tenant's exclusive rented space.

## 5. Must Tenants Use Your Central Antenna or Satellite Dish?

Faced with the prospect of many dishes and antennas adorning an otherwise clean set of balconies, you may install a central antenna or dish for use by all tenants.

This is lawful only when your device provides:

- **Equal access.** The tenant must be able to get the same programming or fixed wireless service that he could receive with his own antenna.
- **Equal quality.** The signal quality to and from the apartment via the landlord's antenna must be as good or better than the tenant could get using his own device.
- **Equal value.** The cost of using your device must be the same or less than the cost of installing, maintaining and using an individual antenna, and
- **Equal readiness.** You can't prohibit individual devices if installation of a central antenna will unreasonably delay the tenant's ability to receive programming or fixed wireless services—for example, if your central antenna won't be available for months.

If you install a central antenna after a tenant has installed her own, you may require removal of the tenant's individual antenna, as long as your device meets the above requirements. In addition, you must pay for the removal of the tenant's device and compensate the tenant for the value of the antenna.

## 6. How to Handle Disputes About Antennas and Satellite Dishes

In spite of the FCC's attempts to clarify tenants' rights to reception and landlords' rights to control what happens on their property, there are many possibilities for disagreements. For example, what exactly is "acceptable" reception? If the landlord requires antennas to be painted, at what point is the expense considered "unreasonable?" Ideally, you can try to avoid disputes in the first place by dealing directly with your tenant. If your own attempts don't resolve the problem, you can call the FCC and ask for oral guidance. You may also formally ask the FCC for a written opinion, called a Declaratory Ruling. For information on obtaining oral or written guidance from the FCC, follow the directions as shown on the FCC website at www.fcc.gov/csb/facts/otard.html.

Chapter **10**

# Landlord's Right of Entry and Tenant's Right to Privacy

Next to disputes over rent or security deposits, one of the most common—and emotion-filled—misunderstandings between landlords and tenants involves conflicts between your right to enter the rental property and a tenant's right to be left alone at home. What is so unfortunate is that many of these problems are un-necessary. Most can be avoided if you adopt fair—and, of course, legal—policies to enter the tenant's unit and then clearly explain these policies to the tenant from the first day of your relationship. (And if you employ a manager or management company, make sure they also follow your guidelines.)

This chapter covers your legal right to enter a tenant's unit and recommends a practical approach to giving advance notice of entry. These sensible practices should help keep you out of legal hot water.

To make sure you and your tenant are operating on the same wavelength, be sure your lease or rental agreement includes a clause explaining your rights and responsibilities regarding access to the property. (See Clause 15 of the form agreements in Chapter 2.)

## A. General Rules of Entry

The tenant's duty to pay rent depends on your proper repair and maintenance of the premises. As explained in Chapter 9, inattention to your property's maintenance can give the tenant the right to with-hold rent, sue, move out and more. But to keep rental property shipshape, you need to see it and work on it. There is no statewide statute that covers a landlord's right of entry. However, rent stabiliza-tion and rent control laws give landlords a right of entry, as does New York City law. (See Sections B and C, below.) In addition, leases and rental agree-ments, both oral and written, that give landlords a reasonable right to enter rented property under certain broad circumstances, such as in an emergency or to make repairs, are routinely enforced by New York courts.

That doesn't mean that you can put something outrageous in your lease, such as landlord announc-ing that the landlord can enter whenever he feels

like it. Your tenant is, after all, entitled to privacy. To be enforceable, your lease or rental agreement entry clause must limit your right of entry to clear and legitimate business reasons and provide for reasonable notice of your intention to enter the unit.

Leases and rental agreements may permit the landlord (and the landlord's employees and agents) to enter for one or more of the following reasons:

- in the event of an emergency or for an emergency repair
- to repair or maintain the rental unit
- to inspect the unit's physical condition, or
- to show the rental unit to prospective tenants, purchasers or mortgagees.

For non-emergencies, most leases and rental agreements require you to provide the tenant with a minimum amount of notice before entering. The form agreements in this book permit you to enter to make repairs, conduct an inspection, or to show the unit on "reasonable" notice, unless it is impractical to do so—for example, in cases of emergency. (See Chapter 2, Clause 15.) As a general rule, at least 24 hours' notice is presumed to be reasonable for non-emergency access. We talk about what's "reasonable" under different circumstances in Section D, below.

Tenants who refuse to let you into their rental units, after proper notice, may be terminated on the ground that they have violated a substantial obligation of the lease. (Chapter 13 explains how to terminate a month-to-month tenancy. Chapters 14 and 15 explain how to terminate a fixed-term tenancy.)

## B. New York City Tenants Must Permit Entry for Repairs and Inspections

**If your property is located outside New York City, you can skip this section.** New York City's "Owner's Right of Access" law (NYC Adm. Code § 27-2008) prohibits tenants from refusing to permit the owner, the owner's agent or employee to enter the tenant's rental unit for the purpose of:

- responding to emergencies
- making repairs or improvements required by law or code, and
- inspecting the rental unit to determine if it complies with applicable laws and codes.

This law is especially helpful to landlords who need access to a unit for which there is no right of entry under the lease or rental agreement or for which there's an oral rental agreement.

New York City tenants must also grant access for the landlord's installation of a fire safety notice on the inside front door of their apartments. For more information on fire safety plans and notices, see Chapter 9, Section B17.

**NYC law does not require tenants to permit entry for the purpose of showing a rental unit to prospective tenants, purchasers or mortgagees.** However, New York City tenants are required to permit entry for this purpose if a) their lease or rental agreement authorizes it (see Section A, above) or 2) if the unit is covered by rent control or rent stabilization law (see Section C, below).

The NYC access law requires landlords to exercise their right of access at a "reasonable time and in a reasonable manner." A city regulation (28 RCNY § 25-101) helps flesh out the reasonableness requirement as follows:

**Emergency repair access** requires no advance notice to the tenant. "Emergency repairs" are any repairs that are urgently needed to prevent injury or property damage, and include items such as gas leaks, leaking pipes or appliances, stopped-up drains, leaking roofs and broken and dangerous ceiling conditions.

**Access for repairs or improvements** requires at least one week's advance written notice to the tenant. The notice should describe the nature of the repair or improvement you plan to make.

**Access for an inspection** requires at least 24 hours' advance written notice to the tenant. If the tenant is rent stabilized, you must give at least five days' written notice of the inspection, so as to enable the tenant to be present.

New York City landlords may use the Notice of Intent to Enter Dwelling Unit form in Section F, below, to provide the required written notice.

 **A tenant can (and usually will) agree to provide access on far less than one week's notice.** In fact, many tenants will expect you to respond to repair requests within 24 to 72 hours after they're reported to management. A pesky tenant may, however, insist on a full week's written notice before letting you in to make needed repairs or improvements.

You can enter a tenant's unit at any mutually convenient time. Except in emergencies, tenants may, however, insist on providing access only between the hours of 9:00 AM and 5:00 PM, Monday through Friday (except holidays). (28 RCNY § 25-101.)

## C. Rent-Regulated Tenants Must Give Access for Repairs, Improvements, Inspections and Showings

You can skip this section if you do not own any rental units that are rent controlled or rent stabilized. If you're not sure if a rental unit is covered by rent regulation, see Chapter 4.

Rent control and rent stabilization laws (9 NYCRR §§ 2104.2(f); 2204.2(a)(6); 2524.3(e), NYC Adm. Code § 26-408(a)(6)) require rent-regulated tenants throughout the state to provide access to you and your agents for the following purposes:

- to make necessary emergency repairs
- to make necessary repairs and improvements
- for apartment inspections, and
- to show the unit to prospective tenants, purchasers or mortgagees.

Rent-regulated tenants who unreasonably refuse to provide access to the landlord, after proper notice, may be terminated. (Chapters 14 and 15 explain this termination ground and procedure).

**Rent-stabilized tenants in New York City must be given at least five days' advance written notice of any inspection or showing to give the tenant a chance to be present at a mutually convenient time.** (9 NYCRR § 2524.3(e).) While the NYC Rent Stabilization Code sets no minimum notice period for repairs, the City's access law, which also applies, does. Access for non-emergency repairs or improvements required by law requires at least one week's advance written notice to the tenant. The notice should describe the nature of the repair or improvement you plan to make (see Section B, above).

Even if advance written notice of entry is not required, it's a good idea to provide it. The Notice of Intent to Enter Dwelling Unit form, in Section F, below, can be used to provide written notice.

Some tenants seek a rent reduction for decreased services from DHCR, and then refuse entry to their apartments for inspection or repair. If you experience access problems with a tenant who has filed a DHCR services complaint, follow the special procedure described in Chapter 9, Section F (under "Access Problems: When Tenants Refuse Entry for Repairs,") to avoid an unfair rent decrease.

## D. The Best Approach to Giving Reasonable Notice

Once you rent residential property, you must respect it as your tenant's home. That means giving the tenant reasonable notice of your intention to enter the unit to make repairs or improvements, to inspect its condition, or to show the unit to a prospective tenant, purchaser or lender. We recommend you provide as much written notice as possible. Try to arrange a mutually convenient time, and only enter for clearly legitimate business reasons, such as to make necessary repairs. Common sense suggests that you be considerate of your tenants' privacy and do your best to accommodate their schedules. You'll go a long way toward keeping tenants and will minimize disputes and legal problems by doing so.

Here's how to avoid having a tenant claim that you violated his legal right of privacy:

- Give the tenant a reasonable amount of notice, at least 24 hours' if at all possible, more if required by law (for example, in New York City).
- Try to reach the tenant at home or at work to give the notice. Make sure you know how to reach the tenant during the day to give notice.

- Provide written notice if possible—either a brief letter or a formal notice of intent to enter a dwelling unit (see samples below).

**Whenever possible, put your access notice in writing—even if you already talked to the tenant about it.** A letter or notice can serve to confirm an access date agreed to over the phone, and help remind the tenant about the appointment. A copy of a written notice can prove that you followed correct procedures before you entered the tenant's unit. And if you're "locked out" (see "Must Tenants Supply Keys to Privately Installed Locks?" below) the notice is proof that you tried to gain access to the tenant's unit to make needed repairs or respond to a reported problem.

- Try to arrange entry at a reasonable time that's convenient to the tenant.
- If you can't reach the tenant personally or by phone, and if your intended date of entry is too soon to enable you to send a letter, it's a good idea to post a note detailing your plan on the tenant's front door. If, despite all of these efforts, your tenant does not receive notice, you are probably on solid ground to enter and do the repair, since you have done all that could reasonably be expected to comply with the notice requirements.
- Keep a copy of all requests for entry (written and oral) in your tenant's file, along with other communications, such as repair request forms (discussed in Chapter 9, Section G).

A sample letter requesting entry and a formal notice of intent to enter a dwelling unit are included in Section F, below.

## E. Entry in Case of Emergency

You can enter a rental unit without giving notice to respond to a true emergency—such as a fire or gas leak—that threatens life or property if not corrected immediately.

Here are some examples of emergency situations when it would be legal to enter without giving the tenant notice:

- Smoke is pouring out the tenant's window. You call the fire department and use your master key—or even break in, if necessary—to try to deal with the fire.
- You see water coming out of the bottom of a tenant's back door. It's okay to enter and find the water leak.
- Your on-site manager hears screams coming from the apartment next door. He knocks on the apartment door, but no one answers. After calling the police, he uses his pass key to enter and see what's wrong.

On the other hand, your urge to repair a problem that's important but doesn't threaten life or property —say, a stopped-up drain that is not causing any damage—isn't a true emergency that would allow entry without proper notice.

If you do have to enter a tenant's apartment in an emergency, be sure to leave a note or call the tenant explaining the circumstances and the date and time you entered. Here's an example:

### Sample Letter Explaining Entry in Emergency

September 2, 200x

Dear Tammy,

Due to your oven being left on, I had to enter your apartment this afternoon around 3 o'clock. Apparently, you left your apartment while bread was still in the oven, and didn't return in time to take it out. Joe, your upstairs neighbor, called me and reported smoke and a strong burning smell coming from your kitchen. I entered your apartment and turned the oven off and removed the bread. Please be more careful next time.

Sincerely,

*Herb Layton*

Herb Layton

To facilitate your right of entry in an emergency, make sure your lease or rental agreement forbids tenants from re-keying, adding additional locks or installing a security system without your permission.

(See Clause 12 of the form agreements in Chapter 2.) If you grant permission to change or add locks, make sure your tenant gives you duplicate keys. If you allow the tenant to install a security system, make sure you get the name and phone number of the alarm company or instructions on how to disarm the system in an emergency.

### Must Tenants Supply Keys to Privately Installed Locks?

There's nothing worse than having an expensive contractor arrive for a scheduled repair, only to be "locked out" of the tenant's unit. While privately installed locks help tenants feel safer, they're a big headache for landlords. Hopefully, your lease or rental agreement (like the one in this book) requires tenants to furnish duplicate keys to privately installed locks. (Chapter 2, Clause 12.) Courts have ruled that a tenant's duty to supply a duplicate key is a "substantial obligation" of the lease. (See, for example, *Lavanant v. Lovelace*, 71 Misc. 2d 974, 337 N.Y.S.2d 962 (App. Term, 2d Dep't 1972) aff'd 41 A.D.2d 905, 343 N.Y.S.2d 559 (1st Dep't 1973).) That means that you can terminate the lease if the tenant refuses, after a demand, to give you a copy of the key.

The state Multiple Dwelling Law (which applies to tenants in buildings with three or more units in New York City and Buffalo) also requires tenants to furnish duplicate keys to privately installed locks. (MDL § 51-c.)

**Don't change locks.** If your tenant installs a lock without your permission, don't change the lock, even if you immediately give the tenant a key. This invites a lawsuit and false claims that you tried to lock the tenant out or stole the tenant's possessions. Section L discusses how to deal with tenants who unreasonably deny entry.

## F.  Entry to Make Repairs

Most leases and rental agreements, as well as New York City law and rent control and rent stabilization laws, allow you and your repair person to enter the tenant's home to make necessary or agreed-upon repairs, alterations or improvements to the rental unit. If you need to make a repair—for example, to fix a broken oven, replace a floor tile or check the point of entry of a persistent ant infestation—you should enter only at reasonable times and you should give a reasonable amount of notice, usually at least 24 hours. However, if this is impracticable—for example, a repair person is available on a few hours' notice—you will probably be on solid ground if you explain the situation to your tenant and then give shorter notice. Of course, if your tenant agrees to a shorter notice period, you have no problem.

 **New York City tenants can insist that you give up to one week's notice of your intent to enter to make required repairs** (see Section B, above). If, however, the tenant agreed to a shorter notice period in the lease or rental agreement, the tenant is obligated to provide access on shorter than one week's notice. As a practical matter though, tenants are usually happy to permit access for needed repairs on far less than one week's notice.

EXAMPLE: Amy told her landlord Tom that her bathroom sink was stopped up and draining very slowly. Tom called the plumber, who said that he had several large jobs in progress, but would be able to squeeze in Amy's repair at some point within the next few days. The plumber promised to call Tom before he came over. Tom relayed this information to Amy, telling her he would give her at least four hours' notice before the plumber came. Amy told Tom that four hours' notice would be fine.

In many situations, the notice period will not be a problem, since your tenant will be delighted that you are making needed repairs and will cooperate with your entry requirements. However, as every experienced landlord knows, some tenants are uncooperative when it comes to providing reasonable

access to make repairs, while at the same time demanding that repairs be made immediately. (Of course, if the time is really inconvenient for the tenant—you want to make a non-emergency repair the day your tenant is preparing dinner for her new in-laws—try to be accommodating and reschedule a more convenient appointment.) Section L, below, discusses how to handle tenants who unreasonably deny entry.

Whenever possible, put your request for access in writing and be sure to describe the nature of the repair or problem. A sample letter follows.

### Sample Letter Requesting Entry

January 6, 200X

Anna Rivera
100 Van Horton Street
Apt. B
Nyack, NY 10960

Dear Ms. Rivera:

In response to your complaint regarding the broken garbage disposal in your apartment, I have arranged to have it repaired tomorrow, Tuesday, January 7, at 2:00 PM. I attempted to reach you today (both at your home and work phone numbers) and notify you of this repair appointment. Because I was unable to reach you by phone, I am leaving this note on your door.

Sincerely,

*Marlene Morgan*

Marlene Morgan, Manager

**Let the tenant know if your plans change.** A tenant may be justifiably annoyed if you or your repair person show up late or not at all—for example, if you're supposed to come at 2 PM and don't show up until 8 AM the next morning. If it isn't possible to come on time in the first place, call the tenant and explain the problem, and ask permission to enter later on. If the tenant denies permission, you'll have to give a second notice.

## Notice of Intent to Enter Dwelling Unit

To: _Anna Rivera_
    Tenant

    _100 Van Horton Street, Apt. B_
    Street address

    _Nyack, NY 10960_
    City and State

THIS NOTICE is to inform you that on _January 7, 200X_ ,

☑ at approximately _1:00_ ~~AM~~/PM the landlord, or the landlord's agent, will enter the

premises for the following reason:

☑ To make or arrange for the following repairs or improvements:

    _fix garbage disposal_

☐ To show the premises to:

    ☐ a prospective tenant or purchaser

    ☑ workers or contractors regarding the above repair or improvement

☐ Other: _____

You are, of course, welcome to be present. If you have any questions or if the date or time is

inconvenient, please notify me promptly at _914-555-7899_ .

                                                               Phone number

_January 5, 200X_              _Marlene Morgan_

Date                        Landlord/Manager

If you don't get cooperation after you send the letter, or you prefer a more formal approach, you can try using the Notice of Intent to Enter Dwelling Unit form, above.

 You will find a Notice of Intent to Enter Dwelling Unit on the Forms CD as well as a blank tear-out copy in Appendix IV.

---

### How to Avoid Tenant Theft Claims

By planning ahead, you can minimize the chances that you or your repair person will be accused of theft. Give plenty of notice of your entry—this gives the tenant the chance to hide valuables. Try to arrange repairs or visit the rental unit only when the tenant is home. If that's not possible, you or your manager should be present. Carefully check references of plumbers and other repair people, and only allow people whom you trust to enter alone.

---

## G. Entry to Inspect Unit

It's an excellent idea to inspect your rental properties at least once a year. That way you can find small problems before they become big ones, and tenants can't claim that they didn't have an opportunity to report complaints to you. (Chapter 9, Section H, discusses inspections.) Inspections may also be necessary to investigate a problem that affects other units in the building, such as an interior wall leak.

The lease and rental agreements in this book (Clause 15 in Chapter 2) give you the right to enter a tenant's unit—after giving reasonable notice—to inspect the unit's physical condition, either for a routine inspection or to evaluate a special problem. Rent control and rent stabilization laws also permit entry for this purpose. (See Section C.) Whenever possible, put your access notice in writing, by using a letter requesting entry or a more formal Notice of Intent to Enter Dwelling Unit, like the ones that appear in Section F, above.

Unless the tenant agrees to a shorter time period, rent-stabilized tenants in New York City are entitled to at least five days' written notice of your intent to enter to inspect the unit (see Section B, above).

**Don't use the right to inspect improperly.** Don't use your right to access to harass or annoy the tenant. Repeated inspections absent a specific reason, even when proper notice is given, are an invitation to a lawsuit.

## H. Entry During Tenant's Extended Absence

Some leases and rental agreements have clauses that give landlords the right to enter the rental unit during a tenant's extended absence, usually defined as two weeks or more. These clauses are intended to permit you to maintain the property as necessary and to inspect for damage and needed repairs. For example, during a period of extreme cold, it makes sense to check the pipes in rental units to make sure they haven't burst when the tenant is away for winter vacation.

Even without such a clause in your lease or rental agreement, you should be on safe legal ground to enter rental property during a tenant's extended absence, as long as there is an immediate and genuine need to protect the property from damage. You should enter only if something really needs to be done right away. For example, if the tenant leaves the windows wide open just before a driving rainstorm, you would be justified in entering to close them.

**Require tenants to report extended absences.** To protect yourself and make sure your tenant knows what to expect, be sure your lease or rental agreement requires the tenant to inform you when he will be gone for an extended time, such as two weeks, and alerts him of your intent to enter the premises during these times if necessary. (See Clause 16 of the form agreements in Chapter 2.)

## I.  Entry to Show Property to Prospective Tenants, Buyers or Lenders

Most leases allow landlords to enter rented property to show it to prospective tenants toward the end of a tenancy, or to prospective purchasers or lenders if you wish to sell or refinance the property. Rent control and rent stabilization laws also permit entry for this purpose. Remember too, that a tenant may always agree to let you show the unit, even if they're not required to do so by a lease or law. So don't be reluctant to ask.

To obtain access, follow the same notice procedures for entry to make repairs, discussed in Section F, above. Simply check off the appropriate box on the Notice of Intent to Enter Dwelling Unit form shown above.

Unless the tenant agrees to less notice, give New York City rent-stabilized tenants at least five days' written notice of your intent to enter. (See Section B, above.)

### 1.  Showing Property to Prospective New Tenants

If you don't plan to renew a tenant's about-to-expire lease, or have given or received a notice terminating a month-to-month tenancy, you may show the premises to prospective new tenants during the last few weeks (or even months) of the outgoing tenant's stay. It is not a good idea, however, to show property if the current tenant is under the impression that his lease or rental agreement will be renewed, or if a dispute exists over whether the current tenant has a right to stay. If there's a chance the dispute will end up in court as an eviction lawsuit, the current tenant may be able to hang on for several weeks or even months. Insisting on showing the property in this situation only causes unnecessary friction at the same time that it's of little value, since you will be unable to tell the new tenants when they can move in.

If you lease a unit that you can't turn over, you may end up paying the new tenant's temporary

housing costs while you and the old tenant duke it out in court. The form lease and rental agreements in this book include a clause that may limit your liability if, for reasons beyond your control, you must delay a new tenant's move-in date after you've signed a lease or rental agreement. (See Clause 17 in Chapter 2.)

### 2.  Showing Property to Prospective Buyers or Lenders

You may also show your property—whether apartments in a multiple-unit building, a rented single-family house or condominium unit—to potential buyers or mortgage companies. Remember to give the required amount of notice to your tenant. It's also a good idea to tell the tenant the name and phone number of the realty company handling the property sale and the particular real estate agent or broker involved.

Problems usually occur when an overeager real estate salesperson shows up on the tenant's doorstep without warning, or calls on very short notice and asks to be let in to show the place to a possible buyer. In this situation, the tenant is within his right to say "I'm busy right now—try again in a few days after we've set a time convenient for all of us." Naturally, this type of misunderstanding is not conducive to good landlord-tenant relations, not to mention a sale of the property. Make sure the real estate salespeople you deal with understand the law and respect your tenants' rights to advance notice.

### 3.  Putting For Sale or For Rent Signs on the Property

Occasionally, friction is caused by landlords who put signs on tenants' homes, such as "For Sale" or "For Rent" signs in front of an apartment building or a rented single-family house. Even if the sign says "Don't Disturb the Occupant" and you are conscientious about giving notice before showing property, prospective buyers or renters may nonetheless disturb the tenant with unwelcome inquiries.

When thinking about this, it pays to put yourself in the tenant's shoes and realize that a tenant who likes where he is living will often feel threatened and insecure about a potential sale. A new owner may mean a rent increase or eviction notice if the new owner wants to move in herself. In this situation, if your tenant's privacy is ruined by repeated inquiries the tenant may even resort to suing you for invasion of privacy, just as if you personally had made repeated illegal entries.

To head off this possibility, consider not putting a For Sale sign on the property. In this age of computerized multiple-listing services, signs aren't always necessary. Indeed, many real estate agents sell houses and other real estate without ever placing a For Sale sign on the property, except when an open house is in progress. If you or your real estate agent must put up a sign advertising sale or rental of the property, make sure it clearly warns against disturbing the occupant and includes a telephone number to call—for example, "Shown by Appointment Only" or "Inquire at 555-1357—Do Not Disturb Occupant Under Any Circumstances." If your real estate agent refuses to accommodate you, find a new one who will respect your tenants' privacy and keep you out of a lawsuit.

**Don't use a lockbox.** Under no circumstances should an owner of occupied rental property that is listed for sale allow the placing of a key-holding "lockbox" on the door. This is a metal box that attaches to the front door and contains the key to that door. It can be opened by a master key held by area real estate salespeople. Since a lockbox allows a salesperson to enter in disregard of notice requirements, it should not be used—period. A lockbox will leave you wide open to a tenant's lawsuit for invasion of privacy. You could also be sued for the value of property that the tenant claims was lost.

## J.  Entry by Others

This section describes situations when other people, such as municipal inspectors, may want entry to your rental property.

### 1.  Health, Safety or Building Inspections

If a health, safety or building inspector has a credible reason to suspect that a tenant's rental unit violates housing codes or local standards—for example, a neighbor has complained about noxious smells coming from the tenant's home or about his 20 cats—they will usually knock on the tenant's door and ask permission to enter. Except in the case of genuine emergency, your tenant has the right to say no.

Inspectors have ways to get around tenant refusals. A logical first step (maybe even before they stop by the rental unit) is to ask you to let them in. Think twice before you do so: If it's not a genuine emergency, you don't have the right to let yourself, or others, into the unit without reasonable notice. Granted, if there's a health or safety hazard in the rental unit, you'll want to know about it, but you can't barge in without notice.

If your tenant refuses entry and you don't hand the inspectors a key, their next step will probably be to get a search warrant based on the information from the tenant's neighbor. The inspectors must first convince a judge that the source of their information—the neighbor—is reliable, and that there is a strong likelihood that public health or safety is at risk. Once you (or the tenant) see a signed, recently-issued warrant, you have to open up. Inspectors who believe that a tenant will refuse entry often bring along police officers who have the right to do whatever it takes to overcome the tenant's objections.

### 2.  Police

Even the police may not enter a tenant's rental unit unless they can show you or your tenant a recently issued search or arrest warrant, signed by a judge. The police do not need a search warrant, however, if they need to enter to prevent a catastrophe, such as an explosion, if they are in hot pursuit of a fleeing criminal or to prevent the imminent destruction of evidence of a significant offense.

### 3. Your Right to Let Others In

You should not give others permission to enter a tenant's home. (Municipal inspections, however, may pose an exception.) Occasionally, you or your resident manager will be faced with a very convincing stranger who will tell a heart-rending story:

- "I'm Nancy's boyfriend and I need to get my clothes out of her closet now that I'm moving to Los Angeles."
- "If I don't get my heart medicine that I left in this apartment, I'll die on the spot," or
- "I'm John's father and I just got in from the North Pole, where a polar bear ate my wallet, and I have no other place to stay."

The problem arises when you can't contact the tenant at work or elsewhere to ask whether it's okay to let the desperate individual in. This is one reason why you should always know how to reach your tenants during the day.

The story the desperate person tells you may be the truth, and chances are that if your tenant could be contacted, she would say "Yes, let Uncle Harry in immediately." But you can't know this, and it doesn't make sense to expose yourself to the potential liability involved should you get taken in by a clever con artist. There is always the chance that the person is really a smooth talker whom your tenant has a dozen good reasons to want kept out. You risk being legally responsible should your tenant's property be stolen or damaged. If you do let a stranger in without your tenant's permission, you may be sued for invasion of privacy as well.

In short, never let a stranger into your tenant's home without your tenant's permission. Even if you have been authorized to allow a certain person to enter, it is wise to ask for identification. Although this no-entry-without-authorization policy may sometimes be difficult to adhere to in the face of a convincing story, stick to it. You have much more to lose in admitting the wrong person to the tenant's home than you would have to gain by letting in someone who's "probably okay."

## K. Other Types of Invasions of Privacy

Entering a tenant's home without his knowledge or consent isn't the only way you can interfere with a tenant's privacy. Here are a few other common situations, with advice on how to handle them.

### 1. Giving Information About the Tenant to Strangers

As a landlord, you may be asked by strangers, including creditors, banks and prospective landlords, to provide credit or other information about your tenant. Did she pay the rent on time? Did she maintain the rental property? Cause any problems?

Basically, you have a legal right to give out truthful and normal business information about your tenant to people and businesses who ask and have a legitimate reason to know—for example, the tenant's bank when she applies for a loan or a prospective landlord who wants a reference. Resist any urges to add helpful personal touches, unless the tenant has given you written permission to release this sort of information. (We discuss release forms in Chapter 1.) You have nothing to gain, and possibly a lot to lose, if you give out information that your tenant feels constitutes a serious violation of her privacy.

And if you give out incorrect information—even if you believe it to be accurate—you can really be in a legal mess if the person to whom you disclose it relies on this (incorrect) information to take some action that negatively affects your tenant.

> EXAMPLE: If you tell others that a tenant has filed for bankruptcy (and this isn't true), the tenant has grounds to sue you for defamation (libel or slander) if he is damaged as a result— for example, if he doesn't get a job.

Some landlords feel that they have a moral duty to communicate information to other prospective landlords, especially if the tenant has failed to pay rent, maintain the premises or has created other serious problems. If you do give out this information, make sure you are absolutely factual and that the information you provide has been requested. If you go out of your way to give out negative information—for example, you try to blackball the tenant with other landlords in your area—you definitely risk legal liability for libeling your tenant.

⚠ **Beware of gossipy managers.** Many landlords have had serious problems with managers and supers who have gossiped about tenants who, for example, paid rent late, were served with an eviction notice, had overnight visitors or drank too much. This sort of gossip may seem innocent, but it can be an invasion of privacy for which you can be liable. Impress on your managers and supers their duty to keep confidential all sensitive information about tenants.

## 2. Calling or Visiting Tenants at Work

Should you need to call your tenant at work (say, to schedule a time to make repairs), try to be sensitive to whether it's permissible for him to receive personal calls. While some people work at desks with telephones and have bosses who don't get upset about occasional personal calls, others have jobs that are greatly disrupted by any phone call. A general rule seems to be that the more physical the type of the work, the more tyrannical employers are about prohibiting personal phone calls at work.

Under no circumstances should you continue to call a tenant at work who asks you not to do so. This is especially true when calling about late rent payments or other problems.

Never leave specific messages with your tenant's employer, especially those that could reflect negatively on her. A landlord who leaves a message like "Tell your deadbeat employee I'll evict her if she doesn't pay the rent" can expect at least a lot of bad feeling on the part of the tenant. A rent-regulated tenant could file a harassment complaint with the state Division of Housing and Community Renewal and even a lawsuit, especially if your conduct results in the tenant losing her job or a promotion.

As for visiting the tenant at work—say to collect late rent—this is something you should absolutely avoid unless invited. What it boils down to is that no matter what you think of your tenant, you

should respect the sensitive nature of the tenant's relationship with her employer.

## 3. Spying on a Tenant

As a result of worrying too much about illegal subtenants, a few landlords have attempted to interrogate tenants' visitors, knock on their tenants' doors at odd hours or too frequently in order to see who answers or even peek through windows. Needless to say, this sort of conduct can render you liable for punitive damages in an invasion of privacy lawsuit. As far as talking to tenants' guests is concerned, keep your conversations to pleasant hellos or nonthreatening small talk.

### Watch Out for Drug Dealing on Your Property

It's crucial that you keep a careful eye on your tenants if you suspect they're engaging in drug dealing or other illegal behavior. Landlords have a responsibility to keep their properties safe—that includes keeping dealers out by carefully screening prospective tenants (see Chapter 1) and kicking them out pronto when they are discovered. (See Chapter 9, Section B, for details on this statutory duty.) Other tenants and neighbors, as well as government agencies, may bring costly lawsuits against landlords who allow drug dealing on their properties. (Chapter 14 explains how to remove tenants who are selling drugs or using their rental unit to engage in other illegal activities.)

### 4. Mail Tampering

In many properties, landlords have access to tenant mail and packages. In smaller buildings, landlords may distribute all or some of the mail, while in high-rises they have the pass key to lobby mail boxes. While most landlords wouldn't consider rifling through their tenants' mail, some of your staff might be tempted to do so. Under federal law, it is a crime for anyone to take a letter, postcard or package out of a tenant's mailbox before it is delivered with the intent to obstruct the letter, pry into the tenant's business or secrets or open, hide or destroy the mail. (18 U.S.C. 1702.)

### 5. Videotaping

Landlords may legally videotape any of the common areas of the property, including lobbies, garages and public hallways. Landlords usually install video cameras because of legitimate security concerns, but occasionally, tenants discover that their landlord or the police have installed a camera pointed at their apartment's entrance door. New York courts have okayed this type of video surveillance since it is not reasonable for tenants to have an expectation of privacy in the common areas of a rental building, and since the camera records the same things that would be seen by a passer-by in the hallway. The secret installation of a video camera in a tenant's apartment, however, would be a clear invasion of privacy for which the tenant could bring a lawsuit against you for money damages. Section M, below, discusses tenant remedies.

### 6. Credit Report Searches

When dealing with prospective tenants, it's perfectly legal for you to obtain the tenant's credit report to investigate creditworthiness. But once the tenant has moved in, you need a legitimate business purpose to obtain credit information. A federal court has ruled that it is illegal for landlords to order credit checks on tenants for non-credit purposes,

such as verifying an address. (*Ali v. Vikar Management Ltd.*, 994 F. Supp. 492 (S.D.N.Y., 1998).) The Manhattan landlord in this case ordered credit reports on rent-stabilized tenants whom he suspected of maintaining a primary residence elsewhere. Since rent laws require the landlord to renew rent-stabilized tenants' leases without regard to the tenants' creditworthiness, the landlord had no legitimate reason to seek credit information.

### 7. "Self-Help" Evictions

It is illegal for you to enter the rental property and do such things as take off windows and doors, turn off the utilities or change the locks. Removing a tenant by force or threat of force is a criminal misdemeanor. Only city marshals and county sheriffs may carry out evictions, in response to a court order.

## L. What to Do When Tenants Unreasonably Deny Entry

Occasionally, even if you give a generous amount of notice and have a legitimate reason, a tenant may refuse to let you in. If you repeatedly encounter unreasonable refusals to let you or your employees enter the premises, you can probably legally enter anyway, provided you do so in a peaceful manner.

Never push or force your way in. Even if you have the right to be there, you can face liability for anything that goes wrong.

For practical reasons, don't enter alone. If you really need entry and the tenant isn't home, it's just common sense to bring someone along who can later act as a witness in case the tenant claims some of her property is missing.

Another problem landlords face is that many tenants add private locks and don't supply you with a duplicate key. In multiple dwellings this is illegal, because it restricts your right of access in a true emergency or when you have given proper notice. As noted in Section E, above, your lease or rental agreement should require tenants to furnish copies of keys for any added locks, as well as notice of any change of locks or the installation of any burglar alarms. (See Clause 12, Chapter 2.)

If you have a serious conflict over access with an otherwise satisfactory tenant, a sensible first step is to meet with the tenant to see if the problem can be resolved. If you come to an understanding, follow up with a note to confirm your agreement. Here's an example:

### Sample Letter to Tenant Confirming Agreement over Access

> Dear Ms. Korda,
>
> This will confirm our telephone conversation of April 5, 200x, regarding access to your apartment for the purpose of making repairs. As agreed, management will give you 24 hours' advance written notice and will enter only on weekdays during business hours. As further agreed, the building superintendent will knock first, and if no one answers the door, may enter the apartment with a passkey. Thank you for your cooperation in this matter.
>
> Very truly yours,
>
> *Donald O'Bergin*
> Landlord

If attempts at compromise fail, you may be able to terminate the tenancy.

**For month-to-month tenants,** simply give the tenant the requisite termination notice (30 days in New York City and one month outside New York City). Chapter 13 explains how to terminate month-to-month tenants.

**For tenants with leases that provide a right of entry,** you may terminate the tenancy on the ground that the tenant has breached a substantial obligation of the lease. (Chapter 14 discusses terminating on this ground. Chapter 15 explains the procedure to follow.)

**For rent-controlled and rent-stabilized tenants,** a refusal to provide access may violate rent control or rent stabilization laws and entitle you to

evict the tenant. (Chapter 14 discusses terminating rent-regulated tenancies. Chapter 15 explains the procedure to follow.)

 **For unregulated New York City tenants without an entry clause in their lease,** a tenant's refusal to permit access for housing-code–related repairs or inspections violates New York City law (see Section B, above). In some cases, a court will permit an eviction where a tenant violates a local law or regulation. If you do end up in court, be prepared to prove that you required access for a legitimate reason and that you gave the tenant the requisite notice. A good recordkeeping system is crucial in this regard.

## M. Tenants' Remedies If a Landlord Acts Illegally

Conscientious landlords should be receptive to a tenant's complaint that her privacy is being violated and work out an acceptable compromise. If you violate a tenant's right to privacy and you can't work out a compromise, the tenant may bring a lawsuit and ask for money damages. You may be held liable for your property manager's disrespect of the tenant's right of privacy even if you never knew about the manager's conduct. A tenant who can show a repeated pattern of illegal activity, or even one clear example of outrageous conduct, may be able to get a substantial recovery.

While there is no state or city law specifically aimed at safeguarding tenant privacy, depending on the circumstances, a tenant may be able to sue you and recover money damages on one or more of the following legal theories:

- trespass: entry without consent or proper authority
- breach of implied covenant of quiet enjoyment: interfering with a tenant's right to the undisturbed use of her home
- breach of the implied warranty of habitability: violating a tenant's reasonable expectation of privacy and right to exclusive possession (Chapter 9 explains the warranty of habitability)

- infliction of emotional distress: any illegal act that the landlord intends to cause serious emotional consequences to the tenant
- violation of fair credit reporting laws: obtaining information from a tenant's credit report for non-credit purposes
- defamation: making an untrue and damaging statement about a tenant to others, or

- unlawful eviction: changing the locks without a court order or removing the tenant from the premises by force or threat of force.

These types of lawsuits are beyond the scope of this book and require expert legal advice. (See Chapter 17 for advice on finding and working with a lawyer.)  ■

Chapter **11**

# Dealing With Environmental Hazards

Landlord liability for environmental hazards has grown dramatically since the 1970s. Tenants have won big damage awards from landlords for injuries from exposure to lead, asbestos and other environmental hazards found in rental properties. At the same time, several laws have been enacted that require you to test for and abate environmental hazards, some of which you may never have heard of, using specially trained workers and expensive techniques.

This chapter provides an overview of the legal and practical issues involving landlord liability for environmental health hazards—specifically lead, asbestos, ozone-depleting refrigerants, radon and mold.

Chapter 9 explains how to maintain habitable property by complying with state and local housing laws. Chapter 9 also examines a tenant's legal options under the warranty of habitability and other statutes for dealing with lead, asbestos or other environmental hazards at your property.

## A. Lead

As we all know, exposure to lead-based paint or lead-contaminated drinking water may lead to serious health problems, particularly in children. Brain damage, attention disorders and hyperactivity have all been associated with lead poisoning. Landlords who are found responsible for lead may face liability for a child's lifelong disability. Jury awards and settlements for lead poisoning are typically enormous, because they cover remedial treatment and education of a child for the rest of his life, and include an award for the estimated "loss of earning" capacity caused by the injury. The cost of a typical "slip and fall" injury pales in comparison to some of the multimillion dollar jury awards and settlements for lead poisoning.

Prior to 1950, lead was a common ingredient in residential interior and exterior paints. Lead was used in pigments to make brighter, more durable paint. The federal government banned the sale of lead-based paint for residential use in 1978. Chances are that a property built before 1979 has at least some surfaces that were finished with lead-based paint. According to the New York State Department of Health, more than 90% of New York's housing stock was built before 1979. Pre-1950 housing in poor and urban neighborhoods that has been allowed to age and deteriorate is by far the greatest source of lead poisonings.

Another source of lead exposure in older structures is from lead drinking water pipes, lead-based solder and lead-contaminated soil. At this time, federal and state legislation has not targeted these sources of lead contamination; consequently, this chapter focuses on lead from paint. Be aware, however, that if you have contaminated soil or deteriorating lead pipes, you may face liability if someone is sickened because of it, and you have not taken steps to eliminate or contain the problem.

In this section, we examine your obligation to disclose lead paint hazards under federal law, and your obligation to abate lead hazards under state law. Finally, we explain some special rules that apply to New York City properties.

### 1. Federal Law: Disclosing Lead Paint Hazards to New and Renewal Tenants

Because of the health problems caused by lead paint poisoning, the Residential Lead-Based Paint Hazard Reduction Act was enacted in 1992 (42 U.S.C. § 4852d). It is commonly referred to as Title X (Ten). Compliance with Title X became the law for all landlords as of December 6, 1996.

The goal of Title X is "lead hazard reduction," which means evaluating the risk of poisoning in each housing situation and taking the appropriate steps to reduce the hazard. The Occupational Safety and Health Administration (OSHA) and the Environmental Protection Agency (EPA) have written regulations explaining the law (24 Code of Federal Regulations Part 35 and 40 Code of Federal Regulations Part 745). For more information see "Lead Hazard Resources," in Subsection 4, below.

## a. Give Disclosure Statement to Rental Applicants, Renewal Tenants

To comply with Title X, you must give rental applicants who plan to sign a lease or rental agreement and current tenants who are renewing their leases at properties built before 1978, any information you possess on lead paint hazards at your property. Your "lead paint disclosure statement" must cover hazards in individual rental units, common areas and garages, tool sheds, other outbuildings, signs, fences and play areas.

The Forms CD includes a Disclosure of Information on Lead-Based Paint or Lead-Based Paint Hazards form and Appendix IV includes a blank tear-out copy. This form meets EPA requirements.

If you have had your property tested for lead (see "Lead Inspections," below), a copy of the report, or a summary written by the inspector, must accompany the disclosure statement.

## b. Lead Information Pamphlet Must Accompany Disclosure Statement

In addition to the disclosure statement, you must also give all rental applicants and tenants the lead hazard information pamphlet, "Protect Your Family From Lead in Your Home," written by the EPA. (See "Lead Hazard Resources" below.) Appendix IV includes a tear-out copy of the pamphlet, which you may reproduce. The graphics in the original pamphlet must be included.

**If the lease is in another language besides English,** landlords must give the applicant or current tenant the disclosure form (and the lead hazard information pamphlet discussed above) in the language of the lease. You can obtain Spanish versions of the disclosure form and pamphlet from the EPA. (See "Lead Hazard Resources," below.)

### Leaded Mini-Blinds

Some imported mini-blinds from China, Taiwan, Indonesia and Mexico are likely to contain lead, but are not banned by the Consumer Product Safety Commission. If your property has leaded mini-blinds, you do not have to tell tenants that they contain lead unless you know that the blinds have begun to deteriorate and produce lead dust. To avoid problems, use mini-blinds from other sources or different kinds of window coverings.

## c. When to Give Tenants the Disclosure Statement and Pamphlet

Landlords must give the disclosure statement and lead information pamphlet to rental applicants and renewal tenants *before* they are "obligated under any contract" to rent housing from the landlord. Rental applicants become "obligated" when they sign a lease, renewal lease or rental agreement for a rental unit. Therefore, tell applicants and renewal tenants to read and sign the disclosure statement and pamphlet *before* they sign the lease or rental agreement.

**Don't overlook rent-controlled tenants and long-term month-to-month tenants.** Compliance with Title X became the law for all landlords as of December 6, 1996. You should have given rent-controlled and non-regulated month-to-month tenants a disclosure statement when you collected your first rent check dated on or after December 6, 1996.

Once a tenant has received a disclosure statement and pamphlet, you don't need to give them to the tenant again at renewal time unless you've never given them one before, or if circumstances change—for example, if an inspection or test alerts you to a lead hazard that you didn't know about. In that case, a revised disclosure statement must be given to the tenant to review and sign. You're not legally required to give the tenant another lead information pamphlet, unless you (or your staff) undertake significant renovations or remodeling that will disturb a leaded surface (see Subsection 2, below).

## Lead Inspections

A lead inspection is a surface-by-surface investigation of the property's painted surfaces, but does not include taking dust or soil samples. A risk assessment gathers paint, dust and soil samples for analysis, and includes a visual inspection of the property. While lead inspections and risk assessments are not required by federal or state law, you may voluntarily arrange an inspection in order to certify that the property is lead free and exempt from federal regulations. (See the list of exemptions, below.) Also, if you take out a loan or buy insurance, your bank or insurance company may require a lead inspection. NYC law requires landlords to conduct a visual inspection of units in pre-1960 multiple dwellings where a child under age six resides.

Federal law requires New York landlords to use only EPA-trained and certified lead inspectors or risk assessors. (15 U.S.C. § 2682.) New York State does not have its own certification or training program. Anyone who performs abatement work must also be EPA trained and certified. For a listing of EPA-trained and certified lead inspectors and risk assessors in your area, contact the National Lead Information Center (800-424-LEAD) or visit the Lead Listing website (www.leadlisting.org).

Any information or reports you obtain from the lead inspector or assessor about lead-based paint hazards in a rental unit or in the common areas of your property must be disclosed to new and renewal tenants under federal law (Section A1 discusses your duty to disclose lead paint hazards).

### d. Enforcement and Penalties

HUD and EPA plan to enforce renters' rights to know about the presence of lead-based paint. They'll use "testers" who pose as rental applicants and who secretly document whether you give tenants the required disclosure statement and information pamphlet.

Landlords who fail to distribute the required information may receive one or more of the following penalties:

- a notice of noncompliance, the mildest form of reprimand
- a civil penalty, which can include fines of up to $11,000 per violation for willful and continuing noncompliance
- an order to pay an injured tenant up to three times his actual damages, or
- a criminal fine of up to $11,000 per violation.

## 2. Federal Law: "Renovators" Must Give Tenants Lead Information When Renovating Units or Common Areas

When you renovate occupied rental units or common areas in buildings constructed before 1978, EPA regulations require that current tenants receive lead hazard information before the renovation work begins. (40 CFR §§ 745.80-88.) The regulations were developed under the federal Toxic Substances Control Act (15 U.S.C. §§ 2681-2692) and became effective on June 1, 1999.

The obligation to distribute lead information rests with the "renovator." If you hire an outside contractor to perform renovation work, the contractor is the renovator. But if you, your property manager, superintendent or other employees perform the renovation work, the landlord is the renovator and is obliged to give out the required information.

The type of information that the renovator must give to tenants depends on where the renovation is taking place. If an occupied rental unit is being worked on, you must give the tenant a copy of the EPA pamphlet "Protect Your Family From Lead in Your Home." If common areas will be affected, you will have to distribute a notice to every rental unit in the building.

### a.  What Qualifies As a Renovation?

According to EPA regulations, a "renovation" is any change to an occupied rental unit or common area of your building that disturbs painted surfaces. Here are some examples:

- removing or modifying a painted door, wall, baseboard or ceiling
- scraping or sanding paint, or
- removing a large structure like a wall, partition or window.

Not every renovation triggers the federal law, though. There are four big exceptions:

1.  **Emergency renovations.** If a sudden or unexpected event, such as a fire or flood, requires that you make emergency repairs to a rental unit or to your property's common areas, there's no need to distribute lead hazard information to tenants before work begins.

2.  **Minor repairs or maintenance.** Minor work that affects two square feet or less of a painted surface is also exempt. Minor repairs include routine electrical and plumbing work, so long as no more than two square feet of the wall, ceiling or other painted surface gets disturbed by the work.

3.  **Renovations in lead-free properties.** If the rental unit or building in which the renovation takes place has been certified as containing no lead paint, you're not required to give out the required information.

4.  **Common area renovations in buildings with three or fewer units.** Only buildings with four or more units are required to give tenants information about common area renovations.

Repainting a rental unit in preparation for a new tenant doesn't qualify as a renovation unless accompanied by sanding, scraping or other surface preparation activities that may generate paint dust. Minor spot scraping or sanding can qualify for the "minor repairs and maintenance" exception if no more than two square feet of paint is disturbed on any surface to be painted. (EPA Interpretive Guidance, Part I, May 28, 1999.)

### b.  Give Out EPA Pamphlet When Renovating Occupied Rental Units

Before starting a renovation to an occupied rental unit, the renovator must give the EPA pamphlet, "Protect Your Family From Lead in Your Home," to at least one adult occupant of the unit being occupied, preferably the tenant. This is the same one you gave new tenants when they signed their lease or rental agreement (see Section 1, above). This requirement applies to all rental properties, including single-family homes and duplexes, unless the property has been certified lead-free by an inspector.

You may mail or hand deliver the pamphlet to the tenant. If you mail it, you must get a "certificate of mailing" from the post office dated at least seven days before the renovation work begins. If you hand deliver it, have the tenant sign and date a receipt acknowledging that the pamphlet was received before renovation work began in the unit. Make sure the tenant will receive the pamphlet 60 days (or less) before the work begins (delivering the pamphlet more than 60 days in advance won't do).

### c.  Give Out Notice When Renovating Common Areas

If your building has four or more units, the renovator—you or your contractor—must notify tenants of all "affected units" about the renovation and tell them how to obtain a free copy of the EPA pamphlet, "Protect Your Family From Lead in Your Home." (40 CFR § 745.85(b)(2).) In most cases, common area renovations will affect all units in your property, meaning that all tenants must be notified about the renovation. But when renovating a "limited use common area" in a large apartment building, such as the 16th floor hallway, you need only notify those units serviced by, or in close proximity to, the limited use common area. The EPA defines large buildings as those having 50 or more units.

To comply, the renovator must deliver a notice to every affected unit describing the nature and location of the renovation work, its location and the dates you expect to begin and finish work (see the sample Common Area Renovations Notice, below). If you can't provide specific dates, you may use terms like "on or about," "in early June" or "in late July," to describe expected starting and ending dates for the renovation. The notices *must be delivered within 60 days before work begins.* The notices may be slipped under apartment doors or given to any adult occupant of the rental unit. (You may not mail the notices, however.) After the notices are delivered, keep a copy in your file, together with a note describing the date and manner in which you delivered the notices to rental units.

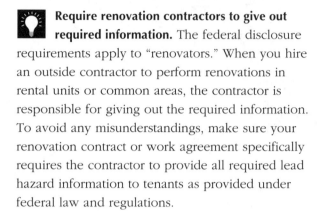 **Require renovation contractors to give out required information.** The federal disclosure requirements apply to "renovators." When you hire an outside contractor to perform renovations in rental units or common areas, the contractor is responsible for giving out the required information. To avoid any misunderstandings, make sure your renovation contract or work agreement specifically requires the contractor to provide all required lead hazard information to tenants as provided under federal law and regulations.

### d. Penalties

Failing to give tenants the required information about renovation lead hazards can result in harsh penalties. Renovators who knowingly violate the regulations can get hit with a penalty of up to $27,500 per day for each violation. Willful violations can also result in imprisonment.

### Sample Common Area Renovations Notice

March 1, 200X

Dear Tenant,

Please be advised that we will begin renovating the hallways on or about March 15 200x. Specifically, we will be removing and replacing the baseboards, wallpaper and trim in the 2nd, 3rd and 4th floor corridors, and sanding and repainting the ceilings. We expect the work to be completed in early May, 200x.

You may obtain a free copy of the pamphlet "Protect Your Family from Lead in Your Home" from Paul Hogan, the building superintendent. Paul may be reached at (212) 555-1212.

We will make every attempt to minimize inconvenience to tenants during the renovation process. If you have questions about the proposed renovation work, feel free to contact Mr. Hogan or me.

Very truly yours,

*Lawrence Levy*

Lawrence Levy, Manager

## Rental Properties Exempt From Federal Lead Regulations

These rental properties are exempt from both the federal lead paint disclosure regulations and the renovation regulations. However, local laws relating to lead hazards may nevertheless apply.

- Housing for which a construction permit was obtained, or on which construction was started, after January 1, 1978. Older buildings that have been completely renovated since 1978 are not exempt, even if every painted surface was removed or replaced.
- Housing certified as lead-free by an accredited lead inspector. Lead-free means the absence of any lead paint, even paint that has been completely painted over and encapsulated.
- Lofts, efficiencies, studios and other "zero-bedroom" units, including dormitory housing and rentals in sorority and fraternity houses. University-owned apartments and married student housing are not exempted.
- Short-term vacation rentals of 100 days or less.
- A single room rented in a residential home.
- Housing designed for persons with disabilities (as explained in HUD's Fair Housing Accessibility Guidelines, 56 Code of Federal Regulations 9472, 3/6/91), unless any child less than six years old resides there or is expected to reside there.
- Retirement communities (housing designed for seniors, where one or more tenant is at least 62 years old) unless children under the age of six are present or expected to live there.

## 3. State Laws on Lead Affecting Landlords

Since 1970, New York has prohibited the use of "leaded paint" on any interior surface, windowsill, window frame or porch of a residential unit. (Pub. Health L. § 1372.) In addition, state law requires that pipes supplying drinking water contain no more

than 8% lead, and solder used to join the pipes contain no more than two-tenths of one percent (.2%) lead. (GBL § 399(g).) Drinking water is considered contaminated if it flows through pipes with more than the permissible lead level. (Pub. Health L. § 1373.)

The state does not require landlords to inspect their properties for lead, nor does it routinely send inspectors to rental properties to test for the presence of lead. At the state level, inspections are triggered *solely* by reports of elevated blood levels in children. State law requires health providers to screen pregnant women and small children for lead. (10 NYCRR Part 67.) In addition, nursery and elementary schools require enrollees to be lead-screened by a health care professional. (Pub. Health L. § 1370-c, d and e.) All lead screening results are reported to the State Department of Health.

If a screening indicates lead contamination, the Department of Health orders an inspection of the child's dwelling for lead poisoning hazards. If the child lives in a municipality that has enacted a local lead paint hazard ordinance (see for example, NYC Adm. Code § 27-2056(h)), the inspection is conducted by a local authority. For municipalities that don't have any lead paint ordinances or lead poisoning control programs in effect (such as in many rural counties upstate), the inspection is carried out by the State Department of Health.

Inspectors look for peeling, cracking, blistering, flaking or chipping lead-based paint, lead-contaminated drinking water and lead-contaminated soil. (10 NYCRR § 67-2.8.) If a lead hazard is found, the inspector issues a violation ordering the landlord to abate the hazard by using a prescribed lead abatement method.

Landlords who fail to abate a lead hazard after getting an official "notice and demand" from a Department of Health inspector can get hit with monetary fines of up to $2,500. The state also has the power to appoint a receiver for your property who will abate the lead hazard at your expense. (10 NYCRR § 67-2.8.) Fines and penalties for failing to comply with lead abatement orders issued by local authorities vary, depending on the locality. For more information on state laws and programs on lead, see "Lead Hazard Resources," below.

Lead paint hazards, and potentially, soil and water hazards, may form the basis of a tenant's claim for a violation of the state warranty of habitability law where a child occupies a rental unit with peeling or chipped lead-based paint. (*German v. Federal Home Loan Mortg. Corp.*, 885 F. Supp. 537 (S.D.N.Y. 1995) clarified on reargument in part, 896 F. Supp. 1385 (S.D.N.Y. 1995).) In such cases, courts are authorized to order the landlord to abate the lead paint condition. (*Laura Goldberg Mgmt. v. Rivera*, N.Y.L.J., 7/28/94, p. 23, col. 1 (Civ. Ct., N.Y. County).) Chapter 9 discusses your repair and maintenance obligations under the warranty of habitability.

## Your Insurance Policy May Not Cover Lead Paint-Poisoning Lawsuits

If you are hit with a lead-poisoning lawsuit, you can't presume that your insurance company will be there to defend you or pay money damages to the victim. Depending on the terms of your policy, your insurer may be able to deny coverage for lead exposure claims—even if the suit is without merit. If you know (or presume) that your property contains lead-based paint, review your lead paint liability coverage with your insurance broker.

In the late 1980s, insurance companies began to deny lead liability claims based on a "pollution exclusion clause" that's buried in the fine print of many liability insurance policies. Fortunately for landlords, courts have held that lead paint liability claims as a result of lead paint exposure do not fall within the definition of pollution. So insurers may not legally use the pollution exclusion clause as a reason to deny coverage.

But since lead liability lawsuits are so expensive, some insurance companies have simply stopped writing general liability insurance on older buildings where there is a presumed lead paint exposure. Others have added lead-based paint liability "exclusions" to their policies, excluding coverage for these types of claims. While you can still get coverage, it might be limited or come at a higher premium.

## 4. New York City Lead-Poisoning and Prevention Law

New York City's lead-poisoning prevention and control law (NYC Adm. Code § 27-2056 and following), also known as Local Law 38 of 1999, places several extra obligations on landlords of pre-1960 multiple dwellings. Since 1960, New York City has banned the use of lead-based paint on the interior surfaces of residential buildings. The 1999 law, aimed at preventing lead poisoning of children, presumes that all paint in a unit of a multiple dwelling built before 1960 is lead-based paint—unless the landlord rebuts this presumption by proving otherwise.

The salient points of the New York City law, which include lead hazard notices to tenants, visual inspections of rental units where children under six reside, and a duty to correct lead paint hazards in occupied and vacant units, are explained in the sections below.

### a. Tenant Notification Requirements

The law places two tenant notification requirements on landlords of pre-1960 multiple dwellings, (that is, buildings with three or more units):

**New Tenants.** As of November 12, 1999, you must provide new tenants with both:

- a notice, in a form approved by the New York City Department of Housing Preservation and Development (HPD), inquiring whether a child under age six resides or will reside in the rental unit, and
- a pamphlet entitled "A Guide to New York City Local Law 38 of 1999, Keeping Your Home Safe From Lead-Based Paint Hazards," developed by the New York City Department of Health (DOH), explaining the hazards associated with lead-based paint and related information.

The notice and pamphlet must be given to the tenant when the lease or rental agreement is signed, or, where there is no written rental agreement, when the tenant takes occupancy of the rental unit.

---

## More Information: Lead Hazard Resources

Information on the evaluation and control of lead hazards may be obtained from the following federal, state and New York City resources.

- **National Lead Information Center.** This federally funded resource provides lists of EPA-certified lead paint professionals in your area, as well as lead hazard documents and publications, including the Disclosure of Information on Lead-Based Paint or Lead-Based Paint Hazards form and the EPA pamphlet "Protect Your Family From Lead in Your Home." All listings, documents and publications may be ordered by mail or by fax. Information specialists are also available to field questions about lead laws, lead regulations and abatement procedures. You can call the Center at 800-424-LEAD or visit its website (www.epa.gov/lead/nlic.htm).
- **HUD.** The U.S. Department of Housing and Urban Development maintains a "Lead Listing" of names, addresses and phone numbers of EPA-trained and certified professionals for lead inspections, risk assessments and abatement work in New York. Call 888-LEAD-LIST or access the list on the web at www.leadlisting.org.

For other HUD information on lead hazards, visit www.hud.gov/lea.

- **EPA.** The U.S. Department of Environmental Protection provides pamphlets, documents, forms and information on lead paint hazards, federal laws, regulations and interpretive guidelines. Contact the EPA at 732-321-6671 or visit its website at www.epa.gov/lead.
- **New York State Department of Health.** The Health Department provides information on lead abatement procedures. Contact the Health Department InfoLine at 800-458-1158 or visit its website at www.health. state.ny.us.
- **New York City Department of Health.** For information on lead hazards, choosing lead professionals and lead abatement techniques, call 212-BAN-LEAD or visit the Department of Health website (www.nyc.gov/html/doh/home.html).
- **New York City Department of Housing Preservation and Development.** For information on lead paint regulations, violations and abatement techniques call 212-863-8000 or visit the HPD website at www.nyc.gov/html/hpd/home.html.

---

**Current Tenants.** Between January 1 and January 16 of each year, you must deliver to all current tenants a notice inquiring whether a child under age six lives in the rental unit. This notice must also meet DOH requirements. Tenants are required to respond no later than March 1 and have a continuing obligation to inform you in writing if any child under age six later takes occupancy.

There are four ways you can deliver the notices to current tenants:

- regular mail
- hand delivery
- by including the notice with the January rent bill, if the rent bill will be delivered after December 15 but no later than January 16, or
- by delivering the notice in conjunction with the annual Window Guard Notice which land-

lords are already obligated to provide to tenants during the same time period each year. (Chapter 2, Section E, covers your obligation to provide window guards and notices.)

All pamphlets and notices must, at minimum, be written in English and Spanish. Section b, below, discusses where to get forms.

The New York City tenant notification requirements don't affect your federal law obligation to provide lead paint hazard information to new tenants who are moving into units with one or more bedrooms. You must still supply a "lead hazard disclosure statement," in a form approved by the EPA, covering hazards in individual rental units, common areas, outbuildings, fences and play areas, and, in addition, provide a lead hazard information pamphlet,

"Protect Your Family From Lead in Your Home," written by the EPA. Section A1, above, explains your federal law lead hazard notice obligations.

### b. Where to Get Lead Hazard Notification Forms and Pamphlets

When you sign leases or rental agreements with tenants, including renewal leases, you must have the tenant sign a form which asks, in English and Spanish, whether a child age six or under will reside in the rental unit. You may obtain a single copy of this inquiry form from the New York City Department of Housing Preservation and Development (HPD), 100 Gold Street, New York, NY 10038, 212-863-8000, or download one from its website (www.nyc.gov/html/hpd/pdf/leadrules.pdf). The form is attached as Appendix A ("Lease/Commencement of Occupancy Notice for Prevention of Leadased Paint Hazards—Inquiry Regarding Child") to an HPD publication called *Notice of Adoption of Final Rule Pertaining to Lead-Based Paint.* You can make copies of Appendix A (in English and Spanish) for new tenants.

When you sign leases or rental agreements with tenants, including renewal leases, you must also provide the tenant with a copy of a pamphlet called "A Guide to New York City Local Law 38 of 1999, Keeping Your Home Safe from Lead-Based Paint Hazards." You can order a single copy of the pamphlet from the New York City Department of Health and Mental Hygiene's Lead-Poisoning Prevention Program, 253 Broadway, 11th Floor, New York, NY 10007, 212-BAN LEAD or download a copy from the agency's website (www.nyc.gov/html/doh/html/lead/lead38.html). You can make copies of the pamphlets for new tenants.

In addition, landlords must send an annual notice to current tenants between January 1 and January 16, asking whether a child age six or under resides or will reside in the rental unit. You may obtain a single copy of this form from the New York City Department of Housing Preservation and Development (HPD), 100 Gold Street, New York, NY 10038, 212-863-8000, or download one from its website (www.nyc.gov/html/hpd/pdf/leadrules.pdf). The form is attached as Appendix B ("Annual Notice for Prevention of Lead-Based Paint Hazards—Inquiry Regarding Child") to an HPD publication called "Notice of Adoption of Final Rule Pertaining to Lead-Based Paint."

### c. Rental Unit Inspection Requirements

Whenever you get written notice from a tenant that a child under six resides in an occupied rental unit, or you otherwise know that a child under six lives there, you must perform an annual visual inspection of the unit for "lead-based paint hazards," defined as peeling paint or deteriorated subsurfaces. Peeling paint is defined as paint or other surface-coating material that is curling, cracking, scaling, flaking, blistering, chipping, chalking or loose. A deteriorated subsurface includes any unstable or unsound surface, such as wood or plaster that has been subject to moisture or disturbance, and which is covered by lead-based paint. HPD must also inspect rental units for lead hazards in response to tenant complaints.

You must also visually inspect any apartments that become vacant, before the unit may be reoccupied.

**Keep good records.** Keep a record of all visual self-inspections (as well as records of all corrective work performed) for a period of at least three years. If corrective work is performed, you must record the name, address and telephone number of the person or company that performed the work, the dates work started and ended, the location of the work performed and a detailed description of the work. Also retain any invoices you paid for the work. You must make these records available to HPD upon request. If you sell or transfer the property, all lead paint hazard inspection and work records must be turned over to the new owner.

### d. Duty to Correct Lead Paint Hazards

The New York City law requires you to voluntarily correct any lead-based paint hazards identified by visual inspection, utilizing the work practices specified in the new law or, alternatively, by using the more stringent work practices specified by the health code. (Health Code of the City of New York § 173.14.) A vacant apartment may not be reoccupied until any lead-based paint hazards identified in the inspection are corrected.

You must also correct lead paint violations issued by HPD within 21 days. Time extensions are available if the tenant won't give you access right away. It pays to jump on these violations right way. If you don't correct the violation within 21 days (and didn't get an extension), you'll be required to follow a more stringent, and expensive, set of work practices, as specified by DOH, within 15 days.

Upon completion of violation-related correction work, the landlord must have a "surface dust test" performed by a DOH-certified tester. If the lead content of dust in the rental unit is satisfactory, the landlord may then certify to HPD that the hazardous condition has been corrected.

The civil penalty for failure to correct a violation is $250 per day. If the landlord doesn't correct the violation, the law requires the City to remove the hazard within a specified time frame, at the landlord's expense. The law sharply increases the fines that may be imposed upon landlords for falsely certifying that a lead hazard violation has been corrected. The fines may range from $10,000 to $25,000, up from $1,000 to $3,000.

### e.  Law Specifies New Work Practices

The 1999 law repeals "Local Law 1 of 1982," which had been interpreted to require landlords to make rental units where small children resided "lead-free" by eliminating all lead-based paint. By contrast, the 1999 law requires landlords to make affected units "lead-safe," which permits intact lead-based paint to remain undisturbed.

There are a total of 13 "interim controls," or work practices, that landlords must follow when correcting a lead paint hazard. The specific number of controls that must be taken in a given situation will depend on whether the rental unit is occupied or vacant and whether the work is being performed in response to a violation. In all cases, dry scraping and dry sanding of lead-based paint or paint of unknown lead content in any dwelling units is prohibited. (NYC Adm. Code § 17-181.)

For more information on the specific work practices to follow to correct a given lead paint hazard, contact HPD.

## B.  Asbestos

Exposure to asbestos has long and definitively been linked to an increased risk of cancer, particularly for workers in the asbestos manufacturing industry or in construction jobs involving the use of asbestos materials. More recently, the danger of asbestos in residential properties has also been acknowledged.

Asbestos was used as a fire retardant insulation in the construction of buildings long before it was known to pose severe environmental and health hazards. Structures built before the mid-1970s often contain asbestos insulation around heating systems, plumbing lines, in ceilings and in other areas. Until 1981, asbestos was also widely used in many other building materials, such as vinyl flooring and tiles.

Asbestos is particularly dangerous in its "friable" state, when it is easily crumbled or flaked by hand. Friable asbestos fibers that become airborne—for example, when it is disturbed during renovation work—have the potential to become a significant health problem to tenants. As a result, federal and state laws require landlords to take special precautions before undertaking renovation or demolition work in buildings with asbestos-containing materials.

In this section, we examine your asbestos-handling responsibilities under federal and state laws. We also explain some special rules that are applicable for New York City properties. We then look at some important OSHA regulations that apply to asbestos-related activities carried out by your maintenance personnel.

## 1. Federal and State Asbestos Handling Requirements

The Federal Clean Air Act requires the EPA to develop and enforce regulations to protect the general public from exposure to airborne contaminants. (CAA § 112.) The EPA established national standards for asbestos, intended to minimize the release of asbestos fibers into the air during renovations and demolition work. ("Federal Asbestos Hazard Emergency Response Act" (15 U.S.C. §2641); "National Emission Standards for Hazardous Air Pollutants," 40 CFR Part 61, Subpart M).)

Outside New York City, the EPA standards are administered by the State Department of Labor and the State Department of Health, and are applicable to all rental buildings.

**New York City landlords may skip to Section 2, below.** Within New York City, the EPA standards are enforced by city agencies.

No testing for asbestos is mandated under federal or state law. Nor is there any requirement that you remove or abate any intact asbestos or asbestos-containing material (ACM) that you know about at your property. The federal and state asbestos laws kick in whenever a repair, renovation or demolition project requires you to remove, disturb, repair, encapsulate or enclose *any* amount of asbestos or ACM. For example, EPA standards apply whenever any job affects asbestos-containing pipe covering, boiler covering, sprayed-on insulation, roofing, flashing, siding or vinyl-asbestos tile.

These are the steps either you or your contractor should follow to minimize your legal liability for asbestos exposure and to comply with federal and state requirements. State regulations refer to such work as an "asbestos project," no matter how little ACM is involved.

1.  **Use trained and certified workers.** Any person who works on an asbestos project must be at least 18, meet the training requirements set by the New York State Department of Health and hold a valid asbestos-handling certificate issued by the New York State Department of Labor, Division of Safety and Health, License and Certificate Unit. For more information call the Unit at 518-457-2735 or visit its website at www.labor.state.ny.us/business_ny/ employer_responsibilities/safety_health.html. (Click Asbestos Control Bureau).

2.  **Use licensed contractors.** Any contractor who engages in or supervises work on an asbestos project must be licensed by the state Department of Labor. The contractor and its employees must also be certified as asbestos handlers. Before awarding work on an asbestos-related project to a contractor, obtain a copy of a valid asbestos-handling license for the contractor issued by the New York State Department of Labor (see contact information at the end of step 1, above).

3.  **Notify tenants.** At least ten days before the work begins, an Asbestos Project Notification must be given to all tenants who live on the same floor as the asbestos project, and to the tenants who live one floor above and one floor below the asbestos project. A sample form is shown below. If the project could potentially affect all of your tenants, such as work on your ventilation system, all tenants must be notified. The notice must describe where in the building the asbestos project is taking place, the amount of ACM being handled (in square feet or linear feet), the project's start and finish dates, the contractor's name and asbestos license number and the name and address of the project's air monitoring contractor and lab. The notice must be posted at all direct means of access to the floor where the tenants live, such as at all stairway doors, elevator doors, ramps and hallways. The notice must remain posted until the work is complete.

4.  **Notify state government.** *For "large" asbestos projects* (that is, those involving at least 160 square feet or 260 linear feet of ACM), at least ten days before the project begins, the contractor or property owner must file an Asbestos Project Notification (DOSH Form 483, see sample, below) in duplicate by mail with the State Department of Labor (Division of Safety and Health, Asbestos Control Bureau,

STATE OF NEW YORK - DEPARTMENT OF LABOR
**DIVISION OF SAFETY AND HEALTH**
ASBESTOS CONTROL BUREAU
State Office Campus
Building 12 - Room 157
Albany, N.Y. 12240

| EMERGENCY NOTIFICATION REQUESTED | |
|---|---|
| a. Date of Request | b. Time of Day |
| c. Name of Person Granting Request | |

### AMENDED NOTIFICATION
a. ☐ Postponed ☐ Cancelled
b. New Start Date _____
c. New End Date _____
d. Submitted By

Refer to Information Sheet or Code Rule 56 for Time Deadlines

## *ASBESTOS PROJECT NOTIFICATION*

*WITHIN TWO WORKING DAYS OF THE EMERGENCY APPROVAL*, you must submit duplicate copies of this form with the appropriate fee to the Asbestos Control Bureau at the address shown.

---

1. NAME AND ADDRESS OF CONTRACTOR

2. FEDERAL EMPLOYER IDENTIFICATION NO.

3. ASBESTOS LICENSE NO.

4. MAILING ADDRESS, (if different than listed in ITEM 1)

5. NAME AND ADDRESS OF PARTY FOR WHOM THE PROJECT IS BEING PERFORMED

6. a. NAME AND TITLE OF DULY AUTHORIZED REPRESENTATIVE

b. TELEPHONE NO.
( )

### PROJECT INFORMATION
*PROVIDE ALL INFORMATION REQUESTED FOR THE BUILDING/SITE AT WHICH THE ASBESTOS PROJECT WILL BE CONDUCTED.*

7. ADDRESS (INCLUDE NAME OF BUILDING, ROOM NO., CITY, TOWN, VILLAGE)

8. NAME OF BUILDING OWNER

9. COUNTY

10. CURRENT USE OF BUILDING

11. AGE OF BUILDING

12. TOTAL CONTRACT AMOUNT

13. PROJECT DATE(S) - List phased project dates in **REMARKS** (Item 28)

a. ACTUAL STARTING DATE
_____

b. PROJECTED ENDING DATE

14. TYPE OF ASBESTOS WORK (*CHECK ALL WHICH APPLY*)
☐ Pipe Related
☐ Sprayed on Insulation
☐ Roofing/Flashing
☐ Vessel Covering
☐ Siding
☐ VAT
☐ Demolition
☐ Other (Specify)

15. WILL WORK ON THE PROJECT BE CONDUCTED UNDER A VARIANCE? If yes, specify the type of variance:
☐ APPLICABLE VARIANCE - NO.: _____
☐ INDIVIDUAL VARIANCE - PETITION NO.: _____

16. WILL SUBCONTRACTORS BE USED ON THE PROJECT? ☐ NO ☐ YES
If yes, please list name and federal employer identification number of each subcontractor in **REMARKS** (Item 28) on reverse of form.

17. ASBESTOS PROCEDURE(S) TO BE USED (*CHECK ALL WHICH APPLY*)

☐ REMOVAL ☐ DEMOLITION
☐ ENCLOSURE ☐ DISTURBANCE
☐ ENCAPSULATION ☐ HANDLING
☐ OTHER (Specify)
_____

18. TYPE OF ASBESTOS MATERIAL

☐ FRIABLE

☐ NON-FRIABLE

19. AMOUNT OF ASBESTOS INVOLVED - *CHECK ALL APPLICABLE BOX(ES)*

| **LINEAR FEET** | **SQUARE FEET** |
|---|---|
| ☐ Less than 260 _____ | ☐ Less than 160 _____ |
| (Specify) | (Specify) |
| ☐ ($100) 260-429 | ☐ ($100) 160-259 |
| ☐ ($200) 430-824 | ☐ ($200) 260-499 |
| ☐ ($500) 825-1649 | ☐ ($500) 500-999 |
| ☐ ($1000) 1650 OR MORE | ☐ ($1000) 1000 OR MORE |
| _____ | _____ |
| (Specify) | (Specify) |

20. METHODS TO BE USED AT PROJECT SITE TO PREVENT ASBESTOS DISSEMINATION (INCLUDING TYPE OF EQUIPMENT AND VENTILATION SYSTEMS USED)

21. I verify that the information specified on this notification is true and accurate and that the project will be conducted in compliance with the requirements of Code Rule 56.

a. *Signature of the Contractor or Duly Authorized Representative*

b. Date

---

### PREPARE THIS APPLICATION IN TRIPLICATE AND SUBMIT:
- An original and one copy (with an ink signature on both copies) to the New York State Department of Labor, Division of Safety and Health, Asbestos Control Bureau, State Office Campus, Building 12-Room 157, Albany, NY 12240; *retain one copy for your records.*
- A check or money order, made payable to the Commissioner of Labor, for the fee due based on the project size as shown in item 19.
  *This notification must be submitted at least 10 days prior to the starting date of the asbestos project.*

SH 483 (3-99)

State Office Campus, Building 12-Room 133, Albany, NY 12240) with the appropriate fee. The fee runs between $100 and $1,000, depending on the amount of asbestos involved. For forms and information, call the Asbestos Control Bureau at 518-457-1255.

5. **Notify federal government.** *For "large" asbestos projects* (that is, those involving at least 160 square feet or 260 linear feet of ACM), at least ten days before the project begins, the contractor or property owner must file a Notification of Demolition and Renovation by mail with the New York regional office of the EPA: EPA Asbestos Department, 290 Broadway, 21st Floor, New York, NY 10007-1866. For forms and information call 212-637-4042.

When an emergency arises which requires you or your contractor to disturb at least 160 square feet or 260 linear feet of ACM, you won't have time to notify the state and federal government by mail about the work. But, you'll still need to get telephone approval from both the state and federal agencies before starting work. For emergency approval from the State Department of Labor Asbestos Control Unit, call 518-457-1255. The Region II EPA office may be contacted at 212-637-4042.

6. **Follow work site standards and procedures.** All asbestos projects must be handled in accordance with the requirements set by the Department of Labor's asbestos regulations. (Industrial Code Rule 56–"Asbestos," 12 NYCCRR Part 56.) The regulations detail work site preparation, ACM handling, removal and encapsulation procedures, waste decontamination and removal rules and air sampling, monitoring and analysis requirements. For a free copy, mail a request to State of New York, Department of Labor, Office of Communications, State Office Building Campus, Albany, NY 12240, or download it from its website (www.labor.state.ny.us).

⚠ **Ask your local government's code enforcement office if there are any additional notification or work site requirements in effect.** New York State law permits municipalities to enact their own asbestos ordinances, so long as they are more stringent than state requirements.

By hiring a licensed and certified asbestos abatement contractor to supervise and perform any ACM-related work, you can leave it up to the contractor to file the necessary agency notification forms, post tenant notification forms, hire certified workers who are equipped with the right clothing and equipment, supervise the manner in which the ACM is removed and discarded and hire a subcontractor to perform any required air monitoring testing.

Landlords and contractors who don't follow the rules on asbestos handling can get hit with violations, monetary fines and "stop-work" orders. Fines of up to $1,500 may be imposed for an initial violation. Subsequent violations carry fines of up to $2,500 each. In addition, you may be held legally liable for a tenant's injuries caused by asbestos exposure if you knew, or should have known about a hazardous asbestos condition at your building, but failed to act. Like lead-based paint lawsuits, these claims can be very expensive to defend and may lead to big damage awards if the victim's suit succeeds. If you know or suspect that your building contains potentially hazardous asbestos or ACM, ask your broker to explain your liability insurance coverage for asbestos exposure lawsuits and money damages.

## 2. New York City Asbestos Laws and Regulations

New York City requires all landlords to hire "certified asbestos investigators" to check for the presence of asbestos-containing material before performing building renovation, alteration or demolition work. (NYC Local Law 76 of 1985.) It doesn't matter how small your property is—the law still applies. If the work involves only boiler room equipment, you can hire a "restricted asbestos investigator" instead of a fully certified one. Licensed plumbers and oil-burning equipment installers are often certified as restricted asbestos investigators also. In New York City, local agencies enforce EPA asbestos standards, not the State Department of Labor.

**Exempt work.** Some types of renovation, alteration and demolition work don't usually disturb asbestos, so they're exempt from the asbestos inspection requirement. Examples of exempt work include awning, sign and fire escape erections, exterior concrete jobs, water tank replacements and work on swimming pools, parapet walls and retaining walls. A full list of exempt projects may be found in the New York City Department of Environmental Protection (DEP) asbestos regulations (Rules of the City of New York, "DEP—Asbestos Control Program," Title 15). For exempt work, have your architect or engineer complete and sign an Asbestos Exemption Certification Letter (DEP Form ACP5). You'll need to file this form when you apply to the Department of Buildings (DOB) for a permit to do your proposed renovation, alteration or demolition work.

If the work is not exempt, you'll need to hire an asbestos investigator before you can get a (DOB) permit for the renovation, alteration, or demolition work. If the investigator finds little or no ACM, the investigator completes and signs a Not an Asbestos Project form (DEP Form ACP5). File this form when you apply for your DOB permit.

If the investigator finds that the proposed work will disturb more than 25 linear feet or ten square feet of friable ACM, the work is classified as an "asbestos project." That means that you must complete an Asbestos Inspection Report (NYC Department of Environmental Protection (DEP) Form ACP7), and file it with your application for a permit from the Department of Buildings (DOB) for your proposed renovation, alteration or demolition work. Filing fees are based on the size of the asbestos project.

For all asbestos projects, landlords are required to follow strict DEP asbestos control program regulations. They involve:

- DEP and tenant notification form requirements
- worker certification and protection requirements
- asbestos handling and disposal methods, and
- air sampling, monitoring and analysis.

Because the asbestos abatement rules are complicated, it pays to hire an experienced, licensed and certified asbestos abatement contractor to perform abatement work at your property. That way, when you sign a contract for the work, you can require the contractor to file the necessary agency notification forms, post any necessary tenant notification forms, hire certified workers who are equipped with special clothing and respirators, supervise the manner in which the ACM is removed or encapsulated and hire a subcontractor to perform any required air monitoring testing.

## More Information: Asbestos Resources

Here are the agencies to contact for copies of asbestos laws, regulations, guidelines and forms.

**Federal Laws and Rules.** The U.S. Environmental Protection Agency (EPA) regulates the list of National Emission Standards for Hazardous Air Pollutants (NESHAP). The NESHAP regulations include the emission of asbestos-containing material. For general information, visit the EPA website (www.epa.gov/asbestos/). Specific questions concerning the federal regulations for asbestos materials may be directed to EPA's Region II asbestos coordinator at 212-637-4042.

**New York State Laws and Rules.** Asbestos-related health issues including public concern about exposure, certification of professional abatement contractors and certification of analytical testing laboratories are included in the New York State Department of Health regulations. Questions concerning health-related issues should be directed to the New York State Department of Health, Division of Occupational Health, in Albany at 518-458-6419. Direct questions concerning asbestos-handling licenses to the New York State Department of Labor, Division of Safety and Health, Licensing and Certification Unit, Room 161, Building 12, State Office Campus, Albany, NY 12240, 518-457-2735.

Asbestos abatement and removal projects are regulated by the New York State Department of Labor (DOL) under Industrial Code Rule 56 which covers installation, removal, encapsulation, application or enclosure of asbestos material. Questions concerning asbestos abatement projects may be directed to the New York State Department of Labor, Building 12, State Office Campus, Albany, NY 12240, at 518-457-1255. Detailed information, including Asbestos Project Notification forms, may be viewed or downloaded from the DOL website (www.labor.state.ny.us/business_ny/employer_responsibilities/safety_health.html; click Asbestos Control Bureau).

The Division of Solid and Hazardous Materials regulations concerning asbestos focus on transportation and disposal after an asbestos abatement and removal project. After the asbestos waste has been abated, the waste must be transported to a solid waste landfill. This process is regulated by 6 NYCRR Part 364 Waste Transporter Permits. The areas covered by Part 364 include concerns about asbestos waste transportation, transport permits, and asbestos transportation tracking. Questions concerning asbestos transportation should be directed to the New York State Department of Environmental Conservation, Division of Solid and Hazardous Materials, Waste Transporter Permit Program, Part 364 Hauler Permits at 518-402-8707. Asbestos waste disposal is regulated by 6 NYCRR Part 360 Solid Waste Management Facilities. The areas covered by Part 360 include a definition of asbestos waste, transfer stations, and land disposal issues. Questions concerning asbestos disposal should be directed to the New York State Department of Environmental Conservation, Division of Solid & Hazardous Materials, Bureau of Solid Waste & Land Management, Albany, NY 12233, at 518-402-8693.

**New York City Laws and Rules.** All areas of asbestos regulatory issues conducted in New York City are regulated by local regulations. Questions concerning asbestos issues in New York City should be directed to the New York City Department of Environmental Protection (DEP), Asbestos Control Program Enforcement at 718-595-3682. Detailed information, including various asbestos abatement activity forms, may be downloaded from the DEP website (www.nyc.gov/html/dep/html/asbestos.html).

### 3. Landlord Liability for Asbestos Exposure to Employees and Contractors: OSHA Regulations

State and local governments aren't the only source of rules concerning the handling and maintenance of asbestos. The federal government has also entered the ring, by the way of the Occupational Safety and Health Administration (OSHA) regulations. These regulations are designed to preserve employees' and contractors' health, though of course there are some benefits to tenants as well when you comply.

OSHA's asbestos regulations apply to landlords in their role as employers of maintenance personnel. The rules must be followed by large landlords who employ maintenance staff (or managers who do maintenance work) and small-scale landlords who have no employees, but who do hire outside contractors for repair and maintenance jobs. They apply to any building constructed before 1981, and apply even if the property owner doesn't plan to remodel or otherwise disturb the structure. Unless the owner rules out the presence of asbestos by having a licensed inspector test the property, it will be *presumed* that asbestos is present and the regulations will apply.

**Asbestos exposure in custodial work.** Employees and contractors whose work involves direct contact with asbestos or materials that are presumed to include it—for example, certain types of floors and ceilings—or who clean in areas near asbestos, are subject to OSHA regulations designed for "general industry." The cleaning service that washes asbestos tiles in the lobby of a pre-1981 building, or the handyman who installs smoke alarms that are embedded in acoustic-tile ceilings made with asbestos, would both fall within the custodial work category.

OSHA's general industry regulations require custodial workers to receive two hours of instruction (including appropriate cleaning techniques) and to use special work procedures under the supervision of a trained superior. The general industry standard does not require testing for asbestos. Of course, if it is known that high levels of asbestos are present, even custodial tasks must be performed with appropriately higher levels of protection, such as special masks and clothing.

**Asbestos exposure in renovation or repair work.** A stricter set of procedures is triggered by any intentional disturbance of asbestos or asbestos-containing materials (for example, in heating systems or ceilings). This invariably happens when asbestos materials are subject to repair or renovation. At this level of activity, you should follow the asbestos-handling requirements set by New York State law (see Section B1, above) or, where applicable, New York City law (see Section B2, above). In addition, employers must conduct medical surveillance of certain employees and maintain specified records for many years.

### Key Aspects of OSHA Asbestos Regulations

Our discussion of the impact of the OSHA regulations on residential rental property owners is not intended to give you all the necessary information to make renovations and otherwise conduct your business safely and within the requirements of the regulations. You'll need to get a copy of the actual regulations for that. To obtain information on asbestos regulations, inspections and control, contact the New York Regional Office of the U.S. Occupational Safety and Health Administration (OSHA), 201 Varrick St., Room 670, New York, NY 10014, or call 212-237-2378. OSHA has also developed interactive computer software, called "Asbestos Advisor," that will walk you through questions designed to help identify asbestos in your property and suggest the most sensible solution. It is available free through the OSHA website: www.osha.gov/oshasoft/asbestos.

## C. Refrigerants

Federal law prohibits landlords from deliberately releasing two types of refrigerants into the air. The targeted refrigerants, hydrochlorofluorocarbons (HCFCs) and chlorofluorocarbons (CFCs), also known by the trade name Freon, are commonly found in cooling equipment such as refrigerators, window air conditioners, dehumidifiers and central air conditioning systems. When released into the atmosphere, HCFCs/CFCs can deplete the earth's protective ozone layer and pose threats to human, animal and plant life.

In 1990, Congress amended the Clean Air Act to prohibit the release of ozone-depleting refrigerants into the air during the service, maintenance or disposal of air conditioning and refrigeration equipment. (42 USC § 7401.) Since 1992, the EPA has required that refrigerants be recovered and recycled during servicing or before disposal.

## 1. Worker Certification Required for Service and Repairs

Anyone who services or repairs appliances or equipment that contain HCFCs/CFCs must be certified as a "technician" by the EPA. Here are some examples of work that the EPA says may only be done by a certified technician:

- attaching and detaching hoses and gauges to and from the equipment or appliance to measure pressure
- adding refrigerant to or removing refrigerant from the equipment or appliance, or
- any other activity that violates the integrity of the appliance or equipment, such as removing a compressor, condenser, evaporator or heat exchanger coil.

The certification requirement applies to your maintenance personnel, as well as to any independent contractors you use to service your refrigerators or air conditioning equipment. Apprentices are exempt from certification requirements provided the apprentice is closely and continually supervised by a certified technician. To become certified, technicians are required to pass a test given by an EPA-approved certifying organization. You can get a list of approved certifying organizations by calling the EPA's CFC Hotline at 800-296-1996.

As proof of certification, each technician is issued a wallet card and certificate. Check to make sure anyone who services refrigerators or air condition-

ing equipment at your property has proof of current certification.

## 2. Refrigerants Must Be Reclaimed and Recycled

Before 1992, refrigerants were often "blown out" or released from refrigerators and air conditioning equipment during service or repairs. Since 1992, certified workers must recapture the refrigerants before they're released into the atmosphere. EPA-approved refrigerant-recovery machines are available which draw the refrigerant into a holding tank. The refrigerant is then purified and may be recycled.

Refrigerants should also be reclaimed from appliances and equipment before they are thrown out. Alternatively, you can make arrangements for a special hauler who will recover the refrigerants for you, for an extra cost. As with all contractors, make sure the hauler is properly certified to recover refrigerants properly.

## 3. Recordkeeping

Owners of air conditioning equipment which contains 50 or more pounds of refrigerant must keep servicing records documenting the date and type of service, as well as the quantity of refrigerant added. Make sure any invoice you get from your air conditioning contractor contains the required information so that the invoice can double as a service record. You must hold onto service records for three years.

Also keep copies of your employees' technician certification wallet cards. That way, you have proof of compliance for EPA, if a problem comes up.

## 4. Enforcement

Landlords who release refrigerants into the air are subject to civil penalties of up to $27,500 per day for each violation. EPA regional field inspectors are authorized to make on-site visits to make sure that service records are properly maintained.

## D. Radon

Radon is a naturally occurring radioactive gas that is associated with lung cancer. It can enter and contaminate a property built on soil and rock containing uranium deposits or enter through water from private wells drilled in uranium-rich soil. Radon becomes a lethal health threat when it is trapped in tightly-sealed homes that have been insulated to keep in heat or have poor ventilation, when it escapes from building materials that have incorporated uranium-filled rocks and soils (like certain types of composite tiles or bricks) or is released into the air from aerated household water that has passed through underground concentrations of uranium. Problems occur most frequently in areas where rocky soil is relatively rich in uranium.

Any property can have elevated radon levels. It doesn't matter if it is old or new, or if it has a basement or is on a slab. You must test to find out if you have a radon problem. For the most professional results, hire an inspector certified by the EPA. Testing takes at least three days, and sometimes months. Do-it-yourself testing kits are also available from the state Department of Health and from many building supply stores (see "More Information: Radon Resources," below). If you use one of these kits, make sure it says "Meets EPA Requirements." The best time to test your property is during the heating season, between the months of October and May, when your property is less ventilated.

Ventilation measures will effectively disperse the gas in most situations. These measures range from the obvious (open the windows and provide cross-ventilation) to the somewhat complex (sealing cracks in the foundation, or sucking radon out of the soil before it enters the foundation and venting it into the air above the door through a pipe). According to the EPA, a typical household radon problem can be solved for $500 to $2,500.

If testing indicates high radon levels, be sure to warn tenants and correct the problem. If you own rental property in an area known to have radon problems, but don't test, warn tenants or take

action, you may be sued on any number of legal theories, including negligence and a violation of the implied warranty of habitability.

### High Radon Risk Counties

The U.S. EPA and New York State Department of Health have designated 37 New York counties as high radon risk areas. That means that a large percentage of properties that have been tested there indicate radon levels above EPA's maximum acceptable level.

| | | |
|---|---|---|
| Albany | Genesee | Schuyler |
| Allegany | Greene | Seneca |
| Broome | Livingston | Steuben |
| Cattaraugus | Madison | Sullivan |
| Cayuga | Monroe | Tioga |
| Chautauqua | Oneida | Tompkins |
| Chemung | Onondaga | Ulster |
| Chenango | Ontario | Washington |
| Columbia | Orange | Wayne |
| Cortland | Otsego | Wyoming |
| Delaware | Putnam | Yates |
| Dutchess | Rensselaer | |
| Erie | Schoharie | |

Do you have to inspect for radon contamination? There are currently no laws that require a private landlord to detect and remedy the presence of radon. This does not necessarily mean, however, that under certain circumstances you would not be found liable for radon poisoning. For example, one trial court held a landlord is strictly liable for radon poisoning—meaning that he was held responsible for the injury regardless of whether he tested or not. (*Kaplan v. Coulston,* 381 N.Y.S.2d 634 (1976).) Whether to test for radon depends on the circumstances of each rental property. Certainly, owners of rental property in areas where radon levels are generally known to be dangerously high should test rental property.

## More Information: Radon Resources

Contact the U.S. EPA for information on the detection and removal of radon, including a booklet, *Consumer's Guide to Radon Reduction*. Call the EPA Radon Hotline at 800-767-7236 or visit the EPA website (www.epa.gov).

Contact the New York State Health Department for the names of local radon repair specialists, to order test kits and to obtain other radon-related information. Call the Health Department's Radon Program at 800-458-1158 or visit its website (www.health.state.ny.us).

in apartments had caused personal injuries, settled for $1.17 million.

Currently, there are no federal, state or New York City regulations defining which molds are harmful or what air concentrations of mold pose a threat to health. Nor are there any prescribed remediation methods. Nevertheless, landlords are increasingly finding they must rebut the presumption that the mere presence of mold renders an apartment uninhabitable. (See, for example, *Clarendon Corp. v. Barnett*, N.Y.L.J., July 28, 1999, p.25, col. 5 (Civ.Ct., Kings County); *Northwood Village, Inc. v. Curet*, N.Y.L.J., May 6, 1998, p. 34, col. 4 (Dist. Ct., Suffolk County). In both cases, the tenant alleged a variety of apartment conditions that violated the warranty of habitability, in addition to mold and mildew.)

## E. Mold

Just when you thought you understood the risks posed by asbestos and lead, in comes the next big indoor environmental pollutant: mold. Mold can grow on virtually any moist substance, including wood, paper and carpet. Most forms of mold are harmless, like the kind that grows on your shower curtain. Yet exposure to certain mold spores may trigger allergic reactions, infections and toxic reactions in susceptible tenants.

While molds have existed longer than mankind, modern construction methods have had the unintended effect of creating a hospitable environment for mold to flourish indoors. Better building insulation keeps cold winter air out, but can seal in moisture from uncured building materials, roof leaks and broken pipes. Mold can be found in older buildings, as well, if water-damaged walls, floors, or carpeting go undiscovered or unfixed and stay damp.

Mold contamination in residential properties has resulted in several big lawsuits claiming damages for personal injuries and property damage. While highly-publicized suits were filed against developers in California and Texas, similar cases are pending far closer to home. For example, a January 11, 2002 article in "Mealey's Litigation Report: Mold" reported that a lawsuit brought by the tenants of Manhattan's Henry Philips Plaza South against the building's owners, which claimed that exposure to toxic mold

## More Information: Mold Hazards

The following government agencies have more information about mold hazards.

**U.S. Environmental Protection Agency (EPA).** The EPA has several publications about mold. The latest, *Mold Remediation in Schools and Commercial Buildings* (Pub. EPA 402-K-01-001, March 2001), is also the most comprehensive. To have a printed version mailed or faxed to you, contact the National Center for Environmental Publications (NSCEP), P.O. Box 42419, Cincinnati, OH 42419 (1-800-490-9198 or 513-489-8695 (fax)). You can also download the publication from the EPA website (www.epa.gov/iaq/pubs/moldresources.html). The website also contains several relevant articles, including "Introduction to Molds," "Basic Mold Cleanup," "Ten Things You Should Know About Mold," and links to mold-related resources at other government and university websites.

**New York City Department of Health (DOH).** DOH first issued "Guidelines on Assessment and Remediation of Fungi in Indoor Environments" in 1993, in response to mold growth problems discovered in several New York City buildings. The current guidelines, revised and expanded in November 2000, focus on mold contamination of building components such as walls, ventilation systems and support beams that are chronically moist or water damaged. The guidelines are intended for use by building engineers and management, but are available to the general public. You can get a copy of the guidelines by contacting the DOH Bureau of Environmental & Occupational Disease Epidemiology, 125 Worth Street, New York, NY 10007 212-788-4290). The guidelines may be also be viewed or downloaded from the agency's website (www.nyc.gov/html/doh/html/epi/moldrptl.html).

Chapter **12**

# Collecting Overdue Rent

Prompt rent collection is essential to a property's cash flow. But sooner or later, you'll get stuck with a tenant who's not paying rent. Before you can sue to evict, you must ask the tenant to pay the amount owed—and give her a chance to pay. In legal terms, this is known as making a "rent demand."

When you make a rent demand, it's important to know and follow all the legal requirements. Even a minor mistake can invalidate the demand, and get a later eviction case against the tenant delayed or thrown out of court. This chapter shows you the right way to demand immediate payment of overdue rent.

 Related topics covered in this book include:
- Drafting lease clauses on paying rent and rent default notices: Chapter 2
- Basic rules governing how much rent you can charge, where, how and when rent is due and accepting partial rent payments: Chapter 3
- Rent regulations governing how much rent you can charge rent-controlled and rent-stabilized tenants, including rules on rent increases, rent registration and overcharge proceedings: Chapter 4
- A tenant's right to withhold or pay less rent for unsafe or unlivable conditions: Chapter 9
- Terminating a tenancy for chronic rent non-payment: Chapter 14
- Using a security deposit to cover unpaid rent after you've evicted a tenant: Chapter 16
- How to get legal help for an eviction lawsuit: Chapter 17.

## A. What's a Rent Demand?

A "rent demand" is exactly what it sounds like. It's a demand by the landlord for the tenant to pay rent for a specific time period—or face eviction. New York landlords have the option of demanding the rent either orally or by written notice. (RPAPL § 711(2).) While we cover both oral and written rent demands in this chapter, we recommend you use a written notice for the reasons explained in Section F, below.

The purpose of the rent demand is to notify the tenant of the rent default so that the tenant can pay up and avoid getting sued for eviction. In most cases, the demand will spur the tenant to pay. But if the tenant doesn't pay, the rent demand lays the groundwork for the landlord's "non-payment" eviction proceeding.

### 1. Tenant Can't Give up Right to Notice of Rent Default

There's no getting around the rent demand requirement. A rent demand is a legal prerequisite to an eviction proceeding against a tenant for failure to pay rent. Judges require landlords to issue rent demands even if the tenant's lease or rental agreement says that a rent demand is unnecessary or that the tenant "waives" the right to receive default notices. (*PAK Realty Associates v. RE/MAX Universal, Inc.*, 157 Misc. 2d 985, 599 N.Y.S.2d 399 (Civ. Ct., N.Y. County, 1993).)

Also unenforceable are clauses that call for *automatic* termination of the agreement for nonpayment of rent. (*Park Summit Realty Corp. v. Frank*, 56 N.Y.2d 1025, 453 N.Y.S.2d 643, 439 N.E.2d 358 (1982).)

No matter what your lease or rental agreement says, you must be able to prove that you demanded the rent before the start of an eviction proceeding. If a judge finds that you failed to make a rent demand, or made it improperly, the eviction case must be dismissed. (RPAPL § 711.)

### 2. When to Demand the Rent

How early in the month can you make a rent demand? You can make an oral or written demand any day after the day rent is due. You're not required to give tenants a "grace period" of a few extra days. If the due date falls on a Saturday, Sunday or legal holiday, the due date is extended to the next business day. (GCL § 25(1).) You can make a rent demand as soon as the day after that.

EXAMPLE: Ronnie's lease says that rent is due on the first day of each month. Since the first day of the month in January is a legal holiday, New Year's Day, the due date for rent gets extended to the next business day. If January 1 falls on a Friday, Ronnie's rent is not due until Monday, January 4. That makes, Tuesday, January 5 the earliest date that the landlord can demand January rent.

! **Making a rent demand on a Sunday is prohibited.** (GBL § 11.) Under New York law, the service of any legal process on a Sunday, including a rent demand, is void. The rationale is secular, not religious. The legislature has deemed Sunday a "day of rest" for the general public. Never issue an oral or written rent demand on a Sunday.

## B. Written Rent Demands: The "Three-Day Notice"

A written rent demand is sometimes referred to as a "three-day notice." That's because legally, a landlord making a written rent demand must give the tenant at least three days' notice to pay the rent before starting a "non-payment" eviction proceeding. (RPAPL § 711(2).)

EXAMPLE: Joe, the landlord's agent, hands Ronnie a rent demand notice on Monday, July 17. Ronnie has three days, until Thursday, July 20, to either pay up or move out. If Ronnie ignores the notice, the landlord can sign and deliver eviction papers to Ronnie as soon as Friday, July 21.

But be careful. Three days' notice is the *minimum* time period provided for by law. Your tenant's lease or rental agreement may require you to give the tenant more time to come up with the rent. (Our lease and rental agreement forms require three days' notice. See Clause 19 in Chapter 2.) For example, a tenant's lease could require you to make a rent demand at least five or ten days before

starting a non-payment eviction proceeding. If your tenant's lease contains such a clause, you must comply with the longer time period set out in the lease.

EXAMPLE: The "Default" clause in Zubeda's lease requires Paul, her landlord, to give at least five days' notice of a rent default. Paul arranges for a written rent demand notice to be personally delivered to Zubeda on Monday, July 17. The notice gives Zubeda five days to either pay or quit. Because the five-day period expires on July 22, a Saturday, the due date is extended until Monday July 24. If Zubeda fails to pay or leave by then, Paul can sign eviction papers as early as Tuesday, July 25.

If the tenant's lease or rental agreement doesn't say how much notice you must give the tenant about rent defaults, you must give at least three days' notice, since that is the minimum notice period permitted under state law. Give at least three days' notice to tenants with oral rental agreements, too, unless you specifically agreed to give the tenant more notice.

💡 **Late rent fees are unaffected by rent demand time periods.** If your lease or rental agreement specifies late fees, they'll kick in as soon as your lease or rental agreement says they can. The number of days specified in your rent demand notice will not affect them. (Chapter 3, Section E, discusses late rent fees.)

Courts are picky about rent demand notices. There are four points that judges look for in the notice. The demand must:
1. Identify the premises for which rent is sought.
2. Require the tenant to either pay a specified amount of rent or surrender possession of the premises. (RPAPL § 711(2).) A notice that fails to give the "pay *or* leave" option is invalid.
3. Specify the time period for which the rent is due, such as the month of June, 2003. (*Kalimian v. Collezoni Fifth Ave, Inc.*, N.Y.L.J., 11/13/98, p. 28, col. 3 (App. Term, 1st Dept).)

4. State that you will begin an eviction proceeding if the tenant fails to pay or leave within three days (or within the longer time period required by the tenant's lease or rental agreement).

**⚠ Use care when preparing a rent demand notice.** Rent demands that contain mistakes are routinely subject to attack by tenants in eviction proceedings, on purely technical grounds. A judge can throw out a rent demand notice that omits the "pay or leave" directive, leaves out the time period for which rent is due or fails to warn that the landlord will evict if the notice is ignored. And judges rarely give landlords a chance to fix any errors or omissions in the notice—they dismiss the eviction proceeding instead. If your proceeding is dismissed because of a defective rent demand, you must start all over again by preparing and serving a new (and correct) rent demand notice.

## C. How to Fill out a Rent Demand Notice

A sample Three-Day Rent Demand Notice appears below. This notice includes all four points (listed in Section B, above) that judges look for in rent demand notices.

 The Forms CD includes the Three-Day Rent Demand Notice and Appendix IV includes a blank tear-out copy of the form.

Here are the steps you must take to properly complete the Rent Demand Notice. Since many of the steps will ask you to refer to provisions in the tenant's lease, it's a good idea to pull out the lease before you get started on the form. That's how lawyers do it.

### Step 1: Fill in Each Tenant's Name

Though not specifically required by statute, the tenant's name is customarily included on a rent

demand notice. If there's more than one tenant listed on the lease or rental agreement, insert the name of each tenant on the form, including husband and wife (if both are named in the lease or rental agreement). Don't fill in the names of any roommates or other occupants who live in the rental unit but aren't listed on the lease or rental agreement.

Make sure the names are spelled the same way as they appear on the lease or rental agreement. A misspelled name could give a tenant ammunition to try and delay or derail a later eviction case.

Sometimes, units are leased by businesses for residential use by employees. When issuing a rent demand to a business, fill in the entire legal name for the business. Don't forget to include endings like, Corp., Inc., P.C. and L.L.P. They're an important part of a business entity's name.

### Step 2: Fill in the Address

The notice must identify the premises for which rent is sought. List the full address for the tenant's premises including the unit number or any other relevant description—for example, "downstairs apartment." The premises address should be at least as detailed as the one that's listed on the tenant's lease or rental agreement. Don't forget the postal Zip code.

### Step 3: Fill in the Outstanding Rent and Other Charges

Insert the total amount of rent and other charges due from the tenant. Rent is almost always due in advance on the first of the month. (See Clause 5 of our form agreements in Chapter 2.) For example, rent is due on June 1 for the period June 1 through June 30. If the tenant has paid you part, but not all of the rent due for the period, your rent demand must reflect this. That is, you would fill in the amount of rent that remains unpaid.

After you fill in the total amount due, supply an item-by-item breakdown of monthly rent and other charges due. The breakdown should identify the period for which rent is due by month and year. And it should also describe the nature and amount of any other charges that are included in the total amount of rent due, such as late fees or returned check fees. The sample notice, below, illustrates how to itemize the total amount of rent due.

A minor calculation error will not make the notice invalid, so long as the mistake is made in good faith and isn't intended to mislead the tenant. To avoid problems, be as accurate as possible. And don't round off numbers—demand every penny.

**For non-regulated tenants,** the total demanded may include unpaid late fees, returned check fees, collection fees, legal fees or other charges if: 1) the charge is authorized by the tenant's lease, and 2) the charge is reasonable (not excessive). Double-check to make sure that the tenant's lease permits the charge or fee before adding it to the total amount due in the notice.

 **For rent-regulated tenants, it can be risky to demand other charges in addition to rent.** Some judges have ruled that rent demands issued to rent-regulated tenants may not include legal fees, late charges or collection costs, for example, because they're not part of the legal regulated rent. (See, for example, *London Terrace v. Stevens,* 159 Misc. 2d 542, 605 N.Y.S.2d 814, 816 (Civ. Ct., N.Y. County, 1993).) These judges rely on laws that forbid landlords to demand or collect rent in excess of the legal regulated rent or maximum rent. Other judges reject that view and permit rent demands on rent-stabilized tenants to include legal fees and collection costs. (*Brusco v. Miller,* 167 Misc. 2d 54, 639 N.Y.S.2d 246 (App. Term, 1st Dep't, 1995).)

To be on the safe side, don't include unpaid late charges, collection fees or other extra charges on a rent-regulated tenant's rent demand notice. You might be better off deducting them from the tenant's security deposit after the tenant moves out. If the charges are substantial, check with an experienced landlord-tenant lawyer before adding them to your rent demand. A good attorney should be able to tell you if it's okay to demand such charges in the jurisdiction where your building is located. (See Chapter 17 for advice on finding a lawyer.)

### Step 4: Fill in Time Period/s

Specify the entire time period for which rent and any other charges are unpaid. Your demand must give a period-by-period breakdown of the total amount due if rent is due for more than one time period (two or more months, for instance) or if you are demanding an extra charge besides base rent.

### Step 5: Calculate and Insert Date Deadline to "Pay or Leave"

Fill in a specific date and amount of the notice required by the statute or the lease (whichever is longer). To calculate the deadline, review the "default" clause in the tenant's lease. It should say how many days' notice you must give to demand the rent. Most leases and rental agreements require three to five days' notice. Our lease and rental agreement provides three days' notice to cure rent defaults. (See Clause 19 in Chapter 2.) If the lease or rental agreement doesn't specify any set amount of notice, you must give the tenant at least three days to pay or leave.

Once you've determined the minimum notice you must give for rent defaults, add several days time to serve the notice. It's a far better practice to give the tenant too much notice than too little. A three-day notice that's served 14 days before the deadline to pay or leave, for instance, is timely and valid. But a three-day notice that's served two days before the deadline is worthless.

Some landlords use rent demand forms that indicate a specific deadline for the tenant to pay or leave. They just require payment within a fixed period of time—for example, "three days from the date of service of this notice." We include a deadline date in our notice because we've come across a few judicial decisions in which nonpayment proceedings have been dismissed because the landlord's rent demand omitted a specific deadline date to pay or leave. The judges in those cases reasoned that the lack of a specific deadline made the demand too ambiguous to be legally enforceable, since the tenant had no way to figure out what date service of the notice was completed. (See, for example, *Parkchester Apartments v. Walker*, N.Y.L.J., 6/28/95, p. 30, col. 1 (Civ.Ct., Bronx County).) To avoid problems down the road, the rent demand form in this book requires you to include a specific date by which the tenant must respond to the notice.

## Step 6:   Sign and Date the Notice

The "pay or leave" ultimatum language is already included in our Rent Demand Notice. All you need to add are your *handwritten* signature and the date you signed the notice (not some future date when you expect the tenant to get the notice).

**Don't make rent demand too early.** The date you sign the notice should not be the same day rent was due, but at least one day later.

### Don't Let Your Lawyer Sign or Send Rent Demand Notices for You

The Fair Debt Collections Practices Act (15 U.S.C. §§ 1692 and following) is a federal law regulating debt collectors. Any notices issued by them must, among other requirements, give consumers a 30-day period in which to dispute the alleged debt. Odd as it may sound, a lawyer who signs or mails a rent demand notice on behalf of a landlord-client may be considered a "debt collector" under the law. (*Romea v. Heiberger & Associates*, 163 F.3d 111 (2d Cir. 1998).) A rent demand notice that's signed or sent by a manager, however, won't violate federal law, so long as it was the manager's job to collect rent before the tenant defaulted in the payment of rent. (*Franceschi v. Mautner-Glick Corp.*, 22 F. Supp. 2d 250 (S.D.N.Y. 1998).)

You'll be taking a chance that your eviction lawsuit will be delayed if your lawyer signs your rent demand but fails to comply with the Fair Debt Collection Practices Act. Housing court judges have not been consistent when asked by tenants to dismiss on this ground. Until the dust settles on this issue, our advice is this: Don't let an attorney sign rent demand notices on your behalf.

The lease and rental agreement forms in this book allow you to designate a manager or other agent to issue notices on your behalf. (See Clause 24 in Chapter 2). Whenever possible though, the landlord should personally sign rent demands. If the tenant's lease or rental agreement specifically requires rent demands to be made by the landlord, a rent demand signed by the landlord's agent is subject to attack, unless accompanied by proof of the signer's authority to bind the landlord. In such cases, a statement signed by the landlord should be attached to the rent demand. It should authorize the manager to sign notices on behalf of the landlord. A sample Authorization to Issue Notices for Landlord follows our sample Three-Day Rent Demand Notice, below.

The Forms CD includes the Authorization to Issue Notices for Landlord and Appendix IV includes a blank tear-out copy of the form.

If the tenant has no lease, as is the case with most rent-controlled tenants, the landlord or an authorized managing agent may sign the rent demand. (*Kwong v. Eng*, 183 A.D.2d 558, 583 N.Y.S.2d 457 (1st Dep't).) No written proof of authorization is necessary. However, attaching proof of authorization is a good practice anyway. Many tenants, seeking to delay their eviction proceedings, will ask the court to dismiss eviction proceedings that are based on notices signed by agents, on the ground that the agent lacked authority to sign the notice for the landlord. When faced with such a request, a judge will often schedule a hearing on that issue before going ahead with the eviction proceeding. By attaching your written authorization to the rent demand notice, you can avoid the delay a hearing on this issue might otherwise create.

### Step 7:  Make Copies of the Notice

You'll need copies of the notice to serve on the tenant. Make at least four copies for each tenant named on the notice. Give the copies to the person who will be serving the notice on the tenant. (The process server will need these extra copies if they are unable to serve the tenant personally as described in Section D, below.) Keep the original notice in your file. You'll need it if you sue the tenant for unpaid rent.

## Note on Tenant Habitability Defenses

In some cases, tenants are entitled to withhold or deduct rent for uninhabitable conditions and serious code violations. (See Chapter 9, Landlord's Duty to Repair and Maintain the Premises.) Of course, if a tenant is clearly right in paying less rent, it doesn't make sense to serve a rent demand notice. On the other hand, when drafting your rent demand notice, you needn't reduce the rent due by any anticipated claims that the tenant's unit was unlivable or unsafe for all or part of the time covered by the rent demand. Include the entire amount of rent due for the period in your demand. It's up to the tenant to request a rent break for defective conditions.

## D. How to Deliver a Rent Demand Notice

A rent demand has important legal consequences. So the law is strict about how landlords deliver rent demand notices to tenants. It's critical that you follow the rules on "serving" the notice. If a court-savvy tenant denies getting your rent demand, or claims that you didn't follow proper procedures, you'll need to prove that you served the notice and did it the right way.

**When to serve the notice.** A rent demand notice can be given to your tenant on any day after the rent is due, but not on the day it is due. As explained in Section A2, above, the due date is extended to the next business day if the due date falls on a Saturday, Sunday or a legal holiday.

**Try to serve the notice at a time of day when you would reasonably expect the tenant to be at home and answer the door.** (*Eight Associates v. Hynes*, 65 N.Y.2d 739, 492 N.Y.S.2d 15.) If you're not sure about the tenant's schedule, make an initial attempt to serve the notice during business hours (usually considered to be between 8:00 AM and

## Three-Day Rent Demand Notice

To: Ronnie Eldridge
_____
Tenant
Apartment 15-C, 280 Mercer Street,
_____
Street address
New York, NY 10012
_____
City and State

Dear Tenant of the above Premises:

PLEASE TAKE NOTICE, that you have failed to pay to the Landlord the sum of $_____ $5,100 _____ for rent and other charges for the period from _____ June 1, 200X to July 31, 200X _____, as follows:

Base Rent

| | |
|---|---|
| June, 200X | $2,500.00 |
| July, 200X | $2,500.00 |
| | |
| | |
| Subtotal Rent | $5,000.00 |

Other Charges

| | |
|---|---|
| June 16, 200X—late fee | $50.00 |
| July 16, 200X—late fee | $50.00 |
| | |
| Subtotal Other Charges | $100.00 |
| Total Amount Due | $5,100.00 |

PLEASE TAKE FURTHER NOTICE, that you are required to pay the total amount of rent and other charges due on or before ____ July 25, 200X ____, that being more than __3__ days from the day of the service of this Notice, or vacate and surrender the possession of the premises to the Landlord. In the event you fail to do so, the Landlord will commence summary proceedings under the Statute to recover the possession of the premises.

July 17, 200X
_____
Date

*Joseph Andrews*
_____
Joseph Andrews, Owner and Landlord
c/o Manhattan Properties, Inc.
1500 Nassau Street
New York, NY 10038
212-555-1212

---

### Authorization to Issue Notices for Landlord

I hereby authorize _____ Rachel Rogovin, my Managing Agent _____

_____, to sign all legal notices on

my behalf relating to the property located at ___ 280 Mercer Street, New York, NY 10012 ___

_____.


January 3, 200X _____          *Joseph Andrews* _____
Date                             Owner and Landlord

---

6:00 PM). If no one's home, make a second attempt to serve the notice before or after business hours. Don't go knocking at a tenant's door during "normal rest hours," though, which are usually considered to be between 10:30 PM and 6:00 AM.

**Who should serve the notice.** Anyone over the age of 18 may deliver a rent demand notice to a tenant, so long as that person is not the landlord. (CPLR § 2103-a.) However, the landlord's agents, officers, and employees are permitted to serve rent demands to tenants.

**Make sure process server is licensed.** In New York City, process servers—that is, people who deliver legal notices for a fee, or who serve process five or more times per year—must be licensed by the City Department of Consumer Affairs. (NYC Adm. Code § 20-403.) There are exceptions: Attorneys and employees of government agencies are exempt from the licensing requirement, as is anyone who delivers legal notices fewer than five times a year. If you're a New York City landlord and use a process server who must be licensed, be sure the server has complied, since some judges have thrown out eviction proceedings based on rent demand notices that were served by unlicensed process servers.

**Whom to serve.** Each tenant listed on the rent demand notice must be individually served. If you rented your property to just one tenant whose name alone appears on any written rental agreement or lease, you should serve that person with the rent demand notice.

If you rent to more than one tenant, serve separate copies of the rent demand notice on each tenant. Husbands and wives who are both named in a lease or rental agreement must each be served separately, too.

**How the notice must be served on the tenant.** The law is very strict about how rent demand notices must be served on tenants. (RPAPL § 735.) Generally, a true copy of the notice (that is, an unaltered photocopy of the original) must be delivered to each tenant as follows:

1. Start by attempting to personally deliver the notice to the tenant. Section 1, below, explains service by personal delivery.

2. If the tenant can't be found and isn't at home, the notice may be left with a person of "suitable age and discretion" who lives (or works) at the rental unit. This is known as "substituted service." Section 2, below, details the requirements for substituted service.

3. If, after at least two tries during different times of day, the notice can't be personally delivered

to the tenant or left with someone else who lives or works at the unit, the notice may be delivered to the tenant by placing it on or in a conspicuous place ("nail and mail") service. Section 3, below, discusses conspicuous place service.

In the sections that follow, we detail the mechanics of each of these three methods, and show you how to put together airtight proof that you served the notice the right way.

**Keep notes.** The person who serves the notice must jot down details on all attempts to serve the tenant at the rental unit, including how, when and where the notice was actually served or attempted to be served, as well as the name and physical description of any person served (age, hair color, height, weight). Licensed process servers keep bound, chronological logs to keep track of their service attempts. You'll need this information when you complete a proof of service form, as described in Section E.

## 1. Personal Delivery

Personal delivery means handing a copy of the notice to the tenant. Don't presume that the person who answers the rental unit door is the tenant—ask for the tenant by name. If the tenant's home, but refuses to take the notice, it can be left at the tenant's feet, for example, or in another location where the tenant can see it. If the tenant's not home, another person who lives or works at the rental unit, like a maid, might be able to accept the notice on behalf of the tenant. Section 2, below, explains when the notice may be left with someone else.

The notice needn't be delivered at the rental unit. It can be delivered to the tenant in the lobby, the elevator or even on the street outside your building. Avoid serving tenants at their workplace, however, since this could be interpreted as a tactic designed to needlessly embarrass or harass them.

If the tenant is a corporation, partnership or other business entity, don't presume that the person who answers the door or who lives in the rental unit is

authorized to accept service on behalf of the business. The person serving the notice must ask the person who lives in the unit or answers the door if she is authorized to accept notices on behalf of the business. If she answers yes, the server should get the name of the person served and her position in the business. If the person who answers the door claims not to be authorized to accept service on behalf of the business, the server should not hand the notice to that person. Instead, the server should ask for the name of a person who is authorized, and attempt to serve that person. If after two tries, the server can't find a person who claims to be authorized to accept the notice, you'll need to resort to conspicuous place service (see Section 3, below).

Once the tenant is handed a copy of the notice, service is complete.

## 2. Substituted Service

If you try to personally deliver the notice to the tenant at the rental unit and the tenant's not home, there's still hope. You're allowed to deliver a copy of the notice to another person who either lives or works at the tenant's unit—if that person will take it. (RPAPL § 735.) This is known as "substituted ser-vice." The person who delivers the notice must get the name and a physical description of the person served, and make sure that that person either lives or works at the rental unit. Then, a copy of the notice must be mailed to the tenant by certified or registered mail plus a copy sent by regular mail. Both copies must be mailed within one business day after the papers are delivered to the rental unit. (Section 4, below, details this mailing requirement.)

The person accepting the notice can be a co-tenant, a roommate or a family member of the tenant who lives at the unit. Anyone who works at the rental unit, such as a maid or nanny, may also accept the notice. Delivering the notice to the tenant's neighbor won't work. Neither will handing the notice to a temporary guest or visitor at the tenant's rental unit. That's why it's important to make sure the person who accepts the notice at the rental unit actually lives or works there.

For substituted service to be valid, the person accepting the notice must be of "suitable age and discretion." The law doesn't set a minimum age for the recipient, and judges have been reluctant to set a benchmark age under which service is deemed defective. In the few cases addressing the issue, the minimum age is generally considered to be 12. (*Durham Productions Inc. v. Sterling Film Portfolio Ltd.*, 537 F. Supp. 1241 (S.D.N.Y. 1982).)

⚠ **Don't serve minors.** Although a court may consider service on a minor to be valid, it's risky. If you sue for rent based on a rent demand that was delivered to someone under 18, the tenant may claim that the rent demand was improperly served and ask for a hearing on that issue. This tenant tactic could needlessly delay your case and cost you extra time and money. To head off this problem, instruct the person serving notices to inquire as to the age of anyone who appears to be a minor, before delivering the notice.

An employee of the landlord is not a "suitable" person with whom to leave the notice either. Courts have ruled that security guards, doormen or concierges who are employed by the landlord to screen visitors and guests at the building should not accept a legal notice on behalf of the tenant. (*Napic, N.V. v. Fverfa Investments, Inc.*, 193 A.D.2d 549, 597 N.Y.S.2d 707 (1st Dep't 1993).)

Substituted service is "complete" as of the date you mail copies of the notice to the tenant. That means that the tenant's deadline to pay or leave begins that day, even if the tenant doesn't actually receive the notice until later. (Section C discusses calculating this deadline.)

## 3. Conspicuous Place ("Nail and Mail") Service

If you've twice tried to deliver the notice to the tenant's unit and have found no one home, nor anyone there willing to accept the notice, there's a third option. A copy of the notice may be "affixed" to a conspicuous part of the premises. (RPAPL § 735.) When this method of service is used, a copy of the notice must be mailed to the tenant by certified or registered mail and by regular mail within one day after the papers are delivered. (See Section 4, below, for a detailed discussion of the mailing requirement.)

How should you affix the notice? You can use adhesive tape to stick the notice to the outside of the tenant's door, or you can slip the notice under the entry door, if it will slide through easily. Squeezing the notice between the door and door knob, or between the door and doorjamb is not permitted.

Nail and mail service is the least reliable form of service. The notice could be removed from the outside of the door, for example, before the tenant ever sees it. Because of that, the law makes this type of service a little tougher for landlords to carry out:

- You can't resort to nail and mail service unless you've made a minimum of two attempts to serve the notice either personally to the tenant or to somebody else who lives or works at the tenant's unit.
- The service attempts must be made at times of day when you could reasonably expect to find the tenant at home. Generally, it's acceptable to make one of the two service attempts during business hours, with another attempt being made during non-business hours.

Nail and mail service is "complete" as of the date you mail copies of the notice to the tenant. That means that the tenant's deadline to pay or leave begins that day, even if the tenant doesn't actually receive the notice until later. (Section C has more on this issue.)

## Rent Demand Dos and Don'ts

When it comes to making rent demands, landlords must "dot the i's and cross the t's." A mistake in the wording of the demand or the manner in which it is made or delivered can end up nullifying the rent demand and prevent you from being able to maintain a non-payment eviction proceeding if the tenant doesn't pay. Keep these dos and don'ts in mind when preparing and serving rent demand notices.

**DO:**

- Properly complete the Rent Demand Notice with the tenant's name, address, outstanding rent and other charges and time periods for which these are due, and include language directing the tenant to "pay or leave."
- Serve rent demand notices the right way by attempting to serve the tenant personally and by trying substituted service on at least two occasions, before resorting to "nail and mail" service.
- Always prepare an affidavit of service immediately after the rent demand notice is either delivered or affixed to the tenant's door and any required mailings have been sent.
- Keep good rent demand records, especially when making an oral rent demand.

**DON'T:**

- Make a rent demand until the day after rent is due.
- Demand rent from a tenant who has legitimately withheld rent or used the "repair and deduct" remedy because of a serious habitability problem you had notice of.
- Serve a rent demand notice on a minor, a visitor to the tenant's rental unit or to the building doorman or concierge.
- Make an oral rent demand unless oral demands are expressly permitted by the tenant's lease or rental agreement.

### 4. How to Fulfill the Mailing Requirement

When either substituted service or nail and mail service is used, copies of the notice must be mailed to each tenant within one day of the date the notice is delivered, affixed to or placed under the entrance door of the rental unit. At minimum, two mailings are required for each tenant. One copy of the notice must be sent to the tenant's unit by regular mail, and the other must be sent by either certified or registered mail.

**Mail extra copies to alternate addresses.** Tenants who are subletting or who are away a lot may direct you to send rent bills and notices to a different or "alternate" address. If so, copies of the notice must be sent there too—one copy by regular mail plus another copy by certified or registered mail.

The landlord must be able to show that certified mail carried the proper postage and was treated as certified mail by the post office. So be sure to get independent evidence that all mailings were made. For regular mailings, the post office issues "certificates of mailing" which reflect the date of mailing and the mailing address. For certified and registered mail, get a receipt showing the postage paid, the mailing date and the mailing address.

## E. Proof of Service

Whenever a rent demand notice is served on a tenant, the person who serves it should make a special record called an affidavit of service. An affidavit is a sworn statement describing how, when and where the notice was delivered to the tenant and, in some cases, a physical description of the person served. It must be signed in front of a person who is a state-licensed notary public.

 You'll also need to prepare proof of service when serving termination notices on tenants (Chapters 13 and 15) and notices to quit on former managers and supers (see Chapter 6).

Your process server should complete the appropriate form immediately after he or she delivers (or attempts to deliver) the rent demand notice. That way, details needed to complete the form, such as the exact time of delivery, the recipient's physical characteristics or the color of the entrance door, are easy to recall.

The affidavit of service will be worth its weight in gold when a tenant claims that she didn't get a copy of the rent demand or tells a judge that you didn't follow the right steps when serving the demand. You can show the affidavit to the judge to help prove that service was properly carried out.

## 1. Types of Affidavits of Service

This book contains three different forms for proof of service. The appropriate form to use depends on how the rent demand notice was served:

- Affidavit of Personal Service—used when the notice is left with the tenant
- Affidavit of Substituted Service—used when the notice is given to another adult who lives or works in the tenant's rental unit, and
- Affidavit of Conspicuous Place Service—used for nail and mail service.

A sample of each affidavit is shown below.

The Forms CD includes the Affidavit of Personal Service, the Affidavit of Substituted Service and the Affidavit of Conspicuous Place Service, and Appendix IV includes blank tear-out copies of each of the three forms.

Complete a separate affidavit form for each tenant named on the rent demand notice. The notary signs the affidavit too, and "stamps" (or writes in) her notary license number and expiration date.

Keep the original affidavit in the tenant's file along with the original rent demand. If you later need to evict the tenant for non-payment, you'll need to bring the original rent demand notice and proof of service with you to court.

## 2. How to Complete Affidavit of Service Form

The person who serves the rent demand notice must complete the appropriate affidavit form. While each form is fairly self-explanatory, here are some general tips for completing the affidavits:

**Dates.** Remember that it's against the law to serve, or attempt to serve, a rent demand notice on a Sunday or other day of religious observance. To be on the safe side, avoid weekends and special religious holidays.

**Times.** When inserting times into the affidavit, be exact. Don't approximate or round off to the nearest quarter hour. Also remember to include "AM" or "PM."

**Names.** When inserting the tenant's name on the affidavit, make sure it matches the name on the rent demand notice. Misspelling or omitting part of the tenant's name can put the whole affidavit in question. For affidavits of substituted service, include the full name of the adult who accepted the affidavit on behalf of the tenant. That person must live or work at the tenant's unit and may not be a visitor or overnight guest.

**Addresses and locations.** Where indicated, insert the tenant's full and complete street address, including the unit number, city, state and zip code. If a tenant was served in a location other than his or her rental unit, describe that location as fully as possible.

**Physical descriptions.** Our affidavits of personal service and substituted service ask for a physical description of the person who received the notice. A detailed description can be an effective weapon against tenants who claim they never received the notice, or that your process server gave the notice to the wrong person. Approximations are acceptable for height, weight and age. One way to make the job easier is to insert a range. Describing a person's height as between 5' and 5' 3", between 100-125 pounds and between the ages of 40 and 50, for example is sufficient. Other physical characteristics that should be noted include eyeglasses, facial hair, baldness or obvious birthmarks and scars.

Our affidavit of conspicuous service asks for a description of the door to which the notice was affixed. Here, insert the color of the door and its material—for example, wood or steel.

**Signature.** The person who serves the notice must sign the notice in the presence of a notary public.

**License number.** Professional process servers in NYC must include their Department of Consumer Affairs license number on the affidavit.

# Affidavit of Service by Personal Delivery

STATE OF NEW YORK )

) ss:

COUNTY OF __New York__ )

The undersigned, being duly sworn deposes and says:

1. I am over 18 years of age and am not the landlord.

2. On the ____17th____ of ____July, 200x____, at __5:30 PM__, I served the within Rent Demand Notice on __Ronnie Eldridge__,

the tenant named on the Notice by delivering and leaving with __Ronnie Eldridge__

_____ personally a true copy of the Notice, and that such service was

made __within the passenger elevator at 280 Mercer Street, New York, NY 10012__

_____.

I knew the person so served to be the person mentioned and described herein.

3. The person served is described as:

Sex: ____Female____ Skin color: ____White____

Height: __5"6"-5'8"__ Approximate age: __40-45__

Weight: __130-140 lbs__ Hair color: ____Brown____

Other distinguishing characteristics: __Red glasses__

_____

*John Bosco*
Signature of Server

John Bosco
Printed or Typed Name of Server

N/A
License Number of Server

Sworn to before me this ____17th____ of ____July, 200x____

*Shelia Matthews*

Shelia Matthews , Notary Public

License No. __109-20-1101__

My Commission Expires __5/1/05__

## Affidavit of Service by Substituted Service

STATE OF NEW YORK                                    )

                                                     ) ss:

COUNTY OF ___New York_____ )

The undersigned, being duly sworn deposes and says:

1. I am over 18 years of age and am not the landlord.

2. After an attempt made on ___July 16, 200X_____, at ___8:30 AM___, I was unable to serve

   the rent demand notice, on _____Ronnie Eldridge_____

   by personal delivery at ___Apt. 15-C, 280 Mercer Street, New York, NY 10012._____.

3. On ___July 16, 200X_____, at ___8: 35 AM___, I served a true copy of the rent demand

   notice by gaining admittance to said premises and delivering to and leaving a copy thereof

   personally with _____Clarence Ford_____,

   a person of suitable age and discretion, who was willing to receive same on behalf of the above-

   named tenant and who resided at said premises.

4. The person served is described as:

   Sex: ____Male_____        Skin color: _____Black_____

   Height:___5'9"-5'10"_____        Approximate age: ___45-50_____

   Weight: ___170-180 lbs._____        Hair color: _____Black/Grey_____

   Other distinguishing characteristics: ___Goatee and moustache_____

   _____

5. Within one day thereafter, I mailed true copies of the rent demand notice by regular, first-class

   mail and by certified mail, enclosed in postpaid properly addressed envelopes to _____

   _____Ronnie Eldridge_____ at the address of the premises sought to be

   recovered and the following additional address(es): ___None_____

   _____. Said mail was deposited

   within a Post Office under the exclusive care and custody of the United States Postal Service.

___John Bosco_____

Signature of Server

___John Bosco_____

Printed or Typed Name of Server

___N/A_____

License Number of Server

Sworn to before me this ____17th____ of _____July, 200x_____

_Shelia Matthews_____

___Shelia Matthews_____, Notary Public

License No.___109-20-1101_____

My Commission Expires___5/1/05_____

# Affidavit of Service by Conspicuous Place Service

STATE OF NEW YORK                                    )

                                                    ) ss:

COUNTY OF ___New York_____            )

The undersigned, being duly sworn deposes and says:

1. I am over 18 years of age and am not the landlord.

2. On the _____19 th_____ of _____July, 200x_____, at _5:30 PM_, I served the
   within Rent Demand Notice on ___Ronnie Eldridge_____,
   the tenant of ___Apartment 15-C, 280 Mercer Street, New York, NY 10012___
   by ___"affixing a copy thereof upon a conspicuous place, to wit," (or) "placing a copy___
   ___thereof under"_____ the entrance door at
   ___Apt. 15-C, 280 Mercer Street, New York, NY 10012_____,
   because I was unable to gain admittance or to find a person of suitable age or discretion willing to
   receive same at that time and on prior attempt(s) made on _____July 18, 200X___ at ___8:10PM___

3. The entrance door to the respondent's premises can be described as follows: ___gray steel door___
   ___with brass hardware_____.

4. Within one day thereafter, I mailed true copies of the rent demand by regular, first-class mail and
   by certified mail, enclosed in postpaid properly addressed envelopes to ___Ronnie Eldridge___
   _____ at the address the premises sought to be recovered
   and the following additional address/es: ___None_____
   _____. This mail was deposited
   within a Post Office under the exclusive care and custody of the United States Postal Service.

                                                            _John Bosco_
                                                     Signature of Server

                                                           _John Bosco_
                                                     Printed or Typed Name of Server

                                                              _N/A_
                                                     License Number of Server

Sworn to before me this _____17th___ of _____July, 200x_____

_Shelia Matthews_

___Shelia Matthews_____, Notary Public

License No.___109-20-1101_____

My Commission Expires _____5/1/05_____

## F. Oral Rent Demands

Rent demands don't necessarily need to be in writing. You can make an oral rent demand instead if the tenant's lease permits it. (RPAPL § 711(2).) If the lease or rental agreement does not specify how rent demands are to be made, you may make the demand orally or in writing. Our rental agreement and lease forms (see Clause 19 in Chapter 2) permit you to make either oral or written rent demands. Nevertheless, we prefer written rent demand notices to oral rent demands for rent for several good reasons:

- It's much harder to prove you made an oral rent demand to a tenant than it is to prove that you served a written rent demand.

- A tenant who gets served with a written rent demand notice is more likely to think you mean business (and respond by paying the rent) than a tenant who is merely asked or reminded to pay the rent by you or your managing agent.

- Courts have consistently ruled that an oral demand is insufficient where the tenant's lease requires notice of rent defaults to be in writing.

- Some leases are vague as to whether the landlord can make an oral demand for rent. In such cases, it's far safer to use a written rent demand.

- If the lease you're using has used fuzzy language (including legalese) to describe the manner in which you must present rent demands, you can't be certain that a judge will interpret it your way. In one case, for example, the lease required that "any bill, statement or notice … be in writing." The court ruled that the landlord's oral rent demand was invalid and dismissed the landlord's eviction case. (*Richardson v. Taylor*, N.Y.L.J., 12/5/90, p. 24, col. 5 (Civ. Ct., Kings County).) While other courts might rule the other way, you can't rely on it.

If there's any question as to whether a particular lease provision bars oral rent demands, the landlord must err on the side of caution and serve a written demand of the rent. But if the tenant's lease clearly permits oral rent demands, you may want to consider making one. Making an oral rent demand is obviously easier and cheaper than serving a written rent demand notice.

## 1. How to Make an Oral Rent Demand

To be binding on the tenant, an oral rent demand must satisfy the following four requirements:

- The demand must be made by the landlord or by an authorized agent of the landlord, such as a property manager. Making a rent demand is one job you can't delegate to your lawyer, secretary or office assistant.

- The demand must be made directly to the tenant. Demanding rent from a tenant's relative, employee or guest won't work. You can make the rent demand over the telephone, so long as person on the other end of the phone identifies herself to you as the tenant. (*Oz v. Stolpen*, N.Y.L.J., 12/9/92, p. 22, col. 6 (Civ. Ct., N.Y. County).)

- The demand must clearly inform the tenant of both the amount of rent due and the specific time period for which rent is due. (*Brusco v. Miller,* 167 Misc. 2d 54, 639 N.Y.S.2d 246 (A.T., 1995).) Supplying details is important. A demand for "all back rent" or "all rental arrears" is too indefinite to be valid.

EXAMPLE: "Ms. Jones, you're a week late with your $500 monthly rent for Apt. 3-B. It was due November 1st and today's November 8th. You also owe a $25 late fee from October. If we don't receive the full $525 within three business days, that is by Thursday, November 11th, we'll be forced to bring an eviction proceeding against you. I sincerely hope that won't be necessary."

- The demand should warn the tenant that you will sue for eviction if the tenant fails to pay. (*Mark Stamping Corp. v. Mark Cabinet Manufacturing*, N.Y.L.J., 9/1/93, p. 24, col. 1 (Civ. Ct., Kings County).) A mere conversation with a tenant about the tenant's practice of paying less than the full amount of rent due each month, for example, doesn't constitute an oral demand of the rent. (*Clair v. Zelner*, N.Y.L.J., 6/28/90, p. 29, col. 3 (App. Term, 2d Dep't).) The demand should clearly inform the tenant of the consequences of his or her refusal to pay up—that is, that you'll sue to evict (see example, above).

The rent demand law doesn't require landlords to give the tenant a time deadline for paying—but some judges do. To avoid problems, give the tenant at least three days to pay. That's the minimum period set by the law for written rent demands. Here too, check the tenant's lease first. It may require you to give the tenant more time. For example, some leases say that a rent demand must be given at least five or ten days before you can start an eviction proceeding Our leases and rental agreements require you to give tenants only three days' notice before going to court. (See Clause 19, Chapter 2.)

## 2. Recordkeeping

It's important to keep a written record of an oral rent demand. If the tenant doesn't pay the rent, you'll need to remember the particulars of the oral demand when you bring the tenant to court. A written record will help refresh your recollection later on and could be admitted into evidence at trial as a "business record" if you make it a practice of always making and keeping written records of oral rent demands.

Make your record as soon as possible after making the demand. Simply jot down the date and time you spoke to the tenant; the place you made the demand; whether it was made in person or by phone; and the words you spoke. Sign and date the note, and tuck it into the tenant's file.

EXAMPLE: "On November 8, 2000, at approximately 10:30 A.M, I spoke to Janet Jones, the tenant of Apartment 1-B at 123 Main Street, Buffalo, New York. I reminded her that I was the landlord's agent and told her that we hadn't gotten her November 2000 rent. I told her that

unless she paid $500 for November rent within three days, the landlord would be forced to go to court to evict her. She assured me that a check would be delivered to my office tomorrow. Dated: November 8, 2000, Signed: Mary Manager"

## G. Accepting Rent After You Deliver a Rent Demand Notice

If the tenant offers the rent in full *at any time* after the rent demand, you must accept it, even after the deadline for payment has expired. New York law permits tenants to pay back rent and preserve their tenancy at any time—right up to the moment the judge signs an eviction order. (RPAPL § 751(1).) Payment may be made in any form specified in the lease or rental agreement, such as cash, certified check, money order or personal check. If there's no written rental agreement, payment may be made in any form you've routinely accepted from the tenant in the past—unless you specified the form of payment in the notice itself.

 **Recoup legal expenses by inserting an "attorney fees" clause in your lease or rental agreement.** Some tenants will pay rent only *after* you've begun a non-payment eviction proceeding. By then, you've already incurred legal fees and court costs. You can recover these expenses from the tenant if you include an attorney fees clause in your lease or rental agreement and demand attorney fees when you sue the tenant for rent. The clause entitles the "prevailing party" in any lease-related legal action or proceeding to recover their legal fees and court costs. If a tenant comes up with the full rent after you sue, the landlord is generally considered the prevailing party—even if the case never goes to trial. That means that you're legally entitled to collect your reasonable attorney fees and costs from the tenant. Our lease and rental agreement forms include an attorney fees clause (Clause 20). If a tenant whom you've sued hands you the rent on the courthouse steps, be sure to remind your lawyer to take the necessary steps that will ensure that you get paid.

If you refuse to accept the rent (or insist on more money than demanded in the notice for late fees, for instance), and bring a nonpayment eviction proceeding anyway, your tenant can request and almost always get the case dismissed. And if the lease or rental agreement contains an attorneys' fees clause, you can be ordered to pay your tenant's legal fees and costs. (We explain how attorneys' fees clauses work in Chapter 2, Clause 20.)

You are not required to accept less than the full amount of rent due from the tenant, however. Accepting partial payment after a rent demand operates to cancel the legal effect of the notice. But you should consider accepting partial payments anyway. Remember that you can pocket your tenant's partial payment and immediately issue a new rent demand directing the tenant to pay the new balance or leave.

> EXAMPLE: Danny's rent of $1,200 was due on the first of the month. Danny didn't pay January's rent and didn't have enough for February, either. On February 2, Ali, the manager for Danny's landlord, gave Danny a three-day notice to pay $2,400 or leave. Danny paid $1,200 on February 3 and thought that he'd saved his tenancy. He was amazed when, later that day, Ali handed him a new notice to pay $1,200 or leave. Ali properly served eviction papers on February 7 when Danny failed to pay.

⚠ **If you sign a written agreement with the tenant setting up a payment schedule for delayed or partial rent (discussed in Chapter 3, Section G), you must comply with this agreement.** If the tenant does not end up honoring this agreement, you may then issue a new rent demand.

## H. If the Tenant Won't Pay Rent (or Leave)

In most instances, your rent demand will spur the tenant to pay. But from time to time, you'll be faced with a tenant who ignores the notice and fails to pay or leave by the deadline. As explained in Chapter 14, Section F, it is illegal to harass the tenant in any way, even if she has no valid reason for not paying. Threatening or forcibly evicting the tenant (or cutting off the utilities) are also illegal and may subject you to severe civil and criminal liability.

The only legal way to evict a nonpaying tenant who won't move voluntarily is to bring a nonpayment eviction proceeding and to obtain a judgment of possession and "warrant" directing the sheriff or marshal to evict the tenant.

⚠ **Don't sue if tenant refuses to pay rent for a valid reason.** If you think that the tenant is refusing to pay rent because of a serious repair or maintenance problem, we urge you to read Chapter 9 before preparing any eviction papers. Judges can give tenants generous rent reductions (legally known as "abatements") for uninhabitable conditions. In addition, a judge may order you pay the tenant's legal fees, and may even award punitive damages to the tenant.

Tenants are also entitled to "repair and deduct" under certain circumstances. (See Chapter 9, Section D.) If the tenant has taken a rent deduction for the actual cost to repair a significant defect you knew about but never got around to fixing, it may be cost-effective to give the tenant a rent credit, if the amount is reasonable. So hold off on bringing a lawsuit until you've first tried to negotiate a rent credit for the cost of the repair.

## I. If the Tenant Is Chronically Late Paying Rent

While most tenants pay their rent promptly, others are habitually late. A recalcitrant few withhold payment until they are served with a landlord's rent demand or nonpayment petition. Late-paying tenants create an administrative and financial burden for landlords—especially small property owners who rely on a steady flow of rental income to meet monthly mortgage payments, cover fuel bills, and keep their buildings up and running.

Unfortunately, landlords have never had a clear-cut remedy to deal with late-paying tenants. Regularly commencing nonpayment proceedings is no answer, since a tenant may simply pay the overdue rent at any point in the proceeding to avoid eviction. Though the landlord ultimately collects rent, legal and administrative expenses connected with serving rent demands and instituting nonpayment proceedings are seldom fully recoverable.

Can't you just evict a tenant for chronic late payment? Technically, you can terminate the tenancy on one of these two theories:

1) the tenant's conduct constitutes a "nuisance," or

2) the tenant's conduct violates a substantial obligation of the tenancy, which can't be cured or remedied, by later prompt payment.

In actuality, attempts by landlords to terminate chronic late payers on the theory that their conduct constitutes a nuisance, or is a substantial violation of the lease, have met with mixed results—due largely to the rapidly developing case law on this issue. Chapter 14, Sections B and D, detail the type of proof you need to proceed against a tenant for chronic nonpayment and the likelihood of success under current case law.

 **You can always terminate a month-to-month tenancy for tenants who are chronically late.** Simply terminate the tenancy with a 30-day termination notice within New York City (or a one-month notice outside New York City). You don't have to give (or prove) a reason for termination. (See Chapter 13 for details on the procedure to terminate periodic tenancies.) ■

Chapter **13**

# Terminating Month-to-Month Tenancies

A periodic tenancy can run from week to week, month to month or even year to year. Unlike a tenancy with a lease, which ends on the date specified in the lease, a periodic tenancy automatically renews itself at the end of each period, and continues on until it's terminated by notice. You (or your tenant) can end a periodic tenancy at any time, as long as you give the required amount of advance notice.

Month-to-month tenancies are the most common form of periodic tenancy. They usually begin by mutual agreement when a tenant first moves in. (Chapter 2, Section A, discusses periodic rental agreements.) Month-to-month tenancies can also be created when you accept monthly rent from a hold-over tenant whose lease has expired. (RPL § 232-c.) In both cases, the tenancy continues month after month until either the landlord or tenant ends it.

This chapter reviews the procedure and notice requirements for terminating month-to-month tenancies within and outside New York City. It explains how much notice you must give, what the notice must say and how the notice must be delivered—everything you need to handle this work yourself. This chapter also covers the situations that permit you and your tenant to end the tenancy without

notice, what happens if a tenant leaves without giving required notice and the consequences of accepting rent after a termination notice is given.

## Restrictions on Ending a Tenancy

The general rules for terminating a tenancy described in this chapter don't apply in these situations:

- **Fixed-term tenants.** You can't evict a tenant with a fixed-term lease before the lease expires, unless the tenant refuses to pay rent or violates a significant term of the lease, such as creating a nuisance or damaging the property. (Chapter 14 discusses the grounds on which fixed-term leases may be terminated.)
- **Rent-regulated tenancies.** As long as the tenant pays rent, rent-controlled and rent-stabilized tenancies can't be terminated except on very specific grounds, such as a tenant's violating a substantial obligation of the tenancy, illegal or objectionable conduct or refusing to provide access to the rental unit. (Chapter 14 details the grounds on which rent-regulated tenancies may be ended.) In some cases, you must get permission from the State Division of Housing and Community Renewal (DHCR) before ending the tenancy. (Chapter 15 discusses when DHCR approval is required.)
- **Discrimination.** It is illegal to end a tenancy because of a tenant's race, religion or other reason constituting illegal discrimination. (Chapter 1 discusses illegal discrimination.)
- **Retaliation.** You cannot legally terminate a tenancy to retaliate against a tenant for exercising any tenant-related right under the law, such as the tenant's right to complain to governmental authorities about defective housing conditions or to organize a tenant association. (Chapter 14, Section I, discusses how to avoid charges of retaliation.)

Related topics covered in this book include:

- How to advertise and rent units before a current tenant leaves: Chapter 1
- Writing clear lease and rental agreement provisions on notice required to end a tenancy: Chapter 2
- How to raise the rent or modify other terms of a month-to-month tenancy: Chapter 3
- Highlighting notice requirements in a move-in letter to the tenant: Chapter 7
- Handling tenant requests to sublet or assign the lease: Chapter 8
- Ending a tenancy on three days' notice for nonpayment of rent: Chapter 12
- Removing a month-to-month tenant for drug dealing or other illegal conduct: Chapter 14
- Grounds for terminating a fixed term or rent-regulated tenancy and penalties for engaging in self-help evictions: Chapter 14
- Notices and procedures for terminating a fixed-term or rent-regulated tenancy: Chapter 15
- Preparing a move-out letter and returning security deposits when a tenant leaves: Chapter 16.

## A. How Month-to-Month Tenancies End

If you want a month-to-month tenant to move out, you must first end the tenancy by giving the proper amount of notice. You don't have to give the tenant a special reason, or any reason at all, for terminating the tenancy. (*Park Summit Realty Corp. v. Frank*, 107 Misc. 2d 318, 434 N.Y.S.2d 73 (App. Term, 1st Dep't, 1980), aff'd 84 A.D.2d 700, 448 N.Y.S.2d 414 (1st Dep't 1981), aff'd 56 N.Y.2d 1025, 453 N.Y.S.22d 643, 439 N.E.2d 358 (1982).) You can end a month-to-month tenancy if the tenant makes too much noise, refuses to permit entry for inspections or repairs, pays rent late in the month or if you simply want the unit back for occupancy by you, a family member or a friend. You can't be forced by a tenant or a judge to give your reason for terminating the tenancy. In fact, you don't even need to *have* a

reason for terminating, as long as you're not ending the tenancy for a discriminatory or retaliatory reason.

All you need do is give the tenant the prescribed amount of notice that the tenancy is ending. After the notice period ends, the tenant no longer has the legal right to occupy the premises. State law specifies the minimum amount of notice you must give to end a month-to-month tenancy and the way you must give notice to the tenant. If the tenant's rental agreement requires more notice than the legal minimum, you must comply with the rental agreement and give the tenant more time to leave.

The procedure for terminating month-to-month tenancies in New York City is more stringent than elsewhere in the state. The following sections describe the termination procedures for rental units located within and outside New York City.

**Be meticulous about preparing termination notices.** Be sure your notice is clear, definite and timely. Defective termination notices are routinely subject to attack by tenants in eviction proceedings. And courts rarely give landlords a chance to fix any errors or omissions in a termination notice. (*185 East 85th St. v. Gravanis*, N.Y.L.J., 1/21/81, p. 6, col. 2 (App. Term, 1st Dep't).) If there's a mistake, your case could get thrown out. That means that you must start all over against the tenant with a new termination notice. To avoid problems, follow the procedures described in this chapter.

## B. Terminating Month-to-Month Tenancies Within New York City

If the rental unit is located in New York City, you're required to give the tenant at least 30 days' *written* notice of termination. To be valid, the notice must:

- state the exact date that you elect to end the month-to-month tenancy (Section 2, below, shows you how to figure out the right termination date), and
- warn the tenant that you will begin eviction proceedings to recover possession of the rental unit if the tenant fails to move out on or before the termination date. (RPL § 232-a.)

The words in the termination notice must be crystal clear. A tenant reading your notice should have no doubt that you're terminating her tenancy as of a definite date, that she's required to move out of the rental unit by this date and that you'll go to court to evict her if she doesn't move out. Any murky, misleading or inconsistent language will invalidate the notice. A sample 30-Day Notice of Termination appears at the end of Section 2, below.

## 1. Fixing the Termination Date for a NYC Tenant

The notice must be served on the New York City tenant at least 30 days prior to the contemplated termination date. (RPL § 232-a.)

If the tenancy runs from the first of the month (as is most common), the termination date must fall on the *last day* of the month. (*Clarke v. Shepard,* 188 Misc. 588, 68 N.Y.S.2d 707 (App. Term, 1st Dep't, 1947).) Here's how it works:

- **For 31-day months,** the termination notice must be served on the tenant by the first day of the month in order to terminate on the last day of the month.
- **For 30-day months,** the termination notice must be served *before* the first of the month.
- **For the month of February,** the notice must be served on or before January 29.

It makes no difference if the termination date falls on a weekend or holiday.

EXAMPLE 1: Justin is a month-to-month tenant who pays rent on the first of each month. Selma, Justin's landlord, wants Justin to move out by November 1. On October 1, Selma's manager hands Justin a 30-day termination notice. The notice tells Justin that he must move out on October 31. Because the notice was served 30 days before the October 31 termination date, the notice is valid under state law. (Based on facts from *Seminole Housing Corp. v. M & M Garages, Inc.,* 78 Misc. 2d 755, 359 N.Y.S.2d 711 (Civ. Ct., Queens County, 1974), modified on other grounds, 78 Misc. 2d 762, 359 N.Y.S.2d 710

(App. Term, 2d and 11th Jud.Dists., 1974), aff'd 47 A.D.2d 651, 364 N.Y.S.2d 26 (2d Dep't 1975).)

EXAMPLE 2: Jayne is a month-to-month tenant who pays rent on the first of each month. Mike, Jayne's landlord, wants Jayne to move out by March 1. On February 1, Mike's building super-intendent hands Jayne a 30-day termination notice. The notice tells Jayne to move out on February 28. Mike's termination notice is invalid under state law because it gave Jayne only 27 days' notice of termination. Jayne may safely ignore the notice. To be valid, Mike's notice should have been served by or before January 29—which would have given Jayne 30 days' notice.

EXAMPLE 3: Kate is a month-to-month tenant who pays rent on the first of the month. Neil, her landlord, wants to terminate Kate's tenancy. Neil's process server hands Kate a termination notice on July 15 that tells Kate that she must vacate the rental unit by August 15. The notice is invalid under state law. To be valid, the termination date for a calendar-month tenant must fall on the last day of the month.

If the tenant pays rent on a day other than the first of the month, such as the 15th of the month, your termination notice should end on the last day of the tenancy month, not the last day of the calendar month. So if the tenant pays rent on the 15th day of the month, for instance, the tenancy runs from the 15th of one month to the 14th of the next month. The termination notice, therefore, must terminate the tenancy as of the 14th day of the month.

> **EXAMPLE:** Roberto is a month-to-month tenant who pays rent on the 15th of the month. Ben, his landlord, wants to end Roberto's tenancy. On May 23 Ben's manager hands Roberto a 30-day termination notice. The notice tells Roberto to move out on June 30. While the notice was served more than 30 days before the termination date, the notice is invalid since it didn't terminate the tenancy as of the 14th day of the month. (*Lindquist v. McAlpin*, N.Y.L.J., 2/22/91, p. 32, col. 2 (App. Term, 9th and 10th Jud. Dists.).)

## 2. How to Complete a 30-Day Termination Notice Form for a NYC Tenant

A sample 30-Day Notice of Termination to end month-to-month tenancies in New York City appears below.

The Forms CD includes the Thirty- (30-) Day Notice of Termination and Appendix IV includes a blank tear-out copy of the form.

Here are the steps you must take to properly complete the 30-day termination notice for NYC tenants. If the tenant has a written rental agreement, it's a good idea to pull out the agreement before you get started on the form.

### Step 1. Fill in Each Tenant's Name

If there's more than one tenant listed on the rental agreement, insert the name of each tenant on the form, including husband and wife if both have signed the lease. Don't fill in the names of any roommates or other occupants who live in the rental unit but aren't listed on the rental agreement.

Make sure the names are spelled the same way as they appear on the rental agreement. A misspelled name could give the tenant ammunition to try and delay or derail a later eviction case.

Sometimes, units are rented by businesses for residential use by employees. When issuing a termination notice to a business, fill in the entire legal name for the business. Don't forget to include endings like Corp., Inc., P.C. and L.L.P. They're an important part of a business entity's name.

### Step 2. Fill in the Address

Insert the full address for the tenant's rental unit including the apartment number or any other relevant description (for example, "downstairs apartment"). The address should be at least as detailed as the one that's listed on the rental agreement, if there is one. A rule of thumb used by courts is that the description of the rental unit in the notice must be clear enough to permit a city marshal or county sheriff carrying out an eviction to easily find the tenant's premises. Don't forget the postal Zip code.

### Step 3. Insert the Termination Date

Fill in the month, day and year in which the tenancy will end. Remember that this date must be at least 30 days prior to the date that the notice is served on the tenant, as described in Section B1, above. If the tenant rents on a calendar month basis (that is, rent is due on the first of each month), the termination date must fall on the last day of the month.

> **Give yourself ample time to serve the termination notice.** Termination notices must be "served" on the tenant in a particular way. If the notice is personally delivered to the tenant, the notice is "served" as of that date. But if the tenant cannot be found at the rental unit, it can take a few days to complete service. To be on the safe side, prepare your notice at least 45 days before the

termination date. That will give you two weeks to get copies of the notice to the person who will be serving them on the tenant and for that person to complete service of the notice on the tenant. (Section 4, below, explains how the notice must be served.) You may give the tenant more than the minimum 30 days' notice, but never less.

### Step 4. Sign and Date the Notice

A warning that you will begin eviction (summary) proceedings to recover possession of the rental unit if the tenant fails to move out by the termination is already included in our 30-Day Notice of Termination. All you need to add are your *handwritten* signature and the date you signed the notice.

State law permits the termination notice to be signed by "the landlord or his agent." That means that either the landlord, the landlord's managing agent or attorney may sign the notice. But if the tenant's rental agreement requires the termination notice to come from the landlord personally, only the landlord should sign the notice. Our rental agreement permits the notice to come from the landlord, his agent or attorney. (See Clause 24, Chapter 2.)

If the tenant's rental agreement requires termination notices to be given by the landlord only, a notice signed by the landlord's agent or attorney is subject to attack, unless it's accompanied by proof of the signer's authority to bind the landlord. (*Siegel v. Kentucky Fried Chicken of Long Island, Inc.*, 108 A.D.2d 218, 488 N.Y.S.2d 744 (2d Dep't 1985)., aff'd 67 N.Y.2d 792, 492 N.E.2d, 501 N.Y.S.2d 317 (1986).) In such cases, attach to the notice a statement signed by the landlord authorizing the managing agent or attorney to sign notices for the landlord. A sample Authorization to Issue Notices for Landlord follows our sample Thirty- (30-) Day Notice of Termination, below.

The Forms CD includes the Authorization to Issue Notices for Landlord and Appendix IV includes a blank tear-out copy of this form.

While not required, it's a good idea to include the signer's address and phone number on the notice. That way, the tenant can contact you if she has any questions about the notice.

### Step 5. Make Copies of the Notice

Once you've prepared and signed the termination notice, make at least four photocopies for each tenant named in the notice. You'll need this many copies if the process server is unable to serve the tenant personally and ends up serving the notice by "nail and mail" service (discussed in Chapter 12, Section D).

Keep the original signed termination notice in a safe file; you'll need it if the tenant refuses to move out and you go to court to evict the tenant. Give the photocopies to the person who will be serving the notice on the tenant.

## 3. Who Should Serve the 30-Day Notice of Termination on a New York City Tenant

Anyone over the age of 18 may serve the notice. The notice must not be served by the owner or landlord. (RPL § 735; *Zamar v. Fair*, 153 Misc. 2d 913, 583 N.Y.S.2d 731 (Civ.Ct., Bronx County, 1991).) Your best bet is to direct your managing agent to serve the notice, or to use a process server licensed by the New York City Department of Consumer Affairs. (To find a process server, look in your telephone directory under "process servers.")

## 4. How to Serve a 30-Day Notice of Termination on a New York City Tenant

Each tenant named on the notice must be served with an exact copy of the termination notice. For example, if the notice identifies the tenants as "John and Mary Pagano," serve both John and Mary with

## Thirty- (30-) Day Notice of Termination

To: _____Gail Brousal and William H. Hogeland_____

("Tenants") and any and all persons occupying the premises

Re: _Apartment "B"_____

_278 Henry Street, Brooklyn, NY 11201_____("Premises")

PLEASE TAKE NOTICE, that the undersigned Landlord elects to terminate your monthly tenancy as of
_____December 31, 200X_____, a date at least 30 days from the date of service of this Notice upon
you.

PLEASE TAKE FURTHER NOTICE, that you must surrender and vacate the Premises on or before
_____December 31, 200X_____, the day on which your tenancy expires. If you fail to do so, the
Landlord will commence summary proceedings to remove you from the Premises for holding over
after the expiration of your term, and will demand the monetary value of your use and occupancy of
the Premises during such holding over.

_____November 5, 200x_____      *Paul Hogan*_____
Date                          Signature

                               Paul Hogan, Managing Agent_____
                               Name and Title of Signer

                               c/o Henry Street Realty_____
                               Address

                               3000 Montague St,_____

                               Brooklyn, NY 11201_____

                               _____

                               718- 555-1212_____
                               Phone

---

## Authorization to Issue Notices for Landlord

I hereby authorize _____ Paul Hogan, my Managing Agent _____

_____, to sign all legal notices on

my behalf relating to the property located at _____ 278 Henry Street, Brooklyn, NY 11201.

_____.


January 3, 200x                              John Ferrara
Date                                         Owner and Landlord

---

their own copy of the notice, even if they're married to each other. If the tenant has sublet the rental unit, you're not required to serve a copy of the termination notice to the subtenant—just serve the tenant. (*70 West 85th Street Tenants Corp. v. Cruz*, 173 A.D.2d 338, 569 N.Y.S.2d 705 (1st Dep't 1991).)

If the rental agreement for the premises names more than one person as tenant, you must name each co-tenant in the termination notice and separately serve each co-tenant with a copy of the notice. It won't be sufficient to name and serve only one of the co-tenants, even if the co-tenants are married.

A 30-day termination notice must be served on a tenant in the same manner as a rent demand notice. (RPL § 232-a). That means that you must deliver a true copy of the notice to each named tenant by any one of three methods:

- personal delivery
- "substituted service" to a person of suitable age and discretion who lives or works at the premises, or
- conspicuous place ("nail and mail") service. (RPAPL § 735.)

The mechanics of each method of service are detailed in Chapter 12, Section D.

## 5. Complete an Affidavit of Service

Whenever a termination notice is served on a tenant, the person who serves it should complete an "affidavit of service"—a sworn statement describing how, when and where the notice was delivered to the tenant. You can find sample Affidavit of Service forms and directions for filling them out in Chapter 12, Section E, of this book.

You'll need an affidavit of service if you're later forced to evict a tenant for refusing to move out. Copies of the affidavit of service and termination notice are attached to the eviction papers that get filed in court.

## C. Terminating Month-to-Month Tenancies Outside New York City

For rental units outside New York City, you're required to give at least *one month's* notice of your election to terminate a month-to-month tenancy.

(RPL § 232-b.) Unlike New York City termination notices, the notice can be short and sweet. It must state a clear and definite termination date, but needn't warn the tenant of the consequences of failing to move out.

The notice may be oral or in writing, but be careful. If your rental agreement requires termination notices to be in writing (as does ours—see Clause 4, Chapter 2), you must follow the terms of the rental agreement and give written notice of termination.

We recommend using a written termination notice in every instance—even when your rental agreement permits oral notice. While a written notice means more paperwork, it's worth the extra effort. Here are a few good reasons to use a written termination notice:

**A written termination notice tells your tenant you mean business.** A tenant who's served with a One-Month Notice of Termination is more apt to respond by promptly moving out than a tenant who's merely asked to move out at the end of the month.

**It's much harder to prove you gave an oral notice to a tenant than it is to prove that you served a written notice on a tenant.** If the tenant refuses to move and you sue to evict, you'll need to prove that you gave the tenant a clear, timely and definite notice of termination. A written termination notice makes this job a breeze.

**Courts have consistently ruled that an oral termination notice is insufficient where the tenant's rental agreement requires notices to be in writing.** Some rental agreements are vague as to whether the landlord can give an oral termination notice. In such cases, it's far safer to use a written notice.

## 1.  Determining the Termination Date

Give the notice to the tenant at least one month prior to the contemplated termination date. (RPL § 232-b.) If the tenancy runs on a calendar month (that is, if the tenant pays rent on the first of the month), you must serve the termination notice at least one month prior to the *last day* of the month.

**EXAMPLE 1:** Art is a month-to-month tenant who pays rent on the first of each month. Lou, Art's landlord, wants Art to vacate his rental unit by November 1. On September 30, Lou hands Art a one-month termination notice. The notice tells Art that he must move out on October 31. Because the notice was served at least one month before the October 31 termination date, the notice is valid under state law.

**EXAMPLE 2:** Geri is a month-to-month tenant who pays rent on the first of each month. Ike, Geri's landlord, wants Geri to move out by March 1. On February 1, Ike hands Geri a one-month termination notice. The notice tells Geri to move out on February 28. Geri's termination notice is invalid under state law because it gave Geri only 27 days' notice of termination. Geri may safely ignore the notice. To be valid, Ike's notice should have been served on Geri by or before January 27—which would have given Geri the minimum one month's notice.

**EXAMPLE 3:** Kelly is a month-to-month tenant who pays rent on the first of the month. Norm, her landlord, wants to terminate Kelly's tenancy. On July 15, Norm hands Kelly a termination notice that tells Kelly to vacate the rental unit by August 15. The notice is invalid under state law. To be valid, the termination date for a calendar month tenancy must fall on the last day of the month.

If the tenant pays rent on a day other than the first of the month, your termination notice should end on the last day of the tenancy month, not the last day of the calendar month. So if the tenant pays rent on the 15th day of the month, for instance, the tenancy runs from the 15th of one month to the 14th of the next month. The termination notice, therefore, must terminate the tenancy as of the 14th day of the month.

**EXAMPLE:** Claudio is a month-to-month tenant who pays rent on the 15th of the month. Lida, his landlord, wants to end Claudio's tenancy.

On May 23, Lida hands Claudio a one-month termination notice. The notice tells Claudio to move out on June 30. While the notice was served more than one month before the termination date, the notice may be attacked by the tenant as invalid since it didn't terminate the tenancy as of the 14th day of the month.

## 2. How to Fill out a One-Month Termination Notice Form

A sample One-Month Notice of Termination appears below.

 The Forms CD includes the One-Month Notice of Termination and Appendix IV includes a blank tear-out copy of the form.

The steps required to properly complete a one-month termination notice (outside New York City) are nearly identical to the steps required to complete a 30-day notice of termination within New York City. These steps are described in Section B2, above. The only difference is the termination date (Step 3). Outside of New York City, the date must be at least one month prior to the date that the notice is served on the tenant.

## 3. Who Should Serve the One-Month Notice of Termination

Anyone over 18, *including the landlord*, can deliver or mail the notice to the tenant. (RPL § 232-b.) There's no need to hire a professional process server to give the notice to the tenant.

## 4. How to Serve a One-Month Notice of Termination

It's easy to serve a termination notice outside of New York City. Just deliver *or* mail a copy of the notice of termination to each tenant whose name is listed on the notice. (*McGloine v. Dominy*, 233

N.Y.S.2d 161 (City Ct., Albany, 1962).) Regular mail is acceptable.

This is a far less exacting standard of service than that which is required for rent demands (discussed in Chapter 12) and eviction notices. There's no obligation for you to attempt to serve the tenant by personal delivery, "substituted" service or "nail and mail" service before mailing the notice. You can mail the notice in the first instance.

**Whenever possible, hand deliver written one-month termination notices to tenants.** While the relaxed rules outside New York City permit landlords to give oral termination notices and to mail written termination notices, judges clearly prefer that termination notices be in writing and delivered personally to the tenant. If you end up bringing eviction proceedings against the tenant, your claim that you mailed the termination notice to the tenant or orally terminated the tenancy might undergo closer scrutiny.

If you mail the termination notice (instead of personally delivering it to the tenant), make sure to get a "proof of mailing" from the post office. This is an official receipt that shows the mailing address and date that your notice was mailed. Keep the receipt in a safe place with the original termination notice.

## 5. Complete an Affidavit of Service

If you deliver the notice to the tenant, complete an "affidavit of personal service" right after delivery. If the tenant ignores the notice and you're forced to evict, you'll need to attach copies of the affidavit of service and termination notice to your eviction papers. A sample Affidavit of Service by Personal Delivery and directions on how to fill out the form are in Chapter 12, Section D.

The Forms CD includes the Affidavit of Service by Personal Delivery and Appendix IV includes a blank tear-out copy of the form.

## One-Month Notice of Termination

To: _Gary and Debbie Hecht_

("Tenants") and any and all persons occupying the premises

Re: _65 Clinton Street, Nyack, NY 10960_

_____ ("Premises")

PLEASE TAKE NOTICE, that the undersigned Landlord elects to terminate your monthly tenancy of

the Premises as of _December 31, 200X_, a date a least one month from the date this

notice is served upon you. You must vacate and surrender the Premises on or before that date.

_November 20, 200X_　　　　_Paul Tappan_
Date　　　　　　　　　　　　Signature

　　　　　　　　　　　　　　_Paul Tappan, Owner and Landlord_
　　　　　　　　　　　　　　Name and Title of Signer

　　　　　　　　　　　　　　_2 Main Street_
　　　　　　　　　　　　　　Address

　　　　　　　　　　　　　　_Nyack, NY 10960_

　　　　　　　　　　　　　　_(914) 422-2000_
　　　　　　　　　　　　　　Phone

---

## Affidavit of Service by Personal Delivery

STATE OF NEW YORK                                    )

                                                     ) ss:

COUNTY OF _____ )

The undersigned, being duly sworn deposes and says:

1. I am over 18 years of age ~~and am not the landlord~~.

---

If the landlord delivers the termination notice to the tenant, modify the first paragraph of the affidavit form by deleting or crossing out the words "and am not the landlord."

---

### When Tenants Request More Time to Move Out

Sometimes, a tenant will ask permission to stay in the rental unit for a few extra days beyond the termination date. If you haven't already re-rented the unit to a new tenant, you may want to accommodate the tenant's request if the tenant agrees to pay pro-rated rent for the extra time period. Just make sure you put your agreement into writing. The Sample Letter Extending Tenant's Move-Out Date in Section D3, below, can be modified for this purpose.

---

## D. How Much Notice the Tenant Must Give to End Tenancy

In some cases, tenants are legally required to give notice in order to end a periodic tenancy. The amount and type of notice depends on two factors: 1) whether your rental property is within or outside of New York City, and 2) if the tenant has a written rental agreement.

### 1. New York City Tenants

There isn't any law requiring New York City tenants to give notice of their intention to terminate a periodic tenancy. That means that the tenant may simply hand you the keys at the end of the month, for instance, and say good-bye—without being responsible for paying any additional rent.

You can change this result, however, by using a written rental agreement that requires the tenant to give you written notice of termination. The rental agreement in this book requires month-to-month tenants to provide at least 30 days' prior notice to terminate the rental agreement. You can require tenants who pay rent more frequently than once a month to give you notice that matches their rent payment interval—for example, tenants who pay rent every two weeks would have to give 14 days' notice. To educate your tenants as to what they can expect, make sure your rental agreement includes the appropriate notice requirements for ending a tenancy. (See Clause 4 of the form agreements in Chapter 2.) It is also wise to list termination notice requirements in the move-in letter you send to new tenants. (See Chapter 7.)

## 2. Tenants Outside New York City

State law requires monthly tenants occupying units outside New York City to provide you with at least one month's notice of termination before they move out. The notice may be oral or written. If the notice is written, the tenant may either hand deliver it or mail it to you. (RPL § 232-b.) If, however, the tenant's rental agreement requires more than one month's notice, or specifies that written notices be sent by certified mail, the tenant is required to follow the extra steps laid out in the lease. Our rental agreement (Clause 4 in Chapter 2) requires tenants to give you at least one month's written notice.

A tenant's oral notice of termination must be clear and definite to be legally sufficient.

> EXAMPLE: When an Albany tenant paid rent on July 14, he told his landlord "I'm going to move." One month later, on August 15, the tenant moved out. The landlord sued the tenant for rent from August 15 to September 14, claiming that the tenant moved out without notice. A judge ruled that the tenant's notice, while timely, was too indefinite to be valid. The tenant owed rent to the landlord for the one-month period after he moved out. (*McGloine v. Dominy*, 233 N.Y.S.2d 161 (1963).)

### Must Tenants Give Notice on the First of the Month?

A tenant can give notice at any time—in other words, they don't have to give notice so that the tenancy will end on the last day of the month. If a tenancy ends mid-month, the tenant must pay until that date of the following month. A tenant who gives short notice—declaring that he'd like to leave (and not be responsible for rent) sooner than 30 days hence—can't change this rule. For example, a tenant who pays rent on the first of the month, but gives notice on the tenth, will be obliged to pay for ten days' rent for the next month, even if the tenant moves out earlier.

To prevent tenants from creating move-out dates that do not correspond to the end of your rental period, you may insert a clause in your rental agreement that requires notice to be given only on a certain date—the date the rent is due, usually the first of the month. This means that if the tenant decides on the fifth that she needs to move, she'll have to wait until the first to give notice, and will be obliged to pay for the entire next month, even if she leaves earlier.

## 3. Always Insist on a Tenant's Written Notice of Intent to Move

It's a good idea to insist that your tenant—whether within or outside New York City—give you notice in writing (as does Clause 4 of the form agreements in Chapter 2). Why bother?

Insisting on written notice will prove useful should the tenant not move as planned after you have signed a lease or rental agreement with a new tenant. If there is a new tenant waiting to move in, she may sue you to recover the costs of temporary housing or storage fees for her belongings because you could not deliver possession of the unit. In turn, you will want to sue the old (holdover) tenant for causing the problem by failing to move out. You will have a much stronger case against the holdover tenant if you can produce a written promise to move on a specific date instead of your version of a conversation (which will undoubtedly be disputed by the tenant).

A sample Tenant's Notice of Intent to Move Out form is shown below. Give a copy of this form to any tenant who tells you he or she plans to move.

 The Forms CD includes the Tenant's Notice of Intent to Move Out, and Appendix IV includes a blank tear-out copy.

If the old tenant asks for more time in the rental, but you don't want to continue the tenancy as before, you may want to give him a few days or weeks more, at pro-rated rent. Prepare a written agreement to that effect and have the tenant sign it. See the sample letter below extending the tenant's move-out date.

### Sample Letter Extending Tenant's Move-Out Date

June 20, 200x

Armand LeFleur
Penthouse A
420 Lexington Avenue
New York, NY 10017

Dear Mr. Le Fleur,

On June 1, you gave me a 30-day notice of your intent to move out on July 1. You have since requested to extend your move-out to July 18 due to last-minute problems with the closing of title to your new house. This letter is to verify our agreement that you will vacate Penthouse A on July 18, instead of July 1, and you will pay a pro-rated rent for 18 days (July 1 through July 18). Prorated rent for 18 days, based on your monthly rent of $2,100 or $70 per day is $1,260.

Sincerely,
*Anne Sakamoto, Owner and Landlord*

Agreed to by: *Armand LeFleur*
　　　　　　　Armand LeFleur

Date: *June 20, 200x*

## 4. When the Tenant Doesn't Give the Required Notice

All too often, a tenant will give you a "too short" notice of intent to move. And it's not unheard of for a tenant to move out with no notice or with a wave as he hands you the keys.

Month-to-month tenants in New York City aren't legally required to give you any advance notice that they plan to move out. But outside New York City, a tenant who leaves without giving enough notice has given up the right to occupy the premises, but is still obligated to pay rent through the end of the required notice period. For example, outside New York City the required notice period is one month. Suppose your tenant moves out after telling you 20 days ago that he intended to move. He still owes you for the remaining ten days.

You have a legal duty to try to re-rent the property before you can charge the tenant for giving you too little notice, but few courts expect a landlord to accomplish this in less than a month. This rule, called the landlord's duty to mitigate damages, is discussed in Chapter 16, Section F.

## E. When No Notice Is Required to End Tenancy

Less than a month's notice is required in two extreme cases. A tenant may move out without notice if you've let conditions in the rental unit deteriorate to such a degree that all or part of the unit has become unsafe or uninhabitable (see Section 1, below). And you may terminate the tenancy without notice if the tenant is using the rental unit for an immoral or illegal purpose (see Section 2, below).

### 1. When the Premises Are Unsafe or Uninhabitable

If you seriously violate the rental agreement and fail to fulfill your legal responsibilities—for example, by not correcting serious health or safety problems—a

## Tenant's Notice of Intent to Move Out

April 30, 200X
_____
Date

Anne Sakamoto
_____
Landlord

c/o Lexie Realty, 420 Lexington Avenue
_____
Street Address

New York, New York 10017
_____
City and State

Dear____Ms. Sakamoto_____,
                Landlord

This is to notify you that the undersigned tenants, ____Patti and Joe Ellis_____

_____ will be moving from

Apt. 21-F, 420 Lexington Avenue, New York, NY_____

_____,

on ____May 31, 200X_____ , ____31 days_____ from today.

This provides at least ____30 days'_____ written notice as required in our

rental agreement.


Sincerely,

Patti Ellis
_____
Tenant

Joe Ellis
_____
Tenant

_____
Tenant

tenant may be able to legally move out with no written notice and no further obligation to pay rent. (RPL § 227.) Called a "constructive eviction," this doctrine typically applies only when living conditions are intolerable—for example, if the tenant has had no heat for an extended period in the winter. What constitutes a constructive eviction varies under the circumstances. Generally, if a rental unit has serious habitability problems for anything but a very short time, the tenant may be entitled to move out without giving notice. A tenant's right to move out because of defective conditions at the property is described in Chapter 9.

## 2. Tenant's Illegal Use or Occupancy

A landlord may immediately sue to evict a tenant who uses a rental unit for an illegal or immoral use, or permits others to use it for an illegal or immoral purpose. (RPL § 231(1); RPAPL § 711(5).) No termination notice is required. Prostitution, illegal gambling and drug sales in the rental unit are the most common grounds for terminating a tenancy on this ground. (See Chapter 14, Section C, for details on terminating a tenancy for illegal or immoral activities.)

## F. Accepting Rent After a Termination Notice Is Given

Accepting rent for any period beyond the termination date can cancel the termination notice and create a new month-to-month tenancy. This means you must start all over again with another termination notice if you wish to end the tenancy.

EXAMPLE: On April 15, George sends his landlord Yuri a 30-day notice of his intent to move out. A few weeks later, however, George changes his mind and decides to stay. He simply pays the usual $500 monthly rent on May 1. Without thinking, Yuri cashes the $500 check. Even though she's already re-rented to a new tenant who plans to move in on May 16th, Yuri is powerless to evict George unless she first gives him a new termination notice to move. Unless the lease Yuri signed with the new tenant limits her liability, she will be liable to the new tenant for failing to turn over the rental as promised.

If you collected "last month's rent" when the tenant moved in, do not accept rent for the last month of the tenancy. You are legally obligated to use this money for the last month's rent. Accepting an additional month's rent may extend the tenant's tenancy.

If the tenant asks for more time but you don't want to continue the tenancy as before, you may want to give the tenant a few days or weeks more, at pro-rated rent. Prepare a written agreement to that effect and have the tenant sign it. A sample letter extending the tenant's move-out date appears at Section D3, above. ■

Chapter **14**

# Grounds for Terminating Fixed-Term and Rent-Regulated Tenancies

Unfortunately, even the most sincere and professional attempts at conscientious landlording sometimes fail, and you need to get rid of a troublesome tenant—someone who keeps a dog in violation of a no-pets clause in the lease, repeatedly disturbs other tenants and neighbors by throwing loud parties or otherwise violates your agreement or the law. But you can't just end a tenant's lease when and as you see fit. You must be legally entitled, either under the lease or under a special law, to terminate the tenancy early.

Most leases permit the landlord to end a tenancy early when a tenant violates an important lease term. State laws give landlords other grounds for termination—for instance, when a tenant uses a rental unit for drug sales or other illegal purposes. You can't go to court to evict a tenant unless you can demonstrate that you had a legal reason for terminating the tenant's lease and that you followed the correct termination procedure.

To make the termination process easier to understand, we've divided the issue into two chapters (Chapters 14 and 15). This chapter describes basic termination notices and terms (Section A), and examines the various grounds upon which landlords may legally terminate a fixed-term or rent-regulated tenancy, including:

- which lease violations justify termination (Section B)
- your right to evict a tenant who uses the rental unit for illegal or immoral activity, such as drug dealing or prostitution (Section C)
- your right to end a tenancy when a tenant continuously acts objectionably or creates a nuisance (Section D), and
- special grounds for terminating rent-regulated tenancies under New York City and New York State rent stabilization and rent control laws (Section E).

For each termination ground, we'll tell you what kind of legal notice you must give to the tenant to end the lease. Once you establish your legal ground for termination, and the type of notice(s) you'll need to end the tenancy, go to Chapter 15 for help on drafting the notice(s) and delivering them to the tenant.

Finally, this chapter covers tenants' rights to break their lease and move out early (Sections F and G), as well as the special issue of succession rights to rent-regulated units (Section H).

 **The lease termination procedures covered in this chapter do not apply to terminating a tenancy because your tenant has failed to pay the rent.** Residential lease clauses that call for *automatic* termination of the lease for non-payment of rent are not enforceable in New York. (*Park Summit Realty Corp. v. Frank,* 56 N.Y.2d 1025, 453 N.Y.S.2d 643, 439 N.E.2d 358 (1982).) If the tenant doesn't pay rent, the landlord must serve a legal rent demand on the tenant requiring the tenant to pay a specified amount of rent within a certain time period (usually, three days) or vacate the unit. If the tenant fails to pay rent or move within the time demanded, the landlord may bring a non-payment eviction proceeding against the tenant. Chapter 12 examines the legal procedures for collecting unpaid rent.

Related topics covered in this book include:
- Drafting default and termination provisions and notice requirements in leases: Chapter 2
- Understanding rent control and rent stabilization laws, including what units are covered: Chapter 4
- How to terminate a resident manager's tenancy: Chapter 6
- How to find out who lives in a rental unit and who's legally entitled to be there: Chapter 8
- Making legal rent demands on tenants who don't pay rent on time: Chapter 12
- How to terminate a month-to-month tenancy: Chapter 13
- Drafting and serving notices to cure, termination notices, notices of non-renewal and other notices required to end fixed-term and rent-regulated tenancies: Chapter 15
- Returning security deposits and collecting unpaid rent from a tenant who breaks a lease early: Chapter 16
- Finding a lawyer and conducting your own legal research: Chapter 17.

⚠ **Don't discriminate or retaliate.** You may not legally terminate a tenancy to retaliate against a tenant for exercising any tenant-related right under the law, such as the tenant's right to complain about housing conditions or to organize or join a tenants' association. (See Section I, below, for details on illegal retaliation.) Nor can you terminate a tenancy because of race, religion, sex, marital status, having children, sexual preference or other discriminatory reasons. (See Chapter 1 for a full discussion on discriminatory housing practices.)

## A. Basic Termination Notices and Terms

Here are brief definitions of the various types of legal notices referred to in this chapter. If you're a new landlord, this may sound a bit overwhelming. But as you read this chapter and Chapter 15, you'll have a better understanding of the termination process, what notices are required for different situations and when and how to serve them.

A **"notice to cure" (also known as "default notice")** is primarily used to terminate a tenancy for a violation of a lease clause, such as a "residential use only" clause. It is a legal warning that tells the tenant how he is violating the lease, and states that you will terminate the lease if the tenant doesn't correct or "cure" the problem within a given time period (usually ten days).

If the tenant doesn't remedy the violation within the time provided, you may then issue a **"notice of termination," (also known as a termination notice or "notice to vacate and surrender"),** ending the tenancy as of a particular date, and advising the tenant that an eviction proceeding will be commenced upon expiration of the notice. The amount of time the tenant has to move out varies (it's usually either seven days or one month) depending upon the reason for termination and, in the case of rent-regulated tenants, the form of rent regulation. In many cases, you don't need to serve a notice to cure, but may immediately serve a termination notice.

If you're ending a rent-stabilized tenancy, you may need to serve the tenant with a **"notice of non-renewal"** informing the tenant that you do not intend to renew the lease. Whether or not you need to send a notice of non-renewal depends on the reason for termination. A notice of non-renewal must be served during a window period prior to the expiration of the tenant's current lease. This window period may range from 90 to 150 days or from 120 to 150 days, depending on the situation; this is the time that you would ordinarily be required to offer the tenant a renewal lease. A notice of non-renewal is often combined in one form with the termination notice.

For some rent-regulated properties, there's more paperwork involved in ending a tenancy. For example, in addition to serving a termination notice on the tenant, you may also need to meet **filing requirements of the State Division of Housing and Community Renewal (DHCR)**. These require delivery of a copy of termination notices to the local DHCR office, along with an affidavit (or proof) of service within a specified amount of time (usually, either 48 hours or seven days).

To complicate the termination process even further, in some situations, you must file a **DHCR "Certificate of Eviction"** (also known as a DHCR Eviction Order) after serving the tenant any necessary notice to cure or termination notices, and before commencing an eviction proceeding to remove the tenant.

If the tenant doesn't move out by the time the termination notice expires, you may begin a **"holdover" eviction proceeding** to remove the tenant from the rental unit. See "Overview of Evictions," below.

To evict a tenant who doesn't move out in response to a termination notice, you or your attorney will need to prepare a "notice of petition" and "petition holdover" asking the court to give you legal possession of the rental unit. These papers must be served on the tenant and filed in the civil court. To be entitled to a judgment of possession, you must be able to demonstrate to a judge that you had a legal reason to terminate the tenancy and that you followed the right procedure. The judge will examine the legal and factual sufficiency of your termination notices (as well as your notice to cure or notice of non-renewal, where applicable). In addition, the court will hear any tenant "defenses," which are legal reasons why the tenancy should not be terminated.

If all goes well, the judge will issue a judgement of possession in your favor and a "warrant of eviction," directing the city marshal, county sheriff or town constable to remove the tenant and occupants. (RPAPL §749 (1).) The issuance of the warrant by the judge officially cancels the tenancy and ends the landlord-tenant relationship between you and your tenant. Before carrying out the eviction, the marshal, sheriff or constable will serve the tenant with a notice giving the tenant at least 72 hours' notice of the impending eviction. Only after the notice period ends may the eviction be carried out.

Eviction proceedings are not covered by this book. For help on preparing the necessary papers, see Chapter 17, Lawyers and Legal Research.

## B. Termination for Violation of Lease Term

You have a right to terminate a lease once there's a substantial breach by the tenant. Most leases spell this out by giving you a right to end the tenancy if the tenant violates any term of the lease. (See Clause 19, Chapter 2.) But since leases include a variety of tenant promises and obligations, courts are reluctant to permit a lease to terminate for a mere technical breach or minor violation.

 **Rent stabilization and rent control laws also permit landlords to terminate the tenancy in the event that the tenant violates a substantial obligation of the tenancy.** These include tenant obligations spelled out in a tenant's current lease or, in the case of most rent-controlled tenants, in the expired lease.

### 1. Kinds of "Substantial" Lease Obligations

To justify termination, the tenant must significantly violate a "substantial obligation" of the tenancy. (*Park West Village v. Lewis*, 62 N.Y.2d 431, 477 N.Y.S.2d 124, 465 N.E.2d 844 (1984).)

What's "substantial"? If the lease expressly states that a certain violation will constitute a substantial obligation of the tenancy, that agreement will usually be enforced. Even when a specific lease term isn't expressly labeled substantial, a breach will be considered substantial if the violation actually harms, damages or causes significant injury to the landlord or to the landlord's property. (*Park East Land Corp. v. Finkelstein*, 299 N.Y. 70, 85 N.E. 869 (1949).) A tenant's violation of a "no-alterations" clause that results in physical damage to the rental unit or in the issuance of a violation citation against the landlord, for example, would likely be considered a substantial lease violation and justify termination of the tenancy. On the other hand, hanging a few pictures on the wall, while technically an "improvement or alteration," usually won't support a landlord's claim that the tenant substantially breached the lease.

The following sections describe examples of substantial obligations taken from New York court cases. Also look at "Substantial Obligations Under Our Form Lease," below, for a list of lease clauses in the form lease in Chapter 2 that qualify as substantial.

## Substantial Obligations Under Our Form Lease

The following tenant actions would in all likelihood be considered substantial lease violations and grounds for terminating the tenancy under the lease in Chapter 2 of this book, as well as the court cases described in Section 1.

- business use of the premises which violates local zoning laws or is inconsistent with the residential character of the property (Clause 2)
- failure to post a security deposit (Clause 8)
- illegal sublet or assignment (Clause 10)
- significant physical alterations, such as removing or adding a partition or wall without permission (Clause 12)
- failure to give duplicate key (Clause 12)
- severe property damage (Clause 13)
- keeping a pet without permission, or when the lease explicitly prohibits pets (Clause 14), and
- failure to permit landlord access to inspect, make repairs or show the unit (Clause 15).

A tenant who engages in illegal or objectionable conduct also violates the lease. However, New York law treats these kinds of violations differently, as explained in Sections C and D of this chapter.

### a.  Access Clause

A clause providing the landlord with a right of entry to inspect the rental unit, make repairs and/or show the unit to prospective tenants and mortgagees is a substantial obligation of the lease. For instance, a tenant who refused the landlord's repeated requests for access to install new windows was found by an appeals court to have breached a substantial obligation of the lease and could be evicted. (*Weiner Equities Associates v. Stambler*, N.Y.L.J., 2/21/91, p. 28, col. 3 (App. Term, 2d & 11th Jud. Dists.).)

Chapter 10 details your right of entry and provides sample forms for requesting access.

 Rent stabilization and rent control laws require tenants to provide access to landlords for inspections, to make necessary repairs or improvements required by law or to show the unit to prospective purchasers or mortgagees. A rent-regulated tenant's unreasonable refusal to permit the landlord access is grounds for eviction. For more information, see Section E1, below.

### b.  No-Alterations Clause

A tenant's violation of an express promise not to make alterations to the rental unit without your prior consent is a substantial lease violation. (*Rumiche Corp. v. Eisenreich*, 40 N.Y.2d 174, 386 N.Y.S.2d 208, 352 N.E.2d 125 (1976).) However, alterations that are non-structural, easily removable and consistent with the residential use of the premises may not be substantial enough to justify a tenancy's forfeiture; it depends on the particular facts and circumstances.

Alterations which courts have characterized as "structural" include the installation or removal of windows, the removal or installation of partition walls and the reconstruction of ceilings.

Non-structural alterations which don't significantly violate the no-alterations clause include the installation of wall mirrors and wall-to-wall carpeting. Most of the time, a tenant's replacement of old or defective bathroom vanities, sinks, stoves, refrigerators, kitchen cabinets and linoleum are considered non-structural alterations and do not significantly violate a no-alterations clause, *unless* the replacement causes permanent or lasting damage to the property. (*Mengoni v. Passy*, N.Y.L.J., 11/28/97, p. 28, col. 3 (App.Term., 1st Dep't).)

> EXAMPLE: A Manhattan tenant replaced a 27-year old stove with a new stove. The landlord terminated the tenancy on the ground that the tenant violated the no-alterations clause in the lease, and sued to evict the tenant. An appeals court refused to allow the tenancy to be terminated because the replacement of the stove "was merely a technical violation" of the no-alterations clause of the lease, as opposed to

a significant violation of a substantial lease obligation. (*Ram I LLC v. Stuart*, N.Y.L.J. 4/25/97, p. 25, col. 2, (App.Term, 1st Dep't) aff'd 248 A.D.2d 255, 668 N.Y.S.2d 888 (1st Dep't 1998).)

Courts are more likely, however, to find that a violation has occurred when the item being replaced has real value—in the example, above, chances are the stove was not a vintage Wedgewood. One court has ruled that a tenant's replacement of a refrigerator and kitchen cabinets, when both were in good condition, constituted a substantial violation of the lease's no-alterations clause. (*Britton v. Yazicioglu*, 190 A.D.2d 734, 592 N.Y.S.2d 737 (1st Dep't 1993).) Tenants who install fixtures and appliances always run the risk that the junker they despise is actually your prized heirloom.

 Tenants have a narrowly defined right to alter or repair the premises in specific situations. Examples include:
- alterations by a disabled person (see Chapter 1, Section C4, for details)
- use of the "repair and deduct" procedure (discussed in Chapter 9, Section D), and
- installation of wireless antennas and small satellite dishes (see Chapter 9, Section I, for details).

### c. Duplicate Key Clause

A lease provision that requires the tenant to give you a duplicate key to any privately installed apartment door lock is a substantial obligation. (*24-26 East 82nd Street Tenants Corp. v. Bell*, 248 A.D.2d 277, 670 N.Y.S.2d 78 (1st Dep't 1998).) Buffalo and New York City tenants who live in buildings with three or more units are required by state law to give you a duplicate key to any privately installed apartment door lock. (MDL § 51-c.)

### d. No-Pets Clause

A lease provision that prohibits the tenant from keeping a dog, cat or other pet in the rental unit without your permission is a substantial obligation of the tenancy. A tenant who harbors a pet in violation of a no-pets clause in the lease can be terminated. (*Rivercross Tenants Corp. v. Galateau*, N.Y.L.J., 11/2/90, p. 21, col. 2 (App.Term, 1st Dep't).) However, you must act promptly against a tenant who keeps a pet. A delay could work to waive, or nullify, the no-pets lease provision.

 **NYC and Westchester laws require landlords to object to pets within three months.** In buildings with three or more units, a no-pets provision in the lease is waived if:

- the tenant "openly and notoriously" keeps a pet for three months or more
- you or your agent know about the pet, and
- you fail to object to the pet within that three-month period. (NYC Adm. Code § 27-2009.1, Westchester County Laws § 694.)

EXAMPLE: Sally moves in to your Brooklyn building on September 1 after signing a lease that includes a no-pets clause. On September 15, Daisy, Sally's new pit bull, moves in. Sally walks Daisy every morning, usually waving hello to your building's doorman as she passes through the lobby with her dog. While inspecting the building on the morning of January 15, you see Sally walking Daisy through the lobby. Later that day, you serve Sally with an official notice to cure, warning her that she's violating the no-pets provision in her lease. Sally can safely ignore your notice. Why? You "knew" about Daisy, but didn't object until more than three months after the pet moved in. You're deemed to "know" about a dog if, for instance, a tenant openly walks the pet every day within sight of your doormen, security guards or other building staff. (*Lewis Morris Associates v. Rodriguez*, N.Y.L.J., 2/25/98, p. 30, col. 6 (Civ.Ct., Bronx County).)

Don't be too hasty about terminating a tenant with a pet. Some disabled tenants are legally entitled to keep "service animals" in spite of your no-pets clause where the animal is necessary to the tenant's use and enjoyment of their home. We cover the rights of disabled tenants to keep service animals in Chapter 1, Section B7.

### e. Residential Use Only Clause

A lease clause that restricts the tenant's use of the rental unit to residential or living purposes only is a substantial obligation. However, not every commercial and professional use of the rental property will constitute a significant violation of a residential use only clause. Courts usually examine whether the tenant's use is consistent with the residential character of the rental property.

For instance, a landlord successfully terminated the lease of a rent-stabilized tenant who conducted her entire psychiatric practice from her apartment. New York's highest court ruled that the tenant "departed significantly" from the lease requirement that the apartment be used solely for residential purposes. (*Park West Village v. Lewis*, 62 N.Y.2d 431, 477 N.Y.S.2d 124, 465 N.E.2d 844 (1984).) Because the tenant had specifically agreed to use and occupy the apartment only as a private dwelling, her professional use of the apartment was at odds with the residential character of the apartment complex in which the unit was located.

By contrast, a tenant who ran a small family day-care business in a rent-stabilized apartment did not significantly violate a substantial obligation of the lease, according to one New York City court. (*Sorkin v. Cross*, N.Y.L.J., 4/24/96, p. 27, col. 3 (Civ.Ct. N.Y. County).) The tenant was registered with the city for the right to care for up to six children in the apartment. The judge hearing her eviction case said that the use of the apartment for child care was consistent with the residential character of the apartment and that of the building, so the tenant didn't significantly violate the residential use only clause.

Sometimes it will be easy to know whether your tenant's business constitutes a substantial violation. Local zoning ordinances usually itemize prohibited

uses for residential property. If your tenant's use of the premises is prohibited under local zoning ordinances, the tenant has significantly violated a substantial lease clause and may be terminated. Contact your municipal clerk's office or local public library for advice on how to obtain a copy of your local zoning ordinance.

**New York City zoning laws specifically prohibit ten "home occupations."** They are: advertising or public relations agencies, barber shops, beauty parlors, commercial stables or kennels, depilatory, electrolysis or similar offices, interior decorators' offices or workshops, ophthalmic dispensing, pharmacy, real estate or insurance offices and veterinary medicine. (NYC Zoning Laws, Art. I, § 12-10.)

### f. Security Deposit Clause

An agreement to furnish a lawful security deposit to the landlord under the terms of a lease is a substantial obligation of the tenancy. (*Sharp v. Norwood*, 89 N.Y.2d 1068, 659 N.Y.S.2d 834 (1997).) (For information on how big a security deposit you may lawfully demand, see Chapter 5.)

### g. Sublet or Assignment Clause

By statute, any sublet or assignment by a residential tenant that does not comply with the requirements of RPL § 226-b, also known as the "Sublet Law," constitutes a breach of a substantial obligation of the tenancy. (Chapter 8 details the procedures that tenants must take to properly sublet or assign their unit).

### h. No–Washing-Machine Clause

Where a lease specifically prohibits the installation of a washing machine or other laundry equipment, the violation of that clause is a violation of a substantial obligation. (*Albert v. Chiesa*, N.Y.L.J., 4/10/98, p. 34, col. 6 (App. Term, 2d & 11th Jrd. Dists.).)

### i. Chronic Nonpayment of Rent

A tenant's covenant to pay rent is a primary lease obligation. Chronic, unjustified, nonpayment of rent has long been held to constitute a breach of a substantial lease obligation. (*Sharp v. Norwood*, 89 N.Y.2d 1068, 659 N.Y.S.2d 834, 681 N.E.2d 1280 (1997).)

## 2. Procedure for Termination for Lease Violation

If you decide to end a tenancy for a violation of a substantial lease obligation, the procedure you'll follow will depend on what the tenant's lease says about default and termination and whether your tenant is protected by rent control or rent stabilization. (If you're using the form lease in this book, see Clause 19 in Chapter 2 to know what to do.)

Leases customarily provide that before the landlord may terminate the tenancy for a lease violation, the landlord must first furnish the tenant with written notice of the default, and provide an opportunity to cure it. The notice is referred to as a Notice to Cure or a Notice of Default. For non-regulated tenants, the length of the cure period is dictated by the lease. All four systems of rent regulation require landlords to issue a written notice to cure before terminating a tenant who is violating a substantial obligation, with a cure period of at least ten days.

If the tenant refuses to correct, or "cure," the violation within the time provided, you may then issue a termination notice ending the tenancy. In some cases, a copy of the termination notice must be filed with the local DHCR within a set amount of time, such as 48 hours.

If you have reason to terminate the tenancy on the ground of tenant violation of a substantial lease obligation, see Chapter 15 to find out what notices you must prepare and serve on the tenant and how and when to do so. Start by looking at the chart "Termination Notices at a Glance," at the beginning of Section B in Chapter 15.

## 3. Are All Lease Violations Curable?

The general rule is that landlords must give tenants an opportunity to "cure," or remedy, lease violations before the tenancy may be terminated. But in some cases, the lease violation may not be curable.

A key issue in chronic nonpayment cases based on a substantial lease violation is whether a cure is even possible. Chronic nonpayment claims are, after all, based on a pattern of past conduct. How may a tenant remedy months, or even years, of bad behavior within, say, a ten-day period? And how may landlords verify any attempts by the tenant to cure?

A tenant who receives a ten-day notice to cure a no-pet lease clause violation, by contrast, may readily effect a cure, and preserve the tenancy, by removing the offending pet from the premises within the ten-day deadline. And, when the cure period expires, the landlord may easily verify whether the tenant has completed, or has at least begun to effect, a cure. But the case is far less clear when the lease violation is based on past nonpayment and late payment of rent.

Recognizing the impossibility of curing past conduct within a matter of days, the Appellate Term, First Department, which covers Manhattan and the Bronx, has repeatedly ruled that a pre-termination notice to cure is not required in chronic nonpayment cases based on a substantial lease violation. Outside those boroughs, there is no clear-cut rule. Our best advice is to always issue a notice to cure, even when it is technically unnecessary. That way, the tenant is foreclosed from raising the issue of whether a notice to cure was necessary—a point that could forestall a final decision in your later eviction proceeding.

Even in Manhattan and the Bronx, where a notice to cure is not technically required for chronic non-payment cases, the court has the discretion to postpone the tenant's eviction (what judges call "staying the possessory judgment") for a probationary period, during which time the tenant must demonstrate prompt rent payment. Long-term, rent-regulated tenants are most apt to be entitled to such stays, so as to avoid a forfeiture of their valuable tenancy.

## C. Termination for Immoral or Illegal Use or Occupancy

State law permits landlords to remove any tenant who uses or occupies the rental unit for an illegal trade, manufacture or other purpose or for an immoral purpose. (RPL § 231(a); RPAPL § 711(5).) Neighbors and law enforcement officials are also entitled to take steps to remove one of your tenants who use the unit for an illegal purpose. (RPAPL § 715.)

### 1. What Tenant Conduct Qualifies As Illegal or Immoral?

New York law enumerates several kinds of activities which fall under the "illegal or immoral use or occupancy" category. They include a tenant's use of the rental unit for:

- any illegal trade or manufacture, including the sale or manufacture of illegal drugs or narcotics
- prostitution (sometimes known as a "bawdy house")
- illegal gambling, or
- a "house or place of assignation for lewd persons."

The meanings of the terms in the list above are fairly well-known, but what's considered lewd? Definitions of lewd run the gamut from indecent to lascivious—all the way to obscene. Obviously, lewdness is a very subjective concept. In one case, a tenant's "sex club," where patrons engaged in acts of sadomasochism, constituted a "house or place of assignation for lewd persons" and subjected the tenant to eviction. (*31 West 21st Street Assoc. v. Evening of the Unusual, Inc.,* 125 Misc. 2d 661, 480 N.Y.S.2d 816 (Civ.Ct., N.Y. County, 1984).) But be careful about trying to evict a tenant on this basis. Tenant conduct that you consider lewd might seem downright wholesome to the judge hearing your eviction case.

To evict a tenant on this ground, you don't need to prove that the tenant himself joined the illegal or immoral activity. You need only prove that the tenant knew what was going on, had the ability to control the situation, yet permitted the unit or common areas to be used for the activity. For example, a grandmother's tenancy was terminated on this ground because she sat by while her grandson sold drugs from her rental unit. (*Levites v. Francisco,* N.Y.L.J., 1/15/93, p. 21, col. 5 (App. Term, 1st Dep't).)

### 2. Drug Dealing, Prostitution and Gambling: Reasons for Which You Must Evict

In cases of drug dealing and other illegal businesses, it's not a question of whether it's permissible to evict a tenant—it's imperative to do so. State law imposes a statutory duty on landlords to evict tenants and other occupants who are known to be engaging in illegal drug, prostitution or gambling activities on the property. (RPL § 231(2).) Landlords who fail to take steps to remove tenants whom they know are engaging in illegal activity are liable for any resulting damage, including money damages for injuries to other tenants, guests and employees that occur on the property. Failing to evict drug-dealing tenants can result in practical problems, too. Good tenants who pay rent on time and maintain the rental property may be difficult to find and keep, and the value of your property will plummet.

Paradoxically, the tenant's illegal use of the rental unit must be for an *ongoing illegal business.* A tenant's personal consumption of a controlled substance in the rental unit, while illegal, is not enough to justify a forfeiture of the tenancy. (See, for example, *1895 Grand Concourse Associates v. Ramos,* N.Y.L.J., 12/20/98, p. 23, col. 1 (Civ.Ct., Bronx County).) When it comes to drug-dealing, judges look for a pattern of commercial narcotics activity, especially when the tenant stands to lose a long-term rent-regulated tenancy. (Believe it or not, some judges have ruled that isolated instances of illegal activity are not enough to warrant a forfeiture of a valuable tenancy. They take the view that the tenant must be engaged in a customary or habitual pattern of criminal activity to justify removal.) (See, for example, *New York County District Attorney's Office v. Betesh,* N.Y.L.J., 11/23/98, p. 30, col. 6 (App. Term., 1st Dep't).)

This means that you can't base an eviction proceeding on a mere suspicion that something illegal is going on. Smelling pot wafting from the tenant's unit or seeing nefarious-looking people visit the tenant's unit at all hours isn't enough. You'll need to obtain certified copies of police records such as search warrants, arrest reports and controlled-substance lab reports, to bolster your claim. For that reason, enlist the help of your local police department if you suspect that a tenant is using the rental unit to sell drugs or to conduct other illegal business. If you don't get the law enforcement backup you need (for an arrest), you might still be able to proceed against the tenant under a nuisance theory. (Section D, below, explains this termination ground.)

Carefully screening potential renters and performing background checks can go a long way toward avoiding (or at least minimizing) this type of problem at your property. Chapter 1 suggests ways to screen rental applicants.

### 3. Other Tenants and Law Enforcement Agencies May Evict, Too

A neighboring tenant who lives within 200 feet of a rental unit used for illegal or immoral purposes is authorized under state law to bring an eviction proceeding against the tenant. (RPAPL § 715(1).) In practice, tenants rarely use this power—probably fearing reprisals from the tenant conducting the illegal activity.

The same law authorizes certain enforcement agencies to order you to evict a tenant who uses a rental unit illegally. The county district attorney (or other officer with similar enforcement authority) may personally serve you or your manager with written notice requiring you to commence an eviction proceeding against the tenant. Ordinarily, this action is triggered by your tenant having been arrested and charged with the sale of a controlled substance from the rental unit. (If you don't initiate a proceeding to remove the tenant within five days, or don't diligently prosecute the proceeding after it begins, the officer may bring the proceeding against the tenant *and you* seeking civil penalties up to five

thousand dollars ($5,000) together with the payment of the municipality's costs and reasonable attorneys' fees.) (RPAPL § 715(4); *Kings County District Attorney's Office v. Freshley*, 160 Misc. 2d 302, 608 N.Y.S.2d 788 (Civ.Ct., Kings County, 1993).)

**Consider calling an experienced landlord-tenant lawyer if you get a notice requiring you to begin an eviction proceeding against a tenant who's dealing drugs or using the rental unit illegally.** So-called "illegal use" eviction proceedings are tricky. An attorney can help you prepare, serve and file the papers you need to initiate the proceeding. Failing to respond to the notice could end up costing you more money than initiating an eviction suit against the tenant yourself. Chapter 17 explains how to find a lawyer and conduct legal research.

### 4. Procedure for Termination for Immoral or Illegal Use or Occupancy

For non-regulated units, you can go straight to court to remove a tenant who uses the rental unit for illegal or immoral purposes, such as drug dealing. There's no need to serve the tenant with either a notice to cure or a notice of termination. (RPAPL § 711(5).)

To remove a rent-regulated tenant on the basis of immoral or illegal use or occupancy, you must serve the tenant with a termination notice (in some cases, preceded by a notice to cure) before going to court. In some situations, a copy of the termination notice must be filed with the local DHCR within a set amount of time, such as 48 hours. For details on what notices you must prepare and serve on rent-stabilized and rent-controlled tenants and how and when to do so, see Chapter 15. Start by looking at the chart "Termination Notices at a Glance," at the beginning of Section B in Chapter 15.

## D. Termination for Nuisance or Objectionable Conduct

Most leases contain a provision permitting termination where a tenant or occupant is committing or permitting a "nuisance." Our form lease contains a provision like this (see Chapter 2, Clause 13).

Rent-controlled and rent-stabilized tenants may be terminated on the basis of nuisance or objectionable conduct, too. (See 9 NYCRR §§ 2524.3(b); 9 NYCRR 2504.2(b); 2104.2(b); 2204.2(a)(2).) All four systems of rent regulation permit the landlord to commence an action or proceeding to recover possession of the regulated premises on the ground that "the tenant is committing or permitting a nuisance in such housing accommodations or the building containing such housing accommodations; or is maliciously, or by reason of gross negligence substantially damaging the housing accommodation ... " The regulations that cover rent-controlled units, add: "conduct (that is) such to interfere substantially with the comfort or safety of the landlord or of other tenants or occupants of the same or other adjacent building or structure." In December 2000, the regulations applicable to rent-stabilized units were amended to add: " . . . or the tenant engages in a persistent or continuous course of conduct evidencing an unwarrantable, unreasonable or unlawful use of the property to the annoyance, inconvenience, discomfort or damage to others, the primary purpose of which is intended to harass the owner or other tenants" of the building.

A "nuisance" is generally defined as tenant conduct that threatens the health, safety or comfort of neighboring tenants or other building occupants. To justify termination, the tenant's objectionable conduct must be continuous or persistent. (*Frank v. Park Summit Realty Corp.*, 175 A.D.2d 33, 573 N.Y.S.2d 655 (1st Dep't 1991), modified on other grounds, 79 N.Y.2d 789, 579 N.Y.S.2d 649, 587 N.E.2d 287 (1991).) That means that you can't terminate a tenant for throwing one loud, late-night party or for accidentally overflowing the tub. But you may terminate a tenant who regularly throws loud parties that interfere with other tenants' sleep or regularly overflows the tub, causing water damage to other rental units.

## 1. What Conduct Is Considered a Nuisance?

Here are some examples of tenant conduct which courts have found to constitute a legal nuisance.

### a. Conduct That Poses a Health or Fire Hazard

An accumulation of newspapers and debris in a tenant's apartment may constitute a nuisance where the condition is a health and fire hazard and the tenant fails or refuses to clean up the condition. (*Stratton Cooperative Inc. v. Fener,* 211 A.D.2d 559, 621 N.Y.S.2d 77 (1st Dep't 1995).)

### b. Objectionable Conduct

Continuous loud music and foul odors are examples of legal nuisances that may disturb nearby neighbors. A pattern of antisocial or outrageous behavior exhibited or condoned by a tenant may also constitute a nuisance and subject the tenant to eviction. For example, a Manhattan landlord was permitted to evict a rent-stabilized tenant who condoned the presence of his schizophrenic nephew, even though his nephew engaged in numerous incidents of public nudity, verbal abuse, profanity and vulgarity toward neighboring tenants and staff. (*Frank v. Park Summit Realty Corp.*, 175 A.D.2d 33, 573 N.Y.S.2d 655 (1st Dep't 1991), modified on other grounds, 79 N.Y.2d 789, 579 N.Y.S.2d 649, 587 N.E.2d 287 (1991).) In another case, a Manhattan landlord was permitted to terminate a rent-stabilized tenant for conduct that substantially interfered with the comfort and safety of other neighbors, despite the involuntary nature of the conduct, which was brought on by mental illness. (*301 East 69th St. Assoc. v. Eskin,* 156 Misc. 2d 122, 600 N.Y.S.2d 887 (App. Term, 1st Dep't 1993).)

To qualify as a nuisance, the tenant's objectionable conduct must be outrageous, egregious or extremely antisocial. Annoying, rude or inconsiderate behavior isn't enough to justify termination, even if the tenant's boorish behavior is continuous.

### c. Pets

Unabated animal-related disturbances may trigger a nuisance. Examples include a pet's incessant barking, property damage, urination and defecation in the common areas and chasing, threatening or attacking other tenants or staff.

 **If you attempt to terminate a tenancy for a pet-related reason, be ready for a fight.** Many New Yorkers treat their pets like children, and will pull out all the stops to keep their cherished pet. In one nuisance case, a Bronx tenant brought a renowned pet psychologist to housing court to testify as to the quiet and docile nature of the tenant's pit bull dog. (*Lewis Morris Associates v. Rodriguez*, N.Y.L.J., 2/25/98, (Civ.Ct., Bronx County).) The tenant won the case.

### d. Property Damage

A pattern of conduct (as opposed to a one-time event) that results in damage to the landlord's property, or that of other tenants, will constitute a nuisance. For example, where a tenant agreed in a court agreement to stop causing water damage, but later intentionally caused a toilet overflow that made the apartment below his uninhabitable, a Manhattan court ordered the tenant's eviction on the basis of nuisance. (*Mengoni v. Carlenberg,* N.Y.L.J., 10/2/91, p. 26, col. 2 (Civ.Ct., N.Y. County).)

### e. Chronic Nonpayment of Rent

Landlords may commence holdover proceedings to oust tenants for chronic nonpayment based on nuisance if they can establish three elements:

1) repeated resort to legal process, in the form of rent demands and nonpayment petitions, over a short time period to collect rent from the tenant

2) a complete lack of any legal justification for nonpayment by the tenant, such as needed repairs to the premises, and

3) the tenant's conduct interfered with others' use and enjoyment of the property (also known as "aggravating circumstances"). (See *Sharp v. Norwood*, 89 N.Y.2d 1068, 659 N.Y.S.2d 834 (1997).)

What are aggravating circumstances? Will tenant conduct that interferes solely with the landlord's use and enjoyment of the property suffice, or must the tenant's conduct affect other tenants as well? Our review of the case law suggests that the answer may turn on the rent-regulatory status of the tenant whose eviction is sought. For rent-regulated tenants, it appears that the landlord needs to show that the tenant is engaging in conduct that threatens the health or safety of other tenants in the property, such as refusing to grant access to the landlord to remedy a condition that threatens other tenants' comfort or safety. (*Winforo Associates v. Maloof,* N.Y.L.J., 8/7/02, p. 20, col. 3 (Civ.Ct., N.Y. County).) For unregulated units, tenant interference with the landlord's use of the property may be sufficient. For instance, a landlord whose tenant had remitted 14 bad rent checks, habitually paid rent late in the month, and forced the landlord to institute five nonpayment proceedings in three years, at which the tenant failed to offer any legal justification for nonpayment, demonstrated an unexcused pattern of chronic nonpayment sufficient to establish nuisance. The judge hearing the case also found that the tenant's conduct detrimentally affected the landlord's use of the property, which satisfied the "aggravating circumstances" element. (*105 West 28th Street v. Freeman*, N.Y.L.J., 2/25/98, p. 29, col. 4 (Civ.Ct., N.Y. County).) In this case, there was no allegation that the non-regulated tenant's conduct interfered with the use and enjoyment of the property by other tenants.

 **Talk to a lawyer about how to terminate a tenant who repeatedly fails to pay rent.** The rules on how and when you may terminate the tenancy for chronic rent non-payment vary depending on where your property is located. To be on the safe side, get legal advice before preparing or serving any termination notices on this ground.

## 2. Proving a Nuisance or Objectionable Conduct

Before you terminate a tenancy on the ground of nuisance or objectionable conduct, make sure you have adequate proof of the tenant's actions. If the tenant refuses to move out and you need to go to court to evict, you'll need proof that the tenant continuously created a nuisance or behaved objectionably prior to termination. Here are different kinds of "evidence" you can gather and keep, just in case you later end up in court:

- date-stamped photos or a videotape of unsafe or unsanitary conditions in the rental unit caused by the tenant, or of property damage caused by the tenant
- certified copies of code violations issued as a result of the tenant-caused unsafe or unsanitary conditions or excessive noise
- affidavits from exterminators describing any infestation posed by unsanitary conditions
- invoices from contractors describing repairs made as a result of your tenant's negligence or vandalism
- letters from other tenants complaining about noise or odors emanating from the tenant's unit or complaining about a tenant's objectionable conduct
- a section of pet-stained public hallway carpeting or other pet-damaged property, and
- names, addresses and phone numbers of any tenants, employees or other witnesses whom you can call on to testify about the tenant's actions in a later eviction proceeding.

## 3. Procedure for Termination for Nuisance or Objectionable Conduct

For non-regulated tenancies, the landlord must follow the default procedure for ending tenancies set forth in the lease. If you're using the form lease in this book, see Clause 19 in Chapter 2. Usually, this requires you to first serve the tenant with a notice to cure, describing the pattern of conduct which is creating the nuisance, and warning the tenant that you'll terminate the tenancy in the event

that the conduct doesn't stop within a specified time period, usually ten days or so. If the conduct continues, you may serve a notice of termination.

**If you're not sure if the lease requires a notice to cure before a notice of termination, err on the side of caution and serve a notice to cure.** The tenant may respond favorably by ending the nuisance or behaving better. And if the tenant doesn't mend his ways, you can still send a termination notice.

**To remove a rent-regulated tenant on the basis of nuisance or objectionable conduct, you must serve the tenant with a termination notice (in some cases, preceded by a notice to cure) before going to court.** For rent-controlled units, a copy of the termination notice must be filed with the local DHCR within 48 hours. For details on what notices you must prepare and serve on rent-stabilized and rent-controlled tenants and how and when to do so, see Chapter 15. Start by looking at the chart "Termination Notices at a Glance," at the beginning of Section B in Chapter 15.

You're not required to serve a notice to cure on a state ("ETPA") rent-stabilized tenant who is inflicting serious and substantial injury to you or to the premises. (9 NYCRR § 2501 (d) (2) (iii).) You need only serve a seven-day termination notice.

## E. Grounds for Removing Rent-Regulated Tenants

So long as the tenant pays rent, rent-controlled and rent-stabilized tenancies may be terminated only for specific reasons. Generally, such tenancies may be terminated by the landlord where:

- the tenant violates a substantial obligation of the tenancy (see Section B, above)
- the tenant uses or occupies the premises for an illegal or immoral use (see Section C, above)
- the tenant engages in objectionable conduct or permits a nuisance (see Section D, above)
- the tenant refuses to provide access for necessary repairs or improvements (see Section 1, below)

- the tenant refuses to renew a written lease agreement (see Section 2, below)
- the tenant has failed to use the premises as a primary residence (see Section 3, below)
- the unit is required for the landlord's personal use (see Section 4, below)
- the landlord seeks to withdraw the unit from the rental market (see Section 5, below), or
- the landlord wishes to demolish the premises (see Section 6, below).

**To remove a rent-regulated tenant on the grounds discussed in the following sections, you must follow the notice requirements set by the applicable rent stabilization or rent control laws.** For details on what notices you must prepare and serve on rent-stabilized and rent-controlled tenants and how and when to do so, and the legal authority for termination on various grounds, see Chapter 15. Start by looking at the chart "Termination Notices at a Glance," at the beginning of Section B in Chapter 15.

## 1.  Refusal to Provide Access

A rent-regulated tenant's unreasonable refusal to permit you access to the unit to make necessary repairs or improvements required by law, or to show the unit to prospective purchasers or mortgagees, is a ground for termination. (Unconsol. L. § 8585.1(f); 9 NYCRR § 2524.3(e); 9 NYCRR § 2504.2(e).) For more information on a landlord's right of entry and sample notices requesting access, see Chapter 10.

The procedure for termination for refusal to provide access varies, depending on the applicable rent regulatory system. Here are the basic rules.

### a.  NYC Rent-Stabilized Tenants

Where the landlord seeks access to a rent-stabilized unit in New York City for the purpose of an inspection or a showing, the tenant must first be given at least five days' advance notice so that the parties may attempt to arrange a mutually convenient appointment. (9 NYCRR § 2524.3(e).) If the tenant

fails or refuses to provide access, in most situations you can serve a termination notice (without a cure option) right away. But, if access is a requirement of the lease, and the lease requires that a notice to cure to be served in the event of a violation, you must give your tenant a second chance by serving him with a ten-day written notice to cure the violation. (9 NYCRR § 2524.3(a); *B.A. Associates Equities Corp. v. Baez*, N.Y.L.J., 1/6/93, p. 25, col. 2 (Civ.Ct., Kings County).) If in doubt, serve the notice to cure.

If the tenant continues to refuse to provide access, you may issue a termination notice at least seven calendar days prior to the intended termination date.

### b.  NYS Rent-Stabilized Tenants

You must first serve the tenant with a ten-day written notice to cure the violation. If access is still refused after the notice to cure expires, you may then issue a seven-day notice of termination. A copy of the notice along with an affidavit of service, must be filed with the local DHCR office within seven days after it gets served on the tenant. A notice to cure is not required if the tenant is inflicting serious and substantial injury to you or your property. (9 NYCRR 2504.2.)

### c.  All Rent-Controlled Tenants

A notice to cure is not required. But you must serve a one-month termination notice, unless the tenant is a weekly tenant, in which case you must serve a seven-day termination notice. A copy of the termination notice, along with an affidavit of service, must be filed with the local DHCR office within 48 hours after it is served on the tenant.

## 2.  Refusal to Renew Lease

Landlords are required to offer renewal leases to rent-stabilized tenants (but not to rent-controlled tenants). Chapter 2, Section H, discusses your obligation to offer renewal leases to rent-stabilized tenants and how to prepare a Notice for Renewal.

Some rent-stabilized tenants, however, refuse to sign renewal leases. Perhaps they think that they can postpone a renewal rent increase by not signing the lease. But a tenant's refusal to renew a written lease is a basis for termination, provided the renewal lease is properly prepared and timely offered.

The procedure for termination is as follows.

### a. Rent-Stabilized Tenants

No notice to cure is required for rent-stabilized tenants within or outside New York City. The landlord need only serve the tenant with a 15-day termination notice. (9 NYCRR § 2524.2c(1). 2504.2(f).)

### b. Rent-Controlled Tenants

Landlords aren't required to offer renewal leases to rent-controlled tenants and there's no advantage to be gained from doing so. Nevertheless, if you offer a renewal lease to a rent-controlled tenant, and the tenant refuses to sign it, rent control laws permit you to end the tenancy by serving the tenant with a one-month termination notice. If the tenant is a weekly tenant, serve a seven-day termination notice. (9 NYCRR §§ 2104.3(d)(2), 2204.3(d)(2).) You are not required to obtain a DHCR Certificate of Eviction.

## 3. Non-Primary Residence

Because rent-regulated units are in such short supply, state law requires rent-regulated tenants to use them as a "primary residence." (9 NYCRR § 2524.4(c); 9 NYCRR § 2504.4(d).) The primary residence rule is intended to prevent tenants from using valuable rent-regulated units as occasional residences or as places for friends to stay. Nevertheless, rent-regulated tenants often try to hold onto their apartments after they've moved to another apartment or purchased a home in the suburbs.

 **Chapter 8, Section C, also covers the primary residence requirement.** Specifically, it discusses how a tenant may not be entitled to share a rental unit with immediate family members or roommates unless the tenant uses his or her rental unit as a primary residence.

### a. Special Proof of Non-Primary Residence Required

Any notice served on a tenant to recover a rental unit on the ground of non-primary residence must be carefully worded, and must include the facts that support your claim. In other words, you can't bring a non-primary residence eviction proceeding if you merely think or suspect that the tenant doesn't live in the rental unit anymore. You must do your homework first. Many landlords who suspect that a tenant no longer uses her unit as a primary residence hire private investigators to gather facts for them. Investigators usually have access to computer databases which may turn up a different address where the tenant registers a car, pays bills or has a family—in short, the address where the tenant really lives.

To recover an apartment on the ground of non-primary residence, you must be able to show that the tenant has not maintained an "ongoing, substantial, physical nexus with the premises for actual living purposes as demonstrated by objective, empirical evidence." (*East End Temple v. Silverman*, 199 A.D.2d 94, 605 N.Y.S.2d 56 (1st Dep't 1993).) Although no single factor is solely decisive, evidence which the DHCR has said may be considered in determining whether an apartment is occupied as a primary residence includes:

(1) specifying an address other than the apartment as a place of residence on any tax return, motor vehicle registration, driver's license or other document filed with a public agency

(2) using an address other than the apartment as a voting address

(3) occupying the apartment for an aggregate of less than 183 days of the most recent calendar year, except for temporary periods of reloca-

tion for military service, enrollment as a full time student, employment requiring temporary relocation, or hospitalization for medical treatment, or

(4) subletting the apartment. (9 NYCRR § 2520.6(u).)

After you begin a "non-primary residence" eviction proceeding against a tenant, you can usually get the court's permission to engage in so-called "discovery" proceedings. During the discovery stage of your eviction proceeding, you can demand copies of the tenant's tax returns, monthly bills and other documents that may establish a different primary residence for the tenant. (Chapter 8, Section C4, provides more details on this type of evidence.) You can even require the tenant to answer oral or written questions under oath. But if you bring a proceeding like this on a hunch and can't come up with proof of a different full-time residence for the tenant, you'll end up losing the case and very possibly paying the tenant's legal fees. (Chapter 2, Clause 20, discusses lease clauses that entitle landlords and tenants to recover attorneys' fees.)

## b. NYC Rent-Stabilized Tenant

If a NYC rent-stabilized tenant does not use the rental unit as a primary residence, you have grounds to refuse to renew the tenant's lease and evict the tenant at the end of the current lease term. To terminate the tenancy, you must first serve a notice of non-renewal during the 90- to 150-day "window period" prior the expiration of the tenant's current lease. In addition, you must provide a 30-day termination notice. You can combine both notices in the notice of non-renewal.

## c. NYS Rent-Stabilized Tenants

If a NYS rent-stabilized (ETPA) tenant does not use the rental unit as a primary residence, you have grounds to refuse to renew the tenant's lease and evict the tenant at the end of the current lease term. You must serve the tenant with a 30-day termination notice. An exact copy of the termination notice,

along with proof of service, must be filed with your local DHCR office within seven days of the day you serve the termination notice on the tenant. It is unsettled whether the landlord must also serve a "notice of non-renewal" during the 90- to 120-day "window period" prior to the expiration of the tenant's lease (at which time a renewal lease would ordinarily be required to be offered). (9 NYCRR § 2503.5(a).) While neither the Emergency Tenant Protection Act nor the Regulations require the landlord to serve a notice of non-renewal, some courts have suggested that such a notice is nevertheless necessary. (*Crow v. 83rd Street Assoc.*, 68 N.Y.2d 796, 506 N.Y.S.2d 858, 498 N.E.2d 422 (1986).)

To be on the safe side, ask an attorney in your area if you must serve both a notice of non-renewal and a notice of termination during the window period.

## d. NYC Rent-Controlled Tenants

If a New York City rent-controlled tenant does not use the unit as a primary residence, you may terminate the tenancy. You must serve the tenant with a 30-Day Notice of Termination. No DHCR Certificate of Eviction is required. (*Berman v. Keeton*, 727 N.Y.S.2d 156 (2nd Dep't, 2001.) The termination notice must not only state the ground for removal—that the tenant does not use the premises as a primary residence—but must also recite the facts that will prove this. In addition, you must file an exact copy of the notice of termination, along with an affidavit of service, with the local DHCR office within 48 hours of service of the notice on the tenant.

## e. NYS Rent-Controlled Tenants

For New York State rent-controlled tenants, you must apply to the DHCR for a Certificate of Eviction to be issued for the removal of a tenant who does not use the unit as his or her primary dwelling. (Unconsol. L. § 8585.2(b).) After the certificate of eviction has been issued, serve the tenant with a one-month termination notice.

## 4. Recovery for Owner's Personal Use

In many cases, an owner-landlord may recover possession of a rent-regulated unit for his or her own use or for the use of an immediate family member. The Rent Reform Act of 2000 broadened the definition of immediate family member for all four systems of rent regulation to include the following relatives of the owner: spouse, son, daughter, stepson, stepdaughter, father, mother, stepfather, stepmother, brother, sister, grandfather, grandmother, grandson, granddaughter, father-in-law, mother-in-law, son-in-law or daughter-in-law. (See, for example, 9 NYCRR (RSC) § 2520.6(n).)

**Exemptions.** *Unless* the tenant is offered equivalent or superior housing at the same or lower regulated rent in a "closely proximate area," the landlord may not recover the unit for owner's use where the tenant or the tenant's spouse is:

- a senior citizen, age 62 or older,
- disabled, or

- depending on the system of rent regulations that apply, a tenant of the apartment for 20 years or more. (Uncon. Laws § 8630, subds. a, b; 9 NYCCR §§ 2204.5, 2504.4(a)(2), 2524.4(a)(2).) This 20-year rule applies to rent-controlled tenants statewide and to ETPA rent-stabilized tenants who live outside New York City. Long-term New York City rent-stabilized tenants are *not* protected by the 20-year rule and may be evicted to make way for the owner. (*Brusco v. Armstrong*, N.Y.L.J., 2/6/02, p. 19, col. 1 (App. Term., 1st Dep't).)

⚠ **Corporate landlords and other business entities may not recover apartments on the ground of recovery for owner's personal use.** The building must be owned by one or more individuals.

### Owners of Co-Op/Condo Buildings, Take Note

If you own a unit that is occupied by a "non-purchasing tenant" in a building that has been converted from a rental building to a cooperative or condominium, you may not recover the apartment for your personal use on or after the date the plan to convert the building to cooperative or condominium ownership is declared effective by the Office of the Attorney General. (9 NYCRR § 2524.4(a)(1); see GBL § 352-eeee.) For more information, contact the Attorney General's office at 120 Broadway, New York, NY 10271, 212-416-8000 (www.oag.state.ny.us).

### a. NYC Rent-Stabilized Tenants

You may refuse to renew the lease and terminate a rent-stabilized tenancy in order to recover possession of the unit for your personal use and occupancy, or for that of an immediate family member, for use as a primary residence. (9 NYCRR § 2524.4(a)(1).) To win an eviction proceeding on this ground, the owner-landlord must demonstrate a "good faith" intention to occupy the apartment for personal or family use. (*Nestor v. Britt*, 213 A.D.2d 255, 624 N.Y.S.2d 14 (1st Dep't 1995).) Once recovered, the landlord or family member must remain in occupancy for at least three years. (9 NYCRR § 2524.4(a)(5).)

Corporate landlords may not recover units on this ground. (*Fanelli v. NYC Conciliation and Appeals Bd.*, 90 A.D.2d 756, 455 N.Y.S.2d 814 (1st Dep't 1982) aff'd 58 N.Y.2d 952, 460 N.Y.S.2d 534, 447 N.E.2d 82 (1983).) The law is not settled, however, as to whether a principal in a partnership may recover a unit for personal use or for use by an immediate family member. While some courts have permitted individual partners of a partnership to recover units for their own occupancy, at least one court has ruled that a partnership landlord may not evict a tenant on this ground. (*Hart Realty v. Schneider*, N.Y.L.J., 5/25/94, p. 28, col. 3 (Civ.Ct. N.Y. County).)

 If your building is owned in a partnership name, ask your attorney for advice before terminating a tenancy on the ground of recovery for owner's use.

**Termination procedure.** You must serve the NYC rent-stabilized tenant with a notice of non-renewal during the 90- to 150-day window period before the expiration of the tenant's current lease. The notice should state the full name of the person who will be occupying the rental unit after it is recovered, and that person's relationship to the owner-landlord. A DHCR Certificate of Eviction is not required.

**Failure to use the unit as a primary residence for three years could jeopardize rent increases.** If you recover a unit for your personal use, or that of an immediate family member, you must use it as a primary residence for at least three years. If the apartment is vacated early, or used as a secondary residence, you may lose the right to any rent increases for other apartments in the same building for a three-year period.

### b.   NYS Rent-Stabilized Tenants

You may refuse to renew a lease of a New York State (ETPA) rent-stabilized tenant when you can establish "an immediate and compelling need" to recover the apartment for you or an immediate family member's personal use and occupancy. (9 NYCRR 2504.4(a).) To be eligible to recover an apartment on this ground, the owner of the property must be a "natural person"—not a corporation or other business entity. If the building is owned by more than one person, only one of the individual owners may recover up to two units in the building. If the same owner seeks an additional unit for her use or the use of an immediate family member, the owner must offer the tenant whose apartment is sought, a comparable unit in the building at the same or lower rent, plus relocation expenses.

**Termination procedure.** Before commencing a holdover eviction proceeding to recover the premises, the landlord must first apply to DHCR for a Certificate of Eviction. File an Owner's Application for Order Granting Approval to Refuse to Renew Lease and/or Proceed for Eviction, DHCR Form RA-54. It's available from your local DHCR office or by calling DHCR's Infoline (718-739-6400).

### c.   All Rent-Controlled Tenants

You must apply for and obtain a DHCR Certificate of Eviction before seeking to remove a rent-controlled tenant on the ground of recovery for owner's use. (9 NYCRR § 2204.5(a); 9 NYCRR § 2104.5(a)(1).) The DHCR will issue a certificate if it finds that you seek in good faith to recover possession of the unit because of "immediate and compelling necessity" for your personal use and occupancy or for that of your immediate family. (Unconsol. L. § 8585.2(a); 9 NYCRR § 2204.5(a); 9 NYCRR § 2104.5(a)(1).)

To be entitled to recover the unit on the basis of owner's use, the owner-landlord must be an individual, and not a corporation or partnership. (*Burke v. Joy*, 99 A.D.2d 952, 472 N.Y.S.2d 643 (1st Dep't 1984); *Henrock Realty v. Tuck*, 52 A.D.2d 871, 383 N.Y.S.2d 47 (2d Dep't 1976).)

Under a complex set of regulations, certain rent-controlled tenants who live in buildings owned by cooperative corporations and condominium associations are also exempt. For more information see 9 NYCRR 2104.5(b) and (c) for NYS rent-controlled units and 9 NYCRR § 2204.2(a)(7) or speak with an attorney who specializes in rent-regulatory law.

## 5. Withdrawal of Unit From Rental Market

Under certain circumstances, a landlord may terminate a rent-regulated tenancy in order to permanently withdraw the unit from the market. The circumstances and procedure depend on the unit's location and whether it's subject to rent stabilization or rent control.

### a. NYC Rent-Stabilized Units

You may refuse to renew a rent-stabilized tenant's lease if you seek in good faith to withdraw the unit from both the housing and non-housing markets. You must have no intention of renting or selling all or part of the land or structure. (9 NYCRR §2524.5(a)(1).) You must be able to establish that:

- you require all or part of the rental unit or the land for use in connection with a business you own and operate, or
- substantial violations which constitute fire hazards or conditions dangerous to the life or health of the tenants have been filed against the building and the cost of removing these violations would equal or exceed the building's assessed valuation.

**Termination procedure.** You should apply to the DHCR for a Certificate of Eviction. While the application is pending, send a notice of non-renewal during the 90- to 150-day window period prior to the expiration of the tenant's lease. (9 NYCRR § 2524.5(a)(1).)

### b. NYS Rent-Stabilized Units

You may refuse to renew a NYS rent-stabilized (ETPA) tenant's lease if you seek in good faith to withdraw the tenant's rental unit from both the housing and non-housing rental markets. You can't have any intent to rent or sell all or any part of the land or structure. (9 NYCRR § 2504.4(b).)

**Termination procedure.** You must apply to the DHCR for a Certificate of Eviction.

### c. All Rent-Controlled Units

You may end a rent-controlled tenancy if you can establish that you seek to permanently withdraw the tenant's rental unit from both the non-housing and housing markets, without any intent to rent or sell all or part of the land or structure. You'll need to obtain a DHCR Certificate of Eviction. (9 NYCRR § 2104.9; 9 NYCRR § 2204.9(a).) To be eligible for the Certificate, you must establish that:

- you require the entire structure containing the unit or the land for your own immediate use in connection with a business you own and operate in the immediate vicinity of the property
- substantial violations affecting tenant health and safety have been placed on the structure and the cost to remove the violations would substantially equal or exceed the building's value, as assessed for property tax purposes
- you are an institution operated exclusively for charitable, religious or educational purposes, and the unit is required for your immediate use in connection with its charitable, religious or educational functions (9 NYCRR § 2104.9(c); 9 NYCRR § 2204.9(a)(3).), or
- continued operation of the rental unit would impose other undue hardship. (9 NYCRR § 2104.9(d); 9 NYCRR § 2204.9(a)(4).)

## 6. Demolition of the Building

In some cases, you may terminate a tenancy in order to demolish your building. There are important limitations to this termination right, depending on whether the tenant is rent-controlled or rent-stabilized, and where the building is located.

## a. All Rent-Stabilized Tenants

You may refuse to renew a tenant's lease if you intend to demolish the entire building. But, before you may seek a tenant's eviction, you must apply for and obtain a DHCR Certificate of Eviction. The Certificate will be granted if you can demonstrate (1) that plans for the new building have been filed with or approved by the New York City Department of Buildings, and (2) a financial ability to complete the project. (NYCRR 2524.5(a)(2).)

For more information, take a look at DHCR Operational Bulletin 2002-1, "Procedures Pursuant to the Rent Stabilization Code for the Filing of an Owner's Application to Refuse to Renew Leases on the Grounds of Demolition, Implementing Emergency Tenant Protection Regulations." It details the eligibility and notice requirements. In many cases, the DHCR may require you to offer tenants relocation assistance, payment of moving expenses and/or a stipend. To obtain a copy of the bulletin, request one from the DHCR Infoline 718-739-6400, download it from the DHCR website (www.dhcr.ny.us) or pick one up at your local DHCR office.

## b. All Rent-Controlled Tenants

You can terminate a rent-controlled tenancy for the immediate purpose of demolishing the building and constructing a new commercial building or a new residential building that contains at least 20 percent more rental units than the building being demolished. (Unconsol. L. § 8585.2(d); 9 NYCRR §§ 2204.8, 2104.8.) DHCR may reduce the 20% requirement where there are outstanding fire and housing code violations issued against the building, which would be prohibitively expensive to correct—that is, if the costs would equal or exceed the value of the building for tax purposes.

Before terminating the tenancy, you must first apply for and obtain a DHCR Certificate of Eviction.

To qualify for the Certificate, you must already have secured the appropriate governmental approvals for the demolition. After the Certificate is granted, you must serve the tenant with a 30-day termination notice if the property is in New York City, and a one-month termination notice if the property is located elsewhere in the State.

DHCR Operational Bulletin 2002-1 details your obligations to pay tenant moving expenses, provide relocation assistance and/or pay a stipend. Subsection a, above, describes how to obtain the Bulletin.

## 7. Roommate Overcharge by Rent-Stabilized Tenant

The rent stabilization regulations now put limits on the amount of rent tenants may charge their roommates. Effective December 2000, tenants may not charge unrelated non-tenant roommates a rent that exceeds the roommate's proportionate share of the legal rent for the unit. (9 NYCRR §§ 2525.7(b); 2502.8.)

A roommate's proportionate share is calculated by dividing the legal regulated rent by the total number of tenants and occupants residing in the unit. The tenant's spouse, family members and dependent children are not counted as occupants under this formula. The formula is based solely on a head count, and does not take into account the actual relative square footage or number of rooms in the unit occupied by the roommate.

The regulations, intended to shield roommates from profiteering tenants, may also be used as a sword by landlords. Rent-stabilized tenants who overcharge their subtenants are subject to eviction, according to one intermediate appellate court decision. (*Ram I. LLC v. Mazzola*, N.Y.L.J., 1/2/02, p. 18, col.1 (App. Term, 1st Dep't).) So if you get wind of a roommate overcharge, both the prime and subtenants are vulnerable to eviction. According to the decision, no prior notice to cure is required, meaning that the rent-stabilized tenant will not get a chance to fix the overcharge before termination. Before going to court to evict a tenant on this ground, you must issue a seven-day termination notice.

## F. Tenant's Right of Termination

If a tenant leaves before a fixed-term lease ends, you are usually entitled to the balance of the rent due under the lease, less any rent you receive from new tenants (or, in certain areas, could have received if you had made a diligent effort to re-rent the property). In legalese, this is known as the landlord's duty to mitigate damages, and is discussed in Chapter 16, Section F2.

If you violate a substantial obligation of the lease, like failing to make repairs, the tenant may sue for money damages or a rent abatement. But if you repeatedly violate the lease, and create a condition that threatens the tenant's health or safety, the tenant would probably have a legal excuse to break the lease and move out without further liability for rent. For example, if the front door lock of your building is continuously in disrepair, through no fault of the tenant, the tenant would probably be justified in moving out if she had a legitimate fear for her safety.

In some cases, state law provides tenants with a specific right of termination. We discuss these laws in Sections 1 through 3, below. Whenever possible, arrange for tenants who have a right of termination under state law to sign a surrender agreement when they move out. (Section G, below, explains how lease surrenders work and supplies a form you can use for this purpose.) By getting a surrender agreement from the tenant, you can safely take steps to immediately re-rent the unit.

## 1. Termination by Tenant Senior Citizens

New York RPL § 227-a permits eligible senior citizens to terminate their leases in order to move in with a relative or relocate to certain types of housing. Here are the rules.

### a. Eligible Tenants

A tenant who is 62 or older, or who will turn 62 during the lease term, is eligible to terminate the lease. So are spouses of tenants who are 62 or who will turn 62 during the lease term.

EXAMPLE: Millie, 58, is the tenant of a Bronx apartment. She shares the unit with her second husband, Herbert, who is 64. Millie is eligible for protection under the statute.

Depending on their destination, eligible tenants may be able to terminate their lease early, without any further rent liability. Moving in with a family member for medical reasons and moving to a specified facility may both qualify for early lease termination.

### b. Moving in with a Family Member for Medical Reasons

For tenants with medical conditions, living alone or dealing with stairs, for instance, can make daily personal activities difficult. At times like this, moving in with a son, daughter or other relative can make life a lot easier. The law permits eligible tenants to terminate their leases to move to a family member's home, if they can satisfy two requirements.

First, the tenant or tenant's spouse must be certified by a physician as no longer being able, for medical reasons, to live independently in the rental unit, because she needs help with basic daily activities, such as cooking or bathing. A letter from a doctor (on his or her letterhead) should suffice. The second requirement is a notarized statement from a family member stating that the tenant (or tenant's spouse) is related, and that the tenant will be moving into the family member's home for at least six months or pending admission to one of the facilities listed below. Notarized means that the family member must sign the statement before a licensed notary public.

The doctor's certification and notarized family statement must be attached to the tenant's termination notice, explained in Subsection d, below.

### c. Moving to a Specified Facility

The statute also permits eligible tenants to terminate their leases if they are moving to one of the following specified facilities:

- an adult care facility

- a residential healthcare facility
- a public or privately-subsidized housing unit, or
- a less expensive unit in a housing project or complex for senior citizens.

### d. Procedure for Termination

To terminate the lease, your tenant must give you or your agent written notice of his intention to end the tenancy. The notice may be delivered personally or by mail. If hand delivered, the termination is deemed effective thirty days after the date that the tenant's next rental payment is due. If mailed, the termination is effective 35 days after the tenant's next rent payment due date.

> **EXAMPLE:** On September 5th, Stanley mails a letter to his landlord Gustavo notifying him that he is moving into an adult care facility. The letter is deemed effective September 10—five days after it is mailed. Stanley's next rent payment is due October 1, so Stanley's termination is effective October 31—30 days later. If Stanley moves out on or before October 31, he is released from any further rent liability under the lease.

If the tenant is moving in with a relative, the notice must be accompanied by a physician's certification and a notarized statement from a family member, as explained in Subsection b, above.

If the tenant is moving to one of the facilities described in Subsection c, above, the tenant must document his admission or pending admission with a copy of an executed lease or contract between him and the facility.

## 2. Termination by Military Tenants

The events of 9/11 and the war in the Middle East have led to the potential call of up to 500,000 reservists into active duty. Tenants entering "military service" may terminate a lease upon written notice to the landlord. (NY Mil. L. § 310.) Military service means active full-time duty in the United States Army, Navy, Marine Corps, Air Force, Coast Guard and the Army National Guard, Air National Guard, and the New York Naval Militia and New York Guard. Any landlord or agent who interferes with the removal of the tenant's property from the rental unit, after proper termination of the tenancy, may be found guilty of a criminal misdemeanor and imprisoned for up to a year, fined up to $1,000 or both.

The tenant may terminate the tenancy at any time after the date active, full-time military service begins. To properly terminate the lease, the tenant must prepare a written notice stating that she has elected to terminate her tenancy under Mil. L. § 310. The statute permits this notice to be personally delivered or sent to you via regular mail.

If the tenant pays rent monthly under a lease, the termination is effective 30 days after the first date on which the next rental payment is due after delivery or mailing of the notice. For all other tenancies, termination is effective on the last day of the month following the month in which such notice is delivered or mailed.

> **EXAMPLE 1:** Upset by the World Trade Center attacks, your tenant Pedro decides to join the Marines. After receiving induction papers, Pedro sends you a notice that he is terminating his lease to enter military service. Pedro mails the letter on April 12. His next rental payment is due May 1. The lease terminates May 31—30 days later.

> **EXAMPLE 2:** On June 29, your tenant Georgette, an Air Force reservist, receives orders to report to McGuire Air Force Base the following month. On June 30, Georgette mails you a letter terminating her lease to enter military service. Georgette's next rent payment is due July 1. The lease terminates July 31—30 days later.

Upon termination, the tenant is released from further rent liability. You must refund any advance rent the tenant paid for a period after the termination date.

### 3. Tenant's Right to Terminate Because of Defective Conditions at the Property

In certain circumstances, tenants are entitled to move out because the property is seriously damaged or destroyed. Chapter 9, Section E3, covers this topic, known as "constructive eviction," in detail.

## G. When a Tenant Volunteers to Leave

Sometimes, a tenant will ask if they can break the lease and move out early. In many situations, you'll want to consent to this arrangement. If the unit is rent-stabilized, a vacancy will entitle you to a hefty rent increase. (Chapter 4 explains how rent-stabilized rents may be increased upon a vacancy.) And even if the unit isn't regulated, you may be able to get a lot more rent from a new tenant in a robust rental market. Finally, if the tenant is a troublemaker, it will be cheaper in the long run to release the tenant from the lease than to be engaged in a possibly protracted eviction proceeding.

Of course, sometimes, you may not want the tenant to break the lease—for example, if you're in a tight rental market where tenants are hard to come by. (Chapter 16, Section F, discusses the tenant's liability for unpaid rent in this situation.)

But don't just collect the keys from the departing tenant and wave good-bye. Require the tenant to sign a Lease Surrender Agreement as a condition to your consent to end the lease early. By signing a Lease Surrender Agreement, the departing tenant agrees to terminate the tenancy and relinquish all tenancy rights, including the right to occupy the unit.

 You will find the Lease Surrender Agreement on the Forms CD and a blank tear-out copy in Appendix IV.

## H. Succession Rights to Rent-Regulated Units

Rent-controlled and rent-stabilized tenants often share their apartments with family members or roommates. If the rent-regulated tenant dies or voluntarily moves out, the remaining occupant may, under certain circumstances, have a "succession right" which entitles them to stay in the unit. If the rent-regulated tenant moves out in response to a termination notice or is evicted, succession rights aren't available to occupants. Occupants who have succession rights to rent-stabilized units are entitled to renewal leases. (9 NYCRR § 2503.5(d)(1); 9 NYCRR § 2523.5(b)(1).) Occupants who have succession rights to rent-controlled units are protected from eviction. (9 NYCRR § 2104.4(d); 9 NYCRR § 2204.6(d).)

This section describes the circumstances in which tenancy rights to a rent-regulated unit may be "passed on" to a non-tenant occupant.

### 1. What Occupants Are Eligible for Succession?

Only certain family members are entitled to stay in a unit. However, the definition of family member also includes non-relatives with whom the tenant shared a close relationship, such as a live-in lover or life companion. (*Braschi v. Stahl Assocs.*, 74 N.Y.2d 201, 544 N.Y.S.2d 784, 543 N.E.2d 49 (1989).)

Family members include a tenant's spouse, children, stepchildren, parents, stepparents, brothers, sisters, grandparents, grandchildren, fathers-in-law, mothers-in-law, sons-in-law or daughters-in-law. (Pub. Housing L. § 14.4.)

 **Nephews, nieces, aunts and uncles are no longer included in the definition of "family members."** The Rent Regulation Reform Act of 1997 limited the types of family members who are entitled to succession rights. Previously, rent-regulated units could be passed on to nephews, nieces, aunts and uncles.

### Lease Surrender Agreement

Max Morganstern _____ (Landlord)

and __ Lili Park _____ (Tenant)

agree as follows:

1. Tenant hereby surrenders all right, title and interest in his/her tenancy of the premises known as and located at __Apartment 3B, 271 Park Avenue, New York, NY 10017__ _____ (Premises), effective __October 31, 200X.__ .

2. Landlord and Tenant agree that the Lease for the Premises entered into on __January 1, 200X__ _____ will terminate on __October 31, 200X.__ .

3. Tenant agrees to vacate the Premises on or before __October 31, 200X__ and to remove all his/her personal property and possession from the Premises on or before that date.


__October 31, 200X__          _Max Morganstern_ _____
Date                                          Landlord

__October 3, 200X__          _Lili Park_ _____
Date                                          Tenant

The definition of "family member" under the succession rules also includes any other person residing with the tenant as a primary resident, who can prove having shared an "emotional and financial commitment and interdependence" with the tenant. (9 NYCRR § 2104.6(d)(3)(i); 9 NYCRR § 2204.6(d)(3)(i); 9 NYCRR § 2500.2(n)(2); 9 NYCRR § 2520.6(o)(2).) Whether the tenant and an unrelated occupant have shared the requisite emotional and financial commitment and interdependence depends on:

- the longevity of the relationship
- a sharing of or relying upon each other for payment of household or family expenses, and/or other common necessities of life
- intermingling of finances, such as joint owner- ship of bank accounts, personal and real property, credit cards and loan obligations and sharing a household budget for purposes of receiving government benefits
- engaging in family-type activities by jointly attending family functions, holidays and celebrations, social and recreational activities
- formalizing legal obligations, intentions and responsibilities to each other, such as execut- ing joint wills, naming each other as executor and/or beneficiary, granting each other a power of attorney and/or conferring upon each other authority to make healthcare decisions each for the other, entering into a personal relationship contract, making a domestic partnership declaration and serving as a representative payee for purposes of public benefits
- holding themselves out as family members to their relatives, friends, members of the com- munity or religious institutions or society in general, through their works or actions
- regularly performing family functions, such as caring for each other's extended family members and/or relying upon each other for daily family services, or
- engaging in any other pattern of behavior, agreement or other action which evidences a long-term, emotionally committed relationship.

The determination of whether an occupant is a "family member" is not limited to any one factor or group of factors. And in no event may questions about any sexual relationship between such persons be requested by the landlord or considered by a court in making a determination as to whether the occupant qualifies as a "family member."

EXAMPLE: A Manhattan occupant was permitted to succeed to a rent-stabilized apartment when it was established that he had lived in the unit with the tenant of record for ten years, that they had vacationed and traveled in common and "held themselves out as a couple." Additionally, the occupant had cared for the tenant during his "final illness" and was designated executor and beneficiary of the tenant's residual estate under a will and the beneficiary of a trust ac- count. (*RSP Realty Associates v. Paegeo*, N.Y.L.J., 8/14/92, p. 21, col. 4 (App.Term, 1st Dep't).)

## 2. Residency Requirements

To be eligible to stay in the unit, the family member must demonstrate that, prior to the tenant's move out or death, he principally resided at the premises for whichever of the following time periods is shorter:

- for at least two years (one year if the occupant is disabled or over 62 years of age)
- from the beginning of his relationship with the tenant, or
- from the inception of the tenancy (9 NYCRR § 2104.6(d)(1); 9 NYCRR § 2204.6(d)(1); 9 NYCRR § 2503.5(d)(1); 9 NYCRR § 2523.5(b)(1).)

Moreover, the minimum periods of required residency are not considered interrupted by any period during which a family member temporarily relocates because he or she is:

- engaged in active military duty
- enrolled as a full-time student
- hospitalized for medical treatment, or
- engaged in employment requiring temporary relocation from the rental unit.

Chapter 8, Section B, explains how to find out who lives in a rental unit, information that is important should you need to remove unauthorized occupants.

### 3. Tenant's Successor May Not Pass on Unit Without Rent Increase

If a successor tenant passes on a rental unit to yet another family member, you're entitled to collect vacancy guideline increases and vacancy "bonuses" from the second successor tenant. (Chapter 4 explains how to calculate these rent increases.) The right of a family member to receive a renewal lease or to be protected from eviction after the tenant leaves, without being required to pay the owner a vacancy increase, is limited to the first family member who receives a renewal lease or is protected from eviction. After that, you're entitled to collect all applicable vacancy increases from any new family member who is entitled to receive a lease or to remain in possession.

EXAMPLE: Greta vacated a rent-stabilized apartment on August 1, 2003. Myra, Greta's granddaughter, who has lived with Greta as a primary resident of the apartment for three years, is entitled to receive a renewal lease for the apartment without paying the landlord any vacancy increases. Myra signs, in Myra's name only, a renewal lease starting September 1, 2003. Paul, Myra's brother, began to live with Greta and Myra shortly before Greta left. If Myra were to leave the apartment after two years, and Paul was entitled to receive a lease in Paul's own name because of the succession rules, Paul would be required to pay to the owner all applicable vacancy increases authorized by the rent stabilization laws.

## I. Retaliatory Evictions Prohibited

The threat of eviction is a powerful weapon. Unfortunately, some landlords misuse it to intimidate tenants from making legitimate housing complaints to government agencies and authorities, filing legal proceedings or lawsuits to enforce tenant rights or organizing tenant associations. To keep landlords from threatening termination, or using eviction proceedings to get even with tenants, the state legisla-

ture enacted New York RPL § 223-b. It prohibits landlords from serving a termination notice or starting an eviction proceeding in retaliation for a tenant's having asserted her rights as a tenant. In this section, we'll explain how the statute works and what is prohibited.

### 1. What the Retaliatory Eviction Statute Says

The statute prohibits landlords from serving a termination notice upon any tenant, or commencing any legal action or proceeding to recover possession of a rental unit in retaliation for a tenant's:

- good faith complaint to a governmental authority about a violation of any housing-related law, regulation code or ordinance, such as a no-heat complaint to a housing code enforcement agency, or a rent-overcharge complaint to the DHCR
- legal action to enforce any rights granted under the lease, the warranty of habitability or any other housing law, or
- participation in the activities of a tenants' organization in their building or community.

If a landlord terminates a tenancy to get even with a tenant for making a complaint, bringing a legal action or participating in a tenants' organization (as explained above), and then starts an eviction proceeding, the tenant may raise "retaliatory eviction" as a defense in her answer to the landlord's eviction petition and seek damages for its violation against the landlord. If the tenant proves retaliation (see Section 2, below), the eviction case is dismissed and the tenant may be entitled to money damages resulting from the landlord's spurious eviction lawsuit.

### 2. Statute Makes It Easier to Prove Retaliation

The statute that protects tenants from landlord retaliation provides certain legal "presumptions" to help a tenant prove that his landlord's motive is retaliatory and defeat eviction. Here's how. Under the statute, a landlord's action to terminate a tenancy or evict is *legally presumed* to be retaliatory if the landlord served a termination notice or began a holdover proceeding within six months after the tenant took any of the following types of action:

- complained to a government agency or authority about an alleged violation of any housing-related law, regulation, code or ordinance
- began a lawsuit or administrative proceeding against you to enforce tenant rights under your rental agreement, under the warranty of habitability or other housing laws or regulations, or
- secured an inspection, order or other action in response to a complaint or won a judgment against the landlord in a lawsuit or administrative proceeding.

The effect of the legal presumption built into the anti-retaliation statute is that, without proving anything else, the tenant will win unless the landlord steps forward with evidence that will knock down the presumption. If the landlord can convince the judge that the tenant violated a substantial tenancy obligation, created a nuisance or used the rental unit for an illegal purpose, the landlord may get beyond the presumption. If a court finds that the landlord's real motive is retaliation, and further finds that the landlord wouldn't otherwise have termi-

nated the tenancy or begun an eviction proceeding against the tenant, the eviction proceeding is dismissed and the landlord is subject to civil damages. (RPL § 223-b (3); see also *Mayfair York LLC v. Zimmerman*, 702 N.Y.S.2d 494 (Civ. Ct., N.Y. County, 1999).)

**Not all tenants are entitled to the legal presumptions created by statute.** The statute applies to all rental units except owner-occupied dwellings with fewer than four units. (RPL § 223-b.) Tenants in these smaller buildings must produce evidence of the landlord's retaliatory motive.

## Tenants' Right to Organize

Tenants have a legal right to organize with other renters in the same property or community. They may form, join and participate in tenants' organizations for the purpose of protecting their rights. Landlords may not harass or penalize tenants who exercise this right. Tenants' groups have the right to meet in any common area in their building, such as lobbies and halls, in a peaceful manner, at reasonable hours, without obstructing access to the premises or facilities. (Real PPL § 230.)

# How to Prepare and Serve Notices Terminating Leases and Rent-Regulated Tenancies

The linchpin of an eviction lawsuit is properly terminating the tenancy before you go to court. You can't proceed with your lawsuit, let alone get a judgment for possession of your property or for unpaid rent, without ending the tenancy first.

This chapter explains how to prepare and serve various types of legal notices that end a lease or rent-regulated tenancy and set the stage for the tenant's eventual eviction. But before drafting any of the notices in this chapter, you must first determine that you have a legal right to end the tenancy. Chapter 14 explains the different grounds upon which you may legally terminate a lease or rent-regulated tenancy. Once you've determined that you are legally entitled to end the tenancy, you can consult this chapter to find out what type of notice or notices you must prepare to end the tenancy and how to deliver or serve them to the tenant.

Terminating a tenancy is tricky business— especially when the tenant has a lease or is covered by rent control or rent stabilization. Landlords must strictly comply with all of the requirements of New York law when it comes to preparing and serving default and termination notices. If you make even a small mistake in a required notice, or if the tenant doesn't receive the notice, the termination might be invalid and you may have to start the process all over again.

**Be meticulous in preparing notices.** Because an eviction judgment means the tenant won't have a roof over his head (and his children's heads), judges presiding over eviction proceedings tend to be very picky about default and termination notices. If your notice isn't letter-perfect, the judge can throw out your eviction proceeding and require you to start all over again with a new notice to the tenant. Our advice is to be meticulous in your business practices and notice preparation. Follow our directions carefully. If you're unsure about notice requirements or have any doubt about the language or validity of your termination notice, consult an attorney specializing in landlord-tenant law.

 **For rent-regulated tenancies, consider hiring an experienced landlord-tenant lawyer to prepare or review your termination notices.** Faced with termination, many rent-controlled and rent-stabilized tenants will make every effort to preserve their tenancy. If you end up suing to evict a rent-regulated tenant who has refused to move out, the tenant may look for every possible way to attack the legal and factual adequacy of your termination notices. Judges tend to put these notices under a microscope. If a notice is found lacking, you won't get a second chance to make it right. Your eviction proceeding will get dismissed, and you'll need to start all over again by serving new termination notices. To avoid this fate, hire an experienced landlord-tenant attorney to prepare the notices you need or, at minimum, to review the adequacy of any notice you've prepared yourself before it's served on the tenant.

### What If the Tenant Won't Leave?

Ideally, once you've served the appropriate notices and legally ended the tenancy, the tenant will move out and you can get back to the business of landlording. In a small percentage of cases, however, things won't go smoothly and the tenant will refuse to leave when the tenancy ends—especially if leaving means giving up a valuable rent-controlled or rent-stabilized tenancy. Tenants who stay in a rental unit without permission after their tenancy ends are called "holdover" tenants, since they hold over in the unit after the expiration of their tenancy. When a tenant refuses to leave, you must go to court and bring a "holdover" proceeding to evict the tenant, as well as any non-tenant occupants, such as roommates, who share the rental unit with the tenant. Holdover eviction proceedings are described in Chapter 14, Section A ("Overview of Evictions").

Related topics covered in this book include:

- Drafting lease default and termination notice requirements: Chapter 2
- Understanding rent control and rent stabilization laws and determining what rental units are covered: Chapter 4
- Evicting a resident manager: Chapter 6
- Tenant options if landlord substantially fails to maintain rental property so that all or part of the premises is unlivable (constructive eviction): Chapter 9
- Starting the tenancy termination process for non-payment of rent: Chapter 12.
- Serving legal notices on tenants and preparing proof of service: Chapter 12
- Ending a month-to-month tenancy: Chapter 13
- Reasons why you or the tenant can legally terminate a fixed-term lease or rent-regulated tenancy: Chapter 14
- Using a security deposit to cover unpaid rent after you've terminated a tenancy: Chapter 16
- How to get legal help for an eviction lawsuit: Chapter 17.

## A. Termination Basics

Generally, you can end a tenancy by serving the tenant with one or more legal notices, such as a "notice to cure" and a "notice of termination." The "Termination Notices at a Glance" chart, below, provides an overview of what kind of notices you need to end a tenancy and how and when to serve them. As you'll see from the chart, the specifics vary depending on whether your property is unregulated, rent stabilized or rent regulated. Later sections in this chapter provide the step-by-step instructions and forms you need to properly terminate a fixed-term or rent-regulated tenancy.

Here's a guide to using the "Termination Notices at a Glance" chart.

### 1. Termination Ground

The first column on the chart lists the legal reasons you may end a tenancy, such as violation of a substantial lease obligation, and refers you to the section of Chapter 14 which provides more detail on this particular termination ground. It's important to read the appropriate section in Chapter 14 in order to understand whether it's the tenant's conduct or your special circumstances that have triggered your right to terminate. You'll also need to know whether the tenant fits into any exemptions from termination that sometimes apply. Diplomats, for example, may be protected from eviction as discussed in Chapter 1, Section C.

### 2. Authority for Termination

The second column lists the legal authority that gives you the right to end a tenancy for a particular reason. In some cases, this will be a specific lease

clause and in others, it will be a specific law or regulation. You'll need to cite this lease clause, statute and/or regulation when filling out termination notices, as explained in Sections C, D and E.

### 3. Notice to Cure

The third column indicates whether or not a notice to cure is required for the particular termination ground.

A "notice to cure," or "default notice" as it's also known, is typically given after a tenant violates a term or condition of the lease, such as a no-pets clause or a promise to keep from making too much noise. The notice gives the tenant a set amount of time in which to correct, or "cure," the lease viola- tion. If the tenant fails to cure the violation within the time provided in the notice (usually ten days, see the chart for details), you may terminate the lease by serving a termination notice.

Section C, below, gives step-by-step instructions on how to prepare a notice to cure.

### 4. Notice of Termination

The fourth column indicates whether or not a termination notice is required for the particular termination ground.

A "notice of termination" or "termination notice" informs a tenant that you have elected to end his tenancy as of a particular date, and gives the reason why you are terminating—for example, because the tenant has failed to timely correct a lease violation. The notice serves to warn the tenant that you will begin an eviction proceeding if he doesn't vacate the rental unit on or before the termination date. This date may range from seven days to one month depending on the termination ground and form of rent regulation (see the chart for details).

Section D, below, gives you step-by-step instruc- tions on how to prepare a termination notice.

As you'll see on the chart, in some cases, you'll need to serve the tenant with a notice to cure, before serving the termination notice. In other

cases, you won't need to serve a notice to cure before serving a termination notice. It depends on the reason you are terminating the tenancy

There's one instance where neither a notice to cure nor a notice of termination is required. If your non-regulated tenant uses the rental unit for an "immoral or illegal purpose," such as dealing drugs or prostitution, you may begin a summary eviction proceeding to remove the tenant without serving any prior notice. (This exception does not apply to rent-controlled and rent-stabilized tenants, though.)

### 5. DHCR Filing Requirements for Termination Notices

The fifth column indicates whether a copy of the termination notice must be filed with the State Division of Housing and Community Renewal (DHCR) and the timeline for doing so (either 48 hours or seven days). (Section G, below, covers DHCR filing requirements.)

### 6. Notice of Non-Renewal

The sixth column, which applies only to rent- stabilized tenants, indicates whether a notice of non-renewal is required for the particular termination ground.

As long as the rent is paid, you must offer renewal leases to rent-stabilized tenants as explained in Chapter 2, Section H. Under certain circumstances (such as the tenant's failure to use the rental unit as a primary residence, see the chart), you may refuse to renew a rent-stabilized tenant's lease. In some cases, you may be required to serve a notice of non-renewal informing the tenant that you do not intend to renew the lease and giving the reasons why. The chart indicates when you must serve this notice, such as 90 to 150 days before the tenant's lease expires. In some cases, you may combine the non-renewal notice with the termination notice, as indicated in this column.

Section E, below, explains how to prepare a notice of non-renewal.

## Termination Notices At a Glance

| Termination Ground | Authority for Termination (Must Be Cited in Notice) |
|---|---|
| **Non-Payment of Rent** | Chapter 12 explains how to prepare and serve a Rent Demand Notice for both regulated and unregulated units. |
| **Violation of Substantial Lease Obligation (See Chapter 14, Section B)** | **Unregulated.** Cite lease clause only. |
| | **NYC Rent Stabilization.** NYC Rent Stabilization Code (9 NYCRR) § 2524.3(a) |
| | **NYS Rent Stabilization.** Emergency Tenant Protection Regulations (9 NYCRR) § 2504.2(a) |
| | **NYC Rent Control.** Emergency Housing Rent Control Law (Uncon.) §8585(1)(a); NYC Rent & Rehabilitation Law § 26-408(a)(2); NYC Rent & Evict. Regs. (9 NYCRR) § 2204.2(a)(1) |
| | **NYS Rent Control.** Emergency Housing Rent Control Law (Uncon.) §8585(1)(a); NYC Rent & Evict. Regs. ( 9 NYCRR) § 2104.2(a) |
| **Illegal or Immoral Use or Occupancy (See Chapter 14, Section C)** | **Unregulated.** Real Property Actions and Proceedings Law § 711(5) |
| | **NYC Rent Stabilization.** NYC Rent Stabilization Code (9 NYCRR) §2524.3(d) |
| | **NYS Rent Stabilization.** Emergency Tenant Protection Regs. (9 NYCRR) §2504.2(d) |
| | **NYC Rent Control.** Emergency Housing Rent Control Law (Uncon.) § 8585(1)(b); NYC Rent & Rehabilitation L. § 26-408(a)(4); NYC Rent & Evict. Regs. (9 NYCRR) § 2204.2(a)(4). |
| | **NYS Rent Control.** Emergency Housing Rent Control Law (Uncon.) §8585(1)(b); NYC Rent & Evict. Regs. (9 NYCRR) § 2104.2(d) |
| **Nuisance or Objectionable Conduct (See Chapter 14, Section D)** | **Unregulated.** Cite lease clause. |
| | **NYC Rent Stabilization.** NYC Rent Stabilization Code (9 NYCRR) § 2524.3(b) |
| | **NYS Rent Stabilization.** Emergency Tenant Protection Regulations (9 NYCRR) § 2504.2(b) |
| | **NYC Rent Control.** Emergency Housing Rent Control Law (Uncon.) §8585(1)(b); NYC Rent & Rehabilitation Law § 26-408(a)(2); NYC Rent & Evict. Regs. (9 NYCRR) § 2204.2(a)(2) |
| | **NYS Rent Control.** Emergency Housing Rent Control Law (Uncon.) §8585(1)(b); NYC Rent & Evict. Regs. (9 NYCRR) § 2104.2(b). |
| **Refusal to Provide Access to Premises (For rent-regulated units, see Chapter 14, Section E1)** | **Unregulated.** Cite lease clause violated. |
| | **NYC Rent Stabilization.** New York City Rent Stabilization Code (9 NYCRR) § 2524.3(e) (requires five days' advance written notice) |
| | **NYS Rent Stabilization.** Emergency Tenant Protection Regs. (9 NYCRR) § 2504.2(e) |
| | **NYS Rent Control.** Emergency Housing Rent Control Law (Uncon.) § 8585.1(f); NYC Rent & Rehabilitation Law § 26-408(a)(6); NYC Rent & Evict. Regs. (9 NYCRR) § 2204.2(a)(6) |
| | **NYC Rent Control.** Emergency Housing Rent Control Law (Uncon.) § 8585.1(f); NYC Rent & Evict. Regs. § 2104.2(f) |
| **Refusal to Renew Lease (See Chapter 14, Section E2)** | **Unregulated.** N/A |
| | **NYC Rent Stabilization.** NYC Rent Stabilization Code (9 NYCRR) § 2524.3(f) |
| | **NYS Rent Stabilization.** Emergency Tenant Protection Regs. (9 NYCRR) § 2504.2(f) |
| | **NYC Rent Control.** Emergency Housing Rent Control Law (Uncon.) §8585(1)(e); 9 NYCRR § 2204.2(a)(5) |
| | **NYS Rent Control.** Emergency Housing Rent Control Law (Uncon.) §8585(1)(e); 9 NYCRR § 2104.2(e) |

| Minimum Notice to Cure | Minimum Notice of Termination | File Copy of Termination Notice w/DHCR | Notice of Non-Renewal | DHCR Certificate of Eviction |
|---|---|---|---|---|
| N/A | N/A | N/A | N/A | N/A |
| Follow lease | Follow lease | N/A | No | N/A |
| Ten days | Seven days | No | No | No |
| Ten days | Seven days | Yes, within seven days of service | No | No |
| Ten days | One month | Yes, within 48 hours of service | No | No |
| Ten days | One month | Yes, within 48 hours of service | No | No |
| No | No | N/A | N/A | N/A |
| No | Seven days | No | No | No |
| Ten days | Seven days | Yes, within seven days of service | No | No |
| No | Ten days | Yes, within 48 hours of service | No | No |
| No | Ten days | Yes, within 48 hours of service | No | No |
| Follow lease | Follow lease | N/A | N/A | N/A |
| Follow lease | Seven days | No | No | No |
| Ten days* | Seven days | Yes, within seven days of service | No | No |
| No | Ten days | Yes, within 48 hours of service | No | No |
| No | Ten days | Yes, within 48 hours of service | No | No |
| See lease | See lease | N/A | N/A | N/A |
| See lease | Seven days | No | No | No |
| Ten days | Seven days | Yes, within seven days of service | No | No |
| No | One month | Yes, within 48 hours of service | No | No |
| No | One month | Yes, within 48 hours of service | No | No |
| N/A | N/A | N/A | N/A | N/A |
| No | 15 days | No | No | No |
| Ten days | 15 days | Yes, within seven days of service | No | No |
| No | One month | Yes, within 48 hours of service | No | No |
| No | One month | Yes, within 48 hours of service | No | No |

* If the tenant is inflicting serious or substantial injury to the landlord or premises, no notice to cure is required. (9 NYCRR § 2504.1(d)(2)(iii).)

## Termination Notice At a Glance (continued)

| Termination Ground | Authority for Termination (Must be Cited in Notice) |
| --- | --- |
| **Non-Primary Residence (See Chapter 14, Section E3)** | **Unregulated.** N/A |
| | **NYC Rent Stabilization.** NYC Rent Stabilization Code (9 NYCRR) § 2524.4(c) |
| | **NYS Rent Stabilization.** Emergency Tenant Protection Regulations (9 NYCRR) § 2504.4(d) |
| | **NYC Rent Control.** Uncon. § 8585.2(b) |
| | **NYS Rent Control.** Uncon. § 8585.2(b) |
| **Recovery for Owner's Use (See Chapter 14, Section E4)** | **Unregulated.** N/A |
| | **NYC Rent Stabilization.** NYC Rent Stabilization Code (9 NYCRR) § 2524.4(a)(1) |
| | **NYS Rent Stabilization.** Emergency Tenant Protection Regulations (9 NYCRR) § 2504.4(a) |
| | **NYC Rent Control.** 9 NYCRR § 2204.5(a) |
| | **NYS Rent Control.** 9 NYCRR § 2104.5(a)(1) |
| **Withdrawal of Unit From Rent Market (See Chapter 14, Section E5)** | **Unregulated.** N/A |
| | **NYC Rent Stabilization.** NYC Rent Stabilization Code (9 NYCRR) § 2524.5(a)(1) |
| | **NYS Rent Stabilization.** Emergency Tenant Protection Regulations (9 NYCRR) § 2504.4(b) |
| | **NYC Rent Control.** 9 NYCRR § 2204.9 |
| | **NYS Rent Control.** 9 NYCRR § 2104.9 |
| **Demolition (See Chapter 14, Section E6)** | **Unregulated.** N/A |
| | **NYC Rent Stabilization.** NYC Rent Stabilization Code (9 NYCRR) § 2524.5(a)(2) |
| | **NYS Rent Stabilization.** Emergency Tenant Protection Regulations (9 NYCRR) § 2504.4(f) |
| | **NYC Rent Control.** 9 NYCRR § 2204.8 |
| | **NYS Rent Control.** 9 NYCRR § 2104.8 |

| Minimum Notice to Cure | Minimum Notice of Termination | File Copy of Termination Notice w/DHCR | Notice of Non-Renewal | DHCR Certificate of Eviction |
|---|---|---|---|---|
| N/A | N/A | N/A | N/A | N/A |
| No | 30 days (may be combined w/notice of non-renewal) | No | Yes. Serve 90 to 150 days before lease expires | No |
| No | 30 days (may be combined w/notice of non-renewal) | Yes, within seven days of service | Yes. Serve 90 to 120 days before lease expires | No |
| No | 30 days | Yes, within 48 hours of service | No | No |
| No | One month | Yes, within 48 hours of service | No | Yes. Obtain Certificate of Eviction before serving termination notice |
| N/A | N/A | N/A | N/A | N/A |
| No | 30 days. May be combined w/notice of non-renewal | No | Yes. Serve 120 to 150 days before lease expires | No |
| No | One month. May be combined w/notice of non-renewal | Yes, within seven days of service | Yes. Serve 90 to 120 days before lease expires | Yes. Apply for Certificate of Eviction before serving Notice of Termination |
| No | 30 days | Yes, within 48 hours of service | No | Yes. Obtain Certificate of Eviction before serving termination notice |
| No | One month | Yes, within 48 hours of service | No | Yes. Obtain Certificate of Eviction before serving termination notice |
| N/A | N/A | N/A | N/A | N/A |
| No | 30 days (may be combined w/notice of non-renewal) | No | Yes. Serve 90 to 150 days before lease expires. | Yes. Apply for Certificate of Eviction before serving notice of non-renewal |
| No | No | No | No | Yes. Apply for Certificate of Eviction before serving notice of non-renewal |
| No | 30 days | Yes, within 48 hours after service | No | Yes. Obtain Certificate of Eviction before serving termination notice |
| No | One month | Yes, within 48 hours of service | No | Yes. Obtain Certificate of Eviction before serving termination notice |
| N/A | N/A | N/A | N/A | N/A |
| No | No | No | Yes. Serve 90 to 150 days before lease expires | Yes |
| No | No | No | Yes. Serve 90 to 120 days before lease expires | Yes. Apply for Certificate of Eviction before serving notice of non-renewal |
| No | 30 days | Yes, within 48 hours of service | No | Yes. Obtain Certificate of Eviction before serving termination notice |
| No | One month | Yes, within 48 hours of service | No | Yes. Obtain Certificate of Eviction before serving termination notice |

### 7. DHCR Certificate of Eviction

The seventh column indicates whether you must obtain a Certificate of Eviction, which is an order issued by the Division of Housing and Community Renewal (DHCR) permitting the landlord to begin an eviction proceeding to remove a rent-controlled or rent-stabilized tenant. Section H explains how to apply for a Certificate of Eviction.

## B. Who May Sign Notices?

Before discussing the specifics of the various legal notices, it's important to understand who should sign them.

Whenever possible, you should sign default and termination notices yourself. Many leases require notices to come from the landlord "personally." In such cases, a notice signed by your attorney, manager or other agent will not be legally sufficient, unless it's accompanied by proof of the signer's authority to bind you to the notice. (*Siegel v. Kentucky Fried Chicken of Long Island, Inc.*, 108 A.D.2d 218, 488 N.Y.S.2d 744 (2d Dep't 1985) aff'd 67 N.Y.2d 792, 501 N.Y.S.2d 317, 492 N.E.2d 390 (1986).) Even when the lease doesn't require notices to come from you, the safest course of action is for all termination and default notices to be signed by you. This includes notices to rent-controlled tenants, who often have no current lease.

Sometimes it won't be feasible for you to sign every notice yourself. If you're frequently out of town or live too far from the property to regularly sign notices, you'll need to authorize your agent or attorney to sign them for you. In such cases, it's critical to attach to the notice a copy of a statement signed by you authorizing your agent or attorney to sign notices on your behalf.

The lease in this book allows you to designate a manager or other agent to issue notices on your behalf. (See Clause 24 in Chapter 2.) If you use a different lease, read the default clause and notices carefully before letting an agent or other person sign a default or termination notice.

A sample Authorization to Issue Notices for Landlord is shown below.

 The Forms CD includes the Authorization to Issue Notices for Landlord and Appendix IV includes a blank tear-out copy of the form.

## C. Preparing a Notice to Cure

In many cases, you are legally required to serve a tenant with a so-called notice to cure (also known

---

### Authorization to Issue Notices for Landlord

I hereby authorize _____Joseph Andrews, my Managing Agent_____

_____, to sign all legal notices on

my behalf relating to the property located at _____280 Mercer Street, New York, NY 10012_____

_____.

_____January 3, 200X_____          _____John Bosco_____
Date                                Owner and Landlord

as a default notice). This is a legal notice that informs the tenant that she is violating a specific lease term, such as keeping a pet in violation of a no-pet clause, or violating a regulation that governs rent-stabilized or rent-controlled tenancies. A notice to cure also demands that the tenant correct the violation by a specific date (usually within ten days) and warns that if the violation is not corrected within the prescribed time, the landlord will terminate the tenancy.

Most leases require you to give the tenant a prior notice to cure before you may terminate the tenancy for a lease violation. And in some cases, rent stabilization and rent control laws require you to give the tenant a notice to cure before terminating the tenancy. If a lease, law or regulation requires you to give the tenant a notice to cure, an eviction proceeding against the tenant based solely on a termination notice is defective and will be dismissed. The "Termination Notices At A Glance" chart, above, explains when a notice to cure is required under New York law and the amount of time it must provide for the tenant to "cure" the violation.

**When in doubt, give a notice to cure.** In some cases, the words of the lease will determine your obligation to give a notice to cure. If the words of the tenant's lease are unclear or leave you uncertain as to whether you are required to give a notice to cure before terminating the tenancy, err on the side of caution by serving a ten-day notice to cure.

## 1.  What the Notice to Cure Must Say

There are three points that a notice to cure must cover. It must:
- specifically describe the nature of the tenancy violation and cite which lease clause or rent law the tenant has violated
- direct the tenant to "cure," or correct, the violation within a specified time period, and
- inform the tenant that you will terminate the tenancy in the event that the tenant fails to

cure the default within the time provided in the notice.

A sample Notice to Cure appears below. It meets all of the criteria required for an effective and legal notice.

 The Forms CD includes the Notice to Cure and Appendix IV includes a blank tear-out copy of the form.

## 2.  How to Fill out a Notice to Cure

These are the steps you must take to properly complete the notice to cure. Since many of the steps will ask you to refer to provisions in the tenant's lease, it's a good idea to pull out the lease before you get started on the form. That's how lawyers do it.

**Use care when preparing the notice to cure.** The notice must be crystal clear. Mistakes and omissions in a notice to cure are routinely attacked by tenants in eviction proceedings. A notice that is unclear, equivocal or is capable of being interpreted by the tenant either as a notice to cure or as a notice to termination is fatally defective. And courts rarely give landlords a chance to fix mistakes in the notice.

### Step 1.  Fill in Tenant's Name

Insert the tenant's full name. If there's more than one tenant listed on the lease, insert the name of each tenant on the form. Make sure the names are spelled the same way as they appear on the lease. A misspelled name could give a tenant ammunition to try and delay or derail a later eviction case.

Sometimes, units are leased by businesses for residential use by employees. When issuing a notice to a business, fill in the entire legal name for the business. Don't forget to include endings like, Corp., Inc., P.C. and L.L.P. They are an important part of a business entity's name.

## Step 2.  Fill in Premises Address

The notice must identify the tenant's rental unit. List the full address for the tenant's premises including the unit number or any other relevant description (e.g., "downstairs apartment"). The premises address should be at least as detailed as the one that's listed on the tenant's lease. Don't forget the postal Zip code.

## Step 3.  Fill in Lease Date and Parties' Names

First, insert the date of the tenant's lease. Usually, the date is on the first page of the lease. (You'll find the date in Clause 1 of the form agreements in Chapter 2.) It may be different from the date you and the tenant signed the lease. If you renewed the tenant's lease for an additional term, also include the date of the tenant's most recent renewal agreement. For rent-stabilized tenants, this is the date in the top right corner of the DHCR Renewal Lease Form (DHCR Form RTP-8).

Then fill in the names of the tenants and landlord on the notice as they appear on the lease. If you acquired the property during the term of the lease, the tenant's former landlord is listed on the lease. When drafting the notice, fill in the former landlord's name, followed by the term "landlord's predecessor."

## Step 4.  Describe Tenancy Violation

Describe the tenant's violation or wrongful act. Describe how and approximately when the tenant illegally sublet, caused a nuisance, performed illegal alterations or otherwise violated the tenancy. This is the most important part of the notice, and must be carefully drafted. The tenant is entitled to a clear statement of what she is doing wrong so she can take action to preserve her tenancy.

If the tenant's conduct violates a lease clause and/or a law or regulation, cite the specific provision, clause, article or paragraph of the lease, law or regulation violated. If the tenant is rent controlled

or rent stabilized, you must cite the specific rent law that the tenant is violating. (*Chinatown Apts. v. Chu Cho Lam*, 51 N.Y.2d 786, 433 N.Y.S.2d 86, 412 N.E.2d 1312 (1980).) If your notice is going to a rent-regulated tenant, review the "Law Authorizing Termination" column on the "Termination Notices at a Glance" chart at Section A, above, to find the right rent law citation to include in the notice.

The sample Notice to Cure shown below includes language for a tenant's refusal to provide access. Here are some examples of language to use for tenant's violation in other situations:

**Illegal sublet by a NYC Rent-Stabilized Tenant.** "You are violating a substantial obligation of your tenancy by illegally subletting the Premises in violation of Paragraph 16 of the Lease and Section 2524.3 of the Rent Stabilization Code. Specifically, since at least February 1, 200X, you are no longer residing at the Premises and have sublet the Premises to Betty Wallace, without the prior written consent of the Landlord."

**Noise-Related Nuisance by a NYS Rent-Controlled Tenant.** "You have committed a nuisance by maliciously or negligently engaging in a continuous course of conduct which has substantially interfered with the comfort and safety of other occupants or tenants in the building, in violation of Emergency Housing Rent Control Law Section 8585(1)(b) and Rent and Eviction Regulations Section 2104.2(b). Specifically, on April 1, April 7 and April 15, 200X, you disturbed other tenants in the building and committed a nuisance by having or allowing loud boisterous parties to be held at the Premises that continued past midnight, at which music was played at an extremely loud volume, and at which intoxicated guests milled about and created loud disturbances in the lobby, the elevator and in the hallway outside the front door to the Premises."

**Illegal Alterations by Unregulated Tenant.** "You are violating a substantial obligation of your tenancy, in that, without the prior written consent of the Landlord, you have performed alterations to the Premises in violation of Clause 12 of the Lease and in violation of applicable building codes. Specifically, you have constructed and installed a permanent floor-to-ceiling partition wall in the master bedroom of the Premises."

# Notice to Cure

To:  Sidney Greenwold                                                                                          ,

   "Tenant," and to all persons occupying the Premises described below

Re: All rooms,   Apartment 4-C                          , in the building known as and located at

   259 West 75th Street, New York, NY 10023                          (the "Premises").

PLEASE TAKE NOTICE, that you are violating a   substantial obligation

of your lease dated   February 10, 200X                by and between                          

   Sidney Greenwold                                                    , as Tenant, and

   West Side Realty                                                    

as Landlord (hereinafter, the "Lease"). Specifically, you have  failed and refused to provide access

to the Premises to the Landlord for purposes of replacing the heating valve in the living room

of the Premises, despite repeated oral requests for access from the Landlord on Feb. 1 and Feb.

3, 200X, and repeated written requests for access from the Landlord dated Feb. 6, Feb. 9, and

Feb. 15, 200X. Your continued refusal to provide access to the Premises to the Land-lord for

the purposes of making repairs and improvements violates Clause 15 of the Lease.         .

PLEASE TAKE FURTHER NOTICE, that you are required to cure the violation within  10

days from the date of this notice by      contacting the Landlord at the telephone number listed

below to make an appointment for access to the Premises no later than five days hence and

providing such access to the Premises for as long as may be necessary to replace the living

room heating valve.

                                                                             .

PLEASE TAKE FURTHER NOTICE, that if you fail to cure the violation on or before  March 15, 200X

                          , that being at least  ten (10)                 days from the

date of this Notice, your tenancy will be terminated and you will be required to remove from and

surrender possession of the Premises to the Landlord.

February 20, 200X                    Rita L. Preen

Date                                 Signature

                                     Rita L. Preen, President
                                     Name and Title of Signer

                                     West Side Realty, Inc., Landlord
                                     Address

                                     255 West 75th Street

                                     New York, NY 10023

                                     212-555-1212
                                     Phone

**Unauthorized Pet by NYS Rent-Stabilized Tenant.**
"You are violating a substantial obligation of your tenancy, in that, without the prior written consent of the Landlord, you have, since February 1, 200X, harbored a pet dog in the Premises in violation of Clause 14 of the Lease, and Section 2504.2(a) of the Emergency Tenant Regulations."

**Business Use of Premises by NYC Rent-Stabilized Tenant.** "You are violating a substantial obligation of your tenancy, in that, without the prior written consent of the landlord, you have, since at least July 1, 200X, used and occupied the premises for the operation of a business in violation of Paragraph 1 of the Lease and Section 2524.3(a) of the Rent Stabilization Code. Specifically, you have regularly operated a beauty parlor and/or hair salon business known as "Faye's Fave Hair Design" from the premises in which you and/or your employees shampoo and/or cut and/or style customers' hair for a fee."

## Step 5.   Insert Length of Time for Cure

The length of the cure period is governed by the default clause in the tenant's lease. The lease in this book (Clause 19, Chapter 2) provides a ten-day cure period. If you're using a different lease, check the default clause.

For rent-regulated tenants, review the "Notice to Cure" column on the "Termination Notices At A Glance" chart," in Section A, above, to see how long a cure period is required by the applicable rent law. If the cure period listed in the tenant's lease is longer than the cure period required by the applicable rent law, you must use the longer cure period in your notice.

EXAMPLE: You get several complaints from tenants that Tamara, a rent-stabilized tenant in your Gramercy Square Park building, has been throwing big loud parties that last into the wee hours. You've discussed the situation with Tamara, but the parties have continued. You decide to get serious. New York City rent stabilization laws permit you to terminate a rent-stabilized tenant who creates a nuisance

without a prior notice to cure. But Tamara's lease requires you to give her a ten-day notice to cure. To properly set the stage for an eventual eviction, you must give Tamara a ten-day notice to cure before terminating her tenancy.

## Step 6.   Suggest Way to Cure Violation

For clarity, your notice should tell the tenant what to do in order to cure the tenancy violation. The sample notice to cure shown above includes language for a tenant's refusal to provide access. Here are some examples for other situations.

**Illegal Sublet.** Tell the tenant to cure the violation by "removing the illegal subtenant from the Premises."

**Noise-Related Nuisance.** Tell the tenant to cure by "ceasing and refraining from disturbing or harassing other tenants and abiding by the terms and conditions of the lease."

**Illegal Alterations.** Tell the tenant to cure by "removing the newly installed partition wall from the master bedroom of the Premises and restoring the floors, walls and ceilings of the master bedroom to their original condition."

**Unauthorized Pet.** Tell the tenant to cure by "permanently removing said dog from the Premises."

**Business Use.** Tell the tenant to cure by "using the premises for residential use only and to cease using the premises for the operation of a business."

## Step 7.   Insert Date by Which Violation Must Be Cured

Insert a specific date by which corrective action must be taken by the tenant. To calculate the date, first determine how many days you must give the tenant to cure the violation (see Step 5, above), then add ample time to serve the notice to the tenant. For example, if you're delivering the notice by mail, add at least five (and preferably seven) more days to the cure period, to allow ample time for the notice to be received in the mail. For a ten-day notice to cure, this would mean a notice period of 15 to 17 days.

### Step 8.  Sign and Date the Notice to Cure

Whenever possible, a notice to cure should be issued and signed by you. If you can't sign it, you'll need to authorize your agent or attorney to sign it for you. In such cases, it's critical to attach to the notice a copy of a statement signed by you which authorizes your agent or attorney to sign notices on your behalf (see discussion and sample Authorization to Issue Notices for Landlord, Section B, above).

### Step 9.  Make Copies of the Notice

Make copies of the notice to serve on the tenant. (The number of copies you'll need depends on how the notice is delivered to the tenant (see Section F).) Keep the original notice to cure in your file. If you end up terminating the tenancy and going to court, you'll need the original notice to cure, along with proof of service, to proceed with your eviction lawsuit.

## D. Preparing a Termination Notice

A termination notice informs the tenant that you are ending the tenancy as of a particular date. The notice also serves as a warning to the tenant that you will sue to evict the tenant if she doesn't move out on or before the termination date (usually within one month) stated in the notice. To be valid, your notice must give the tenant the reason or reasons why you are terminating the tenancy. That's so the tenant can decide whether she should move out or stay and fight your eviction proceeding by putting up a legal defense.

The "Notice of Termination" column on the "Termination Notices at a Glance" chart, above, provides details on when and what kind of termination notice you must use to end a tenancy, including situations which first require a notice to cure.

### 1.  What the Termination Notice Must Say

To be effective, a termination notice must be timely, definite and unequivocal (*Saab Enters v. Bell,* 198 A.D.2d 342, 603 N.Y.S.2d 879 (2nd Dep't 1993).)

To meet these criteria, your termination notice must do all of the following:

- Cite the specific lease obligation or prohibition that the tenant has violated and, if the tenant is rent controlled or rent stabilized, it must also cite the specific rent law authorizing termination.
- Describe the reason why you are terminating the tenancy and, whenever possible, supply the precise dates and times of any tenant misconduct that supports the termination ground.
- If a notice to cure was previously served, state that the violation has continued *beyond* the cure period.
- Give a specific date when the tenancy will terminate and by which the tenant must move out, and
- Warn the tenant that if she doesn't vacate the rental unit by the termination date, you will begin an eviction proceeding to recover the rental unit from the tenant.

(*Chinatown Apts. v. Chu Cho Lam,* 51 N.Y.2d 786, 788, 433 N.Y.S.2d 86, 412 N.E. 2d 1312 (1980); (NYC Rent and Evict. Regs.) 9 NYCRR § 2204.3(a), (b); (NYC Rent and Evict. Regs.) 9 NYCRR § 2104.3(a), (b); (RSC) 9 NYCRR § 2524.2(b).)

A sample Notice of Termination appears below. It meets all of the above criteria.

 The Forms CD includes the Notice of Termination and Appendix IV includes a blank tear-out copy of the form.

### 2.  How to Fill out a Notice of Termination Form

If you have already prepared a notice to cure, you will have already gathered the key information you need to fill out the termination notice form. (Section C, above, explains when you need to first give a notice to cure before giving a termination notice.)

For consistency, keep the notice to cure and the tenant's lease on your desk as you fill in the termination notice form.

⚠ **Use care when preparing the Notice of Termination.** The notice must be crystal clear. Mistakes and omissions in a notice of termination are routinely subject to attack by tenants in eviction proceedings. A notice that is unclear, equivocal or is capable of being interpreted by the tenant either as a notice to cure or as a notice to termination is fatally defective. And courts rarely give landlords a chance to fix mistakes in the notice.

### Step 1.  Fill in Names of Tenants and Occupants

Begin filling out your termination notice by inserting the full names of all the tenants who signed the lease. Make sure the names are spelled the same way as they appear on the lease. A misspelled name could provide a tenant with ammunition to delay or derail a later eviction case.

Sometimes, units are leased by businesses for residential use by employees. When issuing a notice to a business, fill in the entire legal name for the business. Don't forget to include endings like Corp., Inc., P.C. and L.L.P. They are an important part of a business entity's name.

### Step 2.  Fill in Premises Address

Fill in the full address for the premises including the unit number or other relevant description—for example, "downstairs apartment." The address on the termination notice form must be at least as detailed as the one that's listed on the tenant's lease. Don't forget the postal Zip code.

### Step 3.  Fill in Lease Date and Parties' Names

First, insert the date of the tenant's lease. Usually, the date is on the first page of the lease. (You'll find the date in Clause 1 of the form agreements in Chapter 2.) It may be different than the date you and the tenant signed the lease. If you renewed the tenant's lease for an additional term, also include the date of the tenant's most recent renewal agreement. For rent-stabilized tenants, this is the date in the top right corner of the DHCR Renewal Lease Form (DHCR Form RTP-8).

Then fill in the names of the tenants and landlord on the notice as they appear on the lease. If you acquired the property during the term of the lease, the tenant's former landlord is listed on the lease. When drafting the notice, fill in the former landlord's name, followed by the term "landlord's predecessor."

### Step 4.  Insert Rent Control or Rent Stabilization Law and/or Regulation Authorizing Termination

 You may skip this step if you are preparing a termination notice for a non-regulated rental unit.

If the tenant is rent regulated, termination must be permitted under rent control or rent stabilization laws. (Chapter 14 describes the reasons you are permitted to end a rent-regulated tenancy.) Your termination notice must cite the rent law or regulation that authorizes you to terminate the tenancy. (*Chinatown Apts. v. Chu Cho Lam*, 51 N.Y.2d 786, 433 N.Y.S.2d 86, 412 N.E.2d 1312 (1980).) If you already gave the tenant a notice to cure, use the same rent law or regulation you cited in that notice. Otherwise, consult the "Termination Notices at a Glance" chart, above, for the correct legal citation to include in the notice.

### Step 5.  Insert the Lease Clause Violated

If you're terminating the lease because the tenant violated a substantial provision of the lease, created a nuisance or engaged in wrongful conduct, identify the specific lease clause the tenant is violating. If the lease refers to its clauses as articles or paragraphs, describe them the same way in your notice.

## Notice of Termination

To:    Elaine Fronhofer                                                               ,

"Tenant," and to all persons occupying the Premises described below

Premises: Apartment 5-C

300 Fifth Avenue,

New York, NY 10001                               (the "Premises").

Re:    Lease dated ___June 1, 200X___ between ___Elaine Fronhofer___

_____, as Tenant,

and _____Limestone Realty_____

_____, Landlord's predecessor (the "Lease").

PLEASE TAKE NOTICE, that pursuant to _New York City Rent Stabilization Code (9 NYCRR)_
§ 2524.3(a), and Article 11, Rule 9 of the Lease

the Landlord elects to terminate your tenancy on the grounds ___that you are violating a___
substantial obligation of your tenancy in that, without the prior written consent of the
Landlord or Landlord's predecessor, you are harboring a dog in the Premises. Such conduct
has continued beyond the cure period set in the notice to cure previously sent to you, a copy
of which is annexed hereto, along with proof of service, and made a part of this notice.

PLEASE TAKE FURTHER NOTICE, that you are hereby required to quit, vacate and surrender the
Premises on or before ___September 30, 200X___, that being more than ___seven days___
after the service of this notice upon you, pursuant to the terms of your lease and applicable law.

PLEASE TAKE FURTHER NOTICE, that if you fail to vacate or surrender the premises, the landlord will
commence summary proceedings to evict you.

___February 20, 200X___     _Eric Corde_
Date                        Signature

Eric Corde, Secretary
Name and Title of Signer

East Side Realty, Inc, Landlord
Address

300 Fifth Avenue

New York, NY 10001

Tel. 212-555-1212
Phone

## Step 6.   Describe Termination Ground

Describe the nature of the lease violation or the tenant's wrongful act or omission. State how and approximately when the tenant illegally sublet, caused a nuisance, performed illegal alterations or otherwise violated their tenancy. This is an important part of the notice, and must be drafted very carefully to clearly tell the tenant why the tenancy is being terminated.

The sample Notice of Termination shown above, includes language describing a tenant's violation of a no-pet clause. Here are some examples for other situations:

**Noise-Related Nuisance.** "… you have committed a nuisance by maliciously or negligently engaging in a continuous course of conduct which has substantially interfered with the comfort and safety of other occupants or tenants in the building. Specifically, on April 1, April 7 and April 15, 200X, you disturbed other tenants in the building and committed a nuisance by having or allowing loud boisterous parties to be held at the Premises that continued past midnight, at which music was played at an extremely loud volume, and at which intoxicated guests milled about and created loud disturbances in the lobby, the elevator and in the hallway outside the front door to the Premises."

**Health and Safety-Related Nuisance.** "… you have committed a nuisance by maliciously or negligently engaging in a continuous course of conduct which has substantially interfered with the comfort and safety of other occupants or tenants in the building. Specifically, you have allowed significant amounts of garbage, newspapers and other refuse to accumulate in the premises and cause an offensive stench. This unsafe and unsanitary condition poses a health hazard to other occupants in the building and threatens their safety and well-being."

**Refusal to Renew NYC Rent-Stabilized Lease.** " … you have refused to execute a renewal lease offered by the Landlord at the legal regulated rent and otherwise on the same terms and conditions as the expired lease, following Landlord's proper and timely notice of its expiration."

**Illegal Conduct by Rent-Regulated Tenant.** " … you are knowingly permitting the Premises to be used for ongoing illegal drug sales. Specifically: On February 3, 200X, and March 4, 200X, the New York Police Department, while executing search warrants at the Premises, recovered cocaine, scales, plastic bags, drug records and $2,755 in U.S. currency. On March 4, 200X, the New York Police Department arrested Paul W. Mann, an occupant of the Premises, for criminal possession of a controlled substance."

## Step 7.   Add Special Language If Notice to Cure Has Already Been Served

If you already gave the tenant a notice to cure and you're terminating because the tenant didn't correct the violation within the cure period, your termination notice should use the same words as the notice to cure to describe the tenant's violation or wrongful conduct. In such cases, you must also add the following sentence: "Such conduct has continued beyond the cure period set in the notice to cure previously sent to you, a copy of which is annexed hereto, along with proof of service, and made a part of this notice."

## Step 8.   Insert Termination Date and Length of Notice

Fill in a specific termination date and the length of the notice required by the lease or applicable rent regulation. To calculate the termination date, review the "Default" or "Termination" clause in the tenant's lease. It will say how many days' notice you must give the tenant to terminate the tenancy. Most leases require between five and 30 days' notice. Our lease provides 10 days' notice to terminate the tenancy. (See Clause 19 in Chapter 2.)

If the tenant is rent-controlled or rent-stabilized, also check to see how many days' notice of termination you're required to give the tenant under the rent law authorizing termination. (See the "Minimum Notice of Termination" column on the "Termination Notices at a Glance" chart in Section A, above.) If it's different from the notice period provided in the lease, use the longer of the two notice periods.

> EXAMPLE: Ed wants to terminate Berta's rent-stabilized tenancy on the ground that she has refused to permit Ed into the unit to make necessary repairs. The default clause in Berta's lease says that ten days' notice of termination is required. Under NYC Rent Stabilization Laws, seven days' notice is required. Ed must give Berta ten days' notice that her tenancy is terminating.

Once, you've determined the minimum notice you must give to terminate the tenancy, add several days time to serve the notice. It's a far better practice to give the tenant too much notice than too little. A 30-day termination notice that's served 45 days before the termination notice, for instance, is timely and valid. But a 30-day notice that's served 29 days before the termination date is worthless.

### Step 9. Sign and Date the Notice

If possible, sign and date the termination notice yourself. If you can't sign it, you'll need to authorize your agent or attorney to sign the notice for you. In such cases, it's critical to attach to the termination notice a copy of a statement signed by you which authorizes your agent or attorney to sign notices on your behalf (see discussion and sample Authorization to Issue Notices for Landlord in Section B, above).

### Step 10. Make Copies of the Notice

If you gave the tenant a notice to cure, attach a copy of the notice to cure and its affidavit of service to the termination notice after you sign it. Make copies of the termination notice and attached papers for service on the tenant. (The number of copies you'll need depends on how the notice is delivered to the tenant (see Section F).) Keep the original in your file. You'll need the original termination notice if you later go to court to evict the tenant.

## E. Notice of Non-Renewal for Rent-Stabilized Tenants

When a non-regulated tenant's lease expires, you're under no legal obligation to renew it, unless the lease itself gives the tenant a renewal option. But in many cases, you'll wish to offer the tenant a renewal lease anyway. Whatever your decision, try to let the tenant know whether you plan to offer a renewal lease at least 30 days before the lease expires. That way, the tenant can make plans to find new quarters, if necessary, and promptly vacate at the end of the lease.

The situation is very different, though, for rent-stabilized tenants. Generally, as long as the rent is paid, you must offer renewal leases to rent-stabilized tenants. (Chapter 2, Section H, explains how to prepare renewal leases.) Nevertheless, there are a few grounds upon which you may refuse to renew a rent-stabilized tenant's lease, upon proper notice. These grounds include:

- the tenant's failure to use the rental unit as a primary residence (see Chapter 14, Section E3)
- your need to recover the rental unit for your use (or that of an immediate family member) (see Chapter 14, Section E4)
- your wish to withdraw the unit from the rental market (see Chapter 14, Section E5), and
- your wish to demolish the premises (see Chapter 14, Section E6).

In certain cases, you must serve the tenant with a "notice of non-renewal," a special notice informing the tenant that the landlord does not intend to renew the lease. The following sections detail when such a notice is required to be served. A sample Notice of Non-Renewal, based on a tenant's non-primary residence, appears below.

 **Hire an experienced landlord-tenant lawyer to prepare your notice of non-renewal.** Faced with a notice of non-renewal, many rent-stabilized tenants will make every effort to preserve their rent-stabilized tenancy. If you sue to evict a tenant who refuses to move out when the lease ends, you can expect the tenant to attack the legal and factual adequacy of your notice of non-renewal. Judges tend to put these notices under a microscope. If your notice of non-renewal is found lacking, you won't get a second chance to make it right. You will be ordered to offer the tenant a one- or two-year renewal lease, at the tenant's option. Result: You must wait until the tenant's renewal lease draws to a close, a year or two down the road, before you can again attempt to recover the apartment. Because the stakes are so high, it's usually a smart bet to hire an attorney to prepare this notice for you. (Chapter 17 explains how to find a landlord-tenant attorney).

## 1. When Notice of Non-Renewal Must Be Served; Timing

The timing of the notice of non-renewal is critical. This notice (which is sometimes called a "Golub" notice) must be served within a specified window period prior to the expiration of the tenant's lease term. (*Golub v. Frank,* 65 N.Y.2d 900, 493 N.Y.S.2d 451, 483 N.E.2d 126 (1985).) Exactly when the window period falls depends on whether the rent-stabilized unit is located within or outside New York City.

### a.  NYC Rent-Stabilization

In some cases, New York City landlords must serve a rent-stabilized tenant with a notice of non-renewal in order to be entitled to recover the unit. Here are the situations that require a notice of non-renewal:

- your tenant has failed to use the apartment as a primary residence (see Chapter 14, Section E3)
- you wish to recover the tenant's unit for your personal use (or for the use of your immediate family member) (See Chapter 14, Section E4), or
- you intend to demolish the building in which the tenant lives and you have filed a demoli-

tion application with DHCR, which is pending or has been granted.

If you wish to withdraw the unit from the rental market, you must file an application with DHCR seeking a Certificate of Eviction. A notice of non-renewal is not required.

For rent-stabilized tenants who live in New York City, the notice of non-renewal must be served at least ninety (90) days and no more than one hundred and fifty (150) days prior to the expiration of the tenant's lease term. This is the same time period during which you would ordinarily offer the tenant a renewal lease. (A rent-stabilized tenant's right to a renewal lease is explained in Chapter 2, Section H.)

EXAMPLE: Mario's lease for his Brooklyn apartment expires December 31. To be timely, Mario's landlord must serve a notice of non-renewal on Mario during the window period that begins August 3 and ends October 2.

### b.  NY State Rent-Stabilization

In some cases, landlords must serve rent-stabilized tenants who occupy units outside New York City with a notice of non-renewal. Here are the situations in which we suggest you issue a notice of non-renewal:

- your tenant has failed to use the apartment as a primary residence (see Chapter 14, Section E3), or
- you intend to demolish the building in which the tenant lives and you have filed a demolition application with DHCR which is pending or has been granted.

If you intend to recover a tenant's unit for your personal use and occupancy (or for that of an immediate family member), or you wish to withdraw the tenant's unit from the market, you must apply to DHCR for an order granting a Certificate of Eviction by filing an Owner's Application for Order Granting Approval to Refuse Renewal of Lease and/or to Proceed for Eviction (DHCR Form RA-54). Apply for the order before the start of the "window" period in which you would ordinarily offer the tenant a renewal lease—that is, three months or more before

## Sample Notice of Non-Renewal

To:   Bernadette Harrigan                                                                                           ,

"Tenant," and to all persons occupying the Premises described below

Premises: Apartment 3-A

84-44 Cuthbert Road

Kew Gardens, New York 11415                              (the "Premises").

Re:   Lease dated ___November 1, 1998___ between ___Bernadette Harrigan___

_____, as Tenant,

and _____Juan Baez_____

_____,"Landlord," as most recently renewed

by renewal agreement dated ___November 1, 200X___ (the "Lease").

PLEASE TAKE NOTICE, that pursuant to ___New York City Rent Stabilization Code (9 NYCRR)___
§ 2524.4(c)_____ ,

the Landlord does not intend to renew your lease for the Premises, which expires on ___October 31,___
___200X___ , because ___the Premises are not being occupied as your primary residence___
_____ .

PLEASE TAKE FURTHER NOTICE, that the Landlord intends to commence an action or proceeding
seeking to recover possession of the subject premises on the ground that ___the Premises are not being___
occupied as your primary residence._____ .

PLEASE TAKE FURTHER NOTICE, that in the event you fail to vacate or surrender possession of the
subject premises on or before ___October 31, 200X___ , that being at least
___thirty (30)___ days after the service of this notice upon you, the Landlord
intends to commence an action or proceeding to recover possession of the subject premises on the
grounds that ___they are not being occupied by you as your primary residence._____ .

PLEASE TAKE FURTHER NOTICE, that the Landlord reasonably believes the facts necessary to
establish the existence of your non-primary residence_____
_____include, but are not limited to, the
following, and such other facts as may be ascertained in the course of discovery proceedings:

1. You maintain your primary residence at a dwelling other than the subject premises and/or
_____

2. You principally or primarily occupy the premises known as and located at 12 Tomahawk Drive,
   Marlton, NJ 08053, and/or

3. You hold a New Jersey driver's license reciting 12 Tomahawk Drive, Marlton, NJ 08053, as your residence and/or

4. You maintain a telephone listing reciting 12 Tomahawk Drive, Marlton, NJ 08053, as your residence address and/or

5. Voting records reflect 12 Tomahawk Drive, Marlton, NJ 08053, as your residence address and/or

6. Building personnel have not seen you at the subject premises on a regular basis, since on or about January 1, 200X, and/or

7. The subject premises are actually being occupied by Barry Bittlesen.

8. _____

PLEASE TAKE FURTHER NOTICE, that this notice is being served upon you in compliance with the terms of your Lease and applicable provisions of law.

August 1, 200X
Date

Juan Baez
Signature

Juan Baez, General Partner
Name and Title of Signer

Baez Holdings, LLC, Landlord
Address

3 Hanover Square

New York, NY 10004

212-555-1212
Phone

the date the tenant's lease expires. DHCR must grant this certificate before you may proceed in court to evict the tenant.

In those localities outside New York City that are subject to New York State Rent Stabilization (ETPA), the notice of non-renewal must be served during the ninety- (90-) to one-hundred-and-twenty- (120-) day "window period" prior to the expiration of the tenant's lease (at which time a renewal lease would ordinarily be offered to the tenant (9 NYCRR 2503.5(a)). (A NYS rent-stabilized tenant's right to a renewal lease is discussed in Chapter 2, Section H.) Some courts have ruled that a notice of non-renewal is not required for rent-stabilized tenants outside New York City, while others have required them. To be safe, serve the tenant with a notice of non-renewal anyway, or seek the advice of an experienced landlord-tenant attorney before taking any action.

**Don't serve a notice of non-renewal too early or too late.** If you miss the window period, you lose out on being able to recover the apartment. That means that you must offer the tenant a one- or two-year renewal lease (at the tenant's option), and wait until the next window period to attempt to end the tenancy again.

## 2. What Notice of Non-Renewal Must Say

Every notice of non-renewal must state your factual reasons for refusing to renew the lease. (9 NYCRR § 2524.2(b).) Here are a few common examples.

### a. Non-Primary Residence

A landlord who serves a notice of non-renewal on the theory that the tenant does not occupy the apartment as a primary residence must state facts supporting the claim. These facts usually include the address of the house or apartment (other than the rent-stabilized unit) owned or leased by the tenant, or which is listed on the tenant's driver's license, motor vehicle, voter registration, bank, credit card or utility records and tax returns.

Our Sample Notice of Non-renewal, above, shows you the type of facts that must be included in a notice of non-renewal to support a claim that the rental unit is not used by the tenant as a primary residence.

**Make sure your facts support your claim of non-primary residence.** "Conclusory" claims, such as "The premises are not your primary residence" or "You really live at 121 East 18th Street," are *not* a good idea and usually fail. Just give your version of the *facts* in the notice—for example, "You lease an apartment at 121 East 18th Street." Leave the legal conclusion making to the court, if you end up suing to evict.

### b. Recovery for Owner's Use in New York City

Another common reason for non-renewal is when the landlord wishes to recover the apartment for her own occupancy, or for that of an immediate family member. In such cases, the notice of non-renewal must give the name of the intended new occupant and his or her familial relationship to you. Simply saying that you need the apartment for your family's own use won't do.

So, for instance, if you want to recover a rent-stabilized apartment so that your mother can move in, your notice must identify your mother by name, and state her relationship to you—for example:

- "I want the apartment for my mother, Katherine Lee, to be used as her primary residence." (*Lee v. Garcia*, N.Y.L.J., 5/14/91, p.24, col. 6 (App. Term, 2d Dep't) or
- "Your landlord needs the apartment for his brother, Francisco Pichardo, and his family to live in." (*Pichardo v. Tavarez,* N.Y.L.J., 5/30/91, p. 27, col. 5 (App. Term, 2d Dep't).

Simply saying that you need the apartment for your family's own use won't do. (*Landriscina v. Solow*, N.Y.L.J., 2/28/90, p. 25, col. 4 (App. Term, 2d Dep't).)

## F. How to Deliver Notices

Read your tenant's lease carefully before serving a notice. Default and termination notices must be served in the manner described in the tenant's lease. Every lease should have a "notices" clause saying how and where the landlord should deliver notices to the tenant during the tenancy. Usually, the tenant's lease will permit notices from the landlord to be mailed by either certified or registered mail. The lease in this book requires notices to be delivered to the tenant personally or sent by registered or certified mail to the tenant at the premises. (Clause 24 in Chapter 2).

But be careful. Some leases require personal delivery. If so, you must attempt to personally serve the tenant in the same manner as a rent demand. Similarly, if the tenant's lease doesn't cover this issue, we recommend that you serve the notice in the same manner as a rent demand. That means having a process server or employee attempt to personally deliver the notice to the tenant. If the tenant can't be found, the notice may be delivered to the tenant via so-called "substituted service" or, as a last resort, by "nail and mail" service.

 **Serve exact copies of your notice on the tenant and keep the original notice in your file.** If the lease permits service by mail, send each tenant listed on the notice a copy of the notice using the method specified (certified mail, registered mail, etc.). If you are required to personally serve the notice to the tenant, make at least four copies for each tenant named on the notice. That way, the person serving the notice will have enough copies to properly complete "nail and mail" service on the tenant, if necessary. Put the original notice in a safe place, along with proof of service. If the tenant refuses to move out, you'll need the original notice and proof of service in order to bring and win an eviction proceeding against the tenant.

Chapter 12, Section D, provides a detailed description of the different procedures for delivering notices.

When it comes to serving notices, it's okay to do more than is required by the tenant's lease, but never less. You risk losing the entire eviction suit if you don't serve notice properly.

EXAMPLE 1: The notice section in Betty's lease requires notices to be delivered to the tenant by certified mail, return receipt requested. Peter, Betty's landlord, wants to make sure that Betty knows her lease is being terminated. So Peter asks Manny, the building's super, to hand deliver the notice to Betty. When Manny sees Betty in the lobby, he hands her the notice. When Peter learns that Betty got the notice, he doesn't bother to mail another copy to Betty by certified mail. After all, she actually received it. When Peter later tries to evict Betty, the eviction proceeding is dismissed because Peter didn't serve Betty with the notice in the manner prescribed by the lease.

EXAMPLE 2: The notice section in Paul's lease requires notices to be delivered to the tenant by certified mail, return receipt requested. Susan, Paul's landlord, wants to make sure that Paul knows his tenancy is being terminated. So Susan asks the building manager to hand deliver the notice to Paul. The manager hands Paul the notice in the elevator. Then, Susan instructs her secretary to send Paul another copy of the notice by certified mail, return receipt requested. When Susan later sues to evict Paul, she's successful because she can prove that she served the tenant with the notice in the manner prescribed by the lease.

### 1. Rent-Controlled Tenants

Delivering notices to rent-controlled tenants can be problematic, since they often have no current lease. If you have an old expired lease for the tenant's unit, you can serve the notice in the manner described in the notice clause of the expired lease. If you don't have an expired lease for the tenant in your file, the best practice is to serve the notice in the same manner as a written rent demand is served. (Chapter 12, Section D, describes how to serve a written rent demand.)

## 2.  Always Complete Proof of Service

If the tenant's lease permits service by mail, the best practice is to mail the notice at the post office, and request a "certificate of mailing" for regular mail and certified and registered mail receipts. Keep the receipts in a safe place with the original, signed notice.

If you're required to serve the notice in the same manner as a written rent demand is served, it's essential to have the person who mailed or delivered the notice to the tenant complete an affidavit of service, and sign it before a licensed notary public. An affidavit of service is a sworn statement that describes how, when and where your notice was served on the tenant.

Mail receipts and affidavits of service can be worth their weight in gold when a tenant claims that she didn't get a copy of a required notice to cure, for instance, or tells a judge that you didn't follow the lease when serving it. The post office

receipts or affidavits may be used in court to help prove that service was properly carried out.

This book contains three different forms for proof of service: an Affidavit of Service by Personal Delivery to be used when the notice is left with the tenant, an Affidavit of Service by Substituted Service to be used when the notice is given to another adult who lives or works in the rental unit, and an Affidavit of Service by Conspicuous Place Service, to be used for so-called "nail and mail" service. Chapter 12, Section E, provides samples of the three affidavits and detailed instructions on how to complete the forms.

The Forms CD includes the Affidavit of Service by Personal Delivery, the Affidavit of Service by Substituted Service and the Affidavit of Service by Conspicuous Place Service, and Appendix IV includes a blank tear-out copy of each of the three forms.

## G. DHCR Filing Requirements for Rent-Regulated Tenancies

In some cases, copies of termination notices served upon rent-regulated tenants must be filed with the State Division of Housing and Community Renewal (DHCR) within a prescribed time period after service on the tenant. Here are the two situations in which you must file.

### 1.  Notices to NY State Rent-Stabilized ("ETPA") Tenants

An exact copy of any notice to cure, termination notice or notice of non-renewal, together with proof of service, must be delivered to the DHCR local rent office within seven days after service on the tenant. ((ETPR) 9 NYCCR § 2504.3(c).) Appendix I includes a list of local DHCR offices.

You may mail the notice to the DHCR, so long as it arrives within seven days after the date that it's served on the tenants. *(Goldcrest Realty Co. v. Valle,* N.Y.L.J., 1/19/94, p. 26, col. 4 (City Ct., Westchester County).)

## 2. Notices to Rent-Controlled Tenants

Within 48 hours after a termination notice is served upon a rent-controlled tenant, an exact copy of the notice, together with an affidavit of service, must be filed with the local DHCR district rent office. Appendix I includes a list of local DHCR offices.

Saturdays, Sundays and legal holidays extend the 48-hour requirement. ((NYC Rent & Evict. Regs.) 9 NYCRR § 2204.3(a), (c); (NYC Rent & Evict. Regs.) 9 NYCRR § 2104.3(c).)

# H. DHCR Certificates of Eviction

In some cases, you must apply to the DHCR and obtain a Certificate of Eviction before you may end a rent-controlled or rent-stabilized tenancy. Here are the circumstances in which a Certificate of Eviction is required, and the type of application you must file to obtain permission to end the tenancy.

**Rent-controlled tenants.** You will need to obtain a DHCR Certificate of Eviction before attempting to terminate a rent-controlled tenancy within and outside New York City on any of the following grounds:

- withdrawal of the unit from the rental market
- demolition of the entire building
- occupancy by landlord or immediate family, and
- non-primary residence (outside NYC only).

These grounds are explained in Chapter 14, Section E.

To apply for the Certificate, file an Owner's Application for Order Granting Approval to Refuse Renewal of Lease and/or Proceed for Eviction, (DHCR Form RA-54). After DHCR issues the certificate, you may terminate the tenancy by issuing a 30-day termination notice for units within New York City. Use a one-month termination notice for units outside of New York City.

**Rent-stabilized tenants.** You may refuse to renew a rent-stabilized tenant's lease, within and outside New York City, and apply to the DHCR for a Certificate of Eviction on the following grounds:

- withdrawal of the unit from the rental market
- demolition of the entire building, and
- occupancy of the unit by the landlord or the landlord's immediate family (outside NYC only).

These grounds are explained in Chapter 14, Section E.

To apply for the Certificate, complete an Owner's Application for Order Granting Approval to Refuse Renewal of Lease and/or Proceed for Eviction (Form RA-54). The best practice is to apply for the Certificate of Eviction before the window period during which you would offer a tenant a renewal lease.

The DHCR will give the tenant a copy of your application for a certificate of eviction and will hold an informal hearing, where you and the tenant may present your respective cases. After the hearing, the DHCR will issue an order granting the application and issuing a Certificate of Eviction or denying the application. If the application is withdrawn or denied, you must offer the tenant a renewal lease. Both the tenant and the landlord may appeal an adverse order. ■

Chapter **16**

# Returning Security Deposits and Other Move-Out Issues

Tenants are always anxious to get their full security deposit back once they move out. So when you apply all or part of a tenant's security deposit to unpaid rent, necessary repairs or big cleaning bills, there's often some fallout. Some tenants sue their landlords in small claims court for the return of their security deposit. Others file complaints with the New York State Attorney General's Office, which investigates security deposit disputes.

Fortunately, you can take some simple steps to minimize the possibility that you'll spend hours answering complaints or haggling in court over back rent, repair costs and damage to your property. First, it will help a lot if you've followed our advice in Chapter 7 regarding moving the tenant in and documenting the condition of the premises. And, of course, you must follow the law scrupulously when you return security deposits. But it's also wise to send the tenant, before he or she moves out, a letter setting out your expectations for how the unit should be left.

This chapter shows you how to apply and refund security deposits as New York law requires, and how to protect yourself at move-out time. This chapter also covers how to defend yourself against a tenant's lawsuit or complaint, as well as the occasional necessity of taking a tenant to small claims court if the deposit doesn't cover unpaid rent, damage or extraordinary cleaning bills.

We cover key aspects of New York security deposit law in this chapter and in Chapter 5. In addition, be sure to check local ordinances in all areas where you own property, just in case any cover security deposit return procedures. (We're not aware of any local ordinances, but it doesn't hurt to double-check.)

 Related topics covered in this book include:
- How to avoid deposit disputes by using clear lease and rental agreement provisions: Chapter 2
- How much you can charge for deposits and state requirements for keeping deposits in a separate account or paying interest: Chapter 5

- Highlighting security deposit rules in a move-in letter to new tenants, taking photographs and using a Landlord-Tenant Checklist to keep track of the condition of the premises before and after the tenant moves in: Chapter 7.

## A. Preparing a Move-Out Letter

Chapter 7 explains how a move-in letter can help get a tenancy off to a good start. Similarly, a move-out letter can also help reduce the possibility of disputes, especially over the return of security deposits.

Your move-out letter should tell the tenant how you expect the unit to be left, explain your inspection procedures, list the kinds of deposit deductions you may legally make and tell the tenant when and how you will send any refund that is due.

A sample Move-Out Letter is shown below. You may want to add or delete items depending on your own needs and how specific you wish to be.

 The Forms CD includes the Move-Out Letter, and Appendix IV includes a blank tear-out version of the form.

Here are a few points you may want to include in a move-out letter:
- specific cleaning requirements, such as bombing for fleas if the tenant has a dog, what to do about stained draperies that need special cleaning or how to clean crayon or dirt from walls
- suggestions on how best to perform minor repairs such as fixing holes left from picture hooks
- a reminder to restore the walls, floors and ceilings after removing attached fixtures like built-in book shelves
- details of how and when the final inspection will be conducted (see Section B, below), and
- a request for a forwarding address where you can mail the tenant's deposit.

# Move-Out Letter

July 5, 200X
_____
Date

Jane Wasserman
_____
Tenant
113 Hicks Street, Apt. 18-F
_____
Street address
Brooklyn, NY 11201
_____
City and State

Dear_____Jane_____,
                    Tenant

We hope you have enjoyed living here. In order that we may mutually end our relationship on a positive note, this move-out letter describes how we expect your unit to be left and what our procedures are for returning your security deposit.

Basically, we expect you to leave your rental unit in the same condition it was when you moved in, except for normal wear and tear. To refresh your memory on the condition of the unit when you moved in, I've attached a copy of the Landlord-Tenant Checklist you signed at the beginning of your tenancy. I'll be using this same form to inspect your unit when you leave.

Specifically, here's a list of items you should thoroughly clean before vacating:

☑ Floors

    ☑ sweep wood floors

    ☑ vacuum carpets and rugs (shampoo, if necessary)

    ☑ mop kitchen and bathroom floors

☑ Walls, baseboards, ceilings and built-in shelves

☑ Kitchen cabinets, countertops and sink, stove and oven—inside and out

☑ Refrigerator—clean inside and out, empty it of food, and turn it off, with the door left open

☑ Bathtubs, showers, toilets and plumbing fixtures

☑ Doors, windows and window coverings

☑ Other

Microwave oven—clean inside and out

If you have any questions as to the type of cleaning we expect, please let me know.

Please don't leave anything behind—that includes bags of garbage, clothes, food, newspapers, furniture, appliances, dishes, plants, cleaning supplies or other items that belong to you.

Please be sure you have disconnected phone and utility services, canceled all newspaper subscriptions and sent the post office a change of address form.

Once you have cleaned your unit and removed all your belongings, please call me at 718-555-1212 to arrange for a walk-through inspection and to return all keys. Please be prepared to give me your forwarding address where we may mail your security deposit.

It's our policy to return all deposits either in person or at an address you provide within 60 days after you move out. If any deductions are made—for past due rent or because the unit is damaged or not sufficiently clean—they will be explained in writing.

If you have any questions, please contact me at 718-555-1212.

Sincerely,

*Denise Parsons*

Landlord/Manager

## B. Inspecting the Unit When a Tenant Leaves

When the tenant leaves, you will need to inspect the unit to assess its condition and what cleaning and repair work is necessary. At the final inspection, check each item—for example, refrigerator or bathroom walls—on the Landlord-Tenant Checklist you and the tenant signed when the tenant moved in. (An excerpt is shown here. See Chapter 7 for a complete Checklist.) Note any item that needs cleaning, repair or replacement in the middle column, *Condition on Departure*. Where possible, note the estimated cost of repair or replacement in the third column; you can subtract the actual costs from the security deposit.

Many landlords do this final inspection on their own and simply send the tenant an itemized statement with any remaining balance of the deposit. If at all possible, we recommend that you make the inspection with the tenant who's moving out, rather than by yourself. Conducting the final inspection with the tenant present (in a conciliatory, nonthreatening way) should alleviate any of the tenant's uncertainty concerning what deductions (if any) you propose to make from the deposit. It also gives the tenant a chance to present her point of view. This provides you and the tenant an opportunity to discuss a possible deduction and, if appropriate, reach a compromise on the spot. Best of all, this approach (having the tenant present at the final inspection) avoids the risk that a tenant who feels unpleasantly surprised by the amount you withhold from the deposit will promptly take the matter to small claims court.

If you have any reason to expect a tenant to take you to court over deductions you plan to make from a security deposit, have the unit examined by another person, such as an employee, a contractor or another tenant in the same building. Make sure this person will be available to testify in court on your behalf, if necessary, should you end up in small claims court.

**Photograph "before" and "after" conditions.** In Chapter 7, we recommend that you photograph or videotape the unit before the tenant moves in. You should do the same when the tenant leaves, so that you can make comparisons and have visual proof in case you are challenged later in court.

### Landlord-Tenant Checklist

GENERAL CONDITION OF RENTAL UNIT AND PREMISES

922 West End Avenue      18-F      NY, NY 10025

Street Address          Unit Number    City

| | Condition on Arrival | Condition on Departure | Estimated Cost of Repair/Replacement |
|---|---|---|---|
| **LIVING ROOM** | | | |
| Floors & Floor Coverings | OK | OK | 0 |
| Drapes & Window Coverings | Mini-blinds discolored | Mini-blinds missing | $75 |
| Walls & Ceilings | OK | 12 "quarter-sized" holes from bookshelf removed | $60 |
| Light Fixtures | OK | OK | 0 |
| Windows, Screens & Doors | Window rattles | OK | 0 |

Keep your inspection notes, photos, tapes and other inspection records for at least six years after the tenant moves out. Tenants have up to six years to sue you over a security deposit.

### Should You Let the Tenant Do Extra Cleaning or Fix the Damage?

Many tenants, faced with losing a large chunk of their security deposit, may want the chance to do some more cleaning or repair any damage you've identified in the final inspection. You may wish to offer a second chance if the tenant seems sincere and capable of doing the work. This may help avoid arguments and maybe even a small claims action. But if the tenant's term has expired and you need to get the apartment ready quickly for another tenant or doubt the tenant's ability to do the work, just say no. And think twice if repairs are required, not just cleaning. If a tenant does a repair poorly—for example, improperly tacking down a carpet that later causes another tenant to trip and injure herself—you will be liable for the injury.

## C. Applying the Security Deposit to the Last Month's Rent

When giving notice, a tenant may ask you to apply the security deposit towards the last month's rent. (Chapter 5, Section B, discusses last month's rent and deposits.) If no portion of the tenant's deposit was labeled last month's rent, you are not legally obliged to apply it in this way.

Why should you object if a tenant asks to use a deposit you are already holding as payment for the last month's rent? The problem is that you can't know in advance what the property will look like when the tenant leaves. If the tenant leaves his apartment a mess, but the whole security deposit has gone to pay the last month's rent, obviously you will have nothing left to use to make repairs or clean the apartment. You will have to absorb the loss or sue the tenant.

You have two choices if you are faced with a tenant who wants to use a security deposit for last month's rent. The first alternative is to grant the tenant's request. Tell the tenant that you'll need to make a quick inspection first, and then, if you have good reason to believe that the tenant will leave the property clean and undamaged, don't worry about the last month's rent. (But don't forget to send the tenant a written statement setting out what happened to the deposit. You can prepare a brief letter, similar to the one we show in Section G, below, for returning the tenant's entire security deposit.)

Of course, if the tenant ends up leaving the property filthy or damaged, the security deposit may not be sufficient to cover last month's rent plus the damage and cleaning repair. In this case, you may need to sue the tenant in small claims court for the difference. (See Example 1, below.)

Your second choice is to treat the tenant's non-payment (or partial payment) of the last month's rent as an ordinary case of rent nonpayment. (See Example 2, below.) This means preparing and serving a rent demand notice (see Chapter 12), and if the tenant doesn't pay, following up with an eviction lawsuit while the tenant is still in occupancy. But because it typically takes at least several weeks to evict a tenant, this probably won't get the tenant out much sooner than he would leave anyway. However, it will provide you with a court judgment for the unpaid last month's rent. This means that you may use the security deposit to pay for cleaning and repair costs, and apply any remainder to the judgment for nonpayment of rent. You then take your judgment and attempt to enforce it, as discussed in Section J, below.

EXAMPLE 1: Ari paid his landlord, Jack, a $1,200 deposit when he rented his $1,000 per month apartment on a month-to-month basis. The rental agreement required Ari to give 30 days' notice before terminating the tenancy.

Ari told Jack on November 1 that he would be leaving at the end of the month, but he did not pay his rent for November. When Ari left on December 1, he also left $1,000 worth of damages. Jack applied the $1,200 deposit to cover the damage, and sent Ari a letter telling him how the security deposit was applied. This left Jack with $200 for the $1,000 rent due, so he sued Ari in small claims court for the $800 still owing. Jack was awarded a judgment for $800 plus the filing fee.

EXAMPLE 2: Natalie paid her landlord Jack a $1,500 deposit when she rented her $1,500 per month apartment on a month-to-month basis. The rental agreement required Natalie to give 30 days' notice before terminating the tenancy. Natalie told Jack on June 1 that she would be leaving at the end of the month, but she did not pay her rent for June.

Remembering what a hassle it was to track down and sue Ari in small claims court for unpaid rent after he had moved out (see Example 1), Jack decides to take a different strategy. On June 3, Jack's process server delivers a three-day rent demand for June rent to Natalie. When Natalie still doesn't pay, Jack begins a non-payment eviction lawsuit on June 7 and is awarded a default money judgment for $1,500 on June 28.

When Natalie left on June 30, she also left $1,000 worth of damages. Jack applied the $1,500 security deposit to cover the damage, and sent Natalie a letter telling her how the security deposit was applied. This left Jack with $500 to apply to the $1,500 money judgment. Then Jack took the judgment to the city marshal who secured the remaining $1,000 due from Natalie's bank account and wages.

## D. Basic Rules for Returning Deposits

New York law does not require landlords to return tenant security deposits within a prescribed period of time. The general rule is that you have a "reasonable time" after the tenant leaves to return the tenant's deposit, adjusted for any deductions. You are entitled to deduct from a tenant's security deposit whatever amount you need to fix damaged

property (outside of "ordinary wear and tear") or to make up unpaid rent.

We recommend that 30 days is a reasonable time to return deposits, although depending on the circumstances, 60 days would also be reasonable. For example, if the tenant left the property damaged and filthy, you might need more than 30 days to fully assess your repair and cleanup costs. To protect yourself, our lease and rental agreement forms (Clause 8 in Chapter 2) provide up to 60 days to return deposits.

After the tenant moves out, send the following to the tenant's last known address (or forwarding address if you have one):

- the tenant's entire deposit, with any accrued interest (see Chapter 5, Section F, for interest requirements), or
- a written, itemized accounting as to how the deposit has been applied toward back rent and costs of damage repair or extraordinary cleaning, together with payment for any deposit balance, including any accumulated interest.

Promptly returning the deposit or presenting the tenant with a written itemization of all deductions and a clear reason why each was made is an essential part of a savvy landlord's overall plan to avoid disputes with tenants. (Section G, below, includes a form for returning a tenant's entire deposit and shows how to prepare an itemized statement, including how to handle situations when you're not sure of the exact deductions.)

**Send an itemization even if you don't send money.** Quite a few landlords mistakenly believe that they don't have to account for the deposit to a tenant who's been evicted by court order or who breaks the lease. But a tenant's misconduct does not entitle a landlord to pocket the entire deposit without further formality. In general, even if the tenant leaves owing several months' rent—more than the amount of the deposit—you should still notify the tenant in writing, within 30 days, as to how the deposit has been applied toward cleaning or repair charges and unpaid rent. You may then need to sue the tenant if the deposit doesn't cover all the damage and unpaid rent.

# E. Deductions for Repairs and Cleaning

As you can imagine, many disputes over security deposits revolve around whether or not it was reasonable for the landlord to deduct the cost of repairing the premises after the tenant moved. Unfortunately, standards in this area are vague. Typically, you may charge for any damage caused by the tenant or for repairs necessary to restore the rental unit to its condition at the beginning at the tenancy, but you may not deduct for the results of ordinary wear and tear.

## 1. Reasonable Deductions

The general rule is that you may charge for any damage caused by the tenant or for repairs or replacements necessary to restore the rental unit to its condition at the beginning of the tenancy, but may not deduct for the results of ordinary wear and tear.

### a. Repairs or Damage

In general, you may deduct for any necessary repairs caused by your tenant's neglect or abuse (or that of your tenant's roommates or guests). Examples include fixing holes in walls, re-hanging interior doors torn from their hinges, replacing broken medicine cabinet mirrors or fixing chipped sinks and tubs. You may also deduct for such things as exterminating flea infestations left behind by a tenant's pet or cleaning tobacco smoke residue from the surfaces of the rental unit. (*McCormick v. Moran*, N.Y.L.J., 11/24/99, p. 35, col. 3 (Watertown City Ct).)

You may also deduct the cost of replacing any items that were furnished to the rental unit when the tenant moved in but are now missing. Items that are commonly missing from a rental unit at move out include appliance accessories such as ice cube trays, butter dishes, racks, and broiler trays, medicine cabinet or closet shelves, smoke detectors and fire extinguishers.

You can't deduct for repairs that are due to normal wear and tear, such as fixing an ailing appliance, re-polishing wood floors or replacing fallen plaster. (See Subsection b, below.)

### b. Normal Wear and Tear

There are no hard and fast rules on what constitutes wear and tear; nor is there a clear definition of the type of deterioration that is the tenant's responsibility. We can, however, offer you some guidelines:

- A tenant shouldn't be charged for filth or damage that was present at move-in, such as dirty mini-blinds or nail holes in the wall.
- A tenant shouldn't be charged for replacing an item when a repair would be sufficient. For example, a tenant who damaged the kitchen counter by placing a hot pan on it shouldn't be charged for replacing the entire counter if an expertly done patch will do the job.
- The longer the tenant lived in a place, the more wear and tear can be expected. In practical terms, this means that you can't always charge for cleaning carpets, drapes or walls or for repainting.

### c. Cleaning

Security deposit deductions for cleaning costs aren't clear-cut. Generally, New York tenants are expected to return their units in "broom-clean" condition, unless a stricter cleaning standard is spelled out in the tenant's lease. (See, for instance, *Fernandez v. Chapman*, N.Y.L.J., 12/30/98, p. 27, col. 4 (Mt. Vernon Just. Ct.).) A landlord may deduct for extraordinary cleaning charges, such as cleaning (or replacing) pet-stained carpets or removing large amounts of debris and garbage left by the tenant. But taking deductions for routine cleaning of dirty stoves, refrigerators, bathroom fixtures or mildew in the bathroom is questionable. If a tenant fights a deduction for basic cleaning charges in small claims court before a mediator, you may lose.

## 2. Common Disagreements Regarding Deductions

Common areas of disagreement between landlords and tenants concern painting, carpeting and fixture removal.

### a. Painting

Can you always deduct the cost of a new paint job from the tenant's security deposit? It depends. If the paint damage was caused by a building leak or by your repair work, you shouldn't charge the tenant for re-painting. But if the tenant's abuse or neglect caused the paint damage, you may be able to charge the tenant for part of the re-painting cost. It depends on how long the tenant occupied the unit since the last paint job, and how frequently you are required to paint under your local housing maintenance code. Faded paint is always due to normal wear and tear—and should never affect your tenant's security deposit.

 **New York City landlords must repaint rental units every three years.** (NYC Adm. Code § 27-2013.) If your tenant lived in a NYC unit for at least three years since the last paint job, you may not deduct any of the cost to repaint from the tenant's security deposit. It was time for you to re-paint the unit anyway. But if the tenant lived in the unit for less than three years, a court mediator might find that you were right to charge the tenant for a pro-rata portion of the re-painting costs, if the damage to the paint job exceeded normal wear and tear.

EXAMPLE: Andrea's New York City studio apartment was freshly painted when she moved in. After her one-year lease expired, she moved out. Bob, Andrea's landlord, inspects the unit and notes that all four walls of the unit are completely scraped, scuffed and dirty—far beyond anyone's definition of normal wear and tear. Bob pays his building superintendent $300 to re-paint the unit. Bob may reasonably deduct

$200 (two-thirds of $300) from Andrea's security deposit.

### b. Rugs and Carpets

If the living room rug was already threadbare when the tenant moved in a few months ago and looks even worse now, it's pretty obvious that the tenant's footsteps have simply contributed to the inevitable, and that this wear and tear is not the tenant's responsibility. On the other hand, a brand-new good quality rug that becomes stained within months, has been subjected to the type of abuse tenants have to pay for. In between, it's anyone's guess. But clearly the longer a tenant has lived in a unit, and the cheaper or older the carpet was when the tenant moved in, the less likely it is that the tenant should be held responsible for its deterioration.

EXAMPLE: A tenant's dog has ruined an eight-year-old rug that had a life expectancy of ten years. If the rug originally cost $1,000, you would charge the tenant $200 for the two years of life that would have remained in the rug had their dog not damaged it.

### c. Fixture Removal

A fixture is any piece of personal property screwed into or otherwise affixed to the walls, floors or ceilings of your rental unit, such as bookcases, shelves, sconces or mirrors. Most tenants install at least one such fixture during the course of their tenancy. But all too often, tenants damage walls, floors or ceilings during the removal process.

Like most leases and rental agreements, the ones in this book require tenants to remove their fixtures at move out and to restore the walls, floors or ceilings to their original condition. If your tenant doesn't remove their fixtures (or other personal property), you may consider it "abandoned." That means that you can choose to keep it or throw it out. (The lease or rental agreement may authorize you to store any personal property left behind at the tenant's expense, as explained in Chapter 2.) Either way, any damage caused by the removal of fixtures is the tenant's responsibility.

## F. Deductions for Unpaid Rent

You can deduct any unpaid rent from a tenant's security deposit, including any unpaid late fees, utility charges or other financial obligations authorized by the lease or rental agreement. You can also deduct holdover rent (also known as "use and occupancy") for each extra day that a tenant remains in occupancy after the tenancy ends. How much rent you're entitled to depends on the circumstances of the tenant's departure and whether the tenant was renting under a month-to-month rental agreement or a fixed term lease. If the deposit doesn't cover the unpaid rent, you may need to sue the tenant as described in Section J, below.

### What to Do With Abandoned Belongings

Tenants sometimes move out leaving furniture or other belongings behind. For example, suppose that a tenant moves out leaving her bicycle in your basement. Should you store it, chuck it or give it away? There's no clear-cut legal procedure under New York law for landlords to follow. So in most cases, the answer will lie in the tenant's lease or rental agreement. It could give you the right to discard the bike or keep it for yourself—or the obligation to store it at the tenant's expense.

The lease and rental agreements in this book let you choose to either store the property at the tenant's expense or to throw it out. (See Clause 25 of the form agreements in Chapter 2.) The property's size and value and the amount of storage space in your building should guide your decision. It makes sense to dump an ex-tenant's old and frayed sofa. But you may be willing to store an ex-tenant's bike, tennis racquet or boxes for a month or so.

If the lease doesn't address abandoned property, the best practice is to send the ex-tenant a certified letter listing the property you're holding and advising her that you will hold the tenant's property for pick-up for a specified time period, say 30 days or so, after which time you'll discard it. If you don't have the ex-tenant's forwarding address, send your letter to the rental unit itself. Hopefully, the post office will forward the letter to her new address. If the ex-tenant doesn't contact you within the specified period, you should be safe discarding the property. But keep your copy of the letter just in case the ex-tenant shows up a year later looking for the belongings she left behind.

### 1. Month-to-Month Tenancies

If you rent on a month-to-month basis, ideally your tenant will give the right amount of notice and pay for the last month's rent. The notice period is set by the rental agreement or by state law. Then, when the tenant leaves as planned, the only issue with respect to the security deposit is whether the tenant has caused any damage or left the place extremely dirty. But there are three common variations on this ideal scenario, and they all allow you to deduct from the tenant's security deposit for unpaid rent:

- The tenant leaves as announced, but with unpaid rent behind.
- The tenant leaves later than planned, and hasn't paid for the extra days, or
- The tenant leaves as announced, but hasn't given you the right amount of notice.

Let's look at each situation.

## a.  Tenant Leaves With Rent Unpaid

If the tenant has been behind on the rent for months, you are entitled to deduct what is owed from the security deposit when the tenant leaves. If the security deposit does not cover the entire amount owed, you may need to sue the tenant as discussed in Section J.

## b.  Tenant Stays After the Announced Departure Date

A tenant who fails to leave when planned (or when requested, if you have terminated the rental agreement), obviously isn't entitled to stay on rent-free. When the tenant eventually does leave, you can figure the exact amount owed by prorating the monthly rent for the number of days the tenant has failed to pay.

> EXAMPLE: Your tenant, Erin, gives notice on March 1 of her intent to move out. She pays you the rent of $1,200 for March. But because she can't get into her new place on time, Erin stays until April 5 without paying anything more for the extra five days. You are entitled to deduct 5/30 (one-sixth) of the total month's rent, or $200, from Erin's security deposit.

## c.  Tenant Gives Inadequate Notice

A tenant who gives less than the legally required amount of notice before leaving must pay rent for that entire period. How much notice is required? Here's a summary of the basic rules. (Chapter 13, Section D, provides more detail.)

- If the tenant has a written rental agreement, the agreement specifies how much notice the tenant must provide you before moving out.
- If the tenant has an oral month-to-month agreement for a unit located outside New York City, the tenant must give you one month's notice. (RPL § 232-b.)
- If the tenant has an oral month-to-month agreement for a unit located within New York City, the tenant is not required to give notice before moving out. (RPL § 232-a.) This is another good reason why you should have month-to-month tenants sign rental agreements.

If the tenant gave less than the legally required amount of notice and moved out, you are entitled to rent money for the balance of the notice period unless the place is re-rented within the notice period.

> EXAMPLE 1: Your tenant Tom moves out on the fifth day of the month, without giving you any notice or paying any rent for the month. The rental market is flooded and you are unable to re-rent the property for two months. Tom's written rental agreement provides that he must give you 30 days' notice of his intent to move out. You are entitled to deduct an entire month's rent (for the missing 30 days' notice) plus one-sixth of one month (for the five holdover days for which Tom failed to pay rent).

> EXAMPLE 2: On September 1, Sheila pays $900 monthly rent for her Yonkers apartment, which she rents under an oral month-to-month tenancy. State law requires one month's notice to terminate a tenancy. On September 15th, Sheila informs you that she's leaving on the 25th. This gives you only ten days' notice, when you're entitled to one month's notice. You're entitled to collect rent for one month from the date

Sheila gives notice, or October 14, unless you find a new tenant in the meantime. Because the rent is paid through September 30, Sheila owes you the prorated rent for 14 days in October. At $900 per month or $30 a day, this works out to $420, which you can deduct from Sheila's security deposit.

## 2. Fixed-Term Leases

A lease obligates both you and the tenant for a set period of time, such as one year. If a tenant leaves before a fixed-term lease expires, you are usually entitled to the balance of the rent due under the lease, less any rent you receive from new tenants, or could have received if you had made a diligent effort to re-rent the property. A tenant who has a legal right to break the lease does not, however, have the same financial obligation.

⚠ **Make sure every departing tenant signs a lease surrender agreement.** A tenant who leaves before the lease ends should always give written notice acknowledging their tenancy termination and relinquishing their rights to occupy the unit. Chapter 14, Section H, includes a Lease Surrender Agreement for this purpose.

### a. If Tenant Has a Legal Reason to Move Out

If the tenant is legally justified in breaking the lease, you may not recover the balance of rent due under the lease. It is as though the lease expired. Leaving early to enter military service or move into a nursing home are valid reasons, as is moving out because of defective conditions in the rental unit. For details on these situations when a tenant may legally move out before a lease ends, see Chapter 14, Section F.

### b. Landlord's Duty to Mitigate Damages if Tenant Leaves Early

When a tenant moves out a month or more before the lease ends, don't presume that you can sit back

and keep the tenant on the hook for rent until the lease runs out. If you don't try to re-rent the unit to a new tenant, and instead use the security deposit or sue the former tenant for the whole rent, you may be disappointed. To be entitled to all of the rent, many judges require you to first show that you made "diligent efforts" to re-rent the property reasonably quickly and to keep your losses to a minimum. (*Paragon Industries v. Williams,* 122 Misc. 2d 628, 473 N.Y.S.2d 93 (App. T., 2d Dep't, 1983).) In legalese, this is known as your duty to mitigate damages.

Rulings from New York courts are inconsistent as to a residential landlord's duty to mitigate damages in these situations. In 1995, New York's top court made it clear that in a commercial lease, the landlord has no duty to mitigate damages where the tenant has abandoned the premises. (*Holy Properties, Ltd. v. Kenneth Cole Productions,* Inc. 87 N.Y.2d 130, 637 N.Y.S.2d 964 (1995).) A commercial landlord may refuse to re-rent the premises and sit idly by while unpaid rent piles up during the remainder of the lease. Since 1995, courts in Manhattan and Westchester have applied this rule to residential landlords too. (See, for example, *Whitehouse Estates, Inc. v. Post,* 662 N.Y.S.2d 982 (App. Term, 1st Dep't 1997). Courts in other parts of New York City continue to make a distinction between commercial and residential tenancies and require residential landlords to take reasonable steps to re-rent apartments that tenants vacate early.

Reasonable steps include advertising the unit in newspapers or on the Internet, listing the unit with real estate brokers, posting "for rent" signs at the property or making other personal efforts to find a new tenant. Keep in mind though, that the judge hearing the case may not agree that the landlord has any duty to mitigate damages, meaning that the tenant would be responsible for paying rent during the balance of the lease term.

If you don't try to re-rent the unit and instead use the entire deposit plus sue the former tenant for all of the rent, the judge may only award you rent for a period of a month or so after the tenant moved out.

We recommend that you always try to re-rent the unit. This approach is obviously a sound business strategy. It's much better to have rent coming in every month than to wait, leaving a rental unit vacant for months, and then try to sue (and collect from) a tenant who's long gone.

And if you can show that you sincerely tried to find a new tenant for the unit, you'll be on solid legal ground to use the entire deposit and sue the lease-breaker for all lost rent—even if your efforts to find a new tenant don't pan out—and to get reimbursed for your out-of-pocket expenses. If you end up suing a former tenant for rent, you'll want to be able to show the judge that you acted reasonably in your attempts to re-rent the property. Reasonable efforts include advertising the unit in newspapers or on the Internet, listing the unit with real estate brokers, posting "For Rent" signs at the property or making other personal efforts to find a new tenant.

Don't rely on your memory and powers of persuasion to convince the judge. Keep detailed records, including:

- the original lease
- copies of any for-rent ads you ran in the newspaper or on the Internet, together with receipts or invoices
- copies of any listing agreements you made with real estate brokers or apartment listing services, along with any receipts or invoices
- a log of the time you (or your employee) spent showing the property, and a value for that time
- a log of any people who offered to rent, and if you rejected them, documentation as to why and,
- a copy of the new tenant's lease, if the new rent is less than the original tenant paid.

If a tenant leaves less than a month before the lease is scheduled to end, you can be almost positive that, if the case goes to court, a judge will conclude that the tenant owes rent for the entire lease term. It would be unreasonable to expect you to immediately find a new tenant to take over the few days left of the lease. But if the tenant leaves more than 30 days before the end of a lease, your duty to look for a new tenant will be taken more seriously by the courts.

**EXAMPLE:** On January 1, Anthony rents a house from Will for $1,200 a month and signs a one-year lease. Anthony moves out on June 30, even though six months remain on the lease, making him responsible for a total rent of $7,200. Will re-rents the property on July 10, this time for $1,250 a month (the new tenants pay $833 for the last 20 days in July), which means that he'll receive a total rent of $7,083 through December 31. That's $117 less than the $7,200 he would have received from Anthony had he lived up to the lease, so Will may deduct $117 from Anthony's deposit. In addition, if Will spent a reasonable amount of money to find a new tenant (for newspaper ads, rental agency commissions and credit checks), he may also deduct this sum from the deposit.

## 3. Deducting Rent After You've Evicted a Tenant

If you successfully sue to evict a tenant, you will obtain a court order telling the tenant to leave (which you give to a marshal, sheriff or constable to enforce) and a money judgment, ordering the tenant to pay you rent through the date of the judgment. Armed with these court orders, you can subtract from the security deposit all unpaid rent and damage repair costs.

**EXAMPLE:** Marilyn sues to evict a tenant who fails to pay May's rent of $900. She gets an eviction judgment from the court on June 10 for rent prorated through that date. The tenant doesn't leave until the 17th, when the sheriff comes and puts him out. Marilyn can deduct the following items from the deposit: costs of necessary repairs or extraordinary cleaning beyond ordinary wear and tear, rent for the week between judgment and eviction (seven days at $30/day, or $210) and the amount of the judgment (for rent through July 10).

Before you subtract the amount of a court judgment for unpaid rent from a deposit, deduct any repair and cleaning costs and any unpaid rent not included in the judgment. The reason is simple. A judgment can be collected in all sorts of ways—for example, you can go after the former tenant's wages or bank account—if the security deposit is not large enough to cover everything owed you. However, you are much more limited when it comes to collecting money the tenant owes you for damage and cleaning if you don't have a judgment for the amount. If you don't subtract the cost of damage and cleaning repair from the deposit, you'll have to file suit in small claims court. (See Section J, below.) But if you subtract the amount for cleaning, damage and any unpaid rent not covered in the judgment first, you will still have the judgment if the deposit isn't large enough to cover everything.

EXAMPLE 1: Amelia collected a security deposit of $1,200 from Timothy, whom she ultimately had to sue to evict for failure to pay rent. Amelia got a judgment for $160 court costs plus $1,000 unpaid rent through the date of the judgment. Timothy didn't leave until the sheriff came, about five days later, thus running up an additional prorated rent of $100. Timothy also left damage that cost $1,000 to repair.

Amelia (who hadn't read this book) first applied the $1,200 security deposit to the $1,160 judgment, leaving only $40 to apply toward the rent of $100 which was not reflected in the judgment, as well as the repair charges, which totaled $1,100. Amelia must now sue Timothy for the $1,060 he still owes her.

EXAMPLE 2: Now, assume that Monique was Timothy's landlord in the same situation. But Monique applied Timothy's $1,200 deposit first to the damage charges of $1,000 and then to the $100 rent not reflected in the judgment. This left $100 to apply to the $1,160 judgment, the balance of which she can collect by garnishing Timothy's wages or collecting from his bank account.

## G. Preparing an Itemized Statement of Deductions

Once you've inspected the premises and determined what you need to deduct for cleaning, repairs and back rent, you're ready to prepare a statement for the tenant. The statement should simply list each deduction and briefly explain what it's for.

While you're not legally required to furnish a written, itemized statement detailing how you've applied the security deposit, we strongly recommend that you do so anyway. Often, tenants don't realize that they left their units in bad shape. They think you're just putting their security deposit in your pocket. A detailed statement helps explain how the money was applied, and that your deductions were reasonable. That makes it far less likely that a tenant will go to small claims court or the Attorney General's office for relief.

This section includes samples of a security deposit itemization form that you can use to explain your deductions as well as a form for returning the entire deposit.

 The Forms CD includes the Security Deposit Itemization form and the Letter for Returning Entire Security Deposit. You'll also find blank tear-out versions of the forms in Appendix IV.

### 1. Refunding the Full Deposit

If the tenant left the rental unit in good shape and doesn't owe you any money, return the tenant's full security deposit along with any accrued interest within a reasonable time. Thirty days of the tenant's move out date is generally considered a reasonable time period. A sample letter refunding the tenant's security deposit appears below.

### 2. Itemizing Deductions

If you are making any deductions from the tenant's security deposit, use the Security Deposit Itemization form shown below.

## Letter for Returning Entire Security Deposit

October 11, 200X
Date

Melissa Mulholland
Tenant

Apt. 10–B, 11 West 42nd Street
Street address and unit number

New York, NY 10036
City and State

Dear Ms. Mulholland ,
                        Tenant

Enclosed please find our check No. 3739 dated October 11, 2000 in the amount of $1,052.46 . This represents a full refund of your $1,000 security deposit, plus accumulated interest of $52.46 for the rental unit at Apt. 1-A, 116-53 Queens Blvd., Forest Hills, New York, NY 11375 ,

,

which you rented from us on a month-to-month basis on March 1 ,1999 , and vacated on September 30 , 2000 .

Thank you for leaving the rental unit in good condition. We wish you the best of luck in your future endeavors.

Sincerely,

*Tom Stein*
Landlord/Manager

## Security Deposit Itemization
### (Deductions for Repairs, Cleaning and Unpaid Rent)

Date: _December 19, 200X_

From: _Mary Monahan, Monahan Realty Co._

_545 Madison Avenue_

_New York, New York 10022_

To: _John and Alice Costello_

_349 West 49th Street_

_New York, New York 10019_

Property Address: _6 East 43rd St., New York, New York 10017_

_____ Apartment Number: _7-B_

Rental Period: _January 1, 200X, to October 31, 200X_

1. Security Deposit Received                             $ _1850_

2. Interest on Deposit (if required by lease or law):    $ _72_

3. Total Credit (sum of lines 1 and 2)                          $ _1922_

4. Itemized Repairs and Related Losses:

   _Replacement of missing foyer light fixture—$75_

   _Painting of living room—$260 (required by crayon_

   _and chalk marks)_

   _(receipts attached)_                Total Repair Cost:  $ _335_

5. Necessary Cleaning:

   _Professionally shampoo pet-stained_

   _carpeting in rear bedroom_

   _____

   _____              Total Cleaning Cost: $ _$90_

6. Defaults in Rent and Additional Rent Not Covered
   by Any Court Judgment (list dates and rates):

   _Unpaid late fee (October 200X)_

   _____

   _____

   _____              Total Rent Defaults: $ _40_

7. Amount of Court Judgment for Rent, Costs, Attorney Fees: $ _____0_____

8. Amount Owed (line 3 minus the sum of lines 4, 5, 6, and 7)

   ☐ a. Total Amount Tenant Owes Landlord:                     $ _____

   ☒ b. Total Amount Landlord Owes Tenant:                 $ _____1,457_____

Comments: _The security deposit has been applied as follows: $425 damage and cleaning_
_charges, $40 for defaults in rent (not covered by any court judgment)._

_Our check no. 7823, dated December 19, 200X, in the amount of $1,457 is enclosed._

After completing the top of the form, fill in the amount of the security deposit you received from the tenant (line 1) and the amount of interest due, if any, (line 2). The sum of these two items is the total credit you're holding for the tenant (line 3).

Fill in details on deductions for repairs and cleaning in lines 4 and 5. For each deduction for repairs or cleaning, list the item and the dollar amount. If you've already had the work done, attach copies of your receipts to the itemization. If the work was performed by your building staff, state your cost for labor (the number of hours required, multiplied by the worker's hourly wage) and materials. If your receipts are not very detailed, add more information on labor and supplies, for example:

- "Carpet cleaning by ABC Carpet Cleaners, $160, required by several large grease stains and candle wax imbedded in living room rug."
- "Plaster repair, $400, of several fist-sized holes in bedroom wall."
- "$250 to replace drapes in living room, damaged by cigarette smoke and holes."

If you can't get necessary work done within a month, make a reasonable estimate of the cost. But keep in mind that if the tenant subsequently sues you, you will need to produce receipts or work orders justifying the amount you deducted.

When you're trying to put a dollar amount on damages, the basic approach is to determine whether the tenant has damaged or substantially shortened the useful life of an item that does wear out. If the answer is yes, you may charge the tenant the prorated cost of the item, based on the age of the item, how long it might have lasted otherwise and the original cost. (See Section E, above, for specific examples.)

The Security Deposit Itemization form also includes spaces for you to include unpaid rent not covered by a court judgment (line 6) and, if you have won an eviction lawsuit against the tenant, the amount of the court judgment you won (line 7). (Section F, above, shows you how to figure these amounts, and explains why it's better to deduct cleaning and damage costs from the security deposit before deducting any of a court judgment.) If the tenant has left without paying utility charges or another financial obligation required under your lease

or rental agreement, provide details on line 6 (Defaults in Rent and Additional Rent Not Covered by Any Court Judgment). Finally, fill in how much the tenant owes you or vice versa on line 8.

If there's a court judgment involved, explain how you applied the deposit in the Comments section at the bottom of the itemization form. This makes it clear that you are demanding the balance owed and that you can still collect any part of the judgment not covered by the security deposit.

The Comments section is also the place for statements such as:

- "A check for $1,457 is enclosed."
- "Please send me a check for $500 by March 1."
- "The security deposit has been applied as follows: $1,000 for repairs and $100 for unpaid late fees. A check for the balance of the deposit ($226.37) is enclosed."

## H. Mailing the Security Deposit Itemization

Some tenants will want to personally pick up any deposit as soon as possible. If that isn't feasible, mail your security deposit itemization to the tenant's last known address or forwarding address as soon as is reasonably possible, along with payment for any balance you owe. When you have all the information necessary to act, don't put it off, as delay almost guarantees that a large number of anxious tenants will contact you.

To be on the safe side, use certified mail. If the tenant hasn't left you a forwarding address, mail the itemization and any balance to the address of the rental property itself. That, after all, is the tenant's last address known to you. If your former tenant has left a forwarding address with the post office, it will forward the mail.

It will be useful for you to know the tenant's new address if the tenant's deposit doesn't cover all proper deductions and you want to sue in small claims court. (See Section J, below.) It will also help you collect any judgment you have against the tenant.

There are two ways that you can learn the tenant's new address:

- **Set up an account with the Postal Service.** You can pay the Post Office in advance to tell you whenever one of your letters is forwarded. Because of the cost involved, this procedure makes sense for landlords with many rental units.
- **Use Return Receipt Requested.** If you don't have many rental units or rarely face this situation, it may not be worth your while to prepay. Instead, you can send the letter "Return Receipt Requested" and, on the Postal Service form, check the box that tells the carrier to note the address where the letter was delivered. This address will be on the receipt that is sent back to you.

If the tenant has left no forwarding address, the letter will come back to you. The postmarked envelope is proof of your good-faith attempt to notify the tenant, in case the tenant ever accuses you of not returning the money properly.

File the itemization with your other tenant records. The tenant has up to six years after moving out to sue you or file a complaint for the return of the security deposit. Keep your itemization and your receipts (together with the envelope in which they were returned to you) for at least that time.

---

### Security Deposits From Co-Tenants

When you rent to two or more co-tenants (they all sign the same written lease or rental agreement), you do not have to return or account for any of the deposit until they all leave. In other words, you're entitled to the benefit of the entire deposit until the entire tenancy ends. Legally, any question as to whether a departing co-tenant is entitled to any share of the deposit should be worked out among the co-tenants.

---

## I. If a Tenant Files a Complaint or Sues You

No matter how meticulous you are about properly accounting to your tenants for their deposits, sooner or later a tenant who disagrees with your assessment of the cost of cleaning or repairs will file a complaint with the state Attorney General's office or sue you (usually in small claims court). Tenants may also file a complaint or sue if you fail to return the deposit within a reasonable period of time (usually 30 days), or violate other legal requirements, such as paying interest on the deposit (for details, see Chapter 5). Usually, the tenant will first contact you and try to work out a compromise.

This section suggests several strategies for dealing with complaints and lawsuits over security deposits, including how to prepare and present a case in small claims court.

⚠️ **Don't throw out your security deposit itemizations, repair bills or receipts for materials, work orders or photographs that support your deductions.** Tenants have up to six years after the tenancy ends to file a complaint or sue you in small claims court over the security deposit. You don't want to be caught defenseless if a tenant files a complaint or sues you a few years down the road.

## 1. How to Work Out a Compromise

Before filing a complaint with the Attorney General or going to court, the tenant will most likely express dissatisfaction by way of a letter or phone call demanding that you refund more than you did or fix some other problem involving the deposit. If you receive a phone call, letter, complaint or summons from a tenant, your best bet is almost always to try to work out a reasonable compromise. Be open to the idea of returning more of the deposit to the tenant, even if you believe your original assessment of the cost of repairs and cleaning was more than fair and you feel you will surely win in court. For practical reasons, it usually doesn't make sense for you or an employee to prepare a small claims case and spend time in court to argue over $50, $100 or even $200. This is especially true because, fair or not, some judges are prone to split the difference between the landlord's and the tenant's claims.

If you and the tenant can't reach a reasonable compromise, you may wish to get help from a small claims court affiliated mediation service. See "The Mediation Alternative," below.

If you arrive at a compromise settlement with your former tenant, you should insist that your payment be accepted as full and final satisfaction of your obligation to return the deposit. The best way to do this is to prepare and have the tenant sign a brief settlement agreement, like the sample shown below.

### Sample Settlement Agreement

James J. Miller, "Landlord," and Cecile Luan, "Tenant," agree as follows:

Landlord rented the premises at 18-54 42nd St., Astoria, NY 11105, pursuant to a written rental agreement from month to month.

Under the Agreement, Tenant paid landlord $1,000 as a security deposit.

On October 31, 200X, Tenant vacated the premises.

On November 22, 200X, Landlord itemized various deductions from the security deposit totaling $380 and refunded the balance of $620 to the Tenant.

Tenant asserts that she is entitled to the additional sum of $300, only $80 of the deductions being proper. Landlord asserts that all of the deductions were proper and that he owes Tenant nothing.

To settle the parties' entire dispute, and to compromise on Tenant's claim for return of the security deposit, Landlord pays to Tenant the sum of $150, receipt of which is hereby acknowledged by tenant in full satisfaction of her claim.

Date: 12/1/0X    *Jim Miller, Landlord*

Date: 12/1/0X    *Cecile Luan, Tenant*

## Splitting the Difference With Tenants

One landlord we know, with thousands of units, experiences about 250 move-outs each month. In about one-third, he receives a complaint from a tenant who claims too much of the deposit was withheld.

This landlord's general policy is to offer to settle for 70% of the disputed amount. Since the average amount withheld is $175, this means the landlord is willing to reduce this amount by $52.50. If a tenant refuses to accept this compromise, the landlord will often make a second offer of a 50% reduction.

He does this not because he thinks his original assessment was wrong, but because he finds that coming to a settlement with a tenant costs a lot less than fighting in court. However, if the settlement offer isn't accepted promptly by the tenant, he fights to win and almost always does.

## 2. When a Tenant Complains to the Attorney General's Office

The New York State Attorney General's office (AG) investigates tenant complaints about security deposits, including claims that the landlord failed to return the security deposit after the tenant has moved out. When a tenant files a complaint, the AG forwards a copy to the landlord with a request to respond. Your best bet is to respond by forwarding to the AG a copy of the security deposit itemization you sent to the tenant, showing how the tenant's deposit was applied to unpaid rent or to pay for tenant-caused damage to the rental unit. This will generally be sufficient to conclude the investigation.

If you don't respond to the tenant's complaint, or if your response doesn't address the issues raised by the tenant, the AG will urge the tenant to file a small claims court action against you. While the AG's office may prosecute claims that the landlord has failed to place security deposits in trust accounts or

to pay interest when required by statute, the AG isn't authorized to prosecute security deposit refund claims on behalf of tenants, nor penalize landlords who take too long to refund security deposits or withhold too much money. Even if the AG is out of the picture, the tenant may continue to pursue the dispute. If the tenant thinks that your security deposit deductions were unreasonable or excessive the tenant may still sue you in court.

**Security Deposit Complaints to AG's Office.** For more information contact the New York State Office of the Attorney General, Consumer Protection Bureau, 120 Broadway, 3rd Floor, New York, NY 10271 212-416-8345, or visit the AG's website at www.oag.state.ny.us.

## 3. When a Tenant Files a Small Claims Lawsuit

If a tenant is going to sue you over the security deposit, it will probably be in small claims court. Tenants usually sue in small claims court because it's inexpensive, simple and quick. It's cheap to file a small claims case, lawyers aren't required and disputes typically go before a judge (there are no juries) within 30 to 60 days, without formal rules of evidence. See "How It's Done in Small Claims Court," below. The maximum amount someone can sue for in small claims court is currently $3,000 in New York. A tenant who is going to sue will probably do it fairly promptly, but technically has up to six years to do so. (CPLR § 213.)

Once the tenant has filed suit, the court will officially notify you of the date, time and place of the small claims court hearing. It's still not too late at this stage to try to work out a settlement by paying part of what the tenant's suing for. However, if you compromise at this stage, put your settlement in writing and make sure the tenant correctly discontinues the small claims court suit "with prejudice." That means that the tenant can't sue you again over the same issue. See the sample settlement agreement, above.

## a.  Who May Defend a Small Claims Court Case?

If your business is incorporated, you can send a corporate director, officer or employee (such as a property manager) or attorney to defend the suit, as long as the person who appears on behalf of the company is authorized to speak for and bind it to a settlement with the tenant. If you are not incorporated, you (or your attorney) must go. But it's rarely worth the cost of having an attorney represent you. Procedures are simple and designed for non-lawyers. (See Sections 1801 through 1804 of the NYC Civil Court Act, the Uniform Justice Court Act and the Uniform City Court Act; Uniform Rules for the NY State Trial Courts, Secs. 208.41 and 208.41-a.)

### How It's Done in Small Claims Court

Court procedure in small claims court is informal and simplified. Strict rules on presenting and admitting evidence don't apply. In some localities, only judges hear small claims court cases. Both judges and arbitrators are available to hear small claims court cases in New York City, Nassau and Westchester counties, the cities of Buffalo and Rochester, and some other locations. An arbitrator is an experienced lawyer who serves without pay. Your case can be tried by an arbitrator if both you and the tenant agree. The up side of having an arbitrator hear the case is that your case will be called far sooner on the day it is set to be heard, since there are almost always more arbitrators than judges. The down side is that once an arbitrator determines a case, the decision is final. That means that you could get stuck with an unfair decision. Neither you nor the tenant can appeal, as you can with small claims court cases heard by a judge.

## b.  How to Prepare for a Small Claims Court Hearing

If the tenant is disputing your deductions for repairs or clearing, you'll want tangible evidence showing the premises were damaged or excessively dirty when the tenant left. But chances are, you won't know of the tenant's plans to sue until *after* you've cleaned up and done the repairs. For this reason, it's prudent (though a bit paranoid) to treat every move-out that involves more than nominal cleaning, repairs and deductions as a potential lawsuit. If you learn in several weeks' time that you've been invited to court, you'll need to have as many of the following items of evidence as you can:

- Copies of the lease or rental agreement, signed by both you and the tenant.
- Copies of move-in and move-out letters clarifying your rules and policies on cleaning, damage repair and security deposits.
- A copy of the Landlord-Tenant Checklist that you should have filled out with the tenant when the tenant moved in and when she moved out, signed by both you and the tenant. This is particularly important if the tenant

admitted, on the Checklist, to damaged or dirty conditions when she moved out.

- Photos or videos of the premises before the tenant moved in which show how clean and undamaged the place was.

- Photos or videos after the tenant left which show a mess or damage.

- An itemization of hours spent by you or your repair or cleaning people on the unit, complete with the hourly costs for the work, plus copies of receipts for cleaning materials or credit card itemizations or canceled checks.

- Damaged items small enough to bring into the courtroom (a curtain with a cigarette hole or a section of pet-stained rug you needed to replace.

- Receipts or a canceled check for professional cleaning (particularly of carpets and drapes) and repair.

- One, or preferably two, witnesses who were familiar with the property, saw it just after the tenant left and who will testify that the place was a mess or that certain items were damaged. People who helped in the cleaning or repair are particularly effective witnesses. There is no rule that says you can't have a close friend or relative testify for you, but given a choice, it's better to have a witness who's neither a friend nor kin.

- If it's difficult for a witness to come to court, a written statement (a signed letter) or affidavit (a sworn statement signed before a notary public) can be used. Documents, however, usually aren't as effective as live testimony. If you do present a written statement from a witness, make sure the statement includes the date of the event, describes exactly what the witness saw in terms of damage, lists any credentials that make the person qualified to testify on the subject and presents any other facts that have a bearing on the dispute. A sample statement is shown below.

If the tenant is disputing your deductions for unpaid rent or other charges, be sure to read Section F, above, for evidence that will support your deductions.

## Sample Declaration of Paul Stallone, Cleaner

I, Paul Stallone, declare:

1. I am employed at A & B Maintenance Company, a contract cleaning and maintenance service located at 123 15th Street, Brooklyn, New York. Gina Cabarga, the owner of an apartment complex at 456 Seventh Avenue, New York, New York, is one of our accounts.

2. On May 1, 199X, I was requested to go to the premises at 456 Seventh Avenue, Apartment 8, New York, New York, to shampoo the carpets. When I entered the premises, I noticed a strong odor, part of what seemed like stale cigarette smoke. An odor also seemed to come from the carpet.

3. When I began using a steam carpet cleaner on the living room carpet, I noticed a strong smell of urine. I stopped the steam cleaner, moved to a dry corner of the carpet, and pulled it from the floor. I then saw a yellow color on the normally white foam-rubber pad beneath the carpet, as well as smelled a strong urine odor, apparently caused by a pet (probably a cat) having urinated on the carpet. On further examination of the parts of the carpet, I noticed similar stains and odors throughout the carpet and pad.

4. In my opinion, the living room carpet and foam-rubber pad underneath need to be removed and replaced and the floor should be sanded and sealed.

I declare under penalty of perjury under the laws of the State of New York that the foregoing is true and correct.

_6/15/9X_                _Paul Stallone_
Date                     Paul Stallone, Cleaner

**Small Claims Suits Don't Affect Other Lawsuits**

Nothing that happens in small claims court affects the validity of any judgment you already have—for example, from an earlier eviction suit—against the tenant. So, if you got a judgment against a tenant for $1,200 for unpaid rent as part of an eviction action, this judgment is still good, even though a tenant wins $200 against you in small claims court based on your failure to return the deposit.

### 4. Penalties for Violating Security Deposit Laws

In addition to whatever amount you wrongfully withheld, the court will usually order you to pay interest from the date you should have refunded the deposit to the tenant (usually, 30 to 60 days from the date the lease or rental agreement ended). If you deliberately and unreasonably withheld the security deposit, the court *could* order you to pay punitive damages to the tenant to punish you for bad conduct. But if the dispute was reasonable, punitive damages aren't appropriate. If the tenant's lease or rental agreement has an attorney's fees clause, you may also be on the hook for the tenant's court costs and legal fees, if any.

**The Mediation Alternative**

Community dispute resolution centers (under contract to the courts) are available in every county in the state. There is normally no charge or a small filing fee. Cases are heard quickly at a time and place that's convenient to you and your former tenant.

The mediation process is voluntary. You can't be forced to show up and you can't force your ex-tenant to show up. Mediation gives you and your former tenant the opportunity to present your positions and to work together on possible solutions with the help of a professionally trained mediator. A written binding agreement can be drawn up to resolve the dispute.

To find the nearest dispute resolution center, call the State Alternative Dispute Resolution Center at 518-238-2888 or write them at 98 Niver St., Cohoes, NY 12047.

## J. If the Deposit Doesn't Cover Damage and Unpaid Rent

Tenants aren't the only ones who can sue in small claims court. If the security deposit doesn't cover what a tenant owes you for back rent, repairs or extraordinary cleaning, you may be able to file a lawsuit against the former tenant in small claims court, too.

If you plan to file suit in small claims court, be sure your claim doesn't exceed the small claims court limit (currently, $3,000) or, if it does, decide whether it make sense to scale it back to the limit. Given the costs of going to formal court, this can sometimes make sense.

 **If your business is organized as a corporation or partnership, be careful about where you file suit.** The general rule in New York State is that corporations and partnerships may not file suit in small claims court. Corporations and partnerships must use village and town courts instead. However, a "commercial small claims court" is available in every borough of New York City, in some district courts in Nassau and Suffolk Counties and in some of the 61 city courts located outside New York City. Where available, corporations and partnerships may file up to five commercial small claims court claims per month. For the court to have jurisdiction, the claim must be for $3,000 or less and the former tenant must either work or live in the county in which the court is located (Sections 1801-A through 1814-A of the NYC Civil Court Act, the Uniform City Court Act and the Uniform District Court Act.) A landlord who conducts business as a "sole proprietorship" (that is, as a one-person business) should file suit in the "regular" small claims court—not the commercial small claims court.

 Don't forget alternatives to small claims court such as mediation (see "The Mediation Alternative," above) or an outside collection agency (see "Using Collection Agencies," below).

## 1.  The Demand Letter

If you decide that it is worthwhile to go after your tenant for money owed, your first step is to write a letter asking for the amount of your claim. Though not legally required for every small claims court case, demand letters can be useful in trying to settle your dispute and are an excellent opportunity to carefully organize the case you will present in court.

Your demand can consist of a cover letter along with a copy of your earlier written itemization of how you applied the tenant's security deposit to the charges (in which you also requested payment of the balance). (See Section G, above.) The tone of your cover letter should be polite, yet firm. Ask for exactly what you want and be sure to set a deadline. Conclude by stating you will promptly file a lawsuit in small claims court if you don't reach an understanding by the deadline.

## 2.  Should You Sue?

If your demand letter does not produce results, think carefully before you rush off to your local small claims court. Ask yourself three questions: (1) Do you have a strong case? (2) Can you locate the former tenant? (3) Can you collect a judgment if you win? If the answer to any of these questions is no, think twice about initiating a suit.

⚠ **Take care of your reputation.** If you are a landlord with many rental units and regularly use a local small claims court, make particularly sure that every case you bring is a good one. You do not want to lose your credibility with the court by appearing to be unfair or poorly prepared.

### a.  Do you have a strong case?

Review your items of evidence, such as before-and-after photos which show that your tenant damaged the rental unit. If you lack a substantial amount of evidence you may end up losing, even though you are in the right. Small claims court is rarely about justice, but always about preparation and skill.

### b.  Can You Locate the Former Tenant?

To begin your small claims court case, legal papers must be sent to the tenant. So you'll need an address where the tenant lives or works. If the tenant left a forwarding address, locating the tenant won't be an issue. But if the tenant left no forwarding address, you may use the tenant's employer's address instead. If you don't have a home or work address for the tenant, you'll need to do a little detective work if you want to sue.

Start by filing a "skip-trace" form at the Post Office using the tenant's name and last known address. If the tenant asked the Post Office to forward mail to a new address, you'll be supplied with the forwarding address. Or, if you have access to the Internet, use a search engine's "people finder" to check for a new address or phone number.

If the tenant's new address is in New York (or the tenant works in New York), you can sue the tenant in the small claims court for the municipality where the tenant lives or works. If the tenant lives in a neighboring state and doesn't work in New York, you'll need to sue the tenant in the other state's small claims court. If the tenant lives too far away, it obviously won't make economic sense to sue the tenant.

### c. Can You Collect a Judgment If You Win?

Winning a small claims court case won't do you any good if you can't collect a judgment. Suing a person you know to be bankrupt, insolvent or just plain broke may not be worth the effort, since you'll have little chance of transforming your court judgment into cash. When you evaluate the solvency of the tenant, keep in mind that small claims judgments are good for 20 years. (CPLR § 211(b).) So if you have a spat with a student or someone who may get a job soon, it might be worthwhile to get a judgment with the hope of collecting later.

Pay particular attention to the issue of how you will collect a judgment. The best way to collect any judgment against your ex-tenant is to garnish wages. If she's working, there is an excellent chance of collecting if payment is not made voluntarily. Another way is to find out the name and address of the defendant's employer. If you sued an employed person, you may be able to collect your judgment out of his or her salary. You can collect 10% of the ex-tenant's salary until the judgment is paid, provided the tenant's gross earnings are above a certain minimum amount set by federal law (currently $142.50 per week). You can't, however, garnish a welfare, Social Security, unemployment, pension or disability check. So, if the person sued gets income from one of these sources, you may be wasting your time unless you can identify some other asset that you can efficiently get your hands on.

Bank accounts, motor vehicles and real estate are other common collection sources. But people who run out on their debts don't always have much in a bank account (or they may have moved the account to make it difficult to locate), and much of their personal property may be exempt under state debt protection laws.

## Using Collection Agencies

If you don't want to sue in small claims court, consider hiring a licensed local collection agency to try to collect from the tenant. The agency will probably want to keep as its fee anywhere from one-third to one-half of what it collects for you. (The older the debt or the more difficult it is to locate the tenant, the more the agency will want.) If the agency can't collect, you can authorize it to hire a lawyer to sue the ex-tenant, usually in a formal (non-small claims) court. Many collection agencies pay all court costs, hoping to recover them if and when they collect the resulting judgment. In exchange for taking the risk of paying costs and losing the case, however, collection agency commissions often rise an additional 15%–20% when they hire a lawyer to sue.

Of course, turning a matter over to a collection agency doesn't necessarily mean you wash your hands of the matter. The collection agency still takes direction from you. If the tenant defends against a lawsuit filed by a collection agency's lawyer, you must be involved in the litigation. The only way to walk away from it completely is to sell the debt to the collection agency, which may pay you only a fraction of the amount owed.

Chapter **17**

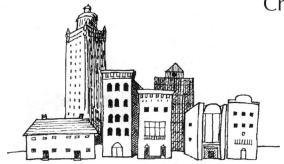

# Lawyers and Legal Research

Landlords should be prepared to deal with most routine legal questions and problems without a lawyer. If you bought all the needed information at the rates lawyers charge—$150 to $350 an hour—it should go without saying that you'd quickly empty your bank account. Just the same, there are times when good advice from a specialist in landlord-tenant law will be helpful, if not essential—for example, in lawsuits by tenants alleging housing discrimination or claiming that dangerous conditions or wrongful acts caused injury. Throughout this book, we point out specific instances when an attorney's advice or services may be useful.

Fortunately, for an intelligent landlord there are a number of other ways to acquire a good working knowledge of the legal principles and procedures necessary to handle problems with tenants, managers, supers and government agencies. Of course, that's the main purpose of this book. But in addition to the information we provide, this chapter specifically recommends a strategy to most efficiently and effectively use legal services and keep up-to-date on landlord-tenant law, so that you can anticipate and avoid many legal problems.

As a sensible landlord, it doesn't make sense to try and run your business without ever consulting a lawyer. When legal problems are potentially serious and expensive, it makes sense to get expert help. But since you almost surely can't afford all the services a lawyer might offer, you obviously need to set priorities. When thinking about a legal problem, ask yourself: "Can I do this myself?" "Can I do this myself with some help from a lawyer?" "Should I simply put this in my lawyer's hands?"

Or, put another way, your challenge isn't to avoid lawyers altogether but rather to use them on a cost-effective basis. Ideally, this means finding a lawyer who's willing to serve as a mentor to help you educate yourself. Then, you can often take care of routine or preliminary matters on your own, turning to your lawyer only when needed for advice and fine-tuning.

**Don't forget small claims court and mediation services.** These are often useful (and less costly) alternatives to hiring a lawyer—for example, in resolving security deposit disputes as discussed in Chapter 16, Section I.

### How Lawyers Can Help Landlords

Here are some important things lawyers can do to help landlords:

- Review key documents you have drafted, such as a lease, lease rider or manager agreement.
- Confirm that you have a good claim or defense vis-a-vis an individual tenant—whether it's a dispute over how much security deposit you must return or your right to raise the rent.
- Make a quick phone call or write a letter to the tenant and get a problem resolved quickly.
- Help you answer an administrative complaint filed by a tenant, such as a DHCR rent overcharge complaint.
- Summarize and point you to the law that applies in a given situation.
- Provide any needed assistance with evictions, including preparing notices and forms, and
- Handle legal problems that are—or are threatening to become—serious, such as a tenant's personal injury lawsuit or discrimination charge.

## A. Finding a Lawyer

How frequently you'll need a lawyer's help will depend on many factors, including the type, number and location of rental units you own, whether your units are rent controlled or rent stabilized, the kinds of problems you run into with tenants, the number of property managers and other employees you hire and your willingness to do some of the legal work yourself.

In looking for a lawyer you can work with, and to manage your subsequent relationship with that person, always remember one key thing—you're the boss. Just because your lawyer has specialized training, knowledge, skills and experience in dealing with legal matters is no reason for you to abdicate control over legal decision making and how much time and money should be spent on a particular legal problem. We say this because despite the fact that you have an intimate knowledge of your business and are in the best position to call the shots, some lawyers will be willing or even eager to try and run your business and charge you dearly for the privilege. The key is to find a lawyer who can provide the amount and type of legal services you need.

## 1. Compile a List of Prospects

Finding a good, reasonably priced lawyer expert in landlord-tenant legal issues is not always an easy task. If you just pick a name out of the telephone book—even someone who advertises as a landlord law expert—you may get someone who's not qualified to deal with your particular problem or someone who will charge too much. If you use an attorney you or a friend has relied on for other legal needs, you will very likely end up with someone who doesn't know enough about landlord-tenant law.

This sorry result is not inevitable—there are good landlords' lawyers who charge fairly for their services. As a general rule, deep experience in landlord-tenant law is most important. As with so many other areas of the law, the information needed to practice effectively in this field has become increasingly specialized in the past two decades—so much so that a general practitioner simply won't do.

### a. Get Recommendations From Other Landlords

The best way to find a suitable attorney is through some trusted person who has had a satisfactory

experience with one. Your best referral sources are other landlords in your area. Ask the names of their lawyers and a little bit about their experiences. Your local landlords' association will likely know of lawyers who have experience in landlord-tenant law too, and other areas of law that affect your business. (Appendix I contains a list of landlord associations throughout the state.) If you talk to a few landlords, chances are you'll come away with several leads on good lawyers experienced in landlord-tenant law.

### b. Contact Lawyer Referral Services

You can also check out lawyer referral services offered by local bar associations. Keep in mind that all lawyer referral services are not created equal. Some services can offer you little more than the names of a few attorneys in your area who may (or may not) have enough experience to meet your needs. Other referral services carefully screen the attorneys they refer to consumers. A good place to start is with the New York State Bar Association Lawyer Referral and Information Service (phone 800-342-3661 or 518-463-3200; www.nysba.org). Appendix I lists 22 other lawyer referral services throughout the state.

## 2. Shop Around

After several reliable people give you the names of hopefully top-notch prospects, your job has just begun. You need to meet with each attorney and make your own evaluation. If you explain that, as a local landlord, you have a continuing need for legal help, many lawyers will be willing to speak to you for a half hour or so at no charge or at a reduced rate so that you can size them up and make an informed selection. Briefly explain your business and legal needs and how much work you plan to do yourself.

Look for experience, personal rapport and accessibility. Some of these traits will be apparent almost immediately. Others may take longer to discover. In addition to the person making the original recommendation, you may want to talk with some of the lawyer's other landlord clients about their satisfaction with the lawyer's work. A lawyer should be able to provide you with such a list of references.

Here are some things to look for in your first meeting:

**Will the lawyer answer all your questions about fees, his experience in landlord-tenant matters and your specific legal problems?** Stay away from lawyers who make you feel uncomfortable asking questions. No matter how experienced and well recommended a lawyer is, if you don't feel rapport with that person during your first meeting or two, you may never achieve an ideal lawyer-client relationship. Trust your instincts and seek a lawyer whose personality is compatible with your own. Be sure you understand how the lawyer charges for services. (Section B discusses various fee arrangements with lawyers.)

**Will the lawyer provide the kind of legal help you want?** If you plan to be actively involved in dealing with your legal business, look for a lawyer who doesn't resent your participation and control. By reading this book all the way through and consulting the legal resources discussed in this chapter, you can answer many of your questions on your own. For example, you might do the initial legal work in making a rent demand or terminating a month-to-month tenancy yourself, but turn over to a lawyer cases which become hotly contested or complicated.

Unfortunately, some lawyers are uncomfortable with the very idea of helping people help themselves. They see themselves as all-knowing experts and expect their clients to accept and follow their advice without question. Obviously, this is not the type of lawyer a self-helper will want.

**Is the lawyer savvy about rent-regulatory issues?** Just because a lawyer handles real estate closings doesn't mean that he knows how to defend a DHCR complaint. If you have any rent-controlled or rent-stabilized units, you'll need a lawyer who can navigate the complex web of laws and regulations that protect rent-regulated tenants.

**Is the lawyer willing to assist you when you have specific questions, billing you on an hourly basis when you handle your own legal work—such as terminations?** One key to figuring out if a lawyer is really willing to help you help yourself is to ask: Is he willing to answer your questions over the phone and charge only for the brief amount of time the conversation lasted? If instead he indicates that he prefers to provide advice in more time-consuming (and therefore profitable) office appointments, you'll want to keep looking.

**Will the lawyer clearly lay out all your options for handling a particular legal problem, including alternate dispute resolution methods such as mediation?**

**Will the lawyer be accessible when you need legal services?** If, every time you have a problem, there's a delay of several days before you can talk to your lawyer on the phone or get an appointment, you'll lose precious time, not to mention sleep. And almost nothing is more aggravating than to leave a legal question or project in a lawyer's hands and then have weeks or even months go by without anything happening. So be sure to discuss with any lawyer whether she will really commit herself to returning your phone calls promptly, work hard on your behalf and follow through on all assignments.

**Does the lawyer represent tenants, too?** Chances are that a lawyer who represents both landlords and tenants can advise you well on how to avoid many legal pitfalls of being a landlord. On the other hand, you'll want to steer clear of lawyers who represent mostly tenants, since their sympathies (world view) are likely to be different from yours.

## B. Types of Fee Arrangements With Lawyers

How you pay your lawyer depends on the type of legal services you need and the amount of legal work you have. Once an agreement is reached, it's a good idea to ask for a written fee agreement— basically an explanation of how the fees and costs will be billed and paid. As part of this, negotiate an overall cap on what you can be billed absent your specific agreement.

If a lawyer will be delegating some of the work on your case to a less experienced associate, paralegal or secretary, that work should be billed at a lower hourly rate. Be sure to get this information recorded in your initial written fee agreement.

There are four basic ways that lawyers charge for their services.

## 1.  Hourly Fees

Usually, you can get competent services for your rental business for $150 to $300 an hour, with most lawyers billing in ten- or 15-minute increments. Comparison shopping among lawyers will help you avoid overpaying. But the cheapest hourly rate isn't necessarily the best. You can often benefit by hiring a more experienced landlord's attorney, even if her hourly rates are high, since she will be further along the learning curve than a general practitioner, and should take less time to review and advise you on the particulars of your legal matter. In many cases, the lawyer will ask you for an advance of a few hundred dollars or more, before she will represent you on an hourly basis.

## 2.  Flat Fees

Sometimes, a lawyer will quote you a flat fee for a specific job. For example, a lawyer may offer to represent you in court for routine eviction cases (such as for nonpayment of rent) that present little trouble, even when they are contested by the tenant. In a flat fee agreement, you pay the same amount regardless of how much time the lawyer spends on a particular job. If you own many rental units and anticipate providing a fair amount of business over the years, you have a golden opportunity to negotiate flat fees that are substantially below the lawyer's normal hourly rate. After all, the lawyer will see you as a very desir-

able client, since you'll generate continuing business for many years to come.

## 3.  Retainer Fees

In some circumstances, it can also make sense to hire a lawyer for a flat annual fee, or retainer, to handle all of your routine legal questions and business, such as noncontested eviction cases. You'll usually pay in equal monthly installments and, normally, the lawyer will bill you an additional amount for extraordinary services—such as representing you in a complicated eviction lawsuit. Since the lawyer can count on a reliable source of income, you can expect lower overall fees. Obviously, the key to making a retainer fee arrangement work is to have a written agreement clearly defining what's routine and what's extraordinary. This type of fee arrangement is more economically feasible for larger landlords (with six or more buildings) with regular legal needs. Also, retainer fee agreements are usually best negotiated after you and your lawyer have worked together long enough to have established a pattern—you know and trust each other well enough to work out a mutually beneficial arrangement.

## 4.  Contingency Fees

This is a percentage (such as one-third) of the amount the lawyer obtains for you in a negotiated settlement or through a trial. If the lawyer recovers nothing for you, there's no fee. Contingency fees are common in personal injury cases, but relatively unusual for the kinds of legal advice and representation landlords need.

## C. Saving on Legal Fees

There are many ways to hold down the cost of legal services. Here is a short list of some of the key ways to save on legal fees.

**Be organized.** Especially when you are paying by the hour, it's prudent to gather important documents, write a short chronology of events and concisely explain a problem to your lawyer. Since papers can get lost in a lawyer's office, keep a copy of everything that's important, such as your lease or rental agreement, move-in letter to new tenants, correspondence with tenants, repair logs and other records. (See the Chapter 7 discussion on organizing tenant records.)

**Be prepared before you meet.** Whenever possible, send your questions in writing to your lawyer before meetings, even phone meetings. That way the lawyer can find answers if he doesn't know them off the top of his head without having to call you back and charge for a separate phone conference. Early preparation also helps focus the meeting so there is less of a chance of digressing into (and having to pay to discuss) unrelated topics.

**Read trade journals in your field, such as publications of your local landlords' association.** Law changes continuously, so you'll want to keep up with specific legal developments affecting your business. Send pertinent articles to your lawyer— and encourage your lawyer to do the same for you. This can dramatically reduce legal research time.

**Show that you're an important client.** Mutual respect is key in an attorney-client relationship. The single most important way to show your lawyer how much you value the relationship is to pay your bills on time. Beyond that, let your lawyer know about plans for expansion and your business's possible future legal needs. And drop your lawyer a line when you've recommended him or her to your landlord colleagues.

**Bundle your legal matters.** You'll save money if you consult with your lawyer on several matters at one time. For example, in a one-hour conference, you may be able to review with your lawyer several items—such as a new lease, anti-age discrimination policy or advertisement for your apartment complex. Significant savings are possible because lawyers commonly divide their billable hours into parts of an hour. For example, if your lawyer bills in 15-minute intervals and you only talk for five minutes, you are likely to be charged for the whole 15 minutes. So it usually pays to gather your questions and ask them all at once, rather than calling every time you have a question.

## Legal Costs Can Mount Up

In addition to the fees they charge for their time, lawyers often bill for some costs as well—and these costs can add up quickly. When you receive a lawyer's bill, you may be surprised at both the amount of the costs and the variety of the services for which the lawyer expects reimbursement. These can include charges for:

- photocopying
- faxes
- overnight mail
- messenger service
- expert witness fees
- court filing fees
- long distance phone calls
- process servers
- work by investigators
- work by legal assistants or paralegals
- deposition transcripts
- online legal research, and
- travel.

Some lawyers absorb the cost of photocopying, faxes, local phone calls and the like as normal office overhead—part of the cost of doing business —but that's not always the case. So, in working out the fee arrangements, discuss the costs you'll be expected to pay. If a lawyer is intent on nickel-and-diming you to death, look elsewhere. For example, if you learn the law office charges $3 or more for each page it faxes, red flags should go up. On the other hand, it is reasonable for a lawyer to pass along costs of things like court costs, process server fees and any work by investigators.

**Carefully review lawyer bills.** Always read your bill. Like everyone else, lawyers make mistakes, and your charges may be wrong. For example, ".1" of an hour (six minutes) may be transposed into "1." (one hour) when the data are entered into the billing system. That's $200 instead of $20 if your lawyer charges $200 per hour. If you have any questions about your bill, feel free to ask your lawyer. You hired him to provide a service and you have the right to expect a clear explanation of your bill.

**Recommended Reading on Lawsuits.** Contact your local apartment or landlords' association for information on any step-by-step guides to evictions in your state. (Appendix I contains a list of landlords' associations throughout the state.) *Represent Yourself in Court*, by Paul Bergman & Sara Berman-Barrett (Nolo), offers more general advice on handling any civil lawsuit on your own or with a lawyer's help.

## D. Resolving Problems With Your Lawyer

If you see a problem emerging with your lawyer, nip it in the bud. Don't just sit back and fume; call or write your lawyer. Whatever it is that rankles, have an honest discussion about your feelings. Maybe you're upset because your lawyer hasn't kept you informed about what's going on in your lawsuit against your tenant for property damage or maybe your lawyer has missed a promised deadline for reviewing your new system for handling maintenance and repair problems. Or maybe last month's bill was shockingly high or you question the breakdown of how your lawyer's time was spent.

Here's one way to test whether a lawyer-client relationship is a good one—ask yourself if you feel able to talk freely with your lawyer about your degree of participation in any legal matter and your control over how the lawyer carries out a legal assignment. If you can't frankly discuss these sometimes sensitive matters with your lawyer, fire that lawyer and hire another one. If you don't, you'll surely waste money on unnecessary legal fees and risk having legal matters turn out badly.

Remember that if you are not satisfied with how your legal matters are being handled, you have the right to withdraw from the attorney-client relationship at any time. Keep in mind, though, that court

approval may be required in some cases, such as when you are in the middle of a contested lawsuit. And, if you owe the attorney legal fees, your attorney may be able to place a "retaining lien" on your files and withhold your legal papers until you've paid for any services rendered to you up to the point of discharge. The attorney must refund the balance of any retainer you've paid that has not been applied to legal fees or expenses.

If you decide to change attorneys, be sure to fire your old lawyer before you hire a new one. Otherwise, you could find yourself being billed by both lawyers at the same time. Also, be sure to get all important legal documents back from a lawyer you no longer employ. Tell your new lawyer what your old one has done to date and pass on the file.

But firing a lawyer may not be enough. Here are some tips on resolving specific problems.

**Mediate.** If you have a dispute over fees, the local bar association may be able to mediate it for you. (Appendix I includes a list of local bar associations.)

**File a complaint.** If a lawyer has violated legal ethics or broken the law—for example, conflict of interest, overbilling, not representing you zealously or stealing money—you can file a written complaint with a New York State Supreme Court attorney grievance committee. The committee will investigate and, if necessary, prosecute your complaint of professional misconduct against the lawyer. Serious violations can result in disciplinary action or even suspension for the lawyer. There are eight attorney grievance committees within the state. (A complete list is in Appendix I.) File your complaint with the committee serving the county where the attorney's office is located.

**Sue for malpractice.** Where a major mistake has been made—for example, a lawyer has missed the deadline for filing a case—you can sue for malpractice. Many lawyers carry malpractice insurance, and your dispute may be settled out of court.

*Mad at Your Lawyer*, by Tanya Starnes (Nolo), shows you in detail how to successfully handle almost every imaginable problem with your lawyer.

## Your Rights As a Client

New York has adopted a "Client Bill of Rights" (22 NYCRR Part 1210). As a client of a New York attorney, you have the following rights:

1. The right to be treated with courtesy and consideration at all times by your lawyer and the other lawyers and personnel in your lawyer's office.

2. The right to an attorney capable of handling your legal matter competently and diligently, in accordance with the highest standards of the profession. If you are not satisfied with how your matter is being handled, you have the right to withdraw from the attorney-client relationship at any time. Keep in mind, though, that court approval may be required in some matters, and your attorney may have a claim against you for the value of services rendered to you up to the point of discharge.

3. The right to your lawyer's independent professional judgment and undivided loyalty uncompromised by personal or professional conflicts of interest, such as your lawyer's own financial or business interests or those of another client.

4. The right to be charged a reasonable fee and to have your lawyer explain at the outset how the fee will be computed and the manner and frequency of billing. You are entitled to request and receive a written itemized bill from your attorney at reasonable intervals. You may refuse to enter into any fee arrangement that you find unsatisfactory.

5. The right to have your questions and concerns addressed in a prompt manner and to have your telephone calls returned promptly.

6. The right to be kept informed as to the status of your case or transaction and to request and receive copies of papers. You are entitled to sufficient information to allow you to participate meaningfully in the development of your legal matter.

7. The right to have your legitimate objectives respected by your attorney, including whether or not to settle your case (court approval of a settlement is required in some matters).

8. The right to privacy in your dealings with your lawyer and to have your secrets and confidences preserved to the extent permitted by law.

9. The right to have your attorney conduct himself or herself ethically in accordance with the New York Code of Professional Responsibility (9 NYCRR § 1200 and following) which sets ethical standards for the legal profession.

10. The right to representation regardless of race, creed, color, religion, sex, sexual orientation, age, national origin or disability.

## E. Attorney Fees in a Lawsuit

If your lease or written rental agreement has an attorney fees provision (see Clause 20 of the form agreements in Chapter 2), you are entitled to recover your "reasonable" attorney fees if you win a lawsuit based on the terms of that agreement. There's no guarantee, however, that a judge will award attorney fees equal to your attorney's actual bill, or that you will ultimately be able to collect the money from the tenant or former tenant. Also, as discussed in Chapter 2, an attorney fees clause in your lease or rental agreement works both ways. Even if the clause doesn't say so, you're liable for the tenant's attorney fees if you lose.

## F. Doing Your Own Legal Research

Using this book is a good way to educate yourself about the laws that affect your business—but one book is not enough by itself. Some landlord associations publish legal updates in their newsletters and on their websites to keep members abreast of new laws and regulations that affect rental property. For instance, the Rent Stabilization Association of New York City, the Real Estate Board of New York and the Community Housing Improvement Program, all keep a close eye on legal developments for their members (see Appendix I for more information on these organizations).

While we recommend that you get copies of state, local and federal laws that affect your landlording business (see Section G, just below), at one time or another you'll probably need to do some further research. For example, you may want to read a specific court case or research a more open-ended question about landlord-tenant law—for instance, your liability for an assault that took place on your rental property.

Lawyers aren't the only source for legal help. There's a lot you can do on your own. Currently, you can get the text of almost every federal and state statute free, online. Rules put out by federal and state regulatory agencies are often available, too, and the Internet's legal resources grow every-day. We list the websites where you can get your hands on legal information in the "Guide to New York Landlord-Tenant Laws," below.

If you don't have access to the Internet, law libraries are full of valuable information, such as state statutes that regulate the landlord-tenant relationship. Your first step is to find a law library that's open to the public. You can find such a library in your county courthouse. Publicly funded law schools generally permit the public to use their libraries, and some private law schools grant access to their libraries—sometimes for a modest fee.

Don't overlook the reference department of the public library if you're in a large city or town. The New York City Public Library, for instance, has a fairly decent legal research collection. Also, ask about using the law library in your own lawyer's office. Some lawyers, on request, will share their books with their clients.

**Keep up-to-date.** Some law compilations, both on the Internet and in print, are out-of-date. Never rely on an old set of laws or regulations, because they are frequently amended. Always make sure the law you're checking contains the most up-to-date legislative amendments.

**Recommended Reading on Legal Research.** We don't have space here to show you how to do your own legal research in anything approaching a comprehensive fashion. To go further, we recommend *Legal Research: How to Find and Understand the Law*, by Stephen Elias & Susan Levinkind (Nolo). This nontechnical book gives easy-to-use, step-by-step instructions on how to find legal information. For an overview of legal research, see Nolo's website at www.nolo.com/lawcenter/statute/index.cfm.

## G. Where to Find State, Local and Federal Laws

Every landlord is governed by state, local and federal law. We refer to the major landlord-tenant laws throughout this book and include citations so that you can do additional research. Because it's so important that you have immediate access to legal information that affects your rental business, we recommend that you get copies of the relevant statutes, codes, and regulations, particularly if your property is rent controlled or rent stabilized. This section summarizes key landlord-tenant laws enacted by state, local and federal governments and explains where to find electronic (online) and paper copies.

**In some areas, like antidiscrimination standards, laws overlap.** When they do overlap, the stricter laws will apply. In practical terms, this usually means that the laws that give tenants the most protection (rights and remedies) will prevail over less protective laws.

## 1. State Laws and Regulations

New York State laws and rules regulate many aspects of the landlord-tenant relationship, including security deposits, discrimination, housing standards, repair and maintenance responsibilities, subletting and eviction procedures.

New York State statutes, which are enacted by the state legislature, are collected in volumes and are available online, in most public libraries and in all law libraries. The statutes are organized by title and section, with each title covering a particular subject matter. The key state laws are the Real Property Law, Real Property Actions and Proceedings Law, Multiple Dwelling Law, Multiple Residence Law, General Obligations Law, Emergency Tenant Protection Act (state rent stabilization laws) and the Emergency Housing Rent Control Act (state rent control laws).

So called "annotated codes," such as *McKinney's Annotated Laws of New York,* contain not only the full text of the laws, but also a brief summary of some of the court decisions interpreting each law. *McKinney's* also supplies references to treatises and articles that discuss the law, has a comprehensive topic index, and is kept up-to-date with annual supplements (often stuck in a pocket inside the back cover of each volume).

State agencies, such as the Division of Housing and Community Renewal (DHCR), the Department of Labor and many others, make their own rules and regulations. Like state laws, landlords are presumed to know about and follow these rules and regulations. To look up a state rule or regulation, ask your librarian for a multi-volume book called the *Official Compilation of Codes, Rules and Regulations of the State of New York* (NYCRR). It's available in most law libraries and in some public libraries.

> EXAMPLE: Emergency Tenant Protection Regulations (companion regulations to the Emergency Tenant Protection Act) may be found at Volume 9 of the NYCRR, starting at Section 2500.1 or 9 NYCRR §2500.1.

The DHCR, which enforces the laws and regulations relating to rent-stabilized and rent-controlled units on a statewide basis has a website (www.dhcr.state.ny.us). Go to the site's "Rent Administration" area to find official fact sheets, advisory opinions, operational bulletins, policy statements and other DHCR publications. Paradoxically, DHCR's site does not have the text of the rent control or rent stabilization laws and regulations you are required to follow. Go figure!

Paperback collections that concentrate on landlord-tenant laws are also available. For instance, *New York Landlord-Tenant Law "Tan Book"* (Matthew Bender), named for the color of its cover, includes all of the current rent stabilization and rent control laws, as well as excerpts from the Real Property and Multiple Dwelling Laws. It is updated annually and is available at any law bookstore or by calling the publisher (800-833-9844). The *"Tan Book"* is a good investment for landlords.

To access state law on the Internet, visit the New York Assembly website www.assembly.state.ny.us. Click "Assembly Legislative Information System," then "New York State Laws," then either "Consolidated" or "Unconsolidated" laws. Finally, click the name of the law you want to see or download. (Rent regulatory laws are part of the Unconsolidated Laws section.) See "Guide to New York Landlord-

Tenant Laws," below for more information on where to find state laws online.

## 2. NYC and Local Ordinances

Local ordinances will also affect your rental property business, particularly if you own rent-regulated property in New York City.

### a. NYC Ordinances

The Administrative Code of the City of New York (NYC Adm. Code) is a collection of all laws enacted by the City Council and signed by the Mayor. It's where you'll find the NYC Building Code, the Housing Maintenance Code (required reading for all NYC landlords!), the Health Code (which includes the window guard law), the Human Rights Law and other city ordinances you're expected to follow with respect to your NYC property.

The "Guide to New York Landlord-Tenant Laws" chart, below, highlights relevant sections of NYC laws, provides a brief description of what each covers and lists online resources, specifically the NYC Rent Guidelines Board (www.housingnyc.com). Here you'll find a current version of the NYC Housing Maintenance Code, guidelines on collecting rent increases from rent-stabilized tenants in New York City, a list of rent-stabilized buildings by Zip code, a "vacancy lease" calculator, and useful information on various housing topics.

 **Current versions of rent control and stabilization regulations are not available online.** See Chapter 4 for more information on keeping up-to-date on rent regulation.

### b. Other Local Ordinances

Outside of NYC, local ordinances, such as health and safety codes, occupancy standards and maintenance and repair requirements, will also affect your business.

EXAMPLE: Albany has a fair housing law (Code of the City of Albany, Chapter 187) that establishes fair housing offices to carry out federal and state fair housing laws. Rochester's property code (Chapter 90 of the Code of the City of Rochester) sets occupancy standards and minimum maintenance and repair standards for housing located within the city of Rochester.

Contact your city supervisor's or local mayor's office for information on local ordinances that affect landlords.

You can often access information on local laws and regulations online at Piper Resources (www.statelocalgov.net/index.cfm). Many counties, towns and villages have staked out turf on the Internet. Sometimes this presence is nothing more than a not-so-slick public relations page, but sometimes it includes a large body of information, including local ordinances available for searching and downloading. PiperInfo is the best source for finding local governments online. First click "New York," then scroll down the page to find your local government's site.

---

### Check out TenantNet— Not Just for Tenants

TenantNet (www.tenant.net) is a rich source of information. Here you can find a searchable database of New York City Housing Court decisions (archived since 1996), as well as over 6,000 administrative decisions of the NYS Division of Housing and Community Renewal (DHCR). The site also has the text of the federal Fair Housing Acts, New York State statutes, the New York City rent stabilization law and code, the NYC rent control law and regulations, the Emergency Tenant Protection Act, the Multiple Dwelling Law and the NYC Housing Maintenance Code. It's best to use TenantNet for news and articles and for reports on latest housing court cases. When checking laws, use the State Assembly website, listed on the "Guide to New York Landlord-Tenant Laws" chart, below, because that is always up-to-date.

## Guide to New York Landlord-Tenant Laws

| Law or Regulation | Relevant Sections | What It Covers | Where to Find Online |
|---|---|---|---|
| **NEW YORK STATE LAWS** | | | |
| Real Property Law (RPL) | Article 7 (§§ 220-238) Article 12-A (§§ 443, 443-a) | Article 7 of the RPL governs landlords' repair and maintenance responsibilities under the state warranty of habitability; delineates a tenant's right to repair and deduct, sublet, assign and share a rental unit with family members and other occupants; covers termination procedures for month-to-month tenancies, as well as other important landlord-tenant issues, including delivery of possession, retaliation, constructive eviction, termination rights of seniors, attorneys' fees and unconscionable lease terms. Article 12-A of the RPL covers: real estate brokers and salesman. | www.assembly.state. ny.us/ALIS |
| Real Property Actions and Proceedings Law (RPAPL) | Article 7 (§§ 701-767) Article 7-A (§§ 769-783) | Article 7 of the RPAPL sets the procedural rules on bringing eviction proceedings against tenants, including what rent demands and eviction petition must say, how eviction notices must be served on tenants, and the circumstances in which judges may issue and stay eviction warrants. Article 7-A of the RPAPL covers so-called rent strikes by tenants. | www.assembly.state. ny.us/ALIS |
| Multiple Dwelling Law (MDL) | All | MDL covers repair and maintenance responsibilities for landlords of buildings with three or more rental units in cities with 325,000 or more people. Applies in NYC and Buffalo only. | www.assembly.state. ny.us/ALIS |
| Multiple Residence Law (MRL) | All | MRL covers repair and maintenance responsibilities for landlords of buildings with three or more rental units in towns and villages and cities with 325,000 or fewer people. Applies to properties outside NYC and Buffalo. | www.assembly.state. ny.us/ALIS |
| General Obligations Law (GOL) | §§ 7-103, 105, 107, 108 | GOL covers rules on collecting, depositing and refunding tenant security deposits. | www.assembly.state. ny.us/ALIS |
| Civil Practice Laws and Rules (CPLR) | §§ 212-215 | CPLR sets time limits for lawsuits relating to leases and rental agreements, negligence and rent overcharge | www.assembly.state. ny.us/ALIS |
| Human Rights Law (HRL), found in Executive Law (Exec. L.) | §§ 296, 296-a | HRL prohibits rental housing discrimination by landlords, owners, lessees, real estate brokers and their employees by reason of race, creed, color, national origin, gender, age, disability, marital status or the presence of children who will reside on the premises. Applies throughout the state except in NYC (see NYC Human Rights Law, below). | www.assembly.state. ny.us/ALIS |
| **Rent Laws & Regulations —Outside NYC** | | | |
| Emergency Housing Rent Control Law | §§ 1-17. Can be found in New York's Unconsolidated Laws, beginning at § 8581. | State rent control law. Applies to rent-controlled units outside NYC. | www.assembly.state. ny.us/ALIS |
| Rent and Eviction Regulations | 9 NYCRR §§ 2100 - 2109 | State rent control regulations. Applies to rent-controlled units outside NYC. | Up-to-date text not currently online. |

## Guide to New York Landlord-Tenant Laws (continued)

| Law or Regulation | Relevant Sections | What It Covers | Where to Find Online |
|---|---|---|---|
| **Rent Laws & Regulations—Outside NYC** | | | |
| Emergency Tenant Protection Act (ETPA) | §§ 1-14. Can be found in New York's Unconsolidated Laws, beginning at § 8621 | State rent stabilization law. Governs all rent-stabilized units outside NYC, granting localities the option of declaring local housing emergencies and instituting rent stabilization. Applies to rent-stabilized units in Nassau, Rockland and Westchester Counties. | www.assembly.state. ny.us/leg |
| Emergency Tenant Protection Regulations (ETPR) | 9 NYCRR §§ 2500 - 2510 | State rent stabilization regulations (companion regulations to ETPA). Applies to rent-stabilized units in Nassau, Rockland and Westchester Counties. | Up-to-date version not currently online. |
| **NEW YORK CITY LAWS** | | | |
| **NYC Rent Laws & Regulations** | | | |
| Local Emergency Housing Rent Control Act | §§ 1(1)-1(17) | New York City rent control law. | www.assembly.state. ny.us/cgi-bin/claws |
| NYC Rent and Rehabilitation Act | NYC Adm. Code §§ 26-401 to 26-415 | New York City rent control law. | Up-to-date version not currently online. |
| NYC Rent and Eviction Regulations | 9 NYCRR §§ 2200-2210 | New York City rent control regulations. | Up-to-date version not currently online. |
| NYC Rent Stabilization Law of 1969 (RSL) | NYC Adm. Code §§ 26-501 to 26-520 | New York City rent stabilization law. | Up-to-date version not currently online. |
| Rent Stabilization Code (RSC) | 9 NYCRR §§ 2520-2530 | New York City rent stabilization regulations (companion to RSL). | www.tenant.net/ Rent_Laws/RSC |
| **Other NYC Laws** | | | |
| NYC Housing Maintenance Code (HMC) | NYC Adm. Code, Title 27, Chapter 2 | Sets repair and maintenance responsibilities for all NYC residential landlords. Also covers safety and security devices, occupancy limits and property registration requirements. | www.housingnyc.com (click housing maintenance code) |
| NYC Window Guard Law | NYC Adm. Code §§ 17-123 | Obligations to notify tenants about law and to supply and install window guards on request. | www.nyc.gov/html/ doh/html/win/win.html |
| NYC Human Rights Law (HRL) | NYC Adm. Code §§ 8-102, 9-107 | Prohibits rental housing discrimination by owners, landlords, lessees, real estate brokers and their employees. Prohibits housing discrimination by reason of race, creed, color, national origin, gender, age, disability, marital status, citizenship, sexual orientation, lawful occupation or the presence of children who will reside on the premises. Also prohibits employment discrimination against certain protected classes. | Not currently online. |
| **FEDERAL LAWS** | | | |
| United States Code (U.S.C.) | Various  Relevant citations are provided throughout this book. | Federal fair housing laws; debt collection practices; lead paint disclosures, employee safety. | www.law.cornell.edu./ federal |
| Code of Federal Regulations (CFR) | Various  Relevant citations are provided throughout this book. | Rules issued by HUD, the EPA and other federal agencies. | www.law.cornell.edu./ federal |

## 3.  Federal Statutes and Regulations

Congress has enacted laws, and federal agencies, such as the U.S. Department of Housing and Urban Development (HUD), have adopted regulations, covering discrimination, wage and hour laws affecting employment of managers and landlord responsibilities to disclose environmental health hazards. We refer to relevant federal agencies throughout this book and suggest you contact them for publications that explain federal laws affecting landlords, or copies of the federal statutes and regulations themselves.

We include citations for many of the federal laws affecting landlords throughout this book. The United States Code (U.S.C.) is the starting place for most federal statutory research. It consists of 50 separate numbered titles. Each title covers a specific subject matter. Two versions of the U.S. Code are published in annotated form: *The United States Code Annotated*, (U.S.C.A.), (West Publishing Co.) and the *United States Code Service* (U.S.C.S.), (Bancroft-Whitney/Lawyer's Co-op). Most law libraries (and many public libraries) carry one or the other. Most federal regulations are published in the Code of Federal Regulations (CFR), organized by subject into 50 separate titles.

To access the U.S. Code online, visit the Cornell Law Information Institute (www.law.cornell.edu). This site provides the entire United States Code, as well as the Code of Federal Regulations. You can also access New York state laws here, as well as decisions of the U.S. Supreme Court and the New York Court of Appeals—New York's highest court.

# H. How to Research Court Decisions

Sometimes the answer to a legal question cannot be found in a statute. This happens when:

- court cases and opinions have greatly expanded or explained the statute, taking it beyond its obvious or literal meaning, or
- the law that applies to your question has been made by judges, not legislators.

## 1.  Court Decisions That Explain Statutes

Statutes and ordinances do not explain themselves. For example, a state law may require you to offer housing that is weatherproofed, but that statute alone may not tell you whether that means you must provide both storm windows and window screens. Chances are, however, that others before you have had the same questions, and they may have come up in the context of a lawsuit. If a judge interpreted the statute and wrote an opinion on the matter, that written opinion, once published, will become "the law" as much as the statute itself. If a higher court (an appellate court) has also examined the question, then its opinion will rule.

To find out if there are written court decisions that interpret a particular statute or ordinance, look in an "annotated code" (discussed in Section G, above). If you find a case that seems to answer your question, it's crucial to make sure that the decision you're reading is still "good law"—that a more recent opinion from a higher court has not reached a different conclusion. To make sure that you are relying on the latest and highest judicial pronouncement, you must use the library research tool known as Shepard's. *Legal Research: How to Find and Understand the Law*, by Stephen Elias & Susan Levinkind (Nolo), has a good, easy-to-follow explanation of how to use the Shepard's system to expand and update your research.

## 2.  Court Decisions That Make Law

Many laws that govern the way you must conduct your business do not even have an initial starting point in a statute or ordinance. These laws are entirely court-made, and are known as "common" law.

Researching common law is more difficult than statutory law, because you do not have the launching pad of a statute or ordinance. With a little perseverance, however, you can certainly find your way to the cases that have developed and explained the legal concept you wish to understand. A good beginning is to ask the librarian for any "practice guides" written in the field of landlord-tenant law.

These are outlines of the law, written for lawyers, that are kept up-to-date and are designed to get you quickly to key information. One particularly useful practice guide is *Landlord and Tenant Practice in New York*, by Daniel Finkelstein and Lucas A. Ferrara (West), a two-volume set which is annually updated. Because practice guides are so popular and easy to use, they are kept in the library reference section and cannot be checked out. More sophisticated research techniques, such as using a set of books called "Words and Phrases," (which sends you to cases based on key words) are explained in the Nolo book *Legal Research*, mentioned above.

## 3. How to Read a Case Citation

If a case you have found in an annotated code (or through a practice guide or key word search) looks important, you may want to read the opinion. You'll need the title of the case and its "citation," which is like an address for the set of books, volume and page where the case can be found.

Although it may look about as decipherable as hieroglyphics, once understood, a case citation gives lots of useful information in a small space. It tells you the names of the people or companies involved, the volume of the reporter (series of books) in which the case is published, the page number on which it begins and the year in which the case was decided.

> EXAMPLE: *Smith Realty Co v. Jones*, 123 N.Y.S.2d 456 (1994). Smith and Jones are the names of the parties having the legal dispute. The case is reported in volume 123 of the New York Supplement, Second Series, beginning on page 456; the court issued the decision in 1994.

New York publishes decisions rendered by all of its appellate courts (and some trial level courts) in so-called "official" state reporters. There are three official case reporters:

**New York Reports (N.Y. and N.Y.2d).** Here, you'll find all of the decisions of New York's highest court, the Court of Appeals. A decision cited as "123 N.Y.2d 456" may be found in Volume 123 of the New York Reports, Second Series, at page 456.

**Appellate Division Reports (App. Div. and App. Div. 2d).** This reporter covers decisions of the state's intermediary appellate courts (which are broken down into four geographic divisions). A decision cited as "123 App. Div. 2d 456" can be found in Volume 123 of the Appellate Division Reports, Second Series, at page 456.

**New York Miscellaneous Reports (Misc. and Misc.2d).** Here you'll find decisions of the Appellate Term, which hears appeals from the NYC Civil Courts, including its housing court part. Certain trial-court–level decisions are also included. A decision cited as "123 Misc. 2d 456" may be found in Volume 123 of NY Miscellaneous Reports, Second Series, at page 456.

A useful resource is **New York Supplement (N.Y.Supp. and N.Y.Supp.2d)**, an "unofficial" case reporter, which collects all of the decisions reported in the three "official" state reporters described above. Many law offices and libraries save space by keeping only *New York Supplement* volumes on its shelves. A case cited as 123 N.Y. Supp. 2d 456 may be found in volume 123 of New York Supplement, Second Series, at page 456.

***The New York Law Journal* (N.Y.L.J.)**, a daily newspaper for lawyers, prints lower court decisions issued in New York City, Nassau, Suffolk, Orange and Rockland Counties that often don't make it into the official reporters or into the *New York Supplement*. Many valuable landlord-tenant decisions are found here (especially on Wednesdays). A decision cited as *Smith Realty Co. v. Jones*, N.Y.L.J., 1/5/99, p. 26, col. 3 (Civ. Ct., N.Y. County) means that you can find the *Smith v. Jones* decision in the January 5, 1999, edition of the newspaper, at page 26, column 3. The case was heard in the New York City Civil Court, in Manhattan (N.Y. County). Old issues of the *New York Law Journal* are available on microfiche at many libraries in the New York City area. You can read excerpts from the *New York Law Journal* on a daily basis for free by visiting its website (www.nylj.com).

For information on court rules, visit New York Courts and Law Guide (www.NYLJ.com/guide.) This site gives you the details on how to file a lawsuit at in the state's county, town and village courts. ■

# Appendix I

# Resources for New York Landlords

Throughout this book, we've mentioned dozens of organizations and government agencies that provide legal information and services to New York landlords. For easy reference, we've pulled together one comprehensive list of contact information (address, phone number and website) for each group. Our list is organized in six major categories:

- real estate industry trade associations, including the Rent Stabilization Association of New York City as well as regional landlords' associations
- Rent Guidelines Boards throughout the state
- federal agencies, such as the U.S. Department of Housing and Urban Development (HUD)
- New York State agencies, such as the Division of Housing and Community Renewal (DHCR)
- New York City agencies, including the Department of Housing Preservation and Development (HPD), and
- bar associations and lawyer referral services.

For more information on the services or resources of a particular organization or agency listed in this Appendix, see the chapters referenced in parentheses.

# A. Real Estate Industry Trade Associations

## National Trade Associations

### National Apartment Association (Introduction)
201 North Union Street, Suite 200
Alexandria, Virginia 22314
703-518-6141
Website: www.naahq.org

### National Multi-Housing Council (Introduction)
1850 M Street NW, Suite 540
Washington, DC 20036
202-974-2300
Website: www.nmhc.org

## New York City Trade Associations

### Rent Stabilization Association of New York City, Inc. (RSA) (Chapters 1, 2 and 4)
123 William Street
New York, NY 10038
212-214-9200
Website: www.rsanyc.com

### The Real Estate Board of New York, Inc. (REBNY) (Chapters 2 and 4)
570 Lexington Avenue
New York, NY 10022
212-532-3100
Website: www.rebny.com

### Community Housing Improvement Program (CHIP) (Chapters 1 and 4)
545 Madison Avenue, 4th Floor
New York, NY 10022
212-838-7442
Website: www.chipnyc.org

### New York Association of Realty Managers (NYARM) (Chapter 6)
29 West 30th St., 4th Floor
New York, NY 10001
212-216-0654
Website: www.nyarm.org

### Small Property Owners of New York (SPONY) (Introduction and Chapter 4)
1681 Third Avenue
New York, NY 10128
212-410-4600
Website: www.spony.org

## Trade Associations Outside of New York City

### Buffalo
### Western New York Real Estate Investors
P.O. Box 637
Grand Island, NY 14072
716-773-2980

### Cortland

**Apartment Owners Association of Cortland**
28 Pleasant Street
Cortland, NY 13045
607-756-7807

### Ithaca

**Landlords Association of Tompkins County**
P.O. Box 337
Ithaca, NY 14851
Website: www.landlordsassociation.com

### Rockland County

**Landlords of Rockland**
Route 9W North
Stony Point, NY 10980
845-942-5675

### Schenectady

**Schenectady Rental Property Owners Association**
P.O. Box 3946
Schenectady, NY 12303
518-374-6367

## B. Rent Guidelines Boards

### New York City Rent Guidelines Board (Chapters 2 and 4)

**NYC Rent Guidelines Board**
51 Chambers Street, Suite 202
New York, NY 10017
212-385-2934
Website: www.housingnyc.com

### Rent Guidelines Boards Outside New York City (Chapters 2 and 4)

**Nassau County Rent Guidelines Board**
50 Clinton Street
Room 605
Hempstead, NY 11550
516-481-9494

**Rockland County Rent Guidelines Board**
9496 North Main Street
Spring Valley, NY 10977
845-425-6575

**Westchester County Rent Guidelines Board**
55 Church Street
White Plains, New York 10601
914-948-4434

## C. Federal Agencies

### U.S. Department of Housing and Urban Development (HUD) (Chapters 1, 8 and 11)

**HUD Headquarters**
451 7th Street
Washington, DC 20410
202-708-1422 (Headquarters)
Website: www.hud.gov

**HUD New York City Local Office**
26 Federal Plaza
Room 3541
New York, NY 10278
212-264-6500

**HUD Albany Local Office**
52 Corporate Circle
Albany, NY 12203
518-464-4200

**HUD Buffalo Local Office**
465 Main Street
Buffalo, NY 14203
716-551-5755

## U.S. Environmental Protection Agency (EPA) (Chapters 2 and 11)

### EPA Headquarters
202 M Street SW
Washington, DC 20460
202-260-2090
908-321-6671 (lead)
800-767-7236 (radon)
Website: www.epa.gov

### EPA New York Regional Office (Region 2)
290 Broadway, 21st Floor
New York, NY 10007-1866
212-637-3000
Website: www.epa.gov/region02

## U.S. Bureau of Citizenship and Immigration Services (BCIS) (formerly INS) (Chapter 6)

### Headquarters
425 I Street NW, Room 3034
Washington, DC 20536
800-375-5283; 357-2099
Website: www.immigration.gov

### New York City District BCIS Office
26 Federal Plaza
New York, NY 10278
800-357-2099

## U.S. Internal Revenue Service (IRS) (Chapter 6)

### IRS Headquarters
Washington, DC
800-829-1040
Website: www.irs.gov

## U.S. Occupational Safety and Health Administration (OSHA) (Chapter 11)

### OSHA New York Regional Office
201 Varick St., Room 670
New York, NY 10014
212-337-2378
Website: www.osha.gov

# D. New York State Agencies

### New York State Attorney General's Office (Chapters 5 and 16)
120 Broadway
New York, NY 10271
212-416-8345
Website: www.oag.state

### New York State Department of Health (Chapter 11)
Corning Tower
Empire State Plaza
Albany, NY 12237
518-486-9002
Website: www.health.state.ny.us

## New York State Division of Housing and Community Renewal (DHCR) (Chapters 2, 4, 9, 14 and 15)

See "DHCR Fact Sheets, Policy Statements and Operational Bulletins," below for a list of useful resources available from the DHCR.

### DHCR Office of Rent Administration
92-31 Union Hall Street, 4th Floor
Jamaica, NY 11433
718-739-6400
Website: www.dhcr.state.ny.us
InfoLine: 718-739-6400

### DHCR Rent Registration Unit
Hampton Plaza, 38-40 State St.
Albany, NY 12207
Website: www.dhcr.state.ny.us

## New York City DHCR Offices

### Lower Manhattan Borough Rent Office

25 Beaver Street, 5th Floor
New York, NY 10004
212-480-6238
(serving properties located on the south side of
110th St. and below)

### Upper Manhattan Borough Rent Office

Adam Clayton Powell, Jr., Office Building
163 W. 125th Street, 5th Floor
New York, NY 10027
212-961-8930
(serving properties located on the north side of
110th St. and above)

### Bronx Borough Rent Office

1 Fordham Plaza, 2nd Floor
Bronx, NY 10458
718-563-5678

### Brooklyn Borough Rent Office

55 Hanson Place, 7th Floor
Brooklyn NY 11217
718-722-4778

### Queens Borough Rent Office

92-31 Union Hall Street, 4th Floor
Jamaica, NY 11433
718-739-6400

### Staten Island Borough Rent Office

60 Bay Street, 7th Floor
Staten Island, NY 10301
718-816-0278

## New York State Regional DHCR Offices

### Albany Rent Office

Hampton Plaza
Albany, NY 12207
518-473-2517
(serving properties located in the counties of
Albany, Columbia, Delaware, Essex, Fulton,
Greene, Hamilton, Montgomery, Orange, Oswego,
Putnam, Rensselaer, Saratoga, Schenectady,
Schoharie, Sullivan, Ulster, Warren and
Washington)

### Buffalo Rent Office

Statler Towers
107 Delaware Avenue, Suite 600
Buffalo, NY 14202
716-842-2244
(serving properties located in the counties of
Allegheny, Cattaraugus, Chautauqua, Chemung,
Erie, Genesee, Livingston, Monroe, Niagara,
Ontario, Orleans, Schuyler, Seneca, Steuben,
Wayne, Wyoming and Yates)

### Nassau County Rent Office

50 Clinton Street, 6th Floor
Hempstead, NY 11550
516-481-9494

### Rockland County Rent Office

Pascack Plaza
9C-Perlman Drive
Spring Valley, NY 10977
845-425-6575

### Syracuse Rent Office

800 South Wilber Avenue
Syracuse, NY 13204
315-473-6930
Mailing address:
P.O. Box 1127
Syracuse, NY 13201
(serving properties in the counties of Broome,
Cayuga, Chenango, Cortland, Franklin, Herkimer,
Jefferson, Lewis, Madison, Oneida, Onondaga,
Oswego, St. Lawrence, Tioga and Tomkins)

## DHCR Fact Sheets, Policy Statements and Operational Bulletins

### DHCR Fact Sheets

*Fact sheets* describe the major elements of rent control and rent stabilization in New York City and New York State. You can order fact sheets from the DHCR's central office (92-31 Union Hall Street, 4th Floor, Jamaica, NY 11433, 718-739-6400) or download them from the DHCR website (www.dhcr.state.ny.us).

#1   Rent Control and Rent Stabilization
#2   Rent Stabilization Lease Rider
#3   Required and Essential Services
#4   Lease Renewal in Rent Stabilized Apartments
#5   Vacancy Leases in Rent Stabilized Apartments
#6   Fair Market Appeals
#7   Sublets, Assignments, and Illusory Tenancies
#8   Emergency Tenant Protection Act of 1974 (ETPA)
#9   Security Deposits
#10  Eviction from an Apartment Based on Owner Occupancy
#11  Rent Increases for Major Capital Improvements (MCI)
#12  Rent Increases for New Services, New Equipment, or Improvements to an Apartment
#13  Fuel Cost Adjustment
#14  Rent Reductions Due to Decreased Services
#15  Heat and Hot Water
#16  Collecting Overcharges in Rent Stabilized NYC Apartments
#17  Harassment
#18  Appealing a Rent Administrator's Order: Petition for Administrative Review
#19  Small Building Owner's Assistance Unit
#20  Special Rights of Disabled Persons
#21  Special Rights of Senior Citizens
#22  Maximum Base Rent Program (MBR) Q&A for Owners
#23  Fuel Cost Adjustment Q&A for Owners
#24  Major Capital Improvements (MCI) Q&A for Owners
#25  Window Guards

#26  Guide to Rent Increase for Rent Stabilized Apartments in NYC
#27  Air Conditioners
#28  Painting Rent Controlled Apartments
#29  Conversion from Electrical Inclusion to Exclusion in Rent Regulated Apartments, State-wide
#30  Succession Rights
#31  Guide to Rent Increases for Rent Stabilized Apartments in Nassau, Rockland and Westchester Counties

### DHCR Policy Statements

*Policy statements* explain how the DHCR interprets various provisions of the rent stabilization and rent control laws and regulations. You can order copies of policy statements from the DHCR Infoline (718-739-6400) or download copies from the DHCR website (www.dhcr.state.ny.us).

No. 89-1   Failure to Maintain Services: Rent Reduction/Restoration
No. 89-2   Application of the Treble Damage Penalty
No. 89-3   MBR Fee Collectibility
No. 89-4   Expedited MCI
No. 89-5   MCI Rent Increases for Replacement Windows after Prior Increase Granted for Storm Windows
No. 89-6   MCI Rent Increases for Replacement of Certain Window Types
No. 89-7   Collection of Administrative Fees: Housing Accommodations Permanently Not Subject to the RSL or ETPA and Application Form
No. 89-8   Asbestos Removal as a Major Capital Improvement/Eligible Costs
No. 89-9   Sponsor Representations, in Cooperative or Condominium Offerings, to Bear Cost of MCIs: Effect on Entitlement to MCI Increases
No. 89-10  Filing Requirements Upon Vacancy of Rent Controlled Apartment

## DHCR Fact Sheets, Policy Statements and Operational Bulletins (continued)

No. 90-1  Effect of Rent Reduction Orders on Maximum Base Rent MBR Increases

No. 90-2  Failure to Maintain Services: Rent Reduction/Restoration Revised 89-1

No. 90-3  Room Count Determination for Major Capital Improvement MCI Application Processing

No. 90-4  Presence of Owners and Tenants at DHCR Inspections

No. 90-5  Arranging Repairs — No Access Inspections

No. 90-6  MCI Eligibility/Roofing

No. 90-7  Processing of 62-B Complaints

No. 90-8  Failure to Maintain Services/Processing MCI Applications

No. 90-9  Late Registration and Failure to Register: Its Effect on MCI Applications

No. 90-10 Major Capital Improvements/Individual Apartment Improvements/Confirmation of Costs/Payments

No. 91-1  Demolition Costs Associated With Individual Apartment Improvements

No. 91-2  MCI Eligibility/Roofing (Revised 90-6)

No. 91-3  Effects of Rent Reductions on Fuel Cost Passalong Adjustments

No. 91-4  Expediting Proceedings

No. 91-5  Limitations of Filing Requests for Reconsideration of Order Issued by Rent Administrators and/or the Commissioner

No. 92-1  Penalties for Failure to Pay Billed Administrative Fees for New York City Rent Stabilized Accommodations for Apartments Covered by the Emergency Tenant Protection Act

No. 92-2  Collectibility of "421-a" Rent Increases

No. 92-3  Proof of Registration

No. 93-1  Responsibility of a Current Owner of a Rent Stabilized Housing Accommodation to Refund Excess Rent Determined Pursuant to a Fair Market Rent Appeal

No. 93-2  Definition of Room for Major Capital Improvements MCI Purposes

No. 93-3  Procedures for Cases Involving 7-A Administrators Appointed by the Housing Court Pursuant to the Real Property Actions and Proceedings Law

No. 93-4  Procedure for Handling Rent Overcharge Awards When the Tenant Has Vacated the Apartment Without Leaving a Forwarding Address

No. 95-1  Rent Overcharge Awards When the Tenant Has Vacated the Apartment Without Leaving a Forwarding Address (Replaces 93-4)

No. 96-1  Third-Person Certification

### DHCR Operational Bulletins

*Operational bulletins* explain how the DHCR intends to implement various provisions of the rent stabilization and rent control laws and regulations. To get the full text of any of the operational bulletins listed below, call the DHCR Infoline (718-739-6400) and ask that a specific bulletin be mailed to you; you may also download operational bulletins from the DHCR website (www.dhcr.state.ny.us).

No. 84-1  New Procedures for Instituting a Proceeding for Administrative Review of an Order Issued by a District Rent Administrator

No. 84-2  Emergency Tenant Protection Act

No. 84-4  Major Capital Improvements / Substantial Rehabilitation / Increased Services and Equipment

No. 84-4  Supplement No. 1 to Operational Bulletin 84-4 (MCI)

No. 84-4  Annual Update of Section B of Supplement No.1 to Operational Bulletin 84-4 (Air Conditioners '86)

No. 84-4  Second Annual Update of Section B of Supplement No. 1 to Operational Bulletin 84-4 (Air Conditioners '87)

## DHCR Fact Sheets, Policy Statements and Operational Bulletins (continued)

No. 84-4  Third Annual Update of Section B of Supplement No. 1 to Operational Bulletin 84-4 (Air Conditioners '88)

No. 84-4  Fourth Annual Update of Section B of Supplement No. 1 to Operational Bulletin 84-4 (Air Conditioners '89)

No. 84-4  Fifth Annual Update of Section B of Supplement No. 1 to Operational Bulletin 84-4 (Air Conditioners '90)

No. 84-4  Sixth Annual Update of Section B of Supplement No. 1 to Operational Bulletin 84-4 (Electrical '91)

No. 84-4  Seventh Annual Update of Section B of Supplement No. 1 to Operational Bulletin 84-4 (Air Conditioners '92)

No. 84-4  Eighth Annual Update of Section B of Supplement No. 1 to Operational Bulletin 84-4 (Electrical '93)

No. 84-4  Ninth Annual Update of Section B of Supplement No. 1 to Operational Bulletin 84-4 (Air Conditioners '94)

No. 84-4  Tenth Annual Update of Section B of Supplement No. 1 to Operational Bulletin 84-4 (Air Conditioners '95)

No. 84-4  Eleventh Annual Update of Section B of Supplement No. 1 to Operational Bulletin 84-4 (Air Conditioners '96)

No. 85-1  Rent Stabilization Rider for Apartment House Tenants in New York City

No. 85-2  Rent Increases for Rent Stabilized Housing Accommodations Based Upon Owner Hardship—Guidelines and Procedures

No. 86-1  Summary of Guideline Rates of Maximum Rent Increases Filed by County and New York City Rent Guidelines Boards for Leases Commencing Between October 1, 1985, and September 30, 1986

No. 87-1  1987 Fuel Cost Adjustment for New York City Rent Controlled Apartments

No. 90-1  Requiring Owners to Submit Sufficient Copies of Designated Applications to the DHCR to Enable the Division to Serve All Affected Tenants With Copies of Such Applications 1990

No. 90-1  Requiring Owners to Submit Sufficient Copies of Designated Applications to the DHCR to Enable the Division to Serve all Affected Tenants With Copies of Such Applications 1992

No. 90-2  Useful Life Schedule for Major Capital Improvements

No. 90-2  Requirement for Application and Extension of the Effective Date of the Waiver Provision of the Useful Life Schedule Addendum

No. 91-2  Penalties for Failure to Pay Billed Administrative Fees for New York City Rent Stabilized Accommodations or for Apartments Covered by the Emergency Tenant Protection Act

No. 92-1  Owner's Notice to New Tenant of Legal Regulated Rent for a Vacant Housing Accommodation Previously Regulated Under the Emergency Tenant Protection Act and Regulations

No. 92-2  Extension of Filing Deadline for PARs and Fuel Cost Reports Due on May 1, 1993

No. 93-1  Procedures for the Implementation of the Freedom of Information Law (FOIL) and Procedures for Responding to Subpoenas Duces Tecum for Files and Records

No. 95-1  Collectibility of MCI/OI Increases where the Rent is Reduced Because of Diminution of Services

No. 95-2  Substantial Rehabilitation

No. 95-3  Implementing the Rent Regulation Reform Act of 1993 and NYC Local Law 1994, No. 4 (Replaces 94-1)

No. 96-1  Procedures Pursuant to the Rent Stabilization Code for the Filing of an Owner's Application to Refuse to Renew Leases on the Grounds of Demolition

**Westchester County Rent Office**

75 South Broadway, Suite 200
White Plains, NY 10601
914-948-4434

## New York State Department of Labor, Employer Services (Chapter 6)

Endicott and the Southern Tier: 607-741-4519
New York City: 212-352-6592
Buffalo and Western New York State: 716-851-2753
Long Island: 516-934-8558
Plattsburgh and North Country: 518-561-0430
Rochester and Finger Lakes area: 716-258-8876
Saratoga and Capital region: 518-587-8443
Syracuse and Central New York: 315-479-3371
Utica and Mohawk Valley: 315-793-2271
Westchester, Rockland and Hudson Valley:
914-997-9543
DOL website: www.labor.state.ny.us.

### NYS Department of Labor, Division of Safety and Health (Chapter 11)

Asbestos Control Bureau
State Office Campus
Building 12, Room 133
Albany, NY 12240
518-457-1255
Website: www.labor.state.ny.us.html/safety

Licensing and Certification Unit
State Office Campus
Building 12, Room 161
Albany, NY 12240
518-457-2735 (for questions on licensing and
certification regarding asbestos)
518-457-1255 (for questions concerning asbestos
abatement projects)
Website: www.labor.state.ny.us/business_ny/
employer_responsibilities/safety_health.html (click
Asbestos Control Bureau).

## New York State Department of Environmental Conservation

Division of Solid & Hazardous Materials
Bureau of Solid Waste & Land Management
Albany, NY 12233
518-402-8693 (for questions about disposal of
hazardous wastes, such as asbestos)

## New York State Division of Criminal Justice Services (Chapters 1 and 6)

4 Tower Place
Albany, NY 12203-3764
900-288-3838 (sex offender registry information
line)
Website: www.criminaljustice.state.ny.us

## New York State Division of Human Rights (Chapters 1 and 6)

One Fordham Plaza, 4th Floor
Bronx, NY 10458
718-741-8400
Website: www.nysdhr.com

## New York State Department of State, Division of Licensing Services (Chapter 6)

84 Holland Avenue
Albany, NY 12208-3490
518-474-4429
Website: www.dos.state.ny.us

## New York State Department of Taxation and Finance (Chapter 6)

P.O. Box 15119
Albany, NY 12212-5119.
800-462-8100
Website: www.tax.state.ny.us

## New York State Workers Compensation Board (Chapter 6)

20 Park Street
Albany, NY 12207
518-474-6967
Website: www.wcb.state.ny.us

## E. New York City Agencies

**New York City Department of Aging (Chapter 4)**
2 Lafayette Street
New York, NY 10007
212-442-1000
Website: www.nyc.gov/html/dfta/home.html

**New York City Commission on Human Rights (Chapters 1 and 6)**
40 Rector Street, 10th Floor
New York, NY 10006
212-306-7500
Website: www.nyc.gov/html/cchr/home.html

**New York City Department of Buildings (Chapters 9 and 11)**
280 Broadway
New York, NY 10007
212-227-7000
Website: www.nyc.gov/html/dob/home.html

**New York City Department of Environmental Protection (Chapter 11)**
96-05 Horace Harding Expressway
Corona, New York
718-337-4357
718-595-3730 (asbestos and lead control, including regulations and forms)
718-595-3682 (asbestos abatement)
Websites: www.nyc.gov/html/dep/home.html;
www.nyc.gov/html/dep/home.html/asbestosf.html
(asbestos abatement activity forms)

**New York City Department of Finance (Chapter 14)**
25 Elm Place
Brooklyn, NY 11201
718-935-6000
Website: www.nyc.gov/html/finance/home.html

**New York City Department of Health (Chapter 11)**
125 Worth Street
New York, NY 10013
212-442-9666 (general number)
212-BAN-LEAD (lead abatement information)
212-788-4290 (mold guidelines)
Website: www.nyc.gov/html/doh/home.html

**New York City Department of Housing Preservation and Development (HPD) (Chapters 6, 9, 10 and 11)**
100 Gold Street
New York, NY 10038
212-863-8000
Website: www.nyc.gov/html/hpd/home.html

## F. Bar Associations and Lawyer Referral Services

Here is a list of 22 bar associations which offer lawyer referral services, the area each serves and whether or not the service meets American Bar Association (ABA) standards. Lawyer referral services that meet ABA standards only refer attorneys who are licensed to practice in New York, maintain adequate malpractice insurance or alternatively, have provided proof of financial responsibility and are experienced in the area of law for which they are being referred.

**New York State Bar Association Lawyer Referral and Information Service**
Albany, NY
800-342-3661
518-487-5909
Serves all counties throughout the state
*Meets ABA standards*

**Albany County Bar Association Lawyer Referral Program**
Albany, NY
518-445-7691
Serves Albany County
*Meets ABA standards*

**Association of the Bar of the City of New York Legal Referral Service**
New York, NY
212-626-7373
212-626-7374 (Spanish)
Serves New York City
*Meets ABA standards*

**Capital District Women's Bar Association**
Albany, NY
518-438-5511
Serves Albany, Schenectady and Troy Counties
*Does not meet ABA standards*

**Bronx County Bar Association Lawyer
 Referral Service**
Bronx, NY
718-293-5600
Serves Bronx County
*Does not meet ABA standards*

**Brooklyn Bar Association Lawyer Referral Service**
Brooklyn, NY
718-624-0843
Serves New York City
*Does not meet ABA standards*

**Broome County Bar Association Lawyer
 Reference Service**
Binghamton, NY
607-723-6331
Serves Broome County
*Does not meet ABA standards*

**Chemung County Lawyer Referral Service**
Elmira, NY
607-734-9687
Serves Chemung County
*Does not meet ABA standards*

**Dutchess County Bar Association Lawyer
 Referral Service**
Poughkeepsie, NY
914-473-7941
Serves Dutchess County
*Does not meet ABA standards*

**Erie County Bar Association**
Buffalo NY
716-852-3100
Serves Erie County
*Meets ABA standards*

**Nassau County Bar Association Lawyer Referral
 Information Service**
Mineola, NY
516-747-4832
Serves Nassau County
*Does not meet ABA standards*

**Monroe County Bar Association**
Rochester, NY
716-546-2130
Serves Monroe, Orleans, Genesee, Stueben,
Wayne, Wyoming and Livingston Counties
*Meets ABA standards*

**Niagara Falls Bar Association**
Niagara Falls, NY
716-284-4101
Serves Niagara County
*Does not meet ABA standards*

**Onondaga County Bar Association Referral Service**
Syracuse NY
315-471-2690
Serves Onondaga County
*Meets ABA standards*

**Orange County Bar Association**
Goshen, NY
914-294-8222
Serves Orange County
*Does not meet ABA standards*

**Putnam County Bar Association Lawyer
 Referral Service**
Carmel, NY
914-225-4904
Serves Putnam, Dutchess and Westchester Counties
*Does not meet ABA standards*

**Queens County Bar Association Lawyer
 Referral Service**
Jamaica, NY
718-291-4500
Serves New York City
*Does not meet ABA standards*

**Richmond County Bar Association**
Staten Island, NY
718-442-4500
Serves Richmond County
*Does not meet ABA standards*

**Rockland County Bar Association Lawyer
 Referral Service**
New City, NY
845-634-2149
Serves Rockland County
*Does not meet ABA standards*

**Suffolk County Bar Association Lawyer
 Referral Service**
Hauppage, NY
516-234-5577
Serves Suffolk County
*Does not meet ABA standards*

**Warren County Bar Association Lawyer
 Referral Service**
Glens Falls, NY
518-792-9239
Serves Warren, Washington, Saratoga and
Essex Counties
*Does not meet ABA standards*

**Westchester County Bar Association Lawyer
 Referral Service**
White Plains, NY
914-761-5151
Serves Westchester County
*Does not meet ABA standards* ■

Appendix **II**

# Sample Lease Forms and Riders for NYC Rent-Stabilized Units

## "ATTACHED RIDER SETS FORTH RIGHTS AND OBLIGATIONS OF TENANTS AND LANDLORDS UNDER THE RENT STABILIZATION LAW." ("LOS DERECHOS Y RESPON-SABILIDADES DE INQUILINOS Y CASEROS ESTÁN DISPONIBLE EN ESPAÑOL").

### STANDARD FORM OF APARTMENT LEASE
**THE REAL ESTATE BOARD OF NEW YORK, INC.**
© Copyright 1988. All Rights Reserved. Reproduction in whole or in part prohibited.

**PREAMBLE:** This lease contains the agreements between You and Owner concerning Your rights and obligations and the rights and obligations of Owner. You and Owner have other rights and obligations which are set forth in government laws and regulations.

You should read this Lease and all of its attached parts carefully. If You have any questions, or if You do not understand any words or statements, get clarification. Once You and Owner sign this Lease You and Owner will be presumed to have read it and understood it. You and Owner admit that all agreements between You and Owner have been written into this Lease. You understand that any agreements made before or after this Lease was signed and not written into it will not be enforceable.

THIS LEASE is made on _____ between
month    day    year

Owner, _____

whose address is _____

and You, the Tenant, _____

whose address is _____

### 1. APARTMENT AND USE
☛ Owner agrees to lease to You Apartment _____ on the _____ floor in the Building at _____ Borough of _____, City and State of New York.

You shall use the Apartment for living purposes only. The Apartment may be occupied by the tenant or tenants named above and by the immediate family of the tenant or tenants and by occupants as defined in and only in accordance with Real Property Law §235-f.

### 2. LENGTH OF LEASE
☛ The term (that means the length) of this Lease is _____ years, _____ months _____ days, beginning on _____
and ending on _____. If you do not do everything You agree to do in this Lease, Owner may have the right to end it before the above date. If Owner does not do everything that owner agrees to do in this Lease, You may have the right to end the Lease before ending date.

### 3. RENT
☛ Your monthly rent for the Apartment is $ _____

until adjusted pursuant to Article 4 below. You must pay Owner the rent, in advance, on the first day of each month either at Owner's office or at another place that Owner may inform You of by written notice. You must pay the first month's rent to Owner when You sign this Lease if the lease begins on the first day of the month. If the Lease begins after the first day of the month, You must pay when you sign this lease(l)the part of the rent from the beginning date of this Lease until the last day of the month and (2)the full rent for the next full calendar month. If this Lease is a Renewal Lease, the rent for the first month of this Lease need not be paid until the first day of the month when the renewal term begins.

### 4. RENT ADJUSTMENTS
If this Lease is for a Rent Stabilized apartment, the rent herein shall be adjusted up or down during the Lease term, including retroactively, to conform to the Rent Guidelines. Where Owner, upon application to the State Division of Housing and Community Renewal ("authorized agency") is found to be entitled to an increase in rent or other relief, You and Owner agree: a. to be bound by such determination; b. where the authorized agency has granted an increase in rent, You shall pay such increase in the manner set forth by the order of the authorized agency; c. except that in the event that an order is issued increasing the stabilization rent because of Owner hardship, You may, within thirty (30) days of your receipt of a copy of the order, cancel your lease on sixty (60) days written notice to Owner. During said period You may continue in occupancy at no increase in rent.

### 5. SECURITY DEPOSIT
☛ You are required to give Owner the sum of $_____ when You sign this Lease as a security deposit, which is called in law a trust. Owner will deposit this security in _____ bank at _____. If the Building contains six or more apartments, the bank account will earn interest. If You carry out all of your agreements in this Lease, at the end of each calendar year Owner or the bank will pay to Owner 1% interest on the deposit for administrative costs and to You all other interest earned on the security deposit.

If You carry out all of your agreements in this Lease and if You move out of the Apartment and return it to Owner in the same condition it was in when You first occupied it, except for ordinary wear and tear or damage caused by fire or other casualty, Owner will return to You the full amount of your security deposit and interest to which You are entitled within 60 days after this Lease ends. However, if You do not carry out all your agreements in this Lease, Owner may keep all or part of your security deposit and any interest which has not yet been paid to You necessary to pay Owner for any losses incurred, including missed payments.

If Owner sells or leases the building, Owner will turn over your security, with interest, either to You or to the person buying or leasing (lessee) the building within 5 days after the sale or lease. Owner will then notify You, by registered or certified mail, of the name and address of the person or company to whom the deposit has been turned over. In such case, Owner will have no further responsibility to You for the security deposit. The new owner or lessee will become responsible to You for the security deposit.

### 6. IF YOU ARE UNABLE TO MOVE IN
A situation could arise which might prevent Owner from letting You move into the Apartment on the beginning date set in this Lease. if this happens for reasons beyond Owner's reasonable control, Owner will not be responsible for Your damages

☛ Space to be filled in.

Page 2

or expenses, and this Lease will remain in effect. However, in such case, this Lease will start on the date when You can move in, and the ending date in Article 2 will be changed to a date reflecting the full term of years set forth in Article 2. You will not have to pay rent until the move-in date Owner gives You by written notice,, or the date You move in, whichever is earlier. If Owner does not give You notice that the move-in date is within 30 days after the beginning date of the term of this Lease as stated in Article 2, You may tell Owner in writing, that Owner has 15 additional days to let You move in, or else the Lease will end. If Owner does not allow You to move in within those additional 15 days, then the Lease is ended. Any money paid by You on account of this Lease will then be refunded promptly by Owner.

### 7. CAPTIONS

In any dispute arising under this Lease, in the event of a conflict between the text and a caption, the text controls.

### 8. WARRANTY OF HABITABILITY

A. All of the sections of this Lease are subject to the provisions of the Warranty of Habitability Law in the form it may have from time to time during this Lease. Nothing in this Lease can be interpreted to mean that You have given up any of your rights under that law. Under that law, Owner agrees that the Apartment and the Building are fit for human habitation and that there will be no conditions which will be detrimental to life, health or safety.

B. You will do nothing to interfere or make more difficult Owner's efforts to provide You and all other occupants of the Building with the required facilities and services. Any condition caused by your misconduct or the misconduct of anyone under your direction or control shall not be a breach by Owner.

### 9. CARE OF YOUR APARTMENT-END OF LEASE-MOVING OUT

A. You will take good care of the apartment and will not permit or do any damage to it, except for damage which occurs through ordinary wear and tear. You will move out on or before the ending date of this lease and leave the Apartment in good order and in the same condition as it was when You first occupied it, except for ordinary wear and tear and damage caused by fire or other casualty.

B. When this Lease ends, You must remove all of your movable property. You must also remove at your own expense, any wall covering, bookcases, cabinets, mirrors, painted murals or any other installation or attachment You may have installed in the Apartment, even if it was done with Owner's consent. You must restore and repair to its original condition those portions of the Apartment affected by those installations and removals. You have not moved out until all persons, furniture and other property of yours is also out of the Apartment. If your property remains in the Apartment after the Lease ends, Owner may either treat You as still in occupancy and charge You for use, or may consider that You have given up the Apartment and any property remaining in the Apartment. In this event, Owner may either discard the property or store it at your expense. You agree to pay Owner for all costs and expenses incurred in removing such property. The provisions of this article will continue to be in effect after the end of this Lease.

### 10. CHANGES AND ALTERATIONS TO APARTMENT

You cannot build in, add to, change or alter, the Apartment in any way, including wallpapering, painting, repainting, or other decorating, without getting Owner's written consent before You do anything. Without Owner's prior written consent, You cannot install or use in the Apartment any of the following: dishwasher machines, clothes washing or drying machines, electric stoves, garbage disposal units, heating, ventilating or air conditioning units or any other electrical equipment which, in Owner's reasonable opinion, will overload the existing wiring installation in the Building or interfere with the use of such electrical wiring facilities by othertenants of the Building. Also, You cannot place in the Apartment water-filled furniture.

### 11. YOUR DUTY TO OBEY AND COMPLY WITH LAWS, REGULATIONS AND LEASE RULES

A. **Government Laws and Orders.** You will obey and comply (1) with all present and future city, state and federal laws and regulations, including the Rent Stabilization Code and Law, which affect the Building or the Apartment, and (2) with all orders and regulations of Insurance Rating Organizations which affect the Apartment and the Building. You will not allow any windows in the Apartment to be cleaned from the outside, unless the equipment and safety devices required by law are used.

B. **Owner's Rules Affecting You.** You will obey all Owner's rules listed in this Lease and all future reasonable rules of Owner or Owner's agent. Notice of all additional rules shall be delivered to You in writing or posted in the lobby or other public place in the building, Owner shall not be responsible to You for not enforcing any rules, regulations or provisions of another tenant's lease except to the extent required by law.

C. **Your Responsibility.** You are responsible for the behavior of yourself, of your immediate family, your servants and people who are visiting You. You will reimburse Owner as additional rent upon demand for the cost of all losses, damages, fines and reasonable legal expenses incurred by Owner because You, members of your immediate family, servants or people visiting You have not obeyed government laws and orders of the agreements or rules of this Lease.

### 12. OBJECTIONABLE CONDUCT

As a tenant in the Building, You will not engage in objectionable conduct. Objectionable conduct means behavior which makes or will make the Apartment or the Building less fit to live in for You or other occupants. It also means anything which interferes with the right of others to properly and peacefully enjoy their Apartments, or causes conditions that are dangerous, hazardous, unsanitary and detrimental to other tenants in the Building. Objectionable conduct by You gives Owner the right to end this Lease.

### 13. SERVICES AND FACILITIES

A. **Required Services.** Owner will provide cold and hot water and heat as required by law, repairs to the Apartment, as required by law, elevator service if the Building has elevator equipment, and the utilities, if any, included in the rent, as set forth in sub-paragraph B. You are not entitled to any rent reduction because of a stoppage or reduction of any of the above services unless it is provided by law.

B. The following utilities are included in the rent _____

C. **Electricity and Other Utilities.** If Owner provides electricity or gas and the charge is included in the rent on Page 1, or if You buy electricity or gas from Owner for a separate (submetered) charge, your obligations are described in the Rider attached to this Lease. If electricity or gas is not included in the rent or is not charged separately by Owner, You must arrange for this service directly with the utility company. You must also pay directly for telephone service if it is not included in the rent.

D. **Appliances.** Appliances supplied by Owner in the Apartment are for your use. They will be maintained and repaired or replaced by Owner, but if repairs or replacement are made necessary because of your negligence or misuse, You will pay Owner for the cost of such repair or replacement as additional rent.

E. **Elevator Service.** If the elevator is the kind that requires an employee of Owner to operate it, Owner may end this service without reducing the rent if: (1) Owner gives You 10 days notice that this service will end; and (2) within a reasonable time after the end of this 10-day notice, Owner begins to substitute an automatic control type of elevator and proceeds diligently with its installation.

F. **Storeroom Use.** If Owner permits You to use any storeroom,laundry or any other facility located in the building but outside of the Apartment, the use of this storeroom or facility will be furnished to You free of charge and at your own risk, except for loss suffered by You due to Owner's negligence. You will operate at your expense any coin operated appliances located in such storerooms or laundries.

### 14. INABILITY TO PROVIDE SERVICES

Because of a strike, labor, trouble, national emergency, repairs, or any other cause beyond Owner's reasonable control, Owner may not be able to provide or may be delayed in providing any services or in making any repairs to the Building.

Space to be filled in.                                                    Rider to be added, if necessary.

Page 3

In any of these events, any rights You may have against Owner are only those rights which are allowed by laws in effect when the reduction in service occurs.

**15.  ENTRY TO APARTMENT**

During reasonable hours and with reasonable notice, except in emergencies, Owner may enter the Apartment for the following reasons:

(A) To erect, use and maintain pipes and conduits in and through the walls and ceilings of the Apartment; to inspect the Apartment and to make any necessary repairs or changes Owner decides are necessary. Your rent will not be reduced because of any of this work, unless required by Law.

(B) To show the Apartment to persons who may wish to become owners or lessees of the entire Building or may be interested in lending money to Owner;

(C) For four months before the end of the Lease, to show the Apartment to persons who wish to rent it;

(D) If during the last month of the Lease You have moved out and removed all or almost all of your property from the Apartment, Owner may enter to make changes, repairs, or redecorations. Your rent will not be reduced for that month and this Lease will not be ended by Owner's entry.

(E) If at any time You are not personally present to permit Owner or Owner's representative to enter the Apartment and entry is necessary or allowed by law or under this lease, Owner or Owner's representatives may nevertheless enter the Apartment. Owner may enter by force in an emergency. Owner will not be responsible to You, unless during this entry, Owner or Owner's representative is negligent or misuses your property.

**16.  ASSIGNING; SUBLETTING; ABANDONMENT**

(a) **Assigning and Subletting.** You cannot assign this Lease or sublet the Apartment without Owner's advance written consent in each instance to a request made by You in the manner required by Real Property Law §226-b. and in accordance with the provisions of the Rent Stabilization Code and Law, relating to subletting. Owner may refuse to consent to a lease assignment for any reason or no reason, but if Owner unreasonably refuses to consent to request for a Lease assignment properly made, at your request in writing, Owner will end this Lease effective as of thirty days after your request. The first and every other time you wish to sublet the Apartment, You must get the written consent of Owner unless Owner unreasonably withholds consent following your request to sublet in the manner provided by Real Property Law §226.b. Owner may impose a reasonable credit check fee on You in connection with an application to assign or sublet. If You fail to pay your rent Owner may collect rent from subtenant or occupant without releasing You from the Lease. Owner will credit the amount collected against the rent due from You. However, Owner's acceptance of such rent does not change the status of the subtenant or occupant to that of direct tenant of Owner and does not release You from this Lease.

(b) **Abandonment.** If You move out of the Apartment (abandonment) before the end of this Lease without the consent of Owner, this Lease will not be ended (except as provided by law following Owner's unreasonable refusal to consent to an assignment or subletting requested by You.) You will remain responsible for each monthly payment of rent as it becomes due until the end of this Lease. In case of abandonment, your responsibility for rent will end only if Owner chooses to end this Lease for default as provided in Article 17.

**17.  DEFAULT**

(1) You default under the Lease if You act in any of the following ways:

(a) You fail to carry out any agreement or provision of this Lease

(b) You or another occupant of the Apartment behaves in an objectionable manner;

(c) You do not take possession or move into the Apartment 15 days after the beginning of this Lease;

(d) You and other legal occupants of the Apartment move out permanently before this Lease ends;

If You do default in any one of these ways, other than a default in the agreement to pay rent, Owner may serve You with a written notice to stop or correct the specified default within 10 days. You must then either stop or correct the default within 10 days, or, if You need more than 10 days, You must begin to correct the default within 10 days and continue to do all that is necessary to correct the default as soon as possible.

(2) If You do not stop or begin to correct a default within 10 days, Owner may give You a second written notice that this Lease will end six days after the date the second written notice is sent to You, At the end of the 6-day period, this Lease will end, You then must move out of the Apartment. Even though this Lease ends, You will remain liable to Owner for unpaid rent up to the end of this Lease, the value of your occupancy, if any, after the Lease ends, and damages caused to Owner after that time as stated in Article 18.

(3) If You do not pay your rent when this Lease requires after a personal demand for rent has been made, or within three days after a statutory written demand for rent has been made, or if the Lease ends, Owner may do the following: (a) enter the apartment and retake possession of it if You have moved out; or (b) go to court and ask that You and all other occupants in the Apartment be compelled to move out.

Once this Lease has been ended, whether because of default or otherwise, You give up any right You might otherwise have to reinstate or renew the Lease.

**18.  REMEDIES OF OWNER AND YOUR LIABILITY**

If this Lease is ended by Owner because of your default, the following are the rights and obligations of You and Owner.

(a) You must pay your rent until this Lease has ended. Thereafter, You must pay an equal amount for what the law calls "use and occupancy" until You actually move out.

(b) Once You are out, Owner may re-rent the Apartment or any portion of it for a period of time which may end before or after the ending date of this Lease. Owner may re-rent to a new tenant at a lesser rent or may charge a higher rent than the rent in this Lease.

(c) Whether the Apartment is re-rented or not, You must pay to Owner as damages:

(1) the difference between the rent in this Lease and the amount, if any, of the rents collected in any later lease or leases of the Apartment for what would have been the remaining period of this Lease; and

(2) Owner's expenses for advertisements, broker's fees and the cost of putting the Apartment in good condition for re-rental; and

∗∗∗ (3) Owner's expenses for attorney's fees.

(d) You shall pay all damages due in monthly installments on the rent day established in this Lease. Any legal action brought to collect one or more monthly installments of damages shall not prejudice in any way Onwer's right to collect the damages for a later month by a similar action. If the rent collected by Owner from a subsequent tenant of the Apartment is more than the unpaid rent and damages which You owe Owner, You cannot receive the difference. Owner's failure to re-rent to another tenant will not release or change your liability for damages, unless the failure is due to Owner's deliberate inaction.

**19.  ADDITIONAL OWNER REMEDIES**

If You do not do everything You have agreed to do, or if You do anything which shows that You intend not to do what You have agreed to do, Owner has the right to ask a Court to make You carry out your agreement or to give the Owner such other relief as the Court can provide. This is in addition to the remedies in Article 17 and 18 of this lease.

**20.  FEES AND EXPENSES**

A. **Owner's Right.** You must reimburse Owner for any of the following fees and expenses incurred by Owner:

(1) Making any repairs to the Apartment or the Building which result from misuse or negligence by You or persons who live with You, visit You, or work for You;

∗∗∗ This may be deleted

Page 4

(2) Repairing or replacing any appliance damaged by Your misuse or negligence.

(3) Correcting any violations of city, state or federal laws or orders and regulations of insurance rating organizations concerning the Apartment or the Building which You or persons who live with You, visit You, or work for You have caused;

(4) Preparing the Apartment for the next tenant if You move out of your Apartment before the Lease ending date;

\*\*\* (5) Any legal fees and disbursements for legal actions or proceedings brought by Owner against You because of a Lease default by You or for defending lawsuits brought against Owner because of your actions;

(6) Removing all of your property after this Lease is ended;

(7) All other fees and expenses incurred by Owner because of your failure to obey any other provisions and agreements of this Lease;

These fees and expenses shall be paid by You to Owner as additional rent within 30 days after You receive Owner's bill or statement. If this Lease has ended when these fees and expenses are incurred, You will still be liable to Owner for the same amount as damages.

B. **Tenant's Right.** Owner agrees that unless sub-paragraph 5 of this Article 20 has been stricken out of this Lease You have the right to collect reasonable legal fees and expenses incurred in a successful defense by You of a lawsuit brought by Owner against You or brought by You against Owner to the extent provided by Real Property Law, section 234.

### 21. PROPERTY LOSS, DAMAGES OR INCONVENIENCE

Unless caused by the negligence or misconduct of Owner or Owner's agents or employees, Owner or Owner's agents and employees are not responsible to You for any of the following: (1) any loss of or damage to You or your property in the Apartment or the Building due to any accidental or intentional cause, even a theft or another crime committed in the Apartment or elsewhere in the Building; (2) any loss of or damage to your property delivered to any employee of the Building (i.e., doorman, superintendent, etc.); or (3) any damage or inconvenience caused to You by actions, negligence or violations of a Lease by any other tenant or person in the Building except to the extent required by law.

Owner will not be liable for any temporary interference with light, ventilation, or view caused by construction by or in behalf of Owner. Owner will not be liable for any such interference on a permanent basis caused by construction on any parcel of land not owned by Owner. Also, Owner will not be liable to You for such interference caused by the permanent closing, darkening or blocking up of windows, if such action is required by law. None of the foregoing events will cause a suspension or reduction of the rent or allow You to cancel the Lease.

### 22. FIRE OR CASUALTY

A. If the Apartment becomes unusable, in part or totally, because of fire, accident or other casualty, this Lease will continue unless ended by Owner under C below or by You under D below. But the rent will be reduced immediately. This reduction will be based upon the part of the Apartment which is unusable.

B. Owner will repair and restore the Apartment, unless Owner decides to take actions described in paragraph C below.

C. After a fire, accident or other casualty in the Building, Owner may decide to tear down the Building or to substantially rebuild it. In such case, Owner need not restore the Apartment but may end this Lease. Owner may do this even if the Apartment has not been damaged, by giving You written notice of this decision within 30 days after the date when the damage occurred. If the Apartment is usable when Owner gives You such notice, this Lease will end 60 days from the last day of the calendar month in which You were given the notice.

D. If the Apartment is completely unusable because of fire, accident or other casualty and it is not repaired in 30 days, You may give Owner written notice that You end the Lease. If You give that notice, this Lease is considered ended on the day that the fire, accident or casualty occurred. Owner will refund your security deposit and the pro-rate portion of rents paid for the month in which the casualty happened.

E. Unless prohibited by the applicable insurance policies, to the extent that such insurance is collected, You and Owner release and waive all right of recovery against the other or anyone claiming through or under each by way of subrogation.

### 23. PUBLIC TAKING

The entire building or a part of it can be acquired (condemned) by any government or government agency for a public or quasi-public use or purpose. If this happens, this Lease shall end on the date the government or agency take title, You shall have no claim against Owner for any damage resulting; You also agree that by signing this Lease, You assign to Owner any claim against the Government or Government agency for the value of the unexpired portion of this Lease.

### 24. SUBORDINATION CERTIFICATE AND ACKNOWLEDGEMENTS

All leases and mortgages of the Building or of the land on which the Building is located, now in effect or made after this Lease is signed, come ahead of this Lease. In other words, this Lease is "subject and subordinate to" any existing or future lease or mortgage on the Building or land, including any renewals, consolidations, modifications and replacements of these leases or mortgages. If certain provisions of any of these leases or mortgages come into effect, the holder of such lease or mortgage can end this Lease. If this happens, You agree that You have no claim against Owner or such lease or mortgage holder. If Owner requests, You will sign promptly an acknowledgement of the "subordination" in the form that Owner requires.

You also agree to sign (if accurate) a written acknowledgement to any third party designated by Owner that this Lease is in effect, that Owner is performing Owner's obligations under this Lease and that you have no present claim against Owner.

### 25. TENANT'S RIGHT TO LIVE IN AND USE THE APARTMENT

If You pay the rent and any required additional rent on time and You do everything You have agreed to do in this Lease, your tenancy cannot be cut off before the ending date, except as provided for in Articles 22, 23, and 24.

### 26. BILLS AND NOTICE

A. Notices to You. Any notice from Owner or Owner's agent or attorney will be considered properly given to You if it (1) is in writing; (2) is signed by or in the name of Owner or Owner's agent; and (3) is addressed to You at the Apartment and delivered to You personally or sent by registered or certified mail to You at the Apartment. The date of service of any written notice by Owner to you under this agreement is the date of delivery or mailing of such notice.

B. Notices to Owner. If You wish to give a notice to Owner, You must write it and deliver it or send it by registered or certified mail to Owner at the address noted on page 1 of this Lease or at another address of which Owner or Agent has given You written notice.

### 27. GIVING UP RIGHT TO TRIAL BY JURY AND COUNTERCLAIM

A. Both You and Owner agree to give up the right to a trial by jury in a court action, proceeding or counter claim on any matters concerning this Lease, the relationship of You and Owner as Tenant and Landlord or your use or occupancy of the Apartment. This agreement to give up the right to a jury trial does not include claims for personal injury or property damage.

B. If Owner begins any court action or proceeding against You which asks that You be compelled to move out, You cannot make a counterclaim unless You are claiming that Owner has not done what Owner is supposed to do about the condition of the Apartment or the Building.

\*\*\* This may be deleted.

Page 5

## 28. NO WAIVER OF LEASE PROVISIONS

A. Even if Owner accepts your rent or fails once or more often to take action against You when You have not done what You have agreed to do in this Lease, the failure of Owner to take action or Owner's acceptance of rent does not prevent Owner from taking action at a later date if You again do not do what You have agreed to do.

B. Only a written agreement between You and Owner can waive any violation of this Lease.

C. If You pay and Owner accepts an amount less than all the rent due, the amount received shall be considered to be in payment of all or a part of the earliest rent due. It will not be considered an agreement by Owner to accept this lesser amount in full satisfaction of all of the rent due.

D. Any agreement to end this Lease and also to end the rights and obligations of You and Owner must be in writing, signed by You and Owner or Owner's agent. Even if You give keys to the Apartment and they are accepted by any employee, or agent, or Owner, this Lease is not ended.

## 29. CONDITION OF THE APARTMENT

When You signed this Lease, You did not rely on anything said by Owner, Owner's agent or superintendent about the physical condition of the Apartment, the Building or the land on which it is built. You did not rely on any promises as to what would be done, unless what was said or promised is written in this Lease and signed by both You and Owner or found in Owner's floor plans or brochure shown to You before You signed the Lease. Before signing this Lease, You have inspected the apartment and You accept it in its present condition "as is," except for any condition which You could not reasonably have seen during your inspection. You agree that Owner has not promised to do any work in the Apartment except as specified in attached "Work" rider.

## 30. RENT INCREASE FOR MAJOR CAPITAL IMPROVEMENT

☞       Owner advises you that an application for increase in stabilized rent on the ground of a building-wide major capital improvement dated _____Docket No. _____is now pending before the State Division of Housing and Community Renewal (Agency). Such application involves the following major capital improvements which are now completed or in progress:

You agree that the stabilized rent herein may be increased during the term of this lease by reason of such improvement as of a date and in the amount permitted by an order from the Agency.

## 31.       DEFINITIONS

A. Owner: The term "Owner" means the person or organization receiving or entitled to receive rent from You for the Apartment at any particular time other than a rent collector or managing agent of Owner. "Owner" includes the owner of the land or Building, a lessor, or sublessor of the land or Building and a mortgagee in possession. It does not include a former owner, even if the former owner signed this Lease.

B. You: The Term "You" means the person or persons signing this Lease as Tenant and the successors and assigns of the signer. This Lease has established a tenant-landlord relationship between You and Owner.

## 32. SUCCESSOR INTERESTS

The agreements in this Lease shall be binding on Owner and You and on those who succeed to the interest of Owner or You by law, by approved assignment or by transfer.

**Owners Rules - a part of this lease - see page 6**

TO CONFIRM OUR AGREEMENTS, OWNER AND YOU RESPECTIVELY SIGN THIS LEASE AS OF THE DAY AND YEAR FIRST WRITTEN ON PAGE 1.

Witnesses

_____          _____ [L.S.]
                                                   Owner's Signature

_____          _____ [L.S.]
                                                   Tenant's Signature

_____          _____ [L.S.]
                                                   Tenant's Signature

### GUARANTY

The undersigned Guarantor guarantees to Owner the strict performance of and observance by Tenant of all the agreements, provisions and rules in the attached Lease. Guarantor agrees to waive all notices when Tenant is not paying rent or not observing and complying with all of the provisions of the attached Lease. Guarantor agrees to be equally liable with Tenant so that Owner may sue Guarantor directly without first suing Tenant. The Guarantor further agrees that his guaranty shall remain in full effect even if the Lease is renewed, changed or extended in any way and even if Owner has to make a claim against Guarantor. Owner and Guarantor agree to waive trial by jury in any action, proceeding or counterclaim brought against the other on any matters concerning the attached Lease or the Guaranty.

Dated, New York City          _____

_____          _____
                       Witness                                                Guarantor

_____          _____
                                                   Address

☞   To be filled in if applicable

Page 6

Apartment

Premises

Tenant

Expires

STANDARD FORM OF APARTMENT

# Lease

The Real Estate Board of New York, Inc.

**ATTACHED RULES WHICH ARE A PART OF THE LEASE
AS PROVIDED BY ARTICLE 11**

**Public Access Ways**
1.  (a) Tenants shall not block or leave anything in or on fire escapes,the sidewalks, entrances, driveways, elevators, stairways, or halls. Public access ways shall be used only for entering and leaving the Apartment and the Building. Only those elevators and passageways designated by Owner can be used for deliveries.
 (b) Baby carriages, bicycles or other property of Tenants shall not be allowed to stand in the halls, passageways, public areas or courts of the Building.
**Bathroom and Plumbing Fixtures**
2.  The bathrooms, toilets and wash closets and plumbing fixtures shall only be used for the purposes for which they were designed or built; sweepings, rubbish bags, acids or other substances shall not be placed in them.
**Refuse**
3.  Carpets, rugs or other articles shall not be hung or shaken out of any window of the Building. Tenants shall not sweep or throw or permit to be swept or thrown any dirt, garbage or other substances out of the windows or into any of the halls, elevators or elevator shafts. Tenants shall not place any articles outside of the Apartment or outside of the building except in safe containers and only at places chosen by Owner.
**Elevators**
4.  All non-automatic passenger and service elevators shall be operated only by employees of Owner and must not in any event be interfered with by Tenants. The service elevators, if any, shall be used by servants, messengers and trades people for entering and leaving, and the passenger elevators, if any, shall not be used by them for any purpose. Nurses with children, however, may use the passenger elevators.
**Laundry**
5.  Laundry and drying apparatus, if any, shall be used by Tenants in the manner and at the times that the superintendent or other representative of Owner may direct. Tenants shall not dry or air clothes on the roof
**Keys and Locks**
6.  Owner may retain a pass key to the apartment. Tenants may install on the entrance of the Apartment an additional lock of not more than three inches in circumference. Tenants may also install a lock on any window but only in the manner provided by law. Immediately upon making any installation of either type, Tenants shall notify Owner or Owner's agent and shall give Owner or Owner's agent a duplicate key. If changes are made to the locks or mechanism installed by Tenants, Tenants must deliver keys to Owner. At the end of this Lease, Tenants must return to Owner all keys either furnished or otherwise obtained. If Tenants lose or fail to return any keys which were furnished to them, Tenants shall pay to Owner the cost of replacing them.
**Noise**
7.  Tenants, their families, guests, employees, or visitors shall not make or permit any disturbing noises in the Apartment or Building or permit anything to be done that will interfere with the rights, comforts or convenience of other tenants. Also, Tenants shall not play a musical instrument or operate or allow to be operated a phonograph, radio or television set so as to disturb or annoy any other occupant of the Building.
**No Projections**
8.  An aerial may not be erected on the roof or outside wall of the Building without the written consent of Owner. Also, awnings or other projections shall not be attached to the outside walls of the Building or to any balcony or terrace.
**No Pets**
9.  Dogs or animals of any kind shall not be kept or harbored in the Apartment, unless in each instance it be expressly permitted in writing by Owner. This consent, if given, can be taken back by Owner at any time for good cause on reasonably given notice. Unless carried or on a leash, a dog shall not be permitted on any passenger elevator or in any public portion of the building. Also, dogs are not permitted on any grass or garden plot under any condition. BECAUSE OF THE HEALTH HAZARD AND POSSIBLE DISTURBANCE OF OTHER TENANTS WHICH ARISE FROM THE UNCONTROLLED PRESENCE OF ANIMALS, ESPECIALLY DOGS, IN THE BUILDING, THE STRICT ADHERENCE TO THE PROVISIONS OF THIS RULE BY EACH TENANT IS A MATERIAL REQUIREMENT OF EACH LEASE. TENANTS' FAILURE TO OBEY THIS RULE SHALL BE CONSIDERED A SERIOUS VIOLATION OF AN IMPORTANT OBLIGATION BY TENANT UNDER THIS LEASE. OWNER MAY ELECT TO END THIS LEASE BASED UPON THIS VIOLATION.
**Moving**
10.  Tenants can use the elevator to move furniture and possessions only on designated days and hours. Owner shall not be liable for any costs, expenses or damages incurred by Tenants in moving because of delays caused by the unavailability of the elevator.
**Floors**
11.  Apartment floors shall be covered with rugs or carpeting to the extent of at least 80% of the floor area of each room excepting only kitchens, pantries, bathrooms and hallways. The tacking strip for wall-to-wall carpeting will be glued, not nailed to the floor.
**Window Guards**
12.  IT IS A VIOLATION OF LAW TO REFUSE, INTERFERE WITH INSTALLATION, OR REMOVE WINDOW GUARDS WHERE REQUIRED. (SEE ATTACHED WINDOW GUARD RIDER)

State of New York
Division of Housing and Community Renewal
Office of Rent Administration
Gertz Plaza
92-31 Union Hall Street
Jamaica, New York 11433
Web Site: www.dhcr.state.ny.us
Email address: dhcrinfo@dhcr.state.ny.us

**Revision Date: April 2001**

**Rent Stabilization Lease Rider For Apartment House Tenants
Residing In New York City**

**FAILURE BY AN OWNER TO ATTACH A COPY OF THIS RIDER TO THE TENANT'S
LEASE WITHOUT CAUSE MAY RESULT IN A FINE OR OTHER SANCTIONS**

**NOTICE**

This Rider, with this Notice, must be attached to all vacancy and renewal leases for rent stabilized apartments. This Rider was prepared pursuant to Section 26-511(d) of the New York City Rent Stabilization Law.

This Rider must be in a print size larger than the print size of the lease to which the Rider is attached. The following language must appear in bold print upon the face of each lease : "**ATTACHED RIDER SETS FORTH RIGHTS AND OBLIGATIONS OF TENANTS AND LANDLORDS UNDER THE RENT STABILIZATION LAW.**" ("**Los Derechos Y Responsabilidades de Inquilinos Y Caseros Están Disponible en Español**".)

**INTRODUCTION**:

This Rider is issued by the New York State Division of Housing and Community Renewal ("DHCR"), pursuant to the Rent Stabilization Law ("RSL"), and Rent Stabilization Code ("Code"). It generally informs tenants and owners about their basic rights and responsibilities under the RSL.

This Rider does not contain every rule applicable to rent stabilized apartments. It is only informational and its provisions are not part of and do not modify the lease. However, it must be attached as an addendum to the lease. It does not replace or modify the RSL, the Code, any order of DHCR, or any order of the New York City Rent Guidelines Board.

The Appendix lists organizations which can provide assistance to tenants and owners who have inquiries, complaints or requests relating to subjects covered in this Rider.

Tenants should keep a copy of this Rider and of any lease they sign.

---

**PROVISIONS**

**1.    GUIDELINES INCREASES FOR RENEWAL LEASES**:

The owner is entitled to increase the rent when a tenant renews a lease ( a "renewal lease"). Each year, effective October 1, the New York City Rent Guidelines Board sets the percentage of maximum permissible increase over the immediately preceding September 30th rent for leases which will begin during the year for which the guidelines order is in effect. The date a lease starts determines which guidelines order applies.

Guidelines orders provide increases for Renewal Leases. The renewing tenant has the choice of the length of the lease. Different percentages are set for rent increases for leases of 1 or 2 years. The guidelines order may incorporate additional provisions, such as a supplementary low-rent adjustment. For additional information see DHCR Fact Sheet #26.

**2.    VACANCY INCREASES FOR VACANCY LEASES**

The owner is entitled to increase the prior legal regulated rent when a new tenant enters into a lease ("vacancy lease"). The legal regulated rent immediately preceding the vacancy may be increased by statutory vacancy increases as follows:

If the vacancy lease is for a term of 2 years, 20% of the prior legal regulated rent; or if the vacancy lease is for a term of 1 year, the increase shall be 20% of the prior legal regulated rent less an amount equal to the difference between:

    a)  The 2 year renewal lease guideline promulgated by the New York City Rent Guidelines Board ("RGB") applied to the prior legal regulated rent and

    b)  The 1 year renewal lease guideline promulgated by the RGB applied to the prior legal regulated rent.

Additional increases are available to owners where the legal regulated rent was last increased by a vacancy allowance eight or more years prior to the entering into of the subject vacancy lease or if no vacancy allowance has been taken, the number of years that the apartment has been subject to stabilization. Generally, this increase equals 0.6%, multiplied by the prior legal regulated rent, multiplied by the number of years since the last vacancy increase.

If the prior legal regulated rent was less than $300, the total vacancy increase shall be as calculated above, **plus** an additional $100. If the prior legal regulated was at least $300, and no more than $500, in no event shall the total vacancy increase be less than $100.

A RGB order may authorize an additional vacancy "allowance," which is separate from the statutory vacancy increase which an owner may charge. The tenant has the choice of whether the vacancy lease will be for a term of 1 or 2 years. For additional information see DHCR Fact Sheets #4 and 26.

## 3.    SECURITY DEPOSITS

An owner may collect a security deposit no greater than one month's rent. However, if the present tenant moved into the apartment prior to the date the apartment first became rent stabilized, and the owner collected more than one month's rent as security, the owner may continue to retain a security deposit of up to two month's rent for that tenant only. When the rent is increased, the owner may charge an additional amount to bring the security deposit up to the full amount of the increased rent to which the owner is entitled.

A security deposit must be deposited in an interest bearing trust account in a banking organization in New York State. The tenant has the option of applying the interest to the rent, leaving the interest in the bank or receiving the interest annually. For additional information see DHCR Fact Sheet #9.

## 4.    OTHER RENT INCREASES:

In addition to guidelines and statutory vacancy increases, the rent may be permanently increased based upon the following:

(A) **New Services, New Equipment, Or Improvements Other Than Repairs - Individual Apartments** - If a new service or new equipment is added or an improvement is made, 1/40th of the cost of the new service, equipment or improvement may be added to the rent. If a new service or new equipment is added or an improvement made while the tenant is in occupancy, the owner must obtain the tenant's written consent to the increase. If a new service or new equipment is provided or an improvement made while the apartment is vacant, consent of the next tenant is not required, but such tenant may challenge the increase if it does not reflect the actual cost of the new service, new equipment or improvement. For additional information see DHCR Fact Sheet #12.

(B) **Major Capital Improvements ("MCI")** - An owner is permitted a rental increase for building-wide major capital improvements, such as the replacement of a boiler, or new plumbing. The owner must receive approval from DHCR which will permit the owner to increase rents pro-rata by 1/84th of the cost of the improvement. The owner is not required to obtain tenant consent. Tenants are served with a notice of the owner's application and have a right to challenge the MCI application on certain grounds. For additional information see DHCR Fact Sheet #11.

(C) **Hardship** - An owner may apply to increase the rents of all rent stabilized apartments based on hardship when:
    1.   the rents are not sufficient to enable the owner to maintain approximately the same average annual net income for a current three-year period as compared with the annual net income which prevailed on the average over the period 1968 through 1970, or for the first three years of operation if the building was completed since 1968, or for the first three years the owner owned the building if the owner cannot obtain records for the years 1968-1970; or
    2.   where the annual gross rental income does not exceed the annual operating expenses by a sum equal to at least 5% of such gross income.

If an application for a rent increase based on a major capital improvement or hardship is granted, the owner may charge the increase during the term of an existing lease only if the lease contains a clause specifically authorizing the owner to do so.

An increase based on a major capital improvement or hardship may not exceed 6% in any 12 month period. Any increase authorized by DHCR which exceeds these annual limitations may be collected in future years.

## 5.    FOR VACANCY LEASES ONLY:

If this Rider is attached to a **RENEWAL LEASE,** the owner is **NOT** obligated to complete this section.

If this Rider is attached to a **VACANCY LEASE,** the owner **MUST** show how the rental amount provided for in such vacancy lease has been computed above the prior legal regulated rent by completing the following chart. The owner is not entitled to a rent which is more than the legal regulated rent. For additional information see DHCR Fact Sheet #5.

ANY INCREASE ABOVE THE PRIOR LEGAL REGULATED RENT MUST BE IN ACCORDANCE WITH ADJUSTMENTS PERMITTED BY THE RENT GUIDELINES BOARD AND THE RENT STABILIZATION

Status of Apartment and Last Tenant
(Owner to Check Appropriate Box - (A), (B), (C), or (D).)

☐  (A)  This apartment was rent stabilized when the last tenant moved out.

Last Legal Regulated Rent                                                    $_____

1.    Statutory Vacancy Increase

(i)  Increase based on (1 year) (2 year) lease (circle one)     (____%)     $_____

(ii) Increase based on length of time (8 years or more)
since last vacancy allowance or if no vacancy alowance
has been taken, the number of years that the apartment
has been subject to stabilization.         (0.6%  x  number of years)    $_____

(iii) Increase based on low rental amount.  If applicable
complete (a) or (b), but not both.

(a)  Prior legal regulated rent was less than $300 -               $_____
additional $100 increase, enter 100

(b)  If the prior legal regulated rent was $300 or more
but less than $500                                      (1)   $100
the sum of (i) and (ii)                                 (2)   _____
(1) minus (2).  If less than zero, enter zero           (3)   _____

Amount from line(3)          $_____

Vacancy Allowance, if permitted by NYC Rent Guidelines Board     (____%)    $_____

Guidelines Supplementary Adjustment, if permitted by NYC Rent
Guidelines Board                                                         $_____

New Equipment, Service, Improvement
for this apartment                                                       $_____

New Legal Regulated Rent                                                 $_____

Separate Charges or Credits:                                             $_____

Surcharge (e.g., 421-a)                                                  $_____

Ancillary Service (e.g., garage)                                         $_____

Other (specify _____)                          $_____

New Tenant's Rent                                                        $_____

or

☐  (B)  This apartment was Rent Controlled at the time the last tenant moved out. This tenant is the first rent
stabilized tenant and the rent agreed to and stated in the lease to which this Rider is attached is $_____.
The owner is entitled to charge a market rent to the first rent stabilized tenant. The first rent charged to
the first rent stabilized tenant becomes the initial legal regulated rent for the apartment under the rent
stabilization system. However, if the tenant has reason to believe that this rent exceeds a "fair market rent",
the tenant may file a "Fair Market Rent Appeal" with DHCR. The owner is required to give the tenant notice,
on DHCR Form RR-1, of the right to file such an appeal. The notice must be served by certified mail. A
tenant only has 90 days, after such notice was mailed to the tenant by the owner by certified mail, to file an
appeal. Otherwise, the rent set forth on the registration form becomes the initial legal regulated rent.

☐  (C)  The rent for this apartment is an Initial or Restructured Rent pursuant to a Government Program.
(Specify Program_____)              $_____.

- or -

☐  (D)  Other_____          $_____.
(Specify - for example, a market or "first" rent after renovation to an individual apartment where the outer
dimensions of the apartment have been substantially altered.)

**6.    RENT REGISTRATION:**

**(A)  Initial**
An owner must register an apartment's rent and services with DHCR within 90 days from when the apartment first becomes subject to the RSL. To complete the rent registration process, the owner must serve the tenant's copy of the registration statement upon the tenant. The tenant may challenge the correctness of the rental as stated in the registration statement within 90 days of the certified mailing to the tenant of the tenant's copy of the registration statement.

**(B)  Annual**
The annual update to the initial registration must be filed with DHCR by July 31st with information as of April 1st of each year. At the time of such filing, the owner must provide each tenant with the tenant's copy. The rental amount registered annually is challengable by the filing with DHCR of a *"Tenant's Complaint of Rent Overcharge and/or Excess Security Deposit"* (DHCR Form RA-89), for a period of 4 years prior to the filing of the complaint.  The rental history prior to this 4 year period will not be examined. Rent charged and paid on the date at the beginning of this 4 year period is the "base date rent."

**(C)  Penalties**
Failure to register shall bar an owner from applying for or collecting any rent increases until such registration has occurred, except for those rent increases which were allowable before the failure to register. However, treble damages will not be imposed against an owner who collects a rent increase, but has not registered where the overcharge results solely because of such owner's failure to file a timely or proper initial or annual registration statement. Where the owner files a late registration statement, any rent increase collected prior to the late registration that would have been lawful except for the failure to timely and properly register will not be found to be an overcharge.

**7.    RENEWAL LEASES:**

A tenant has a right to a renewal lease, with certain exceptions (see section 11 of this Rider, "When An Owner May Refuse To Renew A Lease").

At least 90 days and not more than 150 days before the expiration of a lease, the owner is required to notify the tenant in writing that the lease will soon expire. That notice must also offer the tenant the choice of a 1 or 2 year lease at the permissible guidelines increase. After receiving the notice, the tenant always has 60 days to accept the owner's offer, whether or not the offer is made within the above time period, or even beyond the expiration of the lease term.

Any renewal lease, except for the amount of rent and duration of its term, is required to be on the same terms and conditions as the expired lease, and a fully executed copy of the same must be provided to the tenant within 30 days from the owner's receipt of the renewal lease or renewal form signed by the tenant. If the owner does not return a copy of such fully executed Renewal Lease Form to the tenant within 30 days of receiving the signed renewal lease from the tenant, the tenant is responsible for payment of the new lease rent and may file a *"Tenant's Complaint of Owner's Failure to Renew Lease and/or Failure to Furnish a Copy of a Signed Lease"* (DHCR Form RA-90). DHCR shall order the owner to furnish the copy of the renewal lease or form. If the owner does not comply within 20 days of such order, the owner shall not be entitled to collect a rent guidelines increase until the lease or form is provided.

If a tenant wishes to remain in occupancy beyond the expiration of the lease, the tenant may not refuse to sign a proper renewal lease. If the tenant does refuse to sign a proper renewal lease, he or she may be subject to an eviction proceeding.

An owner may add to a renewal lease the following clauses even if such clauses were not included in the tenant's prior lease:

(A)  the rent may be adjusted by the owner on the basis of Rent Guidelines Board or DHCR Orders;

(B)  if the owner or the lease grants permission to sublet or assign, the owner may charge a sublet vacancy allowance for a sub-tenant or assignee, provided the prime lease is a renewal lease. However, this sublet vacancy allowance may be charged even if such clause is not added to the renewal lease. (Subletting is discussed in section 10 of this Rider);

(C)  (1) if the building in which the apartment is located is receiving tax benefits pursuant to Section 421-a of the Real Property Tax Law, a clause may be added providing for an annual or other periodic rent increase over the initial rent at an average rate of not more than 2.2 % of the amount of such initial rent per annum not to exceed nine, 2.2 percent increases. Such charge shall not become part of the legal regulated rent; however, the cumulative 2.2 percent increases charged prior to the termination of tax benefits may continue to be collected as a separate charge;

(2) provisions for rent increases if authorized under Section 423 of the Real Property Tax Law, a clause may be added to provide for an annual or other periodic rent increase over the legal regulated rent if authorized by Section 423 of the Real Property Tax Law;

(D)  if the Attorney General, pursuant to  Section 352-eeee of the General Business Law, has accepted for filing an Eviction Plan to convert the building to cooperative or condominium ownership, a clause may be added providing that the lease may be cancelled upon expiration of a 3 year period after the Plan is declared effective. (The owner must give the tenant at least 90 days notice that the 3 year period has expired or will be expiring.)

(E)  if a proceeding based on an Owner's Petition for Decontrol ("OPD") is pending, a clause may be added providing that the lease will no longer be in effect as of 60 days from the issuance of a DHCR Decontrol Order, or if a Petition for Administrative Review ("PAR") is filed against such order, 60 days from the issuance of a DHCR order dismissing or denying the PAR, (see section 17 of this Rider, "Renewal Leases Offered During Pendency of High Income Deregulation Proceedings").

## 8.   RENEWAL LEASE SUCCESSION RIGHTS:

In the event that the tenant has permanently vacated the apartment at the time of the renewal lease offer, family members who have lived with the tenant in the apartment as a primary residence for at least two years immediately prior to such permanent vacating (one year for family members who are senior citizens and disabled persons), or from the inception of the tenancy or commencement of the relationship, if for less than such periods, are entitled to a renewal lease.

"Family Member" includes the husband, wife, son, daughter, stepson, stepdaughter, father, mother, stepfather, stepmother, brother, sister, grandfather, grandmother, grandson, granddaughter, father-in-law, mother-in-law, son-in-law or daughter-in-law of the tenant.

"Family member" may also include any other person living with the tenant in the apartment as a primary residence who can prove emotional and financial commitment and interdependence between such person and the tenant. Examples of evidence which is considered in determining whether such emotional and financial commitment and interdependence existed are set forth in the Rent Stabilization Code. Renewal lease succession rights are also discussed in detail in DHCR Fact Sheet #30.

## 9.   SERVICES:

Except for complaints relating to heat, hot water, or other conditions requiring emergency repairs, prior written notification to the owner or managing agent of a service complaint is required. Application for a rent reduction may only be filed between 10 and 60 days after such notification, and a copy of the notification and proof of mailing and delivery must be attached to the application. Applications based on a lack of heat or hot water must be accompanied by a report from the appropriate city agency.

Certain conditions, examples of which are set forth in the Code, which have only a minimal impact on tenants, do not affect the use and enjoyment of the premises, and may exist despite regular maintenance of services. These conditions do not rise to the level of a failure to maintain required services. The passage of time during which a disputed service was not provided without complaint may be considered in determining whether a condition is de minimis. For this purpose, the passage of 4 years or more will be considered presumptive evidence that the condition is de minimis.

The amount of any rent reduction ordered by DHCR shall be reduced by any credit, abatement or offset in rent which the tenant has received pursuant to Sec. 235-b of the Real Property Law ("Warranty of Habitability") that relates to one or more conditions covered by the DHCR Order. For additional information see DHCR Fact Sheets #3 and 14.

## 10.   SUBLETTING AND ASSIGNMENT:

A tenant has the right to sublet his/her apartment, even if subletting is prohibited in the lease, provided that the tenant complies strictly with the provisions of Real Property Law Section 226-b. Tenants who do not comply with these requirements may be subject to eviction proceedings. Compliance with Section 226-b is not determined by DHCR, but by a court of competent jurisdiction. If a tenant in occupancy under a renewal lease sublets his/her apartment, the owner may charge the tenant, the sublet allowance provided by the NYC Rent Guidelines Board. This charge may be passed on to the sub-tenant. However, upon termination of the sublease, the Legal Regulated Rent shall revert to the Legal Regulated Rent without the sublet allowance. The rent increase is the allowance provided by the NYC Rent Guidelines Board available when the tenant's renewal lease commenced, and it takes effect when the subletting takes place. If a tenant in occupancy under a vacancy lease sublets, the owner is not entitled to any rent increase during the subletting.

A tenant who sublets his/her apartment is entitled to charge the sub-tenant the rent permitted under the Rent Stabilization Law, and may charge a 10% surcharge payable to the tenant only if the apartment sublet is fully furnished with the tenant's furniture. Where the tenant charges the sub-tenant any additional rent above such surcharge and sublet allowance, if applicable, the tenant shall be required to pay to the sub-tenant a penalty of three times the rent overcharge, and may also be required to pay interest and attorney's fees. The tenant may also be subject to an eviction proceeding.

**Assignment of Leases**

In an assignment, a tenant transfers the entire remainder of his or her lease to another person (the assignee), and gives up all of his/her rights to reoccupy the apartment.

Pursuant to the provisions of Real Property Law Section 226-b, a tenant may not assign his/her lease without the written consent of the owner, unless the lease expressly provides otherwise. If the owner consents to the assignment of the lease, the owner may charge the assignee, as a vacancy allowance, the rent the owner could have charged had the renewal lease been a vacancy lease. Such vacancy allowance shall remain part of the Legal Regulated Rent for any subsequent renewal lease. The rent increase is the vacancy allowance available when the tenant's renewal lease commenced and it takes effect when the assignment takes place.

An owner is not required to have reasonable grounds to refuse to consent to the assignment. However, if the owner unreasonably refuses consent, the owner must release the tenant from the remainder of the lease, if the tenant, upon 30 days notice to the owner, requests to be released.

If the owner refuses to consent to an assignment and does have reasonable grounds for withholding consent, the tenant cannot assign and the owner is not required to release the tenant from the lease. For additional information see DHCR Fact Sheet #7.

**11. WHEN AN OWNER MAY REFUSE TO RENEW A LEASE:**

As long as a tenant pays the lawful rent to which the owner is entitled, the tenant, except for the specific instances noted, is entitled to remain in the apartment. An owner may not harass a tenant by engaging in an intentional course of conduct intended to make the tenant move from his/her apartment.

**Without DHCR consent**, the owner may refuse to renew a lease and bring an eviction action in Civil Court at the expiration of the lease on any of the following grounds:

(A) the tenant refuses to sign a proper renewal lease offered by the owner;

(B) the owner seeks the apartment in good faith for personal use or for the personal use of members of the owner's immediate family;

(C) the building is owned by a hospital, convent, monastery, asylum, public institution, college, school, dormitory or any institution operated exclusively for charitable or educational purposes and the institution requires the apartment for residential or nonresidential use pursuant to its charitable or educational purposes: or

(D) the tenant does not occupy the apartment as his or her primary residence. The owner must notify the tenant in writing at least 90 and not more than 150 days prior to the expiration of the lease term of the owner's intention not to renew the lease.

**With DHCR consent**, the owner may refuse to renew a lease upon any of the following grounds:

(A) the owner seeks in good faith to recover possession of the apartment for the purpose of demolishing the building and constructing a new building; or

(B) the owner requires the apartment or the land for the owner's own use in connection with a business which the owner owns and operates.

A tenant will be served with a copy of the owner's application and has a right to object. If the owner's application is granted, the owner may bring an eviction action in Civil Court.

**12. EVICTION WHILE THE LEASE IS IN EFFECT:**

The owner may bring an action in Civil Court to evict a tenant during the term of the lease because a tenant:

(A) does not pay rent;

(B) is violating a substantial obligation of the tenancy;

(C) is committing or permitting a nuisance;

(D) is illegally using or occupying the apartment;

(E) has unreasonably refused the owner access to the apartment for the purpose of making necessary repairs or improvements required by law or authorized by DHCR, or for the purpose of inspection or showing. The tenant must be given at least 5 days notice of any such inspection or showing, to be arranged at the mutual convenience of the tenant and owner, so to enable the tenant to be present at the inspection or showing. A tenant cannot be required to permit access for inspection or showing if such requirement would be contrary to the lease; or

(F) is occupying an apartment located in a cooperative or condominium pursuant to an Eviction Plan. (See subdivision (D) of section 7 of this Rider, "Renewal Leases".) A non-purchasing tenant pursuant to a Non-Eviction Plan may not be evicted, except on the grounds set forth in (A) - (E) above.

Tenants are cautioned that causing violations of health, safety, or sanitation standards of housing maintenance laws, or permitting such violations by a member of the family or of the household or by a guest, may be the basis for a court action by the owner.

**13. COOPERATIVE AND CONDOMINIUM CONVERSION:**

Tenants who do not purchase their apartments under a Non-Eviction Conversion Plan continue to be protected by Rent Stabilization. Conversions are regulated by the New York State Attorney General. Any cooperative or condominium conversion plan accepted for filing by the New York State Attorney General's Office will include specific information about tenant rights and protections. An informational booklet about the general subject of conversion is available from the New York State Attorney General's Office.

A Senior Citizen or a Disabled Person in a building which is being converted to cooperative or condominium ownership pursuant to an Eviction Plan is eligible for exemption from the requirement to purchase his/her apartment to remain in occupancy. This exemption is available to Senior Citizens, or to Disabled Persons with impairments expected to be permanent, which prevent them from engaging in any substantial employment. A Conversion Plan accepted for filing by the New York State Attorney General's office must contain specific information regarding this exemption.

**14. SENIOR CITIZENS RENT INCREASE EXEMPTION PROGRAM:**

This program is administered by the New York City Department for the Aging. Tenants or their spouses who are 62 years of age, or older, and whose annual "net" household income does not exceed the established income level may qualify for an exemption from Guidelines rent increases, hardship rent increases, and major capital improvement rent increases. This exemption will only be for that portion of the increase which causes the tenant's rent to exceed one-third of the "net" household income, and is not available for increases based on new services or equipment within the apartment. To ascertain the amount of the net household income limitation, contact the New York City Department for the Aging.

When a Senior Citizen is granted a rent increase exemption, the owner may obtain a real estate tax credit from New York City equal to the amount of the tenant's exemption. Notwithstanding any of the above, a Senior Citizen who receives a rent increase exemption is still required to pay a full month's rent as a security deposit. For additional information see DHCR Fact Sheet #21.

**15. SPECIAL CASES AND EXCEPTIONS:**

Some special rules relating to stabilized rents and required services may apply to newly constructed buildings which receive tax abatement or exemption, and to buildings rehabilitated under certain New York City, New York State, or federal financing or mortgage insurance programs. The rules mentioned in this Rider do not necessarily apply to rent stabilized apartments located in hotels. A separate Hotel Rights Notice informing permanent hotel tenants and owners of their basic rights and responsibilities under the Rent Stabilization Law is available from DHCR.

**16. HIGH INCOME RENT DEREGULATION:**

Upon the issuance of an Order by DHCR, apartments which: (1) are occupied by persons who have a total annual income in excess of $175,000 per annum for each of the two preceding calendar years and (2) have a legal regulated rent of $2,000 or more per month, shall no longer be subject to rent regulation ("High Income Rent Deregulation"). The Rent Stabilization Law permits an owner to file a Petition for High Income Rent Deregulation on an annual basis. As part of the process, the tenant will be required to identify all persons who occupy the apartment as their primary residence on other than a temporary basis, excluding bona fide employees of the tenant(s) and sub-tenants, and certify whether the total annual income was in excess of $175,000 in each of the two preceding calendar years. If the tenant fails to provide the requested information to DHCR, an order of deregulation will be issued. If the tenant provides the requested information and certifies that the total annual income was not in excess of $175,000, the NYS Department of Taxation and Finance will review whether the apartment is occupied by persons who have a total annual income in excess of $175,000 in each of the two preceding calendar years.

**17. RENEWAL LEASES OFFERED DURING PENDENCY OF HIGH INCOME DEREGULATION PROCEEDINGS:**

Where a High Income Deregulation Proceeding is pending before DHCR and the owner is required to offer a renewal lease to the tenant, a separate rider may be attached to and served with the Rent Stabilization Law "Renewal Lease Form" (RTP-8). If so attached and served, it shall become part of and modify the Notice and Renewal Lease. The text of the rider is set forth below and may not be modified or altered without approval of DHCR.

**NOTICE TO TENANT:**

Pursuant to Section 5-a of the Emergency Tenant Protection Act, or Section 26-504.3 of the Rent Stabilization Law, the owner has commenced a proceeding before DHCR for deregulation of your apartment by filing a Petition by Owner for High Income Rent Deregulation on _____, 20_____.
(Date)

That proceeding is now pending before DHCR. If DHCR grants the petition for deregulation, this renewal lease shall be cancelled and shall terminate after 60 days from the date of issuance of an order granting such petition. In the event that you file a Petition for Administrative Review (PAR) the order of deregulation, or if you have already filed such PAR and it is pending before DHCR at the time you receive this Notice, and the PAR is subsequently dismissed or denied, this renewal lease shall be cancelled and shall terminate after 60 days from the issuance by DHCR of an order dismissing or denying the PAR.

Upon such termination of this renewal lease, the liability of the parties for the further performance of the terms, covenants and conditions of this renewal lease shall immediately cease.

**Appendix**

Some agencies which can provide assistance

New York State Division of Housing and Community Renewal (DHCR)

DHCR is a State agency empowered to administer and enforce the Rent Stabilization Law and the Rent Control Law.  Tenants should contact DHCR Public Information Offices listed below for assistance.

**Queens**
92-31 Union Hall Street
Jamaica, NY 11433
(718) 739-6400

**Lower Manhattan** (South side of 110th Street and below)
25 Beaver Street
New York, NY 10004
(212) 480-6700

**Upper Manhattan** (North side of 110th Street and above)
163 West 125th Street
New York, NY 10027
(212) 961-8930

**Bronx**
1 Fordham Plaza,
Bronx, NY 10458
(718) 563-5678

**Brooklyn**
55 Hanson Place, 7th Floor
Brooklyn, NY 11217
(718) 722-4778

**Staten Island**
60 Bay Street, 7th Floor
Staten Island, NY 10301
(718) 816-0277

Attorney General of the State of New York
120 Broadway, New York, NY 10271

Consumer Frauds and Protection Bureau - (212) 416-8345

- investigates and enjoins illegal or fraudulent business practices, including the overcharging of rent and mishandling of rent security deposits by owners.

Real Estate Financing Bureau - (212) 416-8121

- administers and enforces the laws governing cooperative and condominium conversions.  Investigates complaints from tenants in buildings undergoing cooperative or condominium conversion concerning allegations of improper disclosure, harassment, and misleading information.

New York City Department of Housing Preservation and Development (HPD):

Division of Code Enforcement
Principal Office
100 Gold Street, New York, N.Y.  10038 - (212) 863-8000

- enforcement of housing maintenance standards.

New York City Central Complaint Bureau
215 West 125th Street, New York, N.Y.  10038   (212) 824-4328

- receives telephone complaints relating to physical maintenance, health, safety and sanitation standards, including emergency heat and hot water service.  This service is available 24 hours per day.  However, complaints as to emergency heat service are received only between October 1st and May 31st of each year.

New York City Rent Guidelines Board (RGB):
51 Chambers Street, Room 202, New York, N.Y. 10007 - (212) 385-2934

- promulgates annual percentage of rent increases for rent stabilized apartments and provides information on guidelines orders.

New York City Department for the Aging

SCRIE Division
2 Lafayette Street, 6th Floor, New York, New York, 10007 - (212) 442-1000

- administers the Senior Citizen Rent Increase Exemption program.

Copies of New York State and New York City rent laws are available in the business section of some public libraries.  A person should call or write to a public library to determine the exact library which has such legal material.

Appendix **III**

# How to Use the CD-ROM

The tear-out forms in Appendix IV are included on a CD-ROM in the back of the book. This CD-ROM, which can be used with Windows computers, installs files that can be opened, printed and edited using a word processor or other software. It is not a stand-alone software program. Please read this Appendix and the README.TXT file included on the CD-ROM for instructions on using the Forms CD.

**Note to Mac users:** This CD-ROM and its files should also work on Macintosh computers. Please note, however, that Nolo cannot provide technical support for non-Windows users.

### How to View the README File

If you do not know how to view the file README.TXT, insert the Forms CD into your computer's CD-ROM drive and follow these instructions:

- Windows 9x, 2000, Me and XP: (1) On your PC's desktop, double-click the My Computer icon; (2) double-click the icon for the CD-ROM drive into which the Forms CD-ROM was inserted; (3) double-click the file README.TXT.
- Macintosh: (1) On your Mac desktop, double-click the icon for the CD-ROM that you inserted; (2) double-click on the file README.TXT.

While the README file is open, print it out by using the Print command in the File menu.

Two different kinds of forms are contained on the CD-ROM:

- Word processing (RTF) forms that you can open, complete, print and save with your word processing program (see Section B, below), and
- Forms (PDF) that can be viewed only with Adobe Acrobat Reader 4.0 or higher. You can install Acrobat Reader from the Forms CD (see

section C, below). These forms are designed to be printed out and filled in by hand or with a typewriter.

See Appendix IV for a list of forms, their file names and file formats.

## A. Installing the Form Files Onto Your Computer

Before you can do anything with the files on the CD-ROM, you need to install them onto your hard disk. In accordance with U.S. copyright laws, remember that copies of the CD-ROM and its files are for your personal use only.

Insert the Forms CD and do the following:

### 1. Windows 9x, 2000, Me and XP Users

Follow the instructions that appear on the screen. (If nothing happens when you insert the Forms CD-ROM, then (1) double-click the My Computer icon; (2) double-click the icon for the CD-ROM drive into which the Forms CD-ROM was inserted; and (3) double-click the file WELCOME.EXE.)

By default, all the files are installed to the \NY Landlord Forms folder in the \Program Files folder of your computer. A folder called "NY Landlord Forms" is added to the "Programs" folder of the Start menu.

### 2. Macintosh Users

**Step 1:** If the "NY Landlord Forms CD" window is not open, open it by double-clicking the "NY Landlord Forms CD" icon.

**Step 2:** Select the "NY Landlord Forms" folder icon.

**Step 3:** Drag and drop the folder icon onto the icon of your hard disk.

## B. Using the Word Processing Files to Create Documents

This section concerns the files for forms that can be opened and edited with your word processing program.

All word processing forms come in rich text format. These files have the extension ".RTF." For example, the form for the Rental Application form discussed in Chapter 1 is on the file RENTAPP.RTF. All forms and their file names are listed in Appendix IV.

RTF files can be read by most recent word processing programs including all versions of MS Word for Windows and Macintosh, WordPad for Windows, and recent versions of WordPerfect for Windows and Macintosh.

To use a form from the CD to create your documents you must: (1) open a file in your word processor or text editor; (2) edit the form by filling in the required information; (3) print it out; (4) rename and save your revised file.

The following are general instructions on how to do this. However, each word processor uses different commands to open, format, save and print documents. Please read your word processor's manual for specific instructions on performing these tasks.

*Do not call Nolo's technical support if you have questions on how to use your word processor.*

**Step 1:** Opening a File

There are three ways to open the word processing files included on the CD-ROM after you have installed them onto your computer.

• Windows users can open a file by selecting its "shortcut" as follows: (1) Click the Windows "Start" button; (2) open the "Programs" folder; (3) open the "NY Landlord Forms" subfolder; (4) open the "RTF" subfolder; and (5) click on the shortcut to the form you want to work with.

• Both Windows and Macintosh users can open a file directly by double-clicking on it. Use My Computer or Windows Explorer (Windows 9x, 2000, Me or XP) or the Finder (Macintosh) to go to the folder you installed or copied the CD-ROM's files to. Then, double-click on the specific file you want to open.

You can also open a file from within your word processor. To do this, you must first start your word processor. Then, go to the File menu and choose the Open command. This opens a dialog box where you will tell the program (1) the type of file you want to open (*.RTF); and (2) the location and name of the file (you will need to navigate through the directory tree to get to the folder on your hard disk where the CD's files have been installed). If these directions are unclear you will need to look through the manual for your word processing program—Nolo's technical support department will not be able to help you with the use of your word processing program.

---

### Where the Files Are Installed

**Windows and DOS Users:**

• RTF files are installed by default to a folder named \NY Landlord Forms\RTF in the \Program Files folder of your computer.

**Macintosh Users:**

• RTF files are located in the "RTF" folder within the "NY Landlord Forms" folder.

---

**Step 2:** Editing Your Document

Fill in the appropriate information according to the instructions and sample agreements in the book. Underlines are used to indicate where you need to enter your information, frequently followed by instructions in brackets. *Be sure to delete the underlines and instructions from your edited document.* If you do not know how to use your word processor to edit a document, you will need to look through the manual for your word processing program—Nolo's technical support department will not be able to help you with the use of your word processing program.

---

### Editing Forms That Have Optional or Alternative Text

Some of the forms have check boxes before text. The check boxes indicate:
- Optional text, where you choose whether to include or exclude the given text.
- Alternative text, where you select one alternative to include and exclude the other alternatives.

If you are using the tear-out forms in Appendix IV, you simply mark the appropriate box to make your choice.

If you are using the Forms CD, however, we recommend that instead of marking the check boxes, you do the following:

**Optional text**

If you **don't want** to include optional text, just delete it from your document.

If you **do want** to include optional text, just leave it in your document.

In either case, delete the check box itself as well as the italicized instructions that the text is optional.

**Alternative text**

First delete all the alternatives that you do not want to include.

Then delete the remaining check boxes, as well as the italicized instructions that you need to select one of the alternatives provided.

---

**Step 3:** Printing Out the Document

Use your word processor's or text editor's "Print" command to print out your document. If you do not know how to use your word processor to print a document, you will need to look through the manual for your word processing program—Nolo's technical support department will not be able to help you with the use of your word processing program.

**Step 4:** Saving Your Document

After filling in the form, use the "Save As" command to save and rename the file. Because all the files are "read-only" you will not be able to use the "Save" command. This is for your protection. *If you save the file without renaming it, the underlines that indicate where you need to enter your information will be lost and you will not be able to create a new document with this file without recopying the original file from the CD-ROM.*

If you do not know how to use your word processor to save a document, you will need to look through the manual for your word processing program—Nolo's technical support department will *not* be able to help you with the use of your word processing program.

## C. Using U.S. Government Forms

Electronic copies of useful forms from the U.S. Government are included on the CD-ROM in Adobe Acrobat PDF format. You must have the Adobe Acrobat Reader installed on your computer (see below) to use these forms. All forms and their file names are listed in Appendix IV.

These forms cannot be filled out using your computer. To create your document using these files, you must: (1) open the file; (2) print it out; and (3) complete it by hand or typewriter.

## Installing Acrobat Reader

To install the Adobe Acrobat Reader, insert the CD into your computer's CD-ROM drive and follow these instructions:

- Windows 9x, 2000, Me and XP: Follow the instructions that appear on screen. (If nothing happens when you insert the Forms CD-ROM, then (1) double-click the My Computer icon; (2) double-click the icon for the CD-ROM drive into which the Forms CD-ROM was inserted; and (3) double-click the file WELCOME.EXE.)
- Macintosh: (1) If the "NY Landlord Forms CD" window is not open, open it by double-clicking the "NY Landlord Forms CD" icon; and (2) double-click on the "Acrobat Reader Installer" icon.

If you do not know how to use Adobe Acrobat to view and print the files, you will need to consult the online documentation that comes with the Acrobat Reader program.

Do *not* call Nolo technical support if you have questions on how to use Acrobat Reader.

You can also open a PDF file from within Acrobat Reader. To do this, you must first start Reader. Then, go to the File menu and choose the Open command. This opens a dialog box where you will tell the program the location and name of the file (you will need to navigate through the directory tree to get to the folder on your hard disk where the CD's files have been installed). If these directions are unclear you will need to look through Acrobat Reader's help—Nolo's technical support department will *not* be able to help you with the use of Acrobat Reader.

## Where Are the PDF Files Installed?

- Windows Users: PDF files are installed by default to a folder named \NY Landlord Forms\PDF in the \Program Files folder of your computer.
- Macintosh Users: PDF files are located in the "PDF" folder within the "NY Landlord Forms" folder.

**Step 1:** Opening U.S. Government Files

PDF files, like the word processing files, can be opened one of three ways.
- Windows users can open a file by selecting its "shortcut" as follows: (1) Click the Windows "Start" button; (2) open the "Programs" folder; (3) open the "NY Landlord Forms" subfolder; (4) open the "PDF" folder; and (5) click on the shortcut to the form you want to work with.

- Both Windows and Macintosh users can open a file directly by double-clicking on it. Use My Computer or Windows Explorer (Windows 9x, 2000, Me or XP) or the Finder (Macintosh) to go to the folder you created and copied the CD-ROM's files to. Then, double-click on the specific file you want to open.

**Step 2:** Printing U.S. Government Files

Choose Print from the Acrobat Reader File menu. This will open the Print dialog box. In the "Print Range" section of the Print dialog box, select the appropriate print range, then click OK.

**Step 3**: Filling in U.S. Government files

The PDF files cannot be filled out using your computer. To create your document using one of these files, you must first print it out (see Step 2, above), and then complete it by hand or typewriter. ■

Appendix **IV**

# Tear-Out Forms

# Rental Application

*Separate application required from each applicant age 18 or older.*

---

### THIS SECTION TO BE COMPLETED BY LANDLORD

Address of Property to Be Rented: _____

_____

Rental Term: ☐ month-to-month  ☐ lease from _____ to _____

**Amounts Due Prior to Occupancy**

First month's rent ............................................................... $_____

Security deposit .................................................................. $_____

Credit check fee ................................................................. $_____

Other (specify): _____ $_____

TOTAL ...................................... $_____

---

## Applicant

Full Name—include all names you use(d): _____

Home Phone: (_____) _____  Work Phone: (_____) _____

Social Security Number: _____  Driver's License Number/State: _____

Other Identifying Information: _____

Vehicle Make: _____  Model: _____  Color: _____  Year: _____

License Plate Number/State: _____

## Additional Occupants

List everyone, including children, who will live with you:

| Full Name | Relationship to Applicant |
|---|---|
| | |
| | |
| | |
| | |

## Rental History

Current Address: _____

Dates Lived at Address: _____  Reason for Leaving: _____

Landlord/Manager: _____  Landlord/Manager's Phone: (_____) _____

Previous Address: _____

Dates Lived at Address: _____  Reason for Leaving: _____

Landlord/Manager: _____  Landlord/Manager's Phone: (_____) _____

---

Previous Address: _____

Dates Lived at Address: _____     Reason for Leaving: _____

Landlord/Manager: _____      Landlord/Manager's Phone: ( ____ ) _____

## Employment History

Name and Address of Current Employer: _____

_____     Phone: ( ____ ) _____

Name of Supervisor: _____       Supervisor's Phone: ( ____ ) _____

Dates Employed at This Job: _____       Position or Title: _____

Name and Address of Previous Employer: _____

_____     Phone: ( ____ ) _____

Name of Supervisor: _____       Supervisor's Phone: ( ____ ) _____

Dates Employed at This Job: _____       Position or Title: _____

## Income

1. Your gross monthly employment income (before deductions):     $ _____

2. Average monthly amounts of other income (specify sources):    $ _____

_____

_____

TOTAL: _____     $ _____

## Credit and Financial Information

| Bank/Financial Accounts | Account Number | Bank/Institution | Branch |
|---|---|---|---|
| Savings Account: | | | |
| Checking Account: | | | |
| Money Market or Similar Account: | | | |

| Credit Accounts & Loans | Type of Account (Auto loan, Visa, etc.) | Account Number | Name of Creditor | Amount Owed | Monthly Payment |
|---|---|---|---|---|---|
| Major Credit Card: | | | | | |
| Major Credit Card: | | | | | |
| Loan (mortgage, car, student loan, etc.): | | | | | |
| Other Major Obligation: | | | | | |

**Miscellaneous**

Describe the number and type of pets you want to have in the rental property:

_____

_____

Describe water-filled furniture you want to have in the rental property:

_____

_____

Do you smoke?  ☐ yes  ☐ no

Have you ever:   Filed for bankruptcy? ☐ yes  ☐ no      Been sued? ☐ yes  ☐ no

Been evicted? ☐ yes  ☐ no      Been convicted of a crime? ☐ yes  ☐ no

Explain any "yes" listed above: _____

_____


**References and Emergency Contact**

Personal Reference: _____      Relationship: _____

Address: _____

_____      Phone: ( ____ ) _____

Personal Reference: _____      Relationship: _____

Address: _____

_____      Phone: ( ____ ) _____

Contact in Emergency: _____      Relationship: _____

Address: _____

_____      Phone: ( ____ ) _____


I certify that all the information given above is true and correct and understand that my lease or rental

agreement may be terminated if I have made any false or incomplete statement in this application. I authorize

verification of the information provided in this application from my credit sources, credit bureaus, current and

previous landlords and employers and personal references.

_____

Date                          Applicant

Notes (Landlord/Manager): _____

_____

_____

_____

_____

# Consent to Background and Reference Check

I authorize _____
to obtain information about me from my credit sources, court records, current and previous landlords
and employers and personal references. I authorize my credit sources, credit bureaus, current and
previous landlords and employers and personal references to disclose to _____
_____ such information about me as
he or she may request.

\
_____
Name

_____
Address

_____
Phone Number

_____   _____
Date                              Applicant

# Tenant References

Name of Applicant: _____

Address of Rental Unit: _____

## Previous Landlord or Manager

Contact (name, property owner or manager, address of rental unit): _____

_____

Date: _____

## Questions

When did tenant rent from you (move-in and move-out dates)? _____

What was the monthly rent? _____

Did tenant pay rent on time? _____

Was tenant considerate of neighbors—that is, no loud parties and fair, careful use of common areas? _____

_____

Did tenant have any pets? If so, were there any problems? _____

_____

Did tenant make any unreasonable demands or complaints? _____

_____

Why did tenant leave? _____

_____

Did tenant give the proper amount of notice before leaving? _____

Did tenant leave the place in good condition? Did you need to use the security deposit to cover damage?

_____

Any particular problems you'd like to mention? _____

_____

_____

Would you rent to this person again? _____

_____

Other Comments: _____

_____

_____

_____

_____

_____

## Employment Verification

Contact (name, company, position): _____

Date: _____

Salary: _____ Dates of Employment: _____

Comments: _____

_____

_____

_____

_____

_____

_____

## Personal Reference

Contact (name and relationship to applicant): _____

Date: _____ How long have you known the applicant? _____

Would you recommend this person as a prospective tenant? _____

Comments: _____

_____

_____

_____

_____

_____

_____

## Credit and Financial Information

_____

_____

_____

_____

_____

## Notes, Including Reason for Rejecting Applicant

_____

_____

_____

_____

# Month-to-Month Residential Rental Agreement

## Clause 1. Identification of Landlord and Tenant

This Agreement is entered into on _____ between _____

_____ ("Tenant") and

_____ ("Landlord"). Each

Tenant is jointly and severally liable for the payment of rent and performance of all other terms of

this Agreement.

## Clause 2. Identification of Premises

Subject to the terms and conditions in this Agreement, Landlord rents to Tenant, and Tenant rents

from Landlord, for living purposes only, the Premises located at _____

_____ ("the Premises"),

together with the following furnishings and appliances: _____

_____ .

Rental of the Premises also includes _____

_____ .

## Clause 3. Limits on Use and Occupancy

The Premises are to be used for living purposes only for Tenant(s) listed in Clause 1 of this

Agreement, by the immediate family members of the Tenant(s), and by additional occupants as

defined in and only in accordance with RPL § 235-f. For purposes of this clause, immediate family

members include a spouse, a sibling, a child, a stepchild, a grandchild, a parent, parent-in-law,

stepparent or grandparent. In addition to the foregoing, the Premises may be occupied from time to

time by guests of the Tenant(s) for a period of time not exceeding _____ days, unless a

longer period is approved in writing by the Landlord. No immediate family members, additional

occupants or guests may occupy the apartment unless one or more of the Tenants occupy the rental

unit as a primary residence, or unless consented to in writing by the Landlord.

## Clause 4. Term of the Tenancy

The rental will begin on _____, 200___, and continue on a month-to-month

basis. Landlord may terminate the tenancy or modify the terms of this Agreement by giving the

Tenant _____ written notice. Tenant may terminate the tenancy by giving

the Landlord _____ written notice.

## Clause 5. Payment of Rent

### a. Regular monthly rent

Tenant will pay to Landlord a monthly rent of $_____ , and additional rent as set forth

below, payable in advance on the first day of each month, except when that day falls on a weekend

or legal holiday, in which case rent is due on the next business day. Rent will be paid in the
following manner unless Landlord designates otherwise:

**b. Additional rent**

Tenant will pay to Landlord, as additional rent, the following monthly charges: _____,
as well as any other fees or charges defined as additional rent under this Agreement.

**c. Delivery of payment**

Rent and additional rent will be paid:

☐ by mail, to _____

☐ in person, at _____

**d. Form of payment**

Landlord will accept payment in these forms:

☐ personal check made payable to _____

☐ cashier's check made payable to _____

☐ credit card

☐ money order

☐ cash

☐ electronic check or money transfer submitted to: _____

**e. Prorated first month's rent**

For the period from Tenant's move-in date, _____, 200____, through the
end of the month, Tenant will pay to Landlord the prorated monthly rent of $_____.
This amount will be paid on or before the date the Tenant moves in.

## Clause 6. Late Charges

If Tenant fails to pay the rent or additional rent in full before the end of the _____ day
after it's due, Tenant will pay Landlord, as additional rent, a late charge of _____.
Landlord does not waive the right to insist on payment of the rent or additional rent in full on the
date it is due.

## Clause 7. Returned Check and Other Bank Charges

If any check offered by Tenant to Landlord in payment of rent or any other amount due under this
Agreement is returned for lack of sufficient funds, a "stop payment" or any other reason, Tenant will
pay Landlord a returned check charge of $_____.

## Clause 8. Security Deposit

On signing this Agreement, Tenant will pay to Landlord the sum of $_____ as a security
deposit. Landlord will deposit this security deposit in _____
financial institution at _____. If the building in which the
Premises is located contains six or more units, or if the unit is rent-stabilized, the security deposit
will earn interest. Tenant may not, without Landlord's prior written consent, apply this security
deposit to the last month's rent or to any other sum due under this Agreement.

If, within 60 days after Tenant has vacated and left the Premises in as good condition as it was found, except for normal wear and tear, Tenant has returned keys and provided Landlord with a forwarding address, Landlord will return the deposit in full or give Tenant an itemized written statement of the reasons for and dollar amount of any of the security deposit retained by the Landlord. Landlord may withhold all or part of Tenant's security deposit necessary to: (1) remedy any default by Tenant in the payment of rent; (2) repair damage to the Premises, except for ordinary wear and tear caused by Tenant; (3) clean the Premises if necessary, and (4) compensate Landlord for any other losses as allowed under law.

### Clause 9. Utilities

Tenant will pay all utility charges, except for the following, which will be paid by Landlord:

_____

_____ .

### Clause 10. Assignment and Subletting

a. **Assignment.** Tenant will not assign this Agreement without the Landlord's prior written consent. Prior to any assignment, Tenant must request permission to assign from the Landlord, in writing, and in the manner required by Real Property Law § 226-b. Landlord may refuse to consent to an assignment for any reason or for no reason, but if the Landlord unreasonably refuses consent, Tenant may terminate this Agreement upon thirty days' notice.

b. **Subletting.** Tenant will not sublet any part of the Premises without the Landlord's prior written consent.

   1) If the building in which the Premises are located contains fewer than four (4) units, Landlord may refuse to consent to Tenant's sublet request for any reason or for no reason.

   2) If the building in which the Premises are located contains four (4) or more units, Tenant must request permission to sublet from the Landlord, in writing, and in the manner required by New York Real Property Law § 226-b. Landlord may not unreasonably refuse to consent to Tenant's proper request to sublet.

c. **Fees.** Landlord may impose a reasonable fee on Tenant in connection with the review and processing of any Tenant request or application to assign or sublet.

### Clause 11. Tenant's Maintenance Responsibilities

Tenant will: (1) keep the Premises clean, sanitary and in good condition and, upon termination of the tenancy, return the Premises to Landlord in a condition identical to that which existed when Tenant took occupancy, except for ordinary wear and tear; (2) immediately notify Landlord of any defects or dangerous conditions in and about the Premises of which Tenant becomes aware; and (3) reimburse Landlord, on demand by Landlord, for the cost of any repairs to the Premises damaged by Tenant or Tenant's guests or business invitees through misuse or neglect.

Tenant has examined the Premises, including appliances, fixtures, window coverings and carpeting, if any, and has found them to be in good, safe and clean condition and repair, except as noted in the Landlord-Tenant Checklist.

### Clause 12. Repairs and Alterations by Tenant

a. Except as provided by law, or as authorized by the prior written consent of Landlord, Tenant will not make any repairs or alterations to the Premises, including painting, wallpapering or nailing holes in walls. Tenant must not change the plumbing, ventilating, air conditioning or electric or heating systems.

b. If Tenant re-keys or installs any locks to the Premises or installs or alters any burglar alarm system, Tenant will provide Landlord with a duplicate key or keys capable of unlocking all such re-keyed or new locks as well as instructions on how to disarm any altered or new burglar alarm system.

### Clause 13. Violating Laws and Causing Disturbances

Tenant is entitled to quiet enjoyment of the Premises. Tenant and guests or invitees will not use the Premises or adjacent areas in such a way as to: (1) violate any law or ordinance, including laws prohibiting the use, possession or sale of illegal drugs or controlled substances; (2) commit or permit waste (severe property damage); or (3) create a nuisance by annoying, disturbing, inconveniencing or interfering with the quiet enjoyment and peace and quiet of any other tenant or nearby resident, or their safety or comfort, or engage in any other objectionable conduct.

### Clause 14. Pets

No animal, bird or other pet will be kept on the Premises, without the Landlord's written consent, except service animals needed by blind, deaf or disabled persons and _____ under the following conditions: _____
_____ .

### Clause 15. Landlord's Right to Access

Landlord or Landlord's agents may enter the Premises in the event of an emergency, to make repairs or improvements or to show the Premises to prospective buyers or tenants. Landlord may also enter the Premises to conduct an annual inspection to check for safety or maintenance problems. Except in cases of emergency, Tenant's abandonment of the Premises, court order, or where it is impractical to do so, Landlord shall give Tenant reasonable notice before entering the Premises.

### Clause 16. Extended Absences by Tenant

Tenant will notify Landlord in advance if Tenant will be away from the Premises for _____ or more consecutive days. During such absence, Landlord may enter the Premises at times reasonably necessary to maintain the property and inspect for needed repairs.

## Clause 17. Possession of the Premises

**a. Tenant's failure to take possession.** If, after signing this Agreement, Tenant fails to take possession of the Premises, Tenant will still be responsible for paying rent and complying with all other terms of this Agreement.

**b. Landlord's failure to deliver possession.** If Landlord is unable to deliver possession of the Premises to Tenant for any reason not within Landlord's control, including, but not limited to, partial or complete destruction of the Premises, this Agreement shall remain in effect. Tenant's obligation to pay rent shall not begin, however, until such time as the Premises are made available to Tenant for occupancy. Landlord shall notify Tenant of the date that the Premises are available for occupancy. If Landlord fails to deliver possession to the Tenant within 30 days after the date this Agreement begins, Tenant, may elect to terminate the Agreement on written notice to the Landlord, and Landlord shall refund to Tenant any sums previously paid under this Agreement. Landlord shall not be responsible for Tenant's damages or expenses caused by any delay in delivering possession.

## Clause 18. Tenant Rules and Regulations

☐ Tenant acknowledges receipt of, and has read a copy of, tenant rules and regulations, which are attached to and incorporated into this Agreement by this reference. Tenant agrees to obey and comply with these rules and all future reasonable tenant rules and regulations.

## Clause 19. Tenant Default

a. If Tenant fails to pay rent or additional rent after a personal demand for rent has been made by the Landlord or Landlord's agent, or within three days after a written demand for rent has been made by Landlord or Landlord's agent or attorney, Landlord may begin legal proceedings to evict Tenant and Tenant's occupants from the Premises.

b. If Tenant otherwise defaults under this Agreement by:

   1) failing to comply with any other term or rule of this Agreement, or

   2) permanently moving out before this Agreement expires

   then Landlord must give Tenant notice of default stating the type of violation and directing Tenant to cure the violation within 10 days. If Tenant fails to cure the default within the time stated, Landlord shall terminate the Agreement by giving the Tenant a written termination notice. The termination notice will give the date the Agreement will end, which shall not be less than 10 days after the date of the notice. If Tenant and Tenant's occupants fail to move out on or before the termination date, Landlord may begin legal proceedings to evict the Tenant and Tenant's occupants from the Premises.

## Clause 20. Payment of Attorney Fees and Court Costs

In any legal action or proceeding to enforce any part of this Agreement, the prevailing party ☐ shall not ☐ shall recover reasonable attorney fees and court costs.

### Clause 21. Jury Trial and Counterclaims

a. **Jury trial.** Landlord and Tenant agree to give up their right to a trial by jury in any action or proceeding brought by either against the other for any matter concerning the Agreement or the Premises. This does not include actions for personal injury or property damage.

b. **Counterclaims.** Tenant agrees to give up the right to bring a counterclaim or set-off in any action or proceeding by Landlord against Tenant on any matter directly or indirectly related to the Agreement or the Premises.

### Clause 22. Disclosures

Tenant acknowledges that Landlord has made the following disclosures regarding the Premises:

☐ Disclosure of Information on Lead-Based Paint and/or Lead-Based Paint Hazards

☐ Other disclosures:_____

_____

_____

### Clause 23. Damage and Destruction

If all or part of the Premises becomes unusable, in part or totally, because of fire, accident or other casualty, the following shall apply:

a. Unless the Agreement is terminated pursuant to Subparagraphs b or c, below, Landlord will repair and restore the Premises, with this Agreement continuing in full force and effect, except that Tenant's rent shall be abated based upon the part of the Premises which are unusable, while repairs are being made. Landlord shall not be required to repair or replace any property brought onto the Premises by Tenant.

b. In the event that Landlord wishes to demolish or substantially rebuild the building in which the Premises are located, the Landlord need not restore the Premises and may elect instead to terminate this Agreement upon written notice to Tenant within thirty (30) days after such damage. If the Premises are partially usable, this Agreement will terminate 60 days from the last day of the calendar month in which Tenant is given the Landlord's termination notice.

c. If the Premises are completely unusable and the Landlord does repair the Premises within 30 days, Tenant may, upon written notice, elect to terminate this Agreement, effective as of the date the damage occurred.

### Clause 24. Notices

a. **Notices to Tenant.** Any notice from Landlord, or Landlord's agent or attorney will be considered properly given to Tenant if in writing; signed by or in the name of the Landlord or Landlord's agent; and addressed to Tenant at the Premises and delivered to Tenant personally, or sent by registered or certified mail to Tenant at the Premises. The date of service of any written notice by Landlord to Tenant under this Agreement is the date of delivery or mailing of such notice.

**b. Notices to Landlord.** Any notice from Tenant will be considered properly given to Landlord if in writing and delivered or sent to Landlord by registered or certified mail at the following address:

_____

or at another address for which Landlord or Landlord's agent has given Tenant written notice.

## Clause 25. Abandoned Property

When this Agreement expires or is terminated, Tenant must remove all personal property and belongings from the Premises. If any of Tenant's property remains in the Premises after the tenancy ends, Landlord may either discard the property or store it at Tenant's expense. Tenant agrees to pay Landlord for all costs and expenses incurred in removing and/or storing such personal property. The terms of this clause will continue to be in effect after the end of this Agreement.

## Clause 26. Additional Provisions

Additional provisions are as follows: _____

_____

_____

## Clause 27. Validity of Each Part

If any portion of this Agreement is held to be invalid, its invalidity will not affect the validity or enforceability of any other provision of this Agreement.

## Clause 28. Entire Agreement; No Waivers

**a. Entire agreement.** This document constitutes the entire Agreement between the parties, and no promises or representations, other than those contained here and those implied by law, have been made by Landlord or Tenant. Any modifications to this Agreement must be in writing signed by Landlord and Tenant.

**b. No waivers.** Only a written agreement between the Landlord and Tenant may waive an obligation or violation of this Agreement. A waiver may not be implied by the Landlord's acceptance of rent, or failure to take immediate action against the Tenant, while the Tenant is violating one or more provisions of this agreement.

| | | |
|---|---|---|
| Date | Landlord or Landlord's Agent | Title |
| | Street Address | |
| | City, State & Zip | Phone |
| Date | Tenant | Phone |
| Date | Tenant | |
| Date | Witness | |

# Fixed-Term Residential Lease

## Clause 1. Identification of Landlord and Tenant

This Agreement is entered into on _____ between _____

_____ ("Tenant") and

_____ ("Landlord"). Each

Tenant is jointly and severally liable for the payment of rent and performance of all other terms of

this Agreement.

## Clause 2. Identification of Premises

Subject to the terms and conditions in this Agreement, Landlord rents to Tenant, and Tenant rents

from Landlord, for living purposes only, the Premises located at _____

_____ ("the Premises"),

together with the following furnishings and appliances: _____

_____ .

Rental of the Premises also includes _____

_____ .

## Clause 3. Limits on Use and Occupancy

The Premises are to be used for living purposes only for Tenant(s) listed in Clause 1 of this

Agreement, by the immediate family members of the Tenant(s), and by additional occupants as

defined in and only in accordance with RPL § 235-f. For purposes of this clause, immediate family

members include a spouse, a sibling, a child, a stepchild, a grandchild, a parent, parent-in-law,

stepparent or grandparent. In addition to the foregoing, the Premises may be occupied from time to

time by guests of the Tenant(s) for a period of time not exceeding _____ days, unless

a longer period is approved in writing by the Landlord. No immediate family members, additional

occupants or guests may occupy the apartment unless one or more of the Tenants occupy the rental

unit as a primary residence, or unless consented to in writing by the Landlord.

## Clause 4. Term of the Tenancy

The term of the rental will begin on _____ , 200____ , and end on

_____ , 200____ . If Tenant vacates before the term ends, Tenant will be

liable for the balance of the rent for the remainder of the term.

## Clause 5. Payment of Rent

### a. Regular monthly rent

Tenant will pay to Landlord a monthly rent of $_____ , and additional rent as set forth

below, payable in advance on the first day of each month, except when that day falls on a weekend

or legal holiday, in which case rent is due on the next business day. Rent will be paid in the following manner unless Landlord designates otherwise:

**b. Additional rent**

Tenant will pay to Landlord, as additional rent, the following monthly charges: _____, as well as any other fees or charges defined as additional rent under this Agreement.

**c. Delivery of payment**

Rent and additional rent will be paid:

☐ by mail, to _____

☐ in person, at _____

**d. Form of payment**

Landlord will accept payment in these forms:

☐ personal check made payable to _____

☐ cashier's check made payable to _____

☐ credit card

☐ money order

☐ cash

☐ electronic check or money transfer submitted to: _____

**e. Prorated first month's rent**

For the period from Tenant's move-in date, _____, 200_____, through the end of the month, Tenant will pay to Landlord the prorated monthly rent of $_____. This amount will be paid on or before the date the Tenant moves in.

## Clause 6. Late Charges

If Tenant fails to pay the rent or additional rent in full before the end of the _____ day after it's due, Tenant will pay Landlord, as additional rent, a late charge of _____. Landlord does not waive the right to insist on payment of the rent or additional rent in full on the date it is due.

## Clause 7. Returned Check and Other Bank Charges

If any check offered by Tenant to Landlord in payment of rent or any other amount due under this Agreement is returned for lack of sufficient funds, a "stop payment" or any other reason, Tenant will pay Landlord a returned check charge of $_____.

## Clause 8. Security Deposit

On signing this Agreement, Tenant will pay to Landlord the sum of $_____ as a security deposit. Landlord will deposit this security deposit in _____ financial institution at _____. If the building in which the Premises is located contains six or more units, or if the unit is rent-stabilized, the security deposit will earn interest. Tenant may not, without Landlord's prior written consent, apply this security

deposit to the last month's rent or to any other sum due under this Agreement.

If, within 60 days after Tenant has vacated and left the Premises in as good condition as it was found, except for normal wear and tear, Tenant has returned keys and provided Landlord with a forwarding address, Landlord will return the deposit in full or give Tenant an itemized written statement of the reasons for and dollar amount of any of the security deposit retained by the Landlord. Landlord may withhold all or part of Tenant's security deposit necessary to: (1) remedy any default by Tenant in the payment of rent; (2) repair damage to the Premises, except for ordinary wear and tear caused by Tenant; (3) clean the Premises if necessary, and (4) compensate Landlord for any other losses as allowed under law.

## Clause 9. Utilities

Tenant will pay all utility charges, except for the following, which will be paid by Landlord:

_____

_____ .

## Clause 10. Assignment and Subletting

a. **Assignment.** Tenant will not assign this Agreement without the Landlord's prior written consent. Prior to any assignment, Tenant must request permission to assign from the Landlord, in writing, and in the manner required by Real Property Law § 226-b. Landlord may refuse to consent to an assignment for any reason or for no reason, but if the Landlord unreasonably refuses consent, Tenant may terminate this Agreement upon thirty days' notice.

b. **Subletting.** Tenant will not sublet any part of the Premises without the Landlord's prior written consent.

1) If the building in which the Premises are located contains fewer than four (4) units, Landlord may refuse to consent to Tenant's sublet request for any reason or for no reason.

2) If the building in which the Premises are located contains four (4) or more units, Tenant must request permission to sublet from the Landlord, in writing, and in the manner required by New York Real Property Law § 226-b. Landlord may not unreasonably refuse to consent to Tenant's proper request to sublet.

c. **Fees.** Landlord may impose a reasonable fee on Tenant in connection with the review and processing of any Tenant request or application to assign or sublet.

## Clause 11. Tenant's Maintenance Responsibilities

Tenant will: (1) keep the Premises clean, sanitary and in good condition and, upon termination of the tenancy, return the Premises to Landlord in a condition identical to that which existed when Tenant took occupancy, except for ordinary wear and tear; (2) immediately notify Landlord of any defects or dangerous conditions in and about the Premises of which Tenant becomes aware; and (3) reimburse Landlord, on demand by Landlord, for the cost of any repairs to the Premises damaged by Tenant or Tenant's guests or business invitees through misuse or neglect.

Tenant has examined the Premises, including appliances, fixtures, window covering, and carpeting, if any, and has found them to be in good, safe and clean condition and repair, except as noted in the Landlord-Tenant Checklist.

### Clause 12. Repairs and Alterations by Tenant

a.  Except as provided by law, or as authorized by the prior written consent of Landlord, Tenant will not make any repairs or alterations to the Premises, including painting, wallpapering or nailing holes in walls. Tenant must not change the plumbing, ventilating, air conditioning or electric or heating systems.

b.  If Tenant re-keys or installs any locks to the Premises or installs or alters any burglar alarm system, Tenant will provide Landlord with a duplicate key or keys capable of unlocking all such re-keyed or new locks as well as instructions on how to disarm any altered or new burglar alarm system.

### Clause 13. Violating Laws and Causing Disturbances

Tenant is entitled to quiet enjoyment of the Premises. Tenant and guests or invitees will not use the Premises or adjacent areas in such a way as to: (1) violate any law or ordinance, including laws prohibiting the use, possession or sale of illegal drugs or controlled substances; (2) commit or permit waste (severe property damage); or (3) create a nuisance by annoying, disturbing, inconveniencing or interfering with the quiet enjoyment and peace and quiet of any other tenant or nearby resident, or their safety or comfort, or engage in any other objectionable conduct.

### Clause 14. Pets

No animal, bird or other pet will be kept on the Premises, without the Landlord's written consent, except service animals needed by blind, deaf or disabled persons and _____

_____

under the following conditions: _____

_____ .

### Clause 15. Landlord's Right to Access

Landlord or Landlord's agents may enter the Premises in the event of an emergency, to make repairs or improvements or to show the Premises to prospective buyers or tenants. Landlord may also enter the Premises to conduct an annual inspection to check for safety or maintenance problems. Except in cases of emergency, Tenant's abandonment of the Premises, court order, or where it is impractical to do so, Landlord shall give Tenant reasonable notice before entering the Premises.

### Clause 16. Extended Absences by Tenant

Tenant will notify Landlord in advance if Tenant will be away from the Premises for _____ or more consecutive days. During such absence, Landlord may enter the Premises at times reasonably necessary to maintain the property and inspect for needed repairs.

## Clause 17. Possession of the Premises

**a. Tenant's failure to take possession.** If, after signing this Agreement, Tenant fails to take possession of the Premises, Tenant will still be responsible for paying rent and complying with all other terms of this Agreement.

**b. Landlord's failure to deliver possession.** If Landlord is unable to deliver possession of the Premises to Tenant for any reason not within Landlord's control, including, but not limited to, partial or complete destruction of the Premises, this Agreement shall remain in effect. Tenant's obligation to pay rent shall not begin, however, until such time as the Premises are made available to Tenant for occupancy. Landlord shall notify Tenant of the date that the Premises are available for occupancy. If Landlord fails to deliver possession to the Tenant within 30 days after the date this Agreement begins, Tenant, may elect to terminate the Agreement on written notice to the Landlord, and Landlord shall refund to Tenant any sums previously paid under this Agreement. Landlord shall not be responsible for Tenant's damages or expenses caused by any delay in delivering possession.

## Clause 18. Tenant Rules and Regulations

☐ Tenant acknowledges receipt of, and has read a copy of, tenant rules and regulations, which are attached to and incorporated into this Agreement by this reference. Tenant agrees to obey and comply with these rules and all future reasonable tenant rules and regulations.

## Clause 19. Tenant Default

a. If Tenant fails to pay rent or additional rent after a personal demand for rent has been made by the Landlord or Landlord's agent, or within three days after a written demand for rent has been made by Landlord or Landlord's agent or attorney, Landlord may begin legal proceedings to evict Tenant and Tenant's occupants from the Premises.

b. If Tenant otherwise defaults under this Agreement by:

1) failing to comply with any other term or rule of this Agreement, or

2) permanently moving out before this Agreement expires

then Landlord must give Tenant notice of default stating the type of violation and directing Tenant to cure the violation within 10 days. If Tenant fails to cure the default within the time stated, Landlord shall terminate the Agreement by giving the Tenant a written termination notice. The termination notice will give the date the Agreement will end, which shall not be less than 10 days after the date of the notice. If Tenant and Tenant's occupants fail to move out on or before the termination date, Landlord may begin legal proceedings to evict the Tenant and Tenant's occupants from the Premises.

## Clause 20. Payment of Attorney Fees and Court Costs

In any legal action or proceeding to enforce any part of this Agreement, the prevailing party ☐ shall not ☐ shall recover reasonable attorney fees and court costs.

### Clause 21. Jury Trial and Counterclaims

a. **Jury trial.** Landlord and Tenant agree to give up their right to a trial by jury in any action or proceeding brought by either against the other for any matter concerning the Agreement or the Premises. This does not include actions for personal injury or property damage.

b. **Counterclaims.** Tenant agrees to give up the right to bring a counterclaim or set-off in any action or proceeding by Landlord against Tenant on any matter directly or indirectly related to the Agreement or the Premises.

### Clause 22. Disclosures

Tenant acknowledges that Landlord has made the following disclosures regarding the Premises:

☐ Disclosure of Information on Lead-Based Paint and/or Lead-Based Paint Hazards

☐ Other disclosures:_____

_____

_____

### Clause 23. Damage and Destruction

If all or part of the Premises becomes unusable, in part or totally, because of fire, accident or other casualty, the following shall apply:

a. Unless the Agreement is terminated pursuant to Subparagraphs b or c, below, Landlord will repair and restore the Premises, with this Agreement continuing in full force and effect, except that Tenant's rent shall be abated based upon the part of the Premises which are unusable, while repairs are being made. Landlord shall not be required to repair or replace any property brought onto the Premises by Tenant.

b. In the event that Landlord wishes to demolish or substantially rebuild the building in which the Premises are located, the Landlord need not restore the Premises and may elect instead to terminate this Agreement upon written notice to Tenant within thirty (30) days after such damage. If the Premises are partially usable, this Agreement will terminate 60 days from the last day of the calendar month in which Tenant is given the Landlord's termination notice.

c. If the Premises are completely unusable and the Landlord does repair the Premises within 30 days, Tenant may, upon written notice, elect to terminate this Agreement, effective as of the date the damage occurred.

### Clause 24. Notices

a. **Notices to Tenant.** Any notice from Landlord, or Landlord's agent or attorney will be considered properly given to Tenant if in writing; signed by or in the name of the Landlord or Landlord's agent; and addressed to Tenant at the Premises and delivered to Tenant personally, or sent by registered or certified mail to Tenant at the Premises. The date of service of any written notice by Landlord to Tenant under this Agreement is the date of delivery or mailing of such notice.

**b. Notices to Landlord.** Any notice from Tenant will be considered properly given to Landlord if in writing and delivered or sent to Landlord by registered or certified mail at the following address:

_____

or at another address for which Landlord or Landlord's agent has given Tenant written notice.

### Clause 25. Abandoned Property

When this Agreement expires or is terminated, Tenant must remove all personal property and belongings from the Premises. If any of Tenant's property remains in the Premises after the tenancy ends, Landlord may either discard the property or store it at Tenant's expense. Tenant agrees to pay Landlord for all costs and expenses incurred in removing and/or storing such personal property. The terms of this clause will continue to be in effect after the end of this Agreement.

### Clause 26. Additional Provisions

Additional provisions are as follows: _____

_____

_____

### Clause 27. Validity of Each Part

If any portion of this Agreement is held to be invalid, its invalidity will not affect the validity or enforceability of any other provision of this Agreement.

### Clause 28. Entire Agreement; No Waivers

**a. Entire agreement.** This document constitutes the entire Agreement between the parties, and no promises or representations, other than those contained here and those implied by law, have been made by Landlord or Tenant. Any modifications to this Agreement must be in writing signed by Landlord and Tenant.

**b. No waivers.** Only a written agreement between the Landlord and Tenant may waive an obligation or violation of this Agreement. A waiver may not be implied by the Landlord's acceptance of rent, or failure to take immediate action against the Tenant, while the Tenant is violating one or more provisions of this agreement.

| | | |
|---|---|---|
| Date | Landlord or Landlord's Agent | Title |
| | Street Address | |
| | City, State & Zip | Phone |
| Date | Tenant | Phone |
| Date | Tenant | |
| Date | Witness | |

# Guaranty Agreement

1. This Agreement is entered into on _____, between _____
_____ ("Tenant"),
_____, ("Landlord")
and _____ ("Guarantor").

2. Tenant has leased from Landlord the premises located at _____
_____ ("Premises"). Landlord and Tenant signed a lease or
rental agreement specifying the terms and conditions of this rental on _____.
A copy of the lease or rental agreement is attached to this Agreement.

3. Guarantor guarantees to Landlord the full performance of the lease or rental agreement by the Tenant.
Guarantor agrees to be jointly and severally liable with Tenant for Tenant's obligations arising out of
the lease or rental agreement described in Paragraph 2, including but not limited to unpaid rent,
property damage and cleaning and repair costs that exceed Tenant's security deposit. Guarantor further
agrees to waive all notices about any default by Tenant, including nonpayment of rent. (For example, if
Tenant fails to pay the rent on time or damages the premises, Landlord has no duty to warn or notify
Guarantor, and may demand that Guarantor pay for these obligations immediately.)

4. This Guaranty shall remain in full force and effect and will not be changed by any extensions or
renewals of the lease or rental agreement or by an assignment or sublet of the Premises. Guarantor
shall remain liable under the terms of this Agreement for the performance of the Tenant, assignee or
sublessee, unless Landlord relieves Guarantor by express written termination of this Agreement.

5. Owner and Guarantor agree to waive trial by jury in any action or proceeding brought against each
other on any matter arising out of the lease, the rental agreement, or this guaranty.

6. If Landlord and Guarantor are involved in any legal proceeding arising out of this Agreement, the
prevailing party shall recover reasonable attorney fees, court costs and any costs reasonably necessary
to collect a judgment.

_____     _____     _____
Date                        Landlord                     Title

_____     _____
Date                        Tenant

_____     _____
Date                        Guarantor

_____
Guarantor's Address

_____

_____
Witness

# Rent Receipt

_____

_____

_____

_____

Receipt No. _____

Date: _____

Premises address: _____

_____ Unit #: _____

Amount of rent received: _____

Rental period: _____

Form of payment (check one):

☐ Personal check     ☐ Certified check     ☐ Cash

☐ Postal money order     ☐ Bank check     ☐ Other: (specify)_____

Received by: _____

Recipient's name and title: _____

# Agreement for Delayed or Partial Rent Payments

This Agreement is made between _____ "Tenant(s),"

and _____ "Landlord/Manager."

1. _____ "Tenant(s)" has/have paid

   _____

   _____

   on _____, 200____, which was due _____, 200____.

2. _____ (Landlord/Manager)

   agrees to accept all the remainder of the rent on or before _____, 200____,

   and to hold off on any legal proceeding to evict _____

   _____ (Tenant(s))  until that date.


_____        _____
Date                           Landlord/Manager


_____        _____
Date                           Tenant


_____        _____
Date                           Tenant


_____        _____
Date                           Tenant

# Rental Agreement Rider

This Rider shall be attached to and form a part of the Rental Agreement dated _____

between _____ ,

as Landlord, and _____ ,

as Tenant, for the Premises located at _____

_____ .

1. It is hereby agreed that the monthly rent for the Premises shall be increased to $_____
   as of _____ .

2. Tenant agrees to post additional security for the premises in the amount of $_____ on
   or before_____ . Upon receipt of the additional security by landlord,
   the full amount of tenant's security deposit for the premises shall total $_____ .

3. There are no other changes to the Rental Agreement.


_____        _____
Date                                     Landlord/Manager


_____        _____
Date                                     Tenant

# Agreement to Rent Increase for New Equipment or Improvement

Landlord's Name:_____

Address:_____

_____

_____

Tenant's Name:_____

Address:_____

_____

_____

Tenant hereby acknowledges that on or about _____, the Landlord will install into the Tenant's Unit, the new equipment and/or improvements described below:

| Item | Cost |
|------|------|
| _____ | _____ |
| _____ | _____ |
| _____ | _____ |
| _____ | _____ |
| _____ | _____ |
| _____ | _____ |
| Total Cost: | _____ |

Pursuant to applicable law, the Landlord may increase the Unit's legal regulated rent, as of the date of installation, by $_____ per month, which represents 1/40th of the total cost of the equipment and improvements.

_____      _____
Date                      Landlord's Name

_____      _____
Signature                 Title

_____      _____
Date                      Tenant's Name

_____
Signature

# Notice of Security Deposit Transfer

TO:

Tenant: _____ ("Tenant")

Premises: _____ ("Premises")

Rental Unit: _____ ("Rental Unit")

Security Deposit Amount: _____ ("Security Deposit")

PLEASE BE ADVISED, that in connection with the transfer and sale of the Premises from
_____, as Seller,
to _____, as Purchaser,
which sale occurred _____, your Security Deposit for the Rental
Unit, in the amount set forth above, has been transferred and turned over to the Purchaser.

PLEASE BE FURTHER ADVISED that the new Owner and Landlord for the Premises,

_____

is now legally responsible to you for the Security Deposit, and, pursuant to General Obligations Law
§ 7-105, the undersigned has no further responsibility to you for the Security Deposit.


_____        _____
Date                           Seller's Signature


_____        _____
Place                          Seller's Name (Printed)

# Notice of No Security Deposit Record

TO:

Tenant: _____ ("Tenant")

Premises: _____ ("Premises")

Rental Unit: _____ ("Rental Unit")

PLEASE BE ADVISED, that in connection with the transfer and sale of the Premises from

_____, as Seller,

to _____, as Purchaser,

which sale occurred _____, YOU ARE HEREBY NOTIFIED
THAT THERE IS NO RECORD OF ANY SECURITY DEPOSIT FOR YOUR UNIT.

PLEASE BE FURTHER ADVISED, that if you posted a Security Deposit for your Rental Unit, you must,
within 30 days of receipt of this Notice, submit proof of your Security Deposit payment to the
landlord at the following address: _____

_____. Acceptable proof of payment

includes: a receipt from a prior landlord for payment of the security deposit; a cancelled check for
the security deposit payment endorsed by a former owner, or a lease for the Rental Unit signed by a
former landlord acknowledging security deposit payment. Pursuant to General Obligations Law 7-108,
your failure to submit proof that you posted a Security Deposit for the Rental Unit within 30 days
from receipt of this Notice, will release _____

as Owner and Landlord, from any responsibility or liability for a Security Deposit at the end of your
tenancy.

_____     _____
Date                                 Purchaser's Signature


_____     _____
Place                                Purchaser's Name (Printed)

# Building Superintendent/Property Manager Agreement

## 1. Parties

This Agreement is between _____,

Owner of residential real property at _____,

_____, and

_____, (Employee).

## 2. Beginning Date

Employee will begin work on _____.

## 3. Responsibilities

Employee's duties are set forth below:

### Renting Units

☐ answer phone inquiries about vacancies

☐ show vacant units

☐ accept rental applications

☐ select tenants

☐ accept initial rents and deposits

☐ other (specify) _____

☐ _____

### Vacant Apartments

☐ inspect unit when tenant moves in

☐ inspect unit when tenant moves out

☐ clean unit after tenant moves out, including:

    ☐ floors, carpets and rugs

    ☐ walls, baseboards, ceilings, lights and built-in shelves

    ☐ kitchen cabinets, countertops, sinks, stove, oven and refrigerator

    ☐ bathtubs, showers, toilets and plumbing fixtures

    ☐ doors, windows, window coverings and mini-blinds

    ☐ other (specify) _____

    ☐ _____

### Rent Collection

☐ collect rents when due

☐ sign rent receipts

- ☐ maintain rent collection records
- ☐ collect late rents and charges
- ☐ inform Owner of late rents
- ☐ prepare late rent notices
- ☐ serve late rent notices on tenants (when directed by Owner)
- ☐ serve rent increase and tenancy termination notices
- ☐ deposit rent collections in bank
- ☐ other (specify) _____
- ☐ _____

## Maintenance

- ☐ remove garbage, refuse and recycling materials from building for collection
- ☐ inspect heating/hot water system daily
- ☐ inspect fire standpipe/sprinkler system monthly, and complete inspection report
- ☐ vacuum and clean hallways, stairwells and entryways
- ☐ replace lightbulbs in common areas
- ☐ drain water heaters
- ☐ clean exterior stairs, decks, patios, facade and sidewalks
- ☐ clean garage oils on pavement
- ☐ mow lawns
- ☐ rake leaves
- ☐ trim bushes
- ☐ clean up garbage and debris on grounds
- ☐ shovel snow from sidewalks and driveways or arrange for snow removal
- ☐ other (specify) _____
- ☐ _____

## Repairs

- ☐ accept tenant complaints and repair requests
- ☐ inform Owner of extraordinary or unusual maintenance and repair needs
- ☐ maintain written log of tenant complaints
- ☐ handle routine maintenance and repairs, including:
  - ☐ plumbing stoppages
  - ☐ garbage disposal stoppages/repairs
  - ☐ faucet leaks/washer replacement
  - ☐ toilet tank repairs
  - ☐ toilet seat replacement
  - ☐ stove burner repair/replacement

- ☐ stove hinges/knobs replacement
- ☐ dishwasher repair
- ☐ light switch and outlet repair/replacement
- ☐ heater thermostat repair
- ☐ window repair/replacement
- ☐ painting (interior)
- ☐ painting (exterior)
- ☐ replacement of keys
- ☐ window guard installation
- ☐ other (specify)
- ☐ _____

## Other Responsibilities

_____

_____

_____

_____

## 4. Hours and Schedule

Employee will be available to tenants during the following days and times: _____

_____. If the hours required to carry out

any duties may reasonably be expected to exceed _____ hours in any week, Employee

shall notify Owner and obtain Owner's consent before working such extra hours, except in the event

of an emergency. Extra hours worked due to an emergency must be reported to Owner within 24

hours.

## 5. Payment Terms

a. Employee will be paid:

- ☐ $ _____ per hour
- ☐ $ _____ per week
- ☐ $ _____ per month
- ☐ Other: _____

b. Employee will be paid on the specified intervals and dates:

- ☐ Once a week on every _____
- ☐ Twice a month on _____
- ☐ Once a month on _____
- ☐ Other: _____

## 6. Ending the Employee's Employment

Owner may terminate Employee's employment at any time, for any reason that isn't unlawful, with or without notice. Employee may quit at any time, for any reason, with or without notice.

## 7. Rental Unit Occupancy

Owner shall provide Apt. _____ at the property for Employee's occupancy during the term of his or her employment. Employee agrees to occupy the Apartment solely as an incident to employment. Employee's right to occupy the Apartment shall expire when the Employee's employment is terminated or otherwise ends.

## 8. Additional Agreements and Amendments

a. Owner and Employee additionally agree that: _____

_____

_____

_____

_____

_____

_____

_____

_____

_____

_____

_____ .

b. All agreements between Owner and Employee relating to the work specified in this Agreement are incorporated in this Agreement. Any modification to the Agreement must be in writing and signed by both parties.

## 9. Place of Execution

Signed at _____ , _____

_____      _____
Date                                         Owner

_____      _____
Date                                         Employee

# Landlord-Tenant Checklist

## GENERAL CONDITION OF RENTAL UNIT AND PREMISES

Street Address _____     Unit Number _____   City _____

| | Condition on Arrival | Condition on Departure | Estimated Cost of Repair/Replacement |
|---|---|---|---|
| **LIVING ROOM** | | | |
| Floors & Floor Coverings | | | |
| Drapes & Window Coverings | | | |
| Walls & Ceilings | | | |
| Light Fixtures | | | |
| Windows, Screens & Doors | | | |
| Front Door & Locks | | | |
| Fireplace | | | |
| Other | | | |
| Other | | | |
| **KITCHEN** | | | |
| Floors & Floor Coverings | | | |
| Walls & Ceilings | | | |
| Light Fixtures | | | |
| Cabinets | | | |
| Counters | | | |
| Stove/Oven | | | |
| Refrigerator | | | |
| Dishwasher | | | |
| Garbage Disposal | | | |
| Sink & Plumbing | | | |
| Windows, Screens & Doors | | | |
| Other | | | |
| Other | | | |
| **DINING ROOM** | | | |
| Floors & Floor Covering | | | |
| Walls & Ceilings | | | |
| Light Fixtures | | | |
| Windows, Screens & Doors | | | |
| Other | | | |

| | Condition on Arrival | | Condition on Departure | | Estimated Cost of Repair/Replacement |
|---|---|---|---|---|---|
| **BATHROOM(S)** | **Bath 1** | **Bath 2** | **Bath 1** | **Bath 2** | |
| Floors & Floor Coverings | | | | | |
| Walls & Ceilings | | | | | |
| Windows, Screens & Doors | | | | | |
| Light Fixtures | | | | | |
| Bathtub/Shower | | | | | |
| Sink & Counters | | | | | |
| Toilet | | | | | |
| Other | | | | | |
| Other | | | | | |

| | Condition on Arrival | | | Condition on Departure | | | Estimated Cost of Repair/Replacement |
|---|---|---|---|---|---|---|---|
| **BEDROOM(S)** | **Bdrm 1** | **Bdrm 2** | **Bdrm 3** | **Bdrm 1** | **Bdrm 2** | **Bdrm 3** | |
| Floors & Floor Coverings | | | | | | | |
| Windows, Screens & Doors | | | | | | | |
| Walls & Ceilings | | | | | | | |
| Light Fixtures | | | | | | | |
| Other | | | | | | | |
| Other | | | | | | | |
| Other | | | | | | | |
| Other | | | | | | | |

| | Condition on Arrival | Condition on Departure | Estimated Cost of Repair/Replacement |
|---|---|---|---|
| **OTHER AREAS** | | | |
| Heating System | | | |
| Air Conditioning | | | |
| Lawn/Garden | | | |
| Stairs and Hallway | | | |
| Patio, Terrace, Deck, etc. | | | |
| Basement | | | |
| Parking Area | | | |
| Intercom | | | |
| Other | | | |
| Other | | | |
| Other | | | |
| Other | | | |

☐ Tenants acknowledge that all smoke detectors and fire extinguishers, if any, were tested in their presence and found to be in working order, and that the testing procedure was explained to them. Tenants agree to test all detectors at least once a month and to report any problems to Landlord/Manager in writing. Tenants agree to replace all smoke detector batteries as necessary.

**Landlord-Tenant Checklist**

Page 2 of 4

# FURNISHED PROPERTY

| | Condition on Arrival | | | Condition on Departure | | | Estimated Cost of Repair/Replacement |
|---|---|---|---|---|---|---|---|
| **LIVING ROOM** | | | | | | | |
| Coffee Table | | | | | | | |
| End Tables | | | | | | | |
| Lamps | | | | | | | |
| Chairs | | | | | | | |
| Sofa | | | | | | | |
| Other | | | | | | | |
| Other | | | | | | | |
| **KITCHEN** | | | | | | | |
| Broiler Pan | | | | | | | |
| Ice Trays | | | | | | | |
| Other | | | | | | | |
| Other | | | | | | | |
| **DINING AREA** | | | | | | | |
| Chairs | | | | | | | |
| Stools | | | | | | | |
| Table | | | | | | | |
| Other | | | | | | | |
| Other | | | | | | | |
| **BATHROOM(S)** | **Bath 1** | | **Bath 2** | **Bath 1** | | **Bath 2** | |
| Mirrors | | | | | | | |
| Shower Curtain | | | | | | | |
| Hamper | | | | | | | |
| Other | | | | | | | |
| **BEDROOM(S)** | **Bdrm 1** | **Bdrm 2** | **Bdrm 3** | **Bdrm 1** | **Bdrm 2** | **Bdrm 3** | |
| Beds (single) | | | | | | | |
| Beds (double) | | | | | | | |
| Chairs | | | | | | | |
| Chests | | | | | | | |
| Dressing Tables | | | | | | | |
| Lamps | | | | | | | |
| Mirrors | | | | | | | |
| Night Tables | | | | | | | |
| Other | | | | | | | |

| | Condition on Arrival | Condition on Departure | Estimated Cost of Repair/Replacement |
|---|---|---|---|
| Other | | | |
| **OTHER AREAS** | | | |
| Bookcases | | | |
| Desks | | | |
| Pictures | | | |
| Other | | | |
| Other | | | |

Use this space to provide any additional explanation:

_____

_____

_____

_____

_____

_____

_____

_____

_____

_____

_____

Landlord-Tenant Checklist completed on moving in on _____, 200___, and approved by:

_____ and _____
Landlord/Manager                              Tenant

_____
Tenant

_____
Tenant

Landlord-Tenant Checklist completed on moving out on _____, 200___, and approved by:

_____ and _____
Landlord/Manager                              Tenant

_____
Tenant

_____
Tenant

# Move-In Letter

Date _____

Tenant _____

Street address _____

City and State _____

Dear _____,


Welcome to _____

_____. We hope you will enjoy living here. This letter is to explain what you

can expect from the management and what we'll be looking for from you:

**1. Rent:** _____

_____

_____

_____.


**2. Maintenance/Repair Problems:** _____

_____

_____

_____

_____

_____.


**3. Manager or Building Superintendent:** _____

_____

_____

_____

_____

_____.


**4. Landlord-Tenant Checklist:** _____

_____

_____

_____

_____.

**5. Annual Safety Inspection:** _____

_____

_____.

**6. Insurance:** _____

_____

_____

_____

_____.

**7. New Occupants:** _____

_____

_____

_____

_____.

**8. Notice to End Tenancy:** _____

_____

_____.

**9. Security Deposit:** _____

_____

_____.

**10. Moving Out:** _____

_____

_____

_____.

**11. Telephone Number Changes:** _____

_____.

Please let us know if you have any questions.

Sincerely,

_____    _____
Date                                 Owner

I have read and received a copy of this statement.

_____    _____
Date                                 Tenant(s)

# Security Deposit Receipt

_____

_____

_____

_____

Receipt No. _____

Date: _____

Premises address: _____

_____ Unit #: _____

Amount of security deposit received: _____

Form of payment (check one):

☐ Personal check     ☐ Certified check     ☐ Cash

☐ Postal money order     ☐ Bank check     ☐ Other: (specify)_____

Received by: _____

Recipient's name and title: _____

# Request for Identity of Occupants Residing in Rental Unit

_____

Date

_____

Tenant

_____

Rental Unit Address

_____

City and State

Dear_____,

Tenant

New York Real Property Law § 235-f (5) requires you to inform the landlord of the identity of any and all persons, other than yourself, who are living in the rental unit.

Please complete the bottom portion of this letter by inserting the names of all adults and children living in the rental unit and their relationship to you. Then, sign and date this letter where indicated and mail it back to the landlord in the envelope provided. State law (RPL § 235-f) requires you to respond to this request within 30 days of your receipt of this letter.

Thank you in advance for your anticipated cooperation. If you have any questions, feel free to call the undersigned.

Very truly yours,

_____

_____

_____

_____

_____

-- -- -- -- -- -- -- -- -- -- -- -- -- -- -- -- -- -- -- -- -- -- -- -- -- -- -- -- -- -- -- -- -- -- -- -- -- -- -- --

## Statement of Tenant

**Names of adults and names and ages of children (under age 18) other than tenant residing in rental unit**      **Relationship to tenant (family or otherwise)**

1._____      _____

2._____      _____

3._____      _____

For additional persons, check box and attach separate sheet. ☐

Signature of Tenant(s): _____

Date: _____

# Letter Seeking Additional Sublet Information

_____

_____

_____

_____

Dear _____

I have received your request to sublet your apartment, dated _____.
The New York Sublet Law (Real Property Law Section 226-b) permits landlords to ask for information
in addition to that submitted by the tenant in the sublet request.

Accordingly, please instruct your proposed subtenant to complete and sign the attached rental
application. In addition, please provide answers to the following questions:

1. _____

_____

2. _____

_____

3. _____

_____

4. _____

_____

Upon receipt of the requested information, your sublet request will be processed.

Sincerely,

_____

Landlord/Manager

_____

_____

_____

_____

# Consent to Assignment of Lease

_____ ("Landlord") and

_____ ("Tenant") and

_____ ("Assignee")

agree as follows:

1. Tenant has leased the premises at _____

   _____ from Landlord.

2. The lease was signed on _____, 200____, and will expire on

   _____, 200____.

3. Tenant is assigning the balance of Tenant's lease to Assignee, beginning on _____

   _____, 200____, and ending on _____, 200____.

4. Tenant's financial responsibilities under the terms of the lease are not ended by virtue of this

   assignment. Specifically, Tenant understands that:

   a. If Assignee defaults and fails to pay the rent as provided in the lease, namely on

      _____, Tenant will be obligated to do so within

      _____ days of being notified by Landlord; and

   b. If Assignee damages the property beyond normal wear and tear and fails or refuses to pay

      for repairs or replacement, Tenant will be obligated to do so.

5. As of the effective date of the assignment, Tenant permanently gives up the right to occupy the

   premises.

6. Assignee is bound by every term and condition in the lease that is the subject of this assignment.


_____        _____
Date                                   Landlord


_____        _____
Date                                   Tenant


_____        _____
Date                                   Assignee

# Resident's Maintenance/Repair Request

Date: _____

Address: _____

_____ Unit Number_____

Resident's Name: _____

Phone (home): _____ Phone (work): _____

Problem (be as specific as possible):_____

_____

_____

_____

_____

_____

Best time to make repairs: _____

_____

Other comments: _____

_____

_____

_____

I authorize entry into my unit to perform the maintenance or repair requested above, in my absence, unless stated otherwise above.

_____

Resident

- - - - - - - - - - - - - - - - - - - - - - - - - - - - - - - - - - - - - - - - - - - - - - -

FOR MANAGEMENT USE

Work done: _____

Time spent: _____ hours

Date completed: _____, 200____ By: _____

Unable to complete on _____, 200____, because: _____

_____

Notes and comments: _____

_____

Date                    Landlord/Manager/Superintendent

 www.nolo.com                    **Resident's Maintenance/Repair Request**

# Time Estimate for Repair

_____

_____
Date

_____
Tenant

_____
Street Address

_____
Unit Number

_____
City and State

Dear_____,
                      Tenant

Thank you for promptly notifying us of the following problem with your unit:

_____

_____

_____

_____

_____

_____

We expect to have the problem corrected on _____, 200____, due to
the following:

_____

_____

_____

_____

_____

We regret any inconvenience this delay may cause. Please do not hesitate to point out any other
problems that may arise.

Sincerely,

_____
Landlord/Manager/Superintendent

# Annual Safety and Maintenance Update

Please complete the following checklist and note any safety or maintenance problems in your unit or on the premises.

Please describe the specific problems and the rooms or areas involved. Here are some examples of the types of things we want to know about: ceiling leaks, fuses blow out frequently, door lock sticks, water comes out too hot in shower, exhaust fan above stove doesn't work, broken window locks, smoke alarm malfunctions, peeling paint and mice infestation.

Please indicate the approximate date when you first noticed the problem and list any other recommendations or suggestions for improvement.

Please return this form with this month's rent check. Thank you.—THE MANAGEMENT

Name: _____

Address: _____

Unit Number: _____


Please indicate (and explain below) problems with:

☐ Floors and floor coverings _____

☐ Walls and ceilings _____

☐ Windows, screens and doors _____

☐ Window coverings (drapes, mini-blinds, etc.) _____

☐ Electrical system and light fixtures _____

☐ Plumbing (sinks, bathtub, shower or toilet) _____

☐ Heating or air conditioning system_____

☐ Major appliances (stove, oven, dishwasher, refrigerator) _____

☐ Locks or security system _____

☐ Smoke detector _____

☐ Fireplace _____

☐ Cupboards, cabinets and closets _____

☐ Furnishings (table, bed, mirrors, chairs) _____

☐ Laundry facilities _____

☐ Elevator _____

☐ Stairs and handrails _____

☐ Hallway, lobby and common areas _____

☐ Garage _____

☐ Patio, terrace or deck _____

☐ Lawn, fences and grounds_____

☐ Pool and recreational facilities _____

☐ Roof, exterior walls, and other structural _____

☐ Driveway and sidewalks_____

☐ Basement or attic _____

☐ Other _____

_____

Specifics of problems: _____

_____

_____

_____

_____

Other comments: _____

_____

_____

_____

_____

_____        _____

Date                                                    Tenant

- - - - - - - - - - - - - - - - - - - - - - - - - - - - - - - - - - - - - - - - - - - - - - -

FOR MANAGEMENT USE

Action/Response: _____

_____

_____

_____

_____

_____

_____

_____

_____

_____

_____

_____        _____

Date                                                    Landlord/Manager/Superintendent

# Notice of Intent to Enter Dwelling Unit

To: _____
    Tenant

    _____
    Street address

    _____
    City and State

THIS NOTICE is to inform you that on _____,

☐ at approximately _____ AM/PM the landlord, or the landlord's agent, will enter the

premises for the following reason:

☐ To make or arrange for the following repairs or improvements:

_____

_____

_____

_____

_____

☐ To show the premises to:

    ☐ a prospective tenant or purchaser

    ☐ workers or contractors regarding the above repair or improvement

☐ Other: _____

_____

_____

You are, of course, welcome to be present. If you have any questions or if the date or time is

inconvenient, please notify me promptly at _____.
                                                 Phone number

_____    _____
Date                             Landlord/Manager

# Disclosure of Information on Lead-Based Paint or Lead-Based Paint Hazards

## LEAD WARNING STATEMENT

*Housing built before 1978 may contain lead-based paint. Lead from paint, paint chips and dust can pose health hazards if not managed properly. Lead exposure is especially harmful to young children and pregnant women. Before renting pre-1978 housing, lessors must disclose the presence of known lead-based paint and/or lead-based hazards in the dwelling. Lessees must also receive a federally approved pamphlet on lead poisoning prevention.*

### Lessor's Disclosure (initial)

____ (a) Presence of lead-based paint and/or lead-based paint hazards. Check (i) or (ii) below:

    ☐ (i) Known lead-based paint and/or lead-based paint hazards are present in the housing (explain):

      _____

      _____ .

    ☐ (ii) Lessor has no knowledge of lead-based paint and/or lead-based paint hazards in the housing.

____ (b) Records and reports available to the lessor. Check (i) or (ii) below:

    ☐ (i) Lessor has provided the lessee with all available records and reports pertaining to lead-based paint and/or lead-based paint hazards in the housing (list documents below):

      _____

      _____ .

    ☐ (ii) Lessor has no reports or records pertaining to lead-based paint or lead-based paint hazards in the housing.

### Lessee's Acknowledgment (initial)

____ (c) Lessee has received copies of all information listed above.

____ (d) Lessee has received the pamphlet *Protect Your Family From Lead in Your Home.*

### Agent's Acknowledgment (initial)

____ (e) Agent has informed the lessor of the lessor's obligations under 42 U.S.Code 4852d and is aware of his/her responsibility to ensure compliance.

### Certification of Accuracy

The following parties have reviewed the information above and certify, to the best of their knowledge, that the information they have provided is true and accurate.

| | | | |
|---|---|---|---|
| _____ | _____ | _____ | _____ |
| Lessor | Date | Lessor | Date |
| _____ | _____ | _____ | _____ |
| Lessee | Date | Lessee | Date |
| _____ | _____ | _____ | _____ |
| Agent | Date | Agent | Date |

## Are You Planning To Buy, Rent, or Renovate a Home Built Before 1978?

**M**any houses and apartments built before 1978 have paint that contains lead (called lead-based paint). Lead from paint, chips, and dust can pose serious health hazards if not taken care of properly.

By 1996, federal law will require that individuals receive certain information before renting, buying, or renovating pre-1978 housing:

**LANDLORDS** will have to disclose known information on lead-based paint hazards before leases take effect. Leases will include a federal form about lead-based paint.

**SELLERS** will have to disclose known information on lead-based paint hazards before selling a house. Sales contracts will include a federal form about lead-based paint in the building. Buyers will have up to 10 days to check for lead hazards.

**RENOVATORS** will have to give you this pamphlet before starting work.

**IF YOU WANT MORE INFORMATION** on these requirements, call the National Lead Information Clearinghouse at **1-800-424-LEAD.**

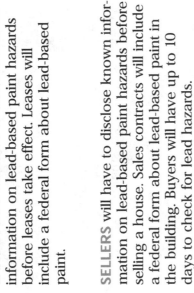

This document is in the public domain. It may be reproduced by an individual or organization without permission. Information provided in this booklet is based upon current scientific and technical understanding of the issues presented and is reflective of the jurisdictional boundaries established by the statutes governing the co-authoring agencies. Following the advice given will not necessarily provide complete protection in all situations or against all health hazards that can be caused by lead exposure.

---

# Protect Your Family From Lead in Your Home

**EPA**
United States
Environmental Protection
Agency

United States Consumer
Product Safety Commission

EPA747-K-94-001
May 1995

U.S. EPA Washington DC 20460
U.S. CPSC Washington DC 20207

# IMPORTANT!

## Lead From Paint, Dust, and Soil Can Be Dangerous If Not Managed Properly

FACT: Lead exposure can harm young children and babies even before they are born.

FACT: Even children that seem healthy can have high levels of lead in their bodies.

FACT: People can get lead in their bodies by breathing or swallowing lead dust, or by eating soil or paint chips with lead in them.

FACT: People have many options for reducing lead hazards. In most cases, lead-based paint that is in good condition is not a hazard.

FACT: Removing lead-based paint improperly can increase the danger to your family.

If you think your home might have lead hazards, read this pamphlet to learn some simple steps to protect your family.

---

## Lead Gets in the Body in Many Ways

People can get lead in their body if they:

◆ Put their hands or other objects covered with lead dust in their mouths.

◆ Eat paint chips or soil that contains lead.

◆ Breathe in lead dust (especially during renovations that disturb painted surfaces).

Lead is even more dangerous to children than adults because:

◆ Babies and young children often put their hands and other objects in their mouths. These objects can have lead dust on them.

◆ Children's growing bodies absorb more lead.

◆ Children's brains and nervous systems are more sensitive to the damaging effects of lead.

1 out of every 11 children in the United States has dangerous levels of lead in the bloodstream.

Even children who appear healthy can have dangerous levels of lead.

## Checking Your Family for Lead

A simple blood test can detect high levels of lead. Blood tests are important for:

- Children who are 6 months to 1 year old (6 months if you live in an older home with cracking or peeling paint).
- Family members that you think might have high levels of lead.

If your child is older than 1 year, talk to your doctor about whether your child needs testing.

Your doctor or health center can do blood tests. They are inexpensive and sometimes free. Your doctor will explain what the test results mean. *Treatment can range from changes in your diet to medication or a hospital stay.*

Get your children tested if you think your home has high levels of lead.

## Where Lead-Based Paint Is Found

Many homes built before 1978 have lead-based paint. The federal government banned lead-based paint from housing in 1978. Some states stopped its use even earlier. Lead can be found:

- In homes in the city, country, or suburbs.
- In apartments, single-family homes, and both private and public housing.
- Inside *and* outside of the house.
- In soil around a home. (Soil can pick up lead from exterior paint, or other sources such as past use of leaded gas in cars.)

In general, the older your home, the more likely it has lead-based paint.

## Lead's Effects

If not detected early, children with high levels of lead in their bodies can suffer from:

- Damage to the brain and nervous system
- Behavior and learning problems (such as hyperactivity)
- Slowed growth
- Hearing problems
- Headaches

Lead is also harmful to adults. Adults can suffer from:

- Difficulties during pregnancy
- Other reproductive problems (in both men and women)
- High blood pressure
- Digestive problems
- Nerve disorders
- Memory and concentration problems
- Muscle and joint pain

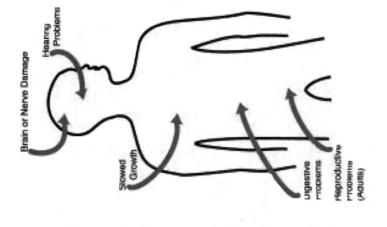

Lead affects the body in many ways.

Brain or Nerve Damage

Hearing Problems

Slowed Growth

Digestive Problems

Reproductive Problems (Adults)

## Where Lead Is Likely To Be a Hazard

Lead-based paint that is in good condition is usually not a hazard.

Peeling, chipping, chalking, or cracking lead-based paint is a hazard and needs immediate attention.

Lead-based paint may also be a hazard when found on surfaces that children can chew or that get a lot of wear-and-tear. These areas include:

◆ Windows and window sills.

◆ Doors and door frames.

◆ Stairs, railings, and banisters.

◆ Porches and fences.

Lead dust can form when lead-based paint is dry scraped, dry sanded, or heated. Dust also forms when painted surfaces bump or rub together. Lead chips and dust can get on surfaces and objects that people touch. Settled lead dust can reenter the air when people vacuum, sweep, or walk through it.

Lead in soil can be a hazard when children play in bare soil or when people bring soil into the house on their shoes. Call your state agency (see page 12) to find out about soil testing for lead.

Lead from paint chips, which you can see, and lead dust, which you can't always see, can both be serious hazards

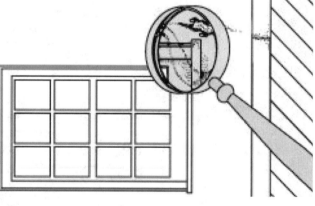

## Checking Your Home for Lead Hazards

You can get your home checked for lead hazards in one of two ways, or both:

◆ A paint inspection tells you the lead content of every painted surface in your home. It won't tell you whether the paint is a hazard or how you should deal with it.

◆ A risk assessment tells you if there are any sources of serious lead exposure (such as peeling paint and lead dust). It also tells you what actions to take to address these hazards.

Have qualified professionals do the work. *The federal government is writing standards for inspectors and risk assessors. Some states might already have standards in place.* Call your state agency for help with locating qualified professionals in your area (see page 12).

Trained professionals use a range of methods when checking your home, including:

◆ Visual inspection of paint condition and location.

◆ Lab tests of paint samples.

◆ Surface dust tests.

◆ A portable x-ray fluorescence machine.

Home test kits for lead are available, but recent studies suggest that they are not always accurate. Consumers should not rely on these tests before doing renovations or to assure safety.

Just knowing that a home has lead-based paint may not tell you if there is a hazard.

## How To Significantly Reduce Lead Hazards

In addition to day-to-day cleaning and good nutrition:

◆ You can **temporarily** reduce lead hazards by taking actions such as repairing damaged painted surfaces and planting grass to cover soil with high lead levels. These actions (called "interim controls") are not permanent solutions and will need ongoing attention.

◆ To **permanently** remove lead hazards, you must hire a lead "abatement" contractor. Abatement (or permanent hazard elimination) methods include removing, sealing, or enclosing lead-based paint with special materials. Just painting over the hazard with regular paint is not enough.

*Removing lead improperly can increase the hazard to your family by spreading even more lead dust around the house.*

*Always use a professional who is trained to remove lead hazards safely.*

Always hire a person with special training for correcting lead problems–someone who knows how to do this work safely and has the proper equipment to clean up thoroughly. If possible, hire a certified lead abatement contractor. Certified contractors will employ qualified workers and follow strict safety rules as set by their state or by the federal government.

Call your state agency (see page 12) for help with locating qualified contractors in your area and to see if financial assistance is available.

## What You Can Do Now To Protect Your Family

**If you suspect that your house has lead hazards, you can take some immediate steps to reduce your family's risk:**

◆ **If you rent, notify your landlord of peeling or chipping paint.**

◆ **Clean up paint chips immediately.**

◆ **Clean floors, window frames, window sills, and other surfaces weekly.** Use a mop or sponge with warm water and a general all-purpose cleaner or a cleaner made specifically for lead. REMEMBER: NEVER MIX AMMONIA AND BLEACH PRODUCTS TOGETHER SINCE THEY CAN FORM A DANGEROUS GAS.

◆ **Thoroughly rinse sponges and mop heads after cleaning dirty or dusty areas.**

◆ **Wash children's hands often, especially before they eat and before nap time and bed time.**

◆ **Keep play areas clean.** Wash bottles, pacifiers, toys, and stuffed animals regularly.

◆ **Keep children from chewing window sills or other painted surfaces.**

◆ **Clean or remove shoes before entering your home to avoid tracking in lead from soil.**

◆ **Make sure children eat nutritious, low-fat meals high in iron and calcium,** such as spinach and low-fat dairy products. Children with good diets absorb less lead.

# Remodeling or Renovating a Home With Lead-Based Paint

Take precautions before you begin remodeling or renovations that disturb painted surfaces (such as scraping off paint or tearing out walls):

◆ **Have the area tested for lead-based paint.**

◆ **Do not use a dry scraper, belt-sander, propane torch, or heat gun** to remove lead-based paint. These actions create large amounts of lead dust and fumes. Lead dust can remain in your home long after the work is done.

◆ **Temporarily move your family** (especially children and pregnant women) out of the apartment or house until the work is done and the area is properly cleaned. If you can't move your family, at least completely seal off the work area.

If not conducted properly, certain types of renovations can release lead from paint and dust into the air.

◆ **Follow other safety measures to reduce lead hazards.** You can find out about other safety measures by calling 1-800-424-LEAD. Ask for the brochure "Reducing Lead Hazards When Remodeling Your Home." This brochure explains what to do before, during, and after renovations.

If you have already completed renovations or remodeling that could have released lead-based paint or dust, get your young children tested and follow the steps outlined on page 7 of this brochure.

# Other Sources of Lead

◆ **Drinking water.** Your home might have plumbing with lead or lead solder. Call your local health department or water supplier to find out about testing your water. You cannot see, smell, or taste lead, and boiling your water will not get rid of lead. If you think your plumbing might have lead in it:

  • Use only cold water for drinking and cooking.

  • Run water for 15 to 30 seconds before drinking it, especially if you have not used your water for a few hours.

*While paint, dust, and soil are the most common lead hazards, other lead sources also exist.*

◆ **The job.** If you work with lead, you could bring it home on your hands or clothes. Shower and change clothes before coming home. Launder your clothes separately from the rest of your family's.

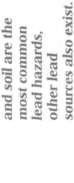

◆ Old painted **toys** and **furniture.**

◆ Food and liquids stored in **lead crystal** or **lead-glazed pottery or porcelain.**

◆ **Lead smelters** or other industries that release lead into the air.

◆ **Hobbies** that use lead, such as making pottery or stained glass, or refinishing furniture.

◆ **Folk remedies** that contain lead, such as "greta" and "azarcon" used to treat an upset stomach.

### The National Lead Information Center

Call **1-800-LEAD-FYI** to learn how to protect children from lead poisoning. For other information on lead hazards, call the center's clearinghouse at **1-800-424-LEAD**. For the hearing impaired, call, **TDD 1-800-526-5456** (FAX: **202-659-1192**, Internet: **EHC@CAIS.COM**).

### EPAÕs Safe Drinking Water Hotline

Call **1-800-426-4791** for information about lead in drinking water.

### Consumer Product Safety Commission Hotline

To request information on lead in consumer products, or to report an unsafe consumer product or a product-related injury call **1-800-638-2772**. (Internet: info@cpsc.gov). For the hearing impaired, call **TDD 1-800-638-8270**.

### Local Sources of Information

## State Health and Environmental Agencies

Some cities and states have their own rules for lead-based paint activities. Check with your state agency (listed below) to see if state or local laws apply to you. Most state agencies can also provide information on finding a lead abatement firm in your area, and on possible sources of financial aid for reducing lead hazards.

| State/Region | Phone Number |
|---|---|
| Alabama | (205) 242-5661 |
| Alaska | (907) 465-5152 |
| Arkansas | (501) 661-2534 |
| Arizona | (602) 542-7307 |
| California | (510) 450-2424 |
| Colorado | (303) 692-3012 |
| Connecticut | (203) 566-5808 |
| Washington, DC | (202) 727-9850 |
| Delaware | (302) 739-4735 |
| Florida | (904) 488-3385 |
| Georgia | (404) 657-6514 |
| Hawaii | (808) 832-5860 |
| Idaho | (208) 332-5544 |
| Illinois | (800) 545-2200 |
| Indiana | (317) 382-6662 |
| Iowa | (800) 972-2026 |
| Kansas | (913) 296-0189 |
| Kentucky | (502) 564-2154 |
| Louisiana | (504) 765-0219 |
| Massachusetts | (800) 532-9571 |
| Maryland | (410) 631-3859 |
| Maine | (207) 287-4311 |
| Michigan | (517) 335-8885 |
| Minnesota | (612) 627-5498 |
| Mississippi | (601) 960-7463 |
| Missouri | (314) 526-4911 |
| Montana | (406) 444-3671 |
| Nebraska | (402) 471-2451 |
| Nevada | (702) 687-6615 |
| New Hampshire | (603) 271-4507 |
| New Jersey | (609) 633-2043 |
| New Mexico | (505) 841-8024 |
| New York | (800) 458-1158 |
| North Carolina | (919) 715-3293 |
| North Dakota | (701) 328-5188 |
| Ohio | (614) 466-1450 |
| Oklahoma | (405) 271-5220 |
| Oregon | (503) 248-5240 |
| Pennsylvania | (717) 782-2884 |
| Rhode Island | (401) 277-3424 |
| South Carolina | (803) 935-7945 |
| South Dakota | (605) 773-3153 |
| Tennessee | (615) 741-5683 |
| Texas | (512) 834-6600 |
| Utah | (801) 536-4000 |
| Vermont | (802) 863-7231 |
| Virginia | (800) 523-4019 |
| Washington | (206) 753-2556 |
| West Virginia | (304) 558-2981 |
| Wisconsin | (608) 266-5885 |
| Wyoming | (307) 777-7391 |

# Simple Steps To Protect Your Family From Lead Hazards

**If you think your home has high levels of lead:**

◆ Get your young children tested for lead, even if they seem healthy.

◆ Wash children's hands, bottles, pacifiers, and toys often.

◆ Make sure children eat healthy, low-fat foods.

◆ Get your home checked for lead hazards.

◆ Regularly clean floors, window sills, and other surfaces.

◆ Wipe soil off shoes before entering house.

◆ Talk to your landlord about fixing surfaces with peeling or chipping paint.

◆ Take precautions to avoid exposure to lead dust when remodeling or renovating (call 1-800-424-LEAD for guidelines).

◆ Don't use a belt-sander, propane torch, dry scraper, or dry sandpaper on painted surfaces that may contain lead.

◆ Don't try to remove lead-based paint yourself.

 Recycled/Recyclable

---

# EPA Regional Offices

Your Regional EPA Office can provide further information regarding regulations and lead protection programs.

**EPA Regional Offices**

**Region 1** (Connecticut, Massachusetts, Maine, New Hampshire, Rhode Island, Vermont)
John F. Kennedy Federal Building
One Congress Street
Boston, MA 02203
(617) 565-3420

**Region 2** (New Jersey, New York, Puerto Rico, Virgin Islands)
Building 5
2890 Woodbridge Avenue
Edison, NJ 08837-3679
(908) 321-6671

**Region 3** (Delaware, Washington DC, Maryland, Pennsylvania, Virginia, West Virginia)
841 Chestnut Building
Philadelphia, PA 19107
(215) 597-9800

**Region 4** (Alabama, Florida, Georgia, Kentucky, Mississippi, North Carolina, South Carolina, Tennessee)
345 Courtland Street, NE
Atlanta, GA 30365
(404) 347-4727

**Region 5** (Illinois, Indiana, Michigan, Minnesota, Ohio, Wisconsin)
77 West Jackson Boulevard
Chicago, IL 60604-3590
(312) 886-6003

**Region 6** (Arkansas, Louisiana, New Mexico, Oklahoma, Texas)
First Interstate Bank Tower
1445 Ross Avenue, 12th Floor, Suite 1200
Dallas, TX 75202-2733
(214) 665-7244

**Region 7** (Iowa, Kansas, Missouri, Nebraska)
726 Minnesota Avenue
Kansas City, KS 66101
(913) 551-7020

**Region 8** (Colorado, Montana, North Dakota, South Dakota, Utah, Wyoming)
999 18th Street, Suite 500
Denver, CO 80202-2405
(303) 293-1603

**Region 9** (Arizona, California, Hawaii, Nevada)
75 Hawthorne Street
San Francisco, CA 94105
(415) 744-1124

**Region 10** (Idaho, Oregon, Washington, Alaska)
1200 Sixth Avenue
Seattle, WA 98101
(206) 553-1200

# CPSC Regional Offices

**Eastern Regional Center**
6 World Trade Center
Vesey Street, Room 350
New York, NY 10048
(212) 466-1612

**Central Regional Center**
230 South Dearborn Street
Room 2944
Chicago, IL 60604-1601
(312) 353-8260

**Western Regional Center**
600 Harrison Street, Room 245
San Francisco, CA 94107
(415) 744-2966

# Three-Day Rent Demand Notice

To:_____

    Tenant

_____

    Street address

_____

    City and State

Dear Tenant of the above Premises:

PLEASE TAKE NOTICE, that you have failed to pay to the Landlord the sum of $_____ for

rent and other charges for the period from _____, as follows:

    Base Rent

    _____    _____

    _____    _____

    _____    _____

    _____    _____

                              Subtotal Rent  _____

    Other Charges

    _____    _____

    _____    _____

    _____    _____

              Subtotal Other Charges  _____

                  Total Amount Due  _____

PLEASE TAKE FURTHER NOTICE, that you are required to pay the total amount of rent and other

charges due on or before _____, that being more than _____ days from the

day of the service of this Notice, or vacate and surrender the possession of the premises to the

Landlord. In the event you fail to do so, the Landlord will commence summary proceedings under

the Statute to recover the possession of the premises.

_____    _____

Date

                                _____

                                _____

                                _____

                                _____

# Authorization to Issue Notices for Landlord

I hereby authorize _____

_____, to sign all legal notices on

my behalf relating to the property located at _____

_____.


_____        _____
Date                                    Owner and Landlord

# Affidavit of Service by Personal Delivery

STATE OF NEW YORK                  )

                                             ) ss:

COUNTY OF _____ )

The undersigned, being duly sworn deposes and says:

1. I am over 18 years of age and am not the landlord.

2. On the _____ of _____, at _____, I served the

   within Rent Demand Notice on _____,

   the tenant named on the Notice by delivering and leaving with _____

   _____ personally a true copy of the Notice, and that such service was

   made _____

   _____.

   I knew the person so served to be the person mentioned and described herein.

3. The person served is described as:

   Sex: _____    Skin color: _____

   Height: _____    Approximate age: _____

   Weight: _____    Hair color: _____

   Other distinguishing characteristics: _____

   _____

    

   _____
   Signature of Server

   _____
   Printed or Typed Name of Server

   _____
   License Number of Server

Sworn to before me this _____ of _____

_____

_____, Notary Public

License No. _____

My Commission Expires _____

---

# Affidavit of Service by Substituted Service

STATE OF NEW YORK                                              )

                                              ) ss:

COUNTY OF _____ )

The undersigned, being duly sworn deposes and says:

1. I am over 18 years of age and am not the landlord.

2. After an attempt made on _____, at _____, I was unable to serve
   the rent demand notice, on _____
   by personal delivery at _____.

3. On _____, at _____, I served a true copy of the rent demand
   notice by gaining admittance to said premises and delivering to and leaving a copy thereof
   personally with _____,
   a person of suitable age and discretion, who was willing to receive same on behalf of the above-
   named tenant and who resided at said premises.

4. The person served is described as:

   Sex: _____ Skin color: _____

   Height:_____ Approximate age: _____

   Weight: _____ Hair color: _____

   Other distinguishing characteristics: _____
   _____

5. Within one day thereafter, I mailed true copies of the rent demand notice by regular, first-class
   mail and by certified mail, enclosed in postpaid properly addressed envelopes to _____
   _____ at the address of the premises sought to be
   recovered and the following additional address(es): _____
   _____. Said mail was deposited
   within a Post Office under the exclusive care and custody of the United States Postal Service.

                   _____
                   Signature of Server

                   _____
                   Printed or Typed Name of Server

                   _____
                   License Number of Server

Sworn to before me this _____ of _____

_____

_____, Notary Public

License No._____

My Commission Expires_____

# Affidavit of Service by Conspicuous Place Service

STATE OF NEW YORK                               )

                                                 ) ss:

COUNTY OF _____ )

The undersigned, being duly sworn deposes and says:

1. I am over 18 years of age and am not the landlord.

2. On the _____ of _____, at _____, I served the

   within Rent Demand Notice on _____,

   the tenant of _____

   by _____

   _____ the entrance door at

   _____,

   because I was unable to gain admittance or to find a person of suitable age or discretion willing to

   receive same at that time and on prior attempt(s) made on _____ at _____.

3. The entrance door to the respondent's premises can be described as follows: _____

   _____.

4. Within one day thereafter, I mailed true copies of the rent demand by regular, first-class mail and

   by certified mail, enclosed in postpaid properly addressed envelopes to _____

   _____ at the address the premises sought to be recovered

   and the following additional address/es: _____

   _____. This mail was deposited

   within a Post Office under the exclusive care and custody of the United States Postal Service.

_____

Signature of Server

_____

Printed or Typed Name of Server

_____

License Number of Server

Sworn to before me this _____ of _____

_____

_____, Notary Public

License No. _____

My Commission Expires _____

---

# Thirty- (30-) Day Notice of Termination

To: _____

("Tenants") and any and all persons occupying the premises

Re:_____

_____ ("Premises")


PLEASE TAKE NOTICE, that the undersigned Landlord elects to terminate your monthly tenancy as of

_____, a date at least 30 days from the date of service of this Notice upon

you.

PLEASE TAKE FURTHER NOTICE, that you must surrender and vacate the Premises on or before

_____, the day on which your tenancy expires. If you fail to do so, the

Landlord will commence summary proceedings to remove you from the Premises for holding over

after the expiration of your term, and will demand the monetary value of your use and occupancy of

the Premises during such holding over.


_____        _____
Date                                 Signature

                                     _____
                                     Name and Title of Signer

                                     _____
                                     Address

                                     _____

                                     _____

                                     _____
                                     Phone

# One-Month Notice of Termination

To: _____

("Tenants") and any and all persons occupying the premises

Re:_____

_____ ("Premises")


PLEASE TAKE NOTICE, that the undersigned Landlord elects to terminate your monthly tenancy of

the Premises as of _____, a date a least one month from the date this

notice is served upon you. You must vacate and surrender the Premises on or before that date.


_____          _____
Date                               Signature

                                   _____
                                   Name and Title of Signer

                                   _____
                                   Address

                                   _____

                                   _____

                                   _____
                                   Phone

# Tenant's Notice of Intent to Move Out

_____

Date

_____

Landlord

_____

Street Address

_____

City and State

Dear _____,

                        Landlord

This is to notify you that the undersigned tenants, _____

_____ will be moving from

_____

_____,

on _____ , _____ from today.
This provides at least _____ written notice as required in our

rental agreement.

Sincerely,

_____

Tenant

_____

Tenant

_____

Tenant

# Lease Surrender Agreement

_____ (Landlord)

and _____ (Tenant)

agree as follows:

1. Tenant hereby surrenders all right, title and interest in his/her tenancy of the premises known

    as and located at _____

    _____ (Premises), effective _____.

2. Landlord and Tenant agree that the Lease for the Premises entered into on _____

    _____ will terminate on _____.

3. Tenant agrees to vacate the Premises on or before _____ and to remove

    all his/her personal property and possession from the Premises on or before that date.


_____     _____
Date                                Landlord


_____     _____
Date                                Tenant

# Notice to Cure

To: _____ ,

    "Tenant," and to all persons occupying the Premises described below

Re: All rooms, _____ , in the building known as and located at

_____ (the "Premises").

PLEASE TAKE NOTICE, that you are violating a _____

of your lease dated _____ by and between _____

_____ , as Tenant, and

_____

as Landlord (hereinafter, the "Lease"). Specifically, you have _____

_____

_____

_____

_____

_____ .

PLEASE TAKE FURTHER NOTICE, that you are required to cure the violation within _____

days from the date of this notice by _____

_____

_____

_____

_____ .

PLEASE TAKE FURTHER NOTICE, that if you fail to cure the violation on or before_____

_____ , that being at least _____ days from the

date of this Notice, your tenancy will be terminated and you will be required to remove from and

surrender possession of the Premises to the Landlord.

_____      _____

Date                    Signature

                    _____

                    Name and Title of Signer

                    _____

                    Address

                    _____

                    _____

                    _____

                    Phone

# Notice of Termination

To: _____,

"Tenant," and to all persons occupying the Premises described below

Premises: _____

_____

_____ (the "Premises").

Re:     Lease dated _____ between _____

_____, as Tenant,

and _____

_____, Landlord's predecessor (the "Lease").

PLEASE TAKE NOTICE, that pursuant to _____

_____

the Landlord elects to terminate your tenancy on the grounds that _____

_____

_____

_____

_____

_____.

PLEASE TAKE FURTHER NOTICE, that you are hereby required to quit, vacate and surrender the

Premises on or before _____, that being more than _____

after the service of this notice upon you, pursuant to the terms of your lease and applicable law.

PLEASE TAKE FURTHER NOTICE, that if you fail to vacate or surrender the premises, the landlord will

commence summary proceedings to evict you.

_____     _____
Date                                          Signature

_____
Name and Title of Signer

_____
Address

_____

_____

_____
Phone

# Move-Out Letter

_____
Date

_____
Tenant

_____
Street address

_____
City and State

Dear_____,
             Tenant

We hope you have enjoyed living here. In order that we may mutually end our relationship on a positive note, this move-out letter describes how we expect your unit to be left and what our procedures are for returning your security deposit.

Basically, we expect you to leave your rental unit in the same condition it was when you moved in, except for normal wear and tear. To refresh your memory on the condition of the unit when you moved in, I've attached a copy of the Landlord-Tenant Checklist you signed at the beginning of your tenancy. I'll be using this same form to inspect your unit when you leave.

Specifically, here's a list of items you should thoroughly clean before vacating:

☐ Floors

    ☐ sweep wood floors

    ☐ vacuum carpets and rugs (shampoo, if necessary)

    ☐ mop kitchen and bathroom floors

☐ Walls, baseboards, ceilings and built-in shelves

☐ Kitchen cabinets, countertops and sink, stove and oven—inside and out

☐ Refrigerator—clean inside and out, empty it of food, and turn it off, with the door left open

☐ Bathtubs, showers, toilets and plumbing fixtures

☐ Doors, windows and window coverings

☐ Other

_____

_____

_____

_____

_____

_____

_____

_____

_____

_____

If you have any questions as to the type of cleaning we expect, please let me know.

Please don't leave anything behind—that includes bags of garbage, clothes, food, newspapers, furniture, appliances, dishes, plants, cleaning supplies or other items that belong to you.

Please be sure you have disconnected phone and utility services, canceled all newspaper subscriptions and sent the post office a change of address form.

Once you have cleaned your unit and removed all your belongings, please call me at _____ to arrange for a walk-through inspection and to return all keys. Please be prepared to give me your forwarding address where we may mail your security deposit.

It's our policy to return all deposits either in person or at an address you provide within _____ after you move out. If any deductions are made—for past due rent or because the unit is damaged or not sufficiently clean—they will be explained in writing.

If you have any questions, please contact me at _____.

Sincerely,

_____
Landlord/Manager

# Security Deposit Itemization
## (Deductions for Repairs, Cleaning and Unpaid Rent)

Date: _____

From: _____

_____

_____

To:  _____

_____

_____

Property Address: _____

_____ Apartment Number: _____

Rental Period: _____

1. Security Deposit Received                              $ _____

2. Interest on Deposit (if required by lease or law):     $ _____

3. Total Credit (sum of lines 1 and 2)                                $ _____

4. Itemized Repairs and Related Losses:

_____

_____

_____

_____     Total Repair Cost:   $ _____

5. Necessary Cleaning:

_____

_____

_____

_____     Total Cleaning Cost:  $ _____

6. Defaults in Rent and Additional Rent Not Covered
   by Any Court Judgment (list dates and rates):

_____

_____

_____

_____     Total Rent Defaults:  $ _____

7. Amount of Court Judgment for Rent, Costs, Attorney Fees:  $ _____

8. Amount Owed (line 3 minus the sum of lines 4, 5, 6, and 7)

    ☐  a. Total Amount Tenant Owes Landlord:                           $ _____

    ☐  b. Total Amount Landlord Owes Tenant:                           $ _____

Comments: _____

_____

_____

_____

_____

_____

_____

_____

_____

_____

_____

_____

_____

_____

_____

_____

# Letter for Returning Entire Security Deposit

_____

Date

_____

Tenant

_____

Street address and unit number

_____

City and State

Dear_____,

                         Tenant

Enclosed please find our check No. _____ dated _____ in the

amount of _____. This represents a full refund of your _____ security deposit,

plus accumulated interest of _____ for the rental unit at _____

_____,

_____,

which you rented from us on a _____ basis on

_____,_____, and vacated on _____, _____ .

Thank you for leaving the rental unit in good condition. We wish you the best of luck in your future
endeavors.

Sincerely,

_____

Landlord/Manager

# Index

## C

Case citations, 17/15
CD-ROM, how to use, Appendix III
Certificate of Eviction, 15/7, 15/9,
 15/26
Checklist, 7/2–7, 16/5
Children, 2/27
CHIP (Community Housing Improvement Program), 4/6
Citizenship, 1/18, 1/19
Codes, 9/9–11
Code violations, 4/19, 9/10
Collection agencies, 16/26
Commissions, 1/38
Common areas, 9/15, 9/20
Community Housing Improvement Program (CHIP), 4/6
Complaint log, 9/47
Complaints, 9/43–47, 9/51–52
Consent to Assignment of Lease, 8/27
Consent to Background and Reference Check, 1/29
Constructive eviction, 13/15, 13/17, 14/24
Consulates, 1/18
Contingency fees, 17/5
Co-signers, 2/37–39
Co-tenants, 8/3–5, 8/6, 8/10
Counterclaim waiver, 2/25
Court costs, 2/24–25
Court decisions, 17/14–15
Credit records and reports, 1/5, 1/33–35
Crime, 9/24–15

## D

Damage, 2/36, 9/31
 See also Repairs and maintenance
Damage control, 7/2–7, 7/8
Dangerous conditions. See Hazardous conditions
Dangers. See Environmental hazards
Default, 2/23–24
Default notice. See Notice to cure
Demand (for occupant names), 8/10–11
Deposits, 1/39–40, 2/20
 See also Security deposits
Deregulation of rental units, 4/23, 4/31, 4/33–34
Destruction, 2/26
DHCR. See New York City Department of Housing and
 Community Renewal
Diplomats, 1/18
Disability, 1/12–15, 2/18, 3/3
Disclosures, 2/5, 11/2–9

Discrimination
 categories of, 1/9–18
 exemptions from laws prohibiting, 1/9
 fair housing laws and, 1/3–4, 1/5, 1/8
 insurance policies and, 1/20
 penalties for, 1/19–20
Dispute resolution, 16/24
Disturbances, 2/18, 2/18–19
DOL (New York State Department of Labor), 6/20–21
Drug dealing, 9/24, 9/25
Drug users, 1/12–13
Duplicate keys, 14/7

## E

EIN (employer identification number), 6/18
Electricity, 9/15–16, 9/20
Elevators, 9/16
Emergency procedures, 6/24–25
Emotional impairments (discrimination for), 1/13
Employee identification number (EIN), 6/18
Employees. See Managers and supers
Employment law
 DOL assistance and, 6/20
 immigration and, 6/21
 managers and supers information needs, 6/5–6, 6/18
 reporting of employees and, 6/21
 tax requirements and ramifications with, 6/18–21
Employment records, 1/5
Employment verification, 1/30, 1/33
Enforcement, 2/27
Entry
 denial of, 10/14–15
 emergencies and, 10/5–6
 general rules of, 1/3
 inspection of unit and, 10/9
 notice for, 10/3, 10/4, 10/5, 10/7
 officials with authority and, 10/11–12
 privately installed locks to units and, 10/6
 rent-stabilized tenants and, 10/4–5
 repairs and, 10/7–9
 repairs and inspections, 10/3–5
 showing for rental or purchase, 10/4, 10/10–11
 See also Access
Environmental hazards
 agencies involving, 11/21
 asbestos, 11/11–17
 lead, 11/2–11
 mold, 11/20
 radon, 11/19–20
 refrigerants, 11/17–18

■

# CATALOG

## ...more from Nolo

|  | PRICE | CODE |
|---|---|---|

## BUSINESS

| | PRICE | CODE |
|---|---|---|
| The CA Nonprofit Corporation Kit (Binder w/CD-ROM) | $59.95 | CNP |
| Consultant & Independent Contractor Agreements (Book w/CD-ROM) | $29.95 | CICA |
| The Corporate Minutes Book (Book w/CD-ROM) | $69.99 | CORMI |
| The Employer's Legal Handbook | $39.99 | EMPL |
| Everyday Employment Law | $29.99 | ELBA |
| Drive a Modest Car & 16 Other Keys to Small Business Success | $24.99 | DRIV |
| Form Your Own Limited Liability Company (Book w/CD-ROM) | $44.99 | LIAB |
| Hiring Independent Contractors: The Employer's Legal Guide (Book w/CD-ROM) | $34.99 | HICI |
| How to Create a Buy-Sell Agreement & Control the Destiny of your Small Business (Book w/Disk-PC) | $49.95 | BSAG |
| How to Create a Noncompete Agreement | $44.95 | NOCMP |
| How to Form a California Professional Corporation (Book w/CD-ROM) | $59.95 | PROF |
| How to Form a Nonprofit Corporation (Book w/CD-ROM)—National Edition | $44.99 | NNP |
| How to Form a Nonprofit Corporation in California (Book w/CD-ROM) | $44.99 | NON |
| How to Form Your Own California Corporation (Binder w/CD-ROM) | $59.99 | CACI |
| How to Form Your Own California Corporation (Book w/CD-ROM) | $34.99 | CCOR |
| How to Get Your Business on the Web | $29.99 | WEBS |
| How to Write a Business Plan | $34.99 | SBS |
| The Independent Paralegal's Handbook | $29.95 | PARA |
| Leasing Space for Your Small Business | $34.95 | LESP |
| Legal Guide for Starting & Running a Small Business | $34.99 | RUNS |
| Legal Forms for Starting & Running a Small Business (Book w/CD-ROM) | $29.95 | RUNS2 |
| Marketing Without Advertising | $24.00 | MWAD |
| Music Law (Book w/CD-ROM) | $34.99 | ML |

Prices subject to change.

|  | PRICE | CODE |
|---|---|---|
| Nolo's Guide to Social Security Disability | $29.99 | QSS |
| Nolo's Quick LLC | $24.99 | LLCQ |
| Nondisclosure Agreements | $39.95 | NAG |
| The Small Business Start-up Kit (Book w/CD-ROM) | $29.99 | SMBU |
| The Small Business Start-up Kit for California (Book w/CD-ROM) | $34.99 | OPEN |
| The Partnership Book: How to Write a Partnership Agreement (Book w/CD-ROM) | $39.99 | PART |
| Sexual Harassment on the Job | $24.95 | HARS |
| Starting & Running a Successful Newsletter or Magazine | $29.99 | MAG |
| Tax Savvy for Small Business | $34.99 | SAVVY |
| Working for Yourself: Law & Taxes for the Self-Employed | $39.99 | WAGE |
| Your Crafts Business: A Legal Guide | $26.99 | VART |
| Your Limited Liability Company: An Operating Manual (Book w/CD-ROM) | $49.99 | LOP |
| Your Rights in the Workplace | $29.99 | YRW |

## CONSUMER

|  | PRICE | CODE |
|---|---|---|
| How to Win Your Personal Injury Claim | $29.99 | PICL |
| Nolo's Encyclopedia of Everyday Law | $29.99 | EVL |
| Nolo's Guide to California Law | $24.95 | CLAW |
| Trouble-Free Travel...And What to Do When Things Go Wrong | $14.95 | TRAV |

## ESTATE PLANNING & PROBATE

|  | PRICE | CODE |
|---|---|---|
| 8 Ways to Avoid Probate | $19.95 | PRO8 |
| 9 Ways to Avoid Estate Taxes | $29.95 | ESTX |
| Estate Planning Basics | $21.99 | ESPN |
| How to Probate an Estate in California | $49.99 | PAE |
| Make Your Own Living Trust (Book w/CD-ROM) | $39.99 | LITR |
| Nolo's Law Form Kit: Wills | $24.95 | KWL |
| Nolo's Simple Will Book (Book w/CD-ROM) | $34.99 | SWIL |

|  | PRICE | CODE |
|---|---|---|
| Plan Your Estate | $44.99 | NEST |
| Quick & Legal Will Book | $15.99 | QUIC |

## FAMILY MATTERS

| | | |
|---|---|---|
| Child Custody: Building Parenting Agreements That Work | $29.95 | CUST |
| The Complete IEP Guide | $24.99 | IEP |
| Divorce & Money: How to Make the Best Financial Decisions During Divorce | $34.99 | DIMO |
| Get a Life: You Don't Need a Million to Retire Well | $24.99 | LIFE |
| The Guardianship Book for California | $39.99 | GB |
| How to Adopt Your Stepchild in California (Book w/CD-ROM) | $34.95 | ADOP |
| A Legal Guide for Lesbian and Gay Couples | $29.99 | LG |
| Living Together: A Legal Guide (Book w/CD-ROM) | $34.99 | LTK |
| Using Divorce Mediation: Save Your Money & Your Sanity | $29.95 | UDMD |

## GOING TO COURT

| | | |
|---|---|---|
| Beat Your Ticket: Go To Court and Win! (National Edition) | $19.99 | BEYT |
| The Criminal Law Handbook: Know Your Rights, Survive the System | $34.99 | KYR |
| Everybody's Guide to Small Claims Court (National Edition) | $26.99 | NSCC |
| Everybody's Guide to Small Claims Court in California | $26.99 | CSCC |
| Fight Your Ticket ... and Win! (California Edition) | $29.99 | FYT |
| How to Change Your Name in California | $34.95 | NAME |
| How to Collect When You Win a Lawsuit (California Edition) | $29.99 | JUDG |
| How to Mediate Your Dispute | $18.95 | MEDI |
| How to Seal Your Juvenile & Criminal Records (California Edition) | $34.95 | CRIM |
| The Lawsuit Survival Guide | $29.99 | UNCL |
| Nolo's Deposition Handbook | $29.99 | DEP |
| Represent Yourself in Court: How to Prepare & Try a Winning Case | $34.99 | RYC |

|  | PRICE | CODE |
|---|---|---|

## HOMEOWNERS, LANDLORDS & TENANTS

| | PRICE | CODE |
|---|---|---|
| California Tenants' Rights | $27.99 | CTEN |
| Deeds for California Real Estate | $24.99 | DEED |
| Dog Law | $21.95 | DOG |
| Every Landlord's Legal Guide (National Edition, Book w/CD-ROM) | $44.99 | ELLI |
| Every Tenant's Legal Guide | $29.99 | EVTEN |
| For Sale by Owner in California | $29.99 | FSBO |
| How to Buy a House in California | $34.99 | BHCA |
| The California Landlord's Law Book: Rights & Responsibilities (Book w/CD-ROM) | $44.99 | LBRT |
| The California Landlord's Law Book: Evictions (Book w/CD-ROM) | $44.99 | LBEV |
| Leases & Rental Agreements | $29.99 | LEAR |
| Neighbor Law: Fences, Trees, Boundaries & Noise | $26.99 | NEI |
| The New York Landlord's Law Book (Book w/CD-ROM) | $39.95 | NYLL |
| New York Tenants' Rights | $27.99 | NYTEN |
| Renters' Rights (National Edition) | $24.99 | RENT |
| Stop Foreclosure Now in California | $29.95 | CLOS |

## HUMOR

| | PRICE | CODE |
|---|---|---|
| Poetic Justice | $9.95 | PJ |

## IMMIGRATION

| | PRICE | CODE |
|---|---|---|
| Becoming A U.S. Citizen: A Guide to the Law, Exam and Interview | $24.99 | USCIT |
| Fiancé & Marriage Visas | $44.99 | IMAR |
| How to Get a Green Card | $29.95 | GRN |
| Student & Tourist Visas | $29.99 | ISTU |
| U.S. Immigration Made Easy | $44.99 | IMEZ |

## MONEY MATTERS

| | PRICE | CODE |
|---|---|---|
| 101 Law Forms for Personal Use (Book w/CD-ROM) | $29.99 | SPOT |

| | PRICE | CODE |
|---|---|---|
| Bankruptcy: Is It the Right Solution to Your Debt Problems? | $19.99 | BRS |
| Chapter 13 Bankruptcy: Repay Your Debts | $34.99 | CH13 |
| Creating Your Own Retirement Plan | $29.99 | YROP |
| Credit Repair (Book w/CD-ROM) | $24.99 | CREP |
| How to File for Chapter 7 Bankruptcy | $34.99 | HFB |
| IRAs, 401(k)s & Other Retirement Plans: Taking Your Money Out | $34.99 | RET |
| Money Troubles: Legal Strategies to Cope With Your Debts | $29.99 | MT |
| Nolo's Law Form Kit: Personal Bankruptcy | $24.99 | KBNK |
| Stand Up to the IRS | $24.99 | SIRS |
| Surviving an IRS Tax Audit | $24.95 | SAUD |
| Take Control of Your Student Loan Debt | $26.95 | SLOAN |

## PATENTS AND COPYRIGHTS

| | PRICE | CODE |
|---|---|---|
| The Copyright Handbook: How to Protect and Use Written Works (Book w/CD-ROM) | $39.99 | COHA |
| Copyright Your Software | $34.95 | CYS |
| Domain Names | $26.95 | DOM |
| Getting Permission: How to License and Clear Copyrighted Materials Online and Off (Book w/CD-ROM) | $34.99 | RIPER |
| How to Make Patent Drawings Yourself | $29.99 | DRAW |
| The Inventor's Notebook | $24.99 | INOT |
| Nolo's Patents for Beginners | $29.99 | QPAT |
| License Your Invention (Book w/CD-ROM) | $39.99 | LICE |
| Patent, Copyright & Trademark | $39.99 | PCTM |
| Patent It Yourself | $49.99 | PAT |
| Patent Searching Made Easy | $29.95 | PATSE |
| The Public Domain | $34.95 | PUBL |
| Web and Software Development: A Legal Guide (Book w/ CD-ROM) | $44.95 | SFT |
| Trademark: Legal Care for Your Business and Product Name | $39.95 | TRD |

|  | PRICE | CODE |
|---|---|---|

## RESEARCH & REFERENCE

| | | |
|---|---|---|
| Legal Research: How to Find & Understand the Law | $34.99 | LRES |

## SENIORS

| | | |
|---|---|---|
| Choose the Right Long-Term Care: Home Care, Assisted Living & Nursing Homes | $21.99 | ELD |
| The Conservatorship Book for California | $44.99 | CNSV |
| Social Security, Medicare & Goverment Pensions | $29.99 | SOA |

## SOFTWARE

**Call or check our website at www.nolo.com
for special discounts on Software!**

| | | |
|---|---|---|
| LeaseWriter CD—Windows | $129.95 | LWD1 |
| LLC Maker—Windows | $89.95 | LLP1 |
| PatentPro Plus—Windows | $399.99 | PAPL |
| Personal RecordKeeper 5.0 CD—Windows | $59.95 | RKD5 |
| Quicken Lawyer 2003 Business Deluxe—Windows | $79.95 | SBQB3 |
| Quicken Lawyer 2003 Personal—Windows | $79.95 | WQP3 |

# Special
# Upgrade Offer

## Order Form

Name _____

Address _____

City _____

State, Zip _____

Daytime Phone _____

E-mail _____

### Our "No-Hassle" Guarantee

Return anything you buy directly from Nolo for any reason and we'll cheerfully refund your purchase price. No ifs, ands or buts.

☐ Check here if you do not wish to receive mailings from other companies

| Item Code | Quantity | Item | Unit Price | Total Price |
|-----------|----------|------|------------|-------------|
|  |  |  |  |  |
|  |  |  |  |  |
|  |  |  |  |  |
|  |  |  |  |  |
|  |  |  |  |  |

**Method of payment**

☐ Check    ☐ VISA    ☐ MasterCard
☐ Discover Card    ☐ American Express

| | |
|---|---|
| Subtotal | |
| Add your local sales tax (California only) | |
| Shipping: RUSH $9, Basic $5 (See below) | |
| "I bought 3, ship it to me FREE!"(Ground shipping only) | |
| TOTAL | |

Account Number _____

Expiration Date _____

Signature _____

## Shipping and Handling

### Rush Delivery—Only $9

**We'll ship any order to any street address in the U.S. by UPS 2nd Day Air\* for only $9!**

\* Order by noon Pacific Time and get your order in 2 business days. Orders placed after noon Pacific Time will arrive in 3 business days. P.O. boxes and S.F. Bay Area use basic shipping. Alaska and Hawaii use 2nd Day Air or Priority Mail.

### Basic Shipping—$5

**Use for P.O. Boxes, Northern California and Ground Service.**

Allow 1-2 weeks for delivery. U.S. addresses only.

## For faster service, use your credit card and our toll-free numbers

**Call our customer service group**
**Monday thru Friday 7am to 7pm PST**

**Phone**    1-800-728-3555
**Fax**      1-800-645-0895
**Mail**     Nolo
             950 Parker St.
             Berkeley, CA 94710

**Order 24 hours a day @**
# www.nolo.com

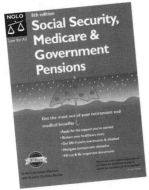

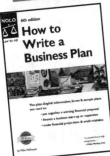
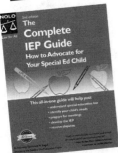

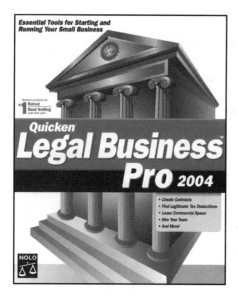

# Remember:

Little publishers have big ears.
We really listen to you.

Take 2 Minutes & Give Us Your 2 cents

**Y**our comments make a big difference in the development and revision of Nolo books and software. Please take a few minutes and register your Nolo product—and your comments—with us. Not only will your input make a difference, you'll receive special offers available only to registered owners of Nolo products on our newest books and software. Register now by:

**PHONE**
1-800-728-3555

**FAX**
1-800-645-0895

**EMAIL**
cs@nolo.com

or **MAIL** us
this registration card

fold here

- - - - - - - - - - - - - - - - - - - - - - - - - - - - - - - - - - - - - - - - - - - - - - - - - - -

## Registration Card

NAME _____ DATE _____

ADDRESS _____

_____

CITY _____ STATE _____ ZIP _____

PHONE _____ E-MAIL _____

WHERE DID YOU HEAR ABOUT THIS PRODUCT? _____

WHERE DID YOU PURCHASE THIS PRODUCT? _____

DID YOU CONSULT A LAWYER? (PLEASE CIRCLE ONE)   YES   NO   NOT APPLICABLE

DID YOU FIND THIS BOOK HELPFUL?   (VERY)   5   4   3   2   1   (NOT AT ALL)

COMMENTS _____

_____

_____

WAS IT EASY TO USE?   (VERY EASY)   5   4   3   2   1   (VERY DIFFICULT)

We occasionally make our mailing list available to carefully selected companies whose products may be of interest to you.

❑   If you do not wish to receive mailings from these companies, please check this box.

❑   You can quote me in future Nolo promotional materials.
    Daytime phone number _____.

**NYLL 2.0**

**Nolo**
*in the*
**NEWS**

"Nolo helps lay people perform legal tasks without the aid—or fees—of lawyers."

**—USA TODAY**

Nolo books are ..."written in plain language, free of legal mumbo jumbo, and spiced with witty personal observations."

**—ASSOCIATED PRESS**

"...Nolo publications...guide people simply through the how, when, where and why of law."

**—WASHINGTON POST**

"Increasingly, people who are not lawyers are performing tasks usually regarded as legal work... And consumers, using books like Nolo's, do routine legal work themselves."

**—NEW YORK TIMES**

"...All of [Nolo's] books are easy-to-understand, are updated regularly, provide pull-out forms...and are often quite moving in their sense of compassion for the struggles of the lay reader."

**—SAN FRANCISCO CHRONICLE**

------------------------------ fold here ------------------------------

Place
stamp here

**Nolo**
**950 Parker Street**
**Berkeley, CA 94710-9867**

Attn: NYLL 2.0